THE KENNEDYS

 For information, write Andrews McMeel Publishing, LLC, an Andrews McMeel Universal company, 1130 Walnut Street, Kansas City, Missouri 64106.

ISBN-13: 978-0-7407-9372-1
ISBN-10: 0-7407-9372-1

Library of Congress Control Number: 2009936122

09 10 11 12 13 RR3 10 9 8 7 6 5 4 3 2 1

www.andrewsmcmeel.com

To all who have dedicated their lives in service to democracy,
especially elected officials and those who hold them accountable.

CONTENTS

Introduction by Bob Schieffer . . . ix

1960s ❦ 1

John F. Kennedy Election and Inauguration ❦ Bay of Pigs ❦ Cuban Missile Crisis
Space Race ❦ Civil Rights ❦ John F. Kennedy Assassination ❦ Robert Kennedy Election
Robert Kennedy Assassination ❦ Chappaquiddick

1970s ❦ 61

Pentagon Papers ❦ Kennedy Center for the Performing Arts ❦ Health Care Reform
Jacqueline Kennedy Onassis Widowed ❦ John F. Kennedy Library and Museum
Edward Kennedy Presidential Run

1980s ❦ 69

Edward Kennedy Presidential Run ❦ Maria Shriver Wedding ❦ Caroline Kennedy Wedding
Joseph Kennedy II Election ❦ Bork Nomination

1990s ❦ 74

William Kennedy Smith Trial ❦ Edward Kennedy Wedding ❦ Health Care Reform
Jacqueline Kennedy Onassis Death ❦ Patrick Kennedy Election ❦ Kathleen Kennedy Townsend Election
Rose Fitzgerald Kennedy Death ❦ John F. Kennedy Jr. Death

Contents

2000s ❦ 86

Caroline Kennedy Convention Address ❦ September 11 Attacks ❦ Michael Skakel Trial
Schwarzenegger Election ❦ Rosemary Kennedy Death ❦ Barack Obama Endorsement
Edward Kennedy Diagnosis ❦ Caroline Kennedy Senate Bid ❦ Eunice Kennedy Shriver Death
Edward Kennedy Death

Eulogies ❦ 111

Tribute to Senator Robert Kennedy Delivered by Senator Edward Kennedy, June 8, 1968
Tribute to Jacqueline Bouvier Kennedy Onassis Delivered by Senator Edward Kennedy, May 23, 1994
Tribute to Rose Fitzgerald Kennedy Delivered by Senator Edward Kennedy, January 25, 1995
Tribute to John F. Kennedy Jr. Delivered by Senator Edward Kennedy, July 23, 1999
Tribute to Senator Edward Kennedy Delivered by President Barack Obama, August 29, 2009

Acknowledgments . . . 123

About The Poynter Institute . . . 125

Introduction

by Bob Schieffer

I spent most of the day Ted Kennedy died asking those who knew him how someone who had such a zest for partisan politics could become so adept at building bipartisan coalitions that had produced so much meaningful legislation.

The best answer came from former Senate Republican Leader Bob Dole, who told me, "Kennedy had this way of saying the most partisan things, but saying it in a way that you never thought he was talking about you personally."

As I drove home that night after reminiscing about Kennedy on the *CBS Evening News*, it occurred to me that I had been writing and asking questions about one Kennedy or another for most of my professional life.

From the 1960s until now, the Kennedy family has dominated American politics and captured America's imagination as no other family ever has.

Year after year, there was always a story to be done about the Kennedys—from tragedy and triumph, to scandal and stories of great compassion. These stories became a saga marked by a string of political yarns, family tragedies, weddings, divorces, and funerals, and Americans never tired of hearing or reading about them.

I never met John Kennedy, but I would become a footnote of sorts to the awful events that befell the young president on that trip to Texas in 1963.

I was the night police reporter at my hometown newspaper, the *Fort Worth Star-Telegram*, and Kennedy had made a breakfast speech in Fort Worth before going to Dallas on that fateful day. When we got word he had been shot, I raced to the office and within minutes heard the radio bulletin: The president was dead.

There was total bedlam in the newsroom. Editors were hollering at people to "get to Dallas and call us when you get there." Every phone was ringing. I grabbed one, only to hear a woman caller ask, "Is there anyone there who can give me a ride to Dallas?"

"Lady," I shouted, "we're not running a taxi service and besides, the president has been shot."

"Yes," the voice responded, "I just heard it on the radio and they said my son is the one they've arrested."

It was Lee Harvey Oswald's mother.

I jotted down her address and assured her I would be there shortly to take her to Dallas.

The paper's auto editor, Bill Foster, was test-driving a Cadillac, so I commandeered Foster and his sedan and the two of us took her to the Dallas police station.

In those days, we never told people who we were unless they asked, and since I always wore a snap-brim hat, the Dallas cops assumed I was a young detective when we told them we had brought Oswald's mother from Fort Worth. When I asked a detective chief if she could talk with her son, I was stunned when he agreed; we were ushered into a holding room off the jail.

As we waited for Oswald to be brought in, I knew I was on the verge of the biggest story of my life—a chance to question the man who had been charged with killing a president.

Alas, it was not to be. After six hours in the police station, an FBI agent finally did what someone should have done when I arrived. He asked who I was, and was not amused to discover I was a reporter. He told me to leave immediately; it seemed he was in a mood to kill me and said something to that effect.

I never got that scoop, but over the years there would be more stories to write about the Kennedys.

John Kennedy's brother Robert would later die at the hands of another assassin. And shortly after I joined CBS News in 1969, Ted Kennedy drove his car off a bridge on Chappaquiddick. As the rookie in the Washington bureau, one of my first assignments was to track down those who had been with him that night and convince them to talk about it. I was never able to do that, nor was anyone else, but the episode would dog Kennedy for the rest of his life.

In the years to come, memories of that night would fade but never be entirely forgotten. As time passed, Americans would watch Ted Kennedy become the family patriarch—the one who walked the nieces down the aisle during the best times and got the nephews out of trouble during the bad times. When John Kennedy Jr. died in a plane crash, it was Ted Kennedy who gave yet another eulogy at yet another Kennedy funeral.

I would come to know and cover Ted Kennedy, first as an unsuccessful presidential candidate and later as one of the Senate's shrewdest negotiators and most effective leaders. I interviewed him countless times in Capitol corridors and on *Face the Nation*. There was always something to ask a Kennedy about because whatever the news, one of them always seemed to be involved.

Ted Kennedy's death ended a career in which he was responsible for a mountain of legislative achievements—reforms touching on everything from women's rights to treatment of the disabled to health insurance for children. It was a remarkable legacy but just one chapter in a family saga that has fascinated Americans for more than half a century.

It is famously said that newspapers are the first draft of history, and it is the first draft of the Kennedy story that has been assembled in this book—the newspaper accounts that recorded the Kennedy story as it happened.

It is a story marked by tragedy, despair, and man's inhumanity to man; but in the end, it is a story of hope and resiliency. It is all here, not fiction as it sometimes reads, but reality as it was recorded by those who were there when it happened.

Bob Schieffer is CBS News chief Washington correspondent and moderator of Face the Nation.

SENATOR JOHN KENNEDY DECLARED PRESIDENTIAL CANDIDACY

"All the News That's Fit to Print"

The New York Times.

LATE CITY EDITION

Occasional rain today; rain ending tonight. Partly cloudy tomorrow.

NEWS SUMMARY AND INDEX, PAGE 91

SECTION ONE

VOL. CIX....No. 37,234. NEW YORK, SUNDAY, JANUARY 3, 1960. TWENTY-FIVE CENTS

MAYOR PLEDGES FULL-SCALE STUDY OF TRANSIT CRISES

One Aim Is to Eliminate Strike Threats—Public Is 'Sick of Them,' He Says

15-CENT FARE PROMISED

Wagner Points to Burden on Budget—Notes Authority Is Creature of the State

By STANLEY LEVEY

President and Aides Work on Messages to Congress

The President with Maurice H. Stans, director of Bureau of the Budget, at Augusta, Ga.

By FELIX BELAIR Jr.

EISENHOWER WARY ON PLAN TO WIDEN CIVIL RIGHTS LAW

Unlikely to Press Congress for U. S. Vote Registrars to Protect Negroes

By ANTHONY LEWIS

Another Democrat Enters Contest

Senator John F. Kennedy at his news conference yesterday

KENNEDY IN RACE; BARS SECOND SPOT IN ANY SITUATION

Formal Announcement Cites Confidence He Will Win Election as President

CHALLENGES SYMINGTON

Insists All Aspirants Should Be Willing to Test Their Strength in Primaries

By RUSSELL BAKER

BORDER BUILD-UP RUSHED IN INDIA

Army Reinforced and Roads Built Near Tibet—Peiping Stand Is Unchanged

By PAUL GRIMES

Bonn Charges Plot To Smear Republic With Anti-Semitism

By ARTHUR J. OLSEN

BENSON DRAFTING 40C CUT IN WHEAT

Price Supports Geared to Open Market Planned to Reduce Surplus

By WILLIAM M. BLAIR

Party's Debate on Kennedy Takes Note of Catholic Vote

By JAMES RESTON

DEMOCRATS PRESS CUT IN STATE TAX

Little Chance Seen for Plan, but It Is Expected to Give Party Campaign Issue

By DOUGLAS DALES

MAN FOUND SLAIN, SECOND WOUNDED

Police Hunt 3 in Shootings at 13th St. and Ave. A

School Integration Has Passed Its Crisis, Negro Leader Says

All-Out Resistance Yielding to Legal Skirmishing, Marshall Declares

By WAYNE PHILLIPS

Thurgood Marshall

Soviet Is Believed Ahead of U.S. In Explosions for Peaceful Use

By GLADWIN HILL

Doctors Find Christmas Strains Make Season Unhappy for Many

By JOHN A. OSMUNDSEN

Today's Sections

Index to Subjects

John Fitzgerald Kennedy, the 42-year-old junior senator from Massachusetts, announced that he would seek the Democratic presidential nomination.

The Kennedys enjoyed sailing around Nantucket Sound near the family compound at Hyannis Port, Massachusetts. (AP Photo)

ALSO IN 1960

Camelot opened on Broadway. *Jacqueline Kennedy later said it was one of her husband's favorite musicals.*

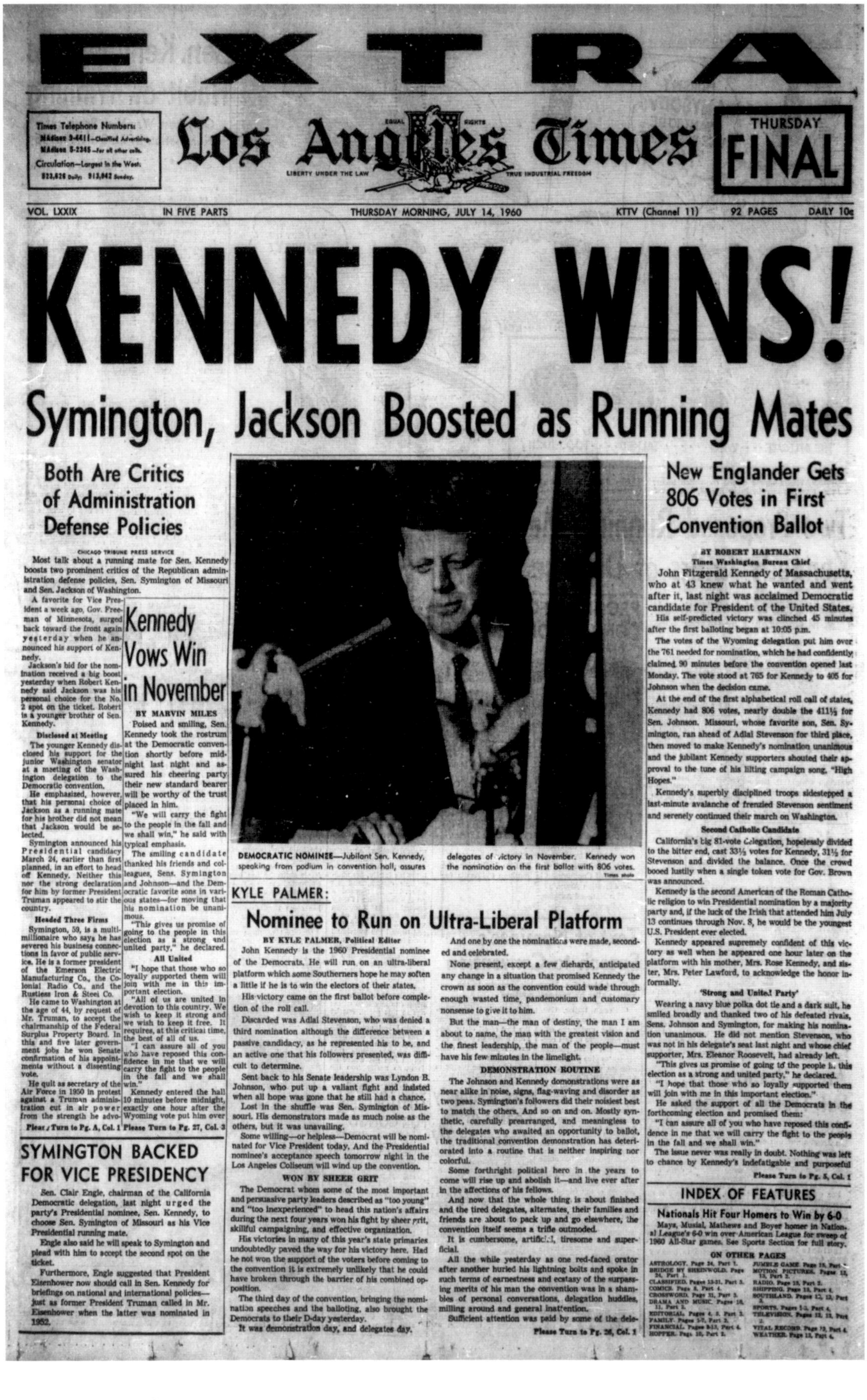

EXTRA

Times Telephone Numbers:
MAdison 9-4411—Classified Advertising.
MAdison 5-2345—For all other calls.
Circulation—Largest in the West:
823,626 Daily; 913,042 Sunday.

Los Angeles Times

EQUAL RIGHTS
LIBERTY UNDER THE LAW · TRUE INDUSTRIAL FREEDOM

THURSDAY FINAL

VOL. LXXIX · IN FIVE PARTS · THURSDAY MORNING, JULY 14, 1960 · KTTV (Channel 11) · 92 PAGES · DAILY 10¢

KENNEDY WINS!

Symington, Jackson Boosted as Running Mates

Both Are Critics of Administration Defense Policies

CHICAGO TRIBUNE PRESS SERVICE

Most talk about a running mate for Sen. Kennedy boosts two prominent critics of the Republican administration defense policies, Sen. Symington of Missouri and Sen. Jackson of Washington.

A favorite for Vice President a week ago, Gov. Freeman of Minnesota, surged back toward the front again yesterday when he announced his support of Kennedy.

Jackson's bid for the nomination received a big boost yesterday when Robert Kennedy said Jackson was his personal choice for the No. 2 spot on the ticket. Robert is a younger brother of Sen. Kennedy.

Disclosed at Meeting

The younger Kennedy disclosed his support for the junior Washington senator at a meeting of the Washington delegation to the Democratic convention.

He emphasized, however, that his personal choice of Jackson as a running mate for his brother did not mean that Jackson would be selected.

Symington announced his Presidential candidacy March 24, earlier than first planned, in an effort to head off Kennedy. Neither this nor the strong declaration for him by former President Truman appeared to stir the country.

Headed Three Firms

Symington, 59, is a multimillionaire who says he has severed his business connections in favor of public service. He is a former president of the Emerson Electric Manufacturing Co., the Colonial Radio Co., and the Rustless Iron & Steel Co.

He came to Washington at the age of 44, by request of Mr. Truman, to accept the chairmanship of the Federal Surplus Property Board. In this and five later government jobs he won Senate confirmation of his appointments without a dissenting vote.

He quit as secretary of the Air Force in 1950 in protest against a Truman administration cut in air power from the strength he advo-

Please Turn to Pg. A, Col. 1

Kennedy Vows Win in November

BY MARVIN MILES

Poised and smiling, Sen. Kennedy took the rostrum at the Democratic convention shortly before midnight last night and assured his cheering party their new standard bearer will be worthy of the trust placed in him.

"We will carry the fight to the people in the fall and we shall win," he said with typical emphasis.

The smiling candidate thanked his friends and colleagues, Sens. Symington and Johnson—and the Democratic favorite sons in various states—for moving that his nomination be unanimous.

"This gives us promise of going to the people in this election as a strong and united party," he declared.

All United

"I hope that those who so loyally supported them will join with me in this important election.

"All of us are united in devotion to this country. We wish to keep it strong and we wish to keep it free. It requires, at this critical time, the best of all of us.

"I can assure all of you who have reposed this confidence in me that we will carry the fight to the people in the fall and we shall win."

Kennedy entered the hall 10 minutes before midnight, exactly one hour after the Wyoming vote put him over

Please Turn to Pg. 27, Col. 3

SYMINGTON BACKED FOR VICE PRESIDENCY

Sen. Clair Engle, chairman of the California Democratic delegation, last night urged the party's Presidential nominee, Sen. Kennedy, to choose Sen. Symington of Missouri as his Vice Presidential running mate.

Engle also said he will speak to Symington and plead with him to accept the second spot on the ticket.

Furthermore, Engle suggested that President Eisenhower now should call in Sen. Kennedy for briefings on national and international policies—just as former President Truman called in Mr. Eisenhower when the latter was nominated in 1952.

DEMOCRATIC NOMINEE—Jubilant Sen. Kennedy, speaking from podium in convention hall, assures delegates of victory in November. Kennedy won the nomination on the first ballot with 806 votes. Times photo

KYLE PALMER:

Nominee to Run on Ultra-Liberal Platform

BY KYLE PALMER, Political Editor

John Kennedy is the 1960 Presidential nominee of the Democrats. He will run on an ultra-liberal platform which some Southerners hope he may soften a little if he is to win the electors of their states.

His victory came on the first ballot before completion of the roll call.

Discarded was Adlai Stevenson, who was denied a third nomination although the difference between a passive candidacy, as he represented his to be, and an active one that his followers presented, was difficult to determine.

Sent back to his Senate leadership was Lyndon B. Johnson, who put up a valiant fight and insisted when all hope was gone that he still had a chance.

Lost in the shuffle was Sen. Symington of Missouri. His demonstrators made as much noise as the others, but it was unavailing.

Some willing—or helpless—Democrat will be nominated for Vice President today. And the Presidential nominee's acceptance speech tomorrow night in the Los Angeles Coliseum will wind up the convention.

WON BY SHEER GRIT

The Democrat whom some of the most important and persuasive party leaders described as "too young" and "too inexperienced" to head this nation's affairs during the next four years won his fight by sheer grit, skillful campaigning, and effective organization.

His victories in many of this year's state primaries undoubtedly paved the way for his victory here. Had he not won the support of the voters before coming to the convention it is extremely unlikely that he could have broken through the barrier of his combined opposition.

The third day of the convention, bringing the nomination speeches and the balloting, also brought the Democrats to their D-day yesterday.

It was demonstration day, and delegates day.

And one by one the nominations were made, seconded and celebrated.

None present, except a few diehards, anticipated any change in a situation that promised Kennedy the crown as soon as the convention could wade through enough wasted time, pandemonium and customary nonsense to give it to him.

But the man—the man of destiny, the man I am about to name, the man with the greatest vision and the finest leadership, the man of the people—must have his few minutes in the limelight.

DEMONSTRATION ROUTINE

The Johnson and Kennedy demonstrations were as near alike in noise, signs, flag-waving and disorder as two peas. Symington's followers did their noisiest best to match the others. And so on and on. Mostly synthetic, carefully prearranged, and meaningless to the delegates who awaited an opportunity to ballot, the traditional convention demonstration has deteriorated into a routine that is neither inspiring nor colorful.

Some forthright political hero in the years to come will rise up and abolish it—and live ever after in the affections of his fellows.

And now that the whole thing is about finished and the tired delegates, alternates, their families and friends are about to pack up and go elsewhere, the convention itself seems a trifle outmoded.

It is cumbersome, artificial, tiresome and superficial.

All the while yesterday as one red-faced orator after another hurled his lightning bolts and spoke in such terms of earnestness and ecstasy of the surpassing merits of his man the convention was in a shambles of personal conversations, delegation huddles, milling around and general inattention.

Sufficient attention was paid by some of the dele-

Please Turn to Pg. 26, Col. 1

New Englander Gets 806 Votes in First Convention Ballot

BY ROBERT HARTMANN
Times Washington Bureau Chief

John Fitzgerald Kennedy of Massachusetts, who at 43 knew what he wanted and went after it, last night was acclaimed Democratic candidate for President of the United States.

His self-predicted victory was clinched 45 minutes after the first balloting began at 10:05 p.m.

The votes of the Wyoming delegation put him over the 761 needed for nomination, which he had confidently claimed 90 minutes before the convention opened last Monday. The vote stood at 765 for Kennedy to 405 for Johnson when the decision came.

At the end of the first alphabetical roll call of states, Kennedy had 806 votes, nearly double the 411½ for Sen. Johnson. Missouri, whose favorite son, Sen. Symington, ran ahead of Adlai Stevenson for third place, then moved to make Kennedy's nomination unanimous and the jubilant Kennedy supporters shouted their approval to the tune of his lilting campaign song, "High Hopes."

Kennedy's superbly disciplined troops sidestepped a last-minute avalanche of frenzied Stevenson sentiment and serenely continued their march on Washington.

Second Catholic Candidate

California's big 81-vote delegation, hopelessly divided to the bitter end, cast 33½ votes for Kennedy, 31½ for Stevenson and divided the balance. Once the crowd booed lustily when a single token vote for Gov. Brown was announced.

Kennedy is the second American of the Roman Catholic religion to win Presidential nomination by a majority party and, if the luck of the Irish that attended him July 13 continues through Nov. 8, he would be the youngest U.S. President ever elected.

Kennedy appeared supremely confident of this victory as well when he appeared one hour later on the platform with his mother, Mrs. Rose Kennedy, and sister, Mrs. Peter Lawford, to acknowledge the honor informally.

'Strong and United Party'

Wearing a navy blue polka dot tie and a dark suit, he smiled broadly and thanked two of his defeated rivals, Sens. Johnson and Symington, for making his nomination unanimous. He did not mention Stevenson, who was not in his delegate's seat last night and whose chief supporter, Mrs. Eleanor Roosevelt, had already left.

"This gives us promise of going to the people in this election as a strong and united party," he declared.

"I hope that those who so loyally supported them will join with me in this important election."

He asked the support of all the Democrats in the forthcoming election and promised them:

"I can assure all of you who have reposed this confidence in me that we will carry the fight to the people in the fall and we shall win."

The issue never was really in doubt. Nothing was left to chance by Kennedy's indefatigable and purposeful

Please Turn to Pg. 5, Col. 1

INDEX OF FEATURES

Nationals Hit Four Homers to Win by 6-0

Mays, Musial, Mathews and Boyer homer in National League's 6-0 win over American League for sweep of 1960 All-Star games. See Sports Section for full story.

ON OTHER PAGES

ASTROLOGY. Page 24, Part 1.
BRIDGE BY SHEINWOLD. Page 24, Part 1.
CLASSIFIED. Pages 13-31, Part 3.
COMICS. Page 8, Part 4.
CROSSWORD. Page 31, Part 3.
DRAMA AND MUSIC. Pages 10, 11, Part 2.
EDITORIAL. Pages 4, 5, Part 2.
FAMILY. Pages 1-7, Part 2.
FINANCIAL. Pages 8-13, Part 4.
HOPPER. Page 10, Part 2.
JUMBLE GAME. Page 18, Part 4.
MOTION PICTURES. Pages 12, 13, Part 2.
RADIO. Page 18, Part 2.
SHIPPING. Page 18, Part 4.
SOUTHLAND. Pages 12, 13, Part 2.
SPORTS. Pages 1-3, Part 4.
TELEVISION. Pages 12, 13, Part 2.
VITAL RECORD. Page 13, Part 4.
WEATHER. Page 13, Part 4.

Kennedy won the Democratic nomination and surprisingly chose for his running mate Senate Majority Leader Lyndon Johnson from Texas, who brought strong southern support to the ticket.

QUOTED

"We stand today on the edge of a New Frontier."

—SENATOR JOHN F. KENNEDY, *July 15, 1960*

SEPTEMBER 12, 1960
SENATOR JOHN KENNEDY DELIVERED SPEECH ABOUT CATHOLICISM

THE WEATHER
Houston and Vicinity: Fair through Wednesday. High today, 90; low tonight, 65; high Wednesday, 90.
East Texas. Fair through Wednesday.
More Data, Sec. 4, Page 17

THE HOUSTON CHRONICLE

FINAL EDITION

Vol. 29 No. 336 "Miss Classified" CA 4-6868 Other Departments CA 7-2211 HOUSTON, TEXAS, TUESDAY, SEPTEMBER 13, 1960 ★★ 44 PAGES PRICE 5 CENTS

Chronicle Photo

U.S. SEN. JOHN KENNEDY FACES PROTESTANT MINISTERS ON RELIGIOUS ISSUE
Democratic Candidate and Audience Turn to Hear Question From Minister Not Shown

Dem Leaders Call Kennedy Visit Triumph

Johnson Says Acclaim 'Couldn't Be Better'

BY BO BYERS AND WALTER MANSELL
Chronicle Staff

Top Texas Democratic leaders were exulting Tuesday over Harris County's reception of Democratic presidential nominee John F. Kennedy.

"It couldn't have been better," Sen. Lyndon B. Johnson, Kennedy's running mate, told The Chronicle. "The Coliseum was filled. It was the most enthusiastic crowd I've ever seen."

Similar opinions were expressed by Speaker Sam Rayburn, Sen. Ralph Yarborough, Lt. Gov. Ben Ramsey, national Democratic committeeman Byron Skelton of Temple, and the party's state chairman, Ed Connally of Abilene.

2000 Greeters at Austin

An estimated crowd of 2000 Austin citizens cheered Kennedy's arrival in Austin shortly before midnight, as he was welcomed at the airport by Gov. and Mrs. Price Daniel and Mayor Tom Miller.

Kennedy was the overnight guest of the governor.

"Houston was wonderful. I think it's been a triumphal march across Texas," said Rayburn.

Kennedy pulls no punches in question and answer session with Ministers' Assn. of Greater Houston. Section 1, Page 8.

"He got bigger crowds than Adlai (Stevenson) or Eisenhower got when they campaigned in Texas," said Yarborough. "The Houston reaction was very, very fine."

Ramsey referred to Kennedy's Coliseum audience as "tremendous," with "a lot of enthusiasm."

"I think Kennedy has done a terrific job and is going to carry the state—no doubt about it," said the lieutenant-governor. "He cleared up the religious issue, which is the only issue that was bothering him in this state."

Gov. Daniel Is Impressed

Daniel, who watched Kennedy's appearance before the Ministers' Assn. of Greater Houston on TV, was impressed.

"I thought he was very good. He handled himself very well," said the governor. "It was a rough thing (the questioning by the ministers), but I thought they treated him very kind."

Kennedy, who walked the length of a long line to shake hands with well-wishers crowding the airport fence in Austin, said he is no longer worried about carrying Texas.

"I came to Texas with some trepidation and some concern. I had read the vice-president's (Nixon's) statements about what they (the Republicans) were going to do in Texas this time, and I thought maybe they were. But now I know he's wrong, and we're going to carry Texas," Kennedy told his cheering audience.

A crowd of 5000 turned out early Tuesday to hear Kennedy speak from the steps of the state capitol in Austin. Gov. Price Daniel, who introduced the candidate, said he is convinced that Texas voters are not going to put the nominee to any "religious test" because he is a member of the Catholic Church.

Communist Question

Kennedy, after praising Johnson's Senate record, turned to the Communist question.

"Khrushchev came to the United States and said our children would be Communists," he said. "Then he went to China and told them we were sick or dying. I do not agree with him."

He then took off on fast moving tour of north Texas.

In Ft. Worth, Dallas

Crowds turned out at the Ft. Worth airport, along the streets leading downtown and

(See KENNEDY, Page 4)

Tropical Storm Loses Force Over Atlantic

Boston — (UPI) — Tropical storm Donna lost hurricane force Tuesday and broke up over the Atlantic.

The dying hurricane plunged across New England in a final orgy of destruction after a 3000-mile rampage which left at least 145 dead.

Twenty seven of the dead were in the United States where the storm's trail of destruction stretched from Florida through New England.

EASTERLY WAVE

Miami — (AP) — Weather forecasters Tuesday watched an easterly wave in the Antilles, some 1200 miles southeast of Miami. The Miami Weather Bureau said the wave showed no circulation "but it does have unusual shower activity and a low barometer."

Scores of coastal towns were shattered and thousands of workers waded into the shambles Tuesday in a gigantic cleanup job.

Donna's winds diminished to only 50 miles per hour as she swirled past Caribou, Maine Tuesday, considerably weaker than the 160-mile gusts which raked the Caribbean and the Atlantic Coast during the past 10 days.

Florida was hardest hit with 11 dead and damage which exceeded $1,000,000,000. Seven persons died in New England; four each in New Jersey and New York state and three in North Carolina.

Puerto Rico counted 106 dead and 10 others died in the Leeward Islands.

Encouraged, Fit Nixon Takes Campaign West

San Francisco — (UPI) — Vice-President Richard M. Nixon carried his "peace without surrender" campaign into the West Tuesday and found himself in encouraging political and physical shape after a rough first day on the presidential stump.

The vice-president's physician reported that Monday's 15-hour work day had caused neither pain nor damage in Nixon's recently infected left knee.

But another bruising day, starting with an early morning news conference, and carrying the Nixon party to Washington, Oregon and Idaho lay in wait.

Power Issue

The G.O.P. candidate planned to discuss the public power issue in the Pacific Northwest today. But he already had spelled out the main theme of his campaign—that peace with the extension of freedom is "the great issue" of 1960 and he hammered hard his point that the Eisenhower administration record had demonstrated the "national maturity" the voters want continued.

An estimated 40,000 persons jammed San Francisco's Union Square at midevening to hear their fellow Californian. Nixon's lieutenants were cheered by this — but far more by the estimated 100,000 who turned out for him in Democratic Dallas.

No Conflict

Nixon said he does not anticipate any situation in which either he or Sen. John F. Kennedy would have to resign the presidency because of a conflict of conscience over religion or any other issue.

The G.O.P. presidential candidate told his news conference that Kennedy's own offer to take such action should be accepted by everyone.

"I respect his statement and I think it could be accepted without further question," Nixon declared.

Khrushchev Curb

The vice-president also made these points:

Restricting Soviet Premier Nikita Khrushchev to Manhattan Island during the forthcoming United Nations session was necessary and taking any other course would be "irresponsible." He said the potential security threat involving Khrushchev's life involves a risk that "in a non-police state we could not afford to take."

He intends to make a "major" civil rights speech in the next two weeks. Nixon said the address is already written but the place at which it will be delivered has not been chosen.

Needled Opponent

Nixon needled Kennedy in

See column by James Reston, New York Times reporter, on the Nixon, campaign. Sec. 1, Page 7.

his campaign checkoff. But he did it politely — following his own admonition that Republicans should try to follow President Eisenhower's own "high standards" of campaigning.

Without mentioning Kennedy, he told his audiences he hoped the "time will never come when any president feels it necessary to apologize for attempting to defend the security of the United States."

This was a reference to the U-2 spy plane incident and Kennedy's suggestion that Eisenhower might have expressed "regret" for the spy plane incident if this could have saved the Paris summit conference.

Evidently lifted by his release to campaign after 11

(See NIXON, Page 4)

U.P.I. Telephoto

WISHING NIXON WELL AT DALLAS' LOVE FIELD
V.-P. and Wife on 14-State Tour

Lumumba Foes Bid for Control

Leopoldville, The Congo—(AP)—The United Nations relaxed its restrictions on airports and broadcasting in the Congo Tuesday, and President Joseph Kasavubu sought quickly to gain the upper hand on the radio.

Congolese troops loyal to the stocky, usually phlegmatic Congo president surrounded the Leopoldville radio station shortly afteh the U.N. ban on political broadcasts was lifted.

The radio station had been Premier Patrice Lumumba's first objective after he was released from a brief internment by troops Monday.

Jean Bolikango, designated as minister of information in the Kasavubu-approved cabinet of Joseph Ileo, broadcast his first appeal to the Congolese.

Bolikango promised an all-out effort to find employment and food for the masses. He announced that Kasavubu has signed new arrest warrants for Lumumba and six of his ministers.

Lumumba was deposed officially as premier eight days ago, by Kasavubu's order, but has held onto the job. Bolikango said Lumumba "is hiding but we will find him for the good of the country."

U. N. soldiers had been withdrawn from the radio station. White-helmeted troops suporting Kasavubu put their own machine guns into position outside the building.

Bolikango later asked 40 newsman for the West's help for the chaotic Congo.

"Independence has brought misery, terror and fear," Bolikango said. "We don't want our people to tell you we had clamored for independence to create starvation."

$3300 COULD PAY PUZZLE ADDICT'S WAY INTO COLLEGE

Working your way through college?

Then $3300 would pay for a lot of tuition. It's yours for the asking if you have the right answers to The Chronicle's Crossword Puzzle. Look in Section 3, Page 3.

Basic Prize	$1300
Regular Subscriber Bonus	500
New Subscriber Bonus	500
Classified Bonus	1000
Total	$3300

Curfew Imposed After Vandalism At Pasadena Zoo

BY DAVE WOODLOCK
Chronicle Staff

Vandalism — including the hacking to death of all five of the city zoo's alligators—prompted the Pasadena city commission Tuesday to order a 10 p.m. curfew at city parks and other municipal recreation facilities.

The commission made it clear the curfew accent was on youth, but it directed the city attorney to draw up an ordinance requiring all persons to vacate such facilities by 10 p.m.

Commissioner J. L. Brammer reported that, in the past year, all five of the city zoo's alligators have been hacked to death, a number of birds have been poisoned and the deer in the zoo have been flushed repeatedly from their pens.

On one occasion, an attempt was made to release the zoo's two Alaskan brown bears.

Brammer also complained that it is costing the city more than $800 a year just to replace broken commode fixtures in park facilities.

In addition to zoo vandalism, Brammer said groups were breaking locks on light controls at baseball fields and tennis courts in order to play nighttime games.

Shooting out the lights also has been a popular sport, he told the council.

The ordinance City Atty. Tom Lay was directed to prepare will call for a misdemeanor penalty with a maximum fine of $200.

Police Commissioner Varreece Berry commented:

"It's a ridiculous situation when we're trying to develop our zoo and beautify our parks and have the kids come in and tear them up."

Laos Revolt Heading Into Full-Size War

Bankok, Thailand — (UPI) The crisis in revolt-torn Laos, now under a state of emergency, threatened Tuesday to turn into a large-scale civil war.

Reports of bitter fighting in Laotian jungle provinces between the counter-revolutionary forces of pro-American Gen. Phoumi Nosavan and Communist-backed troops led to speculation that the Southeast Asia Treaty Organization might send forces into the troubled kingdom.

Radio broadcasts by Phoumis' forces claimed that the Communist Pathet Lao troops had attacked army outposts in Northern Phongsaly and Sam Neua provinces. (See map on page 2).

Texas Draft Quota

Austin —(AP)— The October draft call on Texas is for 450 men, state selective service director Col. Morris S. Schwartz announced Tuesday.

The quota compares with 406 for September.

Butler Is Named To School Board

BY ELMER BERTELSEN
Chronicle Staff

Joe Kelly Butler, 48, an oil well drilling contractor, is a stop-gap member of the Houston school board.

He was appointed by a 4-2 vote Monday night to fill the vacancy created by the resignation of Mrs. Earl Maughmer, Jr.

Butler will serve until Dec. 31. He said he's undecided if he will seek the post in the Nov. 8 election for a four-year term.

The Chronicle said in last Sunday's editions that Butler was the likely board choice for the open seat.

Voting for Butler were board president Henry A. Petersen, Stone Wells, Mrs. H. W. Cullen and Mrs. Frank Dyer.

Mrs. Charles White and W. W. Kemmerer voted for Mrs. A. S. Vandervoort, Jr., a former board member.

Petersen Reluctant

Dr. Petersen was reluctant to Wells' suggestion that the board fill the vacancy of Mrs. Maughmer.

"I believe we ought not to appoint a replacement because I feel it would be wiser and fairer to all possible candidates to let the people pick a board member for the position at the Nov. 8 election," said Petersen. "Let us have an expression from the board on this."

Then the board voted 3-2 to fill the vacancy. Petersen abstained from voting. However, he later voted for Butler.

Mrs. White said she didn't think the board could legally

(See BOARD, Page 5)

IN TODAY'S CHRONICLE

	Sec.	Page
Amusements	4	5
Classified Ads	4	6-17
Comics	4	18, 19
Deaths	4	17
Editorials	1	14
Feature Page	1	15
G.I. Guide	1	11
Markets	2	2, 3
Oil News	2	4
Our City	1	15
Serial Story	4	4
Sports	4	1-4
Women's Section	3	1-3
Radio	1	13
Television	1	12

Recommended Reading

RELIGIOUS ISSUE—Democratic national chairman Henry M. Jackson urges Nixon to reject supporters like Dr. Norman Vincent Peale and his Protestant associates who oppose Kennedy on religious grounds. **Section 1, Page 7.**

SPRINGBOARD IN SPACE—United States scientists are hard at work planning a manned space station which will be the stepping-off place for the last leg of the 186,000-mile trip to the moon. **Section 1, Page 10.**

Sub Sighted Near Ship of Khrushchev

London—(UPI)—The British admiralty has disclosed that an unidentified submarine was sighted Monday "in the vicinity" of the Soviet ship Baltika, which is carrying Premier Nikita Khrushchev to New York and the United Nations general assembly.

The underwater craft was believed by some observers to be Russian.

As the first viable Roman Catholic presidential candidate, Kennedy told a group of ministers that "contrary to common newspaper usage, I am not the Catholic candidate for president. I am the Democratic Party's candidate for president who happens also to be a Catholic."

ALSO IN 1960

The Food and Drug Administration approved the sale of birth control pills, a precursor to the sexual revolution of the 1960s.

FIRST TELEVISED PRESIDENTIAL DEBATE HELD BETWEEN SENATOR JOHN KENNEDY AND VICE PRESIDENT RICHARD NIXON

THE CHRISTIAN SCIENCE MONITOR

AN INTERNATIONAL DAILY NEWSPAPER

VOLUME 52 NO. 257 — BOSTON, TUESDAY, SEPTEMBER 27, 1960 — ATLANTIC EDITION — SEVEN CENTS

Threat to UN Eases; Peking Casts Shadow

U.S. and U.A.R. Presidents Meet

Debate Winner? Voters of Nation

By Godfrey Sperling, Jr.
Chief of the Central News Bureau of The Christian Science Monitor

Chicago

The focal point of some 130,000,000 eyes, the presidential candidates squared off in the first of four unprecedented joint appearances before a vast TV audience.

The winner? The American public was the winner.

The silent Chicago streets, the cavernous ball park, the almost empty theaters. All this attested to the public's intense interest in the two candidates and a clash that centered on the farm, the aged, the schools, the economic growth rate, the lowering of the national debt, the relative maturity and experience of the two men. But the impact naturally spilled over into America's posture in the world today, and who was best qualified to provide leadership for the next four or eight years.

For reporters who have been following the candidates around the United States, there was little that was new in what the two men said. Senator John F. Kennedy, again, was saying that America's performance, vis-à-vis the Soviet Union, was not good enough. Vice-President Richard M. Nixon was saying it had, indeed, been good enough. And both were agreeing that there must be a step up for the future—militarily, scientifically, educationally, economically.

In the main, the verbal exchanges here showed that the objectives of the two candidates are quite similar. The difference lies in the means—and the cost of the means.

Mr. Nixon said, as he has said before, that he has tabulated the Democratic program and thinks it will cost $13,200,000,000 to perhaps $18,000,000,000 while, he said, his own program would cost some $4,000,000,000 to $4,900,000,000.

John F. Kennedy
Resolved . . .

Richard M. Nixon
Resolved . . .

Not One Slip On Banana Peel!

By Richard L. Strout
Staff Correspondent of The Christian Science Monitor

State of the Nations

Who Pays for Reform?

By William H. Stringer
Chief, Washington News Bureau, The Christian Science Monitor

MDC Probe Hears Political Echoes

By Albert D. Hughes

Goldfine Case To Open in Boston

The World's Day

Inside Reading

Just Before the Opening Gavel
Presidential candidates Nixon and Kennedy trade grins

September 27, 1960

About 70 million Americans watched the nation's first televised presidential debate and were struck by the visual contrast. Kennedy looked tan and relaxed; Vice President Richard Nixon, still recovering from a knee injury, refused makeup and appeared tired and nervous, with a five-o'clock shadow.

ALSO IN 1960

At the Summer Olympics, Cassius Clay, who later changed his name to Muhammad Ali, won the gold medal in boxing.

NOVEMBER 8, 1960
JOHN KENNEDY ELECTED THE 35TH U.S. PRESIDENT

WEATHER FORECAST
Bay Area: Fair today, except local morning fog or low clouds. Little change in temperature. Low, 40 to 50; Wednesday, 62 to 67.
Full Report, Page 16

San Francisco Chronicle
THE VOICE OF THE WEST

FINAL

94th YEAR No. 314 | CCCCAAABC | WEDNESDAY, NOVEMBER 9, 1960 | 10 CENTS | GArfield 1-1111

KENNEDY WINS

But His Margin Is Razor-Thin As Nixon Cuts Into Early Lead; Prop. 1 Trails--Prop. 15 Loses

Kennedy Keeps Thin State Lead

By Earl C. Behrens
Political Editor

Democratic presidential nominee John F. Kennedy early today clung to a narrow lead over Republican Vice President Richard M. Nixon in the contest for California's 32 electoral votes.

Vice President Nixon refused to concede the State to Senator Kennedy up to an early hour this morning. The Senator went to bed in his Massachusetts home without claiming a California victory.

Kennedy's supporters, however, held victory celebrations last night.

Returns from 16.250 out of 30,682 gave

Kennedy 1,467,934
Nixon 1,371,425.

Kennedy lead had dropped at one time this morning to less than 70,000 and then rose to nearly 90,000.

S. F. GOES DEMO

More than 50,000 of the Kennedy lead came from San Francisco. Many precincts in Los Angeles and a considerable number in San Diego county were yet to be

See Page D, Col. 5

Karesh Victory

United States Commissioner Joseph Karesh apparently won election to the Superior Court bench yesterday, defeating Municipal Judge Lenore Underwood.

Complete returns from the city's 1286 precincts gave 124,253 votes to 115,813 for Judge Underwood.

Although 18,371 absentee ballots were issued, their tally Monday was not expected to change the outcome.

THE PRESIDENT-ELECT OF THE UNITED STATES
A jubilant John Kennedy held daughter Caroline in his arms

Prop. 1 Falls Behind ---Prop. 15 Beaten

By [illegible]

A tide of "No" votes pushed California's mammoth water bond program out of an early lead today — but the final result may well hinge on the State's absentee ballots.

The referendum measure to reapportion the State Senate was defeated, however, and the lopsided margin of defeat was running heavier than two-to-one.

Proposition 1, to launch a $1.75 billion construction program for water projects, held a narrowing lead during last night's early counting, but dropped behind this morning after 13,165 of the State's 30,682 precincts had been tallied.

The early-morning count on Proposition 1:

Yes—751,502.
No—796,876.

But this abrupt change from the bond issue's earlier lead may have been partly a freak.

Los Angeles county, where the measure was running strong, stopped counting bal-

See Page 2, Col. 3

Mailliard, Shelley Romp To Victory

By Michael Harris

All 14 Northern California Congressmen appeared to have won reelection yesterday — though Representative Clem Miller (Dem-First District) led by only a shaky margin.

Changes in Southern

See Page 8, Col. 1

Democrats Keep Control Of Congress

WASHINGTON, Nov. 9 (Wednesday) (AP) — Democrats easily retained control of Congress in slowly mounting returns early today.

With 32 of the 34 Senate contests decided, the Democrats had won 20 seats to give them a total of 63. They needed 51 to keep the control they had since 1955.

Democratic leaders, claiming an early presidential victory for Senator John F. Kennedy, went ahead with plans to install Senator Mike Mansfield of Montana as the new Senate leader to succeed Lyndon B. Johnson, the Vice President-elect.

In the House, the Republicans made slight inroads into the big Democratic majority of the last session, but were unable to mount a serious

See Page 9, Col. 3

Presidential Race

Nixon Reduces Foe's Early Lead

WASHINGTON (Wednesday), Nov. 9 (AP)—Senator John F. Kennedy early today had the electoral votes necessary for election as the 35th President of the United States, but all was not absolutely certain.

At 2 a. m. (PST), the 43-year-old Massachusetts Senator had a popular vote margin over Republican Vice President Richard M. Nixon of less than 51 per cent.

And the fate of eight States — including the keys to victory or defeat, California (32 electoral votes), Illinois (27) and Minnesota (11) — remained in doubt. Kennedy led in these three States.

With 269 electoral votes needed for victory, Kennedy had definitely won 258. He had won or was leading in a total of 23 States with 331 electoral votes.

Nixon's Total 192

Nixon had taken or was ahead in 26 States with 192 votes.

Kennedy, although trailing in the total number of States in his column by 26-23, had piled up his margin in the populous industrial cities.

At 2:30 a.m. (PST), Kennedy's popular vote was 27,956,222. Nixon had 27,192,815.

Kennedy's percentage was 50.7; Nixon's 49.3.

The Massachusetts Senator went to bed without knowing whether he had actually been elected.

Nixon clutched at hopes that belated tallies in

See Page 1-B, Col. 4

THE INDEX

For complete election coverage, see Pages A, B, C, D and Pages 2 through 14 inside today's Chronicle.

Books	27	Dr. Molner	12	Movies	28-30
Boyd	36	Editorials	26	O'Flaherty	25
Bridge	31	Fashions	11, 12	Pearson	27
Brier	26	Hedda	29	Question Man	16
Caen	15	Hoppe	26	Rosenbaum	33
Chess	31	Jumble	21	Shipping	16
Comics	38	Leiser	34	Sports	33-37
Count Marco	13	Letters	26	TV, Radio	31
Crossword	23, 27	Lively Arts	27	Theaters	28-30
Dear Abby	27	McCabe	27	Want Ads	16
Deaths	16	Millie's Col.	10	Weather	16
Delaplane	25	Mellinkoff	26	Women	10-13

No financial section—Markets closed for election.

Election In Brief

PRESIDENT

Senator Kennedy held a close lead. The popular vote early today showed:

Kennedy 28,443,163
Nixon 27,696,452

Kennedy led in 23 States with 331 electoral votes. Nixon led in 26 States with 192. (A total of 269 is needed for election.)

PROPOSITION 1

Proposition 1, the $1.75 billion water bonds measure, was trailing according to returns from 13,165 of California's 30,682 precincts.

Yes 751,502
No 796,876

PROPOSITION 15

Proposition 15, the State reapportionment measure, was defeated, according to returns from 12,621 precincts.

Yes 393,006
No [illegible]

THE SENATE

Democrats, with 43 holdovers, had elected 20 Senators and were leading in one race.

Republicans, with 23 holdovers, had elected 12 and were leading in one race.

THE HOUSE

At an early hour this morning, with all 437 seats up for election:

Democrats had elected 206, and were leading in 44.

Republicans had elected 98, and were leading in 63.

GOVERNORS

In races for 27 governorships (now held by 14 Democrats and 13 Republicans):

Democrats had won 12 and were leading in 3.

Republicans had won 9 and were leading in 3.

Kennedy watched election returns at the family compound in Hyannis Port. Nixon watched election returns from his suite at the Ambassador Hotel in Los Angeles, where Robert Kennedy would be assassinated in 1968.

ALSO IN 1960

On October 26, John and Robert Kennedy helped secure the release of the Reverend Martin Luther King Jr. from jail after his arrest during an Atlanta sit-in.

JOHN KENNEDY ELECTED THE 35TH U.S. PRESIDENT

Chicago Daily Tribune

FINAL

KENNEDY WINS PRESIDENCY

Kerner and Douglas Easy Victors

VICTOR WAITS OUT RETURNS TO BE CERTAIN

'Jumps with Joy' Sister Says

New President Elect and Vice President

JOHN FITZGERALD KENNEDY

LYNDON BAINES JOHNSON

ILLINOIS FOR KENNEDY BY 85,000 VOTES

3 State Offices Still in Doubt

STATE WINNERS

Adamowski, Ward Are in a Tight Race

WIN IN COUNTY

NIXON SAYS HE CONCEDES POLL DEFEAT

G. O. P. Leads in States Won

Nixon Adds Votes; Says 'We're Dead'

ELECTION BULLETINS

N.Y. Swings to Kennedy in Big Vote

THE WEATHER

MORNING EDITION

The Boston Globe

President Elect KENNEDY

Bay State Splits for Jack, Salty, Volpe, McCormack

ELECTORAL COLLEGE

Texas Endorses Jack and Lyndon

Connecticut First To Go for Kennedy

Democratic Win Surprise in S.C. —First in South To Go for Jack

Mass. Loves Jack But Not His Slate

Democrats Sure Of Senate, House

GP's Gives Its Votes to Nixon

Kennedy Refuses to Claim Victory Despite Rising Lead

Democrats Still Control State Senate, House

VOTE OF STATE FOR PRESIDENT Estimated

Kennedy, D. . . . 1,431,960

Nixon, R. 971,515

Kennedy Wins N.Y. Cats G.O.P. Upstate

Jack on Top Here By Big 4-1 Margin

Auto Insurance Rates Due Today

NO SOAP!!!

Curtis Holds Onto His House Seat, Macdonald Ahead in 8th District

SUFFOLK DOWNS

At age 43, Kennedy became the youngest, and the first Roman Catholic, president of the United States. Kennedy's narrow victory spurred unproven allegations of vote fraud in Texas and Illinois, which joined countless other rumors and conspiracy theories that have fed Kennedy legends over the years.

LARGEST COMBINED DAILY CIRCULATION IN TEXAS

FORT WORTH STAR-TELEGRAM

MORNING

JACK, IKE PLAN PARLEY SOON

Negro Aide Appointed By Senator

Sentimental Gesture Finds Girl Alive

PRESIDENT-ELECT JOHN KENNEDY

This Is West Texas

North Wind Keeps Chill Over Texas

Jack, Nikita Requested To Confer

British Sure 'to Get Along' With Jack, to Miss Ike Ties

THE WEATHER

LATE RETURNS STILL SHOW RAZOR-THIN VOTE MARGIN

Voting Accusations Checked in Texas

NIXON COULD GET POPULAR LEAD

Absentee Vote Can't Change Result

INSIDE INDEX

ST. LOUIS POST-DISPATCH

FINAL

KENNEDY IS ELECTED PRESIDENT

DALTON AND LONG PACE MISSOURI SWEEP

KERNER AND DOUGLAS WIN IN ILLINOIS

DEMOCRATS WIN MAJOR RACES AS STATE LINES UP WITH KENNEDY

Less Than One Vote Per Precinct Puts Kennedy Over in Illinois

KENNEDY ASKS ALL TO HELP NATION 'SAFELY THROUGH' '60S

The President-Elect

MINNESOTA VOTE GIVES SENATOR VICTORY MARGIN

11 Electoral Votes From State Decide Issue—Impact of Democratic Candidate's Catholicism Felt in Many Areas of U.S.

REVENUE PLAN OK'D IN COUNTY; DEMOCRATS WIN

Election Results at a Glance

Start Every Day Right

The Hartford Courant

Weather Forecast
FAIR AND MILDER
Complete Weather, Tides On Page 2

ESTABLISHED 1764, VOL. (DAILY EDITION) CXXIII HARTFORD 1, CONN. SATURDAY MORNING, NOVEMBER 26, 1960—22 PAGES 7 CENTS

Congo Calls Truce With Rebel Katanga

Two Forces May Hold New Talks

Dramatic Turn Follows Meeting

SANTA TO GIVE FREE SLEIGH RIDES

News Briefs

Shoppers Pile into City To See Santa, Yule Lights

Death Pulse Slows; 260 Fall Victim

'LOOK DADDY, ONE HAND': Three-year-old Caroline chats with her father, President-elect John F. Kennedy, as they leave their Georgetown home Friday afternoon for a stroll. Early Friday morning, Kennedy's wife gave birth to a son, John F. Kennedy Jr., at Georgetown University Hospital (AP Wirephoto).

Beaming Kennedy Visits Wife, Tells Caroline of New Brother

Hogback Reservoir Full; New Dam Almost Done

Inside Story

City Man Sought As Impersonator In Gambling Raid

Death Sets Faster Pace On State Roads This Year

Wins Jobless Pay

Store Cashier Who Buys At Rival's Gets in Jam

Today's Index

In Tomorrow's Courant

B.S. or Mrs.?

Quiet, Please!

President-elect Kennedy was flying to Florida when the pilot received word that Jacqueline Kennedy had gone into early labor. Kennedy was headed back to Washington when he learned John F. Kennedy Jr. had been born, slightly underweight but healthy.

Jacqueline Kennedy and President-elect John F. Kennedy posed with his parents, Joseph and Rose Kennedy. (AP Photo)

ALSO IN 1960

The post–World War II baby boom brought the population of the United States to 179.3 million.

At the suggestion of his father, Joseph Kennedy, John F. Kennedy appointed his brother as attorney general. Robert Kennedy, 35, was the youngest member of the cabinet.

ALSO IN 1960

Soon after being discharged from the Army, Elvis Presley appeared on The Frank Sinatra Timex Special.

Kennedy Names Brother, Dillon to Cabinet

The Weather

Today—Mostly sunny, some midday clouds. High in lower 30s. Tonight—Clear and cold. Low near 20. Sunday—Fair and continued cold. Friday's temperatures: High, 42 at 1 p.m.; low, 29 at 8 p.m. Details are on Page B3.

The Washington Post FINAL

Times Herald

84th Year .... No. 12 Phone RE. 7-1234 Copyright, 1960, The Washington Post Co. SATURDAY, DECEMBER 17, 1960 WTOP Radio (1500) TV (Ch. 9) TEN CENTS

Airliner Collision Over N.Y. Kills 134; Boy, 11, Sole Survivor in Flaming Crash

Kennedy's Brother In Cabinet

Robert to Be Head At Justice, Dillon Treasury Chief

By Carroll Kilpatrick
Staff Reporter

President-elect Kennedy yesterday named his brother, Robert, to his Cabinet as Attorney General and picked Under Secretary of State Douglas Dillon, a Republican, as Secretary of the Treasury.

Dillon is the second Republican named to the Kennedy Cabinet, and Robert becomes the first brother of a Chief Executive ever to be appointed to so high an office. The selection of the latter is expected to stir political controversy.

Byron L. (Whizzer) White, a prominent Denver attorney,

Profiles on Day, Dillon and White. Page A11.
Naming of Robert Kennedy is most controversial appointment made by Administration-to-be. Page A13.

was named Deputy Attorney General.

J. Edward Day, Los Angeles insurance executive, who flew to Palm Beach, Fla., with the President-elect last night, is expected to be named Postmaster General today.

Elizabeth Canfield Smith, Democratic National Committeewoman from California, is in line to be named Treasurer of the United States, succeeding Ivy Baker Priest.

Anslinger to Stay On

Mr. Kennedy announced that Harry J. Anslinger, veteran Commissioner of Narcotics, would continue to serve in that post.

The President-elect acknowledged that he was making history in picking a member of his immediate family for the Cabinet, but he called Robert, who was 35 last month, quali-

See KENNEDY, A2, Col. 4

Week's Active Stocks

NEW YORK, Dec. 16 (AP)—Weekly sales, high, low, closing price and net change of the 20 most active stocks for the week. (Add 00 to sales):

[illegible]

Financial News and Tables Pages B6, 7

Wreckage of a United Air Lines jet lies in a residential block in Brooklyn, where it fell after a mid-air collision. United Press International

Seven on Ground Die As Jetliner Sets Afire Entire Brooklyn Block

NEW YORK, Dec. 16 (UPI) — A Jetliner and a Constellation collided over New York in a snowstorm and crashed in the city today in the worst disaster in aviation history.

At least 134 persons were killed in the crashes of a United Air Lines DC-8 jet and a Trans-World Airlines Super-Constellation.

Of the dead, 127 were aboard the planes and 7 were on the ground.

Ten persons in Brooklyn were injured.

It was the first U.S. jet airline crash involving passengers.

One of the planes set afire an entire block in Brooklyn and the other crumpled into pieces over Staten Island and fell in flames.

A high police official said only three of the jet aircraft's four engines were found in the wreckage in Brooklyn. The fourth was found in the wreckage of the Constellation on Staten Island, 12 miles away, along with the Constellation's four piston engines.

Only one passenger survived the crash. He was 11-year-old Stephen Baltz of Wilmette, Ill., son of W. S. Baltz, vice president and general counsel of the Admiral Corp. The youngster was dragged from the jet wreckage in Brooklyn and taken to a hospital in critical condition.

The worst previous airplane crash was that of an Air Force C-124 Globemaster near Tokyo, June 18, 1953, killing 129 persons. The worst previous commercial air disaster was the collision of a United and a

Pictures and map on Page A9
Shocked eyewitnesses recall scene of horror. Page A8.
Passenger lists and crew members' names. Page A8.

TWA plane over the Grand Canyon June 30, 1956, killing 128.

The tragedy set off an immediate massive investigation spearheaded by Elwood R. Quesada, head of the Federal Aviation Agency, who flew here to take personal command.

Quesada said the jet had been in the Preston, N. J., holding pattern, 25 to 30 miles from Idlewild Airport, flying at 5000 feet. The Constellation had been in the Linden, N. J., holding pattern, 20 to 25 miles from La Guardia Airport, flying at 6000 feet.

The TWA plane was in the process of being cleared for an approach to La Guardia and was being tracked on the radarscope, Quesada said. He said investigation had failed to show that the jet had yet been given clearance to fly into Idlewild.

[Police fixed the collision spot above the Narrows, the heavily traveled steamship lane between Brooklyn and Staten

See PLANES, A8, Col. 2

Crowds Hail Selassie on Return Home

By Franca di Sastri
Reuters

ASMARA, Ethiopia, Dec. 16 Emperor Haile Selassie returned here tonight as reports from the Ethiopian capital of Addis Ababa said loyalist troops had crushed a revolt against his regime.

Reports reaching this provincial capital near the Red Sea coast some 450 miles north of Addis Ababa said the leaders of the attempted coup against the Emperor either had been arrested or were in flight.

There was no immediate mention in the reports from the capital on the whereabouts

See ETHIOPIA, A6, Col. 5

Today's Index

52 PAGES—3 SECTIONS
A—24 Pages—News, Church, Sports, Real Estate
B—8 Pages—City Life Obituaries, Women's Financial
C—20 Pages—Classified, TV-Radio, Comics

	Page		Page
Amus'ts	C14	Keep Well	C18
Church	A14-16	Kilgallen	C14
City Life	B1-2	Movie Guide	A8
Classified	C1-12	Music	C14
Comics	C15-19	Obituaries	B3
Crossword	C19	Pearson	C19
Dist. Line	C18	R' Estate	A22-23
Editorials	A12	Sokolsky	A13
Events T'day	C13	Sports	A17-21
Financial	B6-7	TV-Radio	C9
Gardens	B7	Weather	B3
Goren	C15	Women's	B4-5
Horoscope	C16		

Second class postage paid at Washington, D. C. Printed at 1515 L St. N.W., Washington, D. C.

'Tremendous' Barrier Cracked

UGF Drive Exceeds $7 Million Mark For 1st Time but Is Still Short of Goal

By Rasa Gustaitis
Staff Reporter

For the first time in its history, the United Givers Fund passed the seven-million-dollar mark in this year's drive, it was announced yesterday.

Although this still leaves total contributions below the 7.2-million-dollar campaign goal, Daniel W. Bell, general chairman of the 1960 campaign, said "a tremendous psychological barrier" had been cracked.

Like the 4-minute mile, he told the organization's annual meeting, the seven-million-dollar goal will no longer seem impossible after it is proven that it can be attained.

John B. Duncan, District government unit chairman, pushed the total above the mark when he announced that UGF can expect "an additional minimum of $15,000" from his unit, bringing contributions to $7,004,640.

Charles E. Phillips, president of UGF and of Equitable Life Insurance Co., told the members that "the corporation is in excellent shape indeed as the result of the outstanding job done by Dan Bell and the members of his team."

At the annual election, Phillips was renamed president, to serve with the others for a 1-year term. Others reelected were:

John T. Barnett, general manager of Sears Roebuck & Co., senior vice president; Morris Cafritz, president of Cafritz Co., John S. Hayes, president of The Washington Post Broadcast Division, Roger W. Jones, chairman of U. S. Civil Service Commission, and Channing S. Walker, president of George E. Walker, Inc., vice presidents; and John B. Duncan, D. C. Recorder of Deeds, secretary. Douglas R. Smith, president of National Savings and Trust Co., was elected treasurer, replacing the late Bruce Baird.

New Premier Seeks Aid for City

Pro-Western Rebels Clear Vientiane Of Leftist Troops After 4-Day Battle

By Bruce Russell
Reuters

VIENTIANE, Dec. 16—Right-wing rebel leaders Prince Boun Oum and Gen. Phoumi Nosavan entered shattered Vientiane at dusk today and announced its "liberation" from leftist troops.

As the pair drove into this Laotian administrative capital, tanks of their pro-American force were clearing the stubborn remnants of paratroop Capt. Kong Le's leftist troops and pro-Communist Pathet Lao guerillas from their last positions at vital Vientaine airport.

One unofficial report indicated that Kong Le's red-armbanded troops, under attack by Phoumi's white-armbanded men since the battle for Vientiane began Tuesday, were retreating with their heavy artillery supplied by Russia along a road leading north toward the royal capital of Luang Prabang, now held by the rightists.

Boun, Premier of the new rebel Government set up this week, was expected to start trying to restore order here after the retreat by the "red" forces.

[In Washington, the State Department reported that the new rightist Government has appealed to the United States for aid for Vientiane citizens, United Press International reported.

[Prince Boun Oum sent a letter to U. S. Ambassador Winthrop Brown asking for help, "particularly aid for the people of Vientiane, who have suffered greatly because of the Pathet Lao's action." He claimed that major damage to the city had been done by the Communist forces "using artillery airlifted in by the Soviets."]

The capture of the airport was rated highly important by military observers. They said bridges were down between Phoumi's Vientiane forces and his main strong

See LAOS, A5, Col. 1

January 20, 1961
John Kennedy Inaugurated as President

MORNING EDITION

The Boston Globe

TURNIN' BLUE
SATURDAY — Fair, high in mid-teens.
SUNDAY — Sunny, not QUITE so cold.
Full report on Page 2

Vol. CLXXIX No. 21 · © 1961 By Globe Newspaper Co. · BOSTON, SATURDAY, JAN. 21, 1961 · Telephone AV 8-8000 · 22 PAGES—EIGHT CENTS

'Let Us Never Negotiate out of Fear... but Never Fear to Negotiate'

Kennedy Offers World New Start for Peace

(UPI Telephoto)
BEAMING AT HIS SUCCESSOR, outgoing President Eisenhower leaves White House with John F. Kennedy for the swearing-in ceremonies.

Vow to New Nations: Won't Allow Tyranny

Other Inaugural Stories, Pictures on Pages 4, 5, 12, 15 and 22.

By JOHN HARRIS
(Globe Political Editor)

WASHINGTON, Jan. 20—President John F. Kennedy started off his administration with high hopes today, acclaimed by the nation and the entire globe for his inaugural appeal that both sides in the Cold War "begin anew the quest for peace."

Bareheaded despite the 22-degree temperature and icy wind that cut into the shivering throng in Capitol Plaza, the new 43-year-old leader of the free world made peace the rallying cry for the 1960's and the new generation, in his singularly brief, 15-minute speech, which was carried electronically all over the earth.

"To those nations who would make themselves our adversary," declared Mr. Kennedy, his face as solemn as his message, "we offer not a pledge, but a request:

"That both sides begin anew the quest for peace, before the dark powers of destruction unleashed by science engulf all humanity in planned or accidental self-destruction."

INAUGURAL
Page Four

(UPI Telephoto)
PRESIDENT KENNEDY DELIVERS inaugural address. Seated near each other are Mrs. Jacqueline Kennedy and former President Eisenhower.

15 Die, 300 Flee Flood Tides As Blizzard Pounds at N.E.

By EDWARD G. McGRATH

The Inauguration Day blizzard of 1961 howled its way into the history books yesterday by heaping misery on the highways, pounding and flooding coastal homes of New England and plunging the area into an Arctic deep freeze.

Fifteen persons, eight of them from Massachusetts, died in the bitter storm which para in the bitter storm which paralyzed transportation with 12-foot drifts, battered the shore with 35-foot waves and dumped two feet of snow in Western Massachusetts.

It was a blizzard of many contradictions.

City and M.T.A. officials were enthused because Boston generally kept its traffic moving.

But coastal homeowners were stunned by the vicious assault of flood tides which heavily damaged property, disintegrated sea walls and forced the evacuation of more than 300 residents.

Hardest hit was Hull, where at 1:50 yesterday afternoon 250 residents fled their homes on foot and in boats. Civil Defense amphibious ducks and school buses. Heavy seas, pushed by 50-knot winds, flooded the peninsula's lowlands.

Boston measured an official near-record 12.2 inches of snow before the storm tapered off in late afternoon and some of the coldest air of the Winter invaded New England.

Last night, while the six-state area continued the battle to reactivate transportation, temperatures were skidding rapidly to zero on the coast, 10 below in southern interior areas and 15 below in many sections to the north.

STORM
Page Two

STORM PHOTOS, PAGE 7

K Cables Hope For New Peace Under Kennedy

LONDON, Jan. 20 (Reuters)—Russian Premier Nikita Khrushchev and President Leonir Brezhnev today cabled President Kennedy an inauguration day message extending the hope for a "radical improvement" in Soviet-American relations.

They hoped, the Soviet news agency Tass reported, that joint efforts of the United States and Russia would improve relations and therefore "make healthier the entire international climate."

KHRUSHCHEV
Page Twelve

No Mere Snowstorm Curbs Kennedy Magic

By WILFRID C. RODGERS
(Globe Staff Correspondent)

WASHINGTON, Jan. 20—President John Fitzgerald Kennedy sneaked through to another victory today—over a potent snowstorm and other assorted inauguration snags. . . . The 35th President of the United States faced it unflinching.

Other New Englanders weren't so brave. Still chilled from a snow bath the night before, they ran for cover. They found it in hotel lobbies, hotel rooms and in front of TV sets.

WASHINGTON
Page Twelve

Today's Quotes

President Kennedy in his inaugural address—"Let every nation know, whether it wishes us well or ill, that we shall pay any price, bear any burden, meet any hardship, support any friend, oppose any foe to assure the survival and success of liberty."

Dwight D. Eisenhower on how it feels to become a private citizen—"Wonderful, wonderful, fine."

(United Press International)

(AP Wirephoto)
TOO MUCH SUN—Poet Robert Frost, 85, has trouble reading inaugural poem's dedication, even with help of shading hat.

Frost's Eyes Fail Him . . . But His Heart Pinch-Hits

The text of Robert Frost's dedication, which the aging poet was unable to read is on page 4.

By ROBERT L. HEALY
(Globe Washington Correspondent)

WASHINGTON, Jan. 20—The huge crowd on the Capitol grounds had forgot—for the moment—John Fitzgerald Kennedy.

The spectators weren't thinking about Richard M. Nixon and his defeat. They didn't even know—at that one awesome moment—that Dwight D. Eisenhower was on the platform.

Every eye—every hope—and every prayer was centered on one man — white-haired, aged, and bent.

Robert Frost — the nation's most outstanding poet — man whose words may well outlive any deed of many Presidents — was groping, stumbling over words, and hurting inside.

FROST
Page Four

Me Too, Says Fidel; 'Invasion' Alert Off

HAVANA, Jan. 20 (AP)—Prime Minister Fidel Castro tonight called off Cuba's three-week military alert against a "Yankee invasion" that never came and offered to "begin anew" a quest for peace with the administration of President Kennedy.

Castro told a rally of demobilized militiamen at the Presidential Palace that his government noted "with pleasure some positive aspects" of President Kennedy's inaugural address and he promised "no gratuitous attacks and no gratuitous hostile acts" against the United States.

CASTRO
Page Twenty-two

Tax Official's Suicide Note Hints 'Politics'

Acting State Police Capt Michael J. Cullinane said last night he was told that one of two alleged suicide notes left by a Massachusetts Tax Department official in Florida had "political implications."

Cullinane said he was told by Monroe County, Fla., officers that they were seeking authorization to divulge the contents of both notes to Massachusetts authorities.

They were allegedly left by Albert H. Stitt, 48, of Chestnut st., Waban, deputy director of the Tax Department's Alcoholic Excise Division, found dead in his car of carbon monoxide poisoning in Key Largo, Fla., Thursday night.

TAX OFFICIAL
Page Three

Fr. Lally Stands Behind Logue In Row on Staff Reorganization

By ROBERT B. HANRON

Rt. Rev. Francis J. Lally last night took issue with two colleagues on the Boston Redevelopment Authority and came out in full support of Edward J. Logue for the post of development administrator.

The time has come, he said, for the Authority to make up its mind.

"The decision is either in favor of progress or against it," he declared, "and either Boston goes forward with Mr. Logue or remains in a second-class status in the urban renewal effort."

Msgr. Lally, vice-chairman of the Authority and editor of The Pilot, official publication of the Catholic Archdiocese, said that his position, as well as that of Chairman Joseph W. Lund, is well known.

Earlier this week, two other members, James G. Colbert and Stephen J. McCloskey, expressed the opinion that the staff reorganization proposed by Logue is "illegal" and that they could not adopt it in its present form.

RENEWAL ROW
Page Three

GUIDE TO FEATURES

Bridge	17	Financial	10, 11
Churches	8, 9	Obituaries	18
Classified	18-21	Radio-TV	17
Comics	16, 17	Shain	22
Cross-Word	17	Sports	13, 14
Deaths	18	Star Gazer	17
Dr. Crane	17	Theaters	8
Drummond	6	Twistagram	22
Editorials	6	Women	16

Kennedys Open Social Whirl

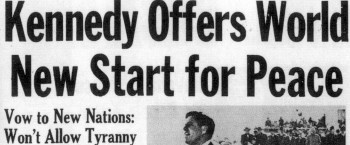

(AP Wirephoto)
HERE'S THAT EVENING DRESS—President and Mrs. John F. Kennedy leave White House for inaugural ball. She's shown for first time in her specially-designed white sheath with puffy overblouse.

Inaugural Dances Cap President's First Day

By FRANCES BURNS
(Globe Staff Correspondent)

President and Mrs. Kennedy entered the Washington social whirl as the nation's first couple tonight by attending five festive inaugural balls.

An evening of champagne, cake and compositions capped the social salute to the new occupants of the White House.

The champagne flowed into glasses held by hundreds of Democrats who gathered in hotels and the local armory. The toasts to Kennedy, Vice President Johnson and their ladies started in the Mayflower Hotel.

John and Jacqueline Kennedy departed from the White House at 9:50 p.m. Mrs. Kennedy wore a white silk sheath by Oleg Cassini, a sheer chiffon lace overblouse, and long white elbow-length gloves.

BALL
Page Twelve

On a bitterly cold Washington, D.C., morning, thousands gathered on the East Front of the U.S. Capitol to watch the swearing-in of the young president. Robert Frost was the first poet to read at a presidential inauguration.

ALSO IN 1961

Five days after taking office, Kennedy held the first live, televised presidential press conference.

January 20, 1961
John Kennedy Inaugurated as President

Kennedy took the oath of office at 12:51 p.m. and delivered the speech that defined his administration, including the line, "Let the word go forth from this time and place, to friend and foe alike, that the torch has been passed to a new generation of Americans."

QUOTED

"Ask not what your country can do for you, ask what you can do for your country."

—President John F. Kennedy, *January 20, 1961*

Pictorial Section B, Other Inaugural Stories, Pictures Pages A2—A8

The Weather

Today—Cloudy and cold. Chance of light snow. High near 25 degrees. Tonight—Fair and cold. Low about 10 degrees. Friday's temperatures: High, 26 degrees at 5 p.m.; low, 20 degrees at 7 a.m. Complete details, Page C4.

The Washington Post

Times Herald

TV Channels

Get this colorful, handy, new booklet size rotogravure TV Magazine preferred by more Washingtonians every Sunday in The Washington Post.

84th Year .. No. 47 Phone RE. 7-1234 Copyright, 1961, The Washington Post Co. SATURDAY, JANUARY 21, 1961 WTOP Radio (1500) TV (Ch. 9) TEN CENTS

Kennedy Takes Oath as President, Proclaims a New 'Quest for Peace'

More Snow Threatens D. C. Area

New Storm Moving In From Midwest To Arrive Today

By Jack Eisen

A second storm that threatens to add a new veneer of snow moved toward the Nation's Capital last night in the wake of a howling blizzard that tied much of the Eastern seaboard in knots.

The new disturbance was sweeping in from the Middle West as the earlier storm, which dropped eight inches of snow here on Inauguration Eve, moved out to sea off New England.

The Weather Bureau forecast that the new storm's center would reach the Virginia capes this afternoon and that "a belt of light snow" would fall to the north of its path.

City's main streets clear; driving elsewhere hazardous; reasons for Thursday traffic snarl; snow shovelers warned to go easy. Page C1.

Mrs. Kennedy's ambulance scores a near-miss. Page C1.

While cities to the north of Washington were digging out of a highway-choking snowfall that ranged up to 29 inches, the Capital made a quick recovery from the traffic nightmare that befell it Thursday night.

Parade Route Cleared

Almost miraculously, it seemed, major streets were fully opened for Inaugural traffic, and the so-called "longest mile in the land"—Pennsylvania ave. from the Capitol to the White House—was cleared for the big parade.

The only activity here that rivaled the Inauguration was the search by owners of thousands of stalled cars they abandoned the night before. Many had been towed away.

The effects of the storm to the north complicated efforts by thousands of Inaugural visitors to get back home. In parts of New England, turnpikes were closed and traffic was at a standstill. Airports were shut down.

Middletown, N. Y., reported a 29-inch fall. New York City schools were closed, and cutting winds whipped the 10-inch snowfall into man-high drifts compounding the woes of a city already snarled by a railroad strike.

Foot in Philadelphia

Philadelphia was blanketed by a foot. Harrisburg, Pa., was buried under 20 inches, the heaviest snowfall in 15 years, but that didn't prevent a special Inaugural train from leaving a mere 30 minutes behind schedule.

Washington's history-making, temper-fraying traffic jam on inaugural eve was largely the product of temperature.

See SNOW, A8, Col. 2

Week's Active Stocks

NEW YORK, Jan. 20 (AP)—Weekly sales, high, low closing price and net change of the 20 most active stocks for the week (add 00 to sales):

Nat Theatre	281.0	[illegible]	[illegible]	[illegible]	[illegible]
Gen Electric	274.9	[illegible]	[illegible]	[illegible]	[illegible]
Sperry Rand	236.1	[illegible]	[illegible]	[illegible]	[illegible]
Stude Pack	217.9	[illegible]	[illegible]	[illegible]	[illegible]
Std Oil NJ	213.8	[illegible]	[illegible]	[illegible]	[illegible]
Fairb Whit	207.5	[illegible]	[illegible]	[illegible]	[illegible]
Balt & Ohio	203.4	[illegible]	[illegible]	[illegible]	[illegible]
Am Motors	188.7	[illegible]	[illegible]	[illegible]	[illegible]
Brunswick	179.1	[illegible]	[illegible]	[illegible]	[illegible]
Ling Temco	176.4	[illegible]	[illegible]	[illegible]	[illegible]
Amer Carp	174.3	[illegible]	[illegible]	[illegible]	[illegible]
Balt & Oh [illegible]	163.7	[illegible]	[illegible]	[illegible]	[illegible]
Westingh El	163.5	[illegible]	[illegible]	[illegible]	[illegible]
Raymond Int	161.8	[illegible]	[illegible]	[illegible]	[illegible]
Un'y Oil Pd	157.8	[illegible]	[illegible]	[illegible]	[illegible]
Unit Fruit	138.3	[illegible]	[illegible]	[illegible]	[illegible]
Gen Motors	130.4	[illegible]	[illegible]	[illegible]	[illegible]
Alumin Ltd	129.4	[illegible]	[illegible]	[illegible]	[illegible]
Beth Steel	119.5	[illegible]	[illegible]	[illegible]	[illegible]
Gen Tel & Tel	119	[illegible]	[illegible]	[illegible]	[illegible]

(*Financial news and tables, Pages A18, 19.*)

By Joe Heiberger, Staff Photographer

Chief Justice Earl Warren administers the oath of office to President Kennedy. Holding the Bible between them is James R. Browning, clerk of the Supreme Court. Mrs. Kennedy, in light coat, and President Eisenhower stand at left. Vice President Lyndon B. Johnson and his predecessor, Richard M. Nixon, stand at right. Former President Harry S. Truman is second from right in the first row.

1 Million Brave Weather To Cheer New President

By Harry Gabbett
Staff Reporter

Hundreds of thousands of enthusiastic well-wishers braved numbing cold and biting winds yesterday to cheer President John F. Kennedy along his Inaugural parade route to the White House.

Officials called the 4-hour parade spectacle a heart-warming tribute to the determination of both the marchers and their watchers—and the hordes of civilian and military

See PARADE, A20, Col. 1

Inaugural Stories On Inside Pages

Senate to act on Cabinet today. Page A2.

Lectern fire adds excitement. Page A3.

Inaugural address gets lavish praise. Page A4.

Ike arrives in Gettysburg. Page A5.

President gets early start on big day. Page A6.

Editorial comment generally favorable. Page A7.

Kennedy Vows to Keep Freedom at 'Any Price'

By Robert C. Albright
Staff Reporter

President Kennedy took office yesterday with a Spartan pledge that Americans will "pay any price, bear any burden" for freedom. But he also softly invited the Communists to "begin anew the quest for peace."

In words of one or two syllables, almost Biblical in their simplicity, he told the quiet people on the snow-frosted Capitol plaza, and the world that listened beyond, that the

See ADDRESS, A3, Col. 1

Eloquence, Pageantry Launch 'New Frontier' In Sunny Wake of Storm

John Fitzgerald Kennedy was inaugurated 35th President of the United States yesterday as the sun glorified Capitol Hill in the happy aftermath of a crippling snow storm.

In his Inaugural address, surely one of the most eloquent in history, the new American leader called on the Communist world to join with the Free World and "begin anew the quest for peace."

He said a live-and-let-live arrangement might not come in his generation's lifetime, and added simply:

"But let us begin."

Leaving the Capitol, President Kennedy and his wife, Jacqueline, travelled westward to the White House in the vanguard of a late-starting Inaugural parade, to the ecstatic cheers of onlookers estimated at a million by Police Chief Robert Murray.

Last night the Chief Executive and the First Lady dashed around the city to a five-site Inaugural ball and it was expected to be well past midnight before they turned in for their first night's sleep in the White House.

The official temperature was 22 degrees, 10 below freezing, as the great drama of the Inauguration began. A sharp 18-mile wind was blowing from the northwest. But the sun, flooding down from a cloudless sky, took some of the bite out of the cold, and gave a radiance to the freshly scrubbed Capitol and to the flags whipping the white marble portico.

Precedents Fall

It was 12:51 p. m. when President-elect Kennedy, great-grandson of Irish immigrants, began repeating the oath of office after Chief Justice Earl Warren. When he uttered the final words, "So help me God," some fascinating precedents tumbled into the history books.

He was the first Roman Catholic and the first man born in the twentieth century to become President of the United States, and at 43 the youngest man ever elected to the great office.

He became the first President since Andrew Johnson with a background of previous service in both the Senate and the House.

And he became the second man in American history to move into the White House while both of his parents were living. The first was Ulysses S. Grant.

Added to all these extraordinary circumstances was the fact that President Kennedy took over the burden from a man who at 70 was the oldest Chief Executive in American history.

Attends Mass

President Kennedy began his fateful day at 8 a. m., although he had been up late the night before. He had a breakfast of orange juice, poached eggs on toast with bacon, and coffee with cream and sugar.

There were 7.7 inches of snow on the ground as he left his Georgetown home at 8:55 a. m. to attend Mass at Holy Trinity Church.

President Eisenhower had telephoned his successor the

See KENNEDY, A6, Col. 6

Transition Snagged By Old Rubber Stamp

Somebody at the White House apparently failed to get the word: the name of the President, as of mid-day yesterday, was John F. Kennedy.

Right after the oath taking ceremony, President Kennedy signed two documents of nomination: one contained the names of his 10 Cabinet officers, the other was for the Ambassador to the U. N., Adlai E. Stevenson.

When the originals plus the usual four or five copies reached the Senate, however, the copies all bore the White House rubber stamp signature "Dwight D. Eisenhower." Discreetly, a Senate clerk struck out "Dwight D. Eisenhower" and put in "John F. Kennedy."

Text of President Kennedy's Inaugural Address

Here is the text of President Kennedy's Inaugural address:

VICE PRESIDENT JOHNSON, Mr. Chief Justice, President Eisenhower, Vice President Nixon, President Truman, reverend clergy, fellow citizens:

We observe today not a victory of a party but a celebration of freedom—symbolizing an end as well as a beginning—signifying renewal as well as change. For I have sworn before you and Almighty God the same solemn oath our forebears prescribed nearly a century and three quarters ago.

The world is very different now. For man holds in his mortal hands the power to abolish all forms of human poverty and all forms of human life. And yet the same revolutionary beliefs for which our forebears fought are still at issue around the globe—the belief that the rights of man come not from the generosity of the state but from the hand of God.

We dare not forget today that we are the heirs of that first revolution. Let the word go forth from this time and place, to friend and foe alike, that the torch has been passed to a new generation of Americans—born in this century, tempered by war, disciplined by a hard and bitter peace, proud of our ancient heritage—and unwilling to witness or permit the slow undoing of those human rights to which this Nation has always been committed, and to which we are committed today at home and around the world.

LET EVERY NATION KNOW, whether it wishes us well or ill, that we shall pay any price, bear any burden, meet any hardship, support any friend, oppose any foe to assure the survival and success of liberty.

This much we pledge—and more.

To those old allies whose cultural and spiritual origins we share, we pledge the loyalty of faithful friends. United, there is little we cannot do in a host of cooperative ventures. Divided, there is little we can do—for we dare not meet a powerful challenge at odds and split asunder.

To those new states whom we welcome to the ranks of the free, we pledge our word that one form of colonial control shall not have passed away merely to be replaced by a far more iron tyranny. We shall not always expect to find them supporting our view. But we shall always hope to find them strongly supporting their own freedom—and to remember that, in the past, those who foolishly sought power by riding the back of the tiger ended up inside.

To those people in the huts and villages of half the globe struggling to break the bonds of mass misery, we pledge our best efforts to help them help themselves, for whatever period is required—not because the Communists may be doing it, not because we seek their votes, but because it is right. If a free society cannot help the many who are poor, it cannot save the few who are rich.

TO OUR SISTER republics south of our border, we offer a special pledge—to convert our good words into good deeds—in a new alliance for progress—to assist free men and free governments in casting off the chains of poverty. But this peaceful revolution of hope cannot become the prey of hostile powers. Let all our neighbors know that we shall join with them to oppose aggression or subversion anywhere in the Americas. And let every other power know that this hemisphere intends to remain the master of its own house.

To that world assembly of sovereign states, the United Nations, our last best hope in an age where the instruments of war have far outpaced the instruments of peace, we renew our pledge of support—to prevent it from becoming merely a forum for invective—to strengthen its shield of the new and the weak—and to enlarge the area in which its writ may run.

Finally, to those nations who would make themselves our adversary, we offer not a pledge but a request: that both sides begin anew the quest for peace, before the dark powers of destruction unleashed by science engulf all humanity in planned or accidental self-destruction.

We dare not tempt them with weakness. For only when our arms are sufficient beyond doubt can we be certain beyond doubt that they will never be employed.

But neither can two great and powerful groups of nations take comfort from our present course—both sides overburdened by the cost of modern weapons, both rightly alarmed by the steady spread of the deadly atom, yet both racing to alter that uncertain balance of terror that stays the hand of mankind's final war.

SO LET US BEGIN ANEW—remembering on both sides that civility is not a sign of weakness, and sincerity is always subject to proof. Let us never negotiate out of fear. But let us never fear to negotiate.

Let both sides explore what problems unite us instead of belaboring those problems which divide us. Let both sides, for the first time, formulate serious and precise proposals for the inspection and control of arms—and bring the absolute power to destroy other nations under the absolute control of all nations.

Let both sides seek to invoke the wonders of science instead of its terrors. Together let us explore the stars, conquer the deserts, eradicate disease, tap the ocean depths and encourage the arts and commerce.

Let both sides unite to heed in all corners of the earth the command of Isaiah—to "undo the heavy burdens . . . (and) let the oppressed go free."

And if a beach-head of cooperation may push back the jungle of suspicion, let both sides join in a new endeavor: creating, not a new balance of power, but a new world of law, where the strong are just and the weak secure and the peace preserved.

ALL THIS WILL not be finished in the first one hundred days. Nor will it be finished in the first one thousand days, nor in the life of this Administration, nor even perhaps in our lifetime on this planet. But let us begin.

In your hands, my fellow citizens, more than mine, will rest the final success or failure of our course. Since this country was founded, each generation of Americans has been summoned to give testimony to its national loyalty. The graves of young Americans who answered the call to service surround the globe.

Now the trumpet summons us again—not as a call to bear arms, though arms we need—not as a call to battle, though embattled we are—but a call to bear the burden of a long twilight struggle, year in and year out, "rejoicing in hope, patient in tribulation"—a struggle against the common enemies of man: tyranny, poverty, disease and war itself.

Can we forge against these enemies a grand and global alliance, North and South, East and West, that can assure a more fruitful life for all mankind? Will you join in that historic effort?

IN THE LONG HISTORY of the world, only a few generations have been granted the role of defending freedom in its hour of maximum danger. I do not shrink from this responsibility—I welcome it. I do not believe that any of us would exchange places with any other people or any other generation. The energy, the faith, the devotion which we bring to this endeavor will light our country and all who serve it—and the glow from that fire can truly light the world.

And so, my fellow Americans: Ask not what your country can do for you—ask what you can do for your country.

My fellow citizens of the world: Ask not what America will do for you, but what together we can do for the freedom of man.

Finally, whether you are citizens of America or citizens of the world, ask of us here the same high standards of strength and sacrifice which we ask of you. With a good conscience our only sure reward, with history the final judge of our deeds, let us go forth to lead the land we love, asking His blessing and His help, but knowing that here on earth God's work must truly be our own.

Today's Index

72 PAGES—4 SECTIONS

A—20 Pages—General News, Sports
B—16 Pages—Inaugural Pictures, Women's, Churches
C—20 Pages—City Life, Classified
D—16 Pages—Real Estate, Comics

	Page		Page
Amus'ts	C19	Herblock	A12
Childs	A12	Horoscope	D13
Churches	B13-15	Keep Well	D12
City Life	C1-3	Kilgallen	C19
Classified	C5-14	Movie Guide	D14
Comics	D11-15	Obituaries	C4
Crossword	D15	Pearson	D15
District Line	D14	Picture Sec.	B1-8
Editorials	A12	R. Estate	D1-10
Events T'day	C18	Sports	A14-17
Federal Diary	C1	Sokolsky	A13
Financial	A18-19	TV-Radio	C18
Gallup	A2	Weather	C4
Goren	D11	Women's	B9-13

Second class postage paid at Washington, D. C. Printed at 1515 L St. N.W., Washington, D. C.

St. Petersburg Times Editorials

"The policy of our paper is very simple — merely to tell the truth"
—Paul Poynter publisher, 1912-1950

Editorial Page 14-A · Phone 5-1111 · Friday, March 3, 1961

Need More Time, Better Package

The needs of St. Petersburg after two decades or more of drift and indecision, are obvious, pressing and staggering. A start must be made to erase the deficits in streets, lighting, drainage and in recreational opportunities, and should be made as soon as possible.

Few would argue against this.

Still, a majority of City Council has acted wisely in deciding that the proposed $26 million bond issue should be postponed and restudied; perhaps repackaged. And means other than the whopping five mill tax increase the whole issue would call for should be exhaustively explored.

HERE ARE SOME of the reasons, despite the unquestioned need of most of the things listed in the package, postponement and further study are wise:

✓ Even if the entire issue had an even chance of being approved—which it would not have, in our estimation—there is no time before the May 16 municipal election to explain it to the public. A campaign to convince the freeholders would take months and a prodigious effort.

✓ Should the package as a whole, or a take-your-choice proposition, be offered without a foundation having been erected, and should all or any part be rejected, it would be a long time before there would be any kind of chance to pass an issue, regardless of merit. A bond issue for some specific project? someone might ask a year or two years hence. Why, the public voted that down in 1961! would be the response.

✓ All other conditions being favorable, the wisdom of holding a referendum in connection with the municipal elections is questionable. The decisions should be made on the basis of what we need and can afford, not in relation to what one candidate might favor and another oppose.

✓ The sum of $26 million for the whole project package, even if broken into selective components for a choice, is staggering and the prospect of a five mill tax increase, to many persons on fixed income, chilling.

✓ The disposition of the $2 million earmarked from the tobacco tax revenue issue for building a Negro wing at Mound Park Hospital is yet to be decided. With Mound Park now integrated, will this be diverted to other uses? Could it be the "nest egg" or activating sum to get things started, while the $26 million in projects are repackaged and spread over a longer length of time, with several bond issues at intervals?

✓ Has City Council actually made a firm policy decision on assessment of drainage costs against the property that is improved by drainage? If not, isn't talk of $8 million for this premature?

✓ And finally, although we should not wait for the two years or more to elapse before the returns are in, what effect will the proposed revaluation of all property for tax purposes have on municipal revenue? Would we need $26 million, or any considerable part of this, if revenue were to increase? And would it be advisable to now increase taxes by five mills, or any considerable part of this, on property which might be assessed at an even higher rate two or three years hence?

THE MOOD OF St. Petersburg presently is something like that of a runner on the starting line, all set and keen to get something started, to fill in the gaps that have accumulated, and to make our city the gracious and beautiful one it should be for our residents and our visitors.

Thus, it took considerable courage for the majority of Council to advise a delay of the issue, we are sure. No one wants to be against progress. Even bona fide "aginners" don't relish the title. But there are right ways and wrong ways to get things done, and the admonition that first things should be done first is still valid. For the foregoing reasons, we feel they have acted wisely, as well as courageously.

New Decoration

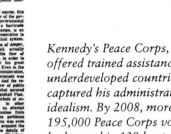

WASHINGTON SCENE

Wide-Open White House Sparkles With Action, But Others Lie Low

By JOSEPH ALSOP

WASHINGTON — The public information policy of the Kennedy Administration is so curious, and may later prove so important, that it cries out for analysis.

It is curious because of the bewildering contrast between the extreme openness of the White House itself, and the cloistered, almost harem - like withdrawal of most of the other government departments. Nothing quite like this contrast has been seen before in political Washington.

The openness of the White House is a calculated policy. Shortly after President Kennedy took office, he and his press secretary, Pierre Salinger, and other leading members of his staff discussed the pros and cons of the kind of rule that would have closed the place up for good. Under the proposed rule, all White House staff members would have had to ask for special permission, as in the Eisenhower era, before talking to any reporter.

The President recognized that such a rule would close the White House. He decided that this was undesirable. As a result, reporters now swarm through the White House staff-offices, briskly asking questions and even quite frequently getting answers about every imaginable subject of public interest.

BY THE SAME token, the President himself, instead of playing the role of a remote, hieratically immobile Byzantine ruler, has been constantly on view, both formally and informally. He has appeared at his televised press conferences, in special television shows of the most un - Byzantine character, and in all sorts of other ways. The effects of this White House openness and presidential accessibility can be seen in the most recent Gallup Poll. Kennedy - the - presidential - personality has had an immense impact.

(Note: This Gallup Poll, published in The Times Wednesday, said 72 per cent of the public approved of President Kennedy's performance during his first month in office. By comparison, 68 per cent approved of President Eisenhower's first - month performance. — The Editors.)

Yet the Democratic congressional leadership and the White House congressional liaison both rather glumly admit that this personal impact of President Kennedy has hardly produced an added vote for his program in the House of Representatives. Somewhere there is a break in the traditional chain of communications, from President, to voters, to the Capitol.

One place to look for the break in the chain is in the government departments, Defense, State, and the rest, whose continued cloistered reticence contrasts so sharply with the new openness of the White House. Nothing could be less like the Eisenhower White House than the Kennedy White House. But the Defense Department under Kennedy, for instance, is exactly like the Defense Department under Eisenhower, only perhaps rather more so.

This departmental reticence, it must be added, is not a calculated policy. It is a natural consequence of the fact that nothing has been done about the innumerable established customs, rules, and prohibitions all intended to prevent free communication of facts to the public. They are all being observed as usual. They are all being taken for granted, as quite proper customs, rules, and prohibitions, which are indeed badly needed to safeguard the delicate electorate from an unsettling flow of public information.

IN REALITY, of course, this cloistered character of the government, this governmental sheltering behind a barricade of classification stamps, is an enormous, recent innovation in the American political system.

In 1939-'41, a time of danger, President Roosevelt actually stimulated a double flow of public information, in order to secure support for his great pre-war measures. Even in the first Truman Administration, the American government was still largely open. And the resulting massive flow of public information was what secured support for the Marshall Plan.

In these past periods of active government, in other words, there was no attempt to prevent the nation from learning about the problems confronting it. There was even an active effort to acquaint the nation with all the details of those problems. Therefore, when the government was ready to act, the nation also was ready. But in the more recent years of passive government, there was an opposite effect — an effort to conceal the mere existence of national problems.

NOT WISHING to take action, any passive government naturally wishes the electorate to feel no need for action. Concealment, in these circumstances, is quite logical. But the habits formed in the years of passivity, though now deep-rooted in our officialdom, are not logical any longer, when the President so clearly wants the government to be active again. What was sauce for the goose, in this case, is plain poison for the gander.

This is one of Kennedy's basic dilemmas. If he resolves the dilemma by restoring the old, traditional government openness, he must pay the price of the numerous embarrassments that always afflict open government. Yet some of those around him are urging payment of this considerable price, because they see that no American government can be successfully active without being open.

THE NATION'S ECONOMY

Looks Like A Long, Troubled Sleep

By WALTER LIPPMANN

There is as yet no evidence, unless it be in the behavior of the stock market, that recovery from the recession is under way or in sight. Unemployment is continuing to increase, steel is operating at half capacity, the automobile business is very poor. All in all there is a growing disposition to ask whether the extremely moderate measures proposed by the President will be sufficient to turn the tide.

The President's task force, ...

... bun." The article discusses the Kennedy program as it has been formulated to date. Professor Samuelson thinks that "when you come to add up in quantitative terms what the whole package of programs can be expected to accomplish, you realize how limited the total package really is."

Professor Samuelson does not say this in criticism of the Administration program. As a matter of fact the current Administration program is about what his task force recommended last January before the President was inaugurated. But the advice at that time was accompanied by the warning, which President Kennedy himself passed on to the country, that the first measures might have to be reinforced by a second set.

IT IS A FAIR inference from Professor Samuelson's article in the Japanese newspaper that he is now rather expecting that a supplementary package will be needed.

These ideas stem from the belief that the present recession, following upon a poor recovery from the recession of 1958, and coming at the end of several years of sluggish economic activity, is much more serious than Congress or the mass of the people who are not unemployed have yet realized. "It is well," says Professor Samuelson, "to have no illusions about the magnitudes of the proposed (Kennedy) measures."

Even, he says, if the economy begins to turn up by the middle of the year, "there is little reason to think that the end of the year will find us with unemployment much better than at the present time." What is more, a quickening of economic growth to the American average rate of 3½ to 4 percent, "will have to wait until the second and third years of President Kennedy's term of office."

THESE ARE HARD judgments of a cool and expert mind. They will be unwelcome to many. They will be unwelcome to those who take the view that with words of confidence and optimism a recession like this one can be talked away, and that the somber truths should be glossed over and suppressed. The more innocent among them go so far as to say that this recession and this slowdown are being prolonged, indeed made worse, because the Kennedy Administration is telling the country that the economy is very sick.

There is everything to be said for keeping up the confidence of a sick patient. But an essential ingredient of that confidence is that the patient be convinced that the doctor is not deceiving himself. If, as seems so probable, we face a long hard effort to revive the American economy, the confidence of the people will best be sustained by convincing them that the economic doctors are not treating nice words as a substitute for real actions.

...ES FORUM

... Can't Write--That Includes Mr. Kennedy

... to millions annually. The Post Office has millions of undelivered letters.

MAX ROSENHAUS
Box 1085
Anna Maria

Affairs Of State

Editor, The Times:

That item about Salinger, 144,000 golf balls and Caroline's cat in last Sunday's Times was sure a beaut, showing the importance of iso-dopes in the space age. I wonder whether it will be reprinted in Moscow, Peiping and Leopoldville.

And let's make sure that w h e n the man from Mars demands, "Take me to your leader," he will be taken to Lucky Pierre without waste of time.

JOHN WORTHING
3020 Park Blvd.
Pinellas Park

Hooligans Of All Ages

Editor, The Times:

Several years ago, while working on the copy desk of the Miami Daily News, I was handed a traffic story covering the period from Christmas Eve through New Year's Day. The number of deaths and injuries was staggering, even to a veteran newspaperman. I thought perhaps a mistake had been made and that the figures were for the state. No mistake. The figures were for the Miami-Miami Beach area.

Bad as the situation was down there, I find it worse today in the St. Petersburg area. This is no revelation, I'm sure. Maybe it is only the voice of one crying in the asphalt jungle. Someone ought to cry, and loud and long, until there is a stop to this senseless slaughter on the streets.

The culprits? Teen-agers my foot. Rather a horde of highway hooligans of all ages, a big percentage of whom deplore the disrespect of today's children and teen-agers and before they catch their breaths set about to exhibit a total disregard for law, not to mention the lives and limbs of their fellow citizens and themselves . . .

JOHN J. WILSON JR.
10005 Bay Pines Blvd.

Fodder Of Our Country

Editor, The Times:

We are continually being solicited for contributions to this and that public health research project. This has always seemed to me to be completely out of order in a society which can and does appropriate huge sums for foreign aid.

If any programs on earth should be in the hands of a strong central government, it should be the programs of physical welfare, if only as an investment in "cannon fodder," for our approaching war with the Soviet Union.

In 1942, I was one in three bus loads of inductees from Pensacola, being sent to Camp Blanding. Less than one - half of us were accepted as physically fit for service. A fine commentary on a typical cross-section of our people, eh? I talked to some of the boys rejected, before they were shipped back to Pensacola. Some told me they had never, in their whole lives, been able to afford seeing a doctor! Troubles which might have been corrected at the outset had to be neglected until they became chronic . . .

MARION A. SMART
3421 15th Ave. S.

'To Joe, The Children Came First'

Editor, The Times:

Recently a plain citizen died most suddenly while in court. His name was Joseph Wenz. His death would be little marked by the average person, naturally, because he was not exactly in the public eye. Yet he left a great void in the hearts of many adults and children, for Joe — as we knew him — was the school patrolman at St. Jude's School for many years.

Everyone's problems were Joe's problems. Yet, although Joe was dear to us, the adults privileged to work with him, still he belonged to the children he helped cross the streets throughout the years; long ago he found the secret to eternal youth, and he was young in heart and spirit himself. To Joe, the school children came first; the rest of us were cogs to keep things running smoothly, but the children — now there was something else — they were really important! If Joe walked by our class rooms we, the teachers, could expect a friendly wave from him and would hear small voices calling, "Hello, Joe," "Hi, Joe," as they wistfully looked out at this kind man, wishing to be with him discussing important things like fishing and baseball.

And Joe tried to teach the boys and girls that duty comes first: duty to one's home, one's school, one's country. His face used to be reverent each morning when we all saluted the flag in the schoolyard. He was a New York patrolman before moving here and delighted us with tales of how devotion to duty must be followed throughout life. Joe might laugh with the children, but their safety was his reason for being.

I doubt if parents could fully realize how truly fine this person was. Now I wonder, as I drive along, how much we appreciate all these kind patrolmen who protect our children. They are all a wonderful, unsung group—but of course to me Joe was the best and "we shall not see his like again."

NANCY S. HOUGHTALING
6455 42nd Ave. N.

(Letters to The Forum delight the editors. We like to receive and publish them. All are read carefully, but to qualify for publication they must bear a name and address, measure up against simple rules involving good taste, libel, accuracy and general interest among our many readers. And, remember, the shorter, the better; only in rare instances will a letter of more than 250 words be used. — The Editors.)

Comic Dictionary

BUSYBODY: A woman who never gets excited over anything until she realizes that it's none of her business.

(Copyright, 1961, by Evan Esar)

Nevertheless, the prospect of a Hoffa loosed — and sure to be elected — to begin industrial organizing drives, take over the air cargo workers and wage war on the AFL - CIO, as he has threatened, is an uncomfortable one.

IT SHOULD BE more uncomfortable, actually, for the rank and file in the labor movement than to the all ...

IF IT WERE ONLY Hoffa who will be on trial with his new-found freedom, it would be of relatively little importance. But we fear that, if his actions and threats even while under monitorship are the criterion, he is going to lead labor into parlous times. The country, and the Congress, is in no mood during a time of soft economy to tolerate costly stoppages and jurisdictional warfare.

A Legion To 'Wage The Peace'

Apparently President Kennedy's conception of a Peace Corps has fired the imagination of a large number of young Americans, men and women alike.

Although the President has repeatedly stressed that life in the Peace Corps "will not be easy", it is obvious, from the immediate response to his announcement that the organization has formally been created, that there will be no lack of volunteers to man the Corps.

That the training course will be rigorous, that there will be no pay, only a living allowance, that Corps members will have to live on the same level as those they are attempting to help — none of these Spartan standards is deterring those who want to "do something for America."

THE REASON FOR this reaction is not hard to trace, we think. There is a real challenge here which offers the greatest possible reward — actually doing something to "wage the peace."

There has been strange irony in the fact that this nation, truly and deeply devoted to world peace, has always been so much more skillful and competent in waging and winning wars than in pursuing and winning the peace.

The past dozen years have been frustrating ones. Instead of being closer to our goal of a world ruled by justice and order than we were at the end of World War II, we are further away from it.

FOR THE YOUNGER generation in particular has this been a maddening process. Except for the additionally frustrating experience of Korea, these young people have not even had the catharsis of fighting a "war to end wars."

They have seen zealous salesmen and missionaries of communism apparently enjoy success after sucess in "selling" what all intelligent young Americans know to be a spurious and inferior product to that of democracy.

So, now that there is an opportunity to do something concrete to meet communism face-to-face in peaceful competition, to demonstrate by precept to the developing nations of the world that the democratic way of life is best, it is no wonder that there is an eager response.

AS ULTRA-IMPORTANT as should be the international effects of the Peace Corps, it may just as profoundly affect us at home.

Perhaps it is because we have won so few international contests with communism that so many seem to fear that democracy here at home can be ideologically defeated.

If the Peace Corps brings about a rebirth of faith in the strength of the democratic ideal, indeed it will be a mighty triumph.

Kennedy's Peace Corps, which offered trained assistance to underdeveloped countries, captured his administration's idealism. By 2008, more than 195,000 Peace Corps volunteers had served in 139 host countries around the world.

ALSO IN 1961

Pete Seeger composed the anti-war song "Where Have All the Flowers Gone?"

About 1,400 Cuban exiles launched the U.S.-sponsored "Bay of Pigs" invasion to overthrow Fidel Castro, who had seized power two years earlier. Within a few days Castro's forces had repelled the invasion, heating up what would become a long-simmering dispute between the two nations.

Magniftyco
Fair today and Wednesday. Mild temperatures. High today 82.
MIAMI TEMPERATURES MONDAY

The Miami Herald

Tuesday, April 18, 1961 — No. 138 — *Florida's Most Complete Newspaper* — 51st Year — 56 Pages — 5 Cents
A Latin American Edition is Published Daily

Eight Great Services
Associated Press — AP Wirephoto
United Press Int'l — UPI Photo
UPI Business Wire — Science Service
New York Times News Service
Chicago Daily News Foreign Service

Invaders Slug Into Interior

* * *

Russia Pledges to Aid Fidel

'Hirelings' From U.S. Blamed

The New York Times Service

MOSCOW — The Soviet Union charged the United States Monday night with responsibility for the invasion of Cuba by what it described as "American hirelings," and promised aid for the Castro regime.

Izvestia, the government newspaper, in the first official reaction contended that plans for landing of anti-Castro forces in Cuba had been worked out and inspired by "American imperialists."

"On all continents voices now are crying out determinedly for an end to the armed aggression against Cuba and from the defense of the freedom and independence of the Cuban people," the Izvestia commentary said.

The official Soviet news agency Tass said the Soviet Union and its allies are prepared to aid Cubans in their battle with anti-Castro revolutionaries. But the nature of such aid was not spelled out.

The Soviet Union and its satellites have provided arms for the Castro regime.

"The U.S.S.R. and other socialist countries, indeed all the peaceloving nations who are her most devoted friends, are prepared to give the Cuban people their help and support," Tass said.

At his vacation retreat in Sochi, on the Black Sea, Premier Nikita Khrushchev conferred on the Cuban crisis with Foreign Minister Andrei Gromyko. A formal government statement on the attack by anti-Castro forces on the Caribbean island is expected today.

An atmosphere of tension gripped the Soviet capital after the announcement by Moscow Radio that "an armed intervention against Cuba had begun."

It was felt by most Western experts that immediate Soviet reaction would be confined to strong diplomatic representations and complaints in the United Nations and propaganda onslaught against the United States.

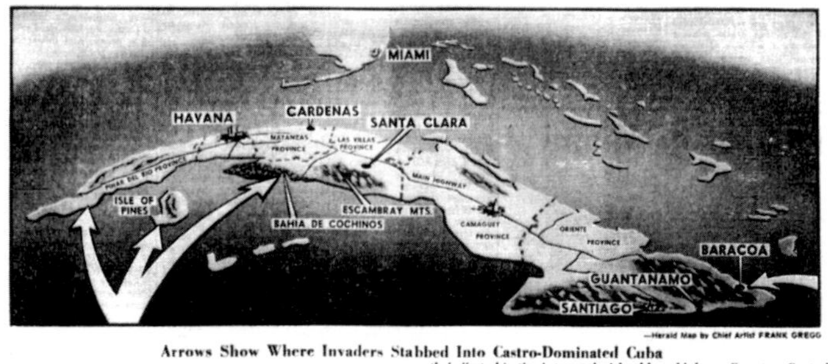

—Herald Map by Chief Artist FRANK GREGG

Arrows Show Where Invaders Stabbed Into Castro-Dominated Cuba
. . . their first objective is to cut the island-long highway, Carretera Central

Casualties Heavy As Battle Rages Throughout Cuba

By DOM BONAFEDE
Herald Staff Writer

Anti-Castro rebels were pushing into the interior of Cuba early today after launching an air-sea assault at several key points along the length of the politically-divided island.

The struggle raged from dawn to dawn, from the marshlands of Las Villas Province to the hill country of Oriente at Cuba's eastern tip.

It was brother against brother as the swiftly striking exile forces made their long awaited bid Monday to overthrow the Communist-oriented regime of Fidel Castro.

A virtual blackout was stretched across Cuba since the first shot of the civil war was fired. Despite early triumphant claims by exile spokesmen in the U.S., it was learned that the rebel troops are paying heavily for every mile gained.

* * *

Aim to Cut Main Highway

Rebels pouring in from Las Villas in the soft underbelly of Cuba were headed towards Central Highway in an apparent attempt to control the strategic road and cut the island in two.

And a report from Castro's own naval observation station at Varadero said that a fleet of eight ships was sighted off Cardenas, the north coast seaport about 90 miles east of Havana.

The station radioed a message, picked up by exile forces in Miami, that it feared the ships were massing for another landing.

At least three beachheads were secured by the invaders.

Under command of Capt. Manuel Artime, 29, the rebels nailed down beachheads at Cochino Bay, at Baracoa in Oriente Province, and in the southwest finger of Pinar del Rio.

* * *

Supplies, Equipment Landed

The rebels said supplies and military equipment had been successfully landed behind the troops.

Casualties were reported heavy on both sides, especially in the Cochino Bay landing area. According to one estimate, 100 Castro militiamen were killed alone in the town of Jaguey Grande, 20 miles inland, during the rebels' trek to the highway.

There were other unconfirmed reports, which spread like a fever throughout Miami and the Caribbean, that the rebels had gained control of the Isle of Pines and had freed the political prisoners there; that Raul Castro, Fidel's brother, had been captured, and that the city of Santiago de Cuba had been taken.

Exiles monitoring the rebel radio reported that skirmishes were staged in the hills of Escambray. Rebel Leader Osvaldo Ramirez was said to be in command of a group of partisans. Evelio Duque, another rebel commandante, is also believed to be in the area but there were no reports on him.

A message delivered on the revolutionary radio indicated that Castro himself was on the scene when rebel airmen attacked the Cochino area.

A Castro army radio dispatcher announced that a bomb fell "where Fidel just was," indicating he was there minutes before the attack.

In an impassioned proclamation, Castro declared a state of emergency throughout the country.

The bearded premier personally assumed charge of the defending forces as commander in chief.

Telephone communication to

Turn to Page 2A Col. 7

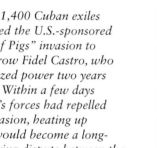

'Apartment' Best Movie

Liz, Lancaster Win Top Oscars

SANTA MONICA, Calif. — (AP) — Elizabeth Taylor, near death two months ago, reached the peak of her career Monday night by winning the award as best actress of 1960 from the Motion Picture Academy.

Burt Lancaster was acclaimed best actor for his role as the shady revivalist of "Elmer Gantry."

"The Apartment" won as best picture, and for best direction by Billy Wilder.

LANCASTER — LIZ

Shirley Jones of "Elmer Gantry" and Peter Ustinov of "Spartacus" won the top supporting roles.

The best song first used in an eligible picture was "Never on Sunday," from "Never on Sunday."

Miss Taylor's victory, for her role as the ill-starred wanton of "Butterfield 8," was one of the most dramatic moments in Oscar's 33 years.

When she heard her name called as winner by Yul Brynner, she clapped both hands over her mouth and stared in apparent astonishment. Then she turned to husband Eddie Fisher, and he helped her to her feet.

Still weakened by her bout with double pneumonia, she was helped to the stage of civic auditorium, walking slowly and uncertainly.

She stood trembling before the audience of 2,500, plus TV onlookers nationwide, and finally said hesitantly in hushed and halting tones:

"I don't really know how to express my gratitude. All I can say is thank you very much."

Other awards:

Best documentary: Features, "The Horse With the Flying Tail," Walt Disney. Short subjects, "Giuseppina," Lester A. Schoenfeld Films (British).

Special Jean Hersholt humanitarian award: Producer Sol Lesser.

Special honary award: Comedian Stan Laurel.

Best short subjects: Cartoons, "Munro," Rembrant Films, William L. Snyder, producer. Live actions subjects, "Day of the Painter," Little Movies, Kingsley-Union Films, Ezra R. Baker, producer.

Best foreign language film, "The Virgin Spring," A. B. Svensk Filmindustri (Sweden).

Rebel Plan: Cut Cuba In Half

By JAMES BUCHANAN
Herald Staff Writer

What is the Cuban rebels' military strategy?

The counter-revolutionary attack to unseat Fidel Castro is a giant pincer movement designed to cut Cuba in two and squeeze its defense forces into surrender.

Between midnight and dawn Monday, rebel forces hit the mountainous east and west ends of Cuba and then threw the main attacking columns at the soft, swampy southern underbelly of the 600-mile-long island.

There are two main objectives for the attackers.

The first is to push northward from the swampland beachhead and cut the Carretera Central, the one and only paved highway which runs the length of the island and over which Castro must move all his army and militiamen.

The second is to push eastward from the Pinar del Rio province landings — toward the capital of Havana and westward from the Oriente Province beachheads to grab Santiago de Cuba, the "capital" of eastern Cuba and the country's second largest city.

The southern column faces the most difficult task under the worst conditions with the least protection.

Its landings, made on the beaches of the Bay of Cochinas, left it just 95 airline miles southeast of Havana and in terrain that resembles the Florida Everglades.

It is the site of the ill-famed Cienaga de Zapata, or the Zapata swamps into which Castro sent hundreds of political prisoners as dawn-to-dusk laborers.

The swamp has no decent roads and is virtually uncharted. The only town giving access to a highway is Jaguey Grande, and it was in this direction that the rebels were last reported. If it can be taken, it would leave them less than 30 miles from their main highway objective.

Because troops landing in the swamp area lacked the cover or defensive positions held by the east and west columns, almost the entire rebel air force — however large that may be — was working over that area.

Reports said the land troops were being supplied with arms and ammunition by air drops, and that small groups of paratroopers had been dropped ahead of the column to soften resistance.

No specific landing points were given for the troops which went into Pinar del Rio province on the west and Oriente province on the east.

However, it is known that

Turn to Page 2A Col. 7

Which Side Do You Believe?

What Rebels Say

Anti-Castro troops have successfully landed by air and sea at several strategic points in Cuba, inflicting heavy casualties among the defending Castro militia.

Fresh troops and supplies are just off the Cuban Shore waiting to be thrown into the fray.

Revolutionary Council President Jose Miro Cardona and Antonio Varona, general coordinator of the Democratic Revolutionary Front, are poised to enter Cuba and set up a provisional government.

Much of Castro's 300,000-member militia has defected and gone over to the side of the invaders.

* * *

What Castro Says

Defending government troops have repulsed a multi-pronged attack by counter-revolutionaries, supplied and directed by "Yankee imperalists."

An appeal for support from the Cuban masses has been met with an overwhelming response in favor of the "Fatherland."

Everything is under control and there is no need for alarm. The business of the revolution should be carried on as usual, although vigilance must be maintained.

In the end, "we shall win."

INVASION STORY

Victory Prayers

More than 5,000 jammed Roman Catholic church to pray for invaders' victory 16A

MATOS

- **PROFILES** of exile leaders Jose Miro Cardona and Tony Varona 7A
- **IT'S FOR REAL,** but is it enough? 17A
- **IN SPANISH** 11A
- **ABLE-BODIED** Cubans swamp anti-Fidel recruiting offices 16A
- **MAJOR HUBERT MATOS,** jailed by Castro for warnings on communism, is one of 3,000 political prisoners invaders hope to free from Isle of Pines prison 17A

—Herald Staff Photos by DAN McCOY

Workers Prepare Gunboat for Invasion of Cuba
. . . ship was once a U.S. Navy subchaser

* * *

Gunboat Loaded at Miami Pier

By JAMES BUCHANAN
Herald Staff Writer

Just 200 feet off busy Biscayne Blvd., a 173-foot Cuban gunboat lay at anchor Monday night, being outfitted to carry men and munitions to the Cuban invasion.

For two weeks, thousands of Miamians have unknowingly passed within sight of the one-time U.S. Navy subchaser Glenwood as dozens of workmen swarmed over her decks and radar-topped superstructure.

The sleek, 450-ton battleship gray hull, carrying a three-inch cannon and ready to receive at least three anti-aircraft weapons, is the personal property of a Cuban industrialist, Santiago Babun.

It was to have been his donation to the anti-Castro fight and was to have made its maiden voyage later this week.

Miami Police Department's harbor patrol and the U.S. Coast Guard were advised of the Glenwood's location some time ago. Neither, however, made any move against the vessel since its status was, and is, completely legal.

Just when and where Babun purchased the 17-year-old PC 1140 is not known. Provisions of the sale call for the old mothballed vessel to be stripped of armament and the guns destroyed in the presence of U.S. officials.

This was to be done at the vessel's present site, the Dade Drydock Co., at 777 Biscayne Blvd.

A three-inch cannon was to come off the foredeck, along with the 40-millimeter and 20-millimeter anti-aircraft guns. These were to be cut into pieces by gas torch in the presence of U.S. agents.

After that, the twin-engined vessel belonged to Babun free and clear, to carry any "merchandise" he chose.

Babun, who owned a cement plant, garages, service stations, virgin timber lands in Cuba's Oriente Province, made no secret of his plans.

The boat, he told associates here, was to be reinforced with additional steel plate in Miami

Turn to Page 2A, Col. 3

Atrocities Cited

Stage Set to Ask Eichmann's Death

JERUSALEM — (AP) — Israel's attorney general resurrected in terrible detail Monday the ghastly record of Nazi atrocities in a powerful prelude to an expected demand for the death penalty for Adolf Eichmann.

Prosecutor Gideon Hausner spoke for nearly six hours after the former Gestapo officer pleaded not guilty 15 times to charges that he slaughtered and tortured Jews by the millions.

Pointing his finger straight at Eichmann, Hausner in his opening statement called him the "zealous executor" of those horrors, the Nazi "specialist in extermination," a man "absolutely devoted to his mission" of exterminating the Jewish people.

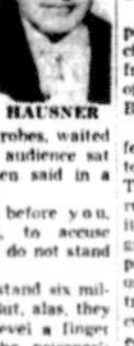

HAUSNER

The attorney-general adjusted the collar of his flowing black robes, waited a moment as the audience sat soundless, and then said in a voice with feeling:

"When I stand before you, judges of Israel, to accuse Adolf Eichmann, I do not stand here alone.

"Here with me stand six million prosecutors. But, alas, they cannot rise and level a finger at the man in the prisoner's dock.

"Their blood cries to heaven

but their voices cannot be heard."

"Only one man in history exists whose hands were exclusively occupied with the extermination of the Jewish people—Adolf Eichmann," Hausner declared.

Eichmann sat without expression in his bullet-proof glass cage as Hausner cited relentlessly the grim evidence left in the wake of Nazi Germany's "final solution to the Jewish problem" and set out to shatter in advance Eichmann's anticipated defense that he directed it on orders.

"We will prove," Hausner told the three judges, "that the accused went far beyond his orders and carried out functions for which he had been given no orders at all."

He charged Eichmann with personally beating a Jewish child to death for stealing fruit from a peach tree in a garden of a home he once owned in Budapest.

The day started with a defeat for Eichmann's defense attorney, Dr. Robert Servatius. The three-judge panel overruled challenges to its authority raised by Servatius on grounds the court might be prejudiced and that the law under which Eichmann is being tried was passed after the crimes with which he is charged.

Then Eichmann stood at attention, his hands straight by his sides, to plead. To each of the 15 counts in the indictment he gave the answer:

"In the spirit of the indictment, I am not guilty."

It was the same answer given by the top Nazi criminals tried at Nuernberg.

Can You Pick Silver Knight?
. . . some nominees . . . 2B

On the Inside

Finch, Carole Get Life Terms
. . . see story Page 8A

Amuse.	5-7C	Kofoed	19C
Bell	1B	Landers	2C
Class.	8-17C	Movies	7C
Comics	18-19C	Pearson	7A
Crossword	18C	Pennekamp	6A
Deaths	8C	Qu'k Quiz	19C
Editorial	6A	Sports	1-7D
Financial	4-7B	Thompson	18C
Goren	19C	TV-Radio	19A
Harris	6A	Weather	2A
Horoscope	18C	Winchell	6C
Jumble	12C	Womens	1-4C

* * *

INSIDE YOUR LEGISLATURE

Districting 14A
Whisky Tax 14A
Urban Renewal 15A
Harness Racing 4D

Today's Chuckle

It's smart to pick your friends, but not to pieces.
—Paris Pups

THE WEATHER
Mostly sunny today and tomorrow. Fair tonight. High today upper 70s to low 80s. Low tonight in 60s. North to northeast winds. For complete weather information see Page 13-A.

FORT LAUDERDALE NEWS

HOME EDITION

AP Wirephoto Photofax — Member Of The Associated Press And UPI — Full NEA Service

51st Year — Four Sections — FORT LAUDERDALE FLORIDA, TUESDAY, APRIL 18, 1961 — 44 Pages — N S — PRICE FIVE CENTS

27 Arrested In Assassination Plot

★ ★ ★ ★ ★ ★ ★ ★ ★ ★ ★ ★ ★ ★ ★ ★

REDS DEMAND U.S. END WAR AS MOBS SHRIEK 'VIVA CUBA'

★ ★ ★ ★

Fidel Nabs 9 Women 'Loyalists'

MIAMI. (AP)—Arrest of 27 persons accused of plotting to assassinate Prime Minister Fidel Castro was announced today by the Cuban government radio in a broadcast heard here.

Among those held, the broadcast said, was Major Humberto Sori Marin, Castro's first minister of agriculture.

SORI

Sori Marin was shot and wounded while trying to flee, the radio added. He was taken to a hospital.

The others, including nine women, are being held for trial by a revolutionary tribunal.

Among them, it was announced, was an American, Rafael Diaz Ottman.

Castro forces seized a large quantity of "arms from Key West" on making the arrests, the broadcast said. Key West is 90 miles from Havana.

The radio also reported that eight terrorists were executed by a firing squad early today in La Cabana prison fortress.

There was no mention in the 30-minute newscast about developments in connection with yesterday's invasion by anti-Castro insurgents, except to repeat a brief communique saying efforts to repel these were continuing.

This communique, issued by Castro, was first read last night and was repeated throughout the night.

The newscast opened with a bulletin from Moscow saying the Soviet government had offered "all help necessary in the just Cuban fight against foreign aggression." This bulletin was repeated twice.

★ ★ ★

Latins Protest Noisily

By THE ASSOCIATED PRESS

Supporters of the Fidel Castro regime staged demonstrations throughout Latin America last night to protest against the Cuban invasion, but the biggest turnout was only 3,000 persons.

The crowd of 3,000 assembled in Montevideo, Uruguay. Steel-helmeted police hurled tear gas bombs to scatter them as they moved on the legislative palace, where a state dinner for visiting Italian President Giovanni Gronchi was getting under way.

Dozens of arrests were made but no serious injuries were reported.

Police broke up other Castro demonstrations in Santiago, Chile, Caracas, Venezuela, and Bogota, Colombia.

In Bogota, the police fired rifles and advanced with fixed bayonets on a crowd of 1,500 trying to attack the U. S. embassy. The demonstrators stoned the building housing the pro-American newspaper El Tiempo, smashed all the windows of the U. S.-operated Colombian-American Institute and

(Continued on Page 12-A, Col. 3)

ON THE WATCH—A U. S. Border Patrolman stands watch at Broward International Airport for any possible movement of soldiers or equipment to Cuba. The Border Patrol and the Broward Sheriff's Department increased the security forces around all airports in the county. Many of the airstrips were used by Castro forces to overthrow Batista.

(News photo by Bill Bates)

Army Asserts

No Danger To Florida

ORLANDO. (AP)—The U. S. Army's top spokesman indicated tonight that the Cuban counter revolution presents no danger to Florida either from the pro-Castro Cubans or from Soviet Union interference.

Army Secretary Elvis J. Stahr Jr. also denied any official knowledge of alleged U. S. government participation in the move to overthrow the government of Premier Fidel Castro.

"This is news to me," Stahr said when asked about the Cuban revolution now under way.

"I assume that Mr. Castro will immediately say, based on past performances of his, that this is a U. S. plot, as has been the case with other plots he accused us of. But in the language of Kentucky vernacular, 'It just ain't so.' It is strictly the propaganda of a desperate man."

Stahr said there is no reason for the United States to be attacked simply because the Cuban people are trying to regain control of their government.

Stahr spoke at the kickoff dinner for the Southeastern Industrial Exposition opening tomorrow and continuing through Thursday.

In his speech, he said the nation must do everything necessary to insure America's freedom and safety.

He echoed President Kennedy's call for a strong, highly mobile force trained in limited warfare with substantial air life and sea lift capacity, and pre-stocked overseas bases.

Gettysburg 'Was Worst Lee Scrap'

ALBANY, N.Y. (UPI) — Bruce Catton, Pulitzer prize-winning Civil War historian, says Gettysburg was "probably the worst battle" Gen. Robert E. Lee fought in the war between the states.

Catton backs British Field Marshal Bernard Montgomery's criticism of the Southern commander's handling of one of the war's major battles.

Montgomery, hero of the World War II battle of El Alamein, said recently that Lee lost his "grip" on his army of Gettysburg.

"That is probably true within limits," Catton said at a news conference yesterday. "When preparing for battle Lee would tell his generals in broad terms what he wanted and then leave them work it out."

Catton, who arrived here for the first assembly of the New York State Civil War Centennial Commission, declined to compare Lee with the North's Gen. U. S. Grant.

More On Cuba

Cuban Recruits	12-A
Castro Days Numbered	13-A
Yanks Look To Swiss	13-A
Free World Hopes	14-A
Guantanamo Security	14-A
Cuba Blockade	14-A

TODAY'S DIRECTORY

Amusements	6, 7-B
Broward County News	1, 2-C
Classified	4 thru 11-C
Comics	12, 13-C
Crossword Puzzle	13-C
Editorial Pages	10, 11-A
Horoscope	13-C
Movie Time Clock	7-C
Sports	1, 2, 3-D
Stocks, Financial	4 thru 7-D
TV	12-C
Weather Report	13-A
Women's Pages	1 thru 4-B

NEWS Phones: JA 2-3711
Classified Ad. JA 3-5425

(AP Wirephoto)

ELIZABETH TAYLOR CLUTCHES OSCAR
. . . she becomes a first-time winner

'Apartment' Wins

Liz And Burt Given Oscars

SANTA MONICA, Calif. (UPI) — Elizabeth Taylor, beset by tragedy and scandal in recent years, stood with her golden Oscar today at the pinnacle of her career—the best actress of 1960.

The dark-haired beauty won the coveted award for her role of a footloose lady in "Butterfield 8."

But her acceptance of the statuette last night at the 33rd annual academy awards presentations was as dramatic a moment as any she had been called upon to play in the movies.

Leaving a sickbed to attend her triumphant hour, Miss Taylor was accompanied by husband Eddie Fisher and her physician. She is still recovering from a near-fatal attack of pneumonia suffered last month in London.

Muscular Burt Lancaster won the best actor award for his performance as the hell-raising preacher in "Elmer Gantry."

After receiving the award Lancaster said, "Next year I

(Continued on Page 12-A, Col. 1)

Invasion Progress In Dark

(From News Wire Services)

LONDON—Soviet Premier Nikita Khrushchev personally appealed to President Kennedy to put an end to the Cuban invasion.

The Tass news agency said Khrushchev warned the President that Russia will give the Castro government all aid necessary to repulse the armed attacks, for which the United States has denied responsibility.

In Moscow, several thousand demonstrators shouting: "Hands off Cuba" smashed windows at the U. S. embassy today with a barrage of rocks.

The demonstrators came in two waves. The first hurled rocks and splattered the yellow facade of the embassy with bottles of green and purple ink.

They plastered signs reading "Viva Cuba" on the high iron fence in front of the embassy and painted anti-American slogans. Mounted police and troops dispersed most of them.

Then about an hour later a second wave arrived, screaming "Viva Cuba," waving Cuban flags and carrying banners saying "hands off Cuba."

They hooted and whistled as they stood in front of the 10-story embassy. They shouted "Cuba da (yes). Yankees nyet (no).

The embassy estimated the crowds at from 3,000 and 5,000. The crowds seemed somewhat smaller to reporters.

NO PANIC

There was no panic inside the embassy. Most of the diplomats' families treated the atack in a "rise-above-it" manner.

With Cuba blacked out for all newsmen except those of the Communist bloc, news of the fighting was confined to sketchy claims by representatives abroad of the anti-Castro forces and vague announcements from Castro's government.

Cuban rebel leaders in the United States claimed the invasion force had struck half-way across Cuba and reached within 90 miles of Havana.

Prime Minister Fidel Castro took personal command of his

(Continued on Page 12-A, Col. 4)

★ ★ ★

Nikita Rattles Saber

Here is the text of Soviet Premier Nikita Khrushchev's statement on the Cuban situation.

The government of the Republic of Cuba has announced that in Cuba on the morning of 16th April, aircraft of the U. S. bomber B26 type subjected to barbarous bombing separate districts of the capital of Cuba, Havana, and a number of other inhabited localities.

There are many killed and injured among the inhabitants of the capital. Following the bombing, early in the morning of 17th April, armed forces of the interventionists landed at various places of the Cuban coast.

The landing took place under the cover of warships and U. S. Air Force. Cuban government troops and the people's militia are engaged in fighting against the invading gangs.

NIKITA

In connection with the invasion of Cuba the Soviet government states the following:

The attack on Cuba is an open challenge to all freedom loving peoples, a dangerous provocation against peace in the area of the Caribbean Sea, and against universal peace. There can be no justification of this criminal invasion.

The organizers of the aggres-

(Continued on Page 12-A, Col. 4)

★ ★ ★ ★

As Cuban Aggressor

Reds Due To Ask UN Denounce U.S.

UNITED NATIONS, N.Y. (AP)—The Soviet Union is expected to demand a UN denunciation of the United States as an aggressor against Cuba and a threat to the peace of the Western Hemisphere. The demand is likely to get a cold reception from most delegations other than Cuba and the nine-nation Soviet bloc.

Some delegates expressed fear that the Castro regime's charges of American aid to the Cuban invaders might lead to Russian intervention. But the general opinion seemed to be that Russia would limit its aid to vocal support and more shipments of arms.

The Soviet news agency Tass said last night that Russia and its allies are prepared to aid the Castro regime in its battle against the revolutionaries, but the Tass commentary did not spell out the nature of such aid.

(Continued on Page 12-A, Col. 4)

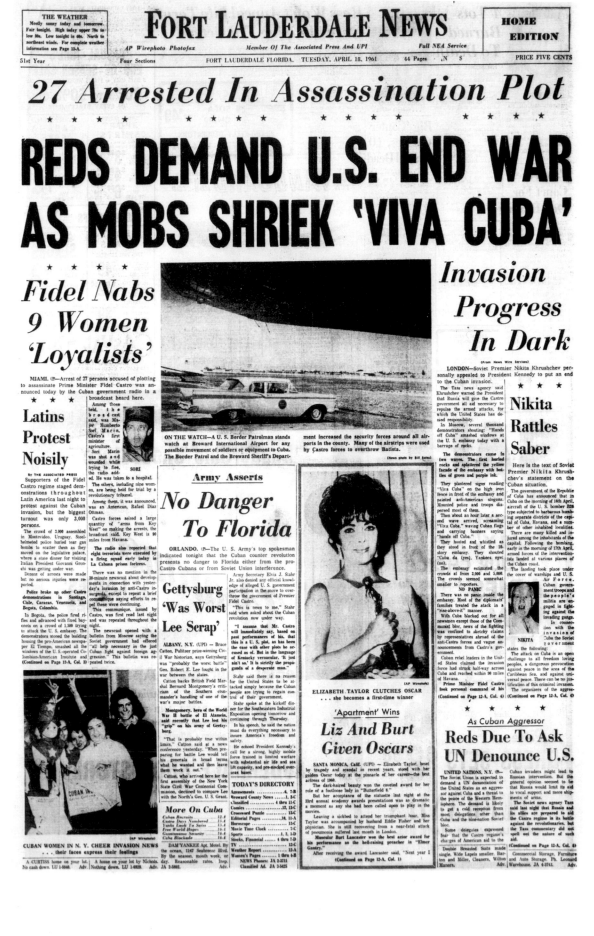

(AP Wirephoto)

CUBAN WOMEN IN N. Y. CHEER INVASION NEWS
. . . their faces express their feelings

Though the invasion was in the works before Kennedy became president, he took responsibility for the failed mission, saying, "Victory has 100 fathers and defeat is an orphan."

ALSO IN 1961

Soviet Premier Nikita Khrushchev ordered construction of the Berlin Wall to seal East Berlin and prevent people from escaping to West Germany.

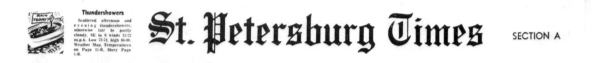

Thundershowers
Scattered afternoon and evening thundershowers, otherwise fair to partly cloudy. SE to S winds 12-22 m.p.h. Low 72-74, high 86-90. Weather Map, Temperatures on Page 11-B. Story Page 1-B.

St. Petersburg Times

SECTION A

Vol. 77—No. 286 • Complete Associated Press, United Press International, New York Times and New York Herald Tribune News Services • ST. PETERSBURG, FLORIDA, SATURDAY, MAY 6, 1961 • PHONE 5-1111 WANT ADS 5-1131 ★ 46 PAGES 10 CENTS

'BOY, WHAT A RIDE!' BEAMS ASTRONAUT SHEPARD

U.S. Takes Giant Step Into Space

JFK To Ask Additional Space Funds

For President's comments on South Viet Nam and Cuba, see Page 2-A.

WASHINGTON (UPI) — President Kennedy yesterday pledged his administration to follow up Cmdr. Alan B. Shepard's historic rocket flight with a request to Congress for funds for a "substantially larger" space program.

The President joined all Americans in rejoicing at the success of the flight and arranged to pay tribute to Shepard — and America's six other astronauts — at a special White House ceremony Monday.

The ceremony with Shepard will be carried live on radio and television, probably about noon, as will a news conference which Shepard will hold at noon (EST).

THE PRESIDENT extended his personal congratulations to Shepard in a telephone call to the astronaut shortly after he completed his successful flight down the Atlantic Missile Range. Later, Kennedy elaborated at a news conference.

At the same time, the President warned that the United States still was behind Russia and had "a long way to go in the field of space." But he declared that the nation was working hard and "we are going to increase our efforts."

He got a prompt promise of Congressional support from Chairman Richard B. Russell, D-Ga., of the Senate Armed Services Committee. Russell said "we must press forward . . . until we have achieved preeminence in space. Congress stands ready to fully support such a program."

SEVERAL members of Congress said they expected the President to award the Medal of Honor to Shepard.

The President will take part in a public ceremony with Shepard on the south lawn of the White House about noon Monday, and then talk privately with the astronaut. He also will meet privately with the nation's other six astronauts after the public ceremony.

SHEPARD, accompanied by the other astronauts, will arrive in Washington from Grand Bahama Island. He will be greeted at nearby Andrews Air Base by his wife, who watched his flight by TV from Virginia Beach, Va., and by his parents, who will come from Derry, N.H.

The astronauts then will fly by helicopter to the White House for their meetings with the President.

HE SAID IT always had been the U.S. custom — and would continue so — to give the infor-

(See KENNEDY, Page 2-A)

SHEPARD DANGLES IN HARNESS AS HE IS LIFTED FROM THE CAPSULE
. . . by cable from helicopter in Atlantic. Space capsule floats at left.

Manned Capsule Blasted 115 Miles Above Earth

CAPE CANAVERAL (AP) — Beaming "Boy, what a ride!" astronaut Alan B. Shepard returned safely to earth yesterday after blasting 115 miles into space — a perfect flight that gave the United States a mighty stride forward in the space race with Russia.

"What a beautiful sight," the 37-year-old test pilot exulted at the top of his 15-minute hop into space and back.

His 6-by-9-foot space capsule reached speeds of 5,100 miles an hour before plunging back down into the Atlantic 302 miles southeast, where it was plucked from the waves by a helicopter.

Shepard was flown immediately to the carrier Lake Champlain, where physicians began checking him over for any ill effects.

"I don't think there's much you'll have to do to me, Doc," he told one of the medicos.

FROM THE carrier Shepard was flown to a hospital on nearby Grand Bahama Island, where a doctor pronounced him "in excellent shape and health."

The physician who monitored his condition by radio during the flight—which subjected him to stresses up to 11 times that of normal gravity — reported the lean, muscular astronaut was probably the calmest man in the whole operation.

President Kennedy telephoned his congratulations to Shepard within minutes after the astronaut's arrival on the carrier and told him of the hero's welcome awaiting him in Washington.

THE PRESIDENT said, "This is an historic milestone in our own exploration into space."

A naval officer who overheard the conversation quoted the astronaut as saying:

"Thank you very much, Mr. President. It was certainly a very thrilling ride. I'd like to thank everyone who made it possible."

A U.S. space agency official said Shepard's feat is only the beginning of America's exploration of space.

The Redstone rocket used as a booster for yesterday's flight

(See U.S., Page 2-A)

★ ★ ★

—AP Wirephoto

SPACEMAN ALAN B. SHEPARD
. . . has smile and wave as he leaves carrier for Grand Bahama Island and a physical checkup in hospital there.

BUT NO CHAMPAGNE

Spirits High, He Looks, Feels Great

GRAND BAHAMA ISLAND (AP) — Spaceman Alan B. Shepard's "perfect flight" was toasted in champagne when he arrived here yesterday, but doctors waiting to check him over did not allow him to participate.

Flashing a Grand Canyon-sized grin, the hungry Shepard enjoyed a huge shrimp cocktail, roast beef sandwich and iced tea.

Hurried into isolation of a hospital guarded by a sentry with holstered pistol, the young astronaut then began at least 24 hours of comprehensive medical and psychological checkups, and detailed reports on all technicalities of his historic mission.

"He looks great, feels great. He is jolly and joking as Al always is," said Capt. Virgil Grissom, a fellow astronaut who admits he was a bit envious and certainly hopes he will be chosen for the next rocket ride.

ASTRONAUT Donald Slayton called the flight "perfect — it couldn't have been any better." he told Shepard, "you pulled it off real good," in a back-slapping greeting at the airport on this pine and palmetto island.

"Everything went fine," Shepard said within earshot of reporters. He waved, but no interviews were permitted.

Within an hour after Shepard arrived here hard rain beat a tattoo on the white roof of the aluminum portable hospital erected especially at Grand Bahama Auxiliary Air Force Base.

If he was harmed in any way, it didn't show. He was in high spirits when he stepped off the plane that brought him here after his space capsule was recovered from the ocean.

"I have to admit I'm a little envious," said Grissom. "I think I have a fair chance of being on the next launch. I certainly do want to be on the next one. I wanted to be on this one."

WHEN SHEPARD reported at the top of his flight how beautiful the earth looked, Slayton said,

(See CHECKUP, Page 2-A)

Legislature Votes To Override Bryant's Vetoes Of Track Bills

Why did Sen. Young walk out of Senate? Page 1-B. Related stories, Page 4-A.

Times-Miami Herald Service

TALLAHASSEE — An incensed legislature yesterday overrode Gov. Farris Bryant's vetoes of harness racetracks for two South Florida Counties and thereby expanded legalized gambling in the state.

The action came after a pointed charge that the governor had double-crossed his own senator, L. K. Edwards of Marion County, a fact which Bryant said resulted from misunderstanding.

Under the new laws, harness racing will be conducted in Broward and Seminole (Sanford) Counties.

The overriding also was made possible by the absence from the chamber of the senators from Miami and St. Petersburg, either of whose vote would have resulted in defeat to the harness tracks.

DADE'S SEN. Cliff Herrell had

(See VETOES, Page 2-A)

Another Bill To Bar Liquor Ads Introduced

Times-Miami Herald Service

TALLAHASSEE — A Senate bill with 17 co-sponsors was introduced yesterday to prohibit the advertising of alcoholic beverages.

It differs with a previous bill only in that it permits small price signs to be displayed inside the store where the liquor is sold.

Sen. Ed Fraser of Macclenny headed the list of sponsors which include almost half the state senators. The Senate total is 38.

Both measures will be taken up by the Temperance Committee of which Fraser is chairman. The committee is expected to meet next week.

First American Voice From Space Is Calm

CAPE CANAVERAL (AP) — The first American voice from space was calm, without waver, with precision.

Only under the mighty forces of a rocket speeding up and suddenly slowing down from 5,160 miles an hour did it become strained.

Here is a partial text of what Astronaut Alan B. Shepard Jr., reported from space, and what the guiding voices — sometimes more excited than his — reported from the ground:

First from the control center before blast off:

"Flight ready to go."

"Flight director on go."

"1:30 and counting."

"1:13, the cherry pickers go."

"All Mercury stations keep clear of your stations unless it is an emergency."

"Suit and cabin temperature control set."

"45 (seconds) and counting."

"Firing command . . . 30 mark."

"10-9-8-7-6-5-4-3-2-1-zero . . . lift off."

Then apparently Shepard's voice: "Roger, lift off and the clock has started."

"Lift off looks very good," from the ground.

"It is A-okay (means perfect). Everything still looks very good."

"This is 7" (Shepard's code

(See FIRST, Page 2-A)

★ ★ ★

Other Astronaut News Inside

Full page of photos of U.S. spaceman and his historic day. Page 10-A.

A Times editorial, "For the Whole World To See", comments on the space flight. Page 8-A.

Domestic and foreign reaction to space flight. Who is the man who gave Shepard the word "Go?" Page 9-A.

Reaction of spaceman's wife. Page 4-B.

The geography of space flight and the eight stages of the flight are shown in illustrations. Page 2-A.

Little New Hampshire town had special reason to celebrate space flight. Page 2-A.

Times Is Cited For Service To Community

The Citation

This is the citation read by Dr. Earl F. English, dean of the University of Missouri School of Journalism, when he presented a medal yesterday designating The St. Petersburg Times as the Distinguished American Newspaper of 1960.

"To THE ST. PETERSBURG TIMES, in recognition of: its record of serving aggressively and courageously the true functions of a daily newspaper for more than three-quarters of a century;

"Its faith in the future of the state of Florida and particularly its own locality, which it has helped develop into an ideal home and business community;

"The development of a planned training program for young journalists, while at the same time providing educational incentive through the granting of Poynter Fund college scholarships; and

"An enlightened employer-employe relationship which has made the production of this newspaper the result of a truly exceptional team effort."

COLUMBIA, Mo. — The Missouri Award for Distinguished Service in Journalism was presented to The St. Petersburg Times, seven journalists and a foreign newspaper here yesterday.

The citation to The Times and others was presented by Dean Earl F. English of the University of Missouri School of Journalism as part of the school's 52nd journalism week activities. Nelson Poynter, editor and president, received the bronze medal in behalf of The Times and its staff.

In presenting the medal, English cited The Times for its record "of serving aggressively and courageously the true functions of a daily newspaper . . . for its faith in the future of the State of Florida and particularly its own locality which it has helped develop . . . the development of a training program for young journalists . . . and an enlight-

(See THE TIMES, Page 2-A)

The Medal

IN TODAY'S TIMES

Queen Of Britain Calls On Pope John

Queen Elizabeth II of Britain yesterday called on Pope John XXIII at the Vatican. For details, photo, see Page 3-A.

RICHARD NIXON, launching a "loyal opposition" campaign, described the recent Cuban invasion a "mistake" and scored President Kennedy for "words," not "deeds." Page 3-A.

PRESIDENT KENNEDY signs minimum wage bill into law. Page 3-A.

★ ★ ★

Bridge	Page 4-C	Horoscope	Page 8-B
Classified	Pages 5-11-C	Jumble	Page 8-B
Comics	Pages 8-9-B	Obituaries	Page 11-B
Crossword	Page 10-B	Outdoors	Page 2-C
Editorial	Page 8-A	Pulse of Pinellas	Page 11-B
Entertainment	Page 10-B	Radio-TV	Page 10-B
Family Today	Pages 4-5-B	Sports	Pages 1-3-C
Financial	Pages 6-7-B	Weather	Pages 1-11-B
Fun	Page 4-C	What's Doing	Page 4-C

Soon after the space flight, Kennedy declared to Congress, "I believe that this nation should commit itself to achieving the goal, before this decade is out, of landing a man on the moon and returning him safely to the earth."

ALSO IN 1961

The movie West Side Story, *with music by Leonard Bernstein and lyrics by Stephen Sondheim, was released four years after the musical opened on Broadway.*

Daily Press

NEWPORT NEWS—HAMPTON, VIRGINIA
HAMPTON ROADS' MORNING NEWSPAPER

NEWPORT NEWS, VIRGINIA, WEDNESDAY MORNING, FEBRUARY 21, 1962 PRICE: 5c BY CARRIER 45c

VIRGINIA WEATHER

Cloudy With Rain In Southwest By This Afternoon, Beginning As Snow Or Sleet In North Or Central Portions. Highs In 40s. Thursday Rain Ending And Warmer, Turning Colder By Night.

Glenn 'Excellent' After Three-Orbit Flight; JFK Will Tender Nation's Thanks Friday

100 SENATORS VOTE

Kennedy Loses On Urban Test

Redistricting Bills Studied By Assembly

Successful Atlantic Landing Climaxes 81,000-Mile Trip

By BEM PRICE

Happy, relaxed Glenn smiles during rest on bunk aboard destroyer Noa Tuesday after recovery from Atlantic.

Glenn's parents talk to grandchildren via TV.

'SUPER GOODWILL TOUR'

World Raises Hearty Cheer For Marine's Epic Journey

FLIGHT PAY GRANTED

'Prayers Answered,' Say Glenn's Parents

By JACK M. BIRCHDILL

Flood Death Toll In Germany 277

U.S. Waits, Then Prays, Then Cheers

'OUR MOST WONDERFUL DAY'

Astronaut's Family Happy, Excited, Proud

By JERRY T. BAULCH

Observers Confident On Flight

By PETER SIGMUND

French Halt Police Leaves As Algerian War Nears End

Namesakes

Mrs. John Glenn Jr. with daughter, Carolyn, and son, David, after husband's flight.

A few days after orbiting the earth, astronaut John Glenn met with Kennedy at Cape Canaveral. Glenn entered politics himself a few years later and became close friends with the Kennedys.

Three out of four television viewers watched A Tour of the White House with Mrs. John F. Kennedy, *the first primetime documentary to draw attention to a first lady. (AP Photo)*

BOSTON GLOBE EXPOSED EDWARD KENNEDY CHEATING INCIDENT

Soon after Edward Kennedy announced his campaign for the Senate, The Boston Globe *published a front-page story detailing his suspension from Harvard for cheating on a Spanish exam in 1951.*

ALSO IN 1962

Telstar, the first space satellite to relay television signals and telephone calls, was launched.

May 19, 1962
Marilyn Monroe Sang at President Kennedy's Birthday Celebration

Crowd Hails Kennedy at N.Y. Rally

'Garden' Jammed; 'Birthday' Salute Aids Party Funds

NEW YORK (AP) — President Kennedy packed Madison Square Garden Saturday night to knock $1 million off the Democrats' national debt and urge strong campaigning for more seats for the party in Congress this year.

The Garden was a sell out for the huge "birthday salute" to Mr. Kennedy, and a great array of theatrical talent provided a two-and-a-half-hour long show for the celebration.

It came on the hottest May day in New York City history, when the temperature had risen to 99. Heat waves still rose in the garden when, after a sultry rendition of "Happy Birthday" by Marilyn Monroe, the President remarked:

"I can now retire from politics."

Joins in Spirit

Discarding most of a prepared speech on his program of "action" and Republican opposition, the President joined in the birthday party spirit.

Thanking the entertainers whose presence helped sell more than $1 million worth of seats at from $10 to $1,000, Mr. Kennedy referred to his father's onetime acid comment on some businessmen.

He added: "When my father was giving his views on business, he always exempted show business."

Johnson Attends

Mr. Kennedy told the crowd that he and Vice President Johnson, who also was present, had run up a $4 million debt in the 1960 campaign.

"That is now gone forever," he said. "Now, all that's left is the national debt."

Mr. Kennedy said some of his legislation had been defeated in the House or Senate by one or two votes, and urged a big push this year to gain additional Democratic seats in Congress.

The party, he said, must not consider 1962 an "off year."

As Miss Monroe, in a slinky white dress, sang her version of "Happy Birthday," two chefs carried around the arena a 5-ft. birthday cake, sparkling with 45 blue candles. The President actually won't be 45 until May 29.

Off to Reception

The party lasted until nearly midnight but the night was not over for the President.

Ending the day that started early with the first of two visits to his ailing father, the President went off to a reception at the home of Arthur Krim, attorney and president of United Artists.

Please Turn to Pg. 3, Col. 1

Los Angeles Times
FINAL
ONE OF THE WORLD'S GREAT NEWSPAPERS
TWENTY SECTIONS—SECTION A
SUNDAY, MAY 20, 1962
KTTV (Channel 11)
408 PAGES
SUNDAY 25c
Peiping 'Won't Tolerate' New U.S. Asia Foothold
Khrushchev Sees A-War Challenge
Warns Kennedy Against 'Pushing Nuclear Button'
Stay Out of Action, Allies Told
Estes Warned by U.S. He Can't Leave Country
Justice Department Serves Order as Senate Group Sets Inquiry for Monday
Orbit Flight Now Delayed Until Thursday
20 Children Injured by Bishop's Auto
New Quake in Mexico Panics Thousands
Three Die as Second Temblor Rocks Capital and Southern Areas of Country
More American Troops Arrive in Thailand
KENNEDY TALK ON MEDICARE ON AIR TODAY
TIMES TO SERIALIZE BOOK BY GOLDWATER
INDEX OF FEATURES
Music Center Reflects Southland Culture
THE WEATHER
...mbers Vote Themselves New Office Building

Marilyn Monroe suggestively sang "Happy Birthday, Mr. President" at a nationally televised Madison Square Garden celebration for the president's 45th birthday, which later fueled rumors about the Kennedy brothers' relationship to the iconic blond bombshell.

This was one of Marilyn Monroe's final public appearances before her death on August 5, 1962. (© Bettmann/CORBIS)

Also in 1962

Johnny Carson became the host of The Tonight Show. *Future* Daily Show *host Jon Stewart was born.*

WEATHER

ATLANTA: Clear and slightly warmer Sunday. Chance of showers Monday. National summary on Page 46.

The Atlanta Journal AND THE ATLANTA CONSTITUTION

FINAL EDITION

Vol. XIII, No. 20 *** Tel. JA. 2-5050—P.O. Box 4689 Atlanta (2), Ga., Sunday, September 30, 1962 206 Pages—12 Sections ***** PRICE 20 CENTS

RALPH McGILL

Ike Properly Condemns . . .

Solemn Oath

Citizen's Duty

Troops Called By President

Mississippi Guardsmen Put Under U.S. Orders

IT'S NAVY CHOW FOR THE ARMY AS MESS TRUCK ROLLS INTO MEMPHIS

Vehicle Brings in Equipment to Feed Army Units Alerted for Possible Use in Mississippi

STREET SCENES

PINEY WOODS PETE Says:

DEAR MISTER EDITOR

Barnett Aide Hit In Contempt Case

NEW ORLEANS, Sept. 29 (AP) — The federal 5th Circuit appeals court declared Mississippi Lt. Gov. Paul B. Johnson in contempt of court Saturday for his part in blocking Negro James H. Meredith from the University of Mississippi.

ARMY TROOPS AIRLIFTED INTO MEMPHIS

200 to 500 Men Join Forces Already on Scene

West Leaders To Huddle on Berlin Crisis

ZERO VANDY, GATORS

Bulldogs, Tech Roll to Victory

New Purge Hits Bosses In Red China

ON INSIDE PAGES

Mercury to Rise As Showers Eyed

OXFORD RULES

Everything Is Settled; It's Now Mongooses

U.S. Demands Soviet Recall Envoys In Sailor-Spy Case

President Kennedy and Attorney General Robert Kennedy ordered federal marshals to accompany James Meredith as he enrolled as the first black student at the University of Mississippi.

Ole Miss 14	Miss. Southern 29	Miss. College 12	Millsaps 7	Auburn 22
Kentucky 0	Southwestern, La. ... 0	Austin 6	Sewanee 7	Tennessee 21
Delta State 41	Ohio State 41	LSU 6	Georgia Tech 17	Texas 34
Jacksonville State .. 13	North Carolina 7	Rice 6	Florida 0	Texas Tech 0

WEATHER

Sunday—increasing cloudiness with a warming trend, low 60, high 88. Winds will be southerly at 10 to 15 miles per hour. Outlook for Monday—mostly cloudy and mild with scattered showers, low near 60, high in the upper 80s.

The Clarion-Ledger
JACKSON DAILY NEWS

PARADE

The annual Parade of Homes opens today. In two sections of today's paper, home builders tell of the houses they will have open along the 32 home route.

ASSOCIATED PRESS UNITED PRESS INTERNATIONAL JACKSON, MISSISSIPPI, SUNDAY, SEPTEMBER 30, 1962 AP WIREPHOTO EIGHT SECTIONS 112 PAGES PRICE 20c

NEGRO REFUSED CREDENTIALS

James L. Hicks, a Negro newsman, is interviewed on the Ole Miss campus at Oxford Saturday after university offficials refused to issue press credentials to him. Hicks, executive editor of the New York Amsterdam News, said he was not asked to leave the campus but would do so on his own accord. — AP Wirephoto.

JFK Takes Over Guard As Army Enters Crisis

Legislature Placed On Stand-By Basis

By CHARLES M. HILLS
Clarion-Ledger Staff Writer

The Mississippi Legislature stands recessed, on a stand-by basis subject to call, until Tuesday afternoon at 2 o'clock.

Any sign of federal invasion of the University of Mississippi or attempted arrest of either Gov. Ross Barnett or Lt. Gov. Paul B. Johnson, is said to be a signal for reconvening of the lawmaking body.

Both Barnett and Johnson are held in contempt of the Fifth Circuit Court of Appeals (Federal) at New Orleans.

Neither appeared in court, Friday and Saturday respectively, as ordered by the court to show cause why they should not be held in contempt.

Barnett and subsequently Johnson, acting as heads of state, have turned back federal marshals attempting to force entry of Negro James Meredith into the University of Mississippi.

CALLED

The legislature, called into extraordinary session two weeks ago to consider reapportionment of the state's legislative seats, has almost completely turned its attention to the Meredith integration debacle.

Saturday morning, the Senate met for more than an hour in executive session, largely to hear a report of progress of the case and possible legal measures to be taken in the event an expected invasion attempt is made by the U. S. Justice Dept. at Oxford.

Gov. Ross Barnett kept his offices open in the New Capitol all morning Saturday, while the Senate met, but the governor himself was not present. Lt. Gov. Johnson did not attend the Senate session.

Meantime, the House of Representatives went home Friday afternoon, also subject to immediate call by Speaker Walter Sillers in case of emergency. Time for end of the recess was set at 2 p.m., Tuesday, the same time that the Senate is expecting to reconvene.

The Senate Thursday morning approved SCR 101, a resolution reapportioning the law-making body by allowing 82 senators, or one from each county and 145 house members.

An inadvertent transposition of names Thursday recorded incorrectly the vote-intentions of Senators Ed Henry of Canton and Herman Camp of Fulton, who were paired on ahe reapportionment measure which passed the Senate. Henry opposes the measure, Camp favors it.

It is expected that the House of Representatives will pass the measure out of committee for attention of the entire body, early next week.

Meantime, with possible comple.

Continued on Page 16A

Armed Volunteers Told Not To Come

MONTGOMERY Ala., (UPI) — The executive secretary to Gov. Ross Barnett Saturday told a Montgomery group of volunteers who had planned a trip to Mississippi not to come immediately.

Elno Smith, leader of the local group which had planned to depart for Oxford Monday Saturday said he had received a call from Hugh Boyd.

Smith said Boyd told him Gov. Barnett was in conference at the present and was planning an important statement later Saturday.

Smith said he and the other volunteers were standing by, awaiting developments.

Unless they heard further from Mississippi officials they would not leave Monday as planned, Smith said.

Earlier Saturday Smith said approximately 57 persons had volunteered to leave here early Monday morning in a motorcade to go directly to Oxford.

Smith said the purpose of the trip was to lend moral and physical support to Barnett in the governor's stand against the federal government.

When asked what he meant by "physical" support, Smith said that if federal marshals tried to "buck" a line made up of volunteers "we'd be willing to let them fellows run into us."

"We plan to stay in Oxford just as long as the situation demands it," Smith said.

OLE MISS MIX CASE

Subcommittee Cites Negro's Lack Of Good Qualifications

By THE ASSOCIATED PRESS

A joint legislative committee charged today Negro James Meredith would have set the University of Mississippi up for expulsion from accrediting association had he been admitted.

The report was issued today after a study of the Meredith situation prior to the recent developments.

The committee said "if the attorney general of the United States is successful" in enrolling a student in the University of Mississippi who does not possess the necessary qualifications under the rules of the university, then "he could" attempt to enroll a select student into the university law school" who had a high school education.

The committee charged Atty. Gen. Robert F. Kennedy could force the registration because "of his race or religion."

The committee, composed of Chairman John C. McLaurin, Rep. Russell L. Fox, Sen. Ben F. Hilbun Jr., Rep. James W. Mathis, and Sen. E. K. Collins, listed three reasons the University of Mississippi originally denied the 29-year-old Kosciusko Negro from the University.

The text in full:

We, the members of your subcommittee, having been duly appointed for the purpose of inquiry into and determining the facts relative to the denial of the application of James H. Meredith by the Registrar of the University of Mississippi on May 25, 1961, do hereby make the following report:

1. The subcommittee has examined under oath, Robert E. Ellis, Registrar of the University of Mississippi; Dr. E. R. Jobe, Executive Secretary of the Board of Trustees of Institutions of Higher Learning of the State of Mississippi; and have examined all minutes and records of the Board of Trustees of Institutions of Higher Learning and other pertinent

Continued On Page 15A

Fall Day Is Lovely In Oxford

Gentle Campus Awaits In Eye Of A Hurricane

By EDMOND LEBRETON

OXFORD, Miss. (AP)—It was a lovely fall day in Oxford, not an intense day of wind and poignant colors like those of a northern fall, but a day of soft greens and golds and warm sun.

The gently spreading campus of the University of Mississippi was awaiting a test of bald force between national and state authority over a Negro's attempt to attend the university.

There were no federal marshals around, and very few state officers. Students — many of whom earlier must have been in the crowd cheering the governor's defiance of federal power — were relaxed and smiling. They went from class to Student Union, chatting and skylarking, boy-attracting and girl-watching in the way of the young everywhere — perhaps with more talent than many not reared in the South.

"Welcome to Ole Miss — Everybody Speaks" said a sign meant for freshman at one door of the building the Negro James H. Meredith hopes to penetrate with the support of federal officers if he is to register.

Even if they didn't say much the students spoke politely when spoken to by the dozens of strangers, newsmen from far places who crowded the halls and wide porch of the same building. The university extended to its uninvited guests the use of a room, typewriters, telephones, coffee, snacks and smiles.

Students and faculty, they met the people from the often critical outside world with its kind of courtesy that is indistinguishable from friendship.

Reporters with nothing much to write watched the girls go by—not one unattractive or lacking taste in dress or grooming. At least half actually pretty and an astonishing number beautiful. It was easy to see how two recent Miss Americas came from this campus in successive years.

On the still green sward of the campus was the ugly brown mark of a cross fashioned of fiber laid on the grass at night and burned.

On a dormitory window sill, carelessly draped like a familiar thing, not flaunted, was a Confederate flag.

Not far from the campus the clay mound over the grave of William Faulkner, a representative of the inside world, who did not always praise the South, was still raw and red but already eroding. There was no marker on it yet, but there were flowers.

The whole enigma of the South somehow was contained in Oxford on a lovely fall day.

Utica Bank Picks Heads

UTICA — It was announced Saturday that G. B. Carmichael has resigned as president of the bank of Utica and has been replaced by Harris Carmichael as the new president.

The same announcement said Ed C. Garrison has been elected executive vice president of the well known financial institution.

Gov. Johnson In Contempt

NEW ORLEANS, La. (AP) — The U. S. 5th Circuit Court of Appeals declared Mississippi Lt. Gov. Paul B. Johnson in contempt of court Saturday for his part in blocking Negro James H. Meredith from the University of Mississippi.

The three-judge panel of the court ordered Johnson fined $5,000 a day unless he shows by 11 a.m. Tuesday that he intends to cooperate with court orders prohibiting interference with Meredith's enrollment.

The same court, with eight judges sitting in, convicted Mississippi Gov. Ross Barnett of contempt Friday for stopping Meredith. It ordered him fined $10,000 a day and taken into custody if he fails to purge himself of contempt by 11 a.m. Tuesday.

The court did not order Johnson taken into custody—under the present circumstances—even if he fails to purge himself.

But it did say that if Johnson acts in place of the governor in violation of court orders he would be committed to custody of the U. S. attorney general, and his fine would be increased to $10,000 a day.

Neither Johnson nor Barnett appeared at their show-cause hearing.

The brief hearing in advance of the ruling was almost a replay of the legal maneuvering in the same court room Friday involving Barnett.

John Doar of the Justice Department told the three-judge panel that Johnson is clearly in contempt for stopping Meredith, 29, and federal marshals at the Ole Miss gates last Wednesday.

ONLY FOR FINE

But he asked only for a fine against Johnson, saying a jail sentence would serve no purpose because Johnson's moves were more or less done in behalf of the governor.

The Justice Department suggested the same deadline for Johnson to purge himself as Barnett received Friday.

Meredith's attorneys, appearing at the hearing along with the Justice Department attorneys to press the action against Johnson, urged a quicker deadline—as they did in the case of Barnett, too.

Against Johnson, the slightly built Meredith took the witness stand—his first testimony since the case was in the U. S. District Court last January.

Calmly, with no show of emotion, he told the court, "I was refused admission to the (university) grounds by the lieutenant governor, Paul Johnson.

A deputy federal marshal, Harry E. Lowe of Washington, told of efforts to serve papers on Johnson. He said he finally stuck the summons in the screen door of Johnson's home at Hattiesburg after Johnson's wife refused to accept them.

He also testified that he tried to serve Johnson with the papers at the lieutenant governor's office in Jackson. But he said one of seven uniformed men who met him in the state office building told him he would be arrested for littering if he left the papers on the floor in front of Johnson's office.

AT THIS POINT

At this point, Judge John R. Brown of Houston, Tex., asked whether it was normal procedure for a federal officer to obey such an order.

Lowe said: "I was instructed not to get arrested."

Along with Brown, judges sitting in on the Johnson hearing were John Minor Wisdom of New Orleans and Richard T. Rives of Montgomery, Ala.

John Satterfield of Yazoo City, Miss., a former president of the American Bar Association, asked permission for himself and other Mississippi attorneys to sit in as friends of the court—representing the State of Mississippi, not Johnson.

As it did with a similar request in the Barnett hearing, the court turned them down.

Satterfield then tried to ask the court to dissolve its sweeping restraining order of last Tuesday prohibiting Barnett and a large number of Mississippi officials from interfering with Meredith's attempts to enroll.

It was this order of the court that the Justice Department accused Barnett and Johnson of ignoring in contempt.

Again, as it did in the Barnett hearing, the court refused.

But at the close of the hearing the court set 1:30 p.m. Monday to hear the State of Mississippi's motion to dissolve the restraining order.

MEREDITH'S WIFE WANTS TO ENTER OLE MISS IN 1963

Mary Meredith, formerly of Gary, Indiana, wife of James "Jay" Meredith, also wants to enter Ole Miss. She is now a student at Jackson State College.

She is quoted by Thomas Buckley in the New York Times as saying she will apply for the graduate school in 1963 to study English for a master's degree.

Her husband's efforts to register at the University of Mississippi are in the limelight this fall.

PARADE OF HOMES OPENS WITH 32 HOMES DISPLAYED

32 Houses Open on Parade of Homes	Section E
Bloody Battle as Reds Cross Potomac	1B
Start Sand Removal Over Chlorine Gas	3A
Meredith Case Pictures, Stories	Section F

REGULAR FEATURES

Affairs	7B	Editorials	6B	On Stage	10B	TV Logs	9B
Books	12B	Gallup	2F	Pearson	7B	Want Ads	Sec F
Crossroads	6B	Gardens	13B	Sports	Sec. C	Weather	2F
Dis-Dat	4B	Hewitt	6B	Stars-Lovers	9B	Women's Sec.	D

16 Pages of Comics
Parade Magazine

Schedules Video Address To U.S.

WASHINGTON (AP) — President Kennedy signed early Sunday a proclamation commanding "all persons engaged in such obstructions of justice" as may interfere with the execution of court desegregation orders to desist immediately.

The President acted as the federal goverment's efforts to get a Negro student into the University of Mississippi neared a climax.

At the same time he signed an executive order authorizing the Secretary of Defense to take whatever steps are necessary to enforce the court decrees.

These included the federation of the Mississippi National Guard.

The President said he placed the Mississippi National Guard under federal control to provide whatever enforcement measures are necessary to carry out desegregation at the university.

The President signed the proclamation at one minute after midnight.

Secretary of Defense Robert S. McNamara, who was at his home waiting for the signal, then signed a Pentagon order which empowered the secretaries of the Army and Air Force to take over Mississippi National Guard units.

In effect, a White House spokesman said, the guard was removed from state control and placed under command of the federal government. It was aimed at taking the guard out of the control of Mississippi's Gov. Ross Barnett.

Neither the proclamation nor the orders—by Kennedy and McNamara—assigned troops into Mississippi.

The strength and authority of the federal government were, however, thrust into the crisis which has developed from Barnett's refusal to admit James H. Meredith, 29, a Negro, to the university.

The White House declined to speculate on what will happen if any Mississippi Guard units refuse to accept orders.

WASHINGTON (AP) — President Kennedy called the Mississippi National Guard into federal service Saturday night as he moved closer to a showdown with Gov. Ross Barnett to get a Negro enrolled into the University of Mississippi.

Putting the National Guard of the state into federal service makes it available for use against the state.

The President acted after making three separate attempts, the White House said, to receive assurance from the governor that "law and order could or would be maintained" in Oxford, Miss., the university town, during the coming week.

The President said he was federalizing the guard "incase they are needer to enforce the orders of the federal court."

TROOPS

Army troops, meanwhile, were ordered moved into a strategic position at Memphis, Tenn., but 50 miles from the campus.

The President announced he will make a 15-minute television-radio broadcast to the nation at 5:15 p.m. Mississippi time Sunday night. The President is expected to outline the steps he has taken or will take in an effort to solve

Continued on Page 16A

MIX NEWS IN BRIEF

Support Massive For Gov. Barnett

COLUMBIA, S. C. (UPI) — Gov. Ross Barnett has been sent a telegram signed by about 700 University of South Carolina students endorsing his stand in the Ole Miss situation.

MIAMI (UPI) — About 500 armed men, members of the Florida White Citizens Council, have been offered to Gov. Ross Barnett to help fight a federal court integration order.

Fred Hockett, executive secretary of the state council, said the men will be in Oxford Monday if Barnett calls for them.

TOPEKA, Kan. (UPI)—If fighting erupts in Mississippi it could spread to other states, Arkansas Gov. Orval Faubus said here.

Faubus told a military gathering of the Missouri-Kansas National Guard that he "left instructions" with his state police and the National Guard to do what was necessary in the event of trouble.

MERIDIAN (UPI) — State officials were urged Saturday by the Lauderdale County Bar Association not to allow the University of Mississippi to lose its academic accreditation.

The association also called on Gov. Ross Barnett not to close the school and "jeopardize and imperil the continued operation of other institutions of higher learning in this state."

COLUMBIA (UPI) — Gov. Ross Barnett has focused the nation's attention on the "federal invasion of the state sovereignty," a leading Republican said here.

William D. Workman JR., GOP candidate for the U. S. Senate, said the Ole Miss issue goes beyond the question of "integration or segregation."

"This involves the basic question of whether the 10th Amendment still means anything, and whether the states of the union still have any of the rights reserved to them under the constitution," he said.

MONTGOMERY, Ala. (UPI) — State Democratic Chairman Roy Mayhall said Saturday he has wired President Kennedy a strong protest on federal handling of the Mississippi crisis.

Mayhall, one of Alabama's leading loyal Democrats, told Kennedy:

"We Democrats in Alabama deplore the use of force against the sovereign power of the State of Mississippi. We believe that control and operation of schools rightfully is vested in the states and the duly elected officials of Mississippi are capabe of determining what is best for the people."

TUSCALOOSA, Ala., (UPI) — The Ku Klux Klan was to meet here Saturday night to show support for resistance of integration efforts at the University of Mississippi.

The announcement was made in Atlanta, Ga., by Calvin F. Craig, Georgia's klan dragon.

The night before Meredith enrolled, two people died and 160 federal marshals were injured in riots.

ALSO IN 1962

Bob Dylan first performed "Blowin' in the Wind," a protest song that became an anthem for the 1960s civil rights movement.

UNITED STATES, SOVIET UNION NEARED WAR OVER CUBAN MISSILE CRISIS

For thirteen days, the United States and the Soviet Union approached the brink of war over the installation of Soviet nuclear-armed missiles in Cuba.

ALSO IN 1962

The Manchurian Candidate, a Cold War–era movie based on a thriller novel about a brainwashed presidential assassin, was released.

Almost Beachy

Northeast Florida For Redistricting ... mood of voters, 18A

CITY EDITION

The Miami Herald

Tuesday, October 23, 1962 — No. 326 — Florida's Most Complete Newspaper — 52nd Year — 56 Pages — 5 Cents

Cuban Blockade Ordered; JFK Warns of War Peril

102 Safe In Plane Ditching

Easy Landing, Calm Sea Help

NUCLEAR-POWERED aircraft carrier Enterprise is among the 40 ships, which were assembled by the Navy for maneuvers in the Caribbean. The exercises were canceled but the ships and men are on station for blockade duty.

Next 48 Hours Decide It: Russian Ships on Way

JFK's 7-Point Program on Cuba

Here is the seven-point program on Cuba enunciated by President Kennedy:

1 — The United States, "to halt this offensive buildup" in Cuba, is imposing "a strict quarantine on all offensive military equipment under shipment to Cuba."

All ships of any kind bound for Cuba are to be turned back if they are found to contain cargoes of offensive weapons. This embargo also will be extended to "other carriers" if need be — meaning airplanes.

2 — Surveillance of Cuba and its military buildup will be stepped up, and the U.S. armed forces have been ordered "to prepare for any eventualities."

3 — U.S. policy will be to regard any nuclear missile launched from Cuba against any nation in the Western Hemisphere as an attack by Russia on the United States requiring full retaliation against the Soviet Union.

4 — The U.S. naval base at Guantanamo, on the eastern tip of Cuba, has been reinforced. U.S. dependents there have been evacuated and additional military units have been ordered to stand by on alert.

5 — An immediate meeting of the Organization of American States has been called to "consider this threat to hemispheric security" and to invoke the Inter-American defense pact provisions "in support of all necessary action."

6 — The United States is asking for an emergency meeting of the United Nations Security Council without delay. The United States will call for "the prompt dismantling and withdrawal of all offensive weapons in Cuba" before it lifts the blockade.

7 — Kennedy called on Soviet Premier Nikita S. Khrushchev "to halt and eliminate this clandestine, reckless and provocative threat to world peace."

Moscow Sleeps Through Speech, Readies Reaction

The Crisis At a Glance

WORLD REACTION varies; Congress, Nixon back President .... Page 1A
NEXT 48 HOURS TELL THE STORY .... Page 1A
FLORIDA GUARD ALERTED, plane schedule interrupted .... Page 1A
HOW DO WE MAKE CUBA DISMANTLE those missiles? .... Page 2A
U.S. HAS CROSSED BORDERS 90 times in the past in hemisphere .... Page 7A
RIO PACT, NOT MONROE DOCTRINE, forms basis for U.S. action .... Page 7A
PHOTOS OF MISSILE BUILDUP in Cuba made Kennedy act .... Page 15A
EXILE LEADERS hope for invasion Page 15A
FAMILIES EVACUATED from Guantanamo .... Page 15A
"WONDERFUL!" exclaims Cuban exiles .... Page 1B
MIAMIANS SAY "It's about time!" Page 1B
WHAT DOES BLOCKADE MEAN? We're on a near-war footing .... Page 1B
BUILDUP IN SOUTH FLORIDA sees planes coming, ships going .... Page 1B
FULL TEXT of President's message Page 2B

Cuban Official Requests Asylum

Interesting Day, Says Kennedy

On the Inside

Hoffa Loses Round to U.S.

Today's Chuckle

Food, Medicine Only Commodities Allowed to Pass

President Kennedy ... ordering blockade

Bryant Alerts Guard, CD

Cuba Quarantined? –It's Still Blockade

UNITED STATES, SOVIET UNION NEARED WAR OVER CUBAN MISSILE CRISIS

★ **DAILY NEWS** 5¢

NEW YORK'S PICTURE NEWSPAPER ®

Vol. 44. No. 103 Copr. 1962 News Syndicate Co. Inc. New York 17, N.Y., Tuesday, October 23, 1962★ WEATHER: Partly cloudy and cool.

JFK THREATENS FORCE AGAINST RED CONVOYS

—Story on Page 3

(NEWS foto by Ed Giorandino)
Grim-faced Gromyko boards airplane.

(Associated Press Wirefoto)

Faces in a Crisis. Presidential Press Secretary Pierre Salinger briefs Washington press corps at the White House. Reporters were told President Kennedy would address nation on world situation of "the highest national urgency" via radio and TV last night. Meanwhile, Soviet Foreign Minister Andrei Gromyko [⟵] left International Airport for East Berlin after four week stay and conference with JFK. —*Story on page 3; other pictures in centerfold*

After a U.S. spy plane photographed the Soviet Union's nuclear missile sites in Cuba, Kennedy met in secret with his advisers for several days because he did not want to disclose to the Soviets that he knew about the missiles.

President John F. Kennedy and Attorney General Robert Kennedy conferred about tensions between the United States and the Soviet Union. (AP Photo)

UNITED STATES, SOVIET UNION NEARED WAR OVER CUBAN MISSILE CRISIS

C.I.S. SKYSCRAPER—pp 9-14

FOR CAR HIRE ROOTES KNOTT MILL MANCHESTER

THE GUARDIAN

36,174 Manchester Tuesday October 23 1962 Price 4d

TYPIST DESKS IN OAK ALL SIZES From £12.10.0 SIMPOLES

US IMPOSES CUBAN ARMS BLOCKADE

Ready to sink Soviet ships if necessary

UN URGED TO ACT

Washington, October 22

The United States is prepared to sink Soviet ships if necessary to prevent offensive weapons reaching Cuba. This was stated by the Defence Department here tonight after President Kennedy had ordered an arms blockade of the island.

Mr Kennedy, announcing in a broadcast "a strict quarantine" to stop an offensive Communist build-up, including the sending of missiles, had said: "All ships of any kind . . . will, if found to contain cargoes of offensive weapons, be turned back." But Cubans would not be denied the necessities of life.

Later a Defence Department spokesman said the United States had placed its forces, including its garrison in Berlin and the Strategic Air Command on a world wide alert. Other officials said a showdown could come with the Soviet Union in 24 hours.

If a ship did not stop when ordered to do so, it was stated, a shot would be fired across its bows. If it still did not stop or turn back, then another shot would be fired at it with the idea of minimising any casualties. The blockade, the formal proclamation of which was expected to be signed by the President tomorrow, would apply to ships of all nations, including Allied vessels.

President Kennedy was taking this and other action because within the past week "unmistakable evidence has established the fact that a series of offensive missile sites is now in preparation on that imprisoned island." The purpose of these bases being built up by Russia could be "none other than to provide a nuclear strike capability against the Western hemisphere."

Threat to peace

Several of the new sites included installations of medium-range ballistic missiles, capable of carrying a nuclear warhead for a distance of more than 1,000 miles—to Washington, the Panama Canal and other places in the Caribbean.

The President announced this seven-point plan of initial action to meet the Soviet move which constituted an "explicit threat to the peace and security of all the Americas":

1. To halt the offensive build-up by a strict quarantine on all offensive military equipment under shipment to Cuba.

Shock for UK

A Foreign Office spokesman said early today that Mr Macmillan had been informed in advance of the contents of Mr Kennedy's announcement on Cuba when the American Ambassador called on him.

British Ministers would consider the matter this morning, he said, adding: "The revelation of the Soviet build-up in Cuba will come as a shock to the whole civilised world."

5. To call tonight for an immediate meeting of the organ of consultation under the Organisation of American States to consider "this threat to hemispheric security and to invoke Articles 6 and 8 of the Rio Treaty in support of all necessary action."

6. To ask tonight for an emergency meeting of the United Nations Security Council to take action "without delay against this latest Soviet threat to world peace."

7. "I call upon chairman (Nikita) Khrushchev to halt and eliminate this clandestine, reckless, and provocative threat to world peace and to stable relations between our two nations. I call upon him further to abandon this course of world domination ..."

Missile bases built up

1,500-MILE RANGE CLAIMED

From MAX FREEDMAN

Washington, October 22

Mr Kennedy emphasised in his broadcast that the programme he was announcing involved no more than "initial measures" which might be extended in coming weeks and months.

He warned the American people that they once again might be required to pay "the price of freedom." But no country in the world, friend or foe, would ever trust the courage or the commitments of the United States if it now refused to honour its obligations in the Western hemisphere.

Mr Kennedy explained that last Tuesday morning he received definite information confirming earlier reports that the nature of the Communist military build-up in Cuba had swiftly and secretly changed. Russia was now shipping missiles there under the cover of secrecy. Already in Cuba were several middle-range ballistic missiles capable of travelling a distance of 1,000 miles and striking.

Text of Mr Kennedy's speech, page 15

The range

In addition Russia had shipped intermediate-range ballistic missiles capable of travelling 1,500 miles. These, now being uncrated and assembled in Cuba, could reach any city from Hudson's Bay and the northernmost tip of Canada to Lima, Peru. Moreover Russia had sent jet bombers to Cuba and these were being uncrated and assembled.

This "urgent transformation of Cuba" constituted a clear and flagrant and dangerous challenge to the security of the hemisphere. It was in clear violation of the Rio pact guaranteeing the security of the Latin American states, and in opposition to the long-standing commitment of the US to the security of Latin America, to the recent resolution passed by Congress and to Mr Kennedy's own statement about American policy should Cuba become an armed Soviet base.

Mr Kennedy, in warning Mr Khrushchev that the US would use its "full retaliatory powers" against the Soviet Union if the Cuban offensive capacity were used against an American country, in effect has given the same commitment to every country in Latin America that has already been given to Western Europe under the NATO treaty. An attack on any one in this hemisphere is regarded as an attack on the United States.

Appeal to Cubans

A hail of radio bulletins

Americans wait for President

From ALISTAIR COOKE

Cabinet to meet today

Members of the secrets inquiry commission. From left to right: Sir Charles Cunningham, Sir Harold Kent, and Sir Burke Trend

Inquiry into security

SEQUEL TO VASSALL TRIAL

By FRANCIS BOYD, our Political Correspondent

Mr Macmillan has ordered a Civil Service inquiry into the circumstances in which the offences, of which John Christopher Vassall, an Admiralty clerk, was found guilty in London yesterday, were committed. The setting up of this inquiry was announced from Admiralty House yesterday shortly after the result of the trial was known.

The Prime Minister decided in this case not to select a chairman from outside the Civil Service because, in the Government's view, the Admiralty's security arrangements were examined adequately by the Romer Committee, and the general security arrangements of the Government were covered in the Radcliffe Committee's report.

The announcement from Admiralty House reads:

"In the light of the conviction of William John Christopher Vassall at the Central Criminal Court today for offences under the Official Secrets Act, the Prime Minister has decided to appoint a committee of inquiry to examine the circumstances in which these offences were committed ..."

"TOTALLY INADEQUATE"

Lord Cobham's silver and paintings in stolen lorry

US air liner ditches: life rafts seen

AMERICA'S CUP RACE IN 1964

UK challenge accepted

Chinese take more posts

McMAHON LINE REPUDIATED

New Delhi, October 22

Mr Nehru today called on the Indian people to prepare to meet the danger of "continuing and unabashed aggression by Chinese forces" on the country's borders.

Chinese use tanks

British Guiana talks start today

FORD'S MAY CUT STAFF

Strike has cost £3m.

By JOHN COLE, our Labour Correspondent

After attempts to spread the strike at the Ford Motor Company's headquarters in Dagenham had failed yesterday, the company said that the disruption already caused has been so severe that it will "not be able to maintain the same labour force as before, at least for some time to come."

Rubbing it in

No question

ELIMINATING ENGLISH FROM 11-PLUS

On other pages

Tomorrow's paper

To prevent the Soviets from delivering more military supplies, Kennedy placed a naval blockade around Cuba and demanded the removal of the missiles.

The Washington Post
Times Herald

The Weather
Today—Considerable cloudiness and cooler, high in low 60s. Tonight—Low in mid 40s. Tuesday—Rather cloudy and cool with some rain likely. Sunday's high, 73, 3 p.m.; low, 42, 7 a.m. *Weather Map and Detail on Page B3.*

First in News
The Washington Post publishes more news and features than any other Washington newspaper and is first in Washington in awards received for journalistic achievement.

85th Year · No. 328 Phone RE. 7-1234 *Copyright © 1962 The Washington Post Co.* **MONDAY, OCTOBER 29, 1962** WTOP-TV (9) Radio (1500) TEN CENTS

Reds Agree to Scrap Bases in Cuba;
U. S. Greets Move as Tension Eases;
U. N. Aides Going to Havana Tuesday

President Flies to Virginia Estate

President Kennedy's helicopter is shown as he took off from the White House lawn yesterday for the family's Glen Ora estate, near Middleburg, Va. The President had lunch with his wife and children. Except for attending church two Sundays, this was the first time he had been out of the White House for more than a week. Story A7.

Castro Bid Is Accepted By Thant

Secretary General To Leave Some of Staff on Island

By Louis B. Fleming
Special to The Washington Post
From The Los Angeles Times

UNITED NATIONS, N. Y., Oct. 28—U. N. Acting Secretary General U Thant will fly to Havana Tuesday on a peace mission without parallel in the 17-year history of the United Nations.

He will take with him some staff members, including his chief military adviser, Brig. Indar Jit Rikhye, and will leave some of them in Cuba—this, in effect, establishing a U.N. presence on the island. U. S. Ambassador Adlai E. Stevenson paid a surprise second visit to Thant tonight, after Thant had announced his trip, to deliver a new letter from President Kennedy.

The letter was in response to yet another note from Thant to the President. The Secretary General said the text would not be released today.

Confer for Hour

Stevenson spent an hour with Thant tonight. He was accompanied by his deputy, Charles W. Yost; John J. McCloy, the Ambassador's special assistant on the Cuban crisis, and Air Force Under Secretary Joseph W. Charyk.

Meanwhile, Soviet First Deputy Foreign Minister Vassily V. Kuznetsov was on his way from Moscow to join in Thant's discussions here. Soviet Premier Nikita S. Khrushchev said he was sending Kuznetsov to help Thant "in his noble efforts aimed at the liquidation of the present dangerous position."

Thant sent a message tonight to Prime Minister Fidel Castro in Havana accepting Castro's invitation of yesterday for a peace mission.

In his reply, Thant asked for personal discussions with Castro of "all important aspects of the problem."

"It would be my hope that, as a result of these discussions, a solution would be reached by which the principle of respects for the sovereignty of Cuba would be assured.

See KREMLIN, A13, Col. 1

Mother, 2 Sons Killed in Fire

CHICAGO, Oct. 28 (UPI)—A mother and her twin boys died today when fire swept through a two-story tenement building. A 15-month-old baby was saved when she was thrown from a second-floor window into the arms of a policeman.

The victims were Mrs. Mary Collins, 32, and her sons, Terry and Perry, 5. Police said the fire began in their second-story dining room.

The child, Sherri Wind Bush, was tossed by Buddy Williams, 15, into the arms of patrolman Michael Pyscznad. She was not hurt.

Caution Is Key Word; K Got U. S. Message: Deadline Was Near

Kremlin Ponders Its Choices After Bad Miscalculation

By Alfred Friendly
Managing Editor,
The Washington Post

Premier Nikita S. Khrushchev got America's message that it was really a matter of "a couple of days"—say a few days—before the United States would move by force to deactivate the Cuban missile bases.

Such action would have risked escalation into nuclear war; at a minimum it would have lost for the Kremlin its one Western Hemisphere satellite, not to mention its prestige and future in Latin America. Accordingly, the Soviets decided to cut their losses, dismantle the missiles themselves and salvage what they could from the situation.

This is how top figures in the U. S. Administration connected with the Cuban crisis explain the proposals and action Khrushchev announced yesterday.

Astonished by Reaction

They believe that Khrushchev made a very bad miscalculation, that he was astonished by the vehemence of the American reaction and by the sheer determination to face nuclear war if necessary to undo the Soviet's arming of Cuba with offensive weapons.

They feel from Khrushchev's public statements (and from a number of still secret messages or conversations that are known to have taken place in the last week) that he came to understand the narrowness of the time dimension the United States was vouchsafing him for action, and the gravity of the kind of action it was prepared to take.

What specific action might have been taken is unclear, quite possibly because the President himself had made no final decision by the time Khrushchev's announcement to dismantle the bases arrived here yesterday.

'Deeper Action' Planned

Whether it would have been bombing of the bases, invasion, or whatever, it was thought of as the Administration as "deeper action." Khrushchev got the message that something of this sort was being prepared from American

See POLICY, A5, Col. 1

Uncertainty Clouds Communists' Next Steps in Cold War

By Murray Marder
Staff Reporter

Utmost caution, with jubilation, was the posture of American strategists yesterday as the Soviet Union and the United States edged back from the brink.

After the gravest crisis of the nuclear age, the next moves are clouded with uncertainty.

If the step back from the abyss is confirmed by physical evidence in the Caribbean, the outcome will be a major advantage to the United States in the Cold War. The United States would have demonstrated that it will risk nuclear war to preserve its vital world interests.

But this in itself will not solve the Berlin crisis. Nor will it necessarily mean that the Soviet Union will not pose an equally crisis confrontation somewhere else, at a time and under circumstances that it finds more favorable.

Kremlin Moves Studied

An immediate dilemma for American policymakers is the current crisis, which is yet to be wholly defused, is the mystery of what has been going on in the Kremlin.

Soviet experts here can only speculate why two apparently directly conflicting messages came from the Kremlin Friday and Saturday. Soviet Premier Nikita S. Khrushchev's Friday letter to President Kennedy set in motion the pullback from the

See KREMLIN, A11, Col. 1

New Notes Stress Aim For Peace

President Calls Soviet Decision 'Statesmanlike'

By Chalmers M. Roberts
Staff Reporter

President Kennedy late yesterday told Soviet Premier Nikita S. Khrushchev that "we step back from danger" now that an agreement is in sight to end the Soviet-American crisis over Cuba.

Mr. Kennedy was responding to the key move, a dramatic announcement Sunday morning by Khrushchev that he had ordered his missile bases on Cuba dismantled. President Kennedy quickly welcomed the move. About

Text of Premier Khrushchev's message on Cuba to President Kennedy and his reply and statement. Pages A6 and 7.

three hours after Khrushchev's message was broadcast early Sunday by Moscow Radio, the White House declared that it was a "statesmanlike decision" and "an important and constructive contribution to peace."

Basis for Accord Seen

The news from Moscow came after 24 hours of uncertainty here over what was going on in the Kremlin. What Khrushchev said in his new letter, a copy of which reached the White House several hours after it had been broadcast, appeared to provide a basis for a firm Soviet-American agreement though there were still many unsettled questions.

The stage is now set for intense diplomatic negotiations with United Nations Secretary General U Thant playing an important role, the President made clear, and the Organization of American States will also be deeply involved.

Just before 5 p.m. Sunday the White House made public the formal presidential response to Khrushchev. It was sent even before the official text of the Khrushchev message reached Mr. Kennedy.

The President reciprocated the conciliatory tone of Khrushchev's Sunday message, saying that "perhaps now, as we step back from danger, we can together make real progress in this vital field." He was re-

See CRISIS, A5, Col. 2

Baltimore Blaze Hurts 3 Firemen

BALTIMORE, Oct. 28 (AP)—Three firemen were injured tonight as some 20 pieces of apparatus battled a 12-alarm blaze in a vacant paper company building in downtown Baltimore.

One of the injured firefighters was in a snorkel basket pouring water on the front of the burning six-story brick structure when a sudden gust of air forced the flames out for some 20 feet, engulfing him.

Officials Blame Communists

Saboteur Bombs Knock Out a Sixth Of Venezuelan Oil-Producing Capacity

From News Dispatches

CARACAS, Venezuela, Oct. 28—Saboteurs believed to be Communists blew up four oil company power stations in Lake Maracaibo early today, knocking out one-sixth of Venezuela's oil producing capacity. Venezuela is the world's leading oil exporter.

Authorities seized two men, believed to be the saboteurs, swimming in debris in the lake. Police said they believed a third man, the apparent ringleader, was killed when one of the saboteurs blew up the saboteurs' motor

boat. Officials said they were Communists.

The attacks on the power substations, situated 55 miles apart along Lake Maracaibo, were termed by "expert sabotage, carefully coordinated," by a company spokesman. One of the saboteurs was identified as an ex-Creole employee.

The blasts were the biggest blow yet struck by the terrorists in their war of nerves and destruction against President Romulo Betancourt. Betancourt is one of the most outspoken foes of Cuban Premier Fidel Castro.

Destruction of the power stations halted production of 525,000 barrels of petroleum a day — one sixth of the nation's total output. The production loss will cost the company and the nation — which

collects about 70 per cent of the proceeds — an estimated $1.10 million a day or as long as it takes to repair the damage.

Preliminary estimates indicate it will take between one and four weeks to restore full production. In the meantime, however, the company has enough crude oil stored to meet its international obligations, a company spokesman said.

The blasts occurred only a few hours after Betancourt had told a nation-wide television and radio audience he had ordered the first armed forces mobilization since 1945. He took the step he said, "because of the obvious gravity" of the situation created by reports that Cuba has been converted into a Soviet base for atomic rockets of medium and intermediate range.

The Government has been cracking down on Communists and pro-Castro sympathizers since Oct. 8 when all constitutional guarantees were suspended.

De Gaulle Is Winner in Referendum But Margin Could Prove Too Thin

By Waverley Root
The Washington Post Foreign Service

PARIS, Oct. 29 (Monday)—The French electorate Sunday approved President Charles de Gaulle's proposal to amend the constitution to elect presidents by popular vote, but his majority in the nation-wide referendum was not substantial enough to rule out the possibility of his resignation.

The semiofficial final results showed that 61.72 per cent of all votes cast—60.98 per cent of valid votes—were "yes" and 38.27 per cent on "no." Semiofficial returns issued early this morning gave these figures:

Registered voters: 27,579,939
Votes cast: 21,306,910.
Abstentions: 6,272,940.
Valid votes: 20,741,247.
"Yes": 12,808,848.
"no": 7,932,399.
Invalid ballots: 665,663.

Thus the amendment carried, but doubt remained as to whether de Gaulle would consider the majority sufficiently decisive to stay in office.

Resignation Proviso

He said in his Oct. 18 broadcast that he would resign, not only if he lost the referendum, but even if he won it by a majority only "small, mediocre or indefinite."

His colleagues — but never

de Gaulle himself—have been defining this as meaning more than half the registered voters —not simply a majority of those actually voting.

One Gaullist who probably does not feel gratified about the results is ex-Prime Minister Michael Debré, whose district voted only 51.2 per cent "yes"—or about 37 per cent of the registered voters.

The referendum was so de Gaulle's proposal to amend which his successors would be chosen directly by the French people rather than by an electoral college of about 50,000 officials.

Acceptance of the constitutional amendment does not necessarily mean that it will now become law. Senate President Gaston Monnerville has announced he will call upon the Constitutional Council to reject the proposal as illegal, and the Council has already ruled once that it was.

Picture on Page A13.

For this reason, a large proportion, if not a majority, of the 300 to 400 government officials and journalists who gathered in the Interior Ministry to receive the returns were predicting an early hour this morning that de Gaulle would resign.

Pompidou View

But Premier Georges Pompidou issued a statement early yesterday professing to find the results gratifying, claiming that the majority could not be considered "mediocre" or indefinite.

If this statement was issued with the approval of de Gaulle, it must mean that the General has decided to stay. But the gloom of some ministers at the Interior building last night suggested that this could be no more than a move

to influence the General's ultimate decision.

Sports Summary

Tittle Stars, Giants Whip Skins, 49-34

The New York Giants, sparked by the magnificent performance of Y. A. Tittle, burst the Redskins' bubble yesterday in New York, handing Washington its first defeat of the season, 49-34.

Tittle tied the National Football League record with seven touchdown passes, completed 27 of 39 attempts and accounted for 505 yards.

Norman Snead tossed four scoring passes for the Redskins and scored a touchdown on a sneak. Snead hit Bobby Mitchell for two of his scoring efforts, covering 44 and 80 yards.

The Green Bay Packers remained the only unbeaten team in the league by defeating the Baltimore Colts, 17-6.

Other pro football scores:

NATIONAL LEAGUE
St. Louis 28		Dallas 24
Cleveland 41		Pittsburgh 14
Detroit 17		Chicago 3
Minnesota 21		Phila. 7
Los. Ang. 18		San Fran. 14

AMERICAN LEAGUE
New York 23		San Diego 3
Dallas 31		Houston 7
Buffalo 45		Denver 38

Today's Index

46 PAGES—2 SECTIONS

A-24 Pages—General News, Editorials, Sports, Financial	B-22 Pages—City Life, Women's, Classified, Comics

Page			Page	
Along	A15	Financial		A23
Art	A22	Comics		B19
Childs	A16	Keep Well		B18
City Life	B19	Movie Guide		A22
Classified	B7, 16	Music		A22
Comics	B17,20	Obituaries		B4
Crossword	B21	Pearson		A21
District Line	B21	Sokolsky		A15
Sports	A15	Sports		A16-21
Editorials	A20	TV-Radio		B6
Ev'th. Today	B19	Wallace		B6
Federal Diary	B1	Women's		B4-5

What Is A Blockade?

Columnist George E. Sokolsky looks at the international meaning of "blockade," and compares the Cuban blockade with those of previous years . . . in his column, "These Days," today on Page A15 of today's Washington Post.

The Washington Post

Police Chase Through Tunnels

Man With Hand Grenade Terrorizes Subway Before Bullets Fell Him

NEW YORK, Oct. 28 (AP)—A man with a live hand grenade terrorized subway passengers and gave police a wild chase across platforms and through tunnels for 40 minutes today before he was brought down by police bullets.

Police had to commandeer a subway train and empty it of passengers at one point in the chase, and a patrolman donned a bulletproof suit to rush the grenade wielder and disarm him.

Tentatively identified as Jerry Hartman, 21, of the Bronx, the man was taken to Fordham Hospital, apparently not seriously wounded.

Police had fired 18 bullets and at least three struck Hartman in the leg, hand and thigh.

As he was taken away, police said, he kept saying: "I want to see Kennedy. I want to see Kennedy."

The man was first involved in a fistfight on an IRT train going through the Bronx to ward Manhattan. At the 149th st. and Third ave. station, he jumped out onto the platform and began waving the grenade.

Then he jumped to the tracks and held off police by threatening: "I'll blow everybody up if you come near me."

All service through the station was cut off throughout the 40-minute chase.

tually took part in the skirmishes up and down the subway tunnel after all subway riders were evacuated from the station.

A sergeant who boarded and cleared an arriving train fired and felled the man once but it was emergency service Patrolman Joseph Goodwin who finally brought him down. Goodwin shot him twice and Third ave. station, he grenade and handcuffed him.

Then Goodwin put the grenade—its pin still in place—in his bulletproof helmet and carried it out.

More than 100 police even-

VOTING IS A RESPONSIBILITY AS WELL AS A RIGHT OF CITIZENSHIP

FAIR

THE BOSTON HERALD

COSTELLO Herter Finally Fires Back Page 18

VOL. CCXXXIII, NO. 129 LATE CITY EDITION HA 6-3000 BOSTON, TUESDAY, NOVEMBER 6, 1962—FORTY PAGES ★★ TEN CENTS

Hot Contests May Draw Record 2,200,000 to Polls

VOTERS TO HAVE SAY TODAY

★ ★ ★ ★ ★ ★ ★ ★ ★

Protest to Moscow

Red Bombers Still in Cuba

By THOMAS J. HAMILTON
(New York Times News Service)

UNITED NATIONS, N. Y.—The United States has protested to the Soviet Union against its failure to dismantle Cuba-based bombers capable of dropping nuclear bombs on the United States.

Grave Matter

According to reliable sources, recent U.S. reconnaissance photos have shown that some of the bombers were still being taken out of packing cases and assembled at an air base near Havana.

These sources said that John J. McCloy, chairman of the U.S. coordinating committee on Cuba policy, protested to Vasily V. Kuznetsov during a luncheon meeting Sunday. It was learned that McCloy told him that the U.S. takes "a most serious view" of the situation.

Members of the Security Council advised U Thant, acting secretary general, Monday that no meeting on the Cuba crisis should be held before next week.

According to reliable sources,

(Continued on Page Fifteen)

India Yields Mountain Pass

Refuelling Delay Hits Arms Airlift

By HENRY S. BRADSHER

NEW DELHI, India (AP)—India disclosed Monday abandonment of a military post controlling Karakoram Pass, one of the most important positions on its long battle line against the troops of Red China.

Quiet Elsewhere

A Defense Ministry spokesman announced the Indian garrison withdrew several days ago from Daulet Beg Oldi, at the foot of the 18,000-foot high pass between disputed Ladakh and Sinkiang Province of Western China.

The garrison was not under fire at the time, but outposts rimming the position had fallen before an offensive the Chinese launched Oct. 20.

Ladakh is at the western end of the Himalayan front, which is an

(Continued on Page Fifteen)

Today's Herald

	Page		Page
Aladdin	31	Krock	19
Alexander	19	Louie	12
Amuse	22	Lyons	31
Boy, Girl	19	Marco	30
Bridge	30	Marriage Int.	21
Caesar	30	Neighbors	19
Class Ads	30, 31	Pearson	18
Comics	38, 39	Porter	28
Commodities	29	Radio-TV	24
Courts	23	Rod, Gun	36
Crossword	31	Society	25
Dahl Cartoon	18	Sports	33-36
Deaths	37	Taylor	31
Editorial	18	TV Gossip	24
Fashion	25	Van Dellen	24
Fin'l	26-29	Waterfront	16
Frazier	12	Women's	24, 25
Horoscope	24		

For Information On Children's Book Fair See Page 9

President Comes to Boston But Only to Vote and Visit

Thousands Cheer Fast Motorcade

By ARTHUR STRATTON

President John F. Kennedy spent election eve in his home city last night, but deliberately applied the soft pedal to campaigning as Massachusetts Democrats know it.

1,000 on Guard

This morning at 9:30 in the Joy Street police station building he will cast a vote for his younger brother, Edward M. Kennedy, U.S. senatorial aspirant.

The brothers visited for about 15 minutes in the President's hotel suite early today. The senatorial candidate came down to the lobby at 12:45 a.m. To newsmen who asked what his brother had said to him, the younger Kennedy replied:

"He wished me luck in today's election."

While hopeful members of his party milled around his hotel, the President slipped out a side entrance and motored to the home of his maternal grandmother, Mrs. John F. Fitzgerald, widow of the legendary "Honey Fitz," in Ashmont.

Extraordinary security provisions — perhaps 1000 officers of several agencies in all — coupled with a Presidential desire to be treated as much as possible like any average American coming home to vote in an important election, dampened the ardor of

(Continued on Page Eleven)

REUNION IN DORCHESTER—President Kennedy took time out from his overnight trip to Massachusetts to make a quick visit to the Dorchester home of Mr. and Mrs. Thomas Fitzgerald where his maternal grandmother, the one-time First Lady of Boston, Mrs. John F. Fitzgerald, 97, resides.

'He's the President!'

'Hi Gram,' He Said, And Kisses Flew

By JAMES F. DRONEY

An elderly lady out Dorchester way received a birthday gift five days late last night.

The gift was a visit from a grandson whose name almost matches hers and who also happens to be President of the United States.

Again and Again

Mrs. John F. Fitzgerald, who was 97 last Wednesday, was obviously keyed up when President Kennedy strode into the second floor south bedroom of the Fitzgerald home at 3 Rundel Park.

Although President Kennedy towers over the fragile first grandlady of the nation, she pulled his head down close to hers and kissed him again and again on the forehead, the hair and cheeks.

"Hi, Gram," the President said.

"Jack," she said, and reached up for him.

(Continued on Page Thirteen)

$1,697,000 Estate

Adlai's Aunt Wills Million to Harvard

The bulk of the $1,697,000 estate of Mrs. Lucy Wallace Porter of Cambridge will go to Harvard University, her will, filed yesterday in Middlesex Registry of Probate, disclosed.

$30,000 for Art

Mrs. Porter, the socially prominent great-aunt of UN Ambassador Adlai Stevenson, left $1,093,000 to Harvard, along with her home, Elmwood, and objects of art and literary value.

Mrs. Porter specified that $30,000 be devoted to the preservation of art and literary matter, and that an A. Kingsley Porter pro-

(Continued on Page Fourteen)

GM Votes Huge Extra Dividend

$1.50 Year-End Totals $425 Million

By WILLIAM F. HOMER, JR.
Financial News Editor

General Motors Corporation Monday made Christmas about $425,000,000 brighter for more than 1,025,000 stockholders, and du Pont.

$1 Year Ago

Directors of the world's largest manufacturing company voted in New York a year-end dividend of $1.50 a share on the common, or $1 a share above the usual quarterly 50 cents payment.

A year ago, the year-end payment was set at $1 a share, or 50

(Cont'd on Page Twenty-Eight)

Of Special Interest

GEORGE MINOT rounds up the national election highlights on **Page 19**

NANCY LODGE, a portrait of the Senate candidates wife **Page 10**

FOR LATEST HERALD-TRAVELER ELECTION RETURNS CALL 423-4545 between 8 P.M. and 2 A.M.

Both Parties See Victory Assured

A promise of clearing weather by noon, the presence of President Kennedy and climactic contests for state and national office will combine today to draw to the polls what is expected to be a record number of Massachusetts voters.

Leaders of both parties predicted confidently last night the total would be easily 2,000,000, of the 2,600,000 enrolled, and some saw more than 2,200,000 turning out, a more massive vote than that of four years ago, when John F. Kennedy was returned to the Senate by the towering margin of 874,000 votes.

That vote helped send Kennedy to the White House, and his younger brother, Edward M. "Ted" Kennedy, goes in to the lists today to test his appeal against that of George Cabot Lodge for a Senate seat contested by the families of the candidates three times in this century.

Kennedy campaign managers predict not only that their man will win, but also that he will win big and launch himself on a brilliant career of his own.

(Continued on Page Fourteen)

Democrats Concentrate On Boston

By RICHARD J. CONNOLLY

Buoyed by the return home of President Kennedy and its anticipated psychological effect on the voters, the Democratic slate appeared confident of complete victory last night amid a flurry of election eve campaigning.

The weary candidates, still using the premise that Massachusetts must elect Democrats if it is to progress with the New Frontier, believed that the

(Continued on Page Twelve)

Candidates Push GOP Drive to Wire

By W. J. McCARTHY

Gov. John A. Volpe visited Boston's city hall yesterday looking for at least a few discerning Democrats and George Cabot Lodge went down to Filene's Basement to offer himself to voters shopping for a good buy in a candidate as Massachusetts Republicans brought to a close their 1962 campaign.

With the old tradition gone by the boards of ending the cam-

(Continued on Page Twelve)

Early Returns Predict Outcome

250,000 Expected At Boston Polls

By ROBERT HANNAN

More than 250,000 Bostonians are expected at the voting machines today.

More Than 10% of State Vote

They make up more than 10 per cent of the state vote and will be the key in determining the outcome of top-of-the-ballot contests.

Two thousand more Boston voters, including Mrs. Jacqueline Kennedy, have voted or will vote by absentee ballots.

Political analysts will be watching the first Boston returns — usually from strong Democratic precincts—to gauge whether Democratic candidates are running strong or headed for trouble.

The Boston vote should give

(Continued on Page Eleven)

At his father's urging, Edward Kennedy ran for the Senate seat vacated by John F. Kennedy. Edward Kennedy's slogan was, "He can do more for Massachusetts," the same one his brother had used when he first ran for the office.

ALSO IN 1962

Vatican II, or the Second Ecumenical Council of the Vatican, opened under Pope John XXIII, an event that would "open the windows" of the Catholic Church to the modern world.

WEATHER
Fair and warm Thursday. National summary on Page 38.

The Atlanta Journal

"COVERS DIXIE LIKE THE DEW"

FINAL
HOME
EDITION

Vol. LXXXI, No. 93 Tel. JA. 2-5050—P.O. Box 4689 Atlanta (2), Ga., Wednesday Evening, June 12, 1963 64 Pages ** Price Five Cents

OLD CUBAN OIL AGAIN

MIAMI, June 12 (AP)—Cuban taxi drivers must turn in their used oil, drained from the crank-case, before being issued new oil, a recently arrived refugee cabby said Wednesday.

The crank case oil is re-refined, he said.

The refugee, Humberto Collazo, of Esmeralda, Camaguey Province, said the government issues oil "of poor quality" every 35 days.

"To get it, drivers also must have a note from the taxicab union certifying that they have done 'voluntary work'," he said. "Voluntary work" means cutting cane on a "volunteer" basis.

Kennedy Asks Golden Rule; Alabama Negroes in Class

NATIONAL GUARD TROOPS STACK ARMS AND GET COMFORTABLE IN TUSCALOOSA
University of Alabama's Foster Auditorium (R) Is Where Vivian Malone and James Hood Registered

Associated Press Wirephoto

Campus Quiet; Wallace Yields

By FRED POWLEDGE
Atlanta Journal Staff Writer

TUSCALOOSA, Ala., June 12—Two Negro students went peacefully to classes at the University of Alabama Wednesday. There were no incidents and most of their fellow students didn't even look twice.

The re-integration of the university came after a time-consuming and elaborate set of speeches, promises, threats, and positions.

In the end, Gov. George Wallace not only stepped aside to let the federal government, backed up by federalized Alabama National Guardsmen, bring two young Negroes into the tax-supported university, but he vacated the "schoolhouse door" and went back to Montgomery.

There, he said in departing, he will carry on the fight for state's

(Text of Gov. Wallace's proclamation on Page 18.)

rights. Five minutes later, two Negroes, Vivian Malone of Mobile and Jimmy Hood of East Gadsden, arrived, went through the same schoolhouse door, and registered as students at the University of Alabama.

THEY WERE the first Negroes here since 1956, when Autherine Lucy put in a brief appearance before she was expelled. Unlike 1956, this desegregation drama was not marred by mobs and violence.

MISS MALONE walked to class Wednesday morning in the company of two young white women.

MONTGOMERY, Ala., June 12 (UPI)—Gov. George Wallace notified President Kennedy Wednesday he would remove all state law enforcement officers from the University of Alabama at Tuscaloosa within the next four days. The governor pulled out 527 officers Wednesday.

Mr. Hood also walked to his first class. Miss Malone noticed a car filled with federal marshals, parked near the classrooms, and shook her head at the marshals.

This was interpreted as being her way of telling the marshals she didn't need any help from them.

The entry of the two Negroes was also lacking in violence or extreme tension.

Tuesday's events unfolded this way:

At 10:54 a.m., Atlanta-time, the governor arrived at Foster Auditorium, where registration of 4,000 summer students has been going on. The auditorium was surrounded by about 250 newsmen and television technicians, a handful of students, and some 300 state law officers. Six highway patrolmen stood on the auditorium roof with automatic weapons in their hands.

The others carried pistols and

Turn to Page 6, Column 4

Would Guarantee Complete Equality

WASHINGTON, June 12 (UPI) — President Kennedy sought national support Wednesday for a racial Golden Rule to put out "fires of frustration and discord" among Negroes by guaranteeing them full equality from lunch counter to polling place.

Warning that there is "a rising tide of discontent that threatens the public safety," Kennedy declared in a radio-television address Tuesday night that "we face . . . a moral crisis as a country and as a people."

"It cannot be met by repressive police action," he said. "It cannot be left to increased demonstrations in the streets. It can-

(Text of President Kennedy's address on Page 20.)

not be quieted by token moves or talk. It is a time to act in the Congress, in your state and local legislative body and, above all, in all of our daily lives."

To carry out his aims, Kennedy said he will send to Congress next week legislation which for the first time in this century would commit this country to the idea that "race has no place in American life or American law."

In a near-paraphrase of the Biblical Golden Rule, the Chief Executive said: "Every American ought to have the right to be treated as he would wish to be treated, as one would wish his children to be treated."

Kennedy spoke from his White House office shortly after he had federalized the Alabama National Guard to enforce integration of the state university. There were these immediate results:

—Senate Democratic Leader Mike Mansfield and other administration backers accepted Kennedy's legislative challenge. Southerners in Congress rejected it.

—Negro leader Martin Luther King Jr. called Kennedy's address "a hallmark in the annals of American history . . . one of the most eloquent, profound and unequivocal pleas for justice and the freedom of all men ever made by a president."

—Roy Wilkins, executive sec-

Turn to Page 10, Column 4

NAACP Aide Shot to Death In Mississippi

JACKSON, Miss. (UPI) — The top integration strategist for the National Association for the Advancement of Colored People in Mississippi was shot to death by a sniper early today while returning from a civil rights rally.

The slaying of Medgar Evers, 37, followed by only hours a plea by President Kennedy for a racial Golden Rule to put out "fires of frustration and discord" among Negroes.

Evers, dying from a rifle slug in the back, was found by police investigating a report of a shooting in the neat, middle class Negro neighborhood where he lived in the Mississippi capital rocked for the past month by racial demonstrations.

The Negro leader died about 15 minutes after being taken to the University of Mississippi medical center.

Evers' neighbor, Houston Wells, said the only coherent thing the state NAACP field secretary said while en route to the hospital was, "Turn me loose." Wells said Evers yelled the words several times.

Police said the shooting happened about 12:40 a.m. CST.

Jackson Detective Chief M. B. Pierce, who sent detectives swarming into the neighborhood, announced that the FBI had been asked to assist the investigation.

The NAACP in New York im-

Turn to Page 10, Column 5

Election Law Revision Panel Goes to Work

Sanders Warns Slanted Statutes Must Be Erased

By CHARLES POU
Atlanta Journal Political Editor

A committee which will attempt an almost complete revision of state election laws—with hopes of doing it by January — was told Wednesday by Gov. Sanders it has a "very, very important" mission.

The governor made his comments as the committee, which includes a Republican leader from Columbus, was sworn in and organized.

The Republican, Attorney William J. Schloth, told reporters one thing he would like to see revised is the law requiring just about all candidates—except Democrats—to compile a petition of 5 per cent of registered voters before they may run.

MR. SCHLOTH suggested an exemption of candidates of the two major parties as one workable revision.

Republicans in Georgia long have complained that this and other election laws have held them back.

Gov. Sanders said the state has been accused of having some unfair elections laws and he said he is tired of hearing such accusations.

He did not admit the charge is true but said any possibly slanted laws should be removed.

Some Rain Due in State

Atlanta and Georgia will have clear to partly cloudy weather Wednesday night. Highs in Atlanta Wednesday and Thursday will be 86 degrees, with low of 65. High Tuesday was 91.

Many sections of Atlanta and North Georgia got showers Tuesday, though officially only a trace Police found homemade fire reau at the Municipal Airport. Emory University received a midday downpour accompanied by high winds. Savannah had .24 of an inch, Alma .26.

Seven in Family Perish in Fire

VASHON, Wash., June 12 (UPI). At least seven members of one family perished when their home was destroyed by fire here early Wednesday morning, the King County coroner's office reported.

There might have been an eighth victim, according to the report, which said one person was saved in the blaze.

Identity of the victims was not known. Vashon is located on Vashon Island a few miles across Puget Sound from Seattle.

Eberhardt Named Athens Ag Chief

The State Board of Regents Wednesday appointed L. W. Eberhardt Jr. as director of the University of Georgia Agricultural Extension Service.

The regents also elected Dr. William B. King, professor of education at Wayne State University in Detroit, as president of Georgia Southwestern College in Americus, effective Aug. 15.

L. W. Eberhardt Jr.

Mr. Eberhardt will succeed W. A. (Bill) Sutton who will retire Aug. 31.

The new director, a native of Jackson County, has been assistant director since 1954. He has previously served as an assistant county agent, county agent and member of the state staff of specialists and supervisors.

He joined the extension service staff in 1936 as assistant county agent in Berrien County. He also served in Emanuel and Truetlen counties before joining the state staff in 1940 as an extension forester.

Dr. O. C. Aderhold, president of the university, pointed out that Mr. Eberhardt, as assistant director, guided the developement of a state agricultural program which outlines specific goals in all areas of extension work and which is expected to result in a $400 million annual increase in Georgia farm income by 1965.

In 1959 Mr. Eberhardt received a superior service award from the U.S. Department of Agriculture for his leadership with the Georgia Extension Service.

In 1962 he was cochairman of a people-to-people agricultural tour of Europe by Georgia farm leaders.

DR. KING will succeed Dr. Lloyd Moll, who has accepted another position in the University System.

He received his master of education degree from the University of Georgia in 1947 and his Ph.D. degree from New York University in 1956.

ON INSIDE PAGES

	Page
Around Town	22
Business	52, 53
Classified Want Ads	54-63
Comics	44
Crossword Puzzle	12
Deaths and Funerals	54
Dorothy Kilgallen	44
Drew Pearson	31
Editorials	30
Feature Page	22
Furman Bisher	46
Mopsy	36
Pat Watters	30
Sports	46-51
Street Poll	33
Television	26
The Ragen Report	7
Theaters	28
Weather Map	38
Wishing Well	19
Women-Society	39-43
Yogi Bear	45

Race Rioting In Maryland Injures Six

CAMBRIDGE, Md., June 12 (AP). Two white men were shot and at least four other persons were injured when a race riot erupted in this small eastern shore community late Tuesday night.

A tense racial situation flared into violence when a crowd of some 150 white persons followed an equal number of Negro integrationist demonstrators back into the Negro section.

The Negroes had just finished their second march on the town's courthouse and jail protesting the sentencing of two teen-age Negro girls. The girls, who had been arrested several times for their participation in racial demonstrations, were committed to state reformatories Monday after they were adjudged to be delinquent.

A HANDFUL of city police tried to keep the two groups separated, but the whites swarmed across the street toward the marchers just as they reached the Negro section of town.

The fight had just started when shots were fired from undetermined locations. One shotgun blast struck the two white men.

Three fires, one a general alarm blaze, broke out after fire bombs were tossed into business establishments operated by whites within the Negro section of town. Police found homemade fire bombs fashioned from beer bottles filled with gasoline in two of these establishments.

JEROME SHENTON, 36, owner of an auto paint and fender shop, and George Bernard Todd, 42, a fire insurance adjuster, were struck by shotgun pellets as they sat in a car in fron of Shenton's shop, located just inside the Negro district. Shenton was struck in the face and Todd was hit in the chest. Both men were treated at Cambridge Maryland Hospital and released.

Desegregated Pools Open Quietly Here

Atlanta's public swimming pools opened on a desegregated basis Wednesday, and Negroes quickly took advantage of the court-enforced move at several places.

There were no reported incidents as idle onlookers watched Negroes enter pools at Piedmont Park, Candler Park and Maddox Park a few hours after the 9 a.m. opening.

In Candler Park, at McLendon Avenue and Candler Park Drive, NE, three Negro youths joined about 40 whites in the pool.

Some white adults near the pool told the white swimmers to prepare to leave when the Negroes were sighted, but a report said most of the whites remained.

The number of Negroes in the Candler Park pool gradually increased during the morning. They appeared in small groups after the first three entered.

By noon, there were 17 Negroes swimming. Whites brought the total in the pool to about 45. A crowd of onlookers around the pool thinned.

IN MADDOX Park, at Bankhead Avenue and Rice Street, a lone Negro appeared during the morning and entered the pool. A witness said he appeared to be "a pretty good swimmer."

Three Negroes swam at Piedmont Park until shortly after noon. They were immediately replaced by four other Negro youths.

Only two whites left the pool when the Negroes first arrived. The number of white swimmers

Turn to Page 19, Column 4

MAN FOUND DEAD AFTER FIRE HERE

A Fulton County school board employe was found dead following a fire at his residence, and his wife, a Fulton schoolteacher, was found apparently overcome by smoke, according to Hapeville police.

The dead man, a maintenance employe for the Fulton County Board of Education, was identified as Lewis O. Mims, 44, of 3845 Atlanta Ave., SE. Police were not immediately sure of the cause of death.

Police said Mrs. Mims was found in a bedroom of their residence, overcome by smoke. Her condition was listed as satisfactory at Grady Hospital Wednesday.

POLICE SAID the fire, which occurred Tuesday night, caused considerable damage. They said the den, kitchen and a bedroom were heavily damaged.

The fire apparently started in the kitchen, which is adjacent to the den, police said. An officer said Mr. Mims fell at the doorway of the kitchen and den as he apparently tried to get out.

Mrs. Mims is a teacher at Red Oak, police said.

PINEY WOODS PETE Says:

DEAR MISTER EDITOR:

The problem of whether or not to paddle obstreperous youngsters is getting attention in Congress. This body of lawmakers for the nation also governs local affairs in Washington, D.C., where unruly pupils appear to have taken charge in some of the city's public schools. Racial tension and idleness aggravate the situation.

The House recently passed and sent to the Senate a bill to permit teachers to wield the rod on unruly pupils, something they are now forbidden to do. One congressman objected, saying the bill "implies that whipping school children is a cure-all for social ills."

No doubt there's something to his argument, but there's another side, too. Someone else has defined juvenile delinquents as "teen-agers who want what they want when they want it and won't wait to get it."

Yours truly,
PINEY WOODS PETE.

From Atlanta to Moscow—No. 4

BRIGHT CLOTHES, SMILES MARK OF FRIENDLY POLES

By HAROLD JOINER
Atlanta Journal Farm Editor

Bright clothes, friendly, smiling faces and a part-way return to a life similar to that back home was the greeting for 49 Georgians on a goodwill tour of Europe when they arrived in Warsaw.

Still a member of the Iron Curtain countries, Poland is nevertheless a maverick, a country of its own mind and different in some of its relationships with Western countries.

The smiles on people's faces was the most impressive sight for us Georgians. We had spent nearly a week in the Soviet Union where smiles were as scarce as rubies.

WE FOUND, too, that the Poles have been friendly toward our country, in a limited sort

Mr. Joiner returned last week from a 20,000-mile tour of Western Europe, three Communist countries and Berlin. He accompanied 48 farmer - businessmen from Georgia on the people-to-people trip. This article is one of a series on what the Georgians did and saw.

of way. Surplus agricultural goods have been sold to them and they have carried on limited trade in certain commodities.

Much of the tension was lifted when we arrived here, although there was still a little evidence of "shadowing." Two of us were followed up the street the first night in Warsaw. The distance was always great, but we knew he was there.

But for the most part there was no strain, no uneasiness.

We found the Poles to be an independent people. One told us that no one will ever have complete control over them. "We will fight for what we believe," he said.

THE POLISH people, with many relatives in this country, feel that they are more Western than the Soviets. They aren't as proud of the Soviets as some might imagine. Or so we found it.

Yet most of the shops in Poland are state owned. They have socialized medicine and schools, too.

The Polish agriculture is different. Most of it, 87 per cent, is privately owned. About 12 per cent is in state-operated farms

Turn to Page 10, Column 1

STREET SCENES

Gentleman in pajamas, goatee and African big game hunting hat watering his lawn on Albemarle Avenue at 6 a.m.

Operator of City Slicker bus going four blocks beyond his turn, saying, "I must have been daydreaming; thank goodness I'm not driving a trolley."

Sharp click-click sounding in Peachtree Sunday school room as prominent Georgian clips his nails during program.

$40 Billion for Moon Race 'Nuts,' Says Ike to GOP

WASHINGTON, June 12 (UPI). Former President Dwight D. Eisenhower said Wednesday "Anybody who would spend $40 billion in a race to the moon for national prestige is nuts."

Eisenhower made the blunt remark at a breakfast meeting with about 160 Republican congressmen. Those attending the gathering said the former chief executive drew sustained applause when he made his "nuts" reference to the Kennedy administration's space program.

THE BREAKFAST was sponsored by the "87th Club," composed of Republican members whose service in the House began with the 87th Congress in 1961. They made Eisenhower an "honorary Republican congressman-at-large."

Looking fit and tan, Eisenhower arrived for the breakfast from Walter Reed Hospital, where he underwent a routine physical checkup. He said he was given a clean bill of health.

The former chief executive called President Kennedy's ad-

DWIGHT EISENHOWER
Makes Blunt Remark

ministration "fiscally irresponsible" for raising the spending budget by more than $27 billion and at the same time proposing to cut taxes.

EISENHOWER cautioned against appropriating unlimited amounts of money for the military services. He said it was up to Congress to determine how much an "adequate" defense would cost, and then refuse to allow "$1 more."

The former president repeated the warning he made on leaving the White House—that the nation should beware of "the military-industrial complex." He said this problem was becoming more acute because "almost every congressman" now has a defense industry or military base in his district. He said he recognized that there was "pressure" on them to vote for ever-higher defense appropriations, but that they should resist approving expenditures beyond necessary needs.

Eisenhower advised the Republicans to work for effective legislation to guarantee Negro voting rights but said he did not think civil rights problems could be solved by "passing a whole bundle of laws."

After Governor George Wallace kept two black students from enrolling at the University of Alabama, Kennedy issued an executive order placing the state's National Guard into federal service.

THE ATLANTA CONSTITUTION

For 95 Years the South's Standard Newspaper

Net Paid Circulation 201,465 For May, 1963

VOL. XCV, No. 305 TEL. JA. 2-5050—P. O. Box 4689 ATLANTA (2), GA., WEDNESDAY, JUNE 12, 1963 48 PAGES, 3 SECTIONS Price Five Cents

Negroes Enter as Wallace Gives In; U.S. in Moral Crisis, Kennedy Says

RALPH McGILL — Of Sad Words, The Saddest—

Inside Today . . .

Must Avert Violence, Nation Told — By TOM WICKER

Governor Yields to Guardsmen — By BILL SHIPP

Macmillan Puts Case to Cabinet — By SYDNEY GRUSON

2 Whites Are Shot in Maryland

"IT IS MY SAD DUTY TO HAVE TO ASK YOU TO STEP ASIDE, SIR"
Gen. Henry Graham Tells Gov. George Wallace That Guard Is Under Federal Control

Congress Lines Up In Sectional Blocs

Wallace Vows to Win in End

5 Die in Storm

Kennedy Selects Harriman To Head Atom Negotiators

Mercury to Slip Back Into 80s

Kennedy's Fair-Hiring Plan Perils Support of Rights Bill — By JACK BELL

Wallace relented once the troops arrived on campus. The same day, Kennedy delivered a televised address about his hopes for new civil rights legislation.

ALSO IN 1963

Betty Friedan's book The Feminine Mystique *helped begin a new era in the history of the women's movement.*

The New York Times.

VOL. CXII..No. 38,505. © 1963 by The New York Times Company. Times Square, New York 36, N. Y. NEW YORK, THURSDAY, JUNE 27, 1963. TEN CENTS

ROBERT KENNEDY OFFERS TO MODIFY CIVIL RIGHTS BILL

Would Exempt Small Stores and Tourist Homes From Public Facilities Clause

HOUSE HEARING OPENED

Attorney General Says That Ending of Discrimination Is Up to Congress

Excerpts from Robert Kennedy's testimony are on Page 18.

By E. W. KENWORTHY
Special to The New York Times

WASHINGTON, June 26—Attorney General Robert F. Kennedy said today that the Administration would be willing to exempt small stores and tourist homes from its proposed ban on discrimination in privately owned public accommodations.

Appearing as the initial witness on President Kennedy's civil rights bill, the Attorney General told the antitrust subcommittee of the House Judiciary Committee that if Congress wanted more explicit language, "we would be happy to work out some cut-off line."

Presumably this would be based on an annual dollar volume of business.

The public accommodations section of the bill is the most controversial. The Attorney General's concession was regarded as greatly improving the chances that the House committee would report a relatively strong bill.

Senate Doubts Noted

In the Senate, however, the doubts of many key members, including the minority leader, Everett McKinley Dirksen of Illinois, go beyond the issue of a cut-off point to the question of whether any ban on public accommodations is not an impairment of property rights.

As the Attorney General was testifying today, Mr. Dirksen predicted that the final bill would contain no ban and would provide simply for voluntary community action with the help of the President's proposed Community Relations Service.

The committee room in the Old House Office Building was jammed, with spectators lining the walls three and four deep, when the Attorney General appeared promptly at 10:30 A.M. He was accompanied by

Continued on Page 19, Column 1

CITY GETS U. S. AID IN COMMUTER TEST

$3,185,000 Granted to Seek New Types of Service

By WARREN WEAVER Jr.
Special to The New York Times

WASHINGTON, June 26—The Federal Government gave New York City $3,185,000 today to try to improve commuter service from Queens and Nassau Counties to the city.

The money, together with $1,593,000 from the city and $1,860,000 in anticipated fare revenue, will be used to finance experiments in transportation by bus, subway and the Long Island Rail Road.

Nautically, the program will underwrite the cost of providing more service at somewhat lower fares for selected routes to determine whether the changes will attract enough new passengers to make the service self-supporting.

Very little, if any, of the money is to be spent on new equipment or facilities. It is to be used to find out how the equipment now in use can be used more productively.

The grant was one of the largest for transit demonstrations made by the Federal Housing and Home Finance Agency, and the air was heavy with Democratic politics at the presentation ceremony.

Mayor Wagner flew down from New York for the occasion, bringing with him Borough President Marks J. Cariello of Queens and Eugene A. Nickerson, the Nassau County Executive.

Continued on Page 41, Column 4

WANT 15% OF MIAMI? Famous Jumbo Airport beach City of Miami lifting, 825 acres. $1,000 under—33 million bonds. Taxes etc. 52% less. Write direct. Phone. Box 12 EX—PLA "A" PARADE, 742 Third Ave.—Advt.

Space Science Fund Cut by House Panel

By JOHN W. FINNEY
Special to The New York Times

WASHINGTON, June 26—The House Science and Astronautics Committee cut back the scientific portion of the space program today, eliminating $134,348,600 in funds for research and exploration.

With the $259,122,000 cut made yesterday in funds for manned space flight, the committee has now cut $393,370,600 from the $5,700,000,000 budget submitted by the National Aeronautics and Space Administration.

Tomorrow, the committee is expected to cut $90,000,000 more from the fund request for the coming year. This would bring the total reduction in the budget authorization bill to $483,000,000.

The committee acted today on two major divisions of the space program—the scientific

Continued on Page 13, Column 7

KENTUCKY FORBIDS BIAS IN BUSINESSES

Governor's Order Affects All Licensed Activities—He Prods School Districts

Special to The New York Times

FRANKFORT, Ky., June 26—Gov. Bert T. Combs signed an executive order today forbidding racial discrimination in all businesses licensed by the state.

The order, which went into effect immediately, covers such businesses as taverns, restaurants, barber shops, beauty parlors, funeral homes and real estate concerns.

His order directed those state agencies empowered to license businesses to prepare reports within 60 days on how they managed to enforce the order.

Mr. Combs suggested that enforcement could be patterned after the procedures of the State Alcoholic Beverage Control Board.

Could Lose License

After an illegal act has been charged, the board cites a licensee and orders him to appear for a hearing to show cause why he should not have his license suspended or revoked.

Hence, the Governor noted, "the penalty under this executive order also would go to a man's pocketbook."

Mr. Combs acted as a special session of the General Assembly, the legislature, met here. Civil rights groups and Mayor William O. Cowger of Louisville had urged the Governor to extend the special session to a state anti-discrimination law.

The session had been called to provide state aid for four eastern Kentucky hospitals owned and operated by the United Mine Workers of America. The union plans to close the hospitals this summer because of economic reasons.

Governor Combs said he had declined to place a civil rights bill before the legislature because many had come to him

Continued on Page 19, Column 3

City Swelters in 96°; Heat Wave to Linger

The temperature rose to 96 degrees at 3:10 P.M. yesterday, but the air yesterday was the hottest day here since last July 9. More of the same was forecast for today.

The temperature edged above Tuesday's high of 95, giving New Yorkers a foretaste of the summer ahead. The temperature, however, stayed below the record of 100 for a June 26 reached in 1952.

A third rail on the New York Central's Harlem Division was buckled by the heat at 6:10 P.M. The rerouting of trains to the single open track delayed 10,000 commuters as much as two hours.

The breakdown occurred just south of Tuckahoe. By midnight, with repairs in progress, more than 25 trains in both directions had been delayed by the trouble.

The railroad said it expected

Continued on Page 67, Column 1

LOANS ON JEWELRY, FURS, CAMERAS Est. 1882. 42 W. 47 St. PL 9-4200.—Advt.

EAST GERMAN CHALLENGE CONFRONTS KENNEDY: President, indicated by arrow, looks across Berlin wall toward sign near the Brandenburg Gate. The sign says: "In the agreements of Yalta and Potsdam U.S. Presidents Roosevelt and Truman undertook: ¶To uproot German militarism and Nazism. ¶To arrest war criminals and bring them to judgment. ¶To prevent the rebirth of German militarism. ¶To ban

all militarists and Nazi propaganda. ¶To ensure that Germany never again menaces her neighbors of world peace. These pledges have been fulfilled in the German Democratic Republic. When will these pledges be fulfilled in West Germany and West Berlin, President Kennedy?" East German officials had had red cloths hung between pillars of gate, blocking off the view for the President's party and East Berliners.

United Press International Radiophoto

Aid for Distressed Areas Revived by Senate, 65-30

By C. P. TRUSSELL
Special to The New York Times

WASHINGTON, June 26—The Senate passed and sent to the House today its own bill to strengthen the program for aid to economically distressed areas. The vote was 65 to 30.

The House, which rejected a similar bill two weeks ago by only five votes, is now expected to reverse itself and approve the job-stimulating program.

¶Increase from $100,000,000 to $250,000,000 the amount authorized at any one time for industrial or commercial loans to create jobs through urban projects.

¶Increase from $75,000,000 to $175,000,000 the authorization for appropriations for public facility grants.

¶Increase from $100,000,000 to $150,000,000 the amount authorized for public facility loans.

The legislation would also permit states or communities to pay the 10 per cent contributions required for the projects at the same time they repaid funds extended by the

Continued on Page 45, Column 4

PAN AM PROPOSES $160 LONDON FARE

Plans Coast-Hawaii Rate of $100 in New Thrift Class Without Liquor or Food

By JOSEPH CARTER

Pan American World Airways proposed a new class of service to Europe and Hawaii yesterday that would radically reduce fares and eliminate meals and liquor aboard the plane.

Under the new year-round first class, the one-way New York-London fare would be $160, a reduction of $103, or $9 per cent, compared with the economy-class rate that now is in effect July 16. There would be no round-trip discount as at present.

Thrift-class service would be provided between California and Hawaii at a one-way fare of $100, compared with the current economy-class rate of $133.

The airline would introduce the service to Hawaii next November, subject to approval of the Civil Aeronautics Board. The service to Europe would start next April if the foreign carriers and Governments concerned and the C.A.B. approve.

Submitted for Study

Juan T. Trippe, Pan American president, announced the new thrift-class rates a month after the trans-Atlantic airlines reached a compromise agreement on fares following a long and bitter dispute.

Airline observers here said this proposal would provide fuel for further heated debate when the International Air Transport Association, the world airlines organization, meets in Europe next fall to set rates and fares. To become effective, they must be agreed upon unanimously at the meeting, tentatively scheduled to open in early September at Salzburg, Austria.

Mr. Trippe said the plans for the new North Atlantic service had been announced at this time "to give all the other airlines concerned time for study" before the meeting at which "future trans-Atlantic fares to be considered and recommended by the airlines to their respective Governments for approval."

Trans World Airlines, Pan

Continued on Page 67, Column 2

47 BILLION VOTED IN HOUSE FOR ARMS

Second Biggest Peacetime Allocation Backed 410 to 1 and Sent to the Senate

Special to The New York Times

WASHINGTON, June 26—The House passed and sent to the Senate today a bill appropriating $47,053,000,000 for defense.

If it is approved by the Senate, it will be the second highest annual military appropriation in peacetime. The $48,350,082,500 allocated last year is the highest thus far.

The House passed the measure, which provides funds for the fiscal year 1964, starting July 1, with one dissent. Representative Thomas B. Curtis, Republican of Missouri, said "we haven't got the money."

"I hope by this vote to call to the people's attention the seriousness of deficit spending," he said.

He said he had no specific objections to the bill, but believed that something should have been cut for economy's sake.

The roll-call vote on the measure was 410 to 1.

The final vote came after two days of discussion but no major debate.

Then the rain came down again, hard. President Kennedy, riding in an open car beside the 80-year-old Mr. de Valera.

The House did not restore a cut of $1,900,000,000 made in the Administration's appropriations

Continued on Page 13, Column 3

Dublin Acclaims Kennedy As One Returning Home

By SYDNEY GRUSON
Special to The New York Times

DUBLIN, June 26—President Kennedy arrived in Dublin this evening and in a sense, he said, it was like coming "home." That was the way the Irish felt about it, too. Mr. Kennedy was hailed by President Eamon de Valera as the "first citizen" of the United States but also by the people

Speeches by de Valera and Kennedy are on Page 13.

of Dublin as the local boy—three generations removed—who made good.

All the Dubliners seemed to be at the airport or lining the road of the 12-mile route to the United States Embassy in Phoenix Park.

If the President was tired after his grueling three days in West Germany, or by the vast emotional outpouring of the West Berliners earlier in the day, he did not show it.

It had rained off and on during the day in and around Dublin, and hailstones had fallen, covering the green fields with short-lasting unseasonable blanket of white.

But the sky was blue and the last of the day's sun was shining when the President's plane landed and for most of the drive to the embassy.

Continued on Page 13, Column 5

MOSCOW WAVERS ON CURBING ARTS

Resistance of Intellectuals Said to Cause Indecision in Party Leadership

By SEYMOUR TOPPING
Special to The New York Times

MOSCOW, June 26 — The Kremlin is wavering in its drive to impose strict ideological curbs on liberal writers and artists.

Western analysts have detected signs of indecision in statements published after the plenary session of the Central Committee of the Soviet Communist party.

The closed four-day plenum, which ended Friday, had been convened to reinforce internal ideological discipline and to find means of insulating the Soviet people against the influx of Western ideas.

The plenum was the first called to deal specifically with ideological questions. Its published results hardly support earlier Soviet statements that the plenum would be a monumental event.

No New Curbs Announced

Statements issued about the meeting have not contained anything substantially new. No further measures were announced that would subject liberal intellectuals to severe organizational controls.

Available evidence, in fact, has indicated to Western analysts that the Soviet leadership has retreated from its announced plan to compel abandonment of all liberal and avant-garde tendencies in literature and art.

In a speech on March 8 Premier Khrushchev asserted that unswerving conformity with the Communist party line would be demanded of literature, fine arts, music, theater, cinema and the press. He de-

Continued on Page 5, Column 3

Annapolis Gets First Academic Dean, a Civilian

Dr. Drought of Marquette Appointed for a Year

By JACK RAYMOND
Special to The New York Times

WASHINGTON, June 26—The Navy appointed a civilian academic dean for the Naval Academy at Annapolis today as part of a major program to improve general education standards for midshipmen.

Dr. Arthur B. Drought, dean of engineering at Marquette University, Milwaukee, was named by Secretary of the Navy Fred Korth for one year.

The 48-year-old professor, who has had wide experience in teaching, research and college administration, will be the 118-year-old Naval Academy's first academic dean.

The United States Military Academy at West Point has an officer as dean of the academic board and he has two civilian advisers. The Air Force Academy at Colorado Springs, Colo., has a brigadier general as dean of faculty.

Heretofore at the Naval Academy, the Superintendent, an officer, was responsible for all courses. The secretary of the

Dr. Arthur B. Drought
Associated Press

Action Follows Settlement of Dispute With Officers

came after a dispute that developed two years ago but was settled last year. The dispute was precipitated by efforts on the part of Secretary Korth to have civilian educators assume virtually all of the nonprofessional instructional positions.

The Navy several years ago had proposed having an academic dean. However, uniformed officers resisted Secretary Korth's sweeping proposals.

If these were carried out, it was said, Navy officers at the academy would be limited to disciplinary and administrative positions. The academy, it was stressed, was a military institution in which habits of command and other military considerations were of considerable importance, more than in an ordinary academic institution.

Secretary Korth subsequently withdrew his proposals for sweeping civilianization of the teaching staff at Annapolis.

Meantime officials at the Naval Academy succeeded in obtaining not only an academic dean

"I am delighted to have such a distinguished educator and administrator accept this appointment."

Dean Drought's appointment

Continued on Page 11, Column 1

PRESIDENT HAILED BY OVER A MILLION IN VISIT TO BERLIN

He Salutes the Divided City as Front Line in World's Struggle for Freedom

LOOKS OVER THE WALL

Says Berliners' Experience Shows Hazard in Trying to Work With Communists

Texts of President's speeches in Berlin, Page 12.

By ARTHUR J. OLSEN
Special to The New York Times

BERLIN, June 26—President Kennedy, inspired by a tumultuous welcome from more than a million of the inhabitants of this isolated and divided city, declared today he was proud to be "a Berliner."

He said his claim to being a Berliner was based on the fact that "all free men, wherever they may live, are citizens of Berlin."

In a rousing speech to 150,000 West Berliners crowded before the City Hall, the President said anyone who thought "we can work with the Communist" should come to Berlin.

However, three hours later, in a less emotional setting, he reaffirmed his belief that the great powers must work together "to preserve the human race."

Warning on Communism

His earlier rejection of dealing with the Communists was a warning against trying to "ride the tiger" of popular fronts that unite democratic and Communist forces. Mr. Kennedy explained in an interpolation in a prepared speech.

The President's City Hall speech was the emotional high point of a spectacular welcome accorded the President by West Berlin. He saluted the city as the front line and shining example of humanity's struggle for freedom.

Those who profess not to understand the great issues between the free world and the Communist world or who think Communism is the wave of the future should come to Berlin, he said.

In his later speech, at the Free University of Berlin, President Kennedy returned firmly to the theme of his address at American University in Washington June 10 in which he called for an attempt to end the cold war.

'Wounds to Heal'

"When the possibilities of reconciliation appear, we in the West will make it clear that we are not hostile to any people or system, provided that they choose their own destiny without interfering with the free choice of others," he said.

"There will be wounds to heal and suspicions to be eased on both sides," he added. "The difference in living standards will have to be reduced—by leveling up, not down. Fair and effective agreements to end the arms race must be reached."

The changes might not come tomorrow, but "our efforts for a real settlement must continue," he said.

Then the President introduced an extemporaneous paragraph into his prepared text.

"As I said this morning, I

Continued on Page 12, Column 1

Berliners' Welcome Filled With Emotion

By TOM WICKER

BERLIN, June 26 — President Kennedy saw the miracle and the tragedy of West Berlin today as the city turned out to greet him and applaud his countrymen.

The reception was one of the largest and most emotional Mr. Kennedy has ever received.

The West Berliners leaped and screamed along the curbs, waved their handkerchiefs and a variety of flags, threw flowers, and broke through police barriers to run beside Mr. Kennedy's car. Some succeeded in shaking his hand. Twice he caught bouquets.

A hand-painted ungrammatical but heartfelt placard spoke the city's heart, reading: "John. I You our best friend." In the Rudolph Wilde Platz, where the President spoke shortly after

Continued on Page 12, Column 6

NEWS INDEX

	Page		Page
Books	29	Music	22-25
Bridge	29	Obituaries	33
Business	43	Real Estate	56
Buyers	52		
Chess	29	Ships and Air	66
Crossword	29	Society	27
Editorial	32	Sports	38-41
Fashions	26	Theaters	22-25
Financial	43-51	TV and Radio	59
Food	20-21	U. N. Proceedings	4
Man in the News	11	Wash. Proceedings	13
		Weather	66

House Summary and Index, Page 33

THE GUARDIAN

36,383 Manchester Thursday June 27 1963 Price 4d

Mr Kennedy's visit a Dublin carnival

Removed from Privy Council

By FRANCIS BOYD, our Political Correspondent

Mr John Profumo has, at his own request, been removed from the Privy Council.

The Queen was present at a meeting of the council at Buckingham Palace yesterday morning at which an order was approved removing him from membership. The order will be published in the "London Gazette" tomorrow.

'Every drop of his blood is Irish . . .'

From ARTHUR HOPCRAFT

Wexford, Wednesday

Home is the hero; fill your glass. This is the Irishman's mood tonight with President Kennedy safely and grandly landed at Dublin Airport in his huge "flying White House," as a television commentator called his Boeing jet AF-1.

He had been told by President de Valera, who would not have been himself nor, for that matter, any Irishman at all, if he had not found time for a reference to old miseries under vanquished tyrants: "We welcome you for yourself. We are proud of you."

President Kennedy's car entering O'Connell Street past the Parnell Monument on arrival in Dublin last night

Yemen may free captives

By CLARE HOLLINGWORTH

The 18 British Servicemen who are still held captive on the Yemeni frontier are hoping to be released today although no agreement between British, Yemeni, and Egyptian officials was reached last night.

Fire cover to cost more

By our Financial Staff

Office and factory fire insurance premiums are to be increased 15 per cent by members of the Fire Offices' Committee from December 1 this year.

TUC fears for winter workless

By JOHN COLE, our Labour Correspondent

Mixed-manned force under fire

Lord Montgomery: 'Poppycock'

By NORMAN SHRAPNEL, our Parliamentary Correspondent

NEW FORCE NOT RULED OUT YET

By Clare Hollingworth

CND vigil at Birch Grove

9 leap off crash plane: 38 killed

On the track of Lord Hailsham...

Coal exports may go up by 40 per cent

More typhoid but outbreak 'mild'

Locomotive works to close

Pardon for 'guinea-pig'

Pearson victory in Budget vote

Elderly admirer tries to kiss Princess

BAOR to be reshaped

By our Defence Correspondent

On other pages

Tomorrow's paper

Kennedy's great-grandparents migrated from Ireland to Boston. Kennedy used the Fitzgerald family Bible, which his ancestors brought from Ireland, when he took the oath of office of president of the United States.

ALSO IN 1963

Popular television programs included The Dick Van Dyke Show, The Beverly Hillbillies, Bonanza, Leave It to Beaver, Perry Mason, *and* The Twilight Zone.

THE NATIONAL OBSERVER

Vol. 2, No. 30 © 1963 Dow Jones & Company, Inc. All Rights Reserved MONDAY, JULY 29, 1963 A Weekly Newspaper Price 25 Cents

Discrimination: How It Works In Labor Unions

A New Drive by Leadership To Enforce Equality Begins to Take Shape

WASHINGTON, D.C.

One day last week, Walter Reuther, the president of the United Auto Workers (UAW) union, accepted an invitation to join the Negro rights march here in Washington. But at the same time, a UAW local in Memphis was accepting donations to pay the lawyers for a Mississippi white man charged with the murder of a Negro integration leader.

And in Cleveland, pressed by Mayor Ralph Locher, a local of the Plumbers and Steamfitters Union agreed to waive certain rules to put two Negro plumbers to work on an underground addition to the downtown convention hall. But as a result, eight white plumbers and 32 other union tradesmen walked off the job.

These contrasting faces of the American labor union movement, one the face of leadership and the other the face of the membership, have worried many leaders and infuriated Negroes for years.

It's the big reason why Negroes and police clashed again last week in New York City, where pickets (who chained themselves together to make their arrest more difficult) claimed Negroes weren't getting as many construction jobs as they should.

Overshadows the Talking

As usual, the bombastic show in the streets overshadowed the earnest talking, negotiating, and long-range planning going on far from the dust and noise. For example, it wasn't widely noted, but President Kennedy last week appointed a Negro lawyer to the five-member National Labor Relations Board, which referees some disputes between unions and management. Howard Jenkins, Jr., 48, who has held several Federal jobs, will take the $20,000-a-year post on Aug. 27.

Negro leaders were cheered, naturally, but they are more interested in the bread-and-better jobs than in status-building appointments. In only 3 of the nation's 25 largest cities does the percentage of Negroes working for the city's [...] equal the proportion of Negroes in the general population.

The Memphis auto workers and the Cleveland plumbers illustrate also the essential difference in discrimination in the North and South. The Memphis workers who gave their money for the defense of the Mississippian, Byron de La Beckwith, were reflecting the basic racial sentiment in their community. In Cleveland the issue seemed really to be a competition for jobs.

Mr. Randolph

Now, for the first time, union leadership seems ready to enforce the written promises in many union constitutions of equal treatment for all workers. "Discrimination is the antithesis of the union concept of brotherhood," an executive of the AFL-CIO said. "I think now the unions are going to do something about it."

The AFL-CIO has always had the power to enforce the anti-discrimination provisions of the union constitutions. But, its critics charge, it never would have considered using this power until forced to do so. The federation's conventions and committees have passed dozens of resolutions. But what, these critics ask, stings less than a watery resolution?

Labor spokesmen argue there's considerable significance to a move last week by AFL-CIO president George Meany. He named four top union presidents to help him start "looking out for the Negroes." Among the members is A. Philip Randolph, a Negro, and a man of whom Mr. Meany once angrily demanded: "Who the

Please Turn to Page 14, Column 4

The Atom and the Ways of Men

Meanings and Dangers in the Nuclear Pact

"Failure to ratify," said Minnesota's Sen. Hubert Humphrey, "would be a tragic dereliction of this nation's political and moral responsibility."

Retorted Virginia's Sen. Willis Robertson: "When have the Russians kept a promise? We've had 52 agreements with them, and they've broken 50."

Reaction to last week's agreement to ban nuclear tests in the atmosphere, in space, and under water was not only swift but divergent.

Some people saw the agreement as a breakthrough in the Cold War; A significant "easing of tensions." They urged the Senate to ratify it. Others, however, were skeptical. They noted the treaty was less than advertised and had notable holes. Given the long history of Soviet perfidy, they doubted whether the pact would hold together. Still others were plain scared. In the Senate and in the Pentagon, some men feared that even a limited test ban would weaken America's nuclear deterrent and present serious dangers to national security.

The Principal Points

The treaty contained four major provisions:

☛ A prohibition on nuclear testing in the atmosphere, in outer space (i.e., beyond the atmosphere, or above 120 miles), and under water. This means that underground tests may continue.

☛ A pledge to "refrain from . . . encouraging" any nuclear explosion in the prohibited environments. This would bar the United States from helping France develop an independent nuclear force, and would prohibit the Soviet Union from giving aid to the nuclear weapons program of Communist China.

☛ An abrogation clause that gives each party the right to "withdraw from the treaty if it decides that extraordinary events . . . have jeopardized the supreme interests of its country." Three months' advance notice of withdrawal is required.

☛ A clause stating that the treaty "shall be open to all (other) states for signature."

Three Sets of Initials

The agreement came on Thursday, at 7:15 p.m. Moscow time, after nearly two weeks of tense and delicate negotiations in Moscow's imitation-Gothic Spridlinovska Palace. At the bottom of the final typewritten page the three principal negotiators—W.A.H. for W. Averell Harriman, U.S. Undersecretary of State for Political Affairs; an ornate, meticulously drawn A.O. for Andrei Gromyko, Russia's foreign minister; a single H. for Viscount Hailsham, British minister for science.

The treaty must still be signed—a ceremonial gesture—by Secretary of State Dean Rusk, the East of Rome, the British foreign secretary, and again by Mr. Gromyko. It must then be submitted for ratification by the U.S. Senate, the Supreme Soviet, and the British Parliament. The British Parliament greeted news of the pact with unqualified joy. The Supreme Soviet will do what Mr. Khrushchev tells them to do. But the U.S. Senate may be troublesome indeed.

With full realization of obstacles in the Senate, President Kennedy went on television Friday night to push his case for the treaty. He called it a "step toward peace, a step away from war," but warned no millennium was at hand. Conjuring up the most extreme views of the horrors of nuclear war, he said, in effect, that the proposed treaty was better than that.

A Time for Banter

Reporters and cameramen had been called to the mansion 3½ hours before the negotiators finally initialed the agreement. When they burst in, they found the three men smiling, obviously happy, indulging in light-hearted banter.

"What took you so long?" asked one reporter.

"Circumstances — we had conversations," replied Mr. Gromyko. "Most agreeable conversations," Lord Hailsham added.

Then it was clear that despite their outward joviality these men were tired indeed. It was equally clear that the final two days of negotiating had been the

most difficult. When the meetings began July 14, Soviet Premier Khrushchev had proposed an East-West nonaggression pact, and during the final stages Mr. Gromyko insisted that the negotiators could not sign a test-ban treaty without also signing a nonaggression pact.

The Western representatives resisted on the grounds that such a pact, in the form outlined by Mr. Khrushchev, would, in effect, recognize the existing boundaries of divided Germany and give diplomatic legitimacy to the East German regime—something neither West Germany nor its Western allies want. Mr. Gromyko finally bowed when the Western delegates assured him that they would discuss such a treaty "fully" with their allies, "with the purpose of achieving agreement satisfactory to all participants."

What About Germany?

But whether they can reach an agreement on Germany is another matter entirely. And if they do not, what becomes of the test-ban treaty? Although Mr. Khrushchev is willing now to sign a treaty without prior resolution of the German question, some skeptics believe that his continued endorsement of such a treaty will depend on future concessions from the West over Germany.

Indeed, the future is full of question marks like these. The treaty itself provides small comfort. Article III says the treaty is "open to all states for signature." But Communist China has already said it would ignore the agreement; and at week's end it was becoming increasingly clear that France's President Charles de Gaulle would too. If either of these two develops a powerful nuclear force—thus increasing the vulnerability of the major powers—Mr. Khrushchev may invoke Article IV, declare that his "supreme interests" have been jeopardized, give his required three-months notice, and resume testing. If Red China develops such a force, the United States might easily feel compelled to break the pact in the same way.

Those who have hailed the pact as a

"major" breakthrough have done so not only because it represents the first significant East-West agreement since the Austrian State Treaty of 1955, but also because they firmly believe that Mr. Khrushchev is being pushed by events into an accommodation with the United States and the other Western powers.

Problems in Russia

They argue, for example, that Mr. Khrushchev is not only having trouble with other powers, from whom he wants to keep the bomb, but that he is also having trouble at home. His economy is a mess, and he is therefore anxious to cut back on military spending and divert funds into industry and agriculture. He said in February that Russia needed a better "balance between the needs of the peace-time economy and the requirements of defense"; apparently, the optimists argue, he now feels that to achieve such a balance he needs a more relaxed atmosphere with the west.

Proponents of this point of view also argue that Mr. Khrushchev became rapidly disenchanted with his "saber-rattling" policy following the Cuba episode, and they too have decided, once and for all, that Russia will win through "peaceful coexistence and competition."

Although this interpretation of Soviet motives is a popular one, critics are quick to point out that one must not assume from all this that Mr. Khrushchev is cozying up to the West on a long-term basis. Sen. Henry M. Jackson, Washington Democrat, points out that Mr. Khrushchev's ultimate goal is still to "bury" the West. He may have had to tailor his tactics to fit the new pressures at home and abroad. But it is just a tailoring job—not a brand new suit of clothes.

If the future gives pause for thought, the past provides equally solid reasons for skepticism—at least in the opinion of some critics. Says Sen. Wallace F. Bennett, Utah Republican:

"I don't like the eagerness of the Russians after years of stalling. Now suddenly

Please Turn to Page 14, Column 3

Kennedy: "Victory for mankind."

De Gaulle: Less than convinced.

Khrushchev: Is he serious?

Mao: Getting own bomb.

Harriman: Happy negotiator.

LeMay: Worried about defense.

Mansfield: Pushing in Senate.

Goldwater: Dubious and balky.

On The Inside

• **E. B. White on the Model T**

Nearly three decades ago E. B. White wrote what has become a classic essay on the Model T, Henry Ford's chief contribution to Americana. July 30 is the 100th anniversary of Mr. Ford's birth. For the occasion, The National Observer has arranged to reproduce Mr. White's fond recollections of the Model T era. The essay, with early-day photos, will be found on Page 18.

☆ ☆ ☆

• **'Madame Minister' and the Reds**

Behind a plain wooden door on a quiet street in Sofia, Bulgaria, a tall, handsome woman presides over one of the toughest jobs in the U.S. diplomatic service. She's Mrs. Eugenie Anderson of Minnesota, the only female U.S. chief of mission to any Communist country. For an account of her adventures, please turn to Page 13.

☆ ☆ ☆

• **Good-by Neighborhood Schools?**

Will school integration swing to the other extreme now—transporting white children to far-away schools so each is carefully mixed? A report from Englewood, N.J., where a plan to end "racial imbalance" is due any day, is on Page 2.

☆ ☆ ☆

• **Focus on the Circus**

What possesses a man to leave college to become a human cannonball for the circus? Does the romantic policeman, smitten by the beautiful serialist, have a chance to win her hand? A writer who traveled with a circus describes the lives of the performers on Page 13.

Kids Are Conned By Turtles' Eggs 'Made in England'

HAMILTON, ONT.

Each summer, officials of the Royal Botanical Gardens in Hamilton conduct a children's program to teach the youngsters to be more aware of nature. This year conservationists concede that the program took an embarrassing turn.

When this summer's study opened, 40 children were sent off on a two-mile hike into forest and marsh. Their group leader pointed out some sassafras trees and then showed them a stream whose soft bank looked like a good spot for turtles to deposit their eggs.

He scratched around in the muddy soil and produced six small, round, white objects, which, he explained, were turtle eggs laid at the end of May and buried so skunks and other marauders would not eat them. The leader then handled the objects.

While the group went on, three of the inquisitive ones decided to take another look at the eggs. They scratched around the soft soil and finally located the cache. But one boy complained the egg he had wasn't leathery the way the leader said it should be. An eight-year-old girl said her egg felt cold and hard. Then a second boy exclaimed that his egg was marked "made in England."

John Lamoureux, chief conservationist at the gardens, admitted that turtle eggs were so scarce this year that his staff substituted ping pong balls. He thought he had sandpapered off all the labels.

Christian Unity Raises Questions At Unity Meeting

Conventioning Clergy Note Compromise Difficulties, Misinformation Trouble

MONTREAL.

Enthusiasm for Christian reunion, so infectious since the late Pope John XXIII convened the historic Vatican Ecumenical Council, has tended to obscure a hard fact. Serious differences obstruct the road to ultimate unity between Protestants and Roman Catholics—and both sides remain adamant on matters of substance.

"If Christians ignore this, if they engage in wishful thinking instead of agonizing analysis, they invite eventual collapse of the unity movement and renewed acrimony between the faiths," said an influential churchman here at the Fourth World Conference on Faith and Order last week. Others among the 287 Protestant and Orthodox theologians here said much the same thing.

True, the ecumenical movement made important headway here. Cardinal Paul Emile Leger, Archbishop of Montreal, worshiped with the Protestant and Eastern Orthodox theologians — the first time a Roman Catholic of his stature had joined other Christians to confess the "sin" of Christian divisions and to ask God to "break our heart of stone and give us a heart able to repent."

But if mutual suspicions lay submerged and doctrinal differences were being played down, these suspicions and genuine differences still existed. "While we are able to recite together a common prayer for unity," said Cardinal Leger, "we are forced to admit that even this unity is in jeopardy because of our hesitation to accept unity as the Lord willed it, because our prejudices set us up one against the other, because our ignorance is unable to penetrate the veil behind which are the unfathomable riches of Christ."

Cardinal Leger

Fear and Prejudice

Some obstacles to Christian unity are emotional, some theological. Each type affects the other. In the local church and community, "fear and prejudice" are the simple, overt obstacles. But theological disputes often lie at their core. On the other hand, when church leaders gather, they haggle mostly over theological differences; yet, as the Protestant and Orthodox theologians found here, prejudice and misunderstanding often exaggerate doctrinal differences.

Prejudice dies hard. "When Protestant parents return home and find their children crying because their Catholic baby sitter has told them that Catholics go to heaven and Protestants go to hell," says one Episcopalian clergyman in whose parish this happened, "they never forget it." The fact that the Roman Catholic Church has specifically repudiated this doctrine—Cardinal Richard Cushing, Archbishop of Boston, excommunicated a Boston priest more than 10 years ago for preaching it—makes little difference to the parents.

Emotions flare up readily on issues of public policy that vitally affect Catholics and Protestants. Hassles over public aid to parochial schools, birth control laws, and tax exemptions for church-owned business properties arise more from the hard facts of social and economic power than from differences in religious doctrine.

Please Turn to Page 9, Column 1

Wonders of Transplants

Surgeons Save Little Claudia Ballay; Bad Kidney Traded for a Good One

NEW ORLEANS.

There didn't seem to be a thing Mr. and Mrs. O. A. Ballay could do but watch their little daughter, Claudia, 8, die. They had first discovered she had a diseased kidney in October 1961. Her deterioration was slow but relentless.

As poisons accumulated in Claudia's body, her mother lost count of the number of times the child had gone into convulsions.

All that kept her alive were blood transfusions, the use of as many as nine drugs simultaneously, and a technique called peritoneal dialysis, in which a fluid is injected into the blood-rich lining of the abdominal cavity. It remains there from 12 to 72 hours, soaking up the blood poisons from the peritoneum. The fluid is then withdrawn.

One Last Chance

The Ballays clung to the hope that somehow their child's weakened kidneys would recover. Last April, however, a dialysis worked only briefly. Claudia's blood urea nitrogen count (doctors call it BUN) soared to 390. A normal count is 8 to 20.

That meant that all hope had gone. There was one last chance—transplantation of a healthy kidney from a donor to Claudia. Transplantation is a swift-moving new surgical development; someday replacement of diseased organs may be as

routine as replacement of worn-out parts in an automobile.

But that day is not here yet; transplantation works occasionally, but more often the patient dies. Knowing the chances, Mr. and Mrs. Ballay hesitated. Claudia had already suffered so much

Please Turn to Page 9, Column 5

At a construction site, protest against job discrimination.

For Claudia, new kidney, new hope.

After years of negotiations between the United States, the Soviet Union, and the United Kingdom, all agreed to the Limited Nuclear Test Ban Treaty, an important step toward greater Cold War arms agreements.

ALSO IN 1963

Jack Nicklaus won his first of six Masters tournaments, more than any other professional golfer to date.

Before a crowd of 200,000 people gathered at the steps of the Lincoln Memorial, the Reverend Martin Luther King Jr. called for racial equality and an end to discrimination.

President John F. Kennedy met at the White House with leaders of the March on Washington, including the Reverend Martin Luther King Jr. (AP Photo)

Arbitration Law Enacted, Halts Rail Strike

The Washington Post
Times Herald

The Weather
Today—Increasing humidity, scattered thundershowers late in day, high 83. Tonight—Low 66. Friday—Clearing, less humid. Wednesday: High 83 at 4:20 p.m.; low, 65 at 5:30 p.m. *Weather Map and Details on Page B3.*

Backyard Bakeout
Instead of bucking the weekend traffic, tempt your family to have a Labor Day stay-at-homes. The lure: a backyard bakeout. Herb-barbecued turkey with the trimmin's is Elinor Lee's tip, but take your pick from many menus—D1.

86th Year -- No. 267 Phone RE. 7-1234 THURSDAY, AUGUST 29, 1963 WTOP-TV (9) Radio (1500) TEN CENTS

200,000 Jam Mall in Mammoth Rally In Solemn, Orderly Plea for Equality

House Vote Postpones Rail Strike

President Signs New Legislation For Arbitration

By Frank C. Porter
Staff Reporter

The House of Representatives yesterday blocked this Century's third Nationwide railroad strike less than eight hours before deadline.

It enacted legislation calling for binding arbitration of the two major issues in the 4-year-old work rules dispute. The Senate voted the measure the day before.

Passage came at 4:42 p.m. on a 286-to-66 standing vote after more than four hours of debate.

Signed by President

President Kennedy signed the measure into law at 6:14 p.m.

Within minutes after House passage, however, the carriers announced they were tearing down notices of new work rules they were to have put into effect unilaterally at 12:01 a.m. today.

Shortly afterward, the heads of the five railroad brotherhoods announced that they were canceling their strike plans.

The brotherhoods, representing 190,000 train crewmen, had stood ready to quit their posts as soon as the new rules were implemented.

Rail Tieup Averted

Thus was averted a transportation tieup which Mr. Kennedy had said would be "intolerable" and a "tragedy."

The new law, however, removes the strike threat for only 180 days. After that, the railroads are free to post new rules—and the unions to walk out—on any of seven issues not covered by arbitration.

Chairman Oren Harris (D-Ark.) of the House Interstate and Foreign Commerce Committee told the Chamber he accepted the good faith of carriers and unions when they told his Committee these or other issues could be settled fairly easily once the two knottiest problems are resolved.

Some members of both Houses failed to share his optimism, claiming the legislation may only postpone a showdown six months rather than end the conflict.

The two big questions involve the 32,500 firemen's jobs on freight and yard diesels, which management says should be eliminated as no longer needed and the crew consist issue—how many conductors...

See RAIL, A6, Col. 1

The March on Washington for Jobs and Freedom moves along Constitution ave. at 21st st. nw, headed for ceremonies at Lincoln Memorial.
By Tom Keller, Staff Photographer

Largest Demonstration On Civil Rights Urges Passage of Legislation

By Robert E. Baker
Staff Reporter

More than 200,000 persons jammed the Mall here yesterday in the biggest civil rights demonstration in the Nation's history.

This was the "March on Washington for Jobs and Freedom," a one-day rally demanding a breakthrough in civil rights for Negroes.

The demonstrators came by special buses and trains in perfect order. They sang and gathered at the Lincoln Memorial to hear their leaders call on Congress to pass civil rights legislation.

In a mammoth display of fervor, they ended the day by pledging to return to their homes and keep up the battle for full equality by more demonstrations, if necessary.

A. Philip Randolph, director of the March and head of the Brotherhood of Sleeping Car Porters, drew great applause in his remarks at the Memorial when he said this was only the beginning of demonstrations here to gain equality for all.

The ten leaders, representing top Negro civil rights organizations, organized labor and religious denominations, visited Capitol Hill in the morning.

Top House and Senate leaders congratulated the marchers on their courteous behavior but were chary about saying that the demonstration would help the passage of pending civil rights legislation. House Speaker John W. Cormack (D-Mass.) did go so far as to say that the impact of the orderly demonstration would help the bill.

After the demonstration, the leaders called on President Kennedy and Vice President Lyndon B. Johnson at the White House.

President's Statement

After the White House meeting, President Kennedy issued a statement in which he said that such demonstrations for equality are not new nor difficult to understand.

"What is different today is the intensified and widespread public awareness of the need to move forward in achieving these objectives—objectives which are older than the Nation," the statement said. It concluded:

"The cause of 20 million Negroes has been advanced by the program conducted so appropriately before the Nation's shrine to the Great Emancipator, but even more significant is the contribution to all mankind."

The estimate of the size of the crowd was made by Police Chief Robert V. Murray. But no definitive estimate could be made of the number of participants which numbered several thousands.

A hand count of 1036 persons in a panoramic photograph of the Washington Monument area, where the participants gathered before

The mood, the effects and the people of the March—in stories and pictures on Pages A12 through A27, Pages D14 and D15.

marching to the Lincoln Memorial, showed 718 Negroes and 320 whites—a Negro percentage of 69.1. A similar check of the area around the Lincoln Memorial yielded an almost identical percentage.

Because the people were rallying around an issue that raises emotions, the city had made unprecedented security arrangements, greater than for presidential inaugurations and for visits of heads of state.

But the crowd, which police said was the biggest within

See MARCH, A12, Col. 1

New Diem Crackdown Reported

By Neil Sheehan

SAIGON, Aug. 28 (UPI)—The Diem government was reported cracking down today on another segment of the populace—the Saigon slum dwellers angered by the arrest of their Budhist clergy and the sacking of their pagodas.

The move came after the government-controlled Viet Nam press agency said the 400 students who carried out demonstrations in Hue had revealed that the supreme leader of the Budhists now supported President Ngo Dinh Diem, and that the military itself ordered the Buddhist Raids.

Informed sources said blue-uniformed members of the Republican Youth Organization, controlled by President Ngo Dinh Diem's brother Ngo Dinh Nhu, were warning slum dwellers not to talk about the government and not to take how many.

See VIET, A8, Col. 1

2 Saved, at Least 5 Others Still Alive Of 25 Trapped by Utah Mine Blast

By R. Greg Nokes

MOAB, Utah, Aug. 28 (AP)—Rescue workers who had almost despaired of hope found at least seven survivors today among the 25 miners trapped 3200 feet underground by an explosion yesterday.

At least three bodies were located by the rescuers.

The first two survivors, haggard and shocked, were brought up from the depths just before noon after a harrowing 17 hours in the pitch black shaft, one of the deepest on the North American continent.

"There are some others down there. I don't know how many," said Paul McKinney, 22. Aside from some acid burns around the eyes, he seemed in good condition.

Recuers who worked throughout the night with tingering hope said they made voice contact with nine men at midmorning.

Hugh Crawford, chief engineer for the Texas Gulf Sulphur Co., operator of the potash mine said:

"There were an undetermined number of survivors. We can't say for certain just how many."

McKinney and Donald Han-na were the first to come up in a "bucket lift" and they were rushed the 23 miles to a hospital here, then taken quickly to an emergency room past a lobby filling with anxious wives and relatives unaware of the fate of their loved ones.

Told there were reports of

Page A3.

at least seven survivors, McKinney and Hanna said they think there might be still more—perhaps four or five more, at least.

Dr. Jay Munsey then put them to bed, but said their general condition was excellent in view of the ordeal.

"They were very thirsty, very hungry and really played out," he said. "But they won't be in the hospital more than 24 hours."

The rescue work was slow going. Debris and damaged equipment clogged the passages. The men were scattered about after the explosion in lateral tunnels beyond and below the main shaft. The blast apparently was triggered by dynamite they were using to inch along through the hard rock toward the main core of potash, used in commercial fertilizer.

Mrs. Robert June, 34, mother of six children, was among the wives keeping the agonizing vigil at the hospital. She knew there were seven survivors; no one waiting with her knew their names.

Everyone strained for a look, a hopeful sign as the first ambulance rolled up to the hospital door.

Hanna was grimy, he seemed of near collapse but he never looked better to Mrs. Donald Hanna.

"Oh, I'm so terribly relieved," she said. "But I felt sure he'd be all right. I knew if there were survivors that Don would be among them. I just had a feeling—it was there, deep down inside."

Hanna and McKinney said they were working at the end of the deepest lateral tunnel at the 3,290 foot level and that they thought most of the trapped miners were in two groups, the others perhaps scattered in ones and twos.

Rally Impact On Congress Still Doubtful

By Robert C. Albright
Staff Reporter

Leaders of the March on Washington yesterday pressed their case for a strengthened civil rights bill and related legislation in a quietly impressive two-hour round of conferences with top House and Senate leaders.

But, on the record anyway, the limited commitments they brought back from the Capitol were substantially those they already had, and there was no indication they made any new converts.

Congressional leaders praised the high tone of the conferences and the conduct of the March.

But many were chary about predicting any net gain for the civil rights legislation from the March. The majority took a wait-and-see attitude.

Speaker John W. McCormack (D-Mass.) told reporters however that if the March was "conducted in such a way as to arouse respect and admiration it will help the bill.

In comment off the floor, ideologically opposed Senators

See HILL, A20, Col. 3

Kennedy watched King's speech on television. Congressman John Lewis recalled the civil rights leaders' meeting with Kennedy after the speech. "He stood in the door and he was beaming like a father," Lewis said.

Today's Index
100 PAGES—7 SECTIONS

	Page		Page
Am'm'ts	G12	Herblock	A16
Buchwald	C9	Keep Well	C16
City Life	B1-2	Lippmann	A17
Classified	G1-14	Movie Guide	G12
Comics	C9-13	Music	G13
Crossword	C13	Obituaries	.B3
Deaths	.A17	Pearson	.13
Editorials	A16	Shoppers' P	B17
Events Today	A19	Sports	F1-7
Federal Diary	B1	TV-Radio	D16
Financial	B4-7	Weather	.B3
Food	D1-15	Women's	.1-7
Games	C9		

Of Special Interest
Premier Khrushchev squelches speculation that he plans trip to United States this year. Page C1.

A28 Pages—News, Editorials
B Pages—City Life, Financial
C14 Pages—General News, Comics
D10 Pages—Food, General News
E Pages—Women's News
F Pages—Sports News
G14 Pages—Classified, Amusements

No Tension, Only a Quiet Sense of Purpose
A Mounting Tide... Toward Lincoln's Temple...

By Marya Mannes
Critic, essayist and author of several books, Miss Mannes is a well-known commentator on the American scene.

At ten o'clock the city was so empty that it looked as if a plague had struck it, or—the streets stretching silently out in the sun, the cops and guardsmen at every corner waiting, as in "High Noon," as if ambush was prepared for an enemy. Shops were closed and the people who normally inhabit Washington presumably fled. Echoes from friends further north assailed the ears: "Wouldn't be there for a million bucks." "Bound to cause harm." "Potentially dangerous."

On the green slopes of the Washington Monument, only a sprinkling of people had gathered. There was an air of bustle and expectancy, but the only drama by 10:30 was that a child had been found at the rest room. His name was Roosevelt Johnson.

What happened then happened slowly but mightily, and by 11:30 a mounting tide of people, placards aloft or handbags hanging, were walking down Constitution Ave. and towards Lincoln's temple.

"Americans just know how to march," said a walking reporter, and then added: "Thank God."

There was, indeed, no attempt at lines, at rhythm, at any formation whatsoever. They did not even stick together, except in the loosest way, by groups or states, or organizations, or bus-loads. They just walked—mostly black, but partly white—like people who know where they are going but are not making a show of it.

By noon two great rivers flowed along either side of the Reflecting Pool until both verges and all the approaches to the Memorial or the man who thought he had freed them were solid with people.

No pomp? No enemy, no plague. A people serious but relaxed; almost festive. Among the neatly suited men, who did not even in the sun take off their coats and ties, were many black and some and stalwart young Negroes, many middle-aged or CORE, and comparatively few "beatniks." These, wet-lipped, sparse-bearded, with hair long on the nape, usually walked with their inevitable counterparts, the girls whose dank straight hair escapes from pins and ribbons, whose toes are dirty. The older white women—and there were many—looked, again, like teachers, or the wives of teachers; more concerned with others than with themselves.

Wherever they were, wherever they sat, there was no look of defiance, only a sort of quiet sense of purpose. They spoke little, they laughed rarely, and when they did they smiled often; they ate their picnics, they listened to their transistors, they clapped their speakers. Brown legs and white legs hung down into the pool, a Negro youth gave final shove to a white boy struggling up the limb of a tree, walked up no matter who jostled or stepped over whom, there was always the low "excuse me..." "excuse me, please."

Great amplified voices sang "Oh Freedom—Oh Freedom"... "before I'll be a slave, I'll be buried in my grave..." and they clapped to that and to "the whole world in my hands" and listened quietly to "How many times must a man look up before he can see the sky?"

The loudest sounds from their throats came in response to the words of Walter Reuther, but only one woman really shouted like a revivalist. She was walking back from the March with a transistor to her ear, and with a voice like a bronchial crow she screeched "Yes!" and "Right!" right into it.

It was a wonderful and immensely important thing that happened here. And the only pity of it was that the people who deplored it, the people who resented it, missed one of the great democratic expressions of this century: a people claiming, with immense control and dignity, the American rights long denied them.

The March had to happen. As Nietzsche said "Great problems are in the street." This one, certainly, can never be swept under the rug.

QUOTED

"I have a dream that my four little children will one day live in a nation where they will not be judged by the color of their skin but by the content of their character."

—REVEREND MARTIN LUTHER KING JR., August 28, 1963

Dr. Martin Luther King's 'Dream' Speech, Full Text

"I Have A Dream"

NEW YORK Amsterdam News

Vol. XLII, No. 36 — 2340 Eighth Ave. New York 27, N. Y. — SATURDAY, SEPTEMBER 7, 1963 — Entered as Second Class Matter, New York City — 15c — Outside NYC 20c

Ray Jones Vs. Adam Can Either One Win?

Inside This Issue!

- Full text of Dr. Martin Luther King's "Dream" speech.
- Two picture pages of March On Washington with 28 other pictures of the March.
- Complete text March On Washington Pledge.
- March On Washington coverage by 12 Amsterdam
- News reporters, including Roy Wilkins' summary.
- Eyewitness account of Ghana Funeral of Dr. W. E. B. DuBois.

Dr. King's Speech

I am happy to join with you today in what will go down in history as the greatest demonstration for freedom in the history of the Nation.

Five score years ago, a great American, in whose symbolic shadow we stand today, signed the Emancipation Proclamation. This momentous decree came as a great beacon of light of hope to millions of Negro slaves who had been seared in the flames of withering injustice. It came as the the joyous daybreak to end the long night of captivity.

But one hundred years later, the Negro still is not free. One hundred years later, the life of the Negro is still sadly crippled by the manacle of segregation and the chain of discrimination. One hundred years later, the Negro lives on a lonely island of poverty in the midst of a vast ocean of matcrial prosperity. One hundred years later, the Negro is still languishing in the corner of American society and finds simseif an exile in his own land. So we have come here today to dramatize a shameful condition.

Promissory Note

In a sense we have come to the capitol to cash a check. When the architects of our republic wrote the magnificent words of the Constitution and the Declaration of Independence, they were signing a promissory note to which every American was to fall heir. This note was a promise that all men — black men as well as wihte men — would be guaranteed the unalienable rights of life, liberty and the pursuit of happiness.

But it is obvious today that America has defaulted on this promissory note insofar as her citizens of color are concerned. Instead of honoring this sacred obligation, America has given the Negro people a bad check. A cneck that has come back marked insufficient funds. But we refuse to believe that the bank of justice is bankrupt. We refuse to believe that there are insufficient funds in the great vaults of opportunity in this Nation.

So we have come to cash this check. A check that will give us the riches of freedom and the security of justice.

We have also come to this hallowed spot to remind America that the fierce urgency is now. This is no time to engage in the luxury of cooling off or to take the tranquilizing drug of gradualism. Now is the time to make real the promise of democracy.

Now is the time to rise from the dark and desolate valley of segregation to the sunlit path of racial justice. Now is the time to lift our Nation from the quick sands of racial injustice to the solid rock of brotherhood. Now is the time to make justice a reality for all of God's children.

It would be fatal for the Nation to overlook the urgency of the moment. This sweltering summer of the Negro's legitimate discount will not pass until there is an invigorating autumn of freedom and equality.

1963 is not an end but a beginning.

Those who hope that the Negro needed to blow off steam and will be content will have a rude awakening if the Nation returns to business as usual. There will be neither rest nor tranquility in America until the Negro is granted his citizenship rights.

The whirlwinds of revolt will continue to shake the foundations of our Nation until the bright day of Justice emerges.

Bars Bitterness

But there is something that I must say to my people who stand on the warm threshold which leads into the palace of justice. In the process of gaining our rightful place, we must not be guilty of wrongful deeds.

Let us not seek to satisfy our thirst for freedom by drinking from the cup of bitterness and hatred.

Dignity, Discipline

We must forever continue our struggle on the high plane of dignity and discipline.

We must not allow our creative protest to de-

(Continued on Page Two)

Read...Remember Marchers' Pledge

WASHINGTON — The more than 250,000 Negro and white civil rights marchers for "jobs and freedom" pledged last Wednesday to continue the fight in their local communities in formal pledges signed by thousands and for which the thousands of others roared approval when read by A. Philip Randolph during the historic demonstrations.

This pledge is as follows:

"Standing before the Lincoln Memorial on the 28th of August, in the centennial year of emancipation, I affirm my complete personal commitment for the struggle for jobs and freedom for all Americans.

"To fulfill this commitment, I pledge that I will not relax until victory is won.

"I pledge that I will join and support all actions undertaken in good faith and in accord with time-honored democratic traditions of nonviolent protest or peaceful assembly and petition, and of redress through the courts and the legislative process.

"I pledge to carry back the message of the March to my friends and neighbors back home and to arouse them to an equal commitment and an equal effort. I will march and I will write letters. I will demonstrate and I will voie. I will work and make sure that my voice and those of my brothers ring clear and determined from every corner of our land.

"I will pledge my heart and my mind and my body, unequivocally and without regard to personal sacrifice, to the achievement of social peace through social justice."

"Purely Personal", Says The NAACP About Charlayne

As far as the NAACP officials are concerned, the surprise secret marriage announcement of pretty Charlayne Hunter to a white classmate at the University of Georgia, Walter Stovall, is "purely a personal matter."

"The NAACP regards this as strictly a private and personal matter between two people," Roy Wilkins, NAACP executive secretary said in a statement to this newspaper.

Mrs. Constance Motley, who was the NAACP Legal Defense Fund's lawyer who aided Mrs. Stovall in entering the Athens, Ga., campus, asserted that she was "indifferent to the whole thing. Personally, I'm glad it was a white man and Negro woman for a change."

While daily newspapers throughout the South were headlining the marriage story and the fact that the couple was expecting a child in December, Mr. Wilkins said that a 1962 survey showed there were 7,000 Negro students in previously all-white colleges in the South, and this was the first interracial marriage that has been reported.

"End Of World"

Meanwhile in a one-room apartment on Cornelia Street in Greenwich Village, the 21 . year old Mrs. Stovall and her 25-year old husband sought to start a new

(Continued on Page 5)

"End Of The World?"

MR. AND MRS. — Charlayne Alberta Hunter, 21, first Negro girl to enter and be graduated from the University of Georgia announced Monday that she had married Walter Stovall, 25, a white student she met on the university campus. The couple, secretly married last spring, is expecting a child in December. Mrs. Stovall is shown as she entered offices of the New Yorker magazine where she is an editorial assistant. Stovall, who still has a year to finish in college is shown outside the building Tuesday. (UPI Photo)

The Big Question

After The March--What?

After the March, what?

In the words of the Big Six, who were responsible for staging the greatest non-violent demonstration in the nation's history, the new drive in the coming months will center on the fight for passage of the President's civil rights bill, voter registration, more street demonstrations in cities throughout the nation and a return to Washington if the civil rights bill develops a filibuster.

Hailing the March as "one of the truly great events in American history," Rev. Martin Luther King told the Amsterdam News that his major fight in the next few months would center on doubling the Negro vote throughout the nation.

Leaders To Meet

King and Roy Wilkins, NAACP executive secretary, both indicated that the sponsors of the March on Washington would meet "on or before September 15" as soon as all the leaders can get a date clear to consider official reactions on the March and plan for areas of possible future cooperation.

John Lewis, the 23-year old young firebrand leader of the Student Non-Violent Coordinating Committee, predicted to this newspaper in a weekend meeting that there would be a "new type of militancy" from members of his group.

"We will leave no stones unturned in seeking to end unemployment and job discrimination in the northern tier of Southern states, and we will continue sitins in restaurants, lunch counters, and movies in the South," he declared. Lewis predicted new militant demonstrations in Atlanta, Ga., Nashville, Tenn., and Durham, N.C., by members of SNCC in the next few weeks.

Dr. King, in New York to rest after the March, said the South-

(Continued on Page 5)

They Are Still At Work On The 'March'

By JAMES BOOKER

In the dimly-lit headquarters at 170 W. 130th St., a small group of workers still toil over the final details of the March on Washington.

"We have a lot of paper work to do, to pay bills, to get all monies in, and we are committed to further activities in Washington if the filibuster develops over the President's civil rights bill, so we will keep this office open with a small crew until we know where things stand," Cleveland Robinson, powerful labor leader and administrative chairman of the March, told the Amsterdam News.

Biggest Task

While the world still marvels over the huge success of the March, few realize that much of the behind scenes credit for this goes to unheralded men like Robinson, Bayard Rustin, deputy director of the March, Mrs. Anna Arnold Hedgeman, who did a yeoman's job getting the support of women's and church groups; Tony Scott, who coordinated New York groups; L. Joseph Overton, Sy Posner, Richard Apter, and scores of others.

"This was the biggest task of our lives, both for Rustin and myself, and my comment on this is that I know that it left the Negro standing ten feet taller," Robinson said.

Right now Robinson estimates that the March cost "well over $100,000," but said he would await a meeting of the administrative committee Thursday before he would know just where they stood financially. He said he feels the headquarters still

(Continued on Page 5)

South Gives Up Again!

BIRMINGHAM, Ala.—The south surrendered to the power of the federal government for the second time in three months Wednesday when Governor George Wallace stood peacefully by and permitted white public schools here to be desegregated for the first time in Alabama's history.

Two Negro students slipped through a back door of the Gray-

(Continued on Page 5)

Ghana Gives State Burial To Dr. DuBois

By WILLIAM BRANCH

ACCRA, Ghana — We were gathering at a secluded spot on a rutted road in the dark of a moonless African night. Our purpose was to hold a torch-light march on the United States Embassy in Ghana to coincide with the mammoth Civil Rights March on Washington back home. An automobile pulled up and its occupant leaned out of the window to pass along the final word: Dr. Du Bois was dead.

The news was not unexpected among the Afro - Americans living and working in Accra, the fast-growing capital of Kwame Nkrumah's hustling West African state of Ghana. It had been known for several days that he was quite ill, and considering his advanced age, that alone could easily have proved fatal. But to those who maintained close contact with "The Father of Pan-Africanism" and his wife,

(Continued on Page 25)

Next Week!

Should Charlayne Hunter have married a white man? The Amsterdam News will poll the people of Harlem on this question next week. What's your answer?

Be sure to read your answer and that of your neighbors in next week's Amsterdam News.

ADAM POWELL — RAY JONES

Is It Money?

Behind The Powell Ray Jones Split?

Absent from Harlem for almost two months apparently ducking a court summons, Rep. Adam Clayton Powell returned Sunday to call for a "Birmingham explosion in New York City" and to announce his formal split with his former associate, City Councilman J. Raymond Jones.

Powell said he was dropping his support of Jones charging him with "selling out to Mayor Wagner" and for abandoning the Black Revolution, terming him "guilty of treason". He said he would support Attorney Henry Williams over Jones in the Sept. 5th Council primary race.

Powell's blasts had not gotten cold, however, before Jones blasted back, accusing Powell of "turning his back on Harlem," and predicting that Powell would be through next year, hinting that a draft movement was being launched behind James Farmer, national director of the Congress on Racial Equality. There was no comment from Farmer.

"The revolution has passed him by and he is angry because they did not ask him to speak at the March on Washington," Jones said in answering Powell's Sunday blasts.

Others

Powell's announcement also included declaring his support for several other candidates, including John Young, for Councilman at-Large and for district leaders, Assemblyman Lloyd E. Dickens and Mrs. Alice Watson, in the 11th A.D. Antonio Rasmus and Mrs. Carrie Thomas, in the 12th A.D., East, opposing Jones and Mrs. Edrie Archibald; and former Manhattan Borough President Hulan Jack and Mrs. Lillian Thompson, in the 14th A.D., West.

The announcement and bitter comments by both Jones and Powell were expected to be the opening guns of a continuing campaign which political observers predict will last long beyond the Sept. 5th primary.

Jones has aligned himself in the primary battle with Attorney Charles Rangel and Mrs. Rosalie Landy, who are seeking the 11th A.D., leadership; and John Edmonds and Mrs. Wilhelmina Adams, seeking the 14th A.D., leadership against Jack and Mrs. Thompson.

All sides have predicted that despite the outcome of this year's leadership primaries, they will battle for legislative seats in next year's primary, and a con-

(Continued on Page 5)

Hey Man! Are You Working?

Are you one of the thousands of jobless Negroes and Puerto Ricans between the ages of 18 and 26 who are interested in learning a skill for the future?

If you are and your interest bends more to the construction industry, then you'd better hurry up and file an application at one of the 18 centers throughout the city.

The City Labor Department has warned that construction applicants have up until Sept. 12, a week from this Thursday, to fil for apprenticeship programs.

The Labor Department's office is at 93 Worth St., just off Centre St. Its telephone number is WAlker 5-1900. If you can't go there and don't know which of the 18 centers is nearest your home, call the department, Monday through Friday, from 9 a.m. to 5 p.m., and ask.

To warn of the Sept. 12 deadline and to heist the number of applications, 200,000 leaflets are being distributed this week in Negro and Puerto Rican com-

(Continued on Page 5)

Merediths Living In D.C.

WASHINGTON — Fresh from receiving his diploma from the University of Mississippi, James Meredith told the Amsterdam News that he would make his residence in the nation's capital for the next year while his wife attends the Howard University graduate school.

Mrs. Mary June Meredith is due to register for the Howard graduate school next week.

The 30-year old first known Negro graduate from "Ole Miss" said he would work on setting up the James Meredith Educational Fund for the next year seeking to raise funds to help Negro high school and college students throughout the South.

He indicated he plans to return to Mississippi, but did not comment on reports that he might enter politics. Asked how he felt after his year's ordeal at the University, Meredith said, "Just like a Negro, nothing else."

Meredith also had no comment on the announcement of the secret marriage of Charlayne Hunter, the recent University of Georgia graduate, but asserted that "I already know about it before I read it in the papers."

As a result of the speech and his other civil rights work, King was named "Man of the Year" by Time *magazine.*

ALSO IN 1963

Pope John XXIII died at age 81 and was succeeded by Pope Paul VI.

Johnson Takes Nation's Helm, Pages 4 and 5

The Dallas Morning News

John F. Kennedy Life History, Pages 16 and 17

VOL. 115—NO. 54 DALLAS, TEXAS, SATURDAY, NOVEMBER 23, 1963—50 PAGES IN 4 SECTIONS ★★★★ PRICE CENTS

KENNEDY SLAIN ON DALLAS STREET

★ ★ ★ ★ ★ ★ ★ ★ ★ ★ ★ ★ ★ ★ ★ ★

JOHNSON BECOMES PRESIDENT

Receives Oath on Aircraft

By ROBERT E. BASKIN
Washington Bureau of The News

In a solemn and sorrowful hour, with a nation mourning its dead President, Lyndon B. Johnson Friday took the oath of office as the 36th chief executive of the United States.

Following custom, the oath-taking took place quickly—only an hour and a half after the assassination of President Kennedy.

Federal Judge Sarah T. Hughes of Dallas administered the oath in a hurriedly arranged ceremony at 2:39 p.m. aboard Air Force 1, the presidential plane that brought Kennedy on his ill-fated Texas trip and on which his body was taken back to Washington.

Mrs. Johnson and Mrs. Kennedy, her stocking still flecked with blood from the assassination, flanked the vice-president as he raised his right hand in the forward compartment of the presidential jetliner at Love Field. About 25 White House staff members and friends were present as Johnson intoned the familiar oath:

"I do solemnly swear that I will perform the duties of President of the United States to the best of my ability, and defend, protect and preserve the Constitution of the United States."

The 55-year-old Johnson, the first Texan ever to become President, turned and kissed his wife on the cheek, giving her shoulders a squeeze. Then he put his arm around Mrs. Kennedy, kissing her gently on her right cheek.

Mrs. Kennedy, in tears, was wearing the same bright pink suit she wore on the fatal ride, a ride in which she had been wildly acclaimed by friendly, cheering crowds in Dallas before rifle shots rang out and the President collapsed in the seat of the car beside her.

Johnson had deliberately delayed the ceremony to give Kennedy's widow time to compose herself for one of the gruelling aspects of her husband's assassination.

CONTINUED ON PAGE 11

Lyndon B. Johnson

Gov. Connally Resting Well

By MIKE QUINN

Gov. John Connally — felled Friday by a sniper's bullet in the back—rested in "quite satisfactory" condition late Friday night at Parkland Hospital following nearly four hours of surgery in the afternoon.

An aide for the governor reported at 10:30 p.m. that the governor was asleep and resting comfortably following the incident which claimed President Kennedy's life.

Meanwhile, Dr. Tom Shires, chief of surgeons at University of Texas Southwestern Medical School, said Connally barely missed a fatal wound.

"After consulting with Mrs. Connally and others on the scene, the consensus is that the governor was quite fortunate that he turned to see what happened to the President. If he had not turned to his right, there is a good chance he probably would have been shot through the heart—as it was, the bullet caused a tangential wound."

Dr. Shires rushed to Dallas by Air Force jet after word of the shooting was flashed.

Connally was operated on by Dr. Robert R. Shaw, thoracic

CONTINUED ON PAGE 3.

Impact Shattering To World Capitals

By the Associated Press

Word of President Kennedy's assassination struck the world's capitals with shattering impact, leaving heads of state and the man in the street stunned and grief-stricken.

While messages of condolence poured into the White House from presidents, premiers and crowned heads, the little people of many lands reacted with numbed disbelief.

Pubs in London and cafes in Paris fell silent as the news came over radio and television.

IN MOSCOW, a Russian girl walked weeping along the street.

At U.N. headquarters in New York, delegates of 11 nations bowed their heads in a moment of silence.

In Buenos Aires, newspapers sounded sirens reserved for news of the utmost gravity.

Britain's Prime Minister Douglas-Home sent condolences, and Sir Winston Churchill branded the slaying a monstrous act.

"The loss to the United States and to the world is incalculable," Sir Winston declared. "Those who come after Mr. Kennedy must strive the more to achieve the ideals of world peace and human happiness and dignity to which his presidency was dedicated."

Douglas-Home issued this terse statement:

"The Prime Minister has learned with the most profound shock and horror of the death

CONTINUED ON PAGE 1.

Pro-Communist Charged With Act

A sniper shot and killed President John F. Kennedy on the streets of Dallas Friday. A 24-year-old pro-Communist who once tried to defect to Russia was charged with the murder shortly before midnight.

Kennedy was shot about 12:20 p.m. Friday at the foot of Elm Street as the Presidential car entered the approach to the Triple Underpass. The President died in a sixth-floor surgery room at Parkland Hospital about 1 p.m., though doctors said there was no chance for him to live when he reached the hospital.

Within two hours, Vice-President Lyndon Johnson was sworn in as the nation's 36th President inside the presidential plane before departing for Washington.

The gunman also seriously wounded Texas Gov. John Connally, who was riding with the President.

Four Hours in Surgery

Connally spent four hours on an operating table, but his condition was reported as "quite satisfactory" at midnight.

The assassin, firing from the sixth floor of the Texas School Book Depository Building near the Triple Underpass sent a Mauser 6.5 rifle bullet smashing into the President's head.

An hour after the President died, police hauled the 24-year-old suspect, Lee Harvey Oswald, out of an Oak Cliff movie house.

He had worked for a short time at the depository, and police had encountered him while searching the building shortly after the assassination. They turned him loose when he was identified as an employe but put out a pickup order on him when he failed to report for a work roll call.

He also was accused of killing a Dallas policeman, J. D. Tippit, whose body was found during the vast manhunt for the President's assassin.

Oswald, who has an extensive pro-Communist background, four years ago renounced his American citizenship in Russia and tried to become a Russian citizen. Later, he returned to this country.

Friendly Crowd Cheered Kennedy

Shockingly, the President was shot after driving the length of Main Street through a crowd termed the largest and friendliest of his 2-day Texas visit. It was a good-natured crowd that surged out from the curbs almost against the swiftly moving presidential car. The protective bubble had been removed from the official convertible.

Mrs. Connally, who occupied one of the two jump seats in the car, turned to the President a few moments before and remarked, "You can't say Dallas wasn't friendly to you."

At Fort Worth, Kennedy had just delivered one of the most well-received speeches of his ca-

CONTINUED ON PAGE 2.

FUNERAL FOR PRESIDENT WILL BE HELD ON MONDAY

WASHINGTON (AP)—President Kennedy's funeral will be held Monday at St. Matthews Roman Catholic Cathedral, the White House announced Friday night.

The body of the slain President will lie in repose at the White House Saturday and will lie in state in the rotunda of the Capitol on Sunday and Monday.

The President's body will be taken a couple of miles to the cathedral at 11 a.m. (EST) Monday. There, Richard Cardinal Cushing, Archbishop of Boston and close friend of the Kennedy family, will celebrate a pontifical requiem Mass at noon.

Acting White House Press Secretary Andrew T. Hatcher said he did not know where Kennedy will be buried. There has been one report, still unconfirmed, that burial would be in the family plot in Brookline, Mass.

The President's body will be moved from the White House in an official cortege to the Capitol rotunda at 1 p.m. Sunday. This ceremony will be attended by members of the

CONTINUED ON PAGE 11.

John F. Kennedy

GRAY CLOUDS WENT AWAY

Day Began as Auspiciously As Any in Kennedy's Career

(Robert E. Baskin, chief of the Washington Bureau of The News, was one of four persons representing the world press in the motorcade which resulted in the President's assassination. This is his account of what happened.)

By ROBERT E. BASKIN
Washington Bureau of The News

It was a day that started as auspiciously as any in the career of John F. Kennedy.

When we boarded the Presidential jetliner, Air Force One, at Fort Worth at midmorning, the White House party was in high spirits. The Fort Worth welcome had been a tremendous one. Shortly before the 15-minute flight to Love Field, ugly gray clouds were swept away by a brisk breeze. The sun was out, and the Texas sky was a vivid blue.

President and Mrs. Kennedy, she strikingly attired in a pink suit with a pert matching hat, made an instant hit at Love Field as they shook hands with hundreds of persons along the fence line.

Then the last journey began.

The big open Lincoln car moved out smoothly, carrying Mr. and Mrs. Kennedy and Gov. John Connally and his wife, Nellie.

Three cars back was the press pool car, in which three other newspapermen and I rode. Just ahead of us were Dallas Mayor and Mrs. Earle Cabell and Rep. Ray Roberts of McKinney.

Malcolm Kilduff, assistant presidential press secretary, was with us, and as we moved into the heart of the city Kilduff expressed elation over the friendly nature of the welcome and the great outpouring of people.

Everyone in the press car agreed it was one of the most cordial receptions the President had received in quite a while.

Buoyed by the cheers of the multitudes on Main Street, our motorcade moved on past the courthouse. Then came the approach to the Triple Underpass, with the leading cars picking up speed as the crowd thinned out somewhat. Over to our right loomed the gaunt structure labeled the Texas State School Book Depository.

It was 12:30 p.m.

The sharp crack of a rifle rang out. But at that moment we couldn't believe it was just that. "What the hell was that?" someone in our car asked.

Then there were two more shots—measured carefully.

We saw people along the street diving for the ground.

CONTINUED ON PAGE 3.

Kennedy was in Texas to patch up divisions within the Texas Democratic Party in preparation for his reelection campaign. The trip was one of Jacqueline Kennedy's first since the death of baby Patrick in August.

November 22, 1963
President Kennedy Assassinated

EXTRA EXTRA

KENNEDY SLAIN

Assassin's Bullet Fells President on Dallas Street

Gravely Wounded, He Slumped Into Wife's Lap; Governor of Texas Also Hit; Nation Is Shocked

The Boston Globe

WASHINGTON (AP) --- Government sources said today that President Kennedy is dead.

DALLAS (UPI) — President Kennedy was shot and gravely wounded by a would-be assassin today as he drove through downtown Dallas in an open car with Texas Gov. John B. Connally.

EXTRA

Shooting Closes Stock Market

News Stops City, Nation — Workers Weep Openly

Ted Got the News Presiding in Senate

Get Tough, Parents Told

Dr. Sutcliffe's Fate In Hands of Jury

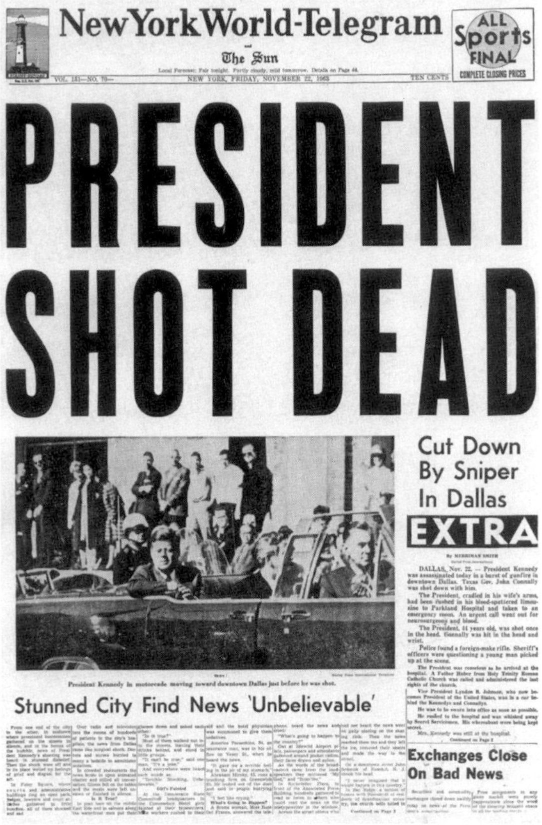
New York World-Telegram

The Sun

ALL Sports FINAL

PRESIDENT SHOT DEAD

Cut Down By Sniper In Dallas

EXTRA

Stunned City Find News 'Unbelievable'

Exchanges Close On Bad News

FORT WORTH STAR-TELEGRAM

MORNING

KENNEDY MURDERED

JOHNSON TAKES OATH AS PRESIDENT

Assassin Wounds Texas Governor

New Chief Executive Returns To Capital With JFK's Body

Connally No Longer In Danger

Defector Admits He Was at Shooting Scene

INSIDE INDEX

Rocky Mountain News

HOME

PRESIDENT IS SLAIN

Suspect Held

DALLAS, Nov. 22 — (UPI) — President Kennedy was assassinated Friday.

John Fitzgerald Kennedy May 29, 1917—Nov. 22, 1963

LBJ Is Sworn In

Some people in Dallas were hostile to Kennedy, though welcoming crowds lined the streets as his convertible passed. The president was shot at 12:30 p.m., and died a half hour later at Parkland Memorial Hospital. Democratic Texas Governor John Connally was also shot, but recovered and was later appointed Secretary of the Treasury under Kennedy's former opponent, Richard Nixon.

NOVEMBER 22, 1963
PRESIDENT KENNEDY ASSASSINATED

THE GUARDIAN

36,511 Manchester Saturday November 23 1963 Price 4d

President Kennedy assassinated

Police arrest suspect

From ALISTAIR COOKE

New York, November 22

President John Fitzgerald Kennedy, the thirty-fifth President of the United States, was shot during a motorcade drive through downtown Dallas this afternoon. He died in the emergency room of the Parkland Memorial Hospital 32 minutes after the attack. He was 46 years old, and is the third President to be assassinated in office since Abraham Lincoln and the first since President McKinley in 1901.

Late this afternoon, the Dallas police took into custody a 24-year-old former marine, Lee H. Oswald, who is alleged to have shot and killed the policeman outside a cinema. He is said to have remarked only : " It is all over now." He is the chairman of a group called the " Fair Play for Cuba Committee," and is married to a Russian girl. He is described at the moment as " a prime suspect."

President Kennedy is succeeded at once by the Vice-President, Lyndon Baines Johnson, a 55-year-old native Texan, who took the oath of office in Dallas at five minutes to four at the hands of a woman Federal Judge.

This is being written in the numbed interval between the first shock and the harried attempt to reconstruct a sequence of fact from an hour of tumult. However, this is the first assassination of a world figure that took place in the age of television ; and every network and station in the country abandoned its daily grind and took up the plotting of the appalling story. At this hour, it begins to form a grisly pattern, contradicted by a grisly preface : the projection on television screens of happy crowd and a grinning President only a few seconds before the gunshots.

The President was almost at the end of his two-day tour of Texas. He was to make a luncheon speech in the Dallas trade mart building and his motor procession had about another mile to go. He had had the warmest welcome of his trip from a great crowd at the airport, and the cries and pleas for a personal touch were so engaging that Mrs Kennedy took the lead and walked from the ramp of the presidential plane to a fence that held the crowd in. She was followed quickly by the President, and they both seized hands and forearms and smiled gladly at the people.

Security precautions

The Secret Service and the police were relieved to get them into their car where Mrs Kennedy sat between the President and John B. Connally, the Governor of Texas. The Dallas police had instituted the most stringent security precautions in the city's history. They wanted no repetition of the small but disgraceful brawl that humiliated Mr Adlai Stevenson in their city when he attended a United Nations rally on October 24.

The motorcade was going along slowly but smoothly when three muffled shots, which the crowd first mistook for fireworks, cracked through the cheers. One hit the shoulder blade and the wrist of Governor Connally, who was taken with the President to the hospital, where his condition is serious. The other brought blood trickling from the back of the head of the sitting President. His right arm flopped from a high wave of greeting and he collapsed into the arms of Mrs Kennedy, who fell unharmed. She was heard to cry, " Oh, no ! " and sat there all the way cradling his head in her lap.

The President was taken to the emergency room of the Parkland Hospital and Governor Connally was taken into surgery. Mrs Kennedy went in with the living President, and less than an hour later came out with the dead man in a bronze coffin, which arrived shortly after two priests had administered the last rites of the Roman Catholic Church. The body was escorted by Generals Clifton and McHugh, the President's chief military and Air Force aides, to the Dallas Airport and flown thence to Washington.

Sniper's nest

Within an hour of the President's death, the Secret Service had found a sniper's nest inside the building from which the first witnesses swore the bullets had been fired. It is a warehouse for a school text book firm, known as the Texas School Depository, on the corner of Elm and Houston Streets. In an upper room, whose open window commanded the route of the Presidential motorcade, the Secret Service men found the remains of a fried chicken and a foreign rifle with a telescopic sight. Alongside it lay three empty cartridge cases.

The Secretary of State, Mr Dean Rusk, and five other Cabinet members were in an aircraft on the way to Japan. The plane turned around in mid-Pacific and headed back to Hawaii and then on to Washington.

In the Senate, it so happened that the President's brother, Edward Kennedy, a freshman Senator from Massachusetts, was presiding, when the Chief Democratic Whip, Senator Mike Mansfield, went to the rostrum and told him the news. The Senator put down his gavel and went from the chamber.

Lying in state

The Speaker of the House, Mr John W. McCormack, who is now the next in line of Presidential succession, and was promptly assigned the Secret Service detail that belongs to the Vice-President, announced that the body of the dead President will be taken tonight to Bethesda Naval Hospital, will go to the White House tomorrow, and thereafter will lie-in-state in the Rotunda under the great dome of the Capitol until noon on Monday.

It will then be removed for the burial service, which will be held in St Matthew's Cathedral in Washington. As a war veteran, the late President could be buried in Arlington National Cemetery, but there was some early talk that he might be taken to the family plot in Boston.

Defector who came back

From RICHARD SCOTT

Washington, November 22.

Lee Oswald, who is under arrest in Dallas as the prime suspect in Mr Kennedy's assassination, went to Russia in 1959 and married a Russian woman who bore him one child. He returned to the United States with his family last year.

Oswald defected after his discharge from the Marines, and later told the US Embassy in Moscow that he had applied for Soviet citizenship. While in Russia he is said to have worked in a Minsk factory.

Last year he applied to be allowed to return to America, and was granted an exit visa by the Soviet authorities. He was recently fined in New Orleans for distributing Communist literature, and is reported to have been chairman of the "Fair Play for Cuba Committee."

Britain to hold national service

It was announced from 10 Downing Street that a national service of commemoration will be held for President Kennedy. The date and place will be decided within the next day or two.

It was also announced that, after consultations with the Opposition, the Government intended to propose that the House of Commons should sit at 2.30 p.m. on Monday for the purpose only of paying tribute to President Kennedy and should thereafter adjourn for the remainder of the day.

The Lord Chamberlain's office has instructed the flying of flags at half mast on public buildings today and again on Monday.

Lee Oswald

Mrs Kennedy bends over the body of her dying husband in the back of the car. An unidentified man is standing on the bumper. Below, Lyndon Johnson is sworn in as the new President in the cabin of the Presidential plane. By his side is Mrs Kennedy

Mrs Kennedy with Mr Robert Kennedy, watching the casket containing the President's body being placed into an ambulance

The Queen sends messages

The Queen has sent messages to Mrs Kennedy and Mr Lyndon Johnson.

The one to Mrs Kennedy was : "I am so deeply distressed to learn of the tragic death of President Kennedy. My husband joins me in sending our heartfelt and sincere sympathy to you and your family. Elizabeth R."

To Mr Johnson, she said : "I am shocked and horrified to learn of the tragic death of President Kennedy. On behalf of my people I send my sincere sympathy to the Government and to the Congress and to the people of the United States of America."

Sir Winston Churchill said : "This monstrous act has taken from us a great statesman and a wise and valiant man." Those coming after Mr Kennedy must strive the more to achieve the ideals of world peace, human happiness, and dignity to which his presidency was dedicated.

MOSCOW : Radio and television programmes were interrupted to give the news, and the radio then played solemn organ music.

PARIS : President de Gaulle said : "President Kennedy died like a soldier, under fire, for his duty and in the service of his country . . . I salute this great example and this great memory."

UNITED NATIONS : Diplomatists from 111 nations stood in silence as the UN General Assembly adjourned.

BONN : The former Chancellor, Dr Adenauer, sent a telegram to Mrs Kennedy saying her husband "will go down in the history of mankind as a martyr for freedom and peace."

Obituary on page 3

Facing the Johnson Administration

From ALISTAIR COOKE

New York, November 22

It is traditional for all Cabinet officers to submit their resignations to the new President, and this will be done when they are all assembled in Washington, tonight or tomorrow.

President Johnson arrived just after six o'clock this evening aboard the Air Force plane that brought the body of the dead President back to Andrews Air Force base in Maryland. He came to a stick of microphones and said :

"We have suffered a loss that cannot be weighed. For me it is a deep personal tragedy. I know that the world shares the sorrow that Mrs Kennedy and her family bear. I'll do my best, that is all I can do. I ask your help and God's."

He will spend the night at the White House seeing some of the Cabinet and the Congressional leaders of both parties.

Uniquely equipped

Once the first blow wore off, the people looked at President Johnson arriving with his new Secret Service detail, and the very unfamiliarity of the title aroused their political instincts which had been anaesthetised with all the rest. We now have to face the Johnson Administration, and after that what ?

After eight years in the House and 12 in the Senate, and three as a Vice-President who was privy to all the business of the National Security Council, the new President, it is being rightly said, is almost uniquely equipped to carry on the Administrative functions of government. In all the crises, from the Bay of Pigs to the civil rights eruptions and the tax bill manoeuvres, he has been always close at hand ; and all the expert advice that Kennedy could command will be his.

But every President rearranges the elements around him. Some influential men will go into decline, other anonymous helpers will come up. There is no cause to fear that the main trend of the Government's policy, either foreign or domestic, will be arrested any more than it has already been arrested by the mulishness of Congress.

Coaxing power

What now begins to stir the politicians, and after them the nation, however, is the identity of the next President. Lyndon Johnson was never a great vote-getter, he has had one moderately severe heart attack, and he has not shown in public at any rate that he has a captivating air of leadership. What he does have is an unrivalled knowledge of how to coax Congressional power. It is possible that the next Congress will move faster under the whip he laid down when he resigned from the Senate.

There is still the question, if one can raise questions in the mournful stupor we are now living through, whether the Democratic Party, once its decent grief is over, will begin to challenge the President's automatic right to be the next nominee. And for the Republicans, after a sombre interval, there is a wholly new prospect of picking a man with some personal dynamism to defeat Johnson.

Running against President Kennedy was a labour that four or five men at most were anxious to undertake, and none of them would relish. Running in an open field, against a fledgling President, is quite another sort of challenge ; and one that may soon quicken more Presidential hopes than we had dreamed of this morning in the happy Texas sunshine.

UN delegates' fears for the future

From HELLA PICK

United Nations (NY), November 22

"The tragedy of this day is beyond instant comprehension. All of us who knew him will bear the grief of his death to the day of ours. And all men everywhere who love peace and justice and freedom will bow their heads."

These were Mr Adlai Stevenson's words today. But in this world kaleidoscope, delegates from every shade of country were expressing the same obviously genuine grief. The General Assembly met briefly at its appointed hour of three o'clock to hear its President "perform the sad duty of announcing the tragic death of President Kennedy and convey the Assembly's sympathy to his family and to the American nation."

U Thant, standing by the side of the Assembly's President, slowly added his profound sorrow, and then for a very long minute, the Assembly stood in deep silence, heads bowed. The public galleries were crowded and from their more uninhibited members came the sounds of sorrow.

With news of his death confirmed, the first reaction of many a delegate was to hope that the assassin was neither a Negro, or, for that matter, a Jew.

"Speechless, terrible, awful, terrifying . . ." The vocabulary may seem dull, but it was genuine as it came from delegate after delegate.

Only Cuba's Ambassador curtly said that he had no comment whatever to make, and even absented himself from the brief Assembly ceremony. But among the other Communist delegates there were hearts as heavy as the rest. And their reason, too, told them that today's loss was grievous for the world.

A Polish delegate said : "We needed his strength to fight the reactionary forces of the world."

Another asked : "What kind of civilisation is this ?"

Ambassador Taied Slim, of Tunisia, echoed a great many others when he called President Kennedy a champion for peace who had slowly helped to win greater equilibrium for the world.

Mr Lyndon Johnson is to most members of the United Nations an unknown factor. Few cared to speculate about the future and some said they would hesitate to make a pronouncement but they greatly feared the consequences of the year which must now elapse before new presidential elections can be held in the United States.

Abraham Zapruder filmed the assassination of President Kennedy with his silent 8mm camera. The Zapruder film was supposed to be a simple home movie of Kennedy's visit to Dallas, but instead became the most complete visual record of the shooting of the president.

At 2:36 p.m., two hours after Kennedy was shot, Lyndon Baines Johnson was sworn in as the 36th president of the United States during a brief ceremony on Air Force One. Next to Johnson during the ceremony was Jacqueline Kennedy, her clothes still bloodstained.

THE OLDEST DAILY NEWSPAPER IN THE UNITED STATES—FOUNDED 1771

The Philadelphia Inquirer

PUBLIC LEDGER

AN INDEPENDENT NEWSPAPER FOR ALL THE PEOPLE

FINAL
CITY EDITION

THE WEATHER
U. S. Weather Bureau Forecast
Philadelphia and vicinity: Mostly cloudy, windy and mild Saturday with showers mostly in the afternoon. High in the lower 60s. Fair and cold Sunday with afternoon cloudiness.
COMPLETE WEATHER DATA ON PAGE 28

October Circulation: Daily, 561,299; Sunday, 972,060 — SATURDAY MORNING, NOVEMBER 23, 1963 — WFIL 560 KC • WFIL-TV CH. 6 — EIGHT CENTS

KENNEDY SHOT TO DEATH

Johnson Is Sworn In as President

Asks Support Of Nation, Divine Help

By ROBERT BARKDOLL

WASHINGTON, Nov. 22 (UPI). — Lyndon B. Johnson assumed the burdens of the Presidency Friday night.

Taking over in the dark shadow of the assassination of President John F. Kennedy, Mr. Johnson asked for the help of the American people and sought the divine help of God.

"I will do my best," he said. "That is all I can do. I ask for your help, and God's."

PLEDGE OF SUPPORT

He won an immediate pledge of bipartisan support from Congressional leaders after a meeting at the White House with leaders of both parties and advisers to the late President.

Mr. Johnson was only a few cars back when an assassin's bullet felled his predecessor in a Dallas, Tex., motorcade. The new Chief Executive held conferences almost immediately after he had arrived back in the capital on the plane which also returned the body of President Kennedy.

After the meeting with Congressional leaders, the White House issued a brief statement saying that President Johnson had asked top Democrats and Republicans for their "united support in the face of the tragedy that has befallen our country."

TIME TO BE UNITED

"He said that it is more essential than ever before that this country be united," the statement said. "The legislative leaders of both parties assured President Johnson of their bipartisan cooperation."

Mr. Johnson, who became the 36th President, also conferred with Secretary of Defense Robert S. McNamara, McGeorge Bundy, White House adviser on national security affairs, and Undersecretary of State George W. Ball.

The Chief Executive also talked by telephone with former Presidents Dwight D. Eisenhower and Harry S Truman. The White House said former President Herbert Hoover also had been contacted. It did not say in what manner.

MEET WITH EISENHOWER

Mr. Eisenhower and Mr. Truman were scheduled to arrive in Washington during the weekend to join mourners when President Kennedy's body will rest in state at the Capitol Sunday and Monday. The White House said Mr. Hoover had indicated he could not get to Washington.

Mr. Johnson scheduled a meeting with Gen. Eisenhower at 11:30 A. M. Saturday.

Last rites for the deceased President will be offered in Washington Monday. A Pontifical Requiem Mass will be cele-

Continued on Page 2, Column 2

In The Inquirer

Departments and Features

Amusements 26, 27
Auctions 40, 41
Bridge 24
Business and Financial 19 to 21
Classified Ads 22 to 41
Church News 28
Comics 24
Death Notices 28
Editorials 18
Obituaries 28
Real Estate 21
Sports 29 to 31
Women's News 25

"The Craft of Intelligence" Page 21

Best of Broadway Page 26
Best of Hollywood Page 26
Washington Background Page 14
Complete Weather Page 28

AP Wirephoto

A moment after assassin's bullet ripped into President Kennedy, the Chief Executive (white half circle) clutches his chest and begins to slump forward in the limousine carrying him in a motorcade through the streets of Dallas, Tex.

Photo from UPI Telephoto by Capt. Cecil Stoughton, Official White House Photographer

Vice President Lyndon Baines Johnson takes oath as 36th President of the United States. In ceremony aboard Presidential plane at Love Field, Dallas, Tex., he is flanked by his wife, Lady Bird (left), and Mrs. John F. Kennedy.

Murder Charged To Pro-Russian Seized in Theater

By FRANK CORMIER

DALLAS, Tex., Nov. 22 (AP).—A gunman assassinated President Kennedy from ambush Friday with a high-powered rifle. Nearly 12 hours later, a 24-year-old man who professed love for Russia was charged with murder.

The charge was filed against Lee Harvey Oswald, 24. Officers said he was the man who hid on the fifth floor of a textbook warehouse and snapped off three quick shots that killed the President and wounded Gov. John B. Connally of Texas.

WIFE CRIES OUT

As the shots reverberated, blood sprang from the President's face. He fell face downward in the back seat of his car. His wife grasped his head and tried to lift it, crying, "Oh, no!"

Half an hour later, John F. Kennedy was dead and the United States had a new President, Lyndon B. Johnson.

Within the hour, police had arrested Oswald following the killing of a Dallas policeman. He was charged with the murder of the officer and several hours later with murder in the assassination of the President.

TOOK RUSSIAN OATH

Four years ago Oswald, of Fort Worth, said he had sworn allegiance to Russia and wanted Russian citizenship. He has a Russian wife.

Oswald denied that he had shot anybody.

Oswald, of Fort Worth, who four years ago said he was applying for Russian citizenship, denied that he had shot anybody.

The assassination occurred just as the President's motorcade was leaving downtown Dallas at the end of a triumphal tour through the city's streets.

His special car—with the protective bubble down — was moving down an incline into an underpass that leads to a freeway route to the Dallas Trade Mart, where he was to speak.

Witnesses heard three shots. One or two bullets struck the President.

GOVERNOR WOUNDED

The third shot wounded Gov. John B. Connally of Texas in the side but his condition was reported not critical.

As the gunfire rang in the street, a reporter in the caravan screamed, "My God, they're shooting at the President!"

The motorcade slowed and then sped forward at breakneck speed to Parkland Hospital near the Trade Mart.

Onlookers, terrified at the sight and sound of the assassination, dived face forward for protection onto a grassy park at the entrance of the

Continued on Page 2, Column 1

Leftist, 24, Charged With Assassination, Slaying of Policeman

By JOHN V. YOUNG

DALLAS, Tex., Nov. 22 (UPI).—Lee Harvey Oswald, 24, a pro-Castro Marxist who defected to Russia in 1959, was charged Friday with the assassination of President Kennedy, who was ambushed with a high-powered rifle.

Oswald made no confession and insisted he knew nothing about the assassination of the President or the serious wounding of Texas Gov. John Connally.

CAUGHT IN THEATER

Manacled, his face battered in a fight with the police who subdued him in a movie theater less than four miles from the assassination scene, Oswald was taken before Justice of the Peace David Johnson for Arraignment.

Police Chief Jesse Curry said he would be brought before a grand jury next week.

Police made paraffin tests on Oswald several hours before he was charged formally.

Police also charged the Marine reject with the murder of a Dallas police officer shortly after the President was slain by a sniper firing a military rifle from the window of a building in downtown Dallas.

DENIES INVOLVEMENT

Police said Oswald, battered and sullen, denied having anything to do with the assassination, but admitted he worked in the building from which the fatal shots were fired. He would not account for his whereabouts at the time of the assassination, police said.

Police said Oswald worked in the Texas School Book Depository building. After the assassination, police found a 7.65 German Army Mauser rifle in the building.

OFFICER SHOT DOWN

Beside it were three empty shells. One cartridge remained in the chamber of the rifle.

A policeman, J. D. Tippitt, 38, was shot down in the street about five blocks from the Texas Theater. The theater cashier, Mrs. Julie Postal, had re-

Continued on Page 2, Column 6

Funeral Rites For President To Be Monday

WASHINGTON, Nov. 22 (AP). —President Kennedy's funeral will be held Monday at St. Matthew's Roman Catholic Cathedral, the White House announced Friday night.

The body of the slain President will be in repose at the White House Saturday and will lie in state in the Rotunda of the Capitol on Sunday and Monday.

FAMILY FRIEND

The President's body will be taken a couple of miles to the Cathedral at 11 A. M. Monday. There, Richard Cardinal Cushing, Archbishop of Boston and a life-long friend of the Kennedy family, will celebrate a Pontifical Requiem Mass at noon.

Acting White House Press Secretary Andrew T. Hatcher said he did not know where Mr. Kennedy would be buried. There has been one report, still unconfirmed, that burial would be in the family plot in Brookline, Mass.

PUBLIC HOURS SET

The President's body will be moved from the White House in an official cortege to the Capitol Rotunda at 1 P. M. Sunday. This ceremony will be attended by members of the Kennedy family, Government leaders, Supreme Court justices, members of Congress and foreign diplomats.

The public will be permitted to file past the bier shortly after its arrival until 9 P. M. Sunday and from 9 until 10 A. M. Monday, the White House said.

Mr. Kennedy's body will lie in

Continued on Page 4, Column 7

Grief Hushes City

Women, Men Weep in Streets

By MIKI MAHONEY

The pace of the city slowed, eyes were moist and voices hushed as stunned Philadelphians tried to accept the reality of President Kennedy's assassination.

The populace reacted as next of kin, informed without warning of a tragic and untimely death. First there was the silence of disbelief, then heartfelt weeping, then shared conversations to ease the initial shock.

Women cried openly, dabbing at tears as they walked on mid-city streets. More than a few men reached for their handkerchiefs, unashamed at the display of emotion.

No one seemed to know what to do next, yet the mood of the city was subdued. The quiet became increasingly loud. Hourly chimes that ordinarily go unnoticed bonged ominously. One could almost hear Flags being lowered to half staff.

At corner newsstands people pressed forward, coins ready to buy the latest editions.

Strangers befriended each other seeking solace in an hour of national sadness. Knots of people along the sidewalks traded bits of information gleaned from early news reports.

Churches, many of them ordinarily closed on Friday, opened their doors for the grieving faithful. In many places of worship, vocal prayers were offered with genuine fervor.

School classes were dismissed or interrupted as pupils witnessed history that would go into future textbooks. At Roman Catholic High School, boys remained after classes to watch television broadcasts in the library. Earlier, they heard the tragic news on the public address sys-

Continued on Page 3, Column 7

On the Inside

John F. Kennedy's life in pictures and text — Pages 7, 8, 9
President Johnson's life in pictures and text — Page 6
A picture story of President Kennedy's last day — Page 3
Background and analytical articles, pictures, map and Philadelphia and world reaction — Pages 2, 4, 5, 10, 11, 12, 13, 14, 15, 16, 21, 22
The President Is Dead—an editorial — Page 18

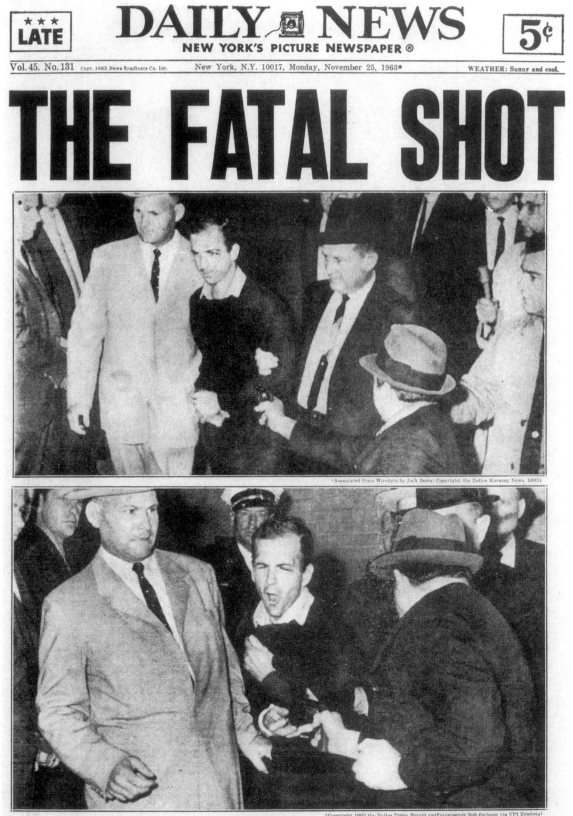

★★★ LATE

DAILY NEWS

NEW YORK'S PICTURE NEWSPAPER ®

5¢

Vol. 45. No. 131 Copr. 1963 News Syndicate Co. Inc. New York, N.Y. 10017, Monday, November 25, 1963★ WEATHER: Sunny and cool.

THE FATAL SHOT

(Associated Press Wirefoto by Jack Beers; Copyright, the Dallas Morning News, 1963)

(Copyright 1963 the Dallas Times Herald and Fotographer Bob Jackson via UPI Telefoto)

ABOVE: Jack Ruby aims at accused Presidential assassin Lee Oswald. BELOW: He shoots.

Story p. 2; six full picture pages

Shortly after the shooting, Lee Harvey Oswald, a self-proclaimed Marxist and former Marine who recently had become an employee at the Texas School Book Depository, was arrested for murdering Kennedy and Dallas police officer J. D. Tippit. Oswald was shot by Jack Ruby, a local nightclub owner, two days after Kennedy's death and died at the same hospital.

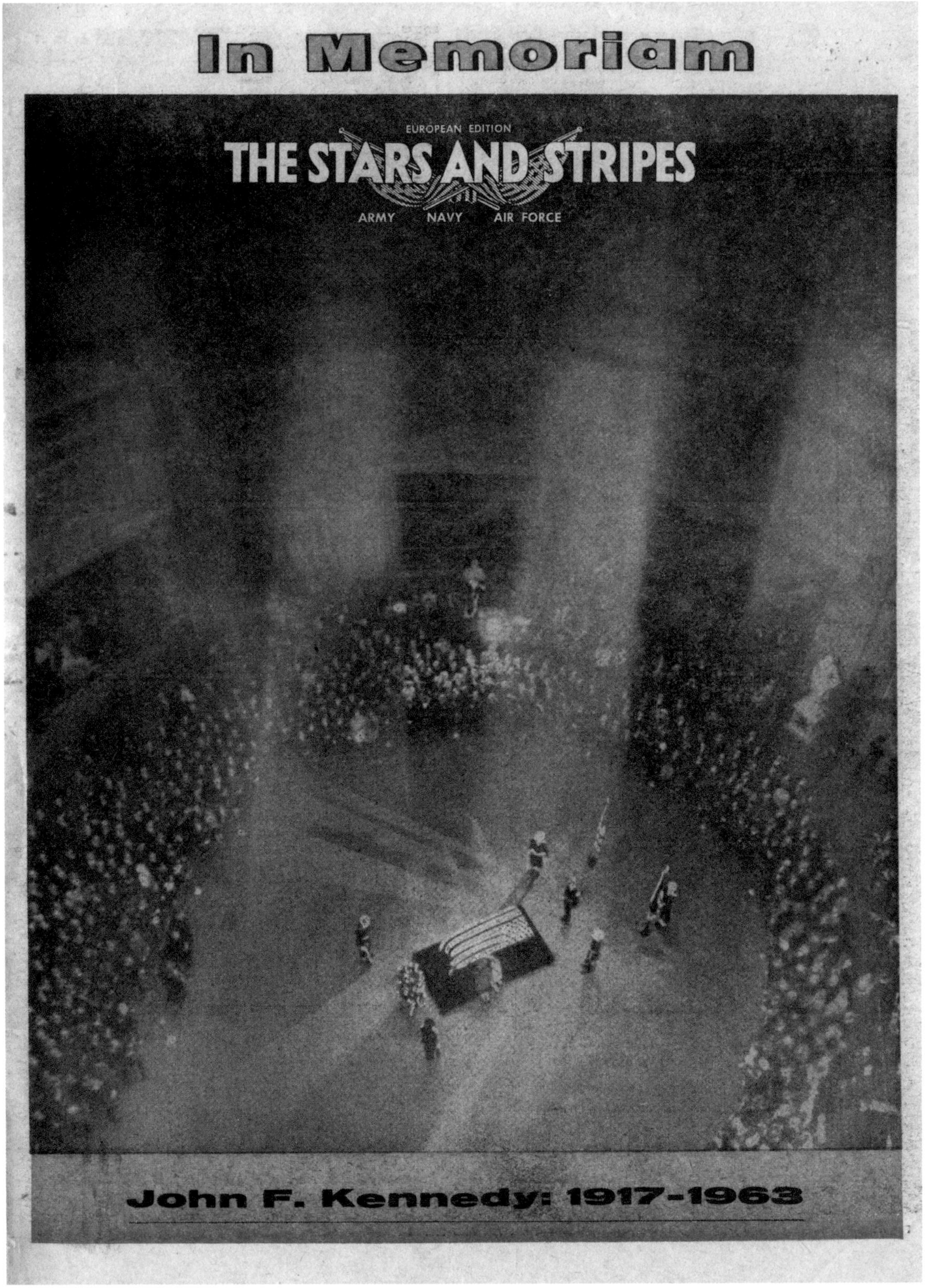
In Memoriam

EUROPEAN EDITION

THE STARS AND STRIPES

ARMY NAVY AIR FORCE

John F. Kennedy: 1917-1963

An honor guard stood by Kennedy's casket as it lay in state in the East Room of the White House for twenty-four hours before being moved to the Capitol Rotunda. Visitors included family and former presidents Dwight D. Eisenhower and Harry S. Truman.

Full Page Color Portrait of the late President—Page 16

GUIDE TO FEATURES

Bridge	26	Obituaries	24
Classified	27-29	Port	23
Cross-Word	26	Shain	26
Deaths	24	Small Worlds	26
Dennis	26	Sports	22-23
Dr. Crane	26	Star Gazer	26
Editorials	10	TV-Radio	26
Financial	23	Theatres	21
McGill	11	Twistagram	28

The Boston Globe
MORNING EDITION
Reg. U.S. Pat. Off.
VOL. 184 NO. 148
© 1963 By GLOBE NEWSPAPER CO.
MONDAY, NOVEMBER 25, 1963
Telephone AV 8-8000
30 PAGES—10c

BEFORE THE DIP
MONDAY—Sunny, in 40s.
TUESDAY—Cloudy, showers.
High Tides
5:36 a.m. 5:59 p.m.
Sun Rises 6:47 Sun Sets 4:16
Full Report on Page 30

'And So, She Took a Ring From Her Finger . . .'

SEN. MANSFIELD:

"There was a man marked with the scars of his love of country, a body active with the surge of a life far, far from spent and, in a moment, it was no more. And so, she took a ring from her finger and placed it in his hands.

"There was a husband who asked much and gave much, and, out of the giving and the asking, wove with a woman what could not be broken in life, and, in a moment it was no more. And so, she took a ring from her finger and placed it in his hands, and kissed him and closed the lid of a coffin."

(Inspiration for giving ring, Page 4)

JUSTICE WARREN:

"John Fitzgerald Kennedy, a great and good President, the friend of all men of good will, a believer in the dignity and equality of all human beings, a fighter for justice, an apostle of peace, has been snatched from our midst by the bullet of an assassin.

"What moved some misguided wretch to do this horrible deed may never be known to us, but we do know that such acts are commonly stimulated by forces of hatred and malevolence, such as today are eating away their way into the bloodstream of American life.

(Full texts of eulogies on Page 8)

All Night Long They Came

Poised on Capitol steps, Mrs. Kennedy and her children prepare to leave. At right, she bends to kiss the President's bier. (AP Photos)

Nine-Mile Line of Mourners

By ROBERT HEALY
Globe Reporter

WASHINGTON — John Fitzgerald Kennedy's last message was carried to Capitol Hill Sunday.

It was a message of sorrow and a nation's shame.

Sunday afternoon and all night the martyred President lay in state in the Capitol Rotunda, while the public filed by the casket.

At midnight close to 100,000 had passed the bier. And still they came. *Despite the chill of the night, the lines grew longer extending at times for nine miles.*

It was apparent that this solemn procession would not be ended until just before the funeral itself today. The Kennedy family had said they would not close the rotunda so long as the public continued to stream inside.

Under a bright Autumn sun on Sunday, some 300,000 persons — who had flooded here from all parts of the nation—watched the body of their assassinated President as it was borne from the White House to the Capitol rotunda.

To the funeral cadence of muffled drums, a caisson, drawn by six white horses, carried the flag-draped casket through this city of sadness.

Today, a day of national mourning, the President's body will be moved back to the White House.

SERVICES
Page 2

Funeral Times

PROCESSION begins: 11 a.m.
SERVICES in St. Matthew's Cathedral: noon
BURIAL in Arlington National Cemetery: 1 p.m.

Jacqueline . . . Courage

By DOROTHY McCARDLE

WASHINGTON—Jacqueline Kennedy Sunday led a grieving people to the bier of her slain husband with matchless courage.

She did not hide her sad, tense face. She never wept. She never faltered as she and her two young children accompanied the body of John F. Kennedy to the Capitol.

Her silent strength was matched by her tender solicitude for her children. She gently clasped the hands of John Jr., who is 3 years old today, and Caroline, who will be 6 years old on Wednesday, in loving reassurance. She leaned down to answer their puzzled questions.

Jacqueline Kennedy makes visit to husband's casket and embraces woman mourning dead President. (Story on Page 4)

She bore the 40-minute ordeal of the procession to the Capitol, the ceremonies and return to the White House with an unspoken sadness and bravery that brought tears to the eyes of spectators and television viewers.

Her beautifully chiseled features were taut with anguish. Her expression was glazed. She seemed to look, not at the crowds, but through them, seeing nothing but the flag-draped coffin of her late husband.

"She is a wonderful mother, she really is," a man whispered.

JACQUELINE Page 2

'. . . And a Flag For My Daddy'

By WILFRID C. RODGERS
Globe Reporter

WASHINGTON — Television viewers watching the services for President Kennedy in the Capitol Rotunda Sunday wondered where the President's 3-year-old son, "John-John," went when he disappeared from his mother's side.

John-John behaved manfully up to a point. He had ascended the steep steps to the Rotunda with his mother and sister, Caroline, without incident. Once inside, John-John wasn't quite sure what to think.

He craned his neck to look up at the high arches of the ceiling, clutched and unclutched his mother's hand and did a couple of half turns to look at the crowd around him.

He wanted to do something, as any 3-year-old would, anything but stand still. Things were just too quiet.

His nurse, Miss Maude Shaw, sensed his plight and walked him to one of the doorways leading from the Rotunda to the House side of the Capitol.

JOHN-JOHN Page 2

Oswald Slain as Millions Gasp

By JAMES S. DOYLE
Globe Reporter

DALLAS—As incredulous millions watched the scene unfold on television, the accused assassin of President Kennedy was shot to death in the basement of the City Jail at 11:15 a.m. Sunday.

Jack Ruby, 52, a portly, balding night club operator and an ardent admirer of the late President, appointed himself executioner of Lee Harvey Oswald.

Ruby stepped through a throng of police and newsmen and wordlessly sent a single bullet from a snub-nosed revolver into Oswald's left side, just below the chest.

"I couldn't help it," Ruby told a relative later.

Oswald, the arrogant, 24-year-old pro-Communist and ex-Marine, died at 2 p.m., 48 hours almost to the minute after John Fitzgerald Kennedy had succumbed to a sniper's bullets.

He died on an operating table at the same Parkland Hospital where doctors had fought in vain to save the President's life.

Oswald, who had steadily denied having anything to do with the assassination — though police said they had an airtight case against him — made no statement as his life ebbed away.

As he was lifted from the oil-stained, cigarette-littered floor of the jail basement, a policeman asked him if he wanted to say anything about the death of the President.

Oswald said no word, just shook his head.

He was shot down while being transferred from the city jail to the county jail.

He was under heavy guard, and police had set up what they considered airtight security precautions to ensure his safety during what was to have been a routine transfer.

How Ruby got into the jail basement unchallenged has not been established.

He was well known to police, both as a hanger-on around headquarters and as a man with a criminal record. Many of the men on the force knew him by sight and name.

SLAYING
Page 6

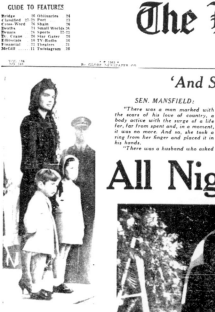

Oswald Cries With Pain as Ruby Fires Fatal Shot

(Copyright, Dallas Times Herald, 1963, via UPI)

Kings, Prime Ministers Pour Into Washington

WASHINGTON—Kings and presidents, prime ministers and other world leaders arrived in Washington Sunday to pay homage to the young President they knew and admired.

Never have so many top foreign leaders gathered in this city of historic events. Perhaps never in history has any event gathered together so many wielders of temporal power.

The subdued procession of the world's mighty moved through Dulles and National Airports as humble Americans silently filed past the bier of John F. Kennedy.

Late Sunday, 67 nations had indicated that they were sending high-ranking representatives and the influx was well under way.

As another long night enveloped the Capitol and the White House, de Gaulle, Erhard, Prince Philip, Douglas-Home, de Valera, Ikeda, King Baudoin, Queen Frederika, Pearson, Macapagal and nearly 100 other rulers of the world slept in Washington.

There were a dozen members of ruling royal families, 18 presidents and heads of government, 29 foreign ministers, five defense ministers.

NOTABLES
Page 2

Crowds lined Pennsylvania Avenue to see a horse-drawn caisson carry Kennedy's flag-draped casket from the White House to the Capitol Rotunda. The procession's ceremonial details were similar to the funeral of President Abraham Lincoln almost 100 years before.

NOVEMBER 25, 1963
PRESIDENT KENNEDY LAID TO REST

For eighteen hours, through the night, people passed silently by Kennedy's casket in the Capitol Rotunda. More than 250,000 waited to pay their respects.

The Forecasts

WICHITA AREA—Fair and a little warmer Tuesday. High 53, low 35.

KANSAS — Mostly fair Tuesday. Highs in 50s.

(Weather map, table Page 15A.)

The Wichita Eagle

Kansas' Leading Home Newspaper for 91 Years

Tributes Paid In Many Ways, Stories, Photos, 8A

91st Year, No. 330 | 36 Pages | WICHITA, KANSAS, 67202, TUESDAY, NOVEMBER 26, 1963 | AM 2-4211 | Price Ten Cents

Ruby Says He Shot on Impulse

Prompt Action On Tax Cuts, Rights Pledged

Johnson Wins Ovation From 35 Governors

WASHINGTON (UPI)—President Johnson told governors of 35 states Monday night that he will seek prompt approval of President Kennedy's tax cut and civil rights programs.

Johnson received a standing ovation from the state leaders after appealing for bipartisan backing in a moment of crisis following the assassination of President Kennedy.

New York Gov. Nelson Rockefeller said Johnson told the group he would speak to Congress and request action on both the tax cut and civil rights measures originally requested by Kennedy.

Johnson has arranged to address a joint session of Congress Wednesday.

ROCKEFELLER said the ovation Johnson received was "a most sincere demonstration of unity in this moment of tragedy."

The governors were hastily assembled following Kennedy's funeral services for the evening meeting. Many were halted at airports and summoned to the Executive Office Building to hear Johnson's appeal.

The President, who was 30 minutes behind schedule, spoke for almost 30 minutes on the nation's problems.

Rockefeller, a leading Republican, and a presidential aspirant, said the new chief executive was "impressive." Pennsylvania Gov. William Scranton, another prominent Republican, praised Johnson's speech and said he was sure that all the governors there would support the new President.

Later, Johnson met with Treasury Secretary Douglas Dillon and budget director Kermit Gordon to discuss the economy and review the budget he will send to Congress in January. Chairman Walter W. Heller of the Council of Economic Advisors sat in on this talk.

JOHNSON ALSO TOLD the governors that the American system is "on trial" in its competition with the Soviet Union.

In an office in the old State Department, the President sat at a desk and faced the seated governors. He told them that "circumstances beyond my con-

(Continued on Page 2A)

De Gaulle Plans Visit Next Year

WASHINGTON (UPI)—President Johnson said Monday night that French President Charles de Gaulle will visit the United States next year for formal talks.

Johnson's announcement followed a private 18-minute chat the two world leaders held with their foreign ministers after Johnson's diplomatic reception for visiting foreign dignitaries.

WIDOW RECEIVES FLAG—Mrs. Jacqueline Kennedy, her face veiled, is handed the American flag which covered the casket bearing her husband, the late President Kennedy, to its final resting place in Arlington National Cemetery Monday.—(AP Photo.)

Nation's Chief Rests In a Hero's Grave

(Related stories on Pages 8A, 12A and 13A)

WASHINGTON (AP)—The peace of eternity came in an Arlington grave Monday to John F. Kennedy, whose quest for enduring peace in a dangerous world was cut short by an assassin's bullet.

And over his resting place will burn an eternal flame.

In death as in life, world statesmen, men of power and renown from half the nations of the world honored the fallen President. They had come here in unprecedented numbers and in mourning.

The new President, Lyndon B. Johnson, and former presidents Dwight D. Eisenhower and Harry S. Truman mourned the passing of the man who had served in the same high office they have held.

BUT IT WAS Mrs. Jacqueline Kennedy, sustained by some unknown strength through three racking days of grief, who touched a torch to the eternal light on the grave of her husband.

But at last this lady in black, with the long veil disguising some of her sorrow and weariness, stumbled just a bit as she left the site of the burial of the 35th President on a gentle slope of Arlington National Cemetery.

The services at the graveside were those of the Roman Catholic Church, for the first Roman Catholic to reach the White House.

Richard Cardinal Cushing, Archbishop of Boston, an old friend of the Kennedy family, said the final ritualistic prayers and sprinkled the casket with holy water before it was lowered into the grave.

And it was Cushing who had celebrated a Requiem Low Mass for the departed President at St. Matthew's Cathedral in the heart of Washington.

IN THE COLORFUL vestments of his high church office, the cardinal invoked the blessings and mercy of God upon Kennedy and his family. And for the family he offered communion and personal words of comfort.

Mrs. Kennedy and others of the family, along with President and Mrs. Johnson, and the assemblage of notables from over the world had marched in the funeral procession the eight blocks from the White House to the cathedral. There were presidents, royalty, chiefs of state, foreign ministers, defense ministers in the gathering.

Towering Charles de Gaulle, president of France, dwarfed diminutive Haile Selassie, emperor of Ethiopia. They were side by side for part of the procession and for all the graveside ceremonies—each in uniform.

There were brilliant red fezes and purple robes worn by some of the foreigners.

For the Cabinet, the Supreme Court and other American dignitaries in the funeral procession, the dress of the day was morning coats and striped trousers.

BUT IT WAS a day for hum-

(Continued on Page 3A)

Family Staying In White House

WASHINGTON (UPI)—Mrs. Jacqueline Kennedy and her children stayed in the White House Monday night.

Press Secretary Pierre Salinger said he will announce plans of the late President's widow Tuesday.

Mrs. Kennedy met with three heads of state in the upstairs family quarters. Coming to express their condolences were President Charles de Gaulle, an old acquaintance; Emperor Haile Selassie of Ethiopia, and President Eamon de Valera of Ireland.

Later, Mrs. Kennedy made an unannounced visit to Arlington National Cemetery and placed a sprig of flowers on the grave of her late husband.

She was accompanied to the cemetery by her brother-in-law, Atty. Gen. Robert F. Kennedy.

They arrived at the main entrance at 11:53 p. m. and left 15 minutes later. Mrs. Kennedy returned to the White House.

Wanted To Avenge Kennedys

DALLAS (UPI)—Flashy Jack Ruby, shorn of his finery and in baggy prison garb, told his lawyer Monday he shot Lee Harvey Oswald on impulse to avenge the sorrowing Kennedy family for what he thought was a Communist assassination plot.

Defense attorney Tom Howard, affirming that the up-from-the slums night club owner would plead temporary insanity, said Ruby told him he had no previous connection with Oswald and never laid eyes on him before his arrest for the assassination last Friday.

Howard said Ruby told him he drove several times around the spot where the President was ambushed and shortly afterward slid into a crowd of newsmen, leaped out and shot Oswald "on the spur of the moment."

RUBY WAS WILLING to take a lie detector test, he said, provided it is confined only to the shooting and the events leading up to it.

Still in an excited state and on the verge of tears, according to Howard, the stocky, balding Ruby declared himself a political neutral, neither Republican nor Democrat. His family said he simply loved all U.S. presidents.

Asked about reports that Ruby was referred to in a document before the House Committee on Un-American Activities, Howard said the 52-year-old vengeance seeker "was sure he had never been called before any committee."

He was never known to be politically biased, according to people in Dallas who knew him socially and professionally.

RUBY TOLD the FBI everything he knew, Howard said.

Huge mounds of bouquets and wreaths, and burning candles line both sides of the street near the spot where the sniper police say was Oswald, fired two bullets into the President's throat and brain last Friday.

Howard said he did not discuss with the onetime penny ante Chicago gambler and street brawler how he slipped past the stringent police security rings Sunday in the basement of the city hall where city jail is located.

HE LEAPED "like a brownish blur," witnesses said, from a huddle of newsmen and protecting police.

Pistol arm outstretched, he fired a .38-caliber bullet into the manacled Oswald at a distance of four inches or less.

Howard quoted Ruby as saying the first time in his life that he saw the 24-year-old Os-

(Continued on Page 2A)

His World Strangely Different

A Brave Little Soldier Salutes Father's Casket

WASHINGTON (UPI)—A little boy at his grieving mother's side saluted the passing casket.

And in that moment, he suddenly became the brave soldier his father would have wanted him to be on this day, of all days.

For Monday, John F. Kennedy Jr. turned three.

His world was strangely different, in little ways a child notices but does not understand.

WHERE WAS HIS DADDY? The tall man with the laughing blue eyes who had a big desk and saw lots of important people and stooped to spank him good-naturedly and took him on helicopter rides and called him John-John."

This was supposed to be the day of The Party. The cake with three candles to blow out, the friends singing boisterous "happy birthdays," the gifts.

He did get a letter, as did his sister Caroline, from Lyndon Johnson, the man they call President now. No one outside the White House knew what the letters said.

But home, the White House, was quiet. Some of the furniture was gone.

AND THE SOLDIERS outside, whose salutes he delighted in trying to return with one of his own, looked different. They didn't glance down at him and sneak a wink or a smile Monday. Their commands barked, their rifles clattered harshly.

His mother, Mrs. Jacqueline Kennedy, left in the morning to go to the Capitol and ride back behind the soldiers and the horses and the wagon with the flag-covered box.

He and his sister, meanwhile dressed and put on their sky blue coats. It was cold outside. Caroline will be six on Wednesday. There was supposed to be a big birthday celebration for everybody at Hyannis Port on Friday, the day after Thanksgiving.

(Continued on Page 3A)

UPI Photo

JOHN KENNEDY JR. . . . A Birthday Farewell . . .

FBI to Give Full Report; Accused Assassin Buried

DALLAS, Tex. (AP) — Lee Harvey Oswald went to his grave almost in secret Monday while the eyes of the nation were turned to the last rites of the chief executive he was accused of killing.

Even as he was being buried investigators were preparing to place on public view the arsenal of evidence they say proves beyond all doubt Oswald was the assassin who took the life of John Fitzgerald Kennedy.

THE FBI IS preparing a detailed report of the assassination, and all the details will be made public, the White House announced Monday night.

President Johnson directed the Justice Department and the FBI "to conduct a prompt and thorough investigation of all the circumstances surrounding the brutal assassination of President Kennedy and the murder of his alleged assassin."

The White House said Johnson has "directed all federal agencies to cooperate, and the people of the nation may be sure that all of the facts will be made public."

THE WASHINGTON announcement came after Rep. Hale Boggs of Louisiana, assistant Democratic House Leader, suggested a high level congressional investigation of Kennedy's assassination be carried out. He said this should be done since the facts cannot be put into the record by a trial of the man accused of firing the fatal shots.

Justice Department officials said they are gathering every shred of evidence and information on the assassination and the subsequent slaying Sunday of Oswald.

In Dallas, District Attorney Henry Wade confirmed that a map, with the site of the assassination clearly plotted, was found in Oswald's Dallas apartment.

AND THE FBI disclosed that an anonymous telephone caller had warned an attempt would be made on Oswald's life during his transfer from City to County Jail.

The FBI said it relayed the tip to Dallas police several hours before the transfer.

It was during the transfer that Oswald was gunned down by night club owner Jack Ruby. Because of the anonymous tip, police said they had an armored car waiting outside for Oswald—but he never made it to the car.

OSWALD, THE 24-year-old

(Continued on Page 2A)

Rededication Services Urged by School Head

By LANCE GILMORE
Eagle Staff Writer

Superintendent of Wichita Public Schools Dr. Lawrence Shepoiser Monday urged principals to conduct rededication exercises in the schools at 8:30 a.m. Tuesday.

He suggested that the exercises include a moment of silence "for each person in his own way to make his personal commitments to the ideals of worthy citizenship."

SHEPOISER ALSO suggested a group commitment be made by giving the Pledge of Allegiance, "thereby reaffirming the impotence of individuals and groups and showing proper restraint for law and order and for government and its officials."

He asked that each principal conduct the exercises appropriate to his school group and the occasion.

Purpose of the exercises is to ask each person "to rededicate himself by making a personal commitment to the ideals of worthy citizenship in American democracy — where love, not hatred, is the guiding light in man's relationship, one to another," Shepoiser said.

THE PUBLIC SCHOOLS and county schools will be in session Tuesday and Wednesday before closing for Thanksgiving Thursday and Friday.

Most Catholic schools are observing a two-day mourning period for President Kennedy and will be closed again Tuesday. After classes Wednesday the schools will close again for Thanksgiving.

Sacred Heart Academy will be in session Tuesday, however.

Lutheran schools will be back in session Tuesday until the Thanksgiving vacation begins Thursday.

Sacred Heart College is closed and will not reopen classes until next Monday.

The University of Wichita and Friends University will resume classes Tuesday morning and continue until the four-day holiday begins Thursday.

State universities in Kansas also will resume Tuesday.

Eagle Highlights

Local News
Wichitans Share in Final Tribute 12A
Business Back to Normal 5A
Deaths 7B

Sports News
WU Cage Test Tonight 4C
Poll Ranks Shocks 5th 4C
Orange Bowl Likes Auburn 5C
Army-Navy Decision Pending 6C

Also Featured
Amusements 3B
Comics 2C
Crossword Puzzle 10A
Editorials 4A
Goren on Bridge 16A
Home Town News 10A
Jumble 11A
Markets 6C
Oil News 3C
Radio-TV Logs 1C
Want Ads 7C-11C
Women's News 14A

(AP Photo)

CAISSON BEARING PRESIDENT KENNEDY'S BODY TURNS TO CROSS POTOMAC
. . . Crowds line Memorial Bridge to watch procession to Arlington National Cemetery . . .

TUESDAY **PREVIEW** EDITION

ONE OF THE WORLD'S GREAT NEWSPAPERS

Los Angeles Times

LATE NEWS

LARGEST CIRCULATION IN THE WEST: 761,481 DAILY; 1,110,295 SUNDAY

VOL. LXXXII SIX PARTS—PART ONE ★★★ TUESDAY MORNING, NOVEMBER 26, 1963 96 PAGES Copyright © 1963 Los Angeles Times DAILY 10c

ENSHRINED

800,000 Mourners on Funeral Route

AT THE FINAL RESTING PLACE—Mourning widow is flanked by husband's b rothers, Robert, left, and Ted as casket is lowered to grave site. AP Wirephoto

Eternal Light to Burn at John F. Kennedy's Tomb in Arlington

ARLINGTON NATIONAL CEMETERY (UPI)—America buried John Fitzgerald Kennedy on Arlington's green slopes today, consigning his body to the land he loved and his soul to the God he worshiped.

After the last rites of a funeral Mass that broke the composure of his grieving widow, the martyred President was borne across the Potomac River to the national shrine of honored dead.

There, before the stricken family and before foreign presidents and princes, he found his final rest. An eternal light will burn at the tomb looking out on the Lincoln Memorial.

An estimated 800,000 hushed mourners lined the streets to pay their respects as the slain President was brought from the Capitol to the White House, from there to St. Matthew's Cathedral, and at last to the still green cemetery.

Other news and pictures of President Kennedy's funeral on pages A, B, C, D, 2, 3, 4, 5, 6 and 7.

Heads of State

Joining the family and all America in its grief were kings, presidents, ministers and princes from nearly every country of the world, Communist as well as free, from Charles de Gaulle of France to Anastas Mikoyan of Russia.

At the grave site, the farewell of "Taps" mourning across the Virginia countryside and the crash of rifle volleys in final salute climaxed a day of sounds. The sounds, above all, convinced those who had refused to believe the young President was dead.

There had been the dirges . . . the muffled drums . . . the sad skirling of bagpipes . . . creaking caisson wheels on hushed streets . . . the cadenced march of military men . . . the sobs of mourners.

At one brief point, it became too much for the veiled Mrs. Jacqueline Kennedy.

She had seen her husband fall before the sniper's bullet Friday. Thrice she visited his bier at the Capitol. She bore up her children in their grief and on foot Monday led the half-mile procession to the funeral Mass.

Moment of Sobbing

It was only at the cathedral that her grief overwhelmed her in public. Upon leaving the Low Pontifical Mass, she suddenly bent forward as though in pain, sobbing into her handkerchief.

Her composure may have been broken by her 5-year-old daughter Caroline. The child began crying inconsolably as she followed her father's casket from the cathedral.

John Jr., whose third birthday fell on this day of grief, broke into cries within the cathedral and was quickly soothed by his mother.

Others wept openly or within.

Under sunny, cloudless skies, but with a chill in the air, the young dead President then was taken across the river and under the trees of Arlington.

Cardinal Officiates

There, in sonorous tones, Richard Cardinal Cushing of Boston, who had married "Jack" Kennedy and his beautiful bride 10 years ago, commended his soul to God.

"Let his soul and all the souls of the faithful departed rest in peace," the archbishop prayed.

At the Mass the Cardinal also had offered the reassuring words and promises of the faithful.

"Life is not taken away . . . Life is but changed."

"I am the resurrection and the life; he who believes in Me, even if he die, shall live."

Through the funeral hours, bells of churches of every faith were tolled in unison.

Some of the most moving moments of the service came

Please Turn to Pg. C, Col. 1

A Little Boy Salutes as Casket Passes

WASHINGTON (UPI)—A little boy at his grieving mother's side saluted the passing casket.

And in that moment, he suddenly became the brave soldier his father would have wanted him to be on this day, of all days.

For Monday, John F. Kennedy Jr. turned 3.

His world was strangely different, in little ways a child notices but does not understand.

Where was his daddy? The tall man with the laughing blue eyes who had a big desk and saw lots of important people and stooped to spank him good-naturedly and took him on helicopter rides and called him "John-John."

Letter From Johnson

This was supposed to be the day of The Party. The cake with three candles to blow out, the friends singing boisterous "happy birthdays," the gifts.

He did get a letter, as did his sister Caroline, from Lyndon Johnson, the man they call President now. No one

Please Turn to Pg. 8, Col. 4

FAREWELL—John Kennedy Jr. salutes the casket of his father as it was carried from cathedral. UPI Telephoto

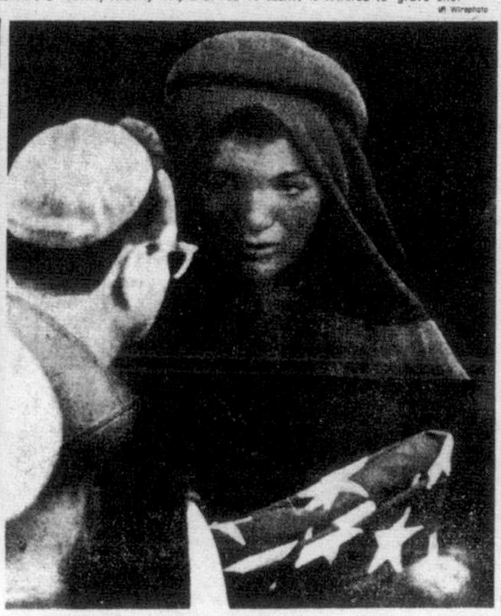

REMEMBRANCE—Mrs. Kennedy, grief showing in her veiled face, is handed the American Flag that covered her husband's casket on journey to the grave. AP Wirephoto

After a funeral Mass at St. Matthew's Cathedral, John F. Kennedy Jr., who was celebrating his third birthday that day, saluted his father's casket. The procession then traveled to Arlington National Cemetery for burial. At the end of the service, Jacqueline Kennedy lit the grave's eternal flame.

QUOTED

"All I keep thinking of is this line from a musical comedy . . . 'Don't let it be forgot, that once there was a spot, for one brief shining moment that was known as Camelot.'"

—*Jacqueline Kennedy*, Life *magazine, December 6, 1963*

"All the News That's Fit to Print"

The New York Times.

LATE CITY EDITION

VOL. CXIII. No. 38,864. NEW YORK, SATURDAY, JUNE 20, 1964. TEN CENTS

CIVIL RIGHTS BILL PASSED, 73-27; JOHNSON URGES ALL TO COMPLY; DIRKSEN BERATES GOLDWATER

U.S. STRESSING IT WOULD FIGHT TO DEFEND ASIA

WARNING TO REDS

Commitment to Laos and South Vietnam Called Unlimited

By MAX FRANKEL

JOHNSON IS FIRM

Vows in California to Oppose Violators of Freedom in World

By TOM WICKER

SENATOR KENNEDY HURT IN AIR CRASH; BAYH INJURED, TOO

Both Are in Fair Condition in Massachusetts Hospital —Pilot of Plane Killed

Senator Edward M. Kennedy

PRESIDENT'S PLEA

He Declares the Task Now Is to Change Law Into Custom

ON HAND FOR THE VOTE: Visitors waiting outside the Capitol yesterday for admittance to the Senate Chamber, before the vote on the civil rights bill was registered.

ACTION BY SENATE

Revised Measure Now Goes Back to House for Concurrence

By E. W. KENWORTHY

ARIZONAN TARGET OF G.O.P. LEADER

Illinoisan, in Speech on the Senate Floor, Scores View Bill Is Unconstitutional

By ANTHONY LEWIS

Rights Bill Roll-Call Vote

North Katanga City Is Seized By Rebels, the Congo Reports

Europeans Flee Albertville, Crossing Lake Tanganyika to Nearby Burundi

By J. ANTHONY LUKAS

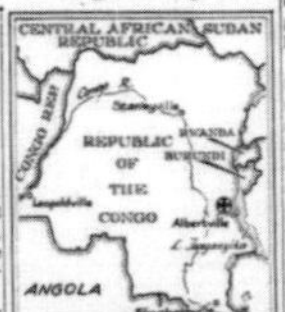

Yanks Woo Cabbies With 20,000 Tickets

By ROBERT LIPSYTE

Erhard Bars Visit To the Soviet Union

Negro Leaders Hail Passage; Some Southerners Voice Anger

CORE Plans Tests

By MARTIN ARNOLD

Region's Reaction Varied

NEWS INDEX

Two people were killed and Kennedy suffered crushed vertebrae, broken ribs, and a collapsed lung when their small airplane crashed in Massachusetts on the way to the state's Democratic Convention.

ALSO IN 1964

An estimated 73 million people watched the Beatles perform "She Loves You" and "I Want to Hold Your Hand" on the Ed Sullivan Show.

THE ATLANTA CONSTITUTION

For 97 Years the South's Standard Newspaper

ATLANTA (2), GA., FRIDAY, JULY 3, 1964

40 PAGES, 3 SECTIONS

Price Five Cents

Net Paid Daily Circulation 202,879 For May, 1964

Humid

RALPH McGILL

From 8-2-2 To 24-24-12

Johnson Signs Civil Rights Bill; Allen Urges All to Obey Law Here

Luci Blows 'Em All Out, All 17!

Mayor Asks Restraint By Negroes

Must Comply, Grand Jury Says

By MARION GAINES

Inside Today . . .

Comply in Peace, Both Races Urge

By TED SIMMONS

President Asks End to Race Hate

Weltner Switches, Votes for Passage

By TED LIPPMAN

U.S. Raises Win, 58-21, In Senate

U.S. Moves Slowly In Enforcing Law

By JOSEPH E. MOHBAT

Buoys to Mark Pollution May Be Placed in Lanier

By BILL SHIPP

A Rainy Fourth In the Offing

U.S. Fights Malaria

Didn't Promise to Nominate Scranton, Ike Is Quoted

Edition for July 4 To Be Combined

Second Ambulance In One Day

Johnson pushed hard to get Congress to pass the Civil Rights Act of 1964, which Kennedy had introduced a few months before he was killed. The sweeping legislation paved the way for the Voting Rights Act, the Fair Housing Act, and the Americans with Disabilities Act.

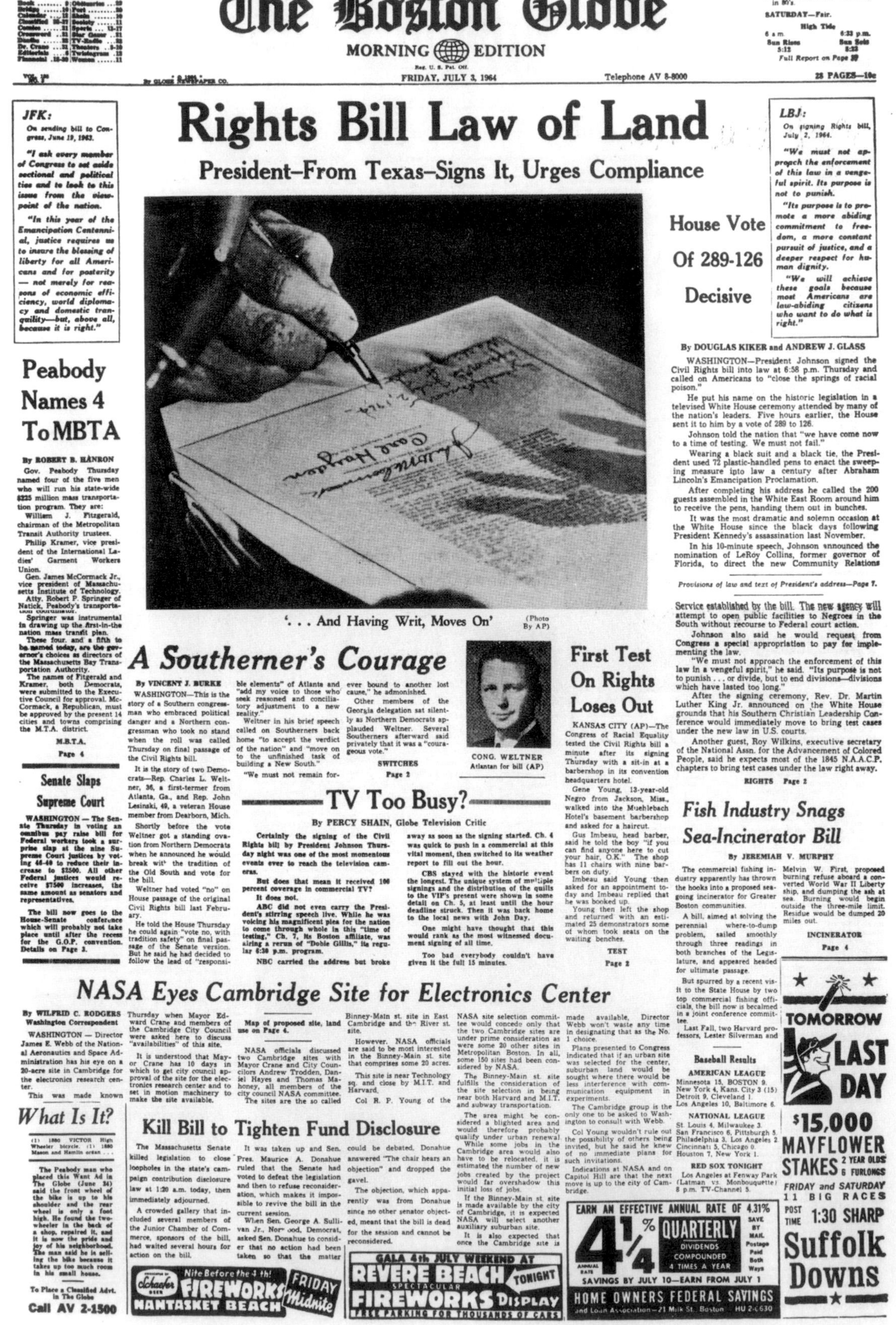

GUIDE TO FEATURES

The Boston Globe

MORNING EDITION

A POOR THIRD

FRIDAY—Scattered showers, in 80's.
SATURDAY—Fair.
High Tide 6 a.m. 6:33 p.m.
Sun Rises 5:12 Sun Sets 8:23
Full Report on Page 19

FRIDAY, JULY 3, 1964 — Telephone AV 8-8000 — 28 PAGES—10c

JFK:

On sending bill to Congress, June 19, 1963.

"I ask every member of Congress to set aside sectional and political ties and to look to this issue from the viewpoint of the nation.

"In this year of the Emancipation Centennial, justice requires us to insure the blessing of liberty for all Americans and for posterity — not merely for reasons of economic efficiency, world diplomacy and domestic tranquility—but, above all, because it is right."

Rights Bill Law of Land

President–From Texas–Signs It, Urges Compliance

'. . . And Having Writ, Moves On' (Photo By AP)

House Vote Of 289-126 Decisive

LBJ:

On signing Rights bill, July 2, 1964.

"We must not approach the enforcement of this law in a vengeful spirit. Its purpose is not to punish.

"Its purpose is to promote a more abiding commitment to freedom, a more constant pursuit of justice, and a deeper respect for human dignity.

"We will achieve these goals because most Americans are law-abiding citizens who want to do what is right."

By DOUGLAS KIKER and ANDREW J. GLASS

WASHINGTON—President Johnson signed the Civil Rights bill into law at 6:58 p.m. Thursday and called on Americans to "close the springs of racial poison."

He put his name on the historic legislation in a televised White House ceremony attended by many of the nation's leaders. Five hours earlier, the House sent it to him by a vote of 289 to 126.

Johnson told the nation that "we have come now to a time of testing. We must not fail."

Wearing a black suit and a black tie, the President used 72 plastic-handled pens to enact the sweeping measure into law a century after Abraham Lincoln's Emancipation Proclamation.

After completing his address he called the 200 guests assembled in the White East Room around him to receive the pens, handing them out in bunches.

It was the most dramatic and solemn occasion at the White House since the black days following President Kennedy's assassination last November.

In his 10-minute speech, Johnson announced the nomination of LeRoy Collins, former governor of Florida, to direct the new Community Relations

Provisions of law and text of President's address—Page 7.

Service established by the bill. The new agency will attempt to open public facilities to Negroes in the South without recourse to Federal court action.

Johnson also said he would request from Congress a special appropriation to pay for implementing the law.

"We must not approach the enforcement of this law in a vengeful spirit," he said. "Its purpose is not to punish . . . or divide, but to end divisions—divisions which have lasted too long."

After the signing ceremony, Rev. Dr. Martin Luther King Jr. announced on the White House grounds that his Southern Christian Leadership Conference would immediately move to bring test cases under the new law in U.S. courts.

Another guest, Roy Wilkins, executive secretary of the National Assn. for the Advancement of Colored People, said he expects most of the 1845 N.A.A.C.P. chapters to bring test cases under the law right away.

RIGHTS Page 2

Peabody Names 4 To MBTA

By ROBERT B. HANRON

Gov. Peabody Thursday named four of the five men who will run his state-wide $225 million mass transportation program. They are:

William J. Fitzgerald, chairman of the Metropolitan Transit Authority trustees.

Philip Kramer, vice president of the International Ladies' Garment Workers Union.

Gen. James McCormack Jr., vice president of Massachusetts Institute of Technology.

Atty. Robert P. Springer of Natick, Peabody's transportation coordinator.

Springer was instrumental in drawing up the first-in-the nation mass transit plan.

These four, and a fifth to be named today, are the governor's choices as directors of the Massachusetts Bay Transportation Authority.

The names of Fitzgerald and Kramer, both Democrats, were submitted to the Executive Council for approval. McCormack, a Republican, must be approved by the present 14 cities and towns comprising the M.T.A. district.

M.B.T.A. Page 4

Senate Slaps Supreme Court

WASHINGTON — The Senate Thursday in voting an omnibus pay raise bill for Federal workers took a surprise slap at the nine Supreme Court justices by voting 46-40 to reduce their increase to $2500. All other Federal justices would receive $7500 increases, the same amount as senators and representatives.

The bill now goes to the House-Senate conference which will probably not take place until after the recess for the G.O.P. convention. Details on Page 3.

A Southerner's Courage

By VINCENT J. BURKE

WASHINGTON—This is the story of a Southern congressman who embraced political danger and a Northern congressman who took no stand when the roll was called Thursday on final passage of the Civil Rights bill.

It is the story of two Democrats—Rep. Charles L. Weltner, 36, a first-termer from Atlanta, Ga., and Rep. John Lesinski, 49, a veteran House member from Dearborn, Mich.

Shortly before the vote Weltner got a standing ovation from Northern Democrats when he announced he would break with the tradition of the Old South and vote for the bill.

Weltner had voted "no" on House passage of the original Civil Rights bill last February.

He told the House Thursday he could again "vote no, with tradition safety" on final passage of the Senate version. But he said he had decided to follow the lead of "responsible elements" of Atlanta and "add my voice to those who seek reasoned and conciliatory adjustment to a new reality."

Weltner in his brief speech called on Southerners back home "to accept the verdict of the nation" and "move on to the unfinished task of building a New South."

"We must not remain forever bound to another lost cause," he admonished.

Other members of the Georgia delegation sat silently as Northern Democrats applauded Weltner. Several Southerners afterward said privately that it was a "courageous vote."

SWITCHES Page 2

CONG. WELTNER
Atlantan for bill (AP)

First Test On Rights Loses Out

KANSAS CITY (AP)—The Congress of Racial Equality tested the Civil Rights bill a minute after its signing Thursday with a sit-in at a barbershop in its convention headquarters hotel.

Gene Young, 13-year-old Negro from Jackson, Miss., walked into the Muehlebach Hotel's basement barbershop and asked for a haircut.

Gus Imbeau, head barber, said he told the boy "if you can find anyone here to cut your hair, O.K." The shop has 11 chairs with nine barbers on duty.

Imbeau said Young then asked for an appointment today and Imbeau replied that he was booked up.

Young then left the shop and returned with an estimated 25 demonstrators some of whom took seats on the waiting benches.

TEST Page 2

TV Too Busy?

By PERCY SHAIN, Globe Television Critic

Certainly the signing of the Civil Rights bill by President Johnson Thursday night was one of the most momentous events ever to reach the television cameras.

But does that mean it received 100 percent coverage in commercial TV?

It does not.

ABC did not even carry the President's stirring speech live. While he was voicing his magnificent plea for the nation to come through whole in this "time of testing," Ch. 7, its Boston affiliate, was airing a rerun of "Dobie Gillis," its regular 6:30 p.m. program.

NBC carried the address but broke away as soon as the signing started. Ch. 4 was quick to push in a commercial at this vital moment, then switched to its weather report to fill out the hour.

CBS stayed with the historic event the longest. The unique system of multiple signings and the distribution of the quills to the VIP's present were shown in some detail on Ch. 5, at least until the hour deadline struck. Then it was back home to the local news with John Day.

One might have thought that this would rank as the most witnessed document signing of all time.

Too bad everybody couldn't have given it the full 15 minutes.

Fish Industry Snags Sea-Incinerator Bill

By JEREMIAH V. MURPHY

The commercial fishing industry apparently has thrown the hooks into a proposed seagoing incinerator for Greater Boston communities.

A bill, aimed at solving the perennial where-to-dump problem, sailed smoothly through three readings in both branches of the Legislature, and appeared headed for ultimate passage.

But spurred by a recent visit to the State House by two top commercial fishing officials, the bill now is becalmed in a joint conference committee.

Last Fall, two Harvard professors, Lester Silverman and Melvin W. First, proposed burning refuse aboard a converted World War II Liberty ship, and dumping the ash at sea. Burning would begin outside the three-mile limit. Residue would be dumped 20 miles out.

INCINERATOR Page 4

NASA Eyes Cambridge Site for Electronics Center

By WILFRID C. RODGERS
Washington Correspondent

WASHINGTON — Director James E. Webb of the National Aeronautics and Space Administration has his eye on a 20-acre site in Cambridge for the electronics research center.

This was made known Thursday when Mayor Edward Crane and members of the Cambridge City Council were asked here to discuss "availabilities" of this site.

It is understood that Mayor Crane has 10 days in which to get city council approval of the site for the electronics research center and to set in motion machinery to make the site available.

Map of proposed site, land use on Page 4.

NASA officials discussed two Cambridge sites with Mayor Crane and City Councilors Andrew Trodden, Daniel Hayes and Thomas Mahoney, all members of the city council NASA committee.

The sites are the so called Binney-Main st. site in East Cambridge and the River st. site.

However, NASA officials are said to be most interested in the Binney-Main st. site that comprises some 20 acres.

This site is near Technology sq. and close by M.I.T. and Harvard.

Col R. P. Young of the NASA site selection committee would concede only that the two Cambridge sites are under prime consideration as were some 20 other sites in Metropolitan Boston. In all, some 150 sites had been considered by NASA.

The Binney-Main st. site fulfills the consideration of the site selection in being near both Harvard and M.I.T. and subway transportation.

The area might be considered a blighted area and would therefore probably qualify under urban renewal.

While some jobs in the Cambridge area would also have to be relocated, it is estimated the number of new jobs created by the project would far overshadow this initial loss of jobs.

If the Binney-Main st. site is made available by the city of Cambridge, it is expected NASA will select another auxiliary suburban site.

It is also expected that once the Cambridge site is made available, Director Webb won't waste any time in designating that as the No. 1 choice.

Plans presented to Congress indicated that if an urban site was selected for the center, suburban land would be sought where there would be less interference with communication equipment in experiments.

The Cambridge group is the only one to be asked to Washington to consult with Webb.

Col Young wouldn't rule out the possibility of others being invited, but he said he knew of no immediate plans for such invitations.

Indications at NASA and on Capitol Hill are that the next move is up to the city of Cambridge.

What Is It?

(1) 1880 VICTOR High Wheeler bicycle. (1) 1880 Mason and Hamlin organ . . .

The Peabody man who placed this Want Ad in The Globe (June 24) said the front wheel of the bike is up to his shoulder and the rear wheel is only a foot high. He found the two-wheeler in the back of a shop, repaired it, and it is now the pride and joy of his neighborhood. The man said he is selling the bike because it takes up too much room in his small house.

To Place a Classified Advt. in The Globe
Call AV 2-1500

Kill Bill to Tighten Fund Disclosure

The Massachusetts Senate killed legislation to close loopholes in the state's campaign contribution disclosure law at 1:20 a.m. today, then immediately adjourned.

A crowded gallery that included several members of the Junior Chamber of Commerce, sponsors of the bill, had waited several hours for action on the bill.

It was taken up and Sen. Pres. Maurice A. Donahue ruled that the Senate had voted to defeat the legislation and then to refuse reconsideration, which makes it impossible to revive the bill in the current session.

When Sen. George A. Sullivan Jr., Norwood, Democrat, asked Sen. Donahue to consider that no action had been taken so that the matter could be debated, Donahue answered "The chair hears an objection" and dropped the gavel.

The objection, which apparently was from Donahue since no other senator objected, meant that the bill is dead for the session and cannot be reconsidered.

Baseball Results

AMERICAN LEAGUE
Minnesota 15, BOSTON 9.
New York 4, Kans. City 3 (15)
Detroit 9, Cleveland 1.
Los Angeles 10, Baltimore 6.

NATIONAL LEAGUE
St. Louis 4, Milwaukee 3.
San Francisco 6, Pittsburgh 5.
Philadelphia 3, Los Angeles 2.
Cincinnati 5, Chicago 0.
Houston 7, New York 1.

RED SOX TONIGHT
Los Angeles at Fenway Park (Latman vs. Monbouquette) 8 p.m. TV-Channel 5.

The bill faced stiff opposition in Congress; the House worked on it for two months and the Senate held it up with a filibuster for nearly two months. Though it passed, the social and political fallout was evident for years to come.

July 2, 1964
Civil Rights Act Became Law

18 • N. Y. AMSTERDAM NEWS, Sat., July 4, 1964

NEW YORK **Amsterdam News**

C. B. POWELL
President & Editor

P. M. H. SAVORY, *Secy-Treas.* - J. L. HICKS, *Executive Editor*

Published weekly by the Powell-Savory Corporation at 2340 Eighth Ave., N. Y. Telephone ACademy 2-7800. Brooklyn office, 1251 Bedford Avenue. Telephone ULster 7-2500

Hail The New Law

(Continued from Page One)

once faltering or failing to plunge headlong toward their goal.

The list goes much further.

For example: Thurgood Marshall's work as head of the NAACP Legal Defense and Educational Fund, Inc., for so many years earned him the appropriate title of "Mr. Civil Rights."

But Mr. Marshall's Herculean efforts would have been to no avail had it not been for the solid backing given him by Allen Knight Chalmers as president of the NAACP Legal Defense Fund, and the strong

WHITNEY YOUNG

A. PHILIP RANDOLPH

support by his two assistants at the time. Attorneys Jack Greenberg and Constance Baker Motley.

The astute A. Philip Randolph, head of the Brotherhood of Sleeping Car Porters, offers another example of the diversified leadership which has been so helpful in this fight. Mr. Randolph, who has a keen sense of the importance of economic independence, has been the elder statesman of the movement from start to finish, and no Bernard Baruch ever advised any group more wisely than he has.

In contrast to Mr. Randolph's seniority and elder statesman's role has been the youthful and vigorous, but still statesmanlike performance of Whitney Young, who in a few short years has emerged as one of the most dynamic fighters in the fight.

And certainly no one can fail to see the important role played by John Lewis of the Students' Non-Violent Coordinating Committee, whose very youth itself went a long way toward marshalling the all-important support of the young people in this fight.

These men have been lions in the fight of the non-legislative organizations but despite their outstanding work, in the final analysis they are only a part of the whole organization to which they belong and it is here that proper credit must also be given.

And, of course, credit cannot be limited to Negro organizations alone. For at various times during the fight this newspaper has had occasion to point out how organizations such as the American Civil Liberties Union, the American Jewish Congress, American Jewish Committee, B'nai B'rith, Anti-Defamation League, various church organizations, both Negro and white, the friendly helpful labor unions, all these organizations have left their mark on whatever monument there is to be erected in the name of civil rights.

JAMES LEWIS

Finally, one can leave the national organizations and go to the local organizations and local leaders stretching across the country from New Jersey to California, from Texas to Boston, and find that the very mention of certain names serves to call to mind a chapter or a page in the book that will eventually be known as "Civil Rights."

For example, read this list of civil rights fighters and record in your mind the incidents in the struggle which they bring into focus:

Rev. Ralph Abernathy, James Baldwin, Daisy Bates, Harry Belafonte, Algernon Black, Dr. Eugene Carson Blake, Dr. Kenneth Clark, Sammy Davis, Jr., Medgar Evers, Rev. Milton Galamison, Dick Gregory, Herbert Hill, Atty. Charles Houston, Walter H. Liebmann, Autherine Lucy, James Meredith, Atty. Robert Ming, Atty. Clarence Mitchell, Harry T. Moore, Rosa Parks, Mrs. Malcolm Peabody, Sidney Poitier, Shad Polier, Adam Clayton Powell, Atty. Andy Ransome, Walter Reuther, Gloria Richardson, Jackie Robinson, Rev. Fred Shuttlesworth, Judge J. Waties Waring, Franklyn Williams, Paul Zuber.

Hail to the Civil Rights Law.

Hail to the Heroes who made it possible!

Planting Freedom's Flag!

People In Action

Why We Can't Wait!

By DR. MARTIN LUTHER KING, JR.
(President, Southern Christian Leadership Conference)

I think it is necessary to set forth the meaning of moderation. If moderation means slowing up in the move for justice and capitulating to the undemocratic practices of the guardians of the status quo, I think moderation is wrong and I would not consider myself a moderate in that manner.

DR. KING

But if moderation means moving on toward the goal of justice with calm reasonableness and wise restraint I think it is a great virtue that all men of good will must seek to achieve during this period of transition.

So when I say "can't wait" I think this is the kind of militant moderation that is necessary to make the American dream a reality. I think it is necessary to solve this problem now. I think the moment is urgent, we have waited more than 344 years for our basic and God-given constitutional rights now only to discover that we are still far from the promised land of civil rights.

I think it is necessary now more than ever before to make it clear that we can't wait because these things are so basic not only for ourselves, because I think this struggle is much larger than the Negro gaining his constitutional rights. I think it is the question now of the destiny of our nation. Our struggle is to save the soul of America.

I think it is necessary for Negro leaders all over the country to stress non-violence more than ever before because there are forces that are seeking to stress violence and in order to counteract this I think it is necessary to make it clear that violence is wrong, it's impractical, it creates more social problems than it solves, and that this is not the way to call the attention of a community to its social ills.

I think we must make it clear that our greatest gains come through non-violence. There is a need for training programs all over the country and in many northern communities right now in the non-violent discipline just as we do in many of the communities in the South. On the other hand I would like to lift the issue to something else because I think it is much deeper than a racial conflict that we have here.

On Hoodlums

It's something that comes from economically deprived individuals. Anti-social responses are environmental and not racial and I think it is necessary to see that these very ugly acts of violence came from individuals who, out of frustration, discontent, bitterness and despair as a result of social isolation and economic deprivation turned to these meaningless and tragic acts because of these conditions.

I think it is necessary to work as hard to get rid of the conditions that bring these behavior patterns into being as it is to condemn the acts.

This is not saying that they must not be condemned. I think it is necessary to condemn them.

I think legal and judicial measures must be used—police action—but after this I think the community must work to get rid of the conditions, get rid of the causal bases instead of merely condemning the effects, because when you develop a generation of people who feel that they have no stake in the society and they see life as little more than a long corridor with no exit sign, than they turn to these behavior patterns which can become tragic to the whole community.

I don't think we have too many leaders advocating violence. The vast majority of Negro leaders are still advocating non-violence. Here and there you get one committed to what is known as "Black Nationalism" and some other ideologies that will say that the Negro should engage in retaliatory or at least defensive violence.

But all of the leaders of the major organizations advocate non-violence and I would say that the leadership is still in the hands of these individuals. Negroes by and large are still willing to follow at least tactical non-violence—that is, they are willing to use non-violence as a technique even though they may not accept it as a way of life.

I am convinced that if we can continue to make meaningful strides and if we make progress and concrete victories are achieved then the leadership will stay in the hands of these persons.

But if we face continued setbacks, then I do think the more extreme elements will gain a greater foothold in the Negro community and will have a greater influence. So I think to a large extent the leadership in the white community of our nation will determine whether there will be wide-spread violence. The response that is given from this leadership and the kind of dramatic program developed by this leadership.

To Be Equal

The Civil Rights Bill

By WHITNEY M. YOUNG, JR.
(Ex. Dir. Nat. Urban League)

Signing of the new civil rights bill by President Johnson may prove to be a "shot heard 'round the world" as famous as the one fired nearly two centuries ago on the Lexington green.

Its ramifications will be international as well as national; for it represents not only a declaration of faith to Negro citizens here that they are "somebody" but it may be "the word" to two billion people of color around the globe that our esteem for them is no less than our friends in Western Europe.

YOUNG

Conceivably, the new declaration could help us rally and inspire the uncommitted nations to our cause. Until now, says Secretary of State Dean Rusk, we have been competing with Russia with "one foot in a cast."

For Negro citizens, especially in the South, the new law will make it possible for them to borrow a book from a library without a court order; to use a playground without picketing; to dine in a restaurant without a sit-in; and to hold their heads higher. The morale uplift of the law alone will motivate countless thousands of men to rise out of poverty as the new opportunities for employment, education and voting are made available to them for the first time.

Until now, the public has expected 20,000,000 Negro citizens to help fight the nation's wars, pay its taxes, and bear themselves in a responsible and loyal manner while denying them the rewards of democracy which the majority takes for granted. However, the best way to insure racial tranquility and peace is to make opportunity and dignity interracial—which is what the bill is all about.

No Blow

Paradoxically, many southerners look upon the new bill as a "blow" to their cause. But it is nothing of the sort. It is the best thing that could happen to Dixie. For every dependent Negro who obtains a better education and a better vocation, relief rolls will decline, purchasing power will perk up, and new lifeblood will be pumped into its cities. On every occasion in which Negroes and whites can meet in public places, strangeness, fear, and hostility will be evaporated by a new sense of mutual effort and interest.

The story of the growth of prosperity and humanity in the South has long paralleled the rise of Negroes up from slavery and toward equality. This is another step. Southerners may complain the most, but they appear certain to benefit the most.

No Cure-All Either

The new law will not be a "cure-all" or panacea. It is now that the most difficult work begins — the struggle of millions to rise out of poverty, illiteracy, slums, and depression into a new world of knowledge, attainment, and prosperity. The law, if effectively enforced, can knock down long-standing roadblocks impeding these ends.

Its very enactment is a meaningful expression of concern for the dreadful injustices and injuries done Negro citizens in the past. To the credit of this nation, it can honestly take stock, face facts, and right old wrongs—and by this shall we measure its greatness and progress.

The leadership of President Johnson and the Senate deserves our warmest thanks — and especially Senators Hubert Humphrey (D.-Minn.), Mike Mansfield (D.-Mont.), Thomas Kuchel (R.-Calif.), and, in particular, Everett M. Dirksen (R.-Ill.). Their leadership produced another long stride on the road to liberty, begun so long ago on the Lexington green. Their work will be known around the world.

Pulse Of New York's Public

The Amsterdam News welcomes letters on either side of any subject. It is preferred that letters not exceed 250 words and they must be signed. Names will be withheld on request. No letters can be returned. All must be addressed to the Editor.

To Mrs. Walker

Sir: This is a reply to Atty. Cora Walker's brainstorm in the Daily News, June 15th issue.

Some constructive points suggested by her are already operative in the Negro community. Some derogatory remarks made by her are false. Her attitude is like a lawyer's out west. Visitor: Who is the best lawyer in town? "I am", replied the lawyer. "Where is your proof", said the visitor. Lawyer: "I don't require proof, I admit it". Atty. Walker doesn't require proof for the points in her interview; she admits them.

After berating her constituents, how does Atty. Walker expect to be elected to the State Senate from the 21st disstrict? If I were in her district, she would not get my vote.

Prophet C. C. Burns
Retired Civil Service employee

Goldwater's Gall

Dear Sir: Please excuse me for taking up your time, but after reading the Daily News dated June 11, 1964, I can not help but express myself.

Our people have been fighting, sacrificing and dying for generations, to enjoy by birthright, what every foreign European gets automatically upon arrival in this country. Namely democracy. I was reading of the U.S. Senate vote to end the filibuster, I can not, for the love of me see how Barry Goldwater had the nerve to vote to retain such a restrictive rule, and at the same time, still have the gall to aspire to the nation's highest office in an election year.

Although his vote was not needed, it was still a slap in the face of more than 20,000,000 citizens. When (if chosen by his party) those very same citizens vote, may decide his politial fate. Therefore I am asking you and every decent and progressive newspaper throughout the nation again: If the Republicans are so nauseous as to choose this man for its 1964 standard bearer, please do all you can to unite every vote at the polls against this reactionary on election day.

Theodore Smith
500 W. 14 St.
New York City

Death Sentence

Dear Sir: Permit me to call your attention to the case of Winston Moseley, who was given a death penalty on June 15, by a jury consisting of eight white and four Negroes. Moseley is guilty and should be killed. Those who kill others can not complain if the same method is used on them. But there are two things about this case I feel deadly important.

1. The crowd in the courtroom of women cheered and applauded the sentence. A clerk said he'd never seen anything like it in 25 years. This was obviously a "lynch mob." I have seen the same spirit in other places.

The judge's remarks were not only unjudicial, but completely insane and illogical.

He literally "gloated" over the death penalty. Some years ago a young fellow went with his girlfriend on a car ride and robbed numerous stores over a period of days, killing eight people. This goodlooking young man got a life sentence.

If Mosely got the chair, so should our goodlooking young white man. Moseley's lawyer was not permitted to introduce a psychiatrist. But when Norman Mailer committed a felonious assault on his wife and she was near the point of death in a hospital, a psychiatrist appeared at 5:00 am in court and Mailer was sent to Bellevue.

When his wife recovered, the psychiatrists at Bellevue decided Mailer was sane. What they would have done if she died, I leave to your imagination.

2. California has the same procedure we have. A jury decides guilt, and a second jury hearing is held for the purpose of determining the sentence, which is then recommended to the judge.

A death penalty in California was reversed by a higher court because the D.A. said that if they didn't give him the chair the man could be out in seven years.

Now the D.A. and the judge at Moseley's hearing both said "life imprisonment isn't that at all; this monster can live to stalk the streets again," and "life imprisonment doesn't mean that at all" (i.e. full life in jail) and added that he might be off in 27 years.

These two statements are clear grounds for appeal. But Judge Shapiro said "I know what I am going to do and the sooner we get him out of Queens County and into the death house the better." He set June 22 as sentencing date, which is rather rapid.

Mosely is an animal who does more harm to the Negroes than the Klu Klux Klan. But, he is entitled to the full benefits of the law, which would be his, if had the money, the good looks, or the right racial background.

I realize that no Negro would want to associate with any movement to have justice done, since it would appear that the Negroes are supporting rapists and murderers.

But the point is you must show the white community that we must have justice-equal for all-at-all-times. It is easy to crusade for civil rights and integration, it takes guts and integrity to fight an unpopular cause. I can't think of any group, other than yours, that would even be slightly interested in Moseley's case, so I send this letter to you.

Mortimer Cohen
10 W. 93 St.
New York City

From Inside Prison

Dear Sir: In 1957, I, as a passenger, was injured while riding a Greyhound Bus. I hired a lawyer to handle my case. On June 14, 1960 my trial was held at the Common Pleas Court in New Haven, Connecticut.

At the trail, I was asked if I had ever had an accident previous to the one in 1957 or after. I said no. I had been hurt while painting on a job, but my understanding was that he meant any motor vehicle accident and I told them so.

Flur months later, I was arrested on the charge of perjury, and given a sentence of 1 to 5 years in the Connecticut State Prison. I think this was an illegal sentence, since the Supreme Court of the United States had made a ruling on perjury and adopted it to the 14th amendment on the Tom Mooney case.

This is why I feel my constitutional rights have been violated. By writ of habeas corpus I have exhausted all my state rights. I'm now ready for the Federal courts, but I need a lawyer. There are many good Negro lawyers in New York, and I think that this case would be worth their effort.

I have not as yet received any money from the Greyhound Bus Company, all I get was 3 years in prison. If you can do anything for me, I would appreciate it very much.

Odell Porter
Box 100
Somers, Connecticut

Senator Edward Kennedy's first major speech as a senator was in support of the civil rights bill. He said, "My brother was the first President of the United States to state publicly that segregation was morally wrong."

QUOTED

"The Great Society rests on abundance and liberty for all. It demands an end to poverty and racial injustice."

—PRESIDENT LYNDON JOHNSON, May 22, 1964

August 25, 1964
Robert Kennedy Declared Senate Candidacy

Although Robert Kennedy had managed John F. Kennedy's campaigns for Senate and the presidency, this was the first time the younger brother ran for office.

The Reverend Martin Luther King Jr. accepted the 1964 Nobel Peace Prize in honor of the nonviolent pursuit of civil rights. (AP Photo)

Miss. Delegation Bolts; Turns Down Loyalty Oath

FINAL EDITION ★ ★ ★ Complete N. Y. Stocks Latest Sports

THE TIMES UNION

109TH YEAR, NO. 128 ALBANY, N. Y., WEDNESDAY, AUGUST 26, 1964 FR TEN CENTS

TWIN ALBANY MUGGINGS

Youth, 18, Is Charged In Murder

By TOM WILKINSON
Times-Union Staff Writer

An Albany youth arrested in New York City yesterday has been charged with first-degree murder in the fatal Clinton Avenue assault on a retired state employee. Theodore R. Burke, 18, of 182 Orange Street was returned to Albany yesterday.

After day-long questioning by Albany police, he was charged with the death of Bert Taber, 80, found unconscious and bleeding on Clinton Avenue Aug. 8.

Burke earlier was charged with second-degree assault in the beating of William Gillette, 40, found unconscious at Swan Street and Clinton Avenue minutes after police discovered Mr. Taber.

Mr. Gillette has remained in a coma and in critical condition since he was admitted to the Albany Medical Center Hospital.

One Victim Died

Mr. Taber died Thursday in the same hospital without regaining consciousness. Coroner Leo Sorel said his skull had been fractured.

Burke will be arraigned in Police Court this morning on the murder and assault charges.

Both Attacked

Albany Police Chief John P. Tuffey said both men had been attacked and robbed sometime in the early morning of Aug. 8. The pockets of both men yielded about $90.

The arrest culminated three weeks of intensive investigation by Albany detectives and led from Albany to Washington, D. C., and New York. De-

See ALBANY YOUTH, Page 2

★ ★ ★ ★ ★ ★ ★ ★ ★ ★ ★ **Saratoga Beat.....** ★ ★ ★ ★ ★ By Bill O'Brien

(Column on Page 3)

Pat Lynch At the Flats

1—Space Conqueror, Pan Pas, Trial By Fire
2—Spike Admiral, Wattana, Scout
3—Bon Nouvel, Sensual, Hustle
4—Atom Smasher, Formal, Johnny, Thirty Knots
5—Look Ma, Chop House, Face The Facts
6—Plaque, Grand Central, Snow House
7—Queen Empress, Grinand Bearit, Candalita
8—Tamerlo, Get Lucky, Greenwich
9—Bully Buffoon, Dry Sails, Traffic Whirl
BEST BET—Space Conqueror

The Lionhearted At Spa Raceway

1—Well Favored, Clever Katherine, Kathy Springwood
2—Borderview Carrie, Lib Genesee, Butternut Everett
3—A.C.'s Magic, Karl Springwood, Spud
4—Ben Adios, Express Pick, Homestretch Susy
5—Rod Oakie, John M. Strong, Nevele Yankee
6—Scothaven Bomber, Judge Dares, Westleigh Boy
7—Audrey Hanover, Ned Rosecroft, Scott Honor
8—Miss Millie Abbe, Forbes Buddy, Bonny Fen
9—Shadydale Air Wings, Runnymede Buzzie, Sarah Smith
BEST BET—A. C.'s MAGIC

Enjoy These Top Columnists

Sylvia Porter	7	Walter Lippmann	22
Dear Abby	21	Bob Considine	22
John McGuire	21	Dr. Carlyle Adams	32

ON THE INSIDE

Stock Market
It takes sharp drop Page 6
Television by Wire
Area stations express caution Page 21

INDEX OF FEATURES

Classified	24-31	News of Women	13-15
Comics	28-30	Obituaries	24
Crossword	29	Radio-TV	16
Editorial	22	Sports	9-12
Financial	6-7	Suburban	8
		Theaters	18-19

Johnson Aids Kennedy In New York Campaign

New York, Aug. 25 (AP)—Atty. Gen. Robert F. Kennedy formally entered the race for the U. S. Senate today as a Democrat from New York, and said President Johnson will campaign for him. The Republican opposition immediately labeled him "The Carpetbagger Candidate."

Mr. Kennedy has had his home in Virginia and his voting residence in Massachusetts. This led his potential Republican opponent Senator Kenneth B. Keating, to gibe:

"I welcome Robert Kennedy to New York. Indeed, as his Senator, I would be glad to furnish him a guide book, road map and other useful literature about the Empire State which any sojourner would find helpful."

Nomination Assured

Nomination of the 38-year-old political head of the Kennedy clan is considered assured of the Sept. 1 Democratic state convention, despite pockets of opposition within party ranks. He said he will resign from the Cabinet if nominated.

KENNEDY: Can he lick label of 'Carpetbagger' and a native New Yorker's strength? Page 2

Mr. Kennedy conceded to newsmen that he has never before ran for public office. The brother of the late President John F. Kennedy added wryly:

"But I've had a couple of relatives who did."

Asked specifically if President Johnson would campaign for him, Mr. Kennedy replied, "yes."

Mr. Kennedy, with the family name an established political drawing card in New York, is generally conceded to be a formidable opponent for Senator Keating, 64, who is seeking his second senatorial term after 18 years in Congress.

Senator Keating has refused to support Senator Barry Goldwater as the GOP candidate for President. As a result, he faces possible opposition from Mrs. Clare Boothe Luce, who has threatened to run for the Senate on the Conservative Party ticket.

Thus Senator Keating's supporters were primed for Mr. Kennedy's announcement, and prepared to hammer hard on twin campaign themes of Democratic carpetbagging and boss control.

Republican State Chairman Fred A. Young claimed "the nomination of this outsider" would mean half a million more votes for Senator Keating.

GOP campaign director Michael N. Scelsi declared:

"Mr. Kennedy, the carpet-

See KENNEDY GETS, Page 2

'Blitz Drive' By Kennedy Seen for State

By DAN BUTTON
Times-Union Executive Editor

Atlantic City, Aug. 25 — A "Kennedy-type blitz" campaign was forecast today for the New York State Democrats' prospective senatorial candidate.

This campaign preview was offered by State Chairman William H. McKeon after Attorney General Robert F. Kennedy, having announced his candidacy in New York City earlier in the day, came here and met with the New York delegation.

Mr. McKeon qualified his observations with "if he's nominated," but there appeared virtually no doubt that Mr. Kennedy will be nominated at the state convention next week. Even those Democrats who are irked by Mr. Kennedy's appearance on the New York scene seemed ready to concede the all-but-inevitable.

The Campaign Upstate

"If he's nominated, he will make an outstanding campaign," Mr. McKeon said. "It will be a Kennedy-type blitz that will carry him into all parts of the state."

The campaign Upstate "especially will be an asset in helping to elect Democratic legislators," the state chairman predicted. He added: "I feel that with a Johnson-Kennedy ticket, we will certainly gain control of at least one house of the Legislature — preparatory to moving Mr. Rockefeller out of office in 1966."

Mr. McKeon hailed the selection of Edwin L. Weisl as the new national committeeman from New York. Mr. Weisl, a friend of President Johnson, was elected by the delegation yesterday to succeed Carmine DeSapio. "He can be a potent force in helping to bring about a strong, unified party," the state chairman commented. He was optimistic about the party's chances of "closing ranks in

See 'BLITZ DRIVE', Page 2

A spotlight over his head focuses attention at Democratic convention on Robert F. Kennedy, with his wife Ethel and Averell Harriman. They were at a reception given for Mr. Kennedy by Mayor Robert F. Wagner of New York. AP Wirephoto

2nd Group Also Rejects Compromise

(C) 1964 New York Times News Service

Atlantic City, N. J., Aug. 25—The Democratic National Convention overwhelmingly approved tonight a compromise that permitted the seating of an all-white Mississippi delegation plus two members of a competing, integrated delegation from that state.

The 1964 platform was read and adopted. Permanent Chairman John W. McCormack took over the gavel, and the stage was set for the nomination tomorrow night of President Johnson and his chosen running mate.

The all-white delegation voted only a short while before to reject the compromise and bolt the convention. Only three of its members signed a required assurance of loyalty to the party and took their seats on the floor.

The integrated Freedom Democratic party also rejected the compromise. But the two designated members, Aaron Henry and the Rev. Edwin King, took seats as "delegates at large."

They sat with the Alaska delegation.

The three members of the Mississippi regular delegation who took their seats did not remain long.

Refuse to Leave

Five members of the Freedom Democrats appeared at the Mississippi section and sat with them. Two more appeared later. Two sergeants-at-arms ordered the unaccredited Freedom Party members to leave but they refused.

As a crush of reporters and photographers got there, the three "loyalists" left, even though one of them had said earlier their purpose was "to keep an unlawfully constituted delegation from having any claim to the seats."

Approval of the seating compromise came on a voice vote. There was a shout of "no" from the section where Alabama was seated and adjacent galleries but Senator John O. Pastore, the temporary chairman, did not hesitate in ruling that "the ayes appear to have it, the ayes do have it."

Voting on the motion was the first order of business after the convention opened and got the preliminaries out of the way.

That was a switch. Programs had scheduled the seating report for late in the evening, after the prime television time had ended.

Adoption of the compromise apparently ended the Mississippi fight, which had at one time threatened a walkout of other Southern delegations, or a divisive floor debate.

Credited to Humphrey

A subcommittee of the credentials committee worked out the arrangement. Senator Hubert H. Humphrey of Minnesota, the man most delegates believe will be chosen to run for vice president, was given substantial credit for the agreement.

His chief rival for the vice-presidency still was believed to be Senator Eugene McCarthy of Minnesota. But President Johnson, who will decide the question, maintained his long silence.

The generally successful

See MISSISSIPPI, Page 4

Killer Cleo Aims At South Florida

Miami, Fla., Aug. 25 — Hurricane Cleo veered straight for Florida tonight after lashing Cuba and leaving a reported 50 or more dead in Haiti. A radio report reaching Port au Prince Haiti, from a businessman in Les Cayes on Haiti's southern peninsula said 50 bodies had been found and a hospital destroyed. Another report from the Dutch freighter Parthenon said 60 per cent of Les Cayes was destroyed and two tugs sunk.

Cleo started its deadly rampage when it hit Guadaloupe Saturday killing at least 14 and injuring 100 others.

The storm made an abrupt turn to the north and took dead aim on Florida after churning westward in the Caribbean with winds of 140 miles an hour. It hit Haiti yesterday.

Florida has been untouched by a hurricane since 1960.

Last year hurricane Flora killed thousands in Haiti before moving on to Cuba. It lashed that island for an unprecedented five days, killing 1,500 persons.

Cleo presented Fidel Castro's reeling economy its second natural disaster in two years. Cuban officials ordered more than 10,000 persons evacuated from low areas. The Cuban Foreign Ministry said a number of homes had been damaged.

There were no immediate reports of casualties in Cuba.

Red Cross headquarters in Atlanta ordered 14 disaster emergency specialists into South Florida to bolster forces already on a standby basis. A spokesman said staff members were on route to district

See CLEO, Page 2

Viet Peace Deal Seen By Goldwater

Cleveland, Aug. 25 (AP)—Republican presidential nominee Barry Goldwater advised Americans today to prepare for word of "a negotiated peace" in South Viet Nam.

He said if the negotiators agree to neutralize the southeast Asian nation, now beset by Red Guerrillas, it would be an open door to Communist infiltration.

Flinging back Democratic charges, he told some 7,000 people at the annual convention of the Veterans of Foreign Wars

See NEGOTIATED, Page 2

Vegas Hotel Hit by Fire

Las Vegas, Nev., Aug. 25 (AP)—Fire today gutted the casino and show lounge of the Sahara Hotel, one of this desert resort's showplaces. Damage was estimated at $1 million.

Fifty firemen fought the blaze. They said there was no danger to guests of the 24-story hotel. The casino and lounge area are separated from the guest rooms.

The fire was believed to have started from a faulty air conditioning unit.

No injuries were reported.

The hotel is worth an estimated $18 million.

THE WEATHER

Clearing and Cooler.

(Map, Details on Page 2.)

WMHT to Renew Sunday Shows With Capital Newspapers Grant

Capitaland's only non-commercial television station will resume Sunday telecasting Sept. 6 under a grant from Capital Newspapers.

Station WMHT, which telecasts on Channel 17, suspended Saturday and Sunday operations a year ago because of a lack of funds.

Donald E. Schein, station manager, said last night the resumption of Sunday programming is possible because of "a generous grant" from The Times-Union and The Knickerbocker News.

The station, operated by Mohawk-Hudson Council on Educational Television, will be on the air Sundays from 5 to 11 p.m. Programs to be announced will come from the Eastern Educational Network, National Educational Television and commercial networks.

Mr. Schein said last night: "I am sure that all Channel 17 viewers will join me in expressing our gratitude to Capital Newspapers for making it possible to present these fine programs on Sunday evenings."

Mr. Schein said that Mohawk-Hudson officials are hopeful that additional funds will be available soon to enable the station to resume Saturday broadcasting.

Channel 17 now broadcasts five nights a week. During the school year, it carries a full schedule of in-school programming during the day, in addition to informational, cultural and sports broadcasts in the evening hours.

Khanh to Resign As Viet President

(C) 1964 New York Times News Service

Saigon, South Vietnam, Aug. 25—Maj. Gen. Nguyen Khanh and the leaders of South Viet Nam's armed forces succumbed to Buddhist and student pressures today. Gen. Khanh and the leaders decided to step down after they elect a head of state who will be charged with the establishment of a new "national structure."

A power struggle ensued as

The civilian explosion in South Viet Nam can prove a serious blow to U.S. efforts in that country. Page 2

United State officials looked on, apparently helpless.

Washington Hopeful

In a deliberate maneuver, Gen. Khanh's partisans expressed the belief that Gen. Khanh would himself be re-elected as chief of state, able to rule with a freer hand. Sources hostile to Gen. Khanh however, doubted this would happen.

(Savage fighting in Da Nang accompanied the Caigon political developments, the Associated Press reported. A mob of predominantly Buddhist rioters sacked and burned a nearby Roman Catholic settlement of

See KHANH, Page 2

Los Angeles Times

LARGEST CIRCULATION IN THE WEST, 812,147 DAILY, 1,149,295 SUNDAY

VOL. LXXXIII 2† FIVE PARTS—PART ONE CC MONDAY MORNING, SEPT. 28, 1964 96 PAGES Copyright © 1964 Los Angeles Times DAILY 10c

OSWALD'S CAPTURE—Lee Harvey Oswald, second from right, struggles with police outside the Texas Theater Nov. 22 after his arrest. This photo was included as an exhibit in the Warren Commission report naming Oswald alone as the killer of President John F. Kennedy and Patrolman J. D. Tippit.

Copyright 1963, Time, Inc. All Rights Reserved

WARREN COMMISSION REPORT:

Oswald Acted Alone in Kennedy Assassination

Historic Crime Found Free of Foreign or Domestic Conspiracy

BY ROBERT E. THOMPSON
Times Staff Writer

WASHINGTON—Lee Harvey Oswald, in a solitary act of violence free of foreign or domestic conspiracy, assassinated President John F. Kennedy in Dallas on Nov. 22, 1963, the Warren Commission ruled Sunday.

The seven-member panel concluded unanimously that Oswald, the murdered 24-year-old Marxist, planned and executed the "cruel and shocking" slaying of Mr. Kennedy without assistance from any individual or group.

Oswald probably was driven to the historic crime, the commission said, by his "overriding hostility" toward society and his "capacity to risk all in cruel and irresponsible actions."

Text of the summary and conclusions of the Warren Commission report starts on Page A. Text of rumors and findings starts on Page C.

But, since Oswald was dead, the commission said it could not make "any definite determination" of the motives of the assassin nor could it judge his "legal guilt" or sanity.

However, the panel said, it was satisfied that "it has ascertained the truth concerning the assassination of President Kennedy to the extent that a prolonged and thorough search makes this possible."

There is no evidence, the commission reported, to substantiate theories that Oswald or his killer, Dallas night club owner Jack Ruby, were associated or involved in any kind of plot.

Nor could the commission find a relationship between Oswald's Communist associations and the murder of Mr. Kennedy. Oswald had gone to the Soviet Union in 1959 and was a fervent partisan of Communist Cuba.

The commission also said in an 888-page report that there "was nothing to support speculation" that Oswald was associated in any way with the Federal Bureau of Investigation, the Central Intelligence Agency or any other U.S. government agency.

In addition, the panel said:

"In its entire investigation the commission has found no evidence of conspiracy, subversion or disloyalty to the U.S. government by any federal, state or local official."

Reports Gleaned From Interviews

These determinations were based upon an exhaustive, 10-month assessment of "all available evidence" and the "reasoned judgment" of all its members, the commission said.

Since President Johnson appointed the bipartisan commission last Nov. 29, its members and staff have studied 2,300 reports from the FBI and 800 from the Secret Service based on some 26,550 interviews of persons having information of possible relevance to the assassination.

Under the chairmanship of Chief Justice Earl Warren, the commission's members are: Sen. Richard B. Russell (D-Ga.), Sen. John Sherman Cooper (R-Ky.) Rep. Hale Boggs (D-La.), Rep. Gerald Ford (R-Mich.), former CIA Director Allen W. Dulles, and New York banker-diplomat John J. McCloy.

They concluded that Oswald, from a sixth-floor window in the Texas School Book Depository building, fired the rifle shots which killed Mr. Kennedy and seriously

Please Turn to Pg. 9, Col. 1

Flaws Found in Security Procedures

Secret Service, FBI and State Dept. Receive Criticism

BY DON IRWIN
Times Staff Writer

WASHINGTON — The Warren Commission has found that security arrangements around the late President John F. Kennedy were "inadequate" and proposes reforms to augment and tighten procedures for Presidential protection.

In the voluminous report it submitted to President Johnson Thursday and made public Sunday, the commission found nothing to reflect on the "courage and devotion to duty" of the Secret Service agents who had primary responsibility for Mr. Kennedy's safety when he was killed by an assassin's bullets last Nov. 22 in Dallas.

Inspection Laxity

But the panel found numerous flaws in procedures that were the foundation of that protection. In criticism that took in not only the Secret Service but the Federal Bureau of Investigation and the State Department, it reported:

1—That the Secret Service placed undue reliance on "standard procedures in use for many years." While the report said that most advance preparations for the Kennedy visit were "soundly planned," it criticized the service for not inspecting buildings along the President's motorcade route and dissented from the Secret Service position that it is "not practical" to make such checks on out-of-town Presidential trips. It held that the service relied on inadequate information and failed to establish effective working procedures with other intelligence and protective agencies.

No Names Listed

2—That files kept by the Protective Research Section of the Secret Service to locate potential attackers of the President listed no names in the Dallas-Ft. Worth area at the time of Mr. Kennedy's visit to Dallas.

3—That the Secret Ser-

Please Turn to Pg. 8, Col. 1

FINDINGS AT A GLANCE

By Associated Press

Here in brief are important finding of the Warren Commission's report on the assassination of President John F. Kennedy:

Lee Harvey Oswald and Jack Ruby acted as loners; there was no conspiracy, domestic or foreign.

Secret Service measures to guard the President were insufficient. Also the FBI failed to tip the Secret Service to Oswald's presence in Dallas.

Dallas police committed errors in the events that led up to the killing of Oswald by Ruby; news media must also "share responsibility for the failure of law enforcement which occurred in connection with the death of Oswald."

Methods for protecting Presidents must be drastically modernized.

British Papers Term Warren Report Honest

LONDON (AP)—The Warren report on President John F. Kennedy's murder won general acceptance in British editorials today as a competent and honest document holding dire lessons for the free world.

Among first commentaries, the only criticism came from the Communist Daily Worker, which called it a whitewash.

News dispatches from Washington headlined the report's criticism of the FBI and Secret Service, long regarded here as models of their trade.

Vulnerability Stressed

Other headlines and editorials stressed the vulnerability of a democratic head of state—something pointed out by the late President himself on the morning of his assassination.

This vulnerability has special meaning here since later this month Queen Elizabeth II is due to tour Canada. Officials believe her life may be in danger there from French Canadian separatists.

The London Times, independent, set the tone of most non-Communist comment by calling the report "thorough, painstaking, voluminous, frank and above all scrupul-

Please Turn to Pg. 6, Col. 4

Troops Leave Saigon After Tension Eases

SAIGON (AP) — Airborne troops and marines loyal to Premier Nguyen Khanh's regime began drifting back to their posts from Saigon Sunday as the threat of a new military coup seemed to ease. But soldiers still held key points in the capital.

There were two other tension-easing developments in this nation torn by Communist guerrilla warfare and an uprising of the Montagnard tribesmen in the central highlands:

Elected Chairman

Phan Khac Suu, a major foe of the late President Ngo Dinh Diem's government, was elected chairman of a new high national council that is supposed to lead the nation back to civilian rule. Student opposition to military rule was a major factor in rioting this summer.

And a fleet of 50 U.S. Army helicopters flew out 60 Vietnamese military and civilian hostages from the main rebel camp at Buon Sar Pa near the border of Cambodia.

The regime made their

Please Turn to Pg. 29, Col. 3

Union Orders Picketing at Three Market Firms

177 Stores of Von, Food Giant, Stater Bros. Selected as First Retail Targets in Strike

Teamster Union officials ordered picketing to begin at midnight Sunday against three supermarket chains and the warehouse of a fourth and predicted food shortages will develop as an inevitable result.

The action was taken on the 15th day of the food industry strike-lockout involving the teamsters and 56 members of the Food Employers Council.

Union attorney Charles Hackler said Teamster locals not involved in the strike-lockout are pledged not to cross the picket lines. This will end deliveries from processors directly to markets in the four chains — and will cut off milk, bread and meat supplies as well, union officials said.

177 Stores Affected

The action is being taken against 177 Von, Food Giant and Stater Bros. stores and against the wholesale operation of Safeway Stores, Inc.

Teamsters in Safeway's creamery, bakery and meat plant, which supply Safeway markets, remained on their jobs during the strike-lockout but now won't cross the picket lines, union officials added.

More than 1,000 Teamster members turned out for a briefing session and picket assignments Sunday at union headquarters, 846 S Union St.

Hand Out Pamphlets

The pickets will hand out pamphlets in which the union contends the markets "illegally locked out teamsters regardless of the warning that such action is illegal."

The picketing, the union literature reads, is "for the sole purpose of protesting the store's unfair practices and inducing it to let its

Please Turn to Pg. 31, Col. 1

2 Sides Seek Speedy End to Strike at GM

DETROIT (AP) — Negotiators for General Motors and the United Auto Workers met for two hours Sunday seeking avenues that might lead to quick settlement of a strike which has cut off the flow of GM's 1965 automobiles.

Deadlocked issues weren't debated anew, only the mechanics of how they should be taken up.

Afterward, the two sides said they would meet again this morning and that procedures had been set up for further bargaining on non-economic union demands that caused the walkout of more than 250,000 GM workers last Friday.

Local Demands, Too

UAW President Walter Reuther told newsmen that efforts would be made to settle some 18,000 local at-the-plant demands at the same time that negotiations are proceeding on a national contract.

Asked if there appeared to be a possibility of settling the nationwide strike before the end of the week, Reuther replied that such a possibility existed—but he declined to make a flat prediction.

Reuther said reaction among workers on the picket lines has been one of "overwhelmingly enthusiastic support" around the country. "They've been pushed around long enough," he said.

GM and the UAW reportedly have reached virtual agreement on an economic package paralleling the ones accepted by the union from Ford and Chrysler. Reuther said these were worth 54

Please Turn to Pg. 21, Col. 8

Group Picked to Help Draft Safety Steps

JOHNSON CITY, Tex. (AP) — President Johnson appointed Sunday a four-man committee to advise him "on the execution of the recommendations of the Warren Commission."

The commission which investigated the assassination of President John F. Kennedy recommended action to tighten the protection of Presidents and to make killing a President or a Vice President a federal crime.

Members of the committee are:

Secretary of the Treasury Douglas Dillon, acting Atty. Gen. Nicholas Katzenbach, Director John A. McCone of the Central Intelligence Agency, and McGeorge Bundy, special assistant to Mr. Johnson for national security affairs.

No Chairman Named

The President named no chairman for the committee. However, it was understood that Dillon, as the ranking member of the panel, would have general supervision over the group.

The panel he selected presumably will canvass the possible need for further measures to be taken to increase protection for the President.

And it was possible that the committee would explore the key question, raised by the commission, as to whether all or part of the protective functions of the Secret Service should be turned over to some other agency.

Train Crash Kills Four; Dozens Hurt

MONTGOMERY, Ill. (AP)—At least four persons were killed and dozens injured late Sunday night when a Chicago, Burlington & Quincy passenger train crashed head-on with a Rock Island Line passenger train standing still on a siding in Montgomery.

A Burlington spokesman said the two-man engine crew of the Rock Island train were among those killed along with a crewman on the Burlington train. Montgomery is located about 40 miles west of Chicago.

TIMES STARTS SERIES BY JOHNSON TODAY

One of the most important political series to be published in The Times this year, "My Hope for America," by President Johnson, begins on Page 2, Part 1, in today's issue.

The Johnson series is appearing as a part of The Times' comprehensive campaign coverage and as a matter of general news interest. The Times earlier published a series based on Barry Goldwater's new book, "Where I Stand."

In "My Hope for America," the President presents his viewpoints on nuclear responsibility, NATO strength, the war on poverty and other national and international issues.

THE WEATHER

U.S. Weather Bureau forecasts: low clouds and local fog in the early morning hours otherwise mostly sunny. High today 77, low 62; high Sunday 75, low 64.

INDEX OF FEATURES

Music Center Site Dedicated Before 3,500

Distinguished gathering of 3,500 pays tribute to "a dreamer and a dream come true" as Music Center site is dedicated to Mrs. Norman Chandler. See Page 1, Part 2.

ON OTHER PAGES

DEAR ABBY. Page 5, Part 4.
ED AINSWORTH. Page 10, Part 3.
DR. ALVAREZ. Page 10, Part 4.
ART NEWS. Page 7, Part 4.
ASTROLOGY. Page 8, Part 4.
BRIDGE. Page 10, Part 4.
BUSINESS. Pages 8-10, Part 3.
CASH WORD. Page 11, Part 3.
CLASSIFIED. Pages 1-20, Part 3.
COMICS. Page 7, Part 2.
CROSSWORD. Page 20, Part 3.
DRAMA AND MUSIC. Pages 13-17, Part 4.
ROSCOE DRUMMOND. Page 5, Part 2.
EDITORIALS. Pages 4-6, Part 2.
ROLAND EVANS and ROBERT NOVAK. Page 5, Part 2.
FAMILY. Pages 1-14, Part 4.
FINANCIAL. Pages 8-10, Part 3.
MAX FREEDMAN. Page 5, Part 2.
CHRISTY FOX. Page 2, Part 4.
HARRY GOLDEN. Page 6, Part 2.
JUMBLE GAME. Page 2, Part 3.
HEDDA HOPPER. Page 16, Part 4.
ROBERT M. HUTCHINS. Page 6, Part 2.
JAMES J. KILPATRICK. Page 6, Part 2.
KIRSCH ON BOOKS. Page 6, Part 4.
MOTION PICTURES. Pages 15-17, Part 4.
"MY HOPE FOR AMERICA," by Lyndon B. Johnson, Page 2, Part 1.
PEANUTS. Page 4, Part 1.
DREW PEARSON. Page 6, Part 2.
RADIO. Pages 18-20, Part 4.
DR. RAFFERTY. Page 5, Part 2.
VICTOR RIESEL. Page 5, Part 2.
ART RYON. Page 8, Part 4.
PHILIP SCHEUER. Page 17, Part 4.
ART SEIDENBAUM. Page 1, Part 4.
SHIPPING. Page 10, Part 3.
CECIL SMITH. Page 18, Part 4.
SOUTHLAND. Page 10, Part 3.
SPORTS. Pages 1-7, Part 3.
TELEVISION. Pages 18-20, Part 4.
VITAL RECORD. Page 11, Part 3.
WEATHER. Page 11, Part 3.
MATT WEINSTOCK. Page 6, Part 2.

Assassination Termed Act of Man 'Alienated' From the Real World

BY VINCENT J. BURKE
Times Staff Writer

WASHINGTON — President John F. Kennedy's assassin was "profoundly alienated from the world in which he lived."

That was one of the big differences between Lee Harvey Oswald and most other men, the Warren Commission reported Sunday.

Unable to find a satisfactory, rational explanation for the assassination, the commission attempted to delve posthumously into Oswald's mental outlook and character.

It found that Oswald was "moved by an overriding hostility to his environment," whatever it happened to be.

"He was never satisfied with anything," the commission reported. "His wife . . . thought that he would not be happy anywhere, 'only on the moon, perhaps.'"

Since Oswald is dead, the commission said it could reach no definite conclusions as to whether he was "sane" under prevailing legal standards.

Summarizing its conclusions, the commission said:

"Many factors were undoubtedly involved in Oswald's motivation for the assassination, and the commission does not believe that it can ascribe to him any one motive or group of motives.

"It is apparent, however, that Oswald was moved by an overriding hostility to his environment. He does not appear to have been able to establish meaningful relationships with other people.

"He was perpetually discontented with the world around him. Long before the assassination he expressed his hatred for American society and acted in protest against it. Oswald's search for what he conceived to be the perfect society was doomed from the start.

"He sought for himself a

Please Turn to Pg. 14, Col. 1

The Warren Commission Report—named for its chairman, Chief Justice Earl Warren—concluded that Lee Harvey Oswald acted alone in the assassination of President Kennedy. Many doubted that conclusion, a skepticism that bred conspiracy theories.

ALSO IN 1964

Stanley Kubrick's movie satirizing the military and the Cold War, Dr. Strangelove, *was released.*

Although many considered Robert Kennedy a carpetbagger from Massachusetts, he won the U.S. Senate seat in New York.

Senator Edward Kennedy and wife, Joan, met children Edward Jr. and Kara at the airport. Son Patrick was born three years later. (AP Photo)

ALSO IN 1964

The NBC game show Jeopardy! *debuted with host Art Fleming.*

State Legislature Democratic

Story in Cols. 1 and 2 Below

Johnson Landslide; Kennedy Is Senator

Sunrise Edition

TIMES UNION

109TH YEAR NO 195 ALBANY N Y WEDNESDAY NOVEMBER 4 1964 TEN CENTS

Johnson Tide Carries Bobby

By ROBERT T. GRAY

New York, Nov. 3 (AP)—President Johnson won New York's giant bloc of 43 electoral votes tonight in a record-smashing victory that carried Robert F. Kennedy, brother of the late president, into the U.S. Senate.

With more than a third of the returns in, President Johnson led Republican Senator Barry Goldwater by more than 2-1, pointing to an all-time high plurality of 2.5 million to 3 million votes.

Mr Kennedy, who encountered "carpetbagger" charges when he came into New York State to run against incumbent Republican Kenneth Keating, ran behind Johnson but nevertheless held a commanding lead.

In returns from 10,757 of 12,439 election districts, President Johnson had 4,014,505 votes to 1,904,670 for Goldwater.

Mr Kennedy led Senator Keating in the same districts, 3,114,638 to 2,616,726.

Legislature Control

Also at stake was control of the legislature, now in the hands of Republicans.

The victory building for President Johnson overshadowed by far the 1.5 million plurality, the previous record, by which former President Eisenhower carried the state in 1956 and the 1.3 million votes, the previous Democratic record, by which Franklin D. Roosevelt won the Empire State in 1936.

A Johnson landslide had been expected and the big suspense of the campaign was in the fight between the 38-year-old Kennedy, former U. S. Attorney General, and the 64-year-old Keating, who was running for a second term.

Mr. Kennedy showed his greatest strength in the Democratic bastion of New York City, but also exhibited surpris-

Robert F. Kennedy

See JOHNSON TIDE, Page 2

Mahoney, Carlino Lose

Democrats Win State Legislature

Walter Mahoney — Joseph Carlino

By TONI ADAMS
Associated Press Staff Writer

The longtime Republican domination of New York's legislature evidently fell into Democratic hands last night, in the tide of President Johnson's victory.

Republican victims in unofficial returns included the legislature's two top Republican leaders.

Republicans had held legislative control for three decades. Democrats ousted Republicans from at least 15 Assembly and six Senate seats.

Mahoney, Carlino Lose

Assembly Speaker Joseph F. Carlino of Nassau County and Senate majority leader Walter J. Mahoney of Buffalo both conceded defeat a few hours after the polls closed.

Democrats evidently captured most of the legislative seats in Senator Mahoney's home county of Erie, where the 56-year-old Mahoney, a legislator for 27 years and majority leader for 10, had been embroiled in local GOP battles. Senator Mahoney lost to John H. Doerr, also a Buffalo attorney. Several races

See LEGISLATURE, Page 2

THE WEATHER
Fair.
(See Map, Details, Page 30)

Albany County, Area Vote Swells Johnson's Margin

By DOC RIVETT
Times-Union Staff Writer

President Lyndon B. Johnson swept Albany County — and most nearby counties — by an unprecedented margin yesterday and in the process pulled a number of local candidates into office by his coattails.

In Albany County, the President erased the four-year-old record for plurality by swamping Senator Barry M. Goldwater by 114,463 to 31,965. That gave the President a margin of 83,498.

The previous high, set four years ago by the late John F. Kennedy, was 30,737.

Robert F. Kennedy, the younger brother of the slain president, carried the county over Republican Senator Kenneth B. Keating by 87,026 to 61,768—a plurality of 25,258.

There had been criticism to the Albany County Democratic organization as "lukewarm" toward Mr Kennedy's candidacy.

Runs Low in City

Whether the organization was as diligent as it might have been is something that only the Democratic leaders know. But Mr. Kennedy did run low on the ticket in the city.

Not only was his city vote 10,000 behind Mr. Johnson's but it even trailed that for State Senator Julian B. Erway, otherwise low man on the ticket.

In other nearby counties, it was much the same story. President Johnson piled up unprecedented totals, and local Democratic candidates managed to outlast their normally victorious Republican opponents.

In Schenectady County, for example, John Kirvin, the Rotterdam supervisor, defeated Clark Wemple by 1,258 votes to become the county's first Democratic assemblyman in 42 years.

In Rensselaer County, Doug-

Congressman Leo W. O'Brien makes a confident victory sign as he casts his ballot at a garage on Melrose Avenue Election Day morning.

Times-Union Staff Photo by Smith

SEE ALBANY, Page 7

Democrats Boost Edge In Congress

Washington, Wednesday, Nov. 4 (UPI) — Democrats scored smashing gains in yesterday's elections, giving President Johnson a better chance of winning passage of items of his controversial ... welfare program.

Riding on the president's coattails, the Democrats nailed down control of the House of Representatives shortly after midnight. Their continued domination of the Senate had been assured hours earlier despite some upsets.

There were some big name changes in Congress.

Former Atty. Gen. Robert F. Kennedy, brother of the late President, defeated Senator Kenneth Keating, R-N. Y., and Representative Robert Taft Jr., R-Ohio, beat aging Democratic Senator Stephen M. Young.

Salinger Beaten

Mr. Johnson's sweep to victory apparently did not rub off on former White House Press Secretary Pierre Salinger in his race for a Senate term on his own in California. Mr.

See DEMOCRATS, Page 2

President's Vote Tops All Records

President Lyndon B. Johnson

Washington, Wednesday, Nov. 4 (UPI)—President Johnson swept back into the White House today on the crest of a landslide victory in which he polled more votes than any other presidential contender in history.

With Americans shattering traditional vote patterns in both north and south, Mr. Johnson won the presidency in his own right by crushing Barry M. Goldwater's conservative challenge everywhere but in the deep south. He even won Maine and Vemont.

The 56-year-old Texan carried back into power with him a Democratic congress, which included a stunning net gain of close to 40 Democratic seats in the House. This was twice the pickup the President had expected in a chamber which caused him the most trouble last session in winning enactment of controversial programs.

With 83 per cent of the ballots counted, Mr. Johnson became the greatest vote getter in U. S. history early this morning when his total topped the 34,227,096 votes received by his slain predecessor, John F. Kennedy.

The figures early today were:

Johnson: 35,694,214
Goldwater: 22,149,413

That gave the Democratic ticket of Johnson and Hubert H. Humphrey 61.7 per cent of the vote against 38.3 per cent for the GOP ticket of Goldwater and Rep. William E. Miller.

Wins 42 States

By then President Johnson had won 43 states for a total of 479 electoral votes and was leading in two states with 7 electoral votes for an indicated total of 486. Goldwater had won 5 states with 47 electoral votes and was leading in one—his home state of Arizona—with five votes for an indicated electoral total of 52.

The President passed the magic figure of 270 electoral votes at 10:11 p. m. when his native state of Texas gave him its 25 electoral votes.

Senator Goldwater did not concede during the night. Instead he announced in Phoenix that he would make a statement at noon EST. A press aide said the Senator wanted to "analyze the vote" that returned him to private life.

May Try Again

His campaign manager, Denison Kitchell, put the Goldwater camp's view this way: "It doesn't look like we're going to win this first round. Four years from now we're going to get the government back to where it belongs."

It was an election in which time-honored political rules were overturned. The President planted the Democratic banner in Vermont for the first time in the state's history and carried Maine, which hadn't gone Democratic since 1912 when it voted for Woodrow Wilson.

Senator Goldwater, on the other hand, broke the long Democratic monopoly in the south and won Mississippi, Alabama, Louisiana, South Carolina and Georgia. Georgia was an unexpected bonus for the GOP candidate.

But that was about all for the 55-year-old Arizonan, who

See JOHNSON, Page 2

Elections at a Glance

ALBANY COUNTY: The Democrats bar our girl from headquarters; the Republicans smile in defeat .... Page 3.

LEGISLATURE: Bill O'Brien analyses a reversal of form where Republican incumbents "tumbled like dominoes." Page 3.

ROCKEFELLER: Doc Rivett reports that the governor steeled himself for the defeat handed his party .... Page 3

CAPITALAND: The old order changeth throughout the area as upsets aplenty dot area results .... Page 4

CONGRESS: Stratton and O'Brien, but Wharton is upset by Ellenville industrialist Joseph Y. Resnick and King is a question mark .... Page 5.

THE RESULTS: Comprehensive tables list the Albany County vote for Assembly and U. S. Senate and county offices ... Pages 3 and 14.

MICHIGAN — Republican Gov. George Romney defeated Representative Neil Staebler, a Democrat. Story on Page 6

TEXAS — Gov. John B. Connolly, a Democrat, won reelection in the race against Republican Jack Critchton. Story on Page 21

VERMONT—Gov. Philip H. Hoff, Democrat, defeated Ralph A. Foote, Republican-Independent. Story on Page 7

OHIO—Republican Robert Taft Jr., son of the late Senator Robert A. Taft, defeated Senator Stephen M. Young. Story on Page 15

California—Former movie actor George Murphy, a Republican, defeated Senator Pierre Salinger, former press secretary under Presidents Kennedy and Johnson. Story on Page 6

MAINE—Senator Edmund S. Muskie, Democrat, won reelection by defeating his Republican opponent, Clifford G. McIntire. Story on Page 6

VERMONT—Senator Winston L. Prouty, Republican-Independent, defeated his Democratic opponent, Frederick J. Fayette. Story on Page 7

CONNECTICUT—Senator Thomas J. Dodd, a Democrat, was reelected, defeating Republican John Lodge. Story on Page 6

Illinois—Gov. Otto Kerner, Democrat, leads Republican Charles H. Percy. Story on Page 7

OKLAHOMA—Fred R. Harris, a Democrat, defeated Republican Bud Wilkinson, former Oklahoma University football coach. Story on Page 7

MASSACHUSETTS—Francis X. Bellotti, Democrat, defeated Republican John A. Volpe, former governor. Story on Page 7

"All the News That's Fit to Print"

The New York Times

LATE CITY EDITION

Weather: Mostly sunny, mild today; fair, mild tonight and tomorrow. Temp. range: today 60-45; Sat. 51-41. Full U.S. report on Page 91.

SECTION ONE

VOL. CXVII..No. 40,230 — NEW YORK, SUNDAY, MARCH 17, 1968 — 40 CENTS

KENNEDY TO MAKE 3 PRIMARY RACES; ATTACKS JOHNSON

CHALLENGE ISSUED

Senator Says Only New Leaders Can Change Divisive Policies

Statement and excerpts from news conference, Page 68.

By TOM WICKER

Robert F. Kennedy speaking in the Senate Caucus Room. At the right are Mrs. Kennedy and two of their children.

LINDSAY DECLARES WELFARE AID CUTS RAISE CITY DEFICIT

Tells Albany His Budget Must Bear $150-Million Cost of Vital Programs

By WILL LISSNER

PRESIDENT READY TO CUT BUDGET TO GAIN TAX RISE

U.S. to Put More Men in Vietnam

CALL-UP MODERATE

35,000-50,000 Men May Go—Reservists Face Active Duty

By ROBERT B. SEMPLE

10 at Washington Parley Seek to Solve Gold Crisis

By NAN ROBERTSON

DROP OF $8-BILLION

Johnson Is Yielding to Congress Pressure —Mills Undecided

By EDWIN L. DALE Jr.

McCarthy Bars Any Deal And Will Continue Drive

By E. W. KENWORTHY

PACT IS REACHED IN MOVERS' STRIKE

15-Day Dispute to End Here if Union Members Vote for Ratification Today

By EMANUEL PERLMUTTER

G.I.'s, in Pincer Move, Kill 128 in a Daylong Battle

STORES HERE HALT GOLD-COIN SELLING

Dealers Cite 'Insane Prices' Being Offered—$98 Bid Reported for $20 Piece

By MURRAY ILLSON

KENNEDY PARADES TO MIXED CHORUS

Draws Boos and Cheers Here in St. Patrick's Day March

By MURRAY SCHUMACH

Survey Shows College Students Back McCarthy Over Kennedy

By LAWRENCE VAN GELDER

Blaiberg Goes Home 74 Days After Heart Transplant

Dr. Philip Blaiberg has a word with Dr. Christiaan N. Barnard, right, at hospital door

First Major Accord Reached on Copper

By DAVID R. JONES

Today's Sections

Index to Subjects

It was clear Robert Kennedy someday would run for president—when the time was right. Growing opposition to the Vietnam War and the weakness of Johnson's support drove Kennedy to campaign in 1968.

ALSO IN 1968

The American public was shocked by the My Lai Massacre in Vietnam.

WEATHER TODAY
Fair And Cool
High, 47; Low, 33
Yesterday
High, 63; Low, 45

THE INDIANAPOLIS STAR

"Where the spirit of the Lord is, there is Liberty"—II Cor. 3-17

VOL. 65, NO. 305 ☆☆ FRIDAY, APRIL 5, 1968 633-1240 10c

MARTIN LUTHER KING SLAIN

★ ★ ★ ★ ★ ★ ★

LBJ, Thant Confer On Peace Move

President Calls Talk 'Helpful, Constructive'

PRESIDENT VISITS U.N.
Secretary U Thant Greets LBJ
(AP Wirephoto)

President Johnson visited Secretary-General U Thant at the United Nations yesterday and will confer with Former President Dwight D. Eisenhower today on his way to Hawaii for a weekend military strategy review of the Vietnam War.

Johnson's spur-of-the-moment discussion with Thant lasted one hour and 16 minutes and dealt with new peace initiatives in Southeast Asia. It also was learned that the President's curtailment of air and sea shelling of North Vietnam was discussed.

Afterwards, the President told newsmen it was a "good meeting" and that Thant was "very helpful and constructive."

Then the President headed back to the White House from New York, where he had flown at midday for a Roman Catholic ceremony, to confer with his two chief peace negotiators, W. Averell Harriman and Llewellyn E. Thompson.

After a planned speech at a Democratic congressional fund-raising dinner in Washington with Vice-President Hubert H. Humphrey, the President scheduled a late evening departure from Andrews Air Force Base, Md., for Honolulu, with an overnight stop in California.

The White House said Mr. Eisenhower would travel by helicopter from his Palm Desert (Calif.) home to March Air Force Base 50 miles away for a breakfast meeting today with the President.

THEY WILL discuss successors to Gen. William C. Westmoreland, the United States war commander, and Adm. Ulyssess S. G. Sharp, commander of U.S. forces in the Pacific. Sharp is retiring July 2, and Westmoreland will be-

Turn to Page 10, Column 3

Marines Seize Khe Sahn Hill

Saigon (UPI)—A battalion of United States Marines pushed 1.5 miles out of Khe Sanh yesterday and seized Hill 471 to the south in the increasingly bloody campaign to lift the North Vietnamese siege of the isolated American position.

Radio Hanoi said "American planes" bombed North Vietnam's extreme northwest corner near Laos, an area far above the U.S. raid limit line, but the Communists did not make a major issue of the charge. The raiders may have been U.S.-built Laotian planes which strayed off course.

THE MARINE battalion, up to 1,500 men, reporting finding 30 freshly killed North Vietnamese bodies as the leathernecks pushed up Hill 471 overlooking the Khe Sanh valley. More were believed killed by U.S. artillery strikes supporting the drive to clear the area of North Vietnamese forces.

Troops of the U.S. 1st Cavalry Division occupied another part of the high ground commanding firing positions into Khe Sanh. Fog and a murderous North Vietnamese artillery barrage inflicted casualties and stalled the big allied push along Highway 9 to relieve the fort.

The allied infantry-tank juggernaut pushing up Highway 9 was reported only 2 miles from the base yesterday in Operation Pegasus, code name for the relief operation.

The U.S. Command said Pegasus, which began Monday, had killed at least 57 North Vietnamese at a cost of nine Americans killed and 78 wounded, most of them by Communist artillery.

Radio Hanoi's report on the

Turn to Page 11, Column 1

Gaining Momentum!

Negro Leader Shot Down At Memphis Hotel

FROM AP AND UPI

Memphis, Tenn. — Dr. Martin Luther King Jr., 1964 Nobel peace prize winner and America's leading exponent of non-violence in the civil rights struggle, was shot to death last night, Assistant Police Chief Henry Lux said.

Two unidentified men were arrested several blocks from where King was shot, while standing on the motel balcony.

The Rev. Andrew Young, executive vice-president of the Southern Christian Leadership Conference headed by King, said the shot hit King in the neck and lower right part of his face.

"He didn't say a word; he didn't move," Young said.

Immediately after the shooting, the civil rights leader was rushed to St. Joseph's Hospital where he was declared dead a short time later.

"It sounded like a firecracker," Young said.

REPORTS OF THE shooting were conflicting. Another source said King was evidently shot in the face. He held a white towel over his face as he was taken into the emergency room.

Memphis police, protecting the city without the aid of national guard troops for the first day since King led a march March 28 in support of striking sanitation workers, immediately moved into the area and sealed off the block surrounding the Lorraine Motel, where King and his party were staying.

City policemen, wearing riot-helmets and carrying shotguns and rifles, blocked newsmen and others from the scene of the shooting.

"We are in a state of emergency here," said Police Director Frank Holloman, who had told a Federal judge earlier in the day that a second mass demonstration planned by King for next Monday could not be held without violence.

"We don't know what happened," he added.

IN WASHINGTON, the FBI said it had begun an investigation of the shooting at the specific request of Attorney General Ramsey Clark.

Police chased a late model, blue car through Memphis and north to Millington. They reported a civilian in a car with a citizens band radio, had closed on the car and opened fire.

Dr. Andrew Young, King's chief lieutenant, reported the Nobel peace prize winner was standing on the balcony of the Lorraine Hotel—evidently alone — when the shot felled him.

YOUNG AND OTHER aides were in King's hotel room. One report said the shot came from a brick building across the street. Police put on a bulletin for a "young white male, well-dressed," who ran out of the building, dropped a weap-

Turn to Page 10, Column 6

Branigin's 'Favorite Son' Race Backed By Indiana Youth Group

A state-wide youth group was formed yesterday to spur the candidacy of Governor Roger D. Branigin in the May 7 presidential preference primary, causing a break among Indiana Young Democrats supporting United States Senators Robert F. Kennedy (D-N.Y.) and Eugene J. McCarthy (D-Minn.)

At the same time, it was announced that Indiana headquarters of the Branigin for President Committee will open tomorrow at 36 South Capitol Avenue.

Gary F. Tyler, state advisor to the Indiana Collegiate Young Democrats, said Youth for Branigin committees already have been formed in 18 counties and on six college campuses.

MEANWHILE, Kennedy was an hour later arriving in Indianapolis after speaking at South Bend and Muncie. He appeared on the University of Notre Dame and Ball State University campuses.

At South Bend, he called for the end of student deferments and at Muncie a crowd estimated at 7,000 heard Kennedy's address in the fieldhouse.

He was accompanied to Indiana by his wife and mother of his 10 children, Mrs. Ethel Kennedy, who also came to Indianapolis with him last week.

At South Bend, Kennedy was greeted at the airport by about 1,500, most of them youths.

"Will you help me win in Indiana?" he asked.

"Yes!" they replied.

His prepared text for a University of Notre Dame audience was devoted to domestic rather than foreign affairs issues and concentrated on the theme that "in the midst of our great affluence, American children are hungry," because "our Federal food programs are simply not doing the job."

Kennedy said he thought the Selective Service System was "inequitable and unfair" and added:

"We should move toward a professional Army as much as possible."

KENNEDY SAID the burdens of war have been carried by the poor and minority groups for to long. Consequently, he thought student deferments should be ended.

When he suggested ending student deferments, Kennedy asked:

"Did I just lose you to Hubert Humphrey?"

Branigin promised an active campaign in his role as Indiana's "favorite son."

"I'm going to get as much exposure as I can, consistent with running the Governor's office," he said.

He declined to say whether he expects to have his name actually placed in nomination at the Democratic Natoinal Convention opening Aug. 26 in Chicago if he wins the primary.

"Right now I'm just think-

Turn to Page 10, Column 1

Mayor Calls For Help On Funds To Build City '500' Festival Float

Mayor Richard G. Lugar called for help yesterday.

The city's chief executive warned that increased citizen participation is needed if the drive for funds to build a City of Indianapolis float for the "500" Festival Parade is to go over the top.

LUGAR SPOKE as the week-long drive closed out its fourth day with contributions for the entire drive standing at $1,735.09—less than half of the minimum $3,500 needed.

Contributions received yesterday totaled $535, including $54.20 collected by the Indianapolis Jaycees today on Monument Circle.

Lugar urged interested citizens and civic groups to send their contributions to:

The Mayor's Float Fund, c/o "500" Festival Associates, 350 North Meridian Street, Indianapolis 46204.

Civic groups making contributions yesterday included the Fraternal Order of Police, $50; Murat Temple Caravan Club, $54.39, and Delta chapter of Beta Sigma Phi Fraternity, $5.

Employes of the City Controller's office contributed $20 and Bryant's Food Shoppe of

Turn to Page 11, Column 4

TODAY'S CHUCKLE

Tolerance is the ability to listen enthusiastically to someone telling your favorite story.

The Weather

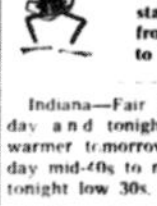

Joe Crow Says: If they discover drugs to improve the intellect will the status change from eggheads to hopheads?

Indiana—Fair and cool today and tonight. Fair and warmer tomorrow. Highs today mid-40s to near 50. Low tonight low 30s.

Indianapolis—Fair and cool today. Sunny and warmer tomorrow.

Dirt-Dust Count: 43 Micrograms of dust per cubic meter of air (average daily count for 1967 was 118).

In's, Out's Of It Plane To See

Not many mothers would put up with having an airplane built in their living room, but for Mrs. Walter Weickert of Kitchener, Ontario, it's just another family project which she enjoys as much as her husband and family. The 19-foot-long aircraft is being built in the living room because it's the only room in the house with enough length and suitable exit—a four-by-six-foot window. The wings will be added after the plane is out of the house, of course. The builders are (from left) Mrs. Weickert; daughters Faith, 12 years old, and Hope, 9; Mr. Weickert and son Chris, 13. (AP Wirephoto)

Inside Today's Star

News Summary On Page 2

Amusement Pages	18-20	Crossword	16	TV-Radio	21, 35
Bridge	17	Editorials	22	Uncle Ray	35
Collins	46	Finance	33, 34	Weather	21
Comics	26	Food	9	Women's Pages	7-9
		Sports	27-32		

The Star's Telephone Numbers

Main Office	633-1240	Sports Results	633-1200
Circulation	633-9211	Want Ads	633-1212

Northside Robbers Grab $50,000 In Gems, Furs

Two men, one armed with a revolver, posed as Internal Revenue Service agents yesterday at a posh Northside home and minutes later fled with more than $50,000 in diamonds and furs, authorities said.

Marion County Sheriff's deputies said the men entered the home of Leonard Farber, 7901 High Drive, Williams Creek, about 9:30 a.m. and bound Mrs. Evelyn Farber, 45 years old, and a nurse with handcuffs and tape before leaving.

Authorities believe the men are the same bandits who beat the owner of the Devington Jewelry Store, 6000 East 46th Street, Wednesday and handcuffed him and an employe to a furnace pipe before escaping with $600 in cash and several watches and diamond rings.

Mrs. Katie Dunston, 42, 3962 Graceland Ave., a nurse in the Farber home, said the men knocked on the front door of the Farber residence, identified themselves as IRS agents and said they wanted to speak with Mrs. Farber.

Earlier, Mrs. Farber said she received a telephone call from a man who asked if her husband was at home. He was not.

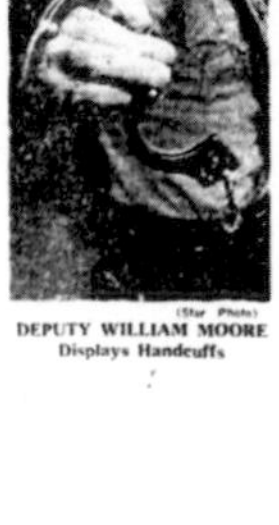

(Star Photo)
DEPUTY WILLIAM MOORE
Displays Handcuffs

Mrs. Farber said when she entered a front room the men ordered her and the nurse to turn their backs and "not to look at us and you won't get hurt."

The bandits then handcuffed each woman's hands behind her back and took Mrs. Dunston to a nearby room where they forced her to lie on the floor and taped her feet.

MRS. FARBER said the men then opened a black attache case, put on black hoods and gloves, and made her take them upstairs where her father, Louis Stein, an invalid, was resting.

The men, Mrs. Farber said, were then satisfied that her father would not bother them, so they ordered her to take them throughout the house and to give them jewelry, money and furs.

Mrs. Ferber said the men collected a 9-carat diamond ring, valued at $36,000, a mink coat, chinchilla stole and other jewelry. She said she told the men that the only money in the house was some

Turn to Page 11, Column 5

Shortly before giving a campaign speech in Indianapolis, Kennedy learned that the Reverend Martin Luther King Jr. had been assassinated, so he informed the crowd and spoke about violence and racial injustice.

QUOTED

"I had a member of my family killed, but he was killed by a white man."

—SENATOR ROBERT KENNEDY, *April 4, 1968*

Photos of Kennedy Shooting

WEDNESDAY FINAL

RACING RESULTS-ENTRIES

Los Angeles Times

LARGEST CIRCULATION IN THE WEST, MORE THAN 950,000 DAILY; MORE THAN 1,250,000 SUNDAY.

VOL. LXXXVII FIVE PARTS—PART ONE WEDNESDAY MORNING, JUNE 5, 1968 104 PAGES Copyright © 1968 Los Angeles Times DAILY 10¢

KENNEDY SHOT

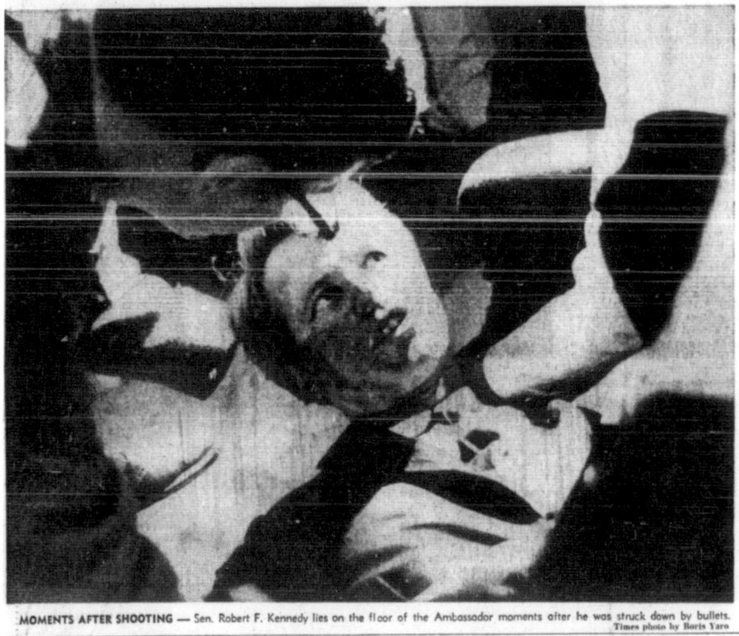

MOMENTS AFTER SHOOTING — Sen. Robert F. Kennedy lies on the floor of the Ambassador moments after he was struck down by bullets.
Times photo by Boris Yaro

Critically Wounded in Head at Victory Fete

BY DARYL E. LEMBKE
Times Staff Writer

Sen. Robert F. Kennedy was shot in the right ear early this morning in a kitchen of the Ambassador only a few moments after he had made a victory statement after capturing the California Democratic presidential primary.

The New York senator's condition was listed as critical at Good Samaritan Hospital, where he was in the intensive care unit.

A suspect in the s hooting was arrested minutes after the shots were fired and was taken to the police administration building downtown under heavy guard. The suspect was not identified.

Inspector Robert Rock of the Los Angeles police said that only one suspect was involved. Rock said there was no reason to believe more than one person was involved.

The police also have the gun that fired the shots, Rock said.

Witnesses nearby said Kennedy's head was covered with blood and a woman standing nearby was also splattered with blood.

Additional photos of Kennedy on Pages 2 and 3.

Also shot was Paul Schrade, UAW official. The extent of his injuries was not known.

The shooting occurred at 12:20 a.m.

Shouts and screams filled the packed hall as the call went out over the public address system for a doctor. Three came to Kennedy's aid as his campaign assistants pleaded for his supporters to be calm and clear the hall.

The senator appeared to be in great pain, but conscious.

As he was lifted into the police ambulance, Kennedy was heard to say:

"Oh, no! No! Don't . . .!"

Mrs. Kennedy whispered to him, apparently trying to comfort and reassure her husband. Then she entered the ambulance, doors were closed behind them and the vehicle sped away.

Kennedy was taken first to Central Receiving Hospital, then was transferred to Good Samaritan, his head wrapped in bandages.

Silence and Shock

Back in the hotel, shocked and silent members of the Kennedy party gathered in small groups around television sets, attempting to clarify their own memories of the event.

Others left in tears.

Kennedy was leaving the Ambassador to attend a party at the Factory in the aftermath of his victory in the Democratic primary.

His path through the kitchen was taken on the spur of the moment.

The assailant fired at the senator at close range and began spraying bullets around the kitchen, witnesses said.

William Barry, a former FBI agent, who is Kennedy's bodyguard, grabbed the gun from the man and wrestled him to the floor.

Roosevelt Grier, the football player, then sat on the assailant until police officers arrived

Please Turn to Page 23, Col. 8

Kennedy Wins Race; Rafferty Apparent Victor Over Kuchel

BY RICHARD BERGHOLZ
Times Political Writer

A late surge of votes from Mexican-American and Negro precincts—particularly in Los Angeles County—made Sen. Robert F. Kennedy the winner in California's Democratic Presidential primary battle Tuesday.

Sen. Eugene McCarthy of Minnesota, Kennedy's major rival in the key primary contest, said he was "reconciled" to a Kennedy triumph. But he said he intended to keep fighting for the party nomination at the Chicago convention Aug. 26.

On the Republican ballot, Dr. Max Rafferty, state superintendent of public instruction, appeared to have ended the political reign of Sen. Thomas H. Kuchel of Anaheim.

The Senate GOP whip and a veteran of 15 years on Capitol Hill ran up leads in Northern and Central California.

Rafferty Vote Projection

But the late surge of votes from Southern California wiped out the Kuchel margin and, on the basis of vote projections, appeared to have swept the conservative Rafferty to an impressive victory.

NBC analysts said their projection of the vote showed Rafferty would get 52% of the Republican vote, and Kuchel would get 45% with the balance going to lesser-known candidates.

The Democratic race for the U.S. Senate nomination was never in doubt.

Former State Controller Alan Cranston easily outdistanced four lesser-known opponents from the very start of the vote-count. For Cranston, it was a political comeback after his defeat two years ago by the current state controller, Republican Houston I. Flournoy.

Tried for Senate in 1964

Cranston had tried for the Democratic nomination for U.S. senator in 1964 but was defeated by Pierre Salinger, who then lost to Republican George Murphy in the finals.

Returns were badly delayed in Los Angeles County, where the old-style paper ballot voting system was changed this year to the IBM-Votomatic punchcard system.

Delays in transporting the punchcard ballots from the precincts to the 93 collection centers and then to the computer counters were blamed for the breakdown in tabulations.

And in Fresno County, a programming error in comp ters was blamed for a breakdown that made their returns lag far behind the rest of the state.

Even before the breakdowns in Los Angeles County, CBS projected Kennedy as the winner over McCarthy by a margin of 52% to

Please Turn to Page 23, Col. 3

L.A. COUNTY RETURNS

PRESIDENTIAL DELEGATION

Democratic
1,805 out of 6,924 Precincts

Kennedy	147,110	50%
McCarthy	115,974	39
Lynch	31,332	11

Republican
1,805 out of 6,924 Precincts

Reagan	123,501	100%

U.S. SENATE

Democratic
1,805 out of 6,924 Precincts

Cranston	143,695	54%
Bellenson	77,739	29
Buchanan	19,681	7
Bennett	16,357	6
Crail	8,358	3

Republican
1,805 out of 6,924 Precincts

Rafferty	109,740	58%
Kuchel	73,898	39
Ware	2,223	1
Jones	1,543	1
Cammack	1,473	1

CONGRESS

13th DISTRICT
Democratic
6 out of 53 Precincts

Horwitz	284	41%
Scheinbaum	277	40
Cole	134	19

13th DISTRICT
Republican
6 out of 53 Precincts

Teague (Inc.)	720	100%

17th DISTRICT
Democratic
22 out of 394 Precincts

Anderson	1,459	32%
Tucker	1,167	25
Gibson	860	19
Hayward	425	9
Frantz	377	8
Griffin	167	4
Pipersky	70	2
Van Petten	67	1

17th DISTRICT
Republican
22 out of 394 Precincts

Howard	443	34%
Blatchford	419	32
Sciarrotta	255	20
Hooper	100	8
Berry	84	6

Please Turn to Page 22, Col. 1

STATEWIDE RETURNS

PRESIDENTIAL DELEGATION

Democratic
7,486 out of 21,301 Precincts

Kennedy	426,917	45%
McCarthy	400,323	42
Lynch	117,928	12

Republican
6,997 out of 21,301 Precincts

Reagan	392,593	100%

U.S. SENATE

Democratic
7,226 out of 21,301 Precincts

Cranston	474,222	59%
Beilenson	175,545	22
Bennett	69,259	9
Buchanan	59,518	7
Crail	23,818	3

Republican
7,267 out of 21,301 Precincts

Kuchel	304,703	52%
Rafferty	264,781	45
Ware	7,502	1
Cammack	6,830	1
Jones	5,141	1

'FIRED AT POINT-BLANK RANGE'

Witness Describes Shooting, Says, 'He Didn't Have Chance'

BY DICK MAIN
Times Staff Writer

"The gunman started firing at point-blank range and Sen. Kennedy didn't have a chance."

Times photographer-reporter Boris Yaro, who was standing only three feet away from the shooting in the kitchen corridor at the Ambassador, fought back tears as he gave this graphic description of the shooting:

"I was getting ready to shoot a picture and I thought the shots were firecrackers going off.

"Kennedy backed up against the kitchen freezers as the gunman fired at him at point-blank range.

"He cringed and threw his hands up over his face.

"I think five shots were fired.

Moved Close to Kennedy

"The gunman was a short, dark-complexioned man. He moved closer toward the senator, holding a short-barrel revolver.

"Three or four people grabbed him but by then it was too late.

"I turned around and saw Sen. Kennedy lying on the floor. Blood seemed to be pouring out of a wound in his head or ear.

"It seemed as though he was trying to say something but you couldn't hear him."

"The gunman was pinned against the freezer and the gun was knocked from his hand.

"People were shouting, 'He's been shot! He's been shot!'

"Others screamed: 'Get a doctor. Bobby has been shot!'"

"The shooting took place less than a minute after Sen. Kennedy stepped off the stage at the Embassy Room. He walked behind the stage through a foyer and into a hotel kitchen corridor.

"He stopped to shake the hand of a bus boy or a waiter who was wearing a white coat.

"Then he moved to shake someone else's hand when the shots rang out."

Karl Eucker, assistant maitre d' at the hotel, helped disarm the gunman. He also witnessed the shooting.

"I heard six shots," he said. "They sounded like Chinese firecrackers.

Please Turn to Page 23, Col. 6

FEATURE INDEX

BOOK REVIEW. Page 9, Part 4.
BRIDGE. Page 11, Part 4.
CLASSIFIED. Pages 1-20, Part 5.
COMICS. Page 7, Part 2.
CROSSWORD. Page 20, Part 5.
EDITORIALS, COLUMNS. Pages 4, 5, Part 2.
ENTERTAINMENT, SOCIETY. Pages 1-21, Part 4.
FINANCIAL. Pages 9-15, Part 3.
METROPOLITAN NEWS. Part 2.
MOTION PICTURES. Pages 15-19, Part 4.
SPORTS. Pages 1-8, Part 3.
TV-RADIO. Pages 20, 21, Part 4.
VITALS, WEATHER. Page 8, Part 2.

Southland elections on Page 9, Part 2.

THE WEATHER

Light smog today.

Heavy night and morning low cloudiness with partial afternoon clearing today and Thursday. High today and Thursday near 73. Low Thursday near 59. High Tuesday, 70; low, 63.

Complete weather information on Page 8, Part 2.

A few minutes after his California primary victory speech at the Ambassador Hotel in Los Angeles, Kennedy was shot and fatally wounded by Sirhan Sirhan, a Palestinian upset over Kennedy's support for Israel.

Index is on Page 2

Classified advertising starts on Page 60

The WASHINGTON DAILY News

Greater Washington Edition **Wednesday, June 5, 1968**

1013 13th St. N.W. (20005) DI. 7-7777
47th Year—No. 181

Second Class Postage at Washington, D. C.
Published Daily Except Sunday

Weather
Sunny today, high 84. Clear tonight, low 62. Tomorrow fair, high 88.

Today at:
12 noon 79
1 a.m. 81
2 a.m. 83

7¢

RFK BATTLING FOR LIFE

Pieces of One Bullet Taken From Head in 4-Hour Surgery; It's 'Extremely Critical'

(Stories and more pictures on Pages 2, 3, 4 and 7)

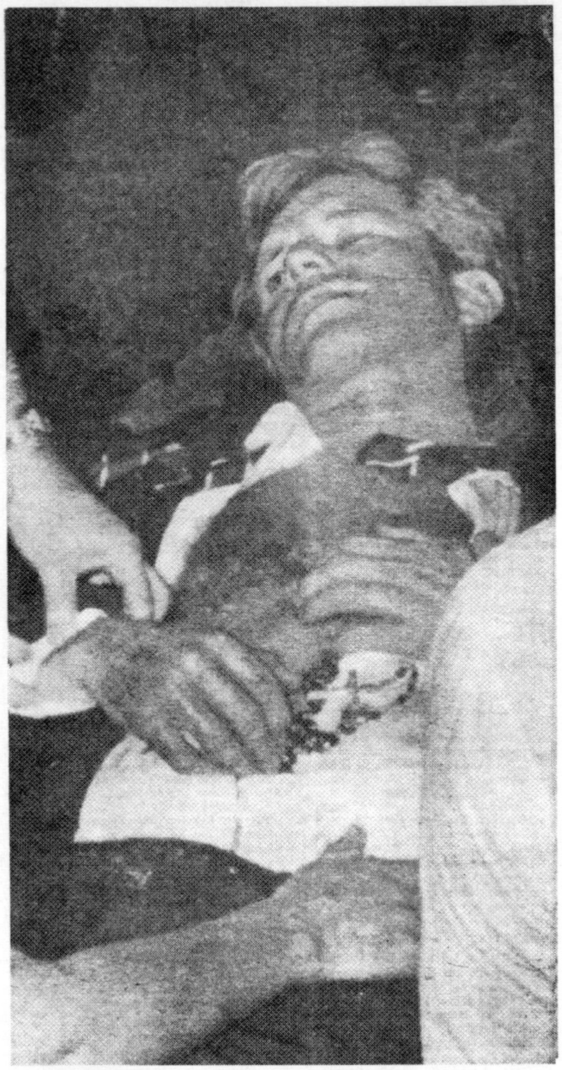

(AN EDITORIAL)

Have We Gone Mad?

At 3:15 a.m. today (Washington time) a gunman critically wounded Sen. Robert F. Kennedy in Los Angeles.

Fifteen minutes earlier, three men had entered the Little Tavern shop at Banks and M Streets in Georgetown, D.C., and, without provocation or warning, shot and killed two Marines, and wounded another Marine and a girl. The story of this other tragedy is on Page 5.

While all Americans humbly pray for the recovery of Sen. Kennedy, and the others wounded in the same fusillade in Los Angeles; and while we mourn the outrageous killings in Georgetown—and try to remain calm withal—certainly all of us must look into ourselves to try to find replies to three searing questions:

- Is our society truly as sick as it seems to be?
- What can we do about it?
- Or, have we gone irrevocably mad?

The First Moments of Tragedy

—UPI Photos

Sen. Kennedy lies wounded on the floor of a Los Angeles hotel kitchen moments after he was shot once in the head and once in the shoulder. He clutches a rosary that was given him by a priest. At left, the suspected assassin at police headquarters after the shooting. Another picture of him on Page 2.

At the time of his death, Kennedy's widow, Ethel, was pregnant with their eleventh child, Rory. Many of Kennedy's children would become politically active in the years to come.

ALSO IN 1968

James Earl Ray, the Reverend Martin Luther King Jr.'s assassin, was captured at London's Heathrow Airport.

"All the News That's Fit to Print"

The New York Times

LATE CITY EDITION

Weather: Partly sunny, warm today. Mostly cloudy tonight, tomorrow. Temp. range: today 82-63; Sat. 82-69. Temp.-Hum. Index 75; Sat. 75. Full U.S. report on Page 91.

SECTION ONE

VOL. CXVII—No. 40,314 © 1968 The New York Times Company NEW YORK, SUNDAY, JUNE 9, 1968 50 CENTS

THOUSANDS IN LAST TRIBUTE TO KENNEDY; SERVICE AT ARLINGTON IS HELD AT NIGHT

Suspect in Assassination of Dr. King Is Seized in London

RAY FOUND ARMED

Arrested at the Airport by Scotland Yard on Way From Lisbon

By FRED P. GRAHAM
Special to The New York Times

WASHINGTON, June 8 — James Earl Ray, accused of the assassination of the Rev. Dr. Martin Luther King Jr., was arrested this morning at London Airport, Attorney General Ramsey Clark announced here today.

Officers of Scotland Yard, acting on information supplied by the Federal Bureau of Investigation, arrested Ray, who the bureau said was masquerading under the name of Eric Starvo Galt at the time of the assassination in Memphis on April 4.

The fugitive's arrest was announced as Americans watched on television the funeral services in New York for Senator Robert F. Kennedy, who was fatally shot Wednesday morning in Los Angeles.

The 40-year-old Ray was apprehended as he disembarked from an airliner bound from Lisbon, Portugal, to Brussels, Belgium. He was traveling on a Canadian passport, obtained under the name of Ramon George Sneyd. The name is that of a Toronto police constable and was used without his knowledge.

Extradition Is Planned

Ray was identified as Sneyd after a search involving photographs for about 200,000 Canadian passport applications from the last year.

Officials here said that extradition proceedings would take at least a week and could be carried out on the basis of the murder charge filed against Ray in Memphis on May 7. Officials in London said it could take three to six weeks.

Ray was indicted for the murder in Memphis on April 23 under the name of Galt and was later re-indicted under his true name.

Ray has also been charged with conspiracy to violate Dr. King's civil rights, a Federal offense. But this is not an extraditable offense under United States treaties with Britain. As a measure of the importance Federal officials attach to the capture, however, Fred M. Vinson Jr., Assistant Attorney General in charge of the Criminal Division, left Washington this afternoon to fly to London.

The Justice Department issued a statement saying that he would "review on behalf of the United States the custody."

Continued on Page 74, Column 1

On Train, Kennedy Élan

By CHARLOTTE CURTIS
Special to The New York Times

WASHINGTON, June 8 — Joseph P. Kennedy 3d was the first of the Kennedys to leave the railroad car that bore his father's coffin, and after him along the aisles came his sister Courtney, his cousin Caroline and his mother, Mrs. Robert F. Kennedy. But Joe, the eldest son, was the first.

Down the swaying train he went, putting out his hand in 19 of the other 20 cars, saying "I'm Joe Kennedy," while outside in the early afternoon sun, the old men of Linden, N. J., stood silently in their undershirts and the women held handkerchiefs to their faces.

"O.K.," said Courtney, who was surrounded by women in black dresses and men in black suits.

And then, on the outskirts of Trenton, where a brass band of teen-agers in brightly colored shorts and shirts had gathered in a grassy field beside the tracks to sound taps, there was Mrs. Kennedy, all in black.

"I'm Joe Kennedy," he said to strangers, his pin-stripe black suit not yet a shambles from the failing air-conditioning, his PT boat tie clip neatly in place. "Thanks for coming," he said, thanks for coming."

Continued on Page 55, Column 4

HARLEM'S ANGUISH EASED BY ARREST

Word of Ray Arrest, on Day of Sorrow, Is Welcomed by Rights Aides Across U.S.

By JOSEPH NOVITSKI

In Harlem yesterday, the sad day of Senator Robert F. Kennedy's funeral turned into an almost happy day with news that the suspect in the death of the Rev. Dr. Martin Luther King Jr. had been captured.

Word of the arrest of James Earl Ray in London, interrupting radio and television broadcasts of the services for Senator Kennedy at 11:45 A.M., spread quickly through the community, carrying with it a sense of relief bordering on joy.

"I am so glad," a woman said as she entered a bar on 125th Street trailing a half-filled shopping cart behind her. "I thought he was dead when they didn't catch him for so long."

At the same time, word of the arrest was welcomed by civil rights leaders here and by officials in the South.

Statement by Young

Whitney M. Young Jr., executive director of the National Urban League, issued the following statement from his offices at 55 East 52d Street:

"We are, of course, gratified that the man accused of Dr. King's assassination has been arrested. The Negro must have such visible evidence that the law will work for him as well as for others if his faith in the American system is to be sustained."

Gov. Lester G. Maddox of Georgia, in Dr. King's home town of Atlanta, said he was delighted at the arrest, according to The Associated Press.

In Memphis, where Dr. King was shot, Chief of Police

Continued on Page 78, Column 3

President Joins Kennedys In Tribute at Graveside

By TOM WICKER
Special to The New York Times

WASHINGTON, June 8 — Senator Robert F. Kennedy was buried tonight in the glow of floodlights, not far from President Kennedy's grave on the hillside at Arlington National Cemetery.

With President and Mrs. Johnson looking on, the flag that draped the murdered Senator's coffin was removed and folded and then handed by John H. Glenn Jr., the former astronaut, to Senator Edward M. Kennedy, now the head of the nation's most prominent political family.

Mr. Kennedy handed the folded flag to Joseph P. Kennedy 3d, the dead man's eldest son, and he gave it to his mother, Mrs. Ethel Kennedy.

The burial at Arlington ended an exhausting day and came about five hours later than originally scheduled. The long delay was caused by the slow pace of the funeral train from New York.

Continued on Page 55, Column 1

CITY-BOUND TRAIN KILLS 2 MOURNERS

5 Others Hurt in Jersey as Crowds Press In to Catch Glimpse of Kennedys

By EDWARD C. BURKS

A man and a woman were killed yesterday as they stood in a crowd watching the Kennedy funeral train pass the Elizabeth, N.J., railroad station.

The train had to be slowed at one point because another train had hit several persons in a waiting crowd at Elizabeth, N.J. Delays in leaving New York's Pennsylvania Station had thrown the 21-car train behind schedule before it started.

Its slow pace all along the line put it further off its expected timetable.

President and Mrs. Johnson and Vice President and Mrs. Humphrey met the train at the edge of the crowd that had overflowed onto one of the four tracks.

The deaths were part of a string of mishaps that plagued the Kennedy train on its 226-mile trip from New York to Washington. Six other persons were injured. The Penn Central Railroad ordered all northbound trains stopped along the route to prevent further harm to

Continued on Page 54, Column 7

JOHNSON AT RITES

Edward Kennedy Pays Tribute to Brother in Crowded Cathedral

Texts of the eulogies are printed on Page 56.

By J. ANTHONY LUKAS

New York bade a solemn but strangely joyful farewell yesterday to Robert Francis Kennedy, who in death had come to symbolize many people's hopes for a fresh breath of life.

A pontifical requiem mass celebrated in the new spirit of the Ecumenical Council by Archbishop Terence J. Cooke of New York, combined anguished moments of grief with the bright Christian expectations of rebirth.

Then the body of the Senator was put aboard a train to Washington for burial in Arlington National Cemetery near the grave of President John F. Kennedy.

More than 2,300 people attending the mass, including President Johnson, heard Richard Cardinal Cushing of Boston cry in his South Boston twang, "Christ have mercy," reminding many of his somber eulogy at the funeral of the Senator's brother five years ago.

'A Good And Decent Man'

But they also heard a white-robed choir high in the loft raise their voices in the exultant "Hallelujah, Hallelujah, Hallelujah" of the chorus from Handel's "Messiah."

And they also heard Senator Edward M. Kennedy of Massachusetts, Robert Kennedy's brother, declare from the white marble sanctuary, just above the African mahogany coffin:

"My brother need not be idealized or enlarged in death beyond what he was in life. He should be remembered simply as a good and decent man, who saw wrong and tried to right it, saw suffering and tried to heal it, saw war and tried to stop it.

"Those of us who loved him and who take him to his rest today pray that what he was to us, and what he wished for others, will someday come to pass for all the world.

"As he said so many times, in many parts of this nation, to

Continued on Page 53, Column 3

REQUIEM: Senator Edward M. Kennedy addressing the congregation at St. Patrick's Cathedral, standing above his brother's coffin. Directly in front of him are members of Robert F. Kennedy's family and relatives. Behind him is Archbishop Terence J. Cooke. At lower left is President Johnson. On the throne at the far left is Richard Cardinal Cushing.

Bidault Returns to France and Is Given Freedom

By JOHN L. HESS
Special to The New York Times

PARIS, June 8 — Georges Bidault of France returned from exile in Brazil today and was given his freedom by the regime that he opposed fiercely during the war in Algeria.

The lifting of an arrest warrant charging him with "insurrectional activities" seemed to strengthen the reconciliation between President de Gaulle and rightist and nationalist Frenchmen in the national election campaign.

The return lent support to reports that amnesty would soon be granted to Gen. Raoul Salan, the last important figure still in prison for the 1962 insurgent movement that opposed ending French control over Algeria.

It was rumored that Jacques Soustelle, former Gaullist who was an associate of Mr. Bidault in his clandestine Council of National Resistance, would also return from exile soon.

Algerian Charge Dropped— Action Viewed as a Step in Reconciliation of Rightists

The resistance council was linked with the Secret Army Organization that Mr. Bidault was said to have headed after March, 1962, when he went into exile after his break with President de Gaulle on plans to grant independence to Algeria.

Mr. Bidault had supported General de Gaulle in 1958, when the general returned to power on what many considered a step toward the division of France into two blocs: the right and center-right behind the regime, the left and center-left in the opposition.

Last week, many of the former colonists in Algeria and other nationalists rallied to the Government after General de Gaulle dissolved the National Assembly and appealed for help

to save France from "totalitarianism."

Their leaders urged, however, that the Government grant amnesty to the last 10 "patriots" still in prison for terrorist acts or rebellion, and lift the arrest warrants against fugitives living abroad. Some ultra-rightists refused to give their blessing to the regime, even in the face of what General de Gaulle termed Communist peril, until this was done.

Mr. Bidault, 68 years old, slight and in poor health, has been living in Brussels after a long sojourn in Brazil.

Accompanied by his wife and two lawyers, he appeared this morning at the frontier post of Baisieux, on the road from Brussels to Lille. A French detachment of gendarmes was waiting for him.

Border formalities were waived and the party drove directly to the Fort de l'Est, the seat of the special State Security Court set up during

Continued on Page 17, Column 1

They Line the Tracks to Say Good-by

By RUSSELL BAKER
Special to The New York Times

Robert F. Kennedy's family brought him back to Washington for the last time today by train, and megalopolis, tan America lined the rails to say good-by.

The journey, slowed by accidents along the way and great crowds that often forced the train to slow almost to a stop, lasted from 1:02 P.M. to 9:08 P.M.— more than twice as long as had been expected.

Drawn by two black electric locomotives of the Penn Central Railroad, the funeral train traveled the 226 miles

from New York through an almost unbroken succession of station throngs, urban street crowds and clusters of small-town mourners.

In the rural stretches separating the great Eastern cities, girls came to the railroad on horseback. Boys sat in the trees. In a desolate swampy section of New Jersey, a lone man knelt in prayer by the trackside. In the loneliest sections, family groups clustered around cars parked in the woods to hold up flags, to wave, or to salute.

It would be idle to guess at how many saw the train bearing the Senator's body.

The train's route took it through the greatest concentration of population on the continent, and in many places it seemed as if whole towns had turned out.

In many places the crowds ignored undermanned police lines and swarmed dangerously onto adjacent tracks to be closer to the train.

The train cortege has been part of the American legend since Walt Whitman immortalized Abraham Lincoln's funeral train back to Illinois in "When Lilacs Last in the Dooryard Bloomed."

There has probably been

Continued on Page 53, Column 3

Today's Sections

Section		
Section 1 (3 Parts)	Section	News
Section 2	Drama, Movies, Garden, Stamps, TV, Radio	
Section 3	Financial and Business	
Section 4	Review of the week	
Section 5	Sports	
Section 6	Magazine	
Section 7	Book Review	
Section 8	Real Estate	
Section 9	Employment Advertising	
Section 10	Resorts and Travel	
Section 11	Advertising	
Section 12	Advertising	

Index to Subjects

	Section	Page
Art	2	21-23
Boating	5	8-12
Bridge	2	148
Camera	2	20
Chess	5	24-35
Coins	2	15
Dance	2	13
Drama	2	1-7
Editorial	4	14
Education	4	11
Fashions	6	94
Ford	6	97
Garden	2	28-40
Home Fashions	6	100
Letters to the Editor	4	15
Movies	2	8-16
Music	2	17-19
News Summary & Index	1	91
Obituaries	1	84-85
Puzzles	2	119
Radio-TV	2	25-30
Records	2	21-24
Science	4	15
Ships and Aviation	5	24-25
Society	1	86-104
Women	2	93
Weather	1	91

JOBS FOR LIBRARIANS AND TEACHERS

The only surviving brother, Senator Edward Kennedy, became the eulogist of the family. Robert Kennedy was buried at Arlington National Cemetery, a short distance from where his brother John had been laid to rest five years before.

Jacqueline Kennedy and children Caroline and John Jr. passed the casket of Senator Robert Kennedy at his funeral. (AP Photo)

QUOTED

"My brother need not be idealized, or enlarged in death beyond what he was in life."

—SENATOR EDWARD KENNEDY, June 8, 1968 (see pages 111–113)

[TRIBUNE Staff Photos]

Youngsters from Kennedy school for retarded children in Palos Park parade past reviewing stand at Chicago Special Olympics.

1,000 Retarded Kids Compete in Chicago Special Olympics

BY SARA JANE GOODYEAR

With pageantry, a parade and bugles, the Chicago Special Olympics opened yesterday in Soldiers' field.

The Olympic torch blazed while runners dashed for the finish line, but it was the smiles and looks of pride by the children that told the story.

The participants were nearly 1,000 retarded children who had come from 23 states and Canada to compete in 200 sports events and to spend a day in the spotlight.

Gov. Shapiro and Mayor Daley welcomed the children, and William McFetridge, president of the park board, called the Olympics a beginning. Mrs. Eunice Kennedy Shriver, wife of the United States ambassador to France, flew in from Paris to represent the Joseph P. Kennedy Jr. Foundation, which co-sponsored the event with the park district.

Amazed at Abilities

Many of the park district officials were amazed at the physical ability shown by the young competitors, whose ages ranged from 8 to 18 and whose I.Q.'s were from 30 to 75.

"Ninety per cent of them seem to run normally," said Ray McDonald, a park district supervisor who was timing the running events. "Their times are almost comparable to the times of normal kids, and they seem to have much more enthusiasm. They don't pick favorites, they cheer everyone."

McDonald said the children didn't get upset by losing. They just seem to enjoy being here and participating," he said.

Mrs. Eunice Kennedy Shriver at reviewing stand with youngsters who participated in sporting events.

The children, well chaperoned by teachers and aprents, participated in the 50-yard dash, 300-yard run, high jump, broad jump, baseball throw a field hockey game, and swimming races. They were grouped by age and skill levels.

Those who finished first thru third were awarded a total of 600 gold, silver, and bronze medallions. All others received sesquicentennial medallions.

They started the events with a parade by states, marching to the music of the Great Lakes Naval Training center band and waving to spectators as they passed the reviewing stand.

They also worked with Stan Mikita, Paul Hornung, Rafer Johnson, George Connor, Bob Mathias, and other famous athletes in sports clinics.

At a press conference before the Olympics began, Mrs. Shriver pledged $75,000 from the Kennedy Foundation for regional Olympics for the retarded during 1969. In 1970, and every two years thereafter, international special Olympics will be held, she said.

"Can Realize Potential"

"The Chicago Special Olympics proves retarded children can be exceptional athletes; that thru sports they can realize their potential for growth," said Mrs. Shriver.

"But they [the children participating yesterday] are only 1,000 out of 1.5 million mentally retarded children who should be given a chance to compete in games like this all over America. Our purpose here today is to secure a pledge that all retarded children will be given this chance in the future."

TRIBUNE, SUNDAY, JULY 21, 1968

TALKS BEGUN BY NIGERIANS AND BIAFRANS

NIAMEY, Niger, July 20 [Reuters] — Federal Nigerian and Biafran delegations began talks here today about a proposed peace conference in Addis Ababa, Ethiopia.

The Niger President, Hamani Diori, was acting as chairman of the talks which were held in a small conference chamber at the presidential palace.

The first session adjourned after 2¾ hours. The delegations will meet again tomorrow.

The five-member Nigerian delegation was led by Aison Ayida, secretary to the economic development ministry. The nine-member Biafran team was headed by Eni Njoku, former Nsukka university vice-chancellor.

Responds to Appeal

The two sides agreed to talk about talks after an appeal by the African Unity Organization consultative committee on Nigeria, meeting here since Monday.

The OAU's committee called on both sides to agree to a "mercy corridor" thru Nigeria for food and medicine for the 500,000 hungry Biafrans.

Each side has made suggestions on how to get the food and drugs into Biafra, but neither has agreed to the other's proposal, leaving the refugees on the verge of starvation, observers said.

The leader of break-away Biafra, Lt. Col. Odumegwu Ojukwu, left for home today after talks with Ethiopian officials including Foreign Minister Ketem Yifru.

No Statement Issued

No statement was issued after the meeting, and Ojukwu refused to speak with newsmen.

In Lagos, Nigeria, Maj. Gen. Yakubu Cowon, federal military ruler, Friday night warned international relief organizations not to meddle in the Nigerian political crisis under the guise of humanitarianism.

Millions May Die in Biafra, Student Seeking Funds Says

BY THOMAS ASKENS

"The lives of 14 million people are at stake. Unless massive help comes soon, this may become the worst tragedy in military history. They are trying to exterminate Biafra."

Jim Bob Achebe spoke angrily because of his personal commitment in the Biafran war.

Achebe, 22, a Biafran, is a Cambridge graduate working on a Ph.D. in engineering at the Illinois Institute of Technology. He is residing temporarily in Hyde Park.

He understands the technology of modern war, and this is a "civilized" war in some respects — one side, Nigeria, fighting with Russian MIG planes; on the other, the breakaway region of Biafra, using oil company helicopters converted into gunships and several other "sides," throwing modern weapons in.

Die of Starvation

The uncivilized aspects are symbolized by Red Cross reports of 12,000 Biafrans dying of starvation every day while governments seem powerless to stop it.

Achebe pointed to what he believed were the roots of the crisis:

"In 1914-1916, the British pulled together Moslem tribes of the north, the Christian tribes of the east, and the mixed Moslem and Christian tribes of the west — all with different languages and ideas of what life should be. They pulled it together and christened it Nigera. Africans have said it's three different West African countries with nothing in common.

"The north held closely to its old feudal system of chiefs and workers, who received no pay except three meals a day and a place to sleep.

Bias Charged

"For years, we easterners couldn't get a job in the north. The first choice for an opening was an Arab; second, a Briton; Arabs-first system would be disrupted and held back from any change.

"Because the east had the second highest level of literacy in Africa, and those in the north were mostly illiterate, this was especially irritating," he went on.

"In the industrial east and west, all competed equally for equal pay.

"From 1948 on, in a push for independence, it appeared the only way to get the British out was to let the north dominate the new government," he explained. "The north feared its Arabs-first system would be disrupted and held back from any change.

Speaking to the osteophatic group's house of delegates in the Drake hotel, Dr. Earl K. Lyons of Chandler, Ariz., criticized the A. M. A. as an annual convention last month in San Francisco, the A. M. A. acted to amalgamate osteopathy with medicine.

[TRIBUNE Staff Photo]

Jim Bob Achebe outside Hyde Park apartment building where he lives.

joined when he declared that discrimination in jobs, even housing, would end in all of Nigeria.

"Five days later, 20,000 Biafrans living in the north were slaughtered . . . university professors, students, and businessmen were killed. Their property was looted and burned, their children killed."

"Ironsi appealed for calm and appointed a commission of inquiry.

"In a month, he was kidnaped and a mass slaughter of the Ibo tribe, the Biafrans, raged thru the whole country except Biafra. Two and a half million Biafrans fled to their homeland, leaving everything behind."

Maj. Gen. Yakubu Gowon, northern Moslem, took control of the country. He ordered all Biafrans back to their jobs and guaranteed their safety.

"Everyone thought it would be the end of the killing," Achebe said. It was not the end. It was the beginning.

Invaded by North

After a try at a peaceful agreement, while the north repudiated, Biafra proclaimed its independence. The north invaded Biafra with 65,000 troops a week later. Biafra pushed them back with 40,000 men, but now the war is in Biafra.

"My family had moved to a country home. All of them sounded optimistic in their last letter, but I don't know how they're living."

Help Is Needed

"What we need, in the short term, is help for the millions of refugees. Two million may die before the end of August unless there is some massive airlift of supplies. The extermination is taking place at a very fast pace. They are trying to starve us in the hope that the civilians will rise up against our Biafran troops.

"The United States can no longer fold its arms. We appeal to the American people to put pressure on their senators and congressmen to ask that the British desist from aggression and to help both sides to a lasting peace."

Jim Bob Achebe has learned that he is getting thru where it counts. More than 20 Chicago church, business, and labor leaders are forming a committee both to raise food and money for Biafra and to demand American political action.

The address will be Emergency Committee for Biafran Relief, suite 838, 33 N. Dearborn st., Chicago, Ill. 60602. Telephone, 236-3125.

MERGER PLAN OF A. M. A. HIT BY OSTEOPATH

The president of the American Osteopathic association has said that the nation's osteopaths would continue to resist efforts of the American Medical association to merge the two groups.

General Takes Power

When an eastern-born general, Maj. Gen. Aguiyi-Ironsi, seized power in 1964 he found that Shell British Petroleum was paying almost nothing in taxes, taking 90 to 95 per cent of its profits out of the country. So he tried to reform the northern-controlled tax system. Then, on May 24, 1966, we re-

PHILIPPINES RECALL AIDS

MANILA, P. I., July 20 [P]— President Ferdinand Marcos today recalled the Philippine ambassador and most of his staff from Malaysia in what the action he termed a "drastic" move in the next step to severing diplomatic relations.

Marcos said the action resulted from Malaysia's rejection of the Philippines' claims to Sabah and the Malaysian delegation's walking out of the lapsed discussions in Bangkok, Thailand.

Sabah, a 29,000 square mile territory on Borneo's northern tip, is rich in rubber, timber, and fishing. Malaysia claims the sultan of Sulu gave up on

the territory in 1878. It became a British protectorate in 1946, declared itself independent after a referendum in 1962 and joined the federation of Malaysia in 1963. The Philippines claim the sultan never gave up Sabah and insists no new Philippine citizens, handed over the rights to Sabah in 1962 to the Philippine government.

South Side Service Station Robbed of $60

Two robbers took $60 yesterday from Lyon's service station, 3636 Vincennes av. An attendant, Jim Tegmeyer of 11614 Nagle av., told police that one of the robbers struck him on the head.

REPORT FROM EUROPE
By Arthur Veysey
CHIEF OF CHICAGO TRIBUNE'S LONDON BUREAU

3,000 Children Die
Daily in Nigeria,
Nurse Reports

LONDON, July 20—An English nurse who has devoted her life to helping Africans in Nigeria says 3,000 children are now dying there every day of famine and disease brought on by a year of civil war.

She says it's high time Britain stops sending guns to Nigeria and starts sending food and medicine. Prime Minister Harold Wilson donated $600,000 from the exchequer and set aside Monday in the house of commons for a discussion of Britain's responsibilities to what was once considered its best ex-colony in Africa.

Nobody knows, even vaguely, how many of Nigeria's 55 million have died since fighting began there last July, but the toll certainly has passed 150,000, and starvation is only beginning to kill. More people are dying in Nigeria than in Viet Nam.

The worst sufferers are the Ibos, long considered the smartest, most energetic people in west Africa. Christian missions, especially Irish Catholics, have had great success among the Ibos, and the Ibos have had great success as business men, bankers, technicians, civil servants, army officers, and as professors throughout Nigeria and along the west African coast.

The Ibos, who a year ago numbered about 10 million, have often been called the Jews of west Africa. Today their leaders say ancient enemies, unleashed after being kept in check by several generations by British rulers, intend to wipe out the Ibos just as the Nazis tried to eliminate Jews from Europe.

Ibos Set Off the Killing

IT WAS, HOWEVER, ambitious Ibos who set off the killing. After Britain left Nigeria in 1960, a Moslem Hausa from the grasslands of northern Nigeria became prime minister and Hausas joined with Christian Yorubas, who lived in the jungled south like the Ibos, to dominate the federal government. Early in 1966 Ibos killed the Hausa premier and Yoruba vice premier and several other officials. An Ibo, Gen. Ironsi, became head of the government.

Among the jealous young-Nigerian supporters was a 31-year-old lieutenant colonel named Odumegwu Ojukwu, whose father had become one of Nigeria's first self-made millionaires. Queen Elizabeth knighted him.

Veysey Gowen Nation Divided Ojukwu

The son grew up in England, studied history at Oxford, drove a young rival lieutenant colonel, Yakubu Gowen, a Methodist lay preacher's son who had grown up in Nigerian mission schools and been trained at Sandhurst, Britain's West Point. He was a northerner but a Christian and a member of a small tribe. He happened to be taking a post-graduate military course in England at the time of the slaughter so he might well have died that night.

Chooses Rival Lieutenant Colonel

TRYING TO PLACATE other areas, the general chose for his chief of staff a young rival lieutenant colonel, Yakubu Gowen, a Methodist lay preacher's son who had grown up in Nigerian mission schools and been trained at Sandhurst, Britain's West Point. He was a northerner but a Christian and a member of a small tribe. He happened to be taking a post-graduate military course in England at the time of the slaughter so he might well have died that night.

After five months, the Hausas and Yorubas struck back, killing Ironsi and thousands of Ibos who lived among them. Surviving Ibos streamed home, abandoning everything. Young Gowon became head of Nigeria, promoting himself, of course, also to major general.

Last summer his rival, Ojukwu, declared eastern Nigeria independent as the new nation of Biafra. Gowon sent troops to arrest him. The rebels counter-invaded into Yoruba country but was gradually driven back. Now, after a year, Gowon's federal army has taken the capital, its port, its oil fields. The Ibos are driven into a forested area about 100 miles square. They are almost out of bullets. Gowon's Capellanism planes landing on a widened road are the only live connection with the rest of the world.

World Church Group Moves to Ecumenism

UPPSALA, Sweden, July 20 [P]— The fourth assembly of the World Council of Churches has closed with some dramatic steps toward ecumenism, particularly with the sometime Roman Catholic church.

The two-week meeting, which ended yesterday, did much to extend the influence of the council beyond its own membership to encompass a major portion of the world's 900 million Christians. Its conciliatory gestures to the Catholic church, represented by 15 official observers, and to conservative Christian nonaffiliates, played a major role.

Take Active Part

In previous meetings, orthodox spokesmen frequently remained aloof from discussion and on occasion even disavowed official decisions. But at Uppsala they gave their active participation and their weight was felt in the group's decisions.

The council, for the first time, also emphasized the voice of youth, accrediting some 150 "youth participants" to the meeting and giving them semi-official status.

The council's new central committee, which was enlarged from 100 to 120 members, met today to choose its new officers. M. M. Thomas of India was named chairman and Mrs. Pauline Webb of London, vice chairman.

The committee will run council affairs until the group's next assembly, probably six or seven years from now.

big all-night sit-in at World Council of Churches assembly in Uppsala, Sweden. Placards contain resolutions demonstrators wanted implemented by churches.

pate in the faith and order commission. This is largely a theological dialog agency which would boost the work of the liberal ecumenical Catholic element.

In another direction, Eastern Orthodox denominations, including a delegation from the Russian church, participated in the meeting for the first time in the group's 20-year history.

Iron Theological Differences

On theological differences, the prospects for agreement were less dramatic but still far from bleak.

Altho the Catholic church still is not a member of the council, it is the only major Christian body remaining outside. Roman Catholics will parti-

ALSO IN 1968

Vietnam War protesters fought police in Chicago's streets and parks during the Democratic National Convention.

Eunice Kennedy Shriver's close friendship with her older, developmentally disabled sister, Rosemary, inspired her to organize camps for people with disabilities. That led to the first Special Olympics Games at Soldier Field in Chicago. (Clipping at right from Chicago Tribune)

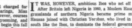

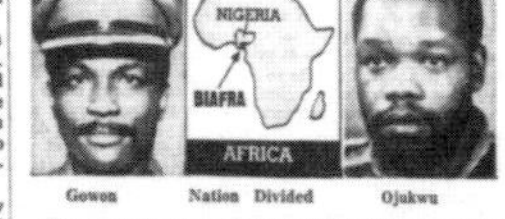

CLOSING STOCKS **Boston Evening Globe** CLOSING STOCKS

© 1968, Globe Newspaper Co. 288-8000 FRIDAY, OCTOBER 18, 1968 • 46 PAGES—10 CENTS

Jacqueline Will Marry Onassis Sunday

Greek Island Sealed Off As Bride-to-Be Arrives | Kennedy Sisters There for Rites | She and Tycoon Will Live In Her N.Y. Apartment

ONASSIS AND JACQUELINE—A wedding on island of Skorpios and a new life. (AP, UPI)

By JOHN RIGOS
United Press International

ANDRAVIDA, Greece—Greek billionaire Aristotle Onassis today greeted Jacqueline Kennedy with a kiss on the cheek and then flew off with her to his private island in the Ionian Sea for their marriage, on Sunday.

A spokesman for Onassis said the wedding would be as private as possible and no reporters or photographers would be permitted.

Honeymoon plans were not disclosed.

In New York, Nancy Tuckerman, Mrs. Kennedy's secretary, said the couple will live later in Mrs. Kennedy's home on Fifth Avenue and the children will continue at their present schools.

Strict security precautions were in effect when Mrs. Kennedy's special jet airliner landed at Andravida after the flight from New York. Heavy police forces kept newsmen, photographers and spectators some distance away from this Greek air force base.

The 62-year-old Onassis greeted Mrs. Kennedy first with a kiss on the cheek, air base sources reported. He then kissed the other members of the family.

The 39-year-old widow of President John F. Kennedy flew here in a DC8 jetliner of Olympia Airlines, owned by her husband-to-be. She was accompanied by her two children, her mother and stepfather, and two of her late husband's sisters.

JACQUELINE
Page 18

Hanoi Replies To Peace Bid

By GEORGE SIBERA
United Press International

PARIS — North Vietnamese diplomatic sources today said Hanoi has replied to the latest U.S. proposals aimed at achieving a breakthrough in the Vietnam war.

The sources gave no further details.

Earlier, the Communist sources had confirmed that the Hanoi regime had received new peace overtures from the United States.

The U.S. suggestions were said by the Hanoi sources to be under urgent review. An answer outlining Hanoi's position will be given shortly by Xuan Thuy, the North Vietnamese negotiator, to Ambassador W. Averell Harriman, the sources said.

It was the first time Hanoi officials had acknowledged in private the existence of an American peace package. Presumably the plan sought assurances that Hanoi will not take advantage of an American bombing halt, and suggested that both Saigon and the National Liberation Front (NLF) be admitted to the peace talks.

The sources said the Hanoi answer would come soon. Presumably, it would be conveyed by Thuy to Harriman at their 27th negotiating meeting at the Majestic Hotel next Wednesday—if not in secret earlier.

Presumably, the decision was a tough one for Hanoi. Observers remarked that North Vietnam hitherto has flatly refused to deal with

BOMBING
Page 22

Apollo 7 Maneuver Jolts Crew

Associated Press

SPACE CENTER, Houston—With a jolting burst of energy, the Apollo 7 astronauts fired their steering engine today in the most powerful maneuver ever made by a manned spaceship.

"Yabba - dubba - doo!" shouted Navy Capt Walter M. Schirra Jr. as the huge engine flashed to life and spurted a steady tail of flame for 66 seconds as Apollo 7 raced 120 miles above the Gulf of Mexico.

"That was a real nice to-do, the machine performed beautifully," spacecraft commander Schirra reported at the completion of this vital test of the engine that one day will guide American astronauts to the moon.

APOLLO
Page 17

Nixon Sees War End in '68

By S. J. MICCICHE

Former Vice President Richard M. Nixon, in Boston today, said he believes that the Vietnam war will end before January 20.

Nixon, addressing a crowd of some 1500 Republican party workers at the Hotel Somerset, said of Vietnam:

". . . and I trust that the war will be brought to an honorable conclusion before the next administration takes office."

The Republican nominee made the statement while discussing what he felt to be the major foreign policy problems confronting the United States.

His reference to Vietnam was merely in passing. He has declined to enter any deep discussion of the Southeast Asian war while the negotiations for its settlement are in progress in Paris.

He urged them to "go out and talk to the fence sitters and to Democrats and Independents." This is essentially the same message he has delivered to similar audiences since he won the nomination.

He said, "We have got to show why people should be voting for" the Nixon-Agnew ticket rather than against Vice President Hubert Humphrey or former Alabama governor George Wallace.

"We don't want to back into it (Presidency). We want to win it going away," said Nixon.

He exhuded a feeling of confidence, saying that his is the analysis of a "candidate who has gone around this country and found there is a feeling we're ahead."

At the same time, he indicated some nervousness, reminding his audience, "I'm the expert on losing the close ones."

NIXON
Page 20

HH Finds Happiness At Home Off Range

By MARTIN F. NOLAN

HARTFORD — Vice President Humphrey is becoming "his own man" in his campaign and finding the process of maturation less traumatic than he thought.

Shedding the adolescent shackles of the Vice Presidency, Humphrey has become increasingly outspoken, heedless of the Eyes of Texas that have inhibited him for the past four years.

"I don't care whether Johnson wanted to debate or not. I do. I want a debate," he told the Detroit Economic Club.

HUMPHREY
Page 21

MRS. KENNEDY

HARLECH

CALLAS

Rose Hopes They'll Be Happy

Mrs. Rose Kennedy said today she hopes Jacqueline Kennedy and Aristole Onassis will be very happy together.

She was approached by newsmen after attending services in St. Francis Xavier Church in Hyannis.

"I wish them great happiness," Mrs. Kennedy said when asked about how she felt about her daughter-in-law's marriage.

She had nothing else to say on the subjejct. Earlier, her secretary said Mrs. Kennedy would have no comment.

In London, Lord Harlech, whose name had been linked romantically with that of President John F. Kennedy's widow, wished the couple well.

"Mrs. Kennedy has been a very close friend for more than 14 years," he said. "I'm very happy about it. I certainly hope they will be happy."

Harlech, 50, a widower and a Roman Catholic, had been considered by many the man most likely to become Mrs. Kennedy's second husband.

In Paris, opera star Maria Callas also said she was happy, though she didn't sound it.

Telephoned for her reaction, the fiery diva said, "Very good. I am delighted for both of them."

Then she slammed down the receiver, and refused all other calls.

REACTION
Page 18

U.S. Drops 2 Blacks; Olympic Mates Shocked

Globe Wire Services

MEXICO CITY — The U.S. Olympic Committee suspended star Negro sprinters Tommie Smith and John Carlos from the U.S. Olympic team after midnight Thursday for "untypical exhibitionism" during an Olympic victory ceremony Wednesday.

The decision followed a complaint by the International Olympic Committee regarding the conduct of Smith when he received the gold medal for winning the 200-meter event and Carlos when he was presented the bronze medal for finishing third in the 200-meter finals Wednesday.

The Committee gave Carlos and Smith 48 hours to leave Mexico.

Both Smith and Carlos raised clenched fists clothed in black gloves during the playing of the Star Spangled Banner and also wore black knee socks without shoes during the presentation ceremony.

They also wore identical buttons on their team uniforms citing demands for racial equality.

The first reaction among American athletes in Olympic Village was one of shock and bewilderment.

"It is unfair, it is ridiculous," said Art Walker, a Negro triple jumper from Los Angeles who already has competed.

"They say they are doing it because of a protest. This is silly. Since the early 1900's the United States team has been protesting similarly by failing to dip its flag when it passes the reviewing stand. All other countries do it. This is strictly political."

Most countries dip their flags when passing in review but it is against government regulations to dip the American flag under any circumstances. Flag bearers in the Olympic parade have always followed Army and Navy protocol in this re pect.

ATHLETES
Page 29

COSTLY GESTURE—Gold and Bronze medal winners Tommie Smith, center, and John Carlos, right, were sent home by the United States Olympic Committee. The Black Power salute was given Thursday after the presentation of medals. (UPI)

Stocks Surge To New Highs

The stock market this afternoon surged to new two-year highs ina renewal of yesterday's "peace rally".

The closing Dow Jones Industrial Average at 967.49 was up 8.58 from yesterday's close. See Page 33.

INSIDE HEADLINES

BOY SCOUTS TO GO COED—Plans are afoot to let Girl Scouts join Boy Scout troops.
Page 3

MALENKOV BACK IN MOSCOW—Former top Russian reappears in capital after years in virtual exile.
Page 17

GLADYS' WINDS LESSEN—But hurricane's tides pose big threat to Florida coast.
Page 17

N.Y. SCHOOL CRISIS—Janitors refuse to cross striking teachers' picket lines.
Page 19

INDEX TO TONIGHT'S GLOBE

Astro-Guide	36	Crossword	36	Society	12
Book	14	Deaths	38	Sports	25-30
Bridge	8	Editorials	10	TV-Radio	37
Churches	30, 31	Financial	32-34	Theaters	14-17
Classified	39-45	Senior Set	14	Twistagram	36
Comics	36	Shain	37	Women	12, 13

THE WEATHER

Tonight—Increasing cloudiness, low in low 60's.

Saturday—Mostly cloudy, chance of rain.

High Tide at 9:18 p.m. Full Reports, Page 22

Jacqueline Kennedy was 39 when she married the 62-year-old Greek billionaire Aristotle Onassis on his private island off the western coast of Greece. About 20 people, including John F. Kennedy Jr., 7, and his sister, Caroline, 10, attended the short service.

Through the lenses of the paparazzi, the stoic widow of President John F. Kennedy became the trendsetting cultural icon "Jackie O." (AP Photo)

ALSO IN 1968

Former Republican Vice President Richard Nixon defeated Democratic Vice President Hubert Humphrey in the presidential election.

July 18, 1969
Senator Edward Kennedy Drove Car into Water off Chappaquiddick

Edward Kennedy drove off the bridge on Chappaquiddick Island near Martha's Vineyard, killing his passenger, Mary Jo Kopechne, a former campaign worker for Robert Kennedy. By the time Kennedy reported the wreck to police the next day, the car already had been discovered with Kopechne's body inside.

Boston Sunday Globe

© 1969, Globe Newspaper Co. • VOLUME 196 NO. 20 SUNDAY, JULY 20, 1969 • 35 CENTS

Police Seek Leaving-the-Scene Complaint

Ted Kennedy Escapes, Woman Dies As Car Plunges Into Vineyard Pond

CAR SEN. KENNEDY DROVE IS PULLED FROM POND ... spectators watch from bridge. (AP)

'There's a Car in the Water'

By TIMOTHY LELAND
Staff Writer

CHAPPAQUIDDICK ISLAND—It was Saturday morning, a day of rest for some people, but not for Tony Bettencourt, caretaker of the island dump.

Every day is a work day for Tony in the Summers, even Sundays, because the folk who come down to the island for their vacations make a mess at the dump, and the sea gulls pick the garbage bags apart and spread the refuse all over the place, and Tony has to rake it all up and shovel it back where it belongs.

Chappaquiddick Island doesn't have any stores on it or gas stations. It has a fire station though, big enough for a single fire truck, pride and joy of the seven families who live on the island year around. And it has the dump, which is a pretty big responsibility for Tony Bettencourt, especially in July and August when there are so many Summer folk on the island.

Yesterday morning Tony drove his four-wheel-drive beach jeep down the dirt road to the dike bridge to pick up Johnny Smith, just as always.

Johnny, who helps Tony rake up the dump, is 14 years old, son of Rev. David Smith, and when Tony drove up to his house at 9 a.m. yesterday he could see the Edgartown police chief's car up ahead, right by the wooden bridge, and Johnny came running down the road toward him, even before he came to a stop.

ISLAND Page 35

Senator Wanders In Daze for Hours

By RICHARD POWERS and ALAN LUPO
Staff Writers

EDGARTOWN—Sen. Edward M. Kennedy, the only surviving brother in a family pursued by tragedy, narrowly escaped death early yesterday when his car plunged into a pond on a sparsely inhabited island off the coast of Martha's Vineyard.

A passenger, Mary Jo Kopechne, 28, of Washington, a former campaign worker for the late Sen. Robert F. Kennedy, was drowned.

The car went off a wooden bridge, turned over and sank to the bottom of Poucha Pond.

Police said the accident occurred between midnight and 1 a.m. yesterday on Chappaquiddick Island, where Kennedy was visiting with friends at a small cottage.

Staffers for Robert and Edward Kennedy had been having a reunion there.

Police Chief James Arena said last night that he will go to the Edgartown District Court tomorrow to file an application for a complaint charging Kennedy with leaving the scene of an accident without making himself known.

He said also he would issue a Registry of Motor Vehicles violation citation against Kennedy on the same complaint.

After the accident, Kennedy swam to safety, although he told Edgartown police he could not remember how he got out of the car.

He told police he repeatedly dived into the pond to see if Miss Kopechne was still trapped but that he was unable to do anything.

Police said Kennedy did not go to the station until about 10 a.m.

"I was exhausted and in a state of shock," he told them.

Dr. Robert D. Watt, the Kennedy family physician, on Cape Cod, reported last night that the senator "has a slight concussion at the back of his head."

Watt said he gave the senator a sedative "to help relieve the pain."

Kennedy then retired and was resting comfortably, Watt said.

He plans to see Kennedy again today.

Edgartown Police Chief Dominick J. Arena said the car was first seen about 8 a.m. yesterday by some boys who were going fishing near the narrow wooden bridge.

KENNEDY Page 47

DEAD — MARY JO KOPECHNE

Mother in Shock

Ted First to Call Victim's Father

By KEN O. BOTWRIGHT
Staff Writer

The phone in the home of Mr. and Mrs. Joseph A. Kopechne at Berkeley Heights, N.J., rang about 10 a.m. yesterday. It was Sen. Edward M. Kennedy, calling to tell them their daughter had been killed in an auto accident the night before.

Mary Jo Kopechne, an attractive 28-year-old blonde and former secretary in the office of the late Robert F. Kennedy, drowned when a car the senator was driving plunged into a pond on Martha's Vineyard about midnight.

Her 50-year-old father, an insurance man, said at 4 p.m. yesterday that his wife, Gwen, took the call and lapsed into shock.

MARY JO Page 34

All Is Go for Moon Landing Today

By VICTOR K. McELHENY
Staff Writer

SPACE CENTER, Houston—Two men will attempt to make man's first landing on the moon today. An event that should make this date—July 20, 1969—ring down through the ages.

America's Apollo 11 moon-ship entered orbit around the moon at 1:22 p.m. EDT yesterday to begin 24 hours of preparation for today's landing, which is to carry astronauts Neil Armstrong and Edwin Aldrin down to a desolate spot in the Sea of Tranquility.

All portents for the scheduled landing are favorable. The equipment of Apollo 11, fruit of a decade of intense engineering effort, has worked flawlessly since takeoff from Cape Kennedy, Fla., at 9:32 a.m. last Wednesday.

So far the voyage of Armstrong, Aldrin and crewmate Michael Collins has been amazingly smooth, with all indications that the scheduled 4:14 p.m. moonship landing today and Armstrong's first step on the moon at 2:16 a.m. will take place as planned.

The three Americans joined Russia's Luna 15, which was in its third day of orbiting the moon. Its mission never disclosed, Luna changed its course slightly during the day. The Soviets have assured U.S. space officials that Luna will not interfere with Apollo 11.

The astronauts made a vital test of the fragile machine named Eagle that two of them will fly to the surface of the moon today.

Aldrin crawled from the command ship into the small lunar lander called Eagle at 6:58 p.m. to test the equipment.

The Air Force colonel powered up the lunar module for the first time since it was rocketed away from Cape Kennedy four days and 250,000 miles ago.

He also tested the communications systems that will carry word and picture of man's first step on another celestial body.

Collins conducted lunar tracking photography.

He also reported that a small pool of water had formed in one corner of the command module. This occurred in previous Apollo flights and officials said it poses no problem.

Earlier, Armstrong and Aldrin reported sighting some mysterious lunar lights in an area where some scientists believe there are volcanoes.

APOLLO Page 61

Did Luna 15 Make First Scoop?

United Press International

MOSCOW—Russia's mysterious Luna 15 moon ship sent out an unusually long burst of signals yesterday and moved into a slightly higher orbit, causing speculation both in Moscow and at Britain's Jodrell Bank Observatory that some sort of landing might already have been made.

The Soviet government maintained the silence it has maintained since Luna 15 was launched last Sunday but scientific sources have predicted it would scoop up some moon soil ahead of Apollo 11. However, there was no confirmation of speculation that this might have been accomplished by a lunar module.

LUNA Page 54

Rain May Fall

SUNDAY — Cool, possible showers. MONDAY — Chance of showers. (Page 65).

High Tides
3:36 a.m. 4:06 p.m.

Stores Open

Massachusetts merchants, in accord with practices in other retail areas, including New York, Philadelphia and Washington, will be open regular hours on "Moon Day," July 21. Banks will also be open. The stock market will be closed.

Baseball Results

AMERICAN LEAGUE
BOSTON 5, Balitimore 3 (n).
Detroit 10, Cleveland 4.
Chicago 5, Kansas City 4.
Oakland 3, California 2.
Minnesota-Seattle (N).
N w York 9, Washington 0.
Washington 4, New York 0

NATIONAL LEAGUE
Philadelphia 5, Chicago 3.
Montreal 5, New York 4.
Cincinnati 10, Houston 9 (11).
Pittsburgh 3, St. Louis 2
San Diego 6, Atlanta 1
San Fran. 5, Los Angeles 4

RED SOX TODAY
Baltimore at Fenway (Cuellar vs. Culp), 2 p.m. TV-Channel 5.

Historical Timetable: From Landing to First Step

United Press International

SPACE CENTER, Houston—The Apollo 11 timetable, based on the revised NASA flight plan. Times are approximate.

TODAY

7:27 a.m. (EDT)—Crew awakens.

9:27 — Aldrin enters Moon lander without his spacesuit.

10:15 — Armstrong enters Moon lander, wearing spacesuit, and starts final check of systems.

10:42 — Aldrin exits lander, puts on spacesuit in command ship and returns to landing craft.

1:42 p.m.—Lunar lander and command ship separate slightly.

3:06 — Astronauts fire descent engine in lunar lander, drop it into lower Moon orbit and begin the long ride down toward the surface.

4:02—Lander's big engine begins final descent approach firing, braking ship out of orbit at 50,000-foot altitude on sloping path toward the selected landing site.

4:14 — Lander touches down on lunar Sea of Tranquillity.

6:58—Two men begin four-hour rest period prior to leaving Moon lander's cabin.

TOMORROW

2:07 a.m. — Armstrong leaves lander and begins five-minute descent of ladder. He pulls on D-ring, opening equipment stowage area door and allowing television camera a view of surface and foot of ladder.

TIMETABLE Page 61

• A $14.70 Tax Hike Predicted For Boston—Pg. 3

• Nixon Will Offer New Domestic Plan At End Of Trip—Pg. 2

HOME ★★★
SUNDAY NEWS
NEW YORK'S PICTURE NEWSPAPER ®
15¢
Vol. 49. No. 12 Copr. 1969 News Syndicate Co. Inc. New York, N.Y. 10017, Sunday, July 20, 1969* WEATHER: Partly cloudy, hot, humid.

TEDDY ESCAPES, BLONDE DROWNS

Kennedy Car Goes Off Bridge

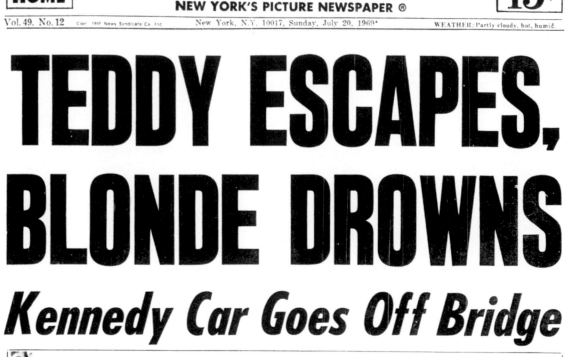

Another Tragedy for Ted. Sen. Edward M. Kennedy's car is pulled out of the water at Chappaquiddick Island, near Martha's Vineyard, after it crashed through side of a bridge and plunged into inlet of Nantucket Sound. Kennedy escaped death, but Mary Jo Kopechne, 25, died. —*Stories on page 2*

Eagle Lands in Moondust Today

Stories on Page 3

A week after the wreck, Kennedy pleaded guilty to a misdemeanor charge of leaving the scene of an accident after causing injury and was given a two-month suspended sentence. At a 1970 inquest into the incident, the judge concluded that Kennedy's negligence contributed to Kopechne's death.

Kennedy went on television, saying it was "indefensible" that he did not immediately report the wreck and denying that he had driven under the influence of alcohol or engaged in "immoral conduct" with Kopechne. He asked Massachusetts's citizens for advice on whether he should resign; media outlets were flooded with calls of support for him.

The Providence Sunday Journal

CITY EDITION ★

● Cooler, Chance of Showers Today .... Page N-40
● Sox Beat Orioles Again, 5-3 .... Page S-1

VOLUME LXXXV. NO. 3. (Copyright 1969 Providence Journal Company) PROVIDENCE, RHODE ISLAND, JULY 20, 1969 218 PAGES PRICE 35c

An 'Ungainly Crate' Challenges Moon

Drawing of lunar module hovering over moon on blast from its rocket engine. —Associated Press Wirephoto

Continued on Page 2, Col. 1

Eager Astronauts Poised For Apollo Effort Climax

Continued on Page 4, Col. 1

Senator Kennedy's car, after being hauled from a pond on Chappaquiddick Island. —UPI Telephoto

Kennedy Car Plunges Off Bridge

Woman Drowns; Police to Charge Senator

Continued on Page 8, Col. 1

Most District Judges To Be Reappointed

By JOHN P. HACKETT

Continued on Page 10, Col. 1

2 Killed, 2 Injured In Dispute at Party

Continued on Page 17, Col. 1

India Nationalizes 14 Top Private Banks

Continued on Page 32, Col. 1

In Today's Sunday Journal

Arts	W-17-22	Gardens	H-6
Books	W-16	State News and Features	N-45-46-47
Death Notices	N-44	Travel	N-41-42-43
Editorials	N-36		
Hobbies, Crossword, Stamps	H-7		
What's Going On and Weather	N-40		

CLASSIFIED ADS ARE IN THE HOME SECTION H-8-20

Free Waterfront Concert Given

By JAMES L. MERRINER

Other Festival Stories On Pages 12, 24

Continued on Page 25, Col. 1

From the deck of the pollution protest yacht Clearwater, Pete Seeger performs for audience on the wharf. —Journal-Bulletin Photo by JACK SPRATT

Atlantic Crossing Completed by English Rower

Continued on Page 18, Col. 1

July 18, 1969

Senator Edward Kennedy Drove Car into Water off Chappaquiddick

The Weather

Today—Variable cloudiness, chance of thunderstorms, high in 90s. Monday — Cloudy, chance of thunderstorms. Probability of rain 30%. Temperature range: Today, 92-75. Yesterday, 95-78. Details, Page D11.

The Washington Post

Times Herald

Index 364 Pages 20 Sections

Amusements	L 1	Gardens	H11
City Life	D 1	Obituaries	C10
Classified	D12	Outdoors	B10
Editorials	B 6	Sports	B 1
Fed. Diary	A33	Style	G 1
Financial	E 1	Travel	L 9

Table of Contents, Page A2

92d Year ·· No. 227 © 1969, The Washington Post Co. SUNDAY, JULY 20, 1969 Phone 223-6000 Circulation 223-6100 Classified 223-6200 30 cents Home delivered 35c

Apollo in Orbit, Set for Landing

Kennedy Passenger Dies in Car Plunge

Sen. Kennedy: 'I was . . . in a state of shock.'

Mary Jo Kopechne: killed in plunge.

By Richard Harwood and Paul Blackwell
Washington Post Staff Writers

A car driven by Massachusetts Sen. Edward M. Kennedy plunged off a narrow bridge on Chappaquiddick Island, Mass., about midnight Friday, killing Kennedy's woman passenger.

She was identified by Kennedy as Mary Jo Kopechne of Washington, a 28-year-old campaign worker who was spending the weekend on nearby Martha's Vineyard island.

The Senator was not physically injured in the accident. But his political career may have been gravely damaged.

Nearly nine hours went by before Kennedy — "exhausted and in a state of shock," according to his statement — walked into police headquarters at Edgartown on Martha's Vineyard to report what had happened.

From Kennedy's statement to police and from other sources, this story emerged:

The Senator flew up to Martha's Vineyard from Washington Friday to take part in the annual Edgartown sailing regatta, and to join his wife and family at Hyannisport this weekend.

Miss Kopechne, once a secretary to the late Sen. Robert F. Kennedy, had gone up to Martha's Vineyard the day before with five girl friends to spend a weekend at the beach.

After sailing in the regatta, Kennedy went to Chappaquiddick to spend the evening at a cottage with friends, whose identities have not been disclosed. Miss Kopechne was among those at the gathering.

Between 11 p.m. and midnight, Kennedy left the cottage in his car to return to his room at the Shiretown Inn in Edgartown.

Miss Kopechne, who was staying at another hotel at Edgartown, rode with him.

As Kennedy approached the road leading to the ferry that connects Chappaquiddick Island with Martha's Vineyard, he made a wrong turn. After driving about a half-mile he came to a small bridge that spans an inlet. The bridge is only 10½ feet wide, has no railings, and is used primarily by fishermen traveling in jeeps and beach buggies.

The car went off the bridge and, according to Kennedy's statement to police, "turned over and sank into the water and landed with the roof resting on the bottom.

"I attempted to open the door and window of the car but have no recollection of how I got out of the car," he reported.

See KENNEDY, A3, Col. 1

Kennedy's Statement

The text of Sen. Kennedy's statement to Edgartown police:

On July 18, 1969, at approximately 11:15 p.m. on Chappaquiddick Island, Martha's Vineyard, I was driving my car on Main Street on my way to get the ferry back to Edgartown. I was unfamiliar with the road and turned right onto Dike Road instead of bearing hard left on Main Street.

After proceeding for approximately one half-mile on Dike Road I descended a hill and came upon a narrow bridge. The car went off the side of the bridge. There was one passenger with me, Miss Mary Jo Kopechne, a former secretary of my brother, Robert Kennedy.

The car turned over and sank into the water and landed with the roof resting on the bottom. I attempted to open the door and window of the car but have no recollection of how I got out of the car.

I came to the surface and then repeatedly dove down to the car in an attempt to see if the passenger was still in the car. I was unsuccessful in the attempt.

I was exhausted and in a state of shock. I recall walking back to where my friends were eating. There was a car parked in front of a cottage and I climbed into the back seat.

I then asked someone to bring me back to Edgartown. I remember walking around for a period of time and then going back to my hotel room. When I fully realized what had happened this morning, I immediately contacted the police.

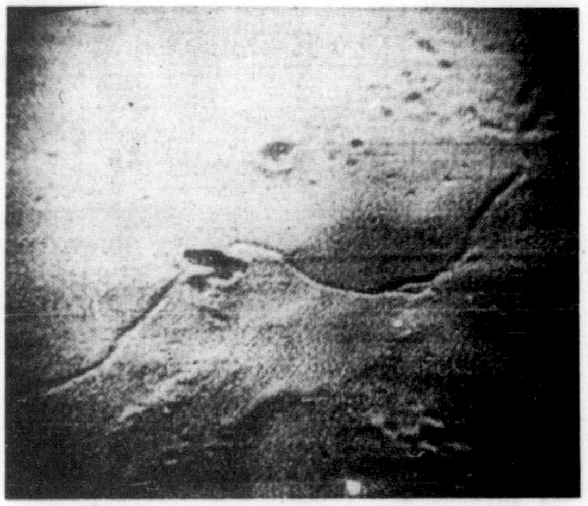

Apollo 11 telecast from lunar orbit shows Sidewinder rill, key landmark to guide astronauts to landing site.

Walk on Moon Poses New Perils

Alien Environment Has Physical, Mental Hazards

By Victor Cohn
Washington Post Staff Writer

HOUSTON—Now man heads toward new perils.

Now he nears a destination, the moon, where:

- A space suit ripped open on a sharp rock—and exposure to lunar vacuum—would mean loss of consciousness in 10 to 15 seconds and death within three minutes as the blood boils for lack of pressure.
- A broken ankle or leg could mean death. If an astronaut could not climb back into his lunar craft, says a top space official, his comrade would "try" to haul him aboard "whether he would succeed or not, I would hesitate to say. It would be difficult."
- Even walking and working may be pathetically clumsy and fatiguing. A man's muscular control on the moon, in one scientist's view, may be "no greater than a child's." A day's work, with present space suits and man's limitations may be only 2½ hours.
- Just seeing may be deceptive and dangerous. "So utterly alien is the lunar environment," believes an Edinburgh University authority, that there will be "a dearth of reliable clues to interpret precisely what the eyes record. Optical illusions will abound—many quite capable of resulting in fatal errors of judgment."
- The mind could falter. "The alien environment of the moon presents a threat to the human mind that is no less than the physical dangers," states the same authority, Prof. Richard L. Gregory, a specialist on the brain and on perception in strange environments.

A good deal of such horror talk may be vastly over-pessimistic. Or it may not be. No one knows.

The first thoughts of astronauts Neil Armstrong and Edwin Aldrin will not be their own physiology but their ship's. This is the first of their perils: its flyability.

See HAZARDS, A14, Col. 1

TV Gives Preview To World

All on Schedule For Touchdown This Afternoon

By Thomas O'Toole
Washington Post Staff Writer

HOUSTON, July 19 — The men of Apollo 11 flew into orbit around the moon today and then took the world on a televised tour of the route they'll follow to land on the moon Sunday.

The epic moment of man's first landing on another heavenly body will be at hand by 4:03 p.m. EDT Sunday, when astronauts Neil Armstrong and Edwin (Buzz) Aldrin start the Lem landing craft called "Eagle" down toward the surface.

Moving on a path that takes them across the moon and down, the two astronauts will reach a low point of 50,000 feet above the western edge of the Sea of Tranquility just after 4 o'clock.

Flying face down and backwards, Armstrong will throttle up Eagle's engine at that point, a move that will slow the spacecraft.

As it starts to slow, it will start to fall—though still flying laterally across the moon toward a chosen landing site 260 miles to the east.

Down and across they'll fly, until about 12 miles from the landing site they'll be flying down almost as fast as they're flying across. Suddenly, their speed will fall—12 miles an hour, 10, 5, until they're almost hovering 50 feet above the surface.

Looking hard at the surface below, they'll pick out the clearest spot and maneuver slowly toward it. Then they'll drop down onto the moon—falling no harder than a three foot jump would be on earth.

At 4:15 p.m. (EDT)., the first humans in history will have landed on the moon's surface.

For 35 minutes today, Armstrong, Aldrin and Michael Collins talked of the moon while panning its bleak and barren surface with the portable color camera they've carried on their historic flight.

The show began at 3:55 p.m. with the spacecraft's window silhouetting the rim of a distant lunar horizon against the black void of space.

Passing westward along the eastern edge of the moon's visible side, the camera recorded the same sights Armstrong and Aldrin will come upon Sunday when they begin their 70-mile descent to the lunar surface.

"It doesn't look very much like a sea," said Collins, "but we're coming up on Smyth Sea right now."

"The area devoid of craters, and that's not much, is very hilly down there," Collins went on.

See APOLLO, A14, Col. 3

Power Crisis Ends in Area

Washington's electric power crisis was over yesterday, as the beginning of a three-day weekend cut commercial and industrial demand.

Mid-afternoon thunderstorms dropped the temperature 15 degrees from the 3 p.m. of 95, easing the load on air conditioners. But the Weather Bureau warned that temperatures will be back in the mid-90's again today.

The humidity—unusual even by Washington's standards—is being kept high by a gentle wind from the Gulf of Mexico, meteorologists said.

Details on Page D1

Nixon Telecast on Aug. 8 To Outline Welfare Plan

By Frank C. Porter
Washington Post Staff Writer

President Nixon will outline "a dramatic new approach" to welfare in a telecast to the Nation on August 8, the White House announced yesterday.

Also to be covered in the roadcast are "new initiatives" for sharing Federal revenues with the states and cities, revisions of the country's manpower training programs and reorganization of the Office of Economic Opportunity, Presidential Press Secretary Ronald L. Ziegler said.

The telecast will come five days after Mr. Nixon returns from his trip around the world.

Earlier, a top White House official said that in the President's view the trip is made necessary, among other things, by a "turning point" in United States relations with the Far East.

Some of the countries along Mr. Nixon's route, particularly Thailand, are concerned about their security in light of predicted U.S. withdrawals from Vietnam, he said.

Others are concerned, he explained, about the possibility that the United States will turn inward and reduce aid and other ties to them once the war in Vietnam is concluded.

The White House spokesman said trade matters will be an important part of the President's discussions with heads of state in many of the countries he visits, particularly in the Philippines and Rumania.

He went out of his way to assure that the visit to Rumania is not intended as an embarrassment or rebuke to the Soviet Union.

"We are willing to have friendly and open relations with any Communist country that is willing to deal on a basis of mutual respect with us," the official said.

At the same time, he expressed disappointment that the Soviet Union doesn't appear to have done all it could to help bring the wars in Vietnam and in Laos to a speedy conclusion.

President Nixon returned to Washington yesterday afternoon by helicopter from a two-day stay at Camp David in the Catoctin Mountains of Maryland. The helicopter was buffeted by the thunderstorm which drenched the D.C. area.

See PRESIDENT, A4, Col. 1

Moon Landing Time Chart

HOUSTON, July 19 — The Apollo 11 timetable for Sunday and Monday:

3:11 p.m. — Astronauts fire Lem descent engines, begin ride to moon's surface.

4:07 p.m.—Lem's engine begins final descent approach firing, braking ship at 50,000-foot altitude on sloping path towards landing site.

4:19 p.m.—Lem lands on moon's surface.

6:23 p.m. to 2:12 a.m. Monday—Astronauts rest, check Lem and eat two meals.

2:12 a.m. Monday—Neil Armstrong opens Lem's hatch and begins descent down ladder.

2:21 a.m. — Armstrong becomes first man to set foot on the moon.

Nixon: Perplexing Problems After 6 Months

By Laurence Stern and Don Oberdorfer
Washington Post Staff Writers

Insight

As Richard M. Nixon's presidency draws to the end of its sixth month today Amricans are descending toward the arid craters of the moon and withdrawing from the steaming paddies of Vietnam.

These are awesomely dramatic milestones for a cautious lawyer-President whose style is deliberately low-keyed and whose penchant is for the undemonstrative.

Tonight's lunar landing represents the commitment of the two Democratic Presidents who preceded Mr. Nixon into office. The actual withdrawal of American troops from Vietnam—though an extension of Lyndon Johnson's diplomatic turnaround in 1968—is an achievement that President Nixon can claim as his own.

"In Vietnam the tide has finally been reversed," says a self-congratulatory White House assessment that is now being circulated privately among high Republican officials. "The question is no longer how fast the war will escalate but how rapidly it will be contracted.

The White House paper then goes on to sound the political keynote that President Nixon and his men are likely to take to the American people in the months—and the elections—ahead.

"After long year during which the American involvement steadily increased, the Nixon Administration has begun the process by which our involvement will be decreased.

"Twenty-five-thousand troops are already being withdrawn; our men are coming home again."

It was perhaps predictable that the first major and most visible landmark of the Nixon Presidency would be in the international arena. "He knows he has to end this—war," said a close student of Mr. Nixon. "Otherwise he will get to a point, like Lyndon Johnson, where he's immobilized."

On Tuesday the President sets off across the world again to five countries on the rim of China and to Rumania, within the sphere of Soviet power. Mr. Nixon and his advisers are hoping for the cheers and toasts that greeted his European tour last February.

At home it is different. The honeymoon between the minority President and the Democratic Congress has ended. Within his own Party political tempers are growing ragged, especially among Republican liberals who voice fears of a sell-out to Southerners and conservatives on programs affecting the urban constituencies—particularly the Negro.

See NIXON, A21, Col. 1

President Nixon's first six months in Vietnam: How has he done? Where is he headed? Story, B1.

Drawing by David Suter

Luna Changes Orbit, May Return Soon

Reuters

Luna 15 made a slight, unexplained change in orbit yesterday, according to British astronomer Sir Bernard Lovell. He said it could not be ruled out that the mysterious Soviet moon probe was transmitting to a capsule on the lunar surface.

Meanwhile, unconfirmed reports circulated Moscow last night indicating that Russian scientists will attempt to bring Luna 15 back to earth soon.

The reports indicated that scientists might try to return the craft to earth Tuesday or Wednesday, which would mark the first time the feat would be achieved with an unmanned ship.

Lovell, head of Jodrell Bank Observatory and space tracking station, said he could not give a definite reason why Luna 15's orbits were suddenly extended by three to six minutes. The change apparently occurred while the probe was behind the moon during its 26th orbit.

Lovell said the probe kept on transmitting as it went behind the moon on the 26th orbit—the first time this had happened. It continued to transmit on its 27th orbit, he said.

[Lovell also reported a 64-minute burst of signals, an unusually long one, from Luna 15 as it changed its orbit, UPI reported.]

The official Russian news agency Tass later confirmed the change in orbit, but said only that it was "according to the program." It said Luna 15 was circling the moon every 123 minutes at a maximum distance of about 138 miles and a minimum of abouh 60 miles.

See LUNA, A14, Col. 6

For decades, Chappaquiddick would be used as evidence of the dark side of Camelot: reckless behavior with alcohol and women, a sense of personal invulnerability, and a political machine ready to cover up even the worst mistakes.

Also in 1969

Jimi Hendrix and others performed at the Woodstock music festival on Max Yasgur's 600-acre dairy farm in upstate New York.

Joseph Kennedy, former U.S. ambassador to Great Britain and patriarch of the Kennedy family, died at 81 from a heart attack, eight years after a debilitating stroke. Six of his grandchildren were honorary pallbearers at his funeral, including John F. Kennedy Jr. and Edward Kennedy Jr.

Neil Armstrong photographed Edwin "Buzz" Aldrin as the Apollo 11 mission achieved President Kennedy's goal of landing a man on the moon. (AP Photo/NASA File)

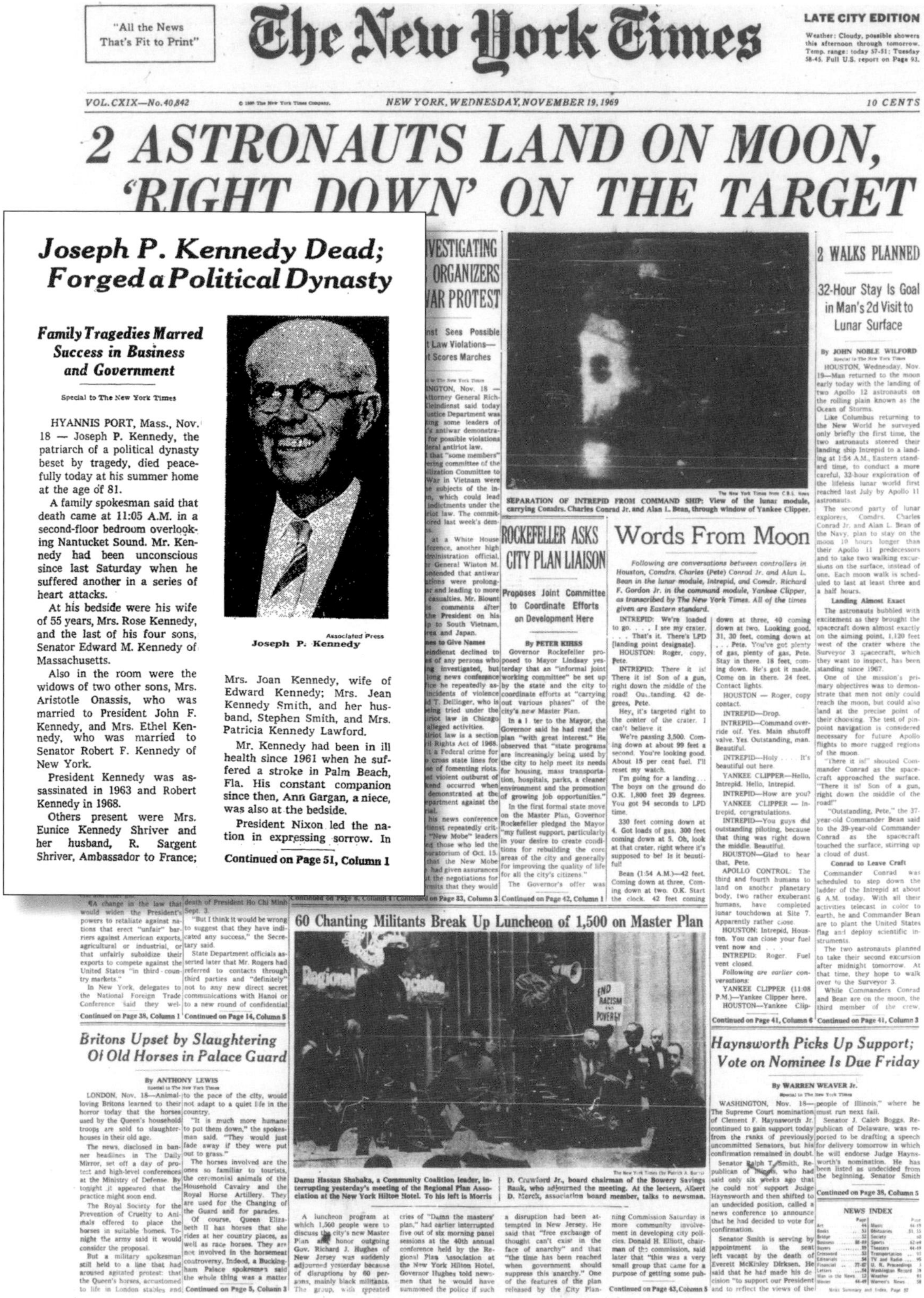

"All the News That's Fit to Print"

The New York Times

LATE CITY EDITION

VOL. CXIX—No. 40,842

NEW YORK, WEDNESDAY, NOVEMBER 19, 1969

10 CENTS

2 ASTRONAUTS LAND ON MOON, 'RIGHT DOWN' ON THE TARGET

Joseph P. Kennedy Dead; Forged a Political Dynasty

Family Tragedies Marred Success in Business and Government

Special to The New York Times

HYANNIS PORT, Mass., Nov. 18 — Joseph P. Kennedy, the patriarch of a political dynasty beset by tragedy, died peacefully today at his summer home at the age of 81.

A family spokesman said that death came at 11:05 A.M. in a second-floor bedroom overlooking Nantucket Sound. Mr. Kennedy had been unconscious since last Saturday when he suffered another in a series of heart attacks.

At his bedside were his wife of 55 years, Mrs. Rose Kennedy, and the last of his four sons, Senator Edward M. Kennedy of Massachusetts.

Also in the room were the widows of two other sons, Mrs. Aristotle Onassis, who was married to President John F. Kennedy, and Mrs. Ethel Kennedy, who was married to Senator Robert F. Kennedy of New York.

President Kennedy was assassinated in 1963 and Robert Kennedy in 1968.

Others present were Mrs. Eunice Kennedy Shriver and her husband, R. Sargent Shriver, Ambassador to France;

Associated Press
Joseph P. Kennedy

Mrs. Joan Kennedy, wife of Edward Kennedy; Mrs. Jean Kennedy Smith, and her husband, Stephen Smith, and Mrs. Patricia Kennedy Lawford.

Mr. Kennedy had been in ill health since 1961 when he suffered a stroke in Palm Beach, Fla. His constant companion since then, Ann Gargan, a niece, was also at the bedside.

President Nixon led the nation in expressing sorrow. In

Continued on Page 51, Column 1

SEPARATION OF INTREPID FROM COMMAND SHIP: View of the lunar module, carrying Comdrs. Charles Conrad Jr. and Alan L. Bean, through window of Yankee Clipper.

ROCKEFELLER ASKS CITY PLAN LIAISON

Proposes Joint Committee to Coordinate Efforts on Development Here

By PETER KIHSS

Governor Rockefeller proposed to Mayor Lindsay yesterday that an "informal joint working committee" be set up by the state and the city to coordinate efforts at "carrying out various phases" of the city's new Master Plan.

Words From Moon

Following are conversations between controllers in Houston, Comdrs. Charles (Pete) Conrad Jr. and Alan L. Bean in the lunar module, Intrepid, and Comdr. Richard F. Gordon Jr. in the command module, Yankee Clipper, as transcribed by The New York Times. All of the times given are Eastern standard.

INTREPID: We're loaded to go. . . . I see my crater. . . . That's it. There's LPD [landing point designated].

2 WALKS PLANNED

32-Hour Stay Is Goal in Man's 2d Visit to Lunar Surface

By JOHN NOBLE WILFORD

HOUSTON, Wednesday, Nov. 19—Man returned to the moon early today with the landing of two Apollo 12 astronauts on the rolling plain known as the Ocean of Storms.

Haynsworth Picks Up Support; Vote on Nominee Is Due Friday

By WARREN WEAVER Jr.

WASHINGTON, Nov. 18—The Supreme Court nomination of Clement F. Haynsworth Jr. continued to gain support today from the ranks of previously uncommitted Senators, but his confirmation remained in doubt.

60 Chanting Militants Break Up Luncheon of 1,500 on Master Plan

Britons Upset by Slaughtering Of Old Horses in Palace Guard

By ANTHONY LEWIS

LONDON, Nov. 18—Animal-loving Britons learned to their horror today that the horses used by the Queen's household troops are sold to slaughterhouses in their old age.

JUNE 22, 1971
BOSTON GLOBE PUBLISHED KENNEDY-ERA PENTAGON PAPERS

Other documents, stories based on Pentagon papers—pgs. 2, 3, 18, 19

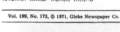

Guide to features

CLASSIFIED ....43-49 FINANCIAL 34-38
COMICS ....51 LIVING 27, 23
CONF. CHAT ....23 OBITUARIES 40, 41
CROSSWORD ....51 SPORTS 25-30
DEATHS ....40 TV RADIO 53
EDITORIALS ....20 THEATERS 31-33

The Boston Globe

Sort of warm

Vol. 199, No. 173, © 1971, Globe Newspaper Co. — TUESDAY MORNING, JUNE 22, 1971 — Telephone 288-8000 — 52 Pages—15c

PRESIDENT KENNEDY speaks at a press conference in November 1961, the year he approved covert actions against North Vietnam.

New Pentagon data brought to light

Ban still on Times, Washington Post

Secret Pentagon Documents bare JFK role in Vietnam war

• Admiral sought nuclear option

By Matthew V. Storin
Globe Staff

Unpublished portions of the 47-Vietnam war were made available yesterday to the Boston Globe.

The Globe is the third US newspaper to report on the 7000 page analysis tracing America's growing involvement in Indochina from World War II through mid-1968.

According to the documents made available to the Globe:

— Gen. Maxwell Taylor advised President Kennedy in 1961 to send 8000 American combat troops into Vietnam but warned the move could lead to increased world tensions and a wider war. There were 1000 US troops in Vietnam at that time.

— As soon as President Johnson announced a partial end to the bombing of North Vietnam on March 31, 1968, he elected to proceed with a policy of Vietnamization similar to that later followed by President Nixon.

—On June 2, 1964, Secretary of Defense Robert S. McNamara in a meeting of top Administration officials in Honolulu discussed the possible use of nuclear weapons in Vietnam. Adm. Harry D. Felt, commander of US forces in the Pacific, openly advocated that American commanders be given this option.

—The Soviet Union, fearing reaction from Communist China, rejected a plea by the United States in May, 1965, that Hanoi be informed that a bombing pause was being undertaken in hopes of prompting negotiations to end the war.

The massive Pentagon study, initiated by Secretary McNamara in June, 1967, was the work of more than 30 authors both inside and outside of government. The first report of the study was published June 13 by the New York Times. The Washington Post began printing reports on June 18.

The people can judge intelligently only if they are given all the facts possible. . . . see Editorial, Page 20.

Yesterday Federal appeals courts in New York and Washington continued their respective temporary bans against publication of further reports by the Times and the Post.

DOCUMENTS, Page 3

• Kennedy OK'd covert action

By Robert Healy
Globe Staff

Gen. Maxwell Taylor in October of 1961 advised President Kennedy in an "eyes only for the President" cable to send 8000 man US military task force into South Vietnam but he warned that the introduction of such a force "may increase tensions and risk escalation into a major war in Aisia."

Gen. Taylor was special adviser to President Kennedy on Vietnam.

At the time of the Taylor mission, which took him and Walt Rostow, later to be President Johnson's chief adviser on national security affairs, and a group of state and defense department officials to South Vietnam, the United States had about 1000 soldiers in South Vietnam. They served as advisers to the South Vietnamese Army.

President Kennedy stepped up covert actions against North Vietnam and increased the number of advisers to 16,000 men before he was assassinated in November of 1963. He never commited a United States ground unit as Taylor recommended.

These disclosures were made in a portion of a secret Pentagon study on the origins of the war in Vietnam started in 1967 by then Secretary of Defense Robert McNamara. They were made available to the Boston Globe yesterday.

For the first time the Globe was making public the role of the Kennedy administration in the escalation of the war. Three earlier reports dealing with other phases of the war were published by the New York Times and two by the Washington Post before publication was halted by court injunctions.

As early as May 11, 1961, President Kennedy, according to the secret report, had approved programs for covert action which had been recommended by a Vietnam Task Force. Among these actions were.

(1) Dispatch of agents into North Vietnam.

(2) Aerial resupply of agents in North Vietnam through the use of civilian mercenary air crews.

(3) Infiltration of special South Vietnam forces into Southeast Laos to locate and attack Communist bases and lines of communication.

KENNEDY, Page 2

Tet offensive turned Johnson toward Vietnamization policy

By Crocker Snow Jr.
Globe Staff

When President Johnson in March 1968 announced publicly that he would not run for re-election, he was also deciding privately that a policy of Vietnamization was the best one for the nation to follow in the war.

The President's speech was also a denial of Gen. William C. Westmoreland's request for an increase of 206,000 American troops.

This change in the President's thinking toward the kind of policy President Nixon has since adopted is evidenced in the concluding portions of the secret Pentagon study viewing the decision-making of American military involvement in Vietnam.

It was March 31, 1968 that President Johnson made his famous peace initiative, in which he announced a limited bombing halt and only a small build-up of 24,500 American troops following the shock of the Tet Offensive two months earlier, and called for Britain and the Soviet Union to take the lead in achieving a peaceful settlement.

In this same speech, the President made an urgent plea for national unity, and took himself out of the 1968 presidential race with the

JOHNSON, Page 2

Court reverses conviction in Pamela Mason case

By S. J. Micchiche
Globe Washington Bureau

WASHINGTON—The conviction of Edward H. Coolidge Jr., serving a life sentence for the 1964 slaying of 14-year-old Manchester, N.H., babysitter Pamela Mason, was reversed by the US Supreme Court yesterday.

A new trial was ordered by the court, which held, 5-to-4, that certain evidence linking Coolidge to the murder had been obtained under a defective search warrant.

The majority view, which evoked a stinging dissent, found it was unconstitutional for the state's attorney general to have issued the search warrant in his capacity as a justice of the peace when he was personally in charge of the police investigation and later served as chief prosecutor.

Since the attorney general "was not the neutral and detached magistrate required by the Constitution, the search stands on no firmer ground than if there had been no warrant at all," wrote Associate Justice Potter Stewart for the majority.

Former US solicitor general, Archibald Cox of Harvard Law School, Coolidge's court-appointed lawyer, argued that the search warrant had not been issued by "a neutral and detached magistrate" and was therefore improper.

MASON, Page 16

Ellsberg promises statement soon on role

DANIEL ELLSBERG
. . . biding his time

By Thomas Oliphant
Globe Staff

SAN DIEGO — Daniel Ellsberg said yesterday he expects to comment publicly in a week or two on his role in the unearthing of the secret Pentagon study of the Indochina war.

The MIT scholar and former top Defense Department and State Department aide spoke through intermediaries known to be close friends of his and to have been in contact with him since he dropped out of sight last week.

The intermediaries insisted on anonymity as a condition for passing on the message from Ellsberg.

While pledging to make a full statement eventually, Ellsberg said he did not wish to do so now.

He said to do so would only further complicate an already complicated situation, in which vast amounts of information are becoming available not just from the Pentagon study but also from the Federal courts where the Nixon Administration is attempting to have the study suppressed.

Ellsberg said he would like to postpone making a complete public statement until the court cases have ended.

He said he did not want to divert public attention from what he termed these important court battles over the public's right to know the truth about the war.

Finally, Ellsberg said he wanted his two children who live in California with his first wife to know that he is well and thinking of them.

He also said he wanted his father, Harry Ellsberg, who lives in a Detroit suburb, to know that he is deeply grateful for the expressions of support he made to the press last week.

The Globe also learned yesterday that Ellsberg had been involved in private efforts to change the country's war policies as far back as 1967.

According to a source close to Ellsberg, he was one of about 35 participants in a private conference in Bermuda, sponsored by the Carnegie Endowment, which brought together several influential Americans, including former top government officials, to talk about the war.

ELLSBERG, Page 6

IN THIS CORNER

Hypnosis enters mind's back-door

By David Lamb
Los Angeles Times

LOS ANGELES—Isadore Cantor, an affable former hearing-aid salesman of 67, teaches self-hypnosis—10 lessons for $250—at the National Hypnosis Institute. The institute has one office and one employee—Cantor, the director.

On the lawn outside his office a large sign placed to attract the eye of passing pedestrians an... tells what his student... plish: control eating... ing; overcome an... fears; improve mem... sleep, bowling, golf

HYPNOSIS, Page 11

In legislative committee report

Welfare residency rule advanced

By David Nyhan
Globe Staff

A special legislative committee investigating welfare in Massachusetts will recommend today adoption of a controversial one-year residency requirement for welfare recipients.

The committee, in an interim report to be released today, will also reportedly recommend:

—Use of Social Security cards to identify recipients and curb fraudulent collection of benefits.

—Creation of an enlarged "fraud squad" to be assigned to the state auditor's office.

—Curtailment of benefits to college students.

Created last spring to recommend changes in welfare laws after phenomenal growth in costs, the committee is headed by Sen. Robert L. Cawley (D-W. Roxbury).

The panel has considered 22 proposals.

Several of the majority report recommendations are expected to cause controversy. All must be aired at public hearings of various committees, including Judiciary, Social Welfare, and Ways and Means.

New York state just adopted a one-year residency requirement that welfare recipients charged is unconstitutional.

As recently as last week, Massachusetts Welfare Comr. Steven A. Minter told the Public Welfare Conference in Plymouth that the residency requirement is unconstitutional, and warned cutbacks might be coming.

Minter said last Friday: "If we think that by imposing residency requirements we will reduce the rolls and thereby cut costs, we are kidding ourselves."

The special committee report, to be detailed at a news conference this afternoon, reportedly recommends college students be trimmed from welfare rolls and families not be allowed to claim college students as dependents.

The recommendation that Auditor Thaddeus Buczko be given control over welfare fraud investigations is expected to be opposed by Gov. Sargent.

REPORT, Page 19

Sargent's tax bill killed again on House rollcall of 119 to 110

By David R. Ellis, Globe Staff

The House killed Gov. Sargent's latest tax bill yesterday, reaffirming an earlier vote by defeating the bill, up for reconsideration, on a 119 to 110 rollcall.

Despite a personal lobbying effort, Sargent could muster only a slight majority of Republicans—32 out of 62—in favor of the $256 million plan.

The major elements of the bill were a 1 percent increase in the state income tax, from 4 to 5 percent; and a variety of business taxes.

Failure of the bill prompted Administration Comr. Charles E. Shepard to order a general belt tightening in state departments and the firing of more than 200 state employees by the end of the week.

The bill was defeated first last Wednesday, by a vote of 129 to 103.

At that time the Republicans voted 22 to 38 against the bill, and the Democrats voted 81 to 91 against it.

A vote to reconsider was taken yesterday following a Republican caucus at which Sargent tried to sell his plan. The reconsideration, which is largely a courtesy, passed 158 to 66.

That meant that the tax bill was alive again, and it touched off nearly two hours of debate.

TAXES, Page 14

After the Nixon administration asked a court to prevent The New York Times *and* The Washington Post *from publishing the Pentagon Papers,* The Boston Globe *began publishing the secret documents, which included details of President Kennedy's role in the escalation of the Vietnam War.*

ALSO IN 1971

All in the Family *debuted, starring Carroll O'Connor as bigot Archie Bunker and offering commentary on controversial social issues.*

SEPTEMBER 8, 1971
THE JOHN F. KENNEDY CENTER FOR THE PERFORMING ARTS OPENED

The Washington Post **STYLE** *Entertainment* / *Travel* **SHOW**

SUNDAY, SEPTEMBER 5, 1971 F1

At Last—A Center Stage for the Arts in Washington

"The life of the arts, far from being an interruption, a distraction, in the life of a nation, is very close to the center of a nation's purpose – and is a test of the quality of a nation's civilization."

—*John F. Kennedy*

By Myra MacPherson

Wednesday's opening of the John F. Kennedy Center for the Performing Arts begins a new era for the arts in the Nation's Capital—and, therefore, in the country.

Even those relentless critics who see the Kennedy Center as that massive white marble Kleenex box along the Potomac will have to say "at last." A Nation's Capital emerged out of the swamps more than 150 years ago, but it took until 1971 for ballet, opera and symphony to find a congenial home here.

For years, listening to music from Washington's inadequate stages was like hearing the latest stereo record on a crank-up victrola. Hand-me-down auditoriums left audiences with vivid, if hardly glorious, memories—orchestras and singers suffering in a Constitution Hall built, not for them, but for the 1930 DAR convention . . . the Kirov or Royal Danish Ballet trooping across Uline Arena's hockey and wrestling emporium . . . Margot Fonteyn taking a pratfall on the unsuitable Constitution Hall stage in her debut before President Harry Truman.

So now, the temptation is to come forth with a little sideshow razzle-dazzle and say: Step right up folks; see this building—the first one ever built in Washington intended specifically for opera concerts, dance, drama.

But there are questions—that only time can answer—as well as promise in the opening of this grand center for the arts.

Of paramount, and genuine, concern to many is whether the center—with all its gilt and chandeliers — will be a palace "for the elite" or whether it will be a "cultural center for the people" in the broader sense of which President Kennedy spoke.

Will the center originate and experiment or be simply a showcase for established productions? What sort of "classical" and "popular" mix in program will be employed to attract the large audiences required to keep the center self-sustaining when the opening furor fades? Can Washington support such an overnight expansion of cultural fare?

If the decor is criticized by some as gaudy, will the large foyers function with an efficiency that more than compensates? And if some are unhappy with the exterior's "slab" design, will the center's interior work so well that these voices will be muted?

There seems to be little quarrel from critics who have listened to rehearsals in both the concert and opera halls that—unlike Lincoln Center where millions have been spent trying

See CENTER, F5, Col. 1

By Tom Allen—The Washington Post

The Kennedy Concert Hall: Beautiful site for beautiful sounds.

Bernstein's Mass

By Paul Hume

Leonard Bernstein and a Mass. The greatest American conductor and one of its foremost composers, a Jew, and the conductor emeritus of the New York Philharmonic writing a Mass for the dedicatory opening of the Kennedy Center with a world premiere.

Memories of Gustav Mahler once a Jew, then a Catholic and conductor of the New York Philharmonic and the composer of the historic Catholic hymn, "Veni, Creator Spiritus," with which he opened his mighty Eighth Symphony.

Both sentiment and logic have their part in the choice of Bernstein to write music to open the Kennedy Center. He was asked to do it by Mrs. Aristotle Onassis, then Mrs. John F. Kennedy, after the death of her husband. Bernstein is particularly characteristic of the younger generation of American artists who were stimulated by the personality and leadership of the late President. And he is, along with his world stature as a conductor, one of the most individual and powerful composers of his country at this time.

But a Mass. Never before has any prominent Jewish composer written a Mass. But, for that matter, never before has a composer written a Mass at all like this one.

It is not merely that Bernstein has set many lines that are purely peripheral to the text of the Mass itself, such as the invitation, "Dominus vobiscum," and its response, "Et cum spiritu tuo," as well as the opening phases, "Asperges me" and "Vidi aquam." He has gone far beyond these and those portions of the Mass that are almost universally composed: Kyrie, Gloria, Credo, Sanctus, Benedictus, and Agnus Dei. These are what you hear in the B Minor Mass of Bach, the Missa Solemnis of Beethoven, or any of the magnificent settings by Palestrina, Mozart, Haydn, or Bruckner.

Bernstein said, a few weeks ago, that he could not simply sit down and write "another Mass" to help celebrate the opening of the Kennedy Center. Not with the world as it is today and with the memory of the Kennedy who is remembered in this Center.

So he has done something like that which he did when he wrote his Third Symphony, which is sub-titled the "Kaddish." In that work, in addition to the text of the ancient Hebrew prayer, Bernstein adds his own commentary, a contemporary look at the world as it is suggested by the words of the Kaddish.

See MASS, F4, Col. 1

On the Inside

- *A "Clip and Save" calendar of upcoming events at the Kennedy Center plus how to get tickets and how to get there by car and bus. Pages F3 and F4.*
- *The sound of music from the Kennedy Center so far promises two halls with "superb acoustics," says Paul Hume. The applause should go to Cyril Harris, on center stage as the acoustical designer. Page F7.*
- *"Why the Kennedy Center?" asks Richard L. Coe and gives the answer through the perspective of the evolution of the performing arts in the nation's capital. Page F2.*
- *The promise and the problems . . . Alan M. Kriegsman reminds critics that "an opening is not an end but a beginning." Page F13.*

I. Prefatory Hymn + Psalm

+ Part KYRIE (quadraphonic tape: Soli, Percussion)

Allegretto con spirito

"Never before has any prominent Jewish composer written a Mass. But, for that matter, never before has a composer written a Mass at all like this one."

Lyrics © 1971 by Leonard Bernstein, reproduced by permission of G. Schirmer, Inc.

Photo by Douglas Chevalier

'Beatrix Cenci'

In May of 1819, Shelley sent his friend, Leigh Hunt, the manuscript of his latest work, a five-act play called "The Cenci." In an accompanying letter, he wrote, "The drama which I now present to you is a sad reality . . . I am content to paint, with such colours as my own heart furnishes, that which has been."

The ghastly story upon which he based his play was, indeed, true. It happened more than two centuries before Shelley reached Rome. But, as he noted in the preface to his play, "On my arrival in Rome, I found that the story of the Cenci was a subject not to be mentioned in Italian society without awakening a deep and breathless interest." Adding that he "had a copy of Guido's picture of Beatrice which is preserved in the Colonna Palace, and my servant instantly recognized it is the portrait of *La Cenci*." Shelley wrote with horror:

"This story of the Cenci is indeed eminently fearful and monstrous: anything like a dry exhibition of it on the stage would be insupportable."

Composer Alberto Ginastera, in choosing the bloody tale as the basis for his third opera, is obviously not going to give his audiences any "dry exhibition."

But where Shelley said "The person who would treat such a subject must increase the ideal, and diminish the actual horror of the events," Ginastera is more likely, if we may judge from the action in his two previous operas, "Don Rodrigo," and the more famous "Bomarzo," to give us the full horror of the events with no relief from their awful impact.

See OPERA, F4, Col. 4

The Kennedy Center in Washington, D.C., opened with a performance featuring the world premiere of a commissioned Requiem Mass by Leonard Bernstein that honored President Kennedy.

ALSO IN 1971

The 26th Amendment to the Constitution, which changed the voting age from 21 to 18, was adopted.

June 17, 1972
Senator Edward Kennedy Proposed National Health Insurance Plan

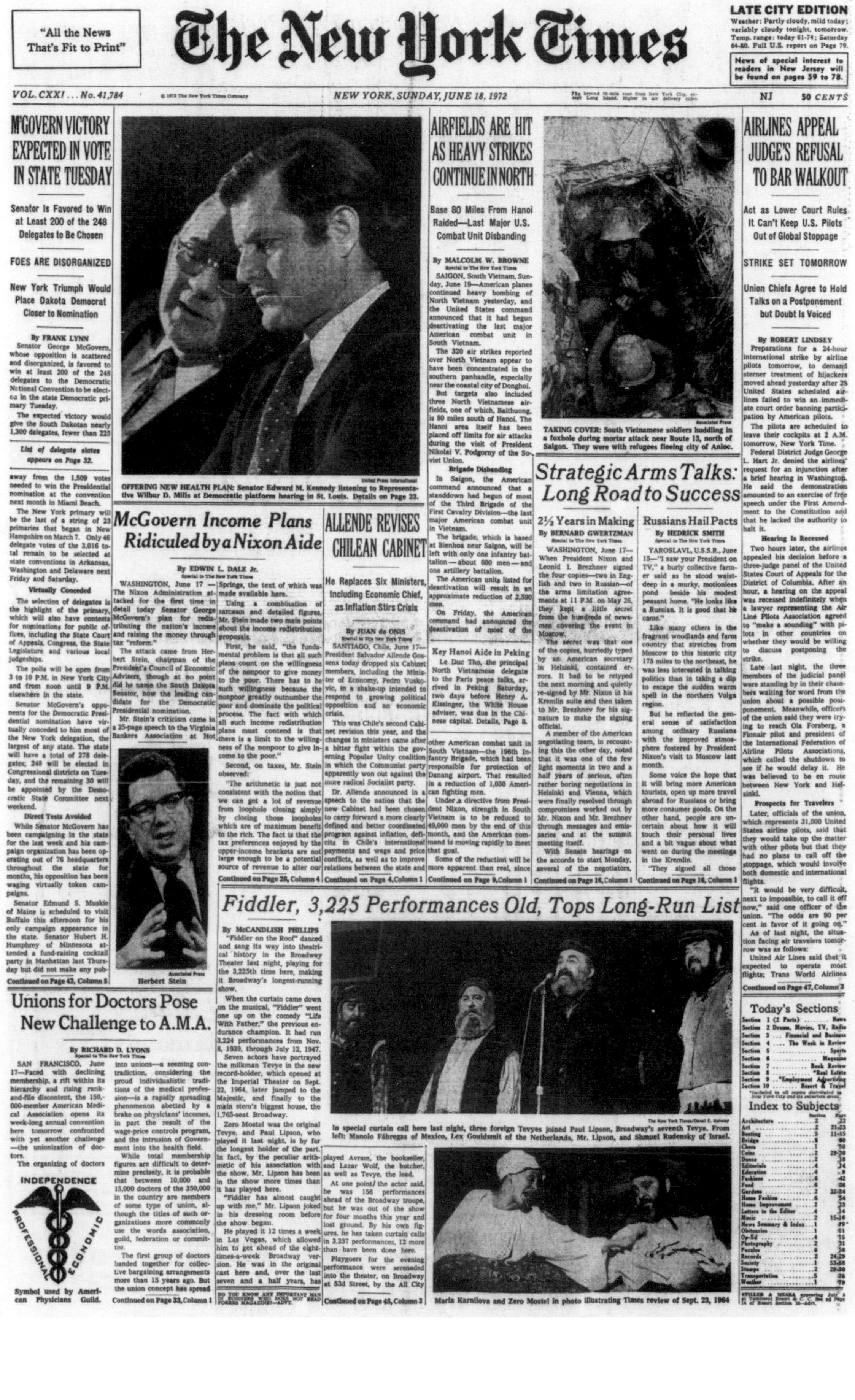

"All the News That's Fit to Print"

The New York Times

LATE CITY EDITION

VOL. CXXI . . . No. 41,784 — NEW YORK, SUNDAY, JUNE 18, 1972 — 50 CENTS

M'GOVERN VICTORY EXPECTED IN VOTE IN STATE TUESDAY

Senator Is Favored to Win at Least 200 of the 248 Delegates to Be Chosen

FOES ARE DISORGANIZED

New York Triumph Would Place Dakota Democrat Closer to Nomination

By FRANK LYNN

OFFERING NEW HEALTH PLAN: Senator Edward M. Kennedy listening to Representative Wilbur D. Mills at Democratic platform hearing in St. Louis. Details on Page 23.

AIRFIELDS ARE HIT AS HEAVY STRIKES CONTINUE IN NORTH

Base 80 Miles From Hanoi Raided—Last Major U.S. Combat Unit Disbanding

By MALCOLM W. BROWNE

TAKING COVER: South Vietnamese soldiers huddling in a foxhole during mortar attack near Route 13, north of Saigon. They were with refugees fleeing city of Anloc.

AIRLINES APPEAL JUDGE'S REFUSAL TO BAR WALKOUT

Act as Lower Court Rules It Can't Keep U.S. Pilots Out of Global Stoppage

STRIKE SET TOMORROW

Union Chiefs Agree to Hold Talks on a Postponement but Doubt Is Voiced

By ROBERT LINDSEY

McGovern Income Plans Ridiculed by a Nixon Aide

By EDWIN L. DALE Jr.

ALLENDE REVISES CHILEAN CABINET

He Replaces Six Ministers, Including Economic Chief, as Inflation Stirs Crisis

By JUAN de ONIS

Strategic Arms Talks: Long Road to Success

2½ Years in Making

By BERNARD GWERTZMAN

Russians Hail Pacts

By HEDRICK SMITH

Key Hanoi Aide in Peking

Herbert Stein

Fiddler, 3,225 Performances Old, Tops Long-Run List

By McCANDLISH PHILLIPS

In special curtain call here last night, three foreign Tevyes joined Paul Lipson, Broadway's seventh Tevye. From left: Manolo Fábregas of Mexico, Lex Gouldsmit of the Netherlands, Mr. Lipson, and Shmuel Rudensky of Israel.

Maria Karnilova and Zero Mostel in photo illustrating Times review of Sept. 23, 1964

Unions for Doctors Pose New Challenge to A.M.A.

By RICHARD D. LYONS

INDEPENDENCE — PROFESSIONAL — ECONOMIC

Symbol used by American Physicians Guild.

Today's Sections

Index to Subjects

At a Democratic Party hearing in St. Louis, Kennedy urged the party to include in its platform national health insurance to cover all Americans.

ALSO IN 1972

The same day, five men were arrested for breaking into Democratic National Committee headquarters at the Watergate Hotel.

JOSEPH KENNEDY II, DAVID KENNEDY INJURED IN JEEP ACCIDENT

David Kennedy was riding in a Jeep driven by his brother Joseph Kennedy II when it overturned, breaking David's back and paralyzing his girlfriend. David Kennedy battled drug addiction throughout his life and died from an overdose in a Palm Beach hotel in 1984.

THE SHIFT INTO PHASE 4

Phone, Gas Rates Increase in N.E. as Freeze Is Lifted

By JOANNA BERKMAN

Gas and telephone rates increased here Monday, the first full day of the lifted price ceilings under Phase IV.

The Boston Gas Company had been allowed a $3.9 million rate hike by the State Dept. of Public Utilities which also approved a $66.6 million rate boost for the New England Telephone Co.

Under the new wage-price regulations, gasoline and petroleum products will remain frozen until Aug. 19 and beef prices will continue to be frozen until Sept. 12.

The 5.5 percent wages increase guidelines are to continue from Phase 3.

Under the new rules, prices set by small and meduim sized business firms may be increased to reflect cost increases since the last quarter of 1972.

Large firms, however, with business of $100 million a year or more will have to give 30 days' notice of any price increases.

Boston Gas Co. spokesman Arthur Sanda said that the minimum increase to residential customers would be 20 cents a month, with an average increase of 50 cents a month. Overall, he said, there will be a 4.45 percent rate increase, with residential heating costs up 3.7 percent and other residential usage up 3.44 percent.

Continued on Page Two

- MEAT PACKERS got another setback in court yesterday when a federal judge denied an injunction to lift the ceiling on beef price before Sept. 12. At about the same time, packers were told by Canada that controls were being placed on beef being exported to U. S. Page 2.
- AUTOMOBILES will cost more this fall. Chrysler applied to the Cost of Living Council for increase in prices on 1974 models. Other manufacturers are expected to follow suit. A number of steel companies said they would also raise prices. Page 2.
- ON THE MONEY FRONT there was a lot of hard news. The stock market dropped 9.18 points. The Federal Reserve Bank increased its discount rate to 7.5 percent. The First National Bank of Boston increased its interest rate to 9¼ percent. Page 13. Page 13.

PARTLY CLOUDY

Report on Page 35

Boston Herald American

Combining the best features of the Herald Traveler and Record American

TELEPHONE 426-3000 ★ TUESDAY, AUGUST 14, 1973 40 PAGES FIFTEEN CENTS

LATE COMPLETE

1 Passenger Feared Paralyzed in Nantucket Accident

2 RFK Sons, 5 Girls in Car Crash

By PAUL CORSETTI and ARSENE DAVIGNON

NANTUCKET—David Kennedy, 18, son of the late Sen. Robert F. Kennedy, suffered a back injury and a friend, Pamela Kelley, 18, a possible broken spine yesterday when a car driven by his brother, Joseph, 20, overturned on Polpis road.

Doctors at Cape Cod Hospital in Hyannis said Miss Kelley, of Centerville on Cape Cod, may be paralyzed and is "seriously ill."

Another of five young women passengers with the Kennedys, Mary Schloff, 22, of Grosse Point, Mich., also was admitted to Cape Cod Hospital with a possible broken pelvis and broken right leg. She was reported in good condition.

Hospital public relations director Torbin Yates said David Kennedy's condition was satisfactory.

Treated and released were Kimberley Kelley, 17, Pamela's sister, right leg injuries; and Patricia Powers, 22, of Spring Lake, N.J., neck and wrist injuries.

The fifth girl, Francesca Deonis, 18, of Centerville, was not listed as injured.

Joseph Kennedy who, police said, escaped with back scratches, was charged with "operating a motor vehicle negligently so that the lives and safety of the public might have been endangered."

Police said all seven young people were thrown "quite a few feet in the air," and landed 20 to 30 feet from the car, a topless sports vehicle.

Sgt. Paul Smith said they were first taken to Nantucket Hospital, and later flown by helicopter ambulance to Cape Cod Hospital.

Mrs. Ethel Kennedy, the senator's widow, went immediately from the family compound in Hyannis to be with her son. She was accompanied by her sister, Eunice Shriver and the latter's husband, Sargent Shriver.

Kimberley Kelley first made headlines in Oct., 1971, when a national publication said she and Robert Kennedy Jr. Planned to wed.

The car was registered to a Peter Van Dyke Emerson of Siasconset, police said.

(Continued on Page Eight)

JOSEPH KENNEDY DAVID KENNEDY

Prince Charles in N.H.

BRITAIN'S PRINCE CHARLES, a lieutenant and deputy gunnery officer, stands on the bow (left), as the H. M. S. Minerva steams into Portsmouth, N. H., harbor. The frigate came to Portsmouth to help the city celebrate its 350th anniversary. The prince has been in the British Navy for two years. (See Story on Page 8) (AP)

Says President 'Not Proper Judge'

Cox Files Tapes Brief, Criticizes Nixon Defense

By WARREN WEAVER
(C) New York Times News Service

WASHINGTON—Archibald Cox, the Watergate special prosecutor, charged yesterday that President Nixon could not be "a proper judge" of whether the public interest requires his making tape recordings of White House conversations available to a grand jury investigation.

In a brief filed in federal district court yesterday, Cox noted that the President's "highest and closest aides and associates have been accused in sworn testimony" before the Senate Committee headed by Sen. Sam. J. Ervin Jr.

The President, Cox declared, "is bound to them not only by the natural emotions of loyalty and gratitude but also by the risk that his present political power and future place in history will be linked to the effect of disclosure to the grand jury on them."

"The evidence on the tapes also may be material to public accusations against the respondent (Nixon) himself," the Cox brief continued, "A question to which he can hardly be indifferent. We call attention to these facts without disrespect to the respondent or his office."

Even if Nixon could disregard his own stake in

(Continued on Page Six)

Nixon to Take Case to Public Within Two Days

Rogers C. B. Morton says President Nixon will be "very candid" when he addresses nation on Watergate. Page 6.

WASHINGTON (UPI) — President Nixon will break his self-imposed silence on Watergate either tomorrow or Thursday and issue a detailed defense against charges that he was aware of efforts to cover up the scandal, White House sources said yesterday.

Sources said Nixon will use the statement, coupled with an appearance on national television, to proclaim he is innocent of any intentional wrongdoing and plead that the scandal cause no further interruption in the work of his administration.

The detailed "white paper," which a team of White House lawyers headed by Leonard Garment and J. Fred Buzhardt have been preparing for several weeks, will be Nixon's first public statement since May 22 on the question of whether he knew about the Watergate break-in or efforts to cover it up.

(Continued on Page Six)

Sargent Says Road Act Frees $800M

Gov. Francis W. Sargent hailed President Nixon's signing of the National Highway Transportation Act yesterday. Almost simultaneously with the Washington signing, the Governor and Transportation Sec. Alan Altschuler, claimed the Act would not only provide the state with new funds for mass transportation, but would free more than $800 million the Governor has not used for highways, for use in extending rapid transit, rail and bus services.

The act calls for spending $23 billion to aid transportation programs, including mass transit, during the next three years. The money will be shared by all 50 states.

According to the Governor's view the $800 million he has not used on Interstate 95, both north and south, or on the inner belt, can now be used for the mass transportation system he proposed last November.

This money, plus the state's normal share of the new Act, according to the Governor will make Massachusetts a national leader in transportation.

"Three years ago we took a gamble in Massachusetts. We were willing to bet that our national transportation policy could not revolve solely around the automobile," he stated.

"Well that gamble paid off.

"First, it will allow us to use highway funds for expansion and improvement in the

(Continued on Page Seventeen)

Grim Toll in Texas Now 27

By JAMES L. OVERTON

HOUSTON (UPI)—Sheriff's deputies unearthed four bodies from shallow graves—including two nude boys buried together—on a Texas beach yesterday, raising to 27 the toll of youngsters tortured and killed in a three-year sex plot that is the worst mass murder in recent U.S. history.

Working under a broiling sun, officers dug up body after body from the sand in a two-mile area that covers two counties near High Island, Tex.

A truck driver, who found one grave Sunday night by poking a stick into the beach until he hit a soft spot, pointed it out to deputies yesterday.

The first body was unearthed during the morning fog. The final two were pulled from a three-foot grave near an embankment parallel to the sea near dusk. Deputies then stopped the search for more victims until today.

The worst previous mass murders in this century were discovered ironically at the same time some of the Texas boys were being slain.

(Continued on Page Ten)

Index

Action Line	11	Mayer	29
Baker	31	Medicare	35
Bishop	32	Mind Mirror	34
Bridge	33	O'Brian	32
Chatter Line	19	Porter	32
Claflin	21	Post Position	40
Classified	37-40	Sports	21-26
Comics	33-35	Theaters	28, 29
Considine	32	TV-Radio	27
Cross Clue	34	Today's Living	18-20
Crossword	33	View From Hill	31
Cryptoquote	33	Walsh	20
Dear Abby	19	White	31
Deaths	36	Weber	34
Dobbins	31	Wishing Well	33
Editorial	30-32		
Financial	14-17		
Gossip	32		
Greenberg	31		
Hart	31		
Heloise	35		
Horgan	21		
Horoscope	34		
Lerner	30		
Mailbag	30		
Manners	28		

U.S. Near UN Vote Against Israel Act

UNITED NATIONS, N.Y. (AP) — The United States was reported yesterday ready to join the UN censure of Israel for forcing down an Arab airliner in an unsuccessful hunt for Palestinian guerrilla leaders.

A U.S. spokesman indicated, however, that any Security Council resolution going beyond censure would face American opposition.

Charging that previous U.S. vetoes of anti-Israel resolutions has spurred "aggression by Israel," Egypt called on the council to impose sanctions.

A mere condemnation of Israel "is not an effective way to restore the balance" in the Middle East, Egyptian Ambassador Ahmed Abdel Meguid declared.

(Continued on Page Ten)

Braintree Couple Happy Millionaires!

PENNIES FROM HEAVEN—Mr. and Mrs. James Gorman of Braintree embrace after winning $1 million Mass. Lottery Prize during drawing in Boston last night. Gorman, 25, is an employe of the telephone company. (Story on Page 36) (AP)

ALSO IN 1973

Spiro Agnew resigned as vice president after pleading no contest to tax evasion charges. Gerald Ford replaced Agnew and later became president when Nixon resigned.

EDWARD KENNEDY JR.'S LEG AMPUTATED DUE TO CANCER

More Of Same
More good weather expected. Highs near 80 degrees. Lows in the middle 50s. Winds will be northerly increasing from 10 to 15 m.p.h. Map, data 2-A.

St. Petersburg Times

Florida's Best Newspaper

Vol. 90—No. 116 · 80 PAGES · ST. PETERSBURG, FLORIDA, SATURDAY, NOVEMBER 17, 1973 · 15 CENTS A COPY

Gulf Oil-Tracts Sale Set

By CHARLES PATRICK
Of The Times Staff

Despite threatened lawsuits and broad public opposition in Florida, Interior Secretary Rogers C. B. Morton announced in Washington Friday that oil-exploration leases on 147 tracts covering 817,000 acres in the Gulf of Mexico off Florida, Alabama and Mississippi will be offered for sale next month.

The tracts will be the first offshore areas opened for oil and gas drilling in the northeastern Gulf and the first off any states other than Louisiana, Texas and California. They include some tracts from 30 to 50 miles west of Clearwater Beach.

THE BIDS WILL be opened in New Orleans Dec. 20 by the Interior Department's Bureau of Land Management. The tracts range from 15 to 90 miles off the coast and are expected to draw bids of from $50,000 to $100-million, depending on size and prospects of finding oil.

Morton said successful bidders will be subject to special stipulations, such as having adequate facilities and equipment for containing and cleaning up oil spills. Environmentalists have opposed the oil-lease sales based on the fear of major oil spills fouling Florida's white beaches and possible long-term damage to the environment from offshore oil rigs.

Don Trusdale, chief of the Bureau of Environmental Analysis of the Interior Department, said that 40 to 50 tracts of land in an area off Fort Walton Beach in the Florida Panhandle have been removed from the sale because of possible conflict with Navy bombing exercises in the area.

TRUSDALE said oil companies will face strict rules, including no barging of oil and use only of designated pipeline corridors. Morton said the governors of Florida, Alabama and Mississippi were being invited to participate in the planning of onshore pipeline corridors to serve the offshore wells.

Jim Barrett, an assistant to Florida Atty. Gen. Robert Shevin, said the state is considering legal steps to prevent drilling. Shevin and other state officials had sought to delay awarding of the leases to further study environmental impact statements.

SHEVIN ON Thursday appealed to Morton for at least a two-year delay in federal approval of the offshore drilling and pleaded with him not to allow the current fuel shortage to prod the federal government into quick action.

U.S. Sen. Lawton Chiles, D-Fla., previously threatened a court suit to delay the drilling.

W. R. Cobb, an exploration engineer for Shell Oil Co. in New Orleans said the new tracts in the Gulf will help solve the energy crisis, but added, "We are still looking at a three-year delay before oil is brought to port, 1974 and 1975 will be severe years."

FEDERAL estimates of the reserves to be developed by the sale range from 1.5-billion to 2.4-billion barrels of oil and 1.8-trillion to 2.9-trillion cubic feet of gas. Tapping those reserves would require 700 to 1,120 wells operating from 75 to 125 platforms and 480 to 800 miles of pipeline.

When production stabilizes, a recent federal report stated, the leases might produce 270,000 to 443,000 barrels of oil per day.

Nixon Signs Alaska Pipeline Bill

New York News Service

WASHINGTON — President Nixon signed the Alaska oil pipeline bill into law Friday, saying at the same time that there is "a reasonable possibility" that the Arab countries might resume petroleum exports to the United States and Europe.

The President gave no timetable for an end to the Arab oil boycott, and he said that "even if it happened tomorrow, we would still have an energy crisis for this year."

BUT HIS COMMENT at an Oval Office signing ceremony for the pipeline bill appeared to reflect some optimism about the Mideast situation.

Nixon also told a group of congressmen and other guests in his office that environmental considerations would have to take second place to efforts to solve the nation's energy crisis in the short run.

WHILE NIXON WAS signing the bill, opening the way for construction to begin next spring on the 789-mile pipeline across Alaska, the Senate continued debate on a measure giving the President powers to cut U.S. energy consumption.

Two amendments were approved providing unemployment and other benefits for workers laid off as a result of fuel shortages and giving the President authority to bar exports of scarce fuels.

AP

Sen. Kennedy And Edward Jr. In 1972

Kennedy Son To Lose Leg To Cancer

WASHINGTON (UPI) — Sen. Edward M. Kennedy's 12-year-old son, Edward Jr., afflicted with bone cancer, will undergo surgery today for amputation of his right leg above the knee, the senator's office disclosed Friday.

The latest tragedy to strike the Kennedy family was announced on the eve of a happy event, the marriage of Kathleen Kennedy, 22, eldest daughter of the late Sen. Robert F. Kennedy, to David Townsend, 25, a Harvard doctoral candidate.

THE FIRST wedding among the newest generation of Kennedys will take place as scheduled a few blocks from Georgetown University Hospital, where the bride's cousin lay stricken.

Shortly after the announcement, President Nixon telephoned the boy's hospital room and spoke to him and his father. A spokesman said the senator and his wife, Joan, were "deeply touched by the President's thoughtfulness."

The younger Kennedy, an athletic-minded seventh-grader, was admitted to the hospital last Friday for diagnostic tests and was re-admitted Tuesday when the tests showed bone cancer.

SEN. KENNEDY AND his wife, who interrupted a European trip and flew back to Washington last weekend, have been at their son's bedside almost constantly. They told the boy Friday morning that he would lose his leg.

The Kennedys' other children are Kara, 13, and Patrick Joseph, 6.

Twelve-year-old Edward Kennedy Jr.'s right leg was amputated above the knee after he was diagnosed with bone cancer. His sister Kara Kennedy would be diagnosed with inoperable lung cancer decades later. Her father would find a surgeon to remove the tumor and she would be cancer-free as of 2009.

3 Knock At Skylab's Door

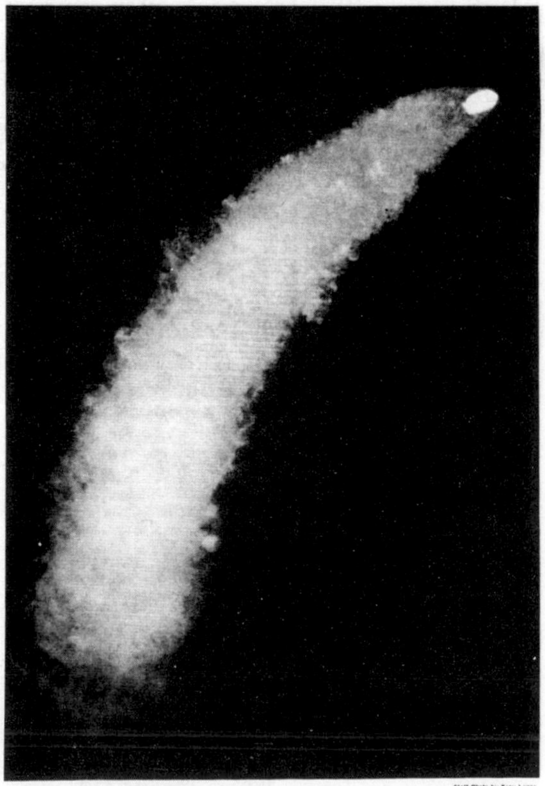

Staff Photo by Tony Lopez

Skylab III Hurtles Upward Trailing A Massive Column Of Smoke

Times Wire Services

HOUSTON — Three rookie astronauts successfully docked with the Skylab space station Friday, overcoming a problem that two times prevented them from linking with the orbiting laboratory where they will live and work for 84 days.

"Whew!" Skylab III commander Gerald P. Carr said as he finally succeeded in the link up. "Glad to be here. Glad to be home."

CARR AND CREWMATES Edward G. Gibson and William R. Pogue, all space first timers, flawlessly sped into orbit aboard a patched-up rocket and then skillfully guided their command ship through a complex series of rocket firings that carried them to a rendezvous with the space station.

As Carr tried to dock with the orbiting lab, however, a docking probe on the point of the cone-shaped command ship failed to latch with a collar-like port on the space station.

The astronaut backed up and rammed the probe into the collar two times but failed to link up.

Finally, he said, he came harder than before and then reported happily moments later: "Houston, we're docked."

"I think what happened is I just hit it too easy," Carr said.

THE FIRST SKYLAB flight last May ran into similar docking problems. It took the fliers eight attempts before they linked the ships.

The three astronauts plan to enter the home-size Skylab space station this morning.

The flawless blastoff and rendezvous will round out a $2.6-billion space program with a holiday voyage of 12 weeks in the last U.S. manned space flight until mid-1975. The three spacemen are scheduled to be in orbit around the Earth during Thanksgiving, Christmas and New Year's Day, with spacewalks planned for the first two holidays.

The astronauts also will have front-row seats for a space-clear view of the comet Kohoutek, which is expected to reach its greatest brilliance during the holiday season.

MEANWHILE, nine astronauts left Houston for Moscow to begin training with Russian space equipment for the joint U.S.-Soviet flight scheduled for July 1975. The pilots will spend two weeks at the Y. A. Gagarin Center of Cosmonaut Training at Star City outside Moscow to learn about the Soyuz spacecraft that will dock with an American Apollo ship in Earth orbit.

A group of Soviet cosmonauts began training in the United States last July. Crewmen from both countries will exchange visits next year for more specific training.

THE NEW Skylab visitors rocketed away from Cape Canaveral precisely on time at 9:01 EST. The Saturn 1B rocket that boosted them into orbit performed perfectly despite numerous tiny cracks that twice delayed the 30th U.S. manned launch.

One of the smallest crowds ever to watch a manned launch included the astronauts' wives and 13 children. The wives had no regrets that the fliers would be away for the holidays and were "simply happy" they had a chance to go into space.

"You've got three happy rookies up here," said Carr as they soared toward Skylab. "It's a great world," added Gibson.

"We can hardly take our eyes away from the window," Pogue said. "There's already nose smears on the window."

Inferno Kills 24 In L.A.

By MARK LOWE

LOS ANGELES (UPI) — Flames swept up an open staircase that acted like a "gigantic chimney" Friday, engulfing an old three-story apartment house and killing 24 persons in the worst residential fire in the city's history. Fifty-two others were injured.

Many of the victims died in their beds or rooms, trapped by the flames and smoke that spread rapidly through the 45-year-old frame-stucco Stratford apartment building.

OTHERS WERE killed when they leaped from windows of the upper floor in a desperate attempt to escape the fire. Nine of the victims were children.

Fire Chief Raymond Hill said he was "99.9 per cent" sure that the fire started in a sofa or chair in the lobby. The first firemen to arrive saw flames shooting from the front of the building "almost into the street." Tragically, the Stratford was under renovation to close the open staircase and comply with an ordinance passed by the City

(See FIRE, 6-A)

Nixon Quoted: Cox Reneged On Tapes

By JAMES M. NAUGHTON
New York Times Service (c)

WASHINGTON — President Nixon reportedly accused Archibald Cox Friday of having reneged at the last minute on a compromise settlement of the Watergate tapes case.

But the report of Nixon's account of events that led to his dismissal of the Watergate special prosecutor last month was challenged by Cox and apparently contradicted by published records of the unsuccessful effort to resolve the tapes controversy out of court.

ACCORDING TO Rep. Charles W. Whalen Jr., R-Ohio, who took notes — which he said included verbatim quotes — on Nixon's eighth and final Watergate meeting with members of Congress Friday, the President gave the following explanation for ordering Cox's dismissal on Saturday, Oct. 20:

"Cox changed his mind on Friday night (Oct. 19) because of lack of confidence in Senator Stennis. We did not know until Saturday he had changed his mind." (The White House, asked to verify the quote attributed to Nixon, did not respond immediately.)

Sen. John C. Stennis, D-Miss. had been chosen by Nixon to authenticate a White House summary of the contents of nine tape recordings subpoenaed by the Watergate Grand Jury. The planned compromise collapsed when Cox refused to accept it and was dismissed. Atty. Gen. Elliot L. Richardson then resigned and Deputy Atty. Gen. William D. Ruckelshaus was dismissed rather than carry out Nixon's order to fire Cox.

COX, REACHED Friday by telephone in Brooksville, Maine, said he had "never questioned Senator Stennis' integrity at all." His objections to the compromise plan, Cox said, were spelled out in a memorandum to Richardson and a letter to Charles Alan Wright, White House lawyer in the tapes case.

Both documents, along with a letter from Wright to Cox, were made public by Cox a few hours before his dismissal on Oct. 20, the date Nixon reportedly said the White House first learned of Cox's objections.

(See COX, 6-A)

Nixon On TV

President Nixon's hour-long press conference with managing editors will be televised live tonight by the three major networks, beginning at 7 p.m. Story, 7-A.

Ann Landers	3-D	Jumble	5-D
Bridge	5-D	Movie & Theatre Times	4-D
Business	13-A	Obituaries	7-B
Classified	7-28-C	People	5-A
Comics	5-D	Public's Page	19-A
Crossword	7-D	Pulse	7-B
Editorial	18-A	Radio-TV	8-D
Financial	12, 14-16-A	Sports	1-7-C
Horoscope	5-D	Weather	2-A

Dow Jones Up 16.78 Points

Story, 13-A

About a month after his leg was amputated, Edward Kennedy Jr. walked with crutches to a nearby car with his parents, Senator Edward Kennedy and Joan Kennedy. (AP Photo)

ALSO IN 1973

The Supreme Court legalized abortion with its controversial decision in Roe v. Wade.

Maryland Wins, Georgetown Loses in NCAA—Page D1

The Washington Post

The Weather

Today—Cloudy, high in the low to mid 50s, low in the 30s. Chance of precipitation is near zero today, 60 per cent tonight. Monday—Rain, high near 50. Yesterday's temperature range, 50-37. Details, Page B3.

Index 360 Pages
 24 Sections
Amusements H 1 Living E 1
Books Sect. H Metro B 1
Classified K 1 Obituaries B 6
Editorial C 6 Sports D 1
Financial F 1 Style G 1
Gardens E11 Travel F11
See Detailed Index A3

98th Year · No. 101 SUNDAY, MARCH 16, 1975 Phone (202) 223-6000 50¢

The Peaceful Cambodians: Innocent Victims of War

By Murrey Marder and Michael Getler
Washington Post Staff Writers

Cambodia is the supreme innocent victim nation in the Indochina war.

Too weak to challenge any intruder, Cambodia first became a highway and a sanctuary for North Vietnamese and Vietcong warfare in South Vietnam. Next, its borders were crossed by American and South Vietnam troops to attack the Communist bases. Finally, Cambodia itself, one of the most peaceful nations in Asia, was pumped into nationwide civil war, with the

opposing Cambodian sides supported by the outside powers.

Few Americans know the full record of overt and covert U.S. involvement in Cambodia. It is a strange mixture of compassion, and strategic exploitation of Cambodian territory as an adjunct of the war in Vietnam. In cold U.S. strategic terms, Cambodia never was more than a target zone for the Vietnamese war.

Out of the Nixon administration's attempt to conceal its original, secret operations in Cambodia from a Congress that feared "another Vietnam,"

came a twisted action-reaction sequence of dissembling, deception and official spying that contributed to the roots of the Watergate scandals, and, ultimately, to President Nixon's resignation.

News Analysis

This corrosive impact, out of all proportion to the actual American strategic stake in Cambodia, accounts for much of the exceptional opposition in Congress to President Ford's appeals for

emergency aid to Cambodia to preserve American "morality" and "credibility."

The Nixon administration's boast that it achieved "peace with honor" by withdrawing all U.S. troops from South Vietnam in early 1973 without surrendering that nation to Communist control, also ended the strategic rationale for American involvement in Cambodia. At the insistence of Congress, American legislation year after year had expressly stated that there was no U.S. "commitment" to Cam-

bodia; the Nixon administration repeatedly agreed.

And yet, the United States for five years did enmesh itself massively in the fate of Cambodia. It armed and greatly expanded the forces of the anti-Communist government in Phnom Penh, while North Vietnam did the same for the Khmer Rouge insurgents, producing a major internal war that did not exist before American troops crossed the Cambodian border in 1970.

Cambodia, U.S. officials maintain, would have been taken over by the Communists in any event because of

its strategic relationship to the war in Vietnam. Perhaps, critics counter, but now Cambodia has had the worst of both worlds, a devastating war plus the prospect of Communist, rule.

There are no accurate statistics on Cambodia for virtually anything, especially on the costs of the war since 1970, in which the dead and wounded run into the hundreds of thousands. Some U.S. experts' estimates go as high as 700,000 Cambodian, military and civilian—one-tenth of the population—

See DECISION, A18, Col. 1

Key Area Taken in Cambodia

Insurgent Rocket Base Recaptured

From News Dispatches

PHNOM PENH, March 15 — Cambodian government forces recaptured the key position of Toul Leap, six miles west of Pochentong airport today, military sources said.

The insurgents had been using the town as a firebase to blast the airport with rockets and field artillery in an attempt to halt the U.S. airlift of arms, rice and fuel to this beleaguered capital.

An official communique said the Khmer Rouge rebels suffered heavy losses when the government troops retook the town.

Meanwhile, insurgents shelled Neak Luong, the government's last position on the Mekong River, a refugee reported. More than 1,000 rounds a day have hit the crowded city for the past three days.

Neak Luong has been cut off from supplies for some time, and a source from the town said starving people "ran like crazy" to get airdropped rice. Hundreds in the town were already dead or dying of starvation, a witness said.

Two children were killed and six adults seriously wounded by rockets fired in Phnom Penh to the insurgents.

The exodus of foreigners from Phnom Penh continued as France reduced its embassy to consulate status and Singapore removed all its diplomats.

The French announced that a consul and a cultural officer would remain here.

Australia flew its diplomats and the Singaporeans to Bangkok on Friday.

Of the 1,100 French citizens living in Cambodia, about 100 have expressed a desire to leave. Cambodia was once a French protectorate and the

See CAMBODIA, A19, Col. 1

Cambodian refugees carry the body of a child killed in a rocket attack Thursday at Phum Cham, about six miles from the capital Phnom Penh.
United Press International

Reporter Is Killed By Saigon Police

By Philip A. McCombs
Washington Post Foreign Service

SAIGON, March 15—Agence France-Presse correspondent Paul Leandri was shot and killed last night as he tried to race his car out of the heavily guarded national police headquarters following a heated and reportedly violent argument with officials, police said today.

Their statement, which places virtually all blame for the incident on Leandri, is the only official version. Many questions remain unanswered but reliable sources with independent access to information about the incident say there is no evidence so far that would significantly contradict the official version.

The argument between Leandri and police that pre-

he wrote several days ago, summons aid. He had been ordered to the police headquarters and threatened with expulsion from the country if he did not reveal his source, they added.

[The French Foreign Ministry said news of Leandri's death was received in Paris with "amazement and indignation," AFP reported. Foreign Minister Jean Sauvagnargues summoned the South Vietnam ambassador to a meeting and instructed the French embassy in Saigon to "raise the very strongest protest" over the newsman's death.

[Leandri, 37, was on his second tour of duty in South Vietnam.]

Leandri telephoned several Western journalists, here, in

Kissinger Renews Bid To Syrians

By Marilyn Berger
Washington Post Staff Writer

AMMAN, March 15—Secretary of State Henry A. Kissinger made another attempt today to win Syrian President Hafez Assad's acquiescence in a new Egyptian-Israeli agreement.

The Palestine Liberation Organization, meeting nearby, announced it had accepted Assad's proposal for setting up joint political and military commands between Syria and the Palestinians.

Following four hours of talks with Assad, Kissinger made the brief hop to Amman for dinner with Jordan's King Hussein.

The confused picture of Mid-East diplomacy was brought into focus during today's stop in Damascus.

Kissinger is trying to persuade Assad to accept a new agreement in which Israel would link the Egyptians to place at Israel's step-by-step the PLO, which calls itself

A Dictator's Death

U.S. Role on Trujillo Examined

By William Greider
Washington Post Staff Writer

On the night they killed Rafael Leonidas Trujillo, an American named Henry Dearborn stayed up until dawn pursuing a bizarre trail of Caribbean intrigue.

Nearly 14 years later, the events of that evening are in the news again because the possibility of U. S. involvement in the death of Dominican Republic dictator Trujillo is a fresh issue confronting the CIA.

Dearborn was the U. S. consul general to the Dominican Republic, the ranking representative of his government, a patient and fastidious man who in both riding in three cars, had caught Generalissimo Trujillo unguarded and gunned him down. They stuffed his body in the trunk of a getaway car and drove off.

At midnight, when Dearborn and his party happened along, the Dominicans were still looking for

See CIA, A6, Col. 1

U.S. Probing Conspiracies On Oil Prices

By Thomas O'Toole
Washington Post Staff Writer

A federal investigation of why oil prices rose so rapidly at the height of the Arab oil embargo has uncovered alleged conspiracies by businessmen and organized criminals to overcharge electric power companies, hospitals, schools and consumers by anywhere from $1 billion to $3 billion.

Grand juries have been convened in Jacksonville, Fla., New York and Los Angeles to examine charges that importers and suppliers falsified U.S. Customs documents and set up dummy corporations to double and triple the price of oil during the embargo. Grand juries may also be convened in Houston, Philadelphia, Baltimore and Boston as the allegations and evidence of illegalities continue to mount.

"This is the biggest investigation of this kind we've ever had," said Robert DiLorenzo of the U.S. Customs Service, one of two federal agencies spearheading the probe into illegal oil pricing. "It is our No. 1 priority right now in fraud investigations."

Customs has as many as 30 agents working full-time in six U.S. ports, poring over tanker records and manifests filed during the embargo, looking for charges. The agents have already uncovered what they believe to be two cases of fraud.

One involved a tanker coming into an East Coast port with a load of what was said to be oil from Venezuela. But the shore road toward George Washington Avenue, Dearborn's car was stopped by Dominican police.

Everyone out, search the car, search the Americans. The roadblock was at an isolated point beside the sea, where waves crash against coral cliffs. It was also near the spot where, less than two hours before, an assassination team of eight men,

In fact, Customs said, the oil carried by the tanker came from Nigeria, where the price was still $5.50 a barrel at the time the tanker reached the United States. The tanker carried an estimated 300,000 barrels of oil, so the alleged overcharge came to more than $2 million.

The second case has reached the Jacksonville grand jury, and involves an oil supplier that sold the Jacksonville Electric Authority between 5 million and 16 million barrels of oil in the six months after the embargo ended for the six months after, most of it at $12 a barrel.

Customs seized records

See PRICING, A13, Col. 1

Portugal Considers Soviet Deal

By Miguel Acoca
Special to The Washington Post

LISBON, March 15—Portugal's revolutionary Armed Forces Movement, which is swiftly imposing a socialist military dictatorship, disclosed today that the government is considering a request from a Portuguese company to provide refueling facilities for the Soviet merchant fleet.

The disclosure came as the ruling revolutionary council announced the takeover of the 33 most important national insurance companies. Only yesterday the council took over Portuguese-owned private banks.

Portugal already has established relations with the Soviet Union following the ouster last April of the right-wing dictatorship, the two countries have been expanding trade and discussing development projects.

Portugal announced an agreement a week ago for the training of fishermen on Soviet ships and for joint ventures in the studies or fishing. Portugal has asked the Soviet Union and other countries for assistance for its depressed fishing industry, once one of its biggest foreign exchange earners.

Dealings with Soviet fishing authorities have aroused concern among the country's NATO partners. The United States is particularly concerned that the left-leaning government may not be a dependable ally.

[NATO Secretary General Joseph Luns said in Naples

See PORTUGAL, A20, Col. 1

ALSO IN 1975

The Vietnam War came to an end on April 30, when the Communist North Vietnamese Army toppled the U.S.-supported Saigon government.

Onassis, 69, Dies in Paris

By Stephen J. Lynton
Washington Post Staff Writer

Aristotle Socrates Onassis, the Greek shipping magnate whose immense wealth brought him a life of jet-set romance and marriage to President John F. Kennedy's widow, died yesterday in Paris at the age of 69.

His wife, the former Jacqueline Bouvier, was reported to be in New York. He died at 12:30 p.m. (7:30 a.m. EDT) at the American Hospital in the Paris suburb of Neuilly. He had been hospitalized since Feb. 6.

Christina Onassis, 23, his daughter by a previous marriage, and his only surviving child, had been at his side during the night.

A hospital communique reported by news agencies attributed his death to a broncho-pulmonary infection not controllable by specific antibiotics. It said he died "without suffering."

He had entered the hospital with various ailments, including myasthenia gravis, a progressive weakening of voluntary muscles. His gall bladder was removed Feb. 9. He was also reported to have heart and respiratory ailments.

Late yesterday, Mrs. Onassis, clad in a black leather coat and a black turtleneck

See ONASSIS, A8, Col. 1

Aristotle S. Onassis in 1973
By Nancy Moran for The Washington Post

Courts, Widow Sort Out Value of a Life

Fourth in a weekly series

By John Saar
Washington Post Staff Writer

The accident happened on a Saturday night when Bob Flowers, 48, went to get the Sunday newspapers. A car from 15th Street NW mounted the Massachusetts Avenue sidewalk on which he was walking and hit him. There followed five lingering days of doctors, surgery, hope and fear before Flowers died of his injuries.

Numb with fatigue, her happy second marriage ended in the stark surroundings of an intensive care unit, Elizabeth Flowers was a widow at 32. It happened in 1970, but she remembers it all like yesterday: the distant crash of glass and metal, her husband's pain, the ordeal of waiting for his or death.

She salvaged her losses with a poetic simplicity: "We were lovers, great friends and big pals." She recoiled from thoughts of suicide and came through a tunnel of depression to make a successful career, but she still feels like "I lost half my life."

Ensuing civil and criminal court proceedings did nothing to ease her grief and very little to compensate her loss. That year, about 55,000 Americans died

THE VICTIMS OF CRIME

on the highways. An unknown number were like Bob Flowers, blameless victims of somebody else's negligence.

The crushing blow from the badly driven 1964 Cadillac killed Flowers as surely as a speeding bullet, yet it was categorized as a traffic offense—somewhat worse than running a stop sign.

District of Columbia police officers investigated the accident as "Death No. 22" and charged the driver, Edward A. Stuart, a city resident. The

widow still thinks of her husband's death as "practically murder."

Under the D.C. Code, the offense of causing the death of another by "careless, reckless, or negligent" driving is a misdemeanor. Stuart later pleaded guilty to the misdemeanor of negligent homicide and received a suspended sentence and probation.

Of 78 traffic fatalities in the District in 1974, nine resulted in prosecutions for negligent homicide. There are no reliable national figures for this category of offense.

His suspended sentence is not uncommonly lenient, according to Warren K. King, deputy chief of the Superior Court Division in the U.S. Attorney's office for the District. "It is only a misdemeanor, so the most you can be sentenced to is a year," King stated. "Generally people think of it as a one-time thing and not really a criminal thing."

"All the homicide statutes have been in existence for 10,000 years," King continued, "and when the automobile explosion took place 30 to 40 years ago the law was not equipped to deal with it."

The concept of vehicular homicide

See VICTIMS, A14, Col. 1

October 20, 1979
John F. Kennedy Library and Museum Dedicated

Priscilla Presley
Out of seclusion
LIVING, Page B1

A special section on President Kennedy
INSIDE

Who is this man named Brando?
ARTS & FILMS, C1

Today's sections
Complete indexes for today's edition on Page 2

Boston Sunday Globe

The weather
Wind, hazy sun, 75-80. Complete details on Page 87

Vol. 217, No. 113© 1979, Globe Newspaper Co. • SUNDAY, OCTOBER 21, 1979 • Telephone 929-2000 Classified 929-1500 Circulation 929-2227 • 75 Cents • 90 cents 30 miles from Boston and beyond

'. . . the essence of President Kennedy's message — the appeal for unselfish dedication to the common good — is more urgent than it ever was.'

—PRESIDENT JIMMY CARTER

'In dedicating this library to Jack, we recall those years of grace, that time of hope. The spark still glows. The journey never ends. The dream shall never die . . . .'

—SEN. EDWARD M. KENNEDY

A day of poetry, politics and wit

In a light moment at yesterday's dedication ceremonies at the John F. Kennedy Library, President Jimmy Carter recalled that JFK once told a reporter that he wouldn't recommend the presidency to others — "at least for a while." That reference, an allusion to a possible bid for the Democratic presidential nomination by Sen. Edward M. Kennedy, brought smiles to the faces of the senator and his wife, Joan. (Globe photos by Stan Grossfeld and William Brett.)

By Martin F. Nolan
Globe Staff

In a gentle Indian Summer haze of music and memories, poetry and politics, the United States government yesterday officially dedicated the presidential library of its 35th President, John Fitzgerald Kennedy.

Jimmy Carter, the fourth President to preside in the shadow of the restoration of a Kennedy dynasty, accepted the keys to the nine-story white structure on behalf of the American people. Carter also used a Kennedy weapon, humor, to defuse a political situation somewhere between delicate and dangerous.

Praising an occasion "at once so solemn and so joyous," Carter also gently suggested that his host for the day, Sen. Edward M. Kennedy, might wait awhile before challenging Carter for the presidency.

Heraldic banners flapping in the breeze at the nearby University of Massachusetts campus suggested the sense of history hovering over the day. "John Kennedy loved politics, he loved laughter, and when the two came together, he loved that best of all," Carter said.

If John Kennedy enjoyed political spontaneity, there was some of that too yesterday, including a kissing confrontation between his widow and President Carter, as well as a feisty speech by his eldest nephew, Joseph Kennedy 2d.

Carter's 17-minute address was prepared in advance except for his historical reference to President Kennedy's comments about the Presidency. Carter had not planned to mention the rivalry between himself and the sole surviving Kennedy son, but the political overtones of Joseph Kennedy's speech apparently allowed Carter to lighten the occasion.

Carter quoted from a Kennedy press conference of March 1962 in which a reporter said, "Mr. President, your brother Ted said recently on television that after seeing the cares of office on you, he wasn't sure he would ever be interested in being President."

At this point, the crowd at Columbia Point stirred, including Kennedy, who had been looking at his own notes. The senator took off his glasses and started to smile as Carter continued with the response of President Kennedy to the second half of the reporter's question. The reporter, Carter said, asked, "I wonder if you could tell us whether, first, if you had it to do over again you would work for the Presidency, and, second, whether you can recommend this job to others?"

President Kennedy, Carter said, replied, "Well, the answer to the first question is yes, and the second is no. I do not recommend it to others — at least for awhile."

By then, Carter had yesterday's crowd with him, transported on the wings of John Kennedy's wit. They were all ready to listen when Carter flashed his own trademark grin and said, "As you can well see, President Kennedy's wit and also his wisdom is certainly as relevant today as it was then."

The day's weather seemed ordered from the libretto of one of the late President's favorite musical shows, Lerner and Loewe's "Camelot." By 8 a.m., the morning fog had cleared. As if by Arthurian edict, rain was banished until sundown and well after. The slightest of southerly breezes wafted across the gathering from the waters of Dorchester Bay.

At 8:30 a.m., the US Coast Guard radio barked out orders requiring all vessels to stay at least 1000 feet from "area Juliet Foxtrot Kilo." The US Secret Service also ordered all airplanes to avoid the air space over the Columbia Point peninsula. Three contingents of Secret Service agents were in the city yesterday, one guarding President Carter, a second guarding Lady Bird Johnson and a third protecting Sen. Kennedy, a move ordered by Carter last month after the senator hinted that he would become a candidate for President.

Most in the crowd of 7000 dressed comfortably and only the most seasoned diplomatic veterans wore hats: W. Averell Harriman, Dean Rusk and John Sherman Cooper. The atmosphere evoked the image of a class reunion in springtime as

JFK, Page 33

THE SPEECHES—Text of speeches by President Jimmy Carter and Sen. Edward Kennedy. Page 2. Other texts. Pages 27, 31.

THE KENNEDYS—It was a great day for the family despite the absence of Mrs. Rose Kennedy who is recuperating in Hyannis Port. Page 29.

THE PRESIDENT—Surrounded by many who yearn to defeat him. President Carter turned to the "wit and wisdom" of John F. Kennedy to relieve some of the tension. Page 36.

THE PEOPLE—The stars of the New Frontier were together again. Some had changed a bit in appearance but for most it was a grand, backslapping reunion. Page 37.

Doyle: Did adults plan school protests?

By Al Larkin
Globe Staff

Boston Police Supt. John Doyle said yesterday that repeated instances in which news reporters were warned in advance of seemingly spontaneous school walkouts have prompted a new investigation into possible behind-the-scenes involvement of adults.

"When the news media starts to get tipped off well in advance of an event, we begin to wonder just how spontaneous it is," he said yesterday in a telephone interview. "It's happened more than once or twice in recent days."

Doyle declined to say which newspapers or radio and television stations received the information, but it was learned that a WEEI radio reporter received an anonymous phone call informing him of a walkout last week well before it happened.

On Friday, Police Comr. Joseph M. Jordan announced plans for the investigation and named Doyle to direct the probe, which is expected to begin Monday morning.

While Jordan indicated that the decision to take a closer look at possible adult involvement was prompted by the recent wave of school walkouts and marches to City Hall, Doyle said, "We're going to look at everything that has happened."

He said the probe would include a closer look at the Sept. 18 stoning of a school bus carrying black students to South Boston High School which, Jordan said earlier this week, is now being viewed as the incident that initiated the current wave of racial violence.

The attack on the bus, which caught city officials by surprise because of the relative absence of racial problems in the schools, prompted speculation that adults might have been involved in planning it because the incident seemed coordinated.

Despite reports that South Boston teenagers met twice with officials from the antibusing South Boston Information Center just before the attack — a charge denied by information center officials — Doyle, at the time, remarked: "I know of no evidence that there was any adult involvement."

Yesterday, the superintendent said he no longer was ruling out adult involvement because " a few things have happened since then to make me reconsider."

However, when asked whether the investigation would focus on the South Boston Information Center, Doyle said "Certainly not. These kids are coming from schools all over the city."

BOSTON, Page 7

SUPT. JOHN DOYLE
Tips to media aroused suspicions

INSIDE

Communist Party backs Salvador junta

The Communist Party, outlawed for more than 30 years, joined two other leftist groups in supporting the new government of El Salvador, and a demonstration against the junta was canceled. Page 77.

Vietnam conciliatory toward Thailand

Vietnamese Minister of State for Foreign Affairs Nguyen Co Thach pledged that Hanoi-led troops hunting Khmer Rouge guerrillas would not cross into Thailand, and he said his government "welcomes all humanitarian aid" to the people of Cambodia and other Indochinese countries. Page 11.

Eisenhower had secret taping system

President Dwight D. Eisenhower for more than five years used a secret Oval Office taping system to record conversations with staff, congressmen, reporters and even Vice President Richard Nixon, the Houston Chronicle reported. Page 1.

The mayoral race in Boston heats up

Mayor Kevin White and his challenger, Joseph Timilty, are entering the final phase of their campaigns for the mayoralty. But the past few weeks, with their increased racial tensions in the city, may prove to be more important to the outcome than will the final two weeks of campaigning. Page 18.

Shortly before his death, Kennedy had discussed the possibility of building a presidential library at Harvard University. The John F. Kennedy Library overlooks the entrance to Boston Harbor and is near the childhood home of Kennedy's mother.

ALSO IN 1979

The China Syndrome, *a movie about a cover-up at a nuclear power plant, was released twelve days before the nuclear accident at Three Mile Island in Pennsylvania.*

NOVEMBER 7, 1979
SENATOR EDWARD KENNEDY DECLARED PRESIDENTIAL CANDIDACY

Kennedy officially announced his candidacy at Boston's Faneuil Hall. The campaign's first challenge was to explain Kennedy's poor performance in an interview with CBS News journalist Roger Mudd, in which the candidate struggled to explain why he wanted to be president.

ALSO IN 1979

Pope John Paul II visited the United States with stops in Boston, New York City, Philadelphia, Des Moines, Chicago, and Washington, D.C.

"All the News That's Fit to Print"

The New York Times

LATE CITY EDITION

Weather: Partly sunny today; cloudy tonight. Chance of showers tomorrow. Temperature range: today 43-55; yesterday 47-59. Details on page D20.

VOL. CXXIX . . . No. 44,395

25 CENTS

The New York Times/George Tames

Senator Edward M. Kennedy and his wife, Joan, in Boston. The bust is of John Quincy Adams, the sixth President.

Kennedy Declares His Candidacy, Vowing New Leadership for Nation

By HEDRICK SMITH

Special to The New York Times

BOSTON, Nov. 7 — Senator Edward M. Kennedy, who had declined entreaties to run for President in the last three campaigns, formally declared his candidacy for election in 1980 today with a pledge to provide a "forceful, effective Presidency" that would get the nation "on the march again."

To an ardently partisan crowd of three generations of the Kennedy family and political allies such as Mayor Jane M. Byrne of Chicago, Gov. Joseph E. Brennan of Maine and Senator John A. Durkin of New Hampshire, as well as to 5,000 Bostonians, he declared in Faneuil Hall that he felt "compelled by events and my commitment to public life" to oppose President Carter. And he contended that the contest would strengthen rather than divide the Democratic Party.

Here and in later campaign appearances today, the 47-year-old Massachusetts Democrat charged that President Carter had "taken the single most inflationary step" by lifting price controls from domestic crude oil last spring, and he attacked the President for saying that the American people were suffering a crisis of spirit.

'Malaise' of Leadership

"I say it is not the American people who are in a malaise," he told a crowd of several hundred supporters in nearby Manchester, N.H. "It's the political leadership that's in a malaise."

Mr. Kennedy issued his 1978 tax return, as well as a medical report saying he was in "excellent health." [Page A17.] The White House response to the announcement was muted, but a memorandum has begun circulating among senior officials with advice on rebutting the Senator's challenge. [Page A17.]

Mr. Kennedy also accused Mr. Carter of letting bureaucrats and subordinates

Continued on Page A17, Column 1

HOUSE PASSES A BI[LL] MANDATING MINIM[UM] FOR WELFARE CHE[CKS]

SENATE OPPOSITION EXPE[CTED]

800,000 Families Would Re[ceive] More Money in 13 States — Other Changes Included

By DAVID E. ROSENBAUM

G.O.P. Gaine[d]

By RICHARD J. MEISLIN

[K]HOMEINI WON'T SEE [E]NVOYS SENT BY U.S.; [S]ILENT ON P.L.O. BID

[CAR]TER TEAM WAITS

[Adm]inistration Clings to Slim Hope Teheran Will Admit Aides

By BERNARD GWERTZMAN

IRAN DEMANDS SHAH

Concern Spreads Among Americans in Capital — 2 More Seized

By JOHN KIFNER

Special to The New York Times

TEHERAN, Iran, Nov. 7 — Ayatollah Ruhollah Khomeini tonight rebuffed an American attempt to negotiate the release of the American Embassy and the scores of staff members and others seized by students, but he appeared to leave open a possibility of a mediation effort by the Palestine Liberation Organization.

The Islamic leader said that neither he nor any other Iranian official would meet with the special envoys, Ramsey Clark, a former Attorney General, and William G. Miller, staff director of the Senate Select Committ on Intelligence. President Carter had sent them by plane toward Iran bearing a message to Teheran's leaders.

The two Americans got as far as Turkey and, according to the State Department, would remain there "pending clarification" from Iran's authorities.

Ayatollah Silent on P.L.O.

The Ayatollah said nothing about the Palestine Liberation Organization. But the state radio reported that a Palestinian delegation was on the way.

[The organization's observers at the United Nations in New York said that a two-member delegation, including Abu Jihad, a leader of Al Fatah, had arrived in the Iranian capital and had begun efforts to protect the lives of American hostages. But in Washington, a high State Department official said the indications were that the Palestinians had not yet reached Teheran and that the Iranians were not interested in discussing with them the seizure of the American Embassy. Page A10.]

In a speech from the Islamic holy city of Qum, broadcast by state television, Ayatollah Khomeini said of the United States and its leaders: "They should just give up the Shah to Iran. That's all."

That was the demand made Sunday by about 500 students when they seized the embassy and about 90 hostages, most of them Americans. The deposed Shah, Mohammed Riza Pahlevi, is hospitalized in New York for cancer and gallstone treatment.

Embassy Called 'Espionage Place'

Noting that the United States had "opposed returning the Shah" and that the embassy was said to be "an espionage place against us," the Ayatollah declared: "Thus my meeting with the envoy is by no means possible."

In Teheran, two American employees of the Bell Helicopter Company were removed from the Hilton Hotel by angry Iranians and taken to the American Embassy to be turned over to the students.

The students, who call themselves "Followers of the Imam's Line," issued a statement saying they would refuse to accept more Americans, and they urged Iranians not to detain any because such actions were part of a "conspiracy set by the C.I.A."

It was not known whether the Bell employees were still being held tonight.

The incident spread fear through the small American community left from the days before the Islamic revolution, when foreign companies had major activities here. It was estimated that 200 Ameri-

Continued on Page A10, Column 5

The New York Times/Neal Boenzi

POLICE RECRUITS SWORN IN: The first recruits hired in five years in New York City were lectured on self-control by Mayor Koch, who said he wanted "to kill" those who assaulted him Monday, but had exercised restraint. Page B3.

One Fight for Women's Rights: A Coal Miner's Life and Death

By WILLIAM SERRIN

Special to The New York Times

COALPORT, Pa., Nov. 2 — What he would not forget, after he had left the hospital where she lay, still in her sweatshirt and long underwear and coveralls, on an emergency room cart, was that there was nothing to suggest she was dead.

The only marks he could see were a small bump and a cut on her left temple. A trickle of blood from the cut matted a bit of her hair. It was like a scrape from striking a car door or a kitchen cabinet. She looked as she did when she was alive.

There was one other thing. Her hands.

Her face, like all coal miners' faces, was black with coal. But her hands had been covered with gloves. And, as she lay on the hospital cart, the gloves removed, her hands were as white as snow.

And the coroner came and pronounced her dead.

The next day the autopsy was performed, and the undertaker took her body to a small, one-story, brick funeral home on Main Street in this small, stark town, stuck into a long hollow between two steep, wooded ridges. They laid her out there, and afterward her body was flown to her home town, Utica, N.Y., and she was buried in Clayville Cemetery.

Death and coal have always gone together. In this century, some 103,000 people have been killed in mine accidents in the United States. Nearly 1,300 miners have been killed in underground mines in the last 10 years.

But the death of this woman, Marilyn McCusker, was different. She was the first woman killed in an underground mine in the United States, and that is bringing a great deal of attention to the accident and to this heavily wooded highlands area, along Moshannon Creek, in the mountains of central Pennsylvania.

There is more to the story than a statistic, though.

Until a few years ago, women could

Continued on Page A16, Column 1

42% in Poll Favor U.S. Talks With P.L.O. on Mideast

Nearly half the Americans who have heard of the Palestine Liberation Organization believe the United States should negotiate with the group despite the objections of Israel. This conclusion emerges from a New York Times/CBS News survey.

Of those asked, three-fifths said they had some knowledge of the P.L.O. Within this group, 42 percent favored talks and 45 percent opposed them. The rest had no opinion.

The P.L.O., a Beirut-based umbrella organization of Palestinian Arab forces, has been waging a strong campaign to gain acceptance as a legitimate political grouping. President Carter, however, has insisted that there can be no talks with the P.L.O. until it recognizes Israel's right to exist behind secure borders. He restated this position at a news conference as recently as Oct. 10.

Support for Treaty Declines

The chief United States delegate to the United Nations, Andrew Young, resigned this summer after he held unauthorized conversations with the P.L.O. representative here. But the Palestinian group has indicated it has had frequent informal contacts with United States aides and has hinted that the aides are aware of the P.L.O.'s plan to send a mission to Teheran on behalf of the Americans being held hostage in the United States Embassy there.

The poll also showed some decline in support for the strategic arms treaty with the Soviet Union.

The poll reached 1,385 people, selected

Continued on Page A5, Column 1

INSIDE

Bolivia Ends Martial Law

The colonel who proclaimed himself President of Bolivia ended martial law and press censorship and said he might form a junta with civilians. Page A2.

3 Seized in Lawyer's Slaying

Three Westchester teen-agers were arrested on charges of murdering Herbert B. Finn, a prominent Phoenix lawyer, last month. Page B1.

No Records on Scotto Gifts

Campaign records were presented at the trial of Anthony M. Scotto to show there were no reports of the political contributions he said he gave. Page B1.

About New York ... B2
Around Nation ... A16
Books ... C19, C21
Bridge ... C22
Crossword ... C20
Dance ... C24
Editorials ... A22
Going Out Guide ... C20
Home Section ... C1-15
Letters ... A22
Man in the News ... A17
Movies ... C17
Music ... C19-20, C24
Notes on People ... B16
Obituaries ... D21
Op-Ed ... A23
Shipping ... D20
Sound ... C9
Sports ... D23-28
Theaters ... C17, C20
TV/Radio ... C23
U.N. Events ... A12
Weather ... D20

News Summary and Index, Page B1

"All the News That's Fit to Print"

The New York Times

LATE CITY EDITION

Weather: Chance of showers today; clear tonight. Sunny, pleasant tomorrow. Temperature range: today 73-86; yesterday 75-93. Details on page B16.

VOL.CXXIX . . No. 44,673 | NEW YORK, TUESDAY, AUGUST 12, 1980 | 25 CENTS

DEMOCRATS BACK CARTER ON NOMINATION RULE; KENNEDY WITHDRAWS FROM PRESIDENTIAL RACE

BETTER PROTECTION OF LEADERS IN WAR ORDERED BY CARTER

Aim Is Faster Evacuation of Capital as Part of New Atom Strategy in a Conflict With Soviet

By RICHARD BURT

Special to The New York Times

WASHINGTON, Aug. 11 — President Carter has ordered more effective procedures for protecting civilian and military leaders in event of nuclear war, including plans for the rapid evacuation of key Government personnel from Washington to airborne and underground command posts, officials said today.

The officials said that the order, Presidential Directive 58, complemented a new nuclear targeting strategy disclosed last week. The strategy gives priority to pinpointing military and political targets in the Soviet Union rather than cities.

In an effort to head off a potentially divisive conflict in the Administration, Secretary of Defense Harold Brown sent a special messenger to Secretary of State Edmund S. Muskie in Maine to explain the new targeting strategy. Mr. Muskie complained on Friday that he had not even known of the existence of the directive when it was signed by Mr. Carter. [Page A10.]

The order on governmental protection, together with the targeting strategy, known as Presidential Directive 59, is said to be part of an effort to strengthen nuclear deterrence by convincing the Soviet Union that the United States could wage an extended nuclear conflict.

Officials said the directive on protection was concerned with maintaining the "continuity of government." It is said to

Continued on Page A9, Column 1

Senator Edward M. Kennedy conceding defeat after rules vote. With him were his wife, Joan, and son Edward Jr.

CALL TO PRESIDENT

The Senator Apparently Surprised His Family by Dropping Out

By B. DRUMMOND AYRES Jr.

Senator Edward M. Kennedy apparently surprised even close members of his family and staff last night when he announced he was pulling out of the race for the Democratic Presidential nomination.

"It wasn't something that had been tried out before, that had really been laid out as an option," a close campaign aide said. "Some suggestions had been made earlier about what he might say, but I don't believe that was one of them."

Transcript of Kennedy withdrawal statement, page B9.

The fact that Mr. Kennedy's political director, Paul Kirk, told reporters just after the rules fight was settled that the Senator would not withdraw was evidence of the apparent surprise in the Kennedy circle.

Later, a Kennedy aide, who asked not to be identified, said the Massachusetts Democrat decided to quit the race in the wake of almost 10 months of nonstop campaigning, after watching the results of the rules fight on television with close family members and aides. The aide said the group, which gathered to munch on a cold supper buffet in the Senator's suite at the Waldorf Astoria Hotel, included his wife, Joan, a sister, Jean Smith, as well as several speech writers and long-time Senate office assistants.

Call to the President

The results of the vote on the rules fight were discussed in a general manner when the balloting was over, the aide reported, then the Senator announced to the gathering that he was going to call President Carter and withdraw.

The Senator's aides refused flatly late last night to discuss whether he might support Mr. Carter in his race against Ronald Reagan, the Republican nominee. One aide said privately, however, that the degree of support might well depend upon the ultimate shape of the platform, which is to be discussed today.

The aide who recounted the events surrounding Mr. Kennedy's withdrawal could supply no details on the call to the President, except that it was placed shortly before 10 P.M. and that Mr. Carter was reached at Camp David, the White House weekend and vacation retreat.

Mr. Kennedy publicly announced his withdrawal from the race a few minutes later in a brief statement read to reporters and campaign workers assembled at his convention headquarters two floors above his suite at the Waldorf. The campaign workers had been subdued

Continued on Page B9, Column 1

LOSER IN SHOWDOWN

1,936-to-1,390 Vote Easily Assures the President of Renomination

By HEDRICK SMITH

President Carter cleared his last obstacle to renomination last night with a surprisingly easy victory in the crucual fight over the rules of the Democratic National Convention that immediately prompted Senator Edward M. Kennedy to end his quest for the nomination.

For all practical purposes, the opening-day showdown vote on the rules assured the President of victory on the nominating roll-call tomorrow night because it bound a comfortable majority of the convention delegates to vote for Mr. Carter.

Excerpts from economic plank and minority report, page B12.

Mr. Kennedy quickly bowed to that reality with a telephone call to President Carter at Camp David, Md., and a public statement saying that "my name will not be placed in nomination."

"President Carter's forces have won an impressive victory," the Senator told a crowd of partisans at the Waldorf Astoria Hotel at 10 P.M., less than two hours after the rules vote.

Assessment by Kennedy

"I'm a realist and I know what this result means," the Massachusetts challenger said to cries of "no" from his backers. "I have called President Carter and congratulated him. The effort on the nomination is over. My name will not be placed in nomination."

That set the stage for moves toward unity by the two rival camps in the party. Although the Senator has lately edged in that direction, he stopped short of pledging all-out support for Mr. Carter in the fall campaign and repeated his earlier intention to lead the debate tonight on economic plans of the platform.

"I continue to care deeply about the ideals of the Democratic Party," Senator Kennedy said. "I continue to care deeply about where this party stands and I hope the delegates will stand with me for a truly Democratic platform."

Differences on Issues

But Vice President Mondale, immediately praising Senator Kennedy for "a class act" in moving so quickly to settle the nomination issue, contended that remaining differences on economic issues were "not fundamental." He noted that the rules debate had not been contentious and that, with Senator Kennedy's gesture, "I think the animosity will be very largely removed."

Robert S. Strauss, the Carter chairman, said there were "still stacks of differences" on the economic issues but

Continued on Page B9, Column 3

Chile's Military Ruler To Ask Voters to Back Extension of His Power

By JUAN de ONIS

President Augusto Pinochet of Chile, his Government shaken by scandal in the security forces and by tax frauds, has summoned voters to a plebiscite next month that is designed to maintain his authoritarian rule for at least eight years.

General Pinochet has been in power for nearly seven years at the head of a military junta that overthrew the left-wing Government of the late President Salvador Allende Gossens.

On Sunday night, in Santiago, General Pinochet said that the plebiscite will be held on Sept. 11, the seventh anniversary of the coup, and was intended to win popular approval of a new constitution.

It provides that after an eight-year period in which General Pinochet would continue to be President, the junta will nominate a presidential candidate, who might or might not be General Pinochet. That candidate, if accepted in a national plebiscite, would serve the next eight years. If he were rejected, there would be an election with candidates nominated in other ways.

The constitution, which has been under study for five years, was rushed to completion by the junta last week because of

Continued on Page A7, Column 1

MAYOR INTRODUCES HIS FINANCIAL PLAN

Asserts President Broke Promises On Federal Aid to U.S. Cities

By CLYDE HABERMAN

Mayor Koch announced his new financial plan for New York City yesterday, using the occasion to accuse the Carter Administration of "broken promises" on Federal aid to the nation's cities.

"If you don't carry the cities of the country, Mr. President, you ain't going to be the next President," Mr. Koch said at a crowded news conference at City Hall.

Technically, the purpose of the session was to disclose details of the Mayor's fiscal program for the next four years, in particular his plans to eliminate a budget deficit for 1982 that he calculated as $733 million.

Text of Mayor's remarks, page B16.

In reality, on the opening day of the Democratic National Convention at Madison Square Garden, Mr. Koch seized a singular political opportunity to press a longstanding plea that the Federal Government do more for urban America.

He made a direct appeal to the delegates last night, addressing them in his capacity as host Mayor. "When Mount St. Helens exploded, Congress appropriated $850 million," he said. "But while New York's South Bronx or Los Angeles's Watts or Boston's Roxbury crumbles and

Continued on Page B16, Column 5

A Graceful Withdrawal

Kennedy's Way of Quitting Should Unify Party Against Reagan and Limit Delegates' Quarreling

By ADAM CLYMER

Senator Edward M. Kennedy quit the Presidential race last night in the style of a man who wanted to unite the Democratic Party against Ronald Reagan.

News Analysis

By announcing his withdrawal at a news conference away from the convention hall he foreclosed any impassioned demonstration by his followers that could have embarrassed President Carter. By calling Mr. Carter first, he made the end of his candidacy seem as graceful as its final weeks had sometimes seemed peevish.

Hamilton Jordan, President Carter's chief political adviser, said Sunday night, expressing hopes for Mr. Kennedy's support: "It will be easier with him. We could do it without him, but it will be easier with him. He doesn't matter so much himself, but his people do."

Much to Offer Campaign

While Mr. Kennedy's active efforts do not guarantee the votes of his followers, they can certainly help. And at a time when only 23 percent of Mr. Kennedy's Democratic followers say they plan to vote for Mr. Carter, according to the latest New York Times/CBS News poll, the Senator's personal participation in the campaign would be immensely helpful.

In the primaries, the Massachusetts Senator defeated Mr. Carter in nine states with 164 electoral votes. Without most of those states it would be impossible to count up enough electoral votes for Mr. Carter to win the election.

As word spread in the convention hall last night, there was a beginning of the reaction that Mr. Carter's forces, and probably Mr. Kennedy's as well, hope for.

Mardee Xifaras, co-chairman of the Massachusetts Kennedy delegation, told a reporter, "If you ask me, the question is where we are going to go now? For me that question was answered a month ago, when the Republicans nominated Ronald Reagan and adopted a platform against the equal rights amendment and for the MX missile."

While Mr. Kennedy's public statement congratulating Mr. Carter on an "impressive victory" on the rules question last night did not commit himself to campaigning for Mr. Carter in the fall, or even to appearing with him on the podium Thursday night, the feeling in the hall was that both would follow from last night's decisions.

Representative Paul Simon, one of Mr. Kennedy's loyal supporters in Illinois,

Continued on Page B9, Column 4

For Kennedy Supporters, Time for Reality and Tears

By FRANCIS X. CLINES

In one swift night of heartfelt discord and sudden concession, the Democrats saw Senator Edward M. Kennedy cap his long, persistent quest for the Presidency last night, within hours of the opening of their convention.

"Oh, no!" the Senator's supporters shouted as the Senator went on television to pronounce himself a "realist" who no longer wanted his name in nomination.

As he spoke, delegates in the other, nonelectronic arena of reality at the convention had no idea the fight was not to be carried forward.

But within minutes the scene outside the Kennedy camp's red, white and blue headquarters was filled with dazed Kennedy partisans. Some cried. Others wandered off, having been ordered by their candidate to quit the fight, a year after he was tempted into the contest.

The turnaround was perhaps a wrenching event for the nation's viewers, but it was a virtual secret for the delegates themselves, who were locked into the elaborately secure convention hall. The Senator's use of television meant his delegates had no immediate forum in which to object, and even as he spoke they were reviewing the bitter scene that followed the opening of the convention.

At 5:03 last evening, the word went forth from the podium: "Shhhhhhh . . ." And for a brief instant the Democrats were silent in a token sanctuary of peace that was dashed to the floor of their convention as soon as prime time arrived.

The shushing — a preliminary kindness to the chairman that preceded a heartfelt party showdown — soon gave way to a cacophony of discord as the forces of Senator Kennedy made what proved to be an unsuccessful last stand against President Carter in a fight over convention rules.

A great hooting and hollering crisscrossed the convention as the two camps finally got together in the same room after eight months of state-by-state clawing for delegates.

Crossing the floor like an anxious general entering the trenches, Tim

Continued on Page B10, Column 2

Delegates demonstrating on the floor of the Democratic National Convention before the vote on binding delegates

INSIDE

Jackson Hits 400th Homer

Reggie Jackson of the Yankees became the 19th major league baseball player to hit 400 home runs in a 3-1 victory over the Chicago White Sox. Page D17.

U.S. Asks Korea to Spare Kim

American officials have asked South Korean leaders to spare Kim Dae Jung, the opposition leader who is facing trial on sedition charges. Page A3.

Around Nation	A12	Music	C6
Art	C9	Notes on People	B4
Books	C8,C10	Obituaries	B17
Bridge	C10	Op-Ed	A19
Business Day	D1-14	Science	C1-5
Crossword	C10	Shipping	A16
Dance	C6	Sports	D16-19
Editorials	A18	Style	B18
Education	C1,C4	Theaters	C7
Going Out Guide	C6	TV/Radio	C19
Letters	A18	U.N. Events	A3
Man in the News	B11	Weather	B16

News Summary and Index, Page B1

Classified Ads	C10-18	Auto Exchange	D19

Kennedy delivered one of his most memorable speeches at the 1980 Democratic National Convention in New York City, saying ". . . the work goes on, the cause endures, the hope still lives, and the dream shall never die."

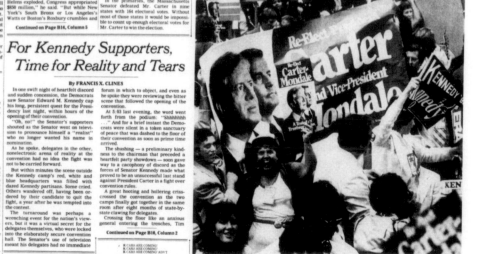

Caroline Kennedy graduated from Harvard University on June 5, 1980, forty years after her father graduated from there. (AP Photo)

ALSO IN 1980

Ronald Reagan defeated President Jimmy Carter in the presidential election.

APRIL 26, 1986
MARIA SHRIVER MARRIED ARNOLD SCHWARZENEGGER

Maria Shriver, daughter of Eunice Kennedy Shriver, married actor and former bodybuilder Arnold Schwarzenegger in a Cape Cod church. The bride's cousin Caroline Kennedy was maid of honor.

Jacqueline Kennedy Onassis and son John F. Kennedy Jr. attended Maria Shriver's wedding to Arnold Schwarzenegger. (AP Photo/Charles Krupa)

ALSO IN 1986

Rupert Murdoch's News Corporation, created in 1980, launched Fox Broadcasting Company.

---

2 Part I/Sunday, April 27, 1986 **R** — Los Angeles Times

The News in Brief

In Part One

Oscar winner Broderick Crawford, who starred in TV's "Highway Patrol" series, died at age 74 in Palm Springs. (Page 3.)

The games people play and the jokes they tell say much about society, says UC Berkeley Prof. Alan Dundes. (Page 3.)

School reforms have swept almost every state since a 1983 report warned of "a rising tide of mediocrity." (Page 4.)

The U.S. drug distribution system still lacks safeguards to curb the introduction of substandard products, a report said. (Page 5.)

Emperor Hirohito draws a variety of emotions from Japanese as he prepares to celebrate his 60th year on the throne. (Page 7.)

President Reagan telephoned former Philippine President Ferdinand E. Marcos, but details were not disclosed. (Page 8.)

In Orange County

Helicopter activity at John Wayne Airport pose a danger to jet airliners, says the Air Line Pilots Assn. (Page 1.)

Nathan Rosenberg is brother of est founder Werner Erhard, and that's an issue in Rosenberg's campaign for Congress. (Page 1.)

In Opinion

The products of the postwar baby boom begin to turn 40 this year, and no one in politics seems to know how to reach the Pepsi generation. (Page 1.)

Mayor Tom Bradley's gubernatorial campaign continues to struggle for a theme—a reason for Californians to toss out Gov. George Deukmejian. (Page 1.)

In Sports

Wally Joyner's two-run homer capped a six-run ninth-inning rally that gave the Angels a 7-6 win over the Minnesota Twins. (Page 1.)

Magic Johnson may be the best player in the NBA, but the MVP award will probably again go to Boston's Larry Bird. (Page 1.)

Al Holbert and Derek Bell are favored to drive their Porsche 962 to victory in today's Grand Prix of Endurance. (Page 1.)

Sprinter Tommie Smith is still remembered, according to Jim Murray, but for the wrong reason. (Page 1.)

In Business

A labor-cost squeeze is on in meatpacking, as the industry tries to weather a prolonged slump with layoffs and pay cuts. (Page 1.)

Controversy is rising over buyouts of nonprofit health maintenance organizations for conversion to the for-profit sector. (Page 1.)

In Calendar

James Aubrey, the mysterious executive who once headed both CBS and MGM, is back after a long absence—as a producer of low-budget exploitation films. (Page 1.)

In View

Margaret Truman Daniel has written a personal memoir of her mother, former First Lady Bess Truman. (Page 1.)

Author Maxine Hong Kingston encouraged Asian students at UC Irvine to rebel against suppression of their artistic spirits. (Page 1.)

In Book Review

David A. Stockman's "The Triumph of Politics: Why the Reagan Revolution Failed" says it failed because President Reagan chose not to save it. (Page 1.)

The World

Afghan Rebels Kill POWs

Afghan guerrillas have put to death at least 13 captured officers and two soldiers of the Kabul government army for being Communists, rebel officials said in Pakistan. They added that dozens of other prisoners from fighting in southeastern Afghanistan are on trial. The officials, who refused to be further identified, said the convicted prisoners were killed by firing squad in Paktia province, where Soviet and Afghan forces have conducted a major offensive.

Soviet President Andrei A. Gromyko, reported to be hospitalized with a high fever, is back at work, according to the Soviet news media. Reports of his ill health were fueled when he failed to attend last week's Kremlin ceremony commemorating the 116th anniversary of the birth of Soviet founder V.I. Lenin. Reports in the party newspaper Pravda, and from the official news agency Tass, said Gromyko, 76, attended Friday's meeting of the Presidium of the Supreme Soviet. Gromyko who served as foreign minister for 28 years before becoming Soviet president last July, is believed to have coronary problems.

British troops shot and killed a leading Irish Republican Army gunman in Northern Ireland as he and an accomplice prepared to launch an attack on security forces, officials said in Belfast. Sinn Fein, the legal political wing of the outlawed IRA, identified the dead man as Seamus McElwaine, 25, a convicted double murderer. He was serving a life sentence when he broke out of Maze Prison near Belfast along with 37 others in September, 1983. McElwaine's companion, who sources identified as Kevin Lynch, was in serious condition with gunshot wounds.

Chinese economic reforms have increased the output of consumer goods but have also caused high inflation, a worsened trade balance and a drop in grain production, a CIA study said. The assessment, released by the congressional Joint Economic Committee, noted that inflation, as measured by Chinese price indexes, tripled in 1985 to 8.8%. Production of such consumer items as washing machines, television sets and refrigerators increased more than 50%, the CIA said. Grain output dropped 7%, the result of reduced acreage, flooding and bureaucratic confusion.

U.S. special envoy Philip C. Habib told Panamanian President Eric A. Delvalle that the Reagan Administration is willing to try to find a way to gain passage of the Contadora peace plan. The 45-minute meeting was "very positive," Foreign Minister Jorge Abadia Arias said. He said Habib had expressed "in a very clear and precise way" U.S. interest in "adding flexibility" to the Administration's position on peace efforts by the Contadora Group—Mexico, Colombia, Venezuela and Panama.

Ecuadorean air force planes and helicopters, under the personal direction of President Leon Febres Cordero, searched the cloud-shrouded Andes for a missing plane carrying Education Minister Camilo Gallegos and four other government officials. Gallegos' 21-year-old son was also on board. The Piper Aztec is believed to have gone down near the 19,352-foot Cotopaxi volcano, 25 miles southeast of Quito, the capital.

Norwegian naval vessels and aircraft combed the inner reaches of the Hardanger Fjord in search of a foreign submarine that was spotted during daylight from a low-flying plane. A Defense Ministry spokesman said the military had neither seen nor heard the unidentified submarine since Friday when it was spotted near Varaldsoy, an island 20 miles inside the fjord.

United Press International

Aloha—Seventh-grader Kathleen Yonohana gives President Reagan a kiss at Hickam Air Force Base, Hawaii, where Reagan stopped on his way to Tokyo economic summit. (Story, Page 8)

The Region

138 Aliens Apprehended

More than 138 people, all believed to be in the U.S. illegally from Mexico, were apprehended at a San Diego house by Border Patrol agents, said Ed Pyeatt, a spokesman for the Border Patrol. Acting on a tip from San Diego police, agents swooped down on the three-bedroom house on the 2100 block of National Avenue in the Logan Heights district in southern San Diego, he said. The group, 134 men and 4 women, had been crammed into the small house for at least eight hours. Some of the aliens told agents that they had paid smugglers about $275 to be taken to Los Angeles. No smuggling suspects were arrested in the raid, Pyeatt said. All the aliens voluntarily returned to Mexico, he said.

Demonstrations for more minority employment at CBS Inc. might begin within two weeks at the Hollywood studios of KCBS-TV Channel 2, the Rev. Jesse Jackson said. After a morning meeting in Beverly Hills with area civil-rights leaders and CBS minority employees, Jackson said supporters of a national network boycott led by his Operation PUSH and Rainbow Coalition would include picketing of the Los Angeles station and, "if that doesn't work," acts of civil disobedience. Similar demonstrations at the CBS-owned station in Chicago over the past seven months have resulted in one instance of arrests of demonstrators attempting to enter the network's building there. Jackson said the demonstrations in Los Angeles will be "synchronized" with demonstrations at CBS-owned TV stations in New York, Chicago, Philadelphia and St. Louis. PUSH is also attempting to persuade minorities in the five cities to stop watching CBS until it increases its number of minority managers, on-air personalities and other employees.

To protect the endangered Coachella Valley fringe-toed lizard, the California Nature Conservancy has spent $25 million to acquire a 13,000-acre preserve on which the creature lives, just east of Palm Springs. Ranging from 3 inches to 10 inches long, the lizard has seen 95% of its sandy habitat destroyed by development over the years. The acquisition money came from a combination of private donations and state and federal grants.

U.S. immigration authorities have exonerated a Border Patrol agent accused of using excessive force last year when he shot a 12-year-old Mexican in the back as the youth stood a few feet from the border but on Mexican soil. For the third time since the incident, officials ruled that six-year Border Patrol Agent Edward Cole was justified in shooting Humberto Carrillo Estrada of Tijuana, who allegedly had been throwing rocks at the agent. The youth recovered, but has limited use of his left arm. Still pending is a $3-million damage suit that the boy's family filed against the U.S. government.

Marcia Herrman, a volunteer at the child advocate's office of the Los Angeles Superior Court, was named Volunteer of the Year from among 43,000 volunteers who donated 2.86-million hours of work on behalf of the county government. Herrman, a Studio City resident, works with children in the court's shelter care facility as they await dependency hearings. "What I do most want to do is support the children and make them feel better about themselves," she said.

Two women were sentenced to nine years in state prison for bilking 100 friends and acquaintances out of $300,000 after persuading them to invest in a secret will that apparently never existed. Julianna Onesty, 64, and Sally Ann Scarpinata, 46, who were convicted in March, each received the maximum possible sentence from Pomona Superior Court Judge Thomas Nuss, Deputy Dist. Atty. Jim Green said. Nuss ordered that restitution be made to victims, and told the women he would reconsider their sentences if the money were recovered within six months, Green said. The two women, neither of whom had a criminal background, duped the victims into believing they were heirs to millions in a secret will that was hung up in probate, Green said. They told the victims their money was needed to pay fees or taxes on the estate, and that investors would double their money.

Great Western Financial has delayed an announcement about the status of its offer to acquire the stock of Citadel Holding, the parent company of Fidelity Federal Savings. The offer expired Friday night. A Great Western spokesman said an announcement will be made early Monday. Great Western has offered to buy Citadel through an exchange of stock, but it is up to Citadel's shareholders to decide if they want to sell.

Southern California Edison Co. is spending $5 million over the next three years to study how future population growth in the rural desert Southwest—and the need for more electrical generation—is likely to affect the region's now basically pristine air. The Desert Research Institute, associated with the University of Nevada, will make the study. It also will monitor and analyze air over parts of Nevada, Arizona, New Mexico and Utah.

The Nation

Haiti Emigrants Rescued

About 150 Haitians stranded on an uninhabited Bahamian island were on their way back to Haiti after being rescued by the U.S. Coast Guard. Coast Guard Lt. Warren Haskovec said that the cutter Bear picked up the emigrants from Cay Lobos, about 250 miles south of Florida, after each was interviewed by agents of the Immigration and Naturalization Service at the request of the Bahamian government. Haskovec said the Haitians, who all seemed to be in good health, were expected to arrive back at Port-au-Prince today.

Officials of Atlanta's predominantly black Spelman College said they will sell approximately $1 million worth of the women's school's holdings in companies that do business in South Africa. The announcement came the day after a rally at which Atlanta Mayor Andrew Young urged Spelman's trustees to vote for the divestiture. School Treasurer Jonathan Smith, a senior vice president of the New York investment firm Mitchell Hutchins Inc., said that the remainder of the school's $41-million endowment is in real estate, other international investments, bonds and cash.

The president of Teamsters Union Local 407 in Cleveland said he plans to run against Jackie Presser for the presidency of the 1.7-million-member national union, it was reported. C. Sam Theodus said he will have his name placed in nomination at the union's convention in Las Vegas next month, the Cleveland Plain Dealer reported. Theodus has said that he is opposed to the union's election process, by which presidents of locals automatically become delegates to the national convention that names the remaining 2,000 delegates.

A federal judge in Boston ordered 3,500 striking transportation workers back to work, temporarily ending a walkout that had stranded an estimated 25,000 commuters for one day. The 10-day restraining order, issued by U.S. District Judge Robert Keeton, will restore commuter service that halted Friday on lines in and out of the city operated by the Boston & Maine Railroad for the Massachusetts Bay Transportation Authority.

The grumbling of Alaska's Augustine Volcano prompted school and church groups to cancel weekend clam digs, and authorities warned against camping on Kenai Peninsula beaches because of the danger from new eruptions. The 4,025-foot volcano southwest of the peninsula was releasing steam, and scientists said that a violent eruption is imminent.

Tremendous expansion in sales of deadly weapons among nations has prompted a growing number of Americans to favor a U.N. resolution against such traffic. The latest Gallup poll found that 61% of Americans would approve of a resolution requesting all nations to refrain from giving or selling arms to other nations—up 9 percentage points since 1981. The findings also suggested that, while Americans tend to favor a militant U.S. posture in dealing with immediate, "brush fire" situations—such as the recent bombing raid on Libya and the 1983 Grenada incursion—they are less bellicose on long-range, global affairs.

Authorities in Missouri said that a trail of spent ransom money led them to the unemployed man they have arrested and charged with murdering a bank president's wife and shooting her husband and another bank officer. Roy G. White, 40, was held without bond in the Texas County Jail on murder and assault charges in the slaying of Wanda Byler and the shooting of her husband, James Byler, and the other bank executive, Kay Jordan, police said.

The State

Youth Dope Ring Alleged

A former Little League baseball coach in San Leandro has been charged with running a marijuana ring that used former players to distribute the drug. Anthony Vergez, 40, was freed on bail after being arrested on charges of marijuana possession and employing minors for illegal purposes. Alameda County sheriff's deputies raided his home and seized $3,360 worth of marijuana and $1,300 in cash. A sheriff's spokesman said Vergez was not a "major" dealer but "was doing a lot of dealing to juveniles and young adults."

The Berkeley Police Assn. urged the City Council to rescind a resolution that barred the police chief from sending officers to anti-apartheid protests on the University of California campus there. The measure adopted this week directed the chief "not to respond to any request for assistance by UC directly or under mutual aid for any anti-apartheid demonstrations providing such response is discretionary." "We don't want our police to basically stifle protest about the university's investments in South Africa," Councilwoman Nancy Skinner said.

Participants in the Great Peace March gathered in Snowfield, Utah, to mourn a member of the mobile community who was killed in a traffic accident. Cynthia I. Carlson, 24, of Rancho Palos Verdes, who left the march temporarily for some sightseeing, died Friday. Another marcher, George W. Mattingly III, 28, Parkhill, Ky., was also injured in the accident. The 300 marchers moved 18 miles Saturday to Hamilton Fort, near Cedar City.

Newsmakers

Stars Come Out for Schwarzenegger-Shriver Wedding

—Before a gathering of guests that rivaled "Who's Who in America," **Maria Shriver** and **Arnold Schwarzenegger** were married in a traditional Roman Catholic ceremony in a Hyannis, Mass., church that was surrounded by hundreds of cheering fans. The bride, anchorwoman on the "CBS Morning News" and a niece of President **John F. Kennedy,** waved to the crowd as she and her body-builder-turned-actor husband departed by limousine for an outdoor reception at the Kennedy compound in nearby Hyannis Port. Earlier, Shriver posed for pictures with her 12 bridesmaids on the steps of St. Francis Xavier Church. The groom arrived minutes later in a silver stretch limousine. Cheers and applause rippled through the throng as celebrities such as pop singer **Andy Williams,** tennis champion **Arthur Ashe** and Sen. **Edward M. Kennedy** (D-Mass.), the bride's uncle, arrived. The crowd's loudest roar, however, was for Shriver's aunt, **Jacqueline Kennedy Onassis,** who emerged from a limousine in a navy-and-white dress with her son, **John F. Kennedy Jr.** The pastor, Father **Edward Duffy,** described the floral displays that bedecked the altar, sanctuary and pews "all the way from the front of the sanctuary right to the door. It's a melange of roses and very, very select flowers," he said.

Associated Press

Arnold Schwarzenegger presents his new wife, Maria Shriver.

—Students at a Pittsburgh high school said they have a greater appreciation of the problems of elderly people since they spent a day limping along hallways with popcorn in their shoes—to simulate bunions—squinting through distorting lenses and trying to pick up coins with their fingers taped together. "Doing this helped open my eyes to see that old people really are people," said **Michelle Berard,** as she limped through a Langley High School hallway. About 40 students participated in the project, which was the idea of health teacher **Carol Gamble.** Gamble said that too many young people view retired people as machines that have been turned off. "They think they just shut down and mind their own business," Gamble told her class. "They don't fall off the Earth and disappear at a certain age."

—Clarke College in Dubuque, Iowa, will offer full tuition to displaced farmers who wish to return to college. "The Sisters of Charity who founded Clarke College made their home among the farmers 153 years ago, so we owe a great deal to them," said Sister **Catherine Dunn,** Clarke's president. "It is incumbent upon Clarke to assist those who have had the misfortune of losing their livelihoods."

—ANN HEROLD

JULY 19, 1986
CAROLINE KENNEDY MARRIED EDWIN SCHLOSSBERG

Index on page 2
Telephone 929-2000
Classified 929-1500
Circulation 929-2222
• © 1986 Globe Newspaper Co.

Boston Sunday Globe

The weather
Sunday: Cloudy, 75
Monday: Ditto
Details page 90

Vol. 230; No. 20 — SUNDAY, JULY 20, 1986 — •$1.25 at newsstands beyond 30 miles from Boston — $1.00

CIA-backed force aided contras, sources say

By Robert Healy
and Stephen Kurkjian
Globe Staff

SAN JOSE, Costa Rica – The CIA hired mercenaries to aid rebels fighting to overthrow the Nicaraguan government in 1984 and 1985, circumventing a congressional ban on such covert aid, according to sources here and in the United States.

In the end, the operation – part of which was located in the neighboring country of Costa Rica – became such a political liability to the Costa Rican government that five of the mercenaries were arrested and jailed. Despite the close ties that the CIA and the US State Department maintained with the government of Costa Rica, no effort was made to free the agency's surrogate operatives.

From the beginning, the operation, in the words of one US intelligence figure, was a "fiasco" of mirrors within mirrors in which one group of mercenaries was hired under CIA contract to watch another group also under contract.

Over the course of almost 18 months, the CIA surrogates were kicked out of base camps of the rebels, known as contras, in Honduras and sent back to New Orleans. Some were then sent to Costa Rica, where they were arrested and still face trial. Honduras is the base for the northern operations by the contras against Nicaragua. Costa Rica is the base for the southern operations.

The main surrogate group consisted of approximately 20 mercenaries recruited by a private Alabama-based group called Civilian Military Assistance to provide men and nonmilitary supplies to contra operations in both Honduras and Costa Rica. While the group's leader, Thomas Posey, has denied that he was sponsored by the CIA, sources both in Costa Rica and the United States said the CIA oversaw the group's activities.

Ultimately, Posey's group was treated with distrust by US intelligence officers, who considered its members unreliable and dangerous to the success of the anti-Sandinista operation. In fact, the Globe has been told that US intelligence was so concerned about the group that the CIA contracted with a second, smaller group, to join the Posey group in order to spy on its operation.

Most of the activity by the mercenary groups came during a period – which continues – when the CIA was prohibited from providing military assistance to the contras. Congressional opposition focused on the agency's bungling in 1983 and 1984 of the mining of several harbors in Nicaragua, which Costa Rican leaders and a US intelligence source, inter-

CONTRAS, Page 12

Globe staff photo/John Tlumacki

Caroline Kennedy and her new husband, Edwin A. Schlossberg, smile as they leave Our Lady of Victory Church in Centerville yesterday after their wedding. More photos, pages 20 and 22.

A Kennedy is wed, an era remembered

By Teresa M. Hanafin
Globe Staff

CENTERVILLE – With the style and grace that typified the Kennedy White House years, the only daughter of one of the nation's most popular presidents was married yesterday.

For millions of Americans who watched Caroline Kennedy frolic in the Oval Office as a child to the delight of her father, President John F. Kennedy, her marriage to Edwin A. Schlossberg, 41, was a joyous scene tinged with nostalgia.

The consensus of the crowd of more than 4,000 that gathered outside Our Lady of Victory Church here was that she was a beautiful bride: "Isn't she gorgeous" was the comment most heard amid a chorus of oohs and aahs.

The crowd also was impressed by Caroline's younger brother, John F. Kennedy Jr., 25, who almost stole the show when he arrived with the bridegroom, for whom he served as best man.

"Isn't he handsome!" one woman exclaimed as he gave onlookers a thumbs-up sign. "He looks like his father," said her friend. "I bet the president would have liked to have seen this."

And when the bride's mother, Jacqueline Kennedy Onassis, 56, came out of the church fighting back tears and lay her head for comfort on the

CAPE, Page 20

Amirault found guilty on all counts

By Paul Langner
Globe Staff

CAMBRIDGE – Twelve Middlesex Superior Court jurors, speaking firmly, loudly and in unison, pronounced 15 guilty verdicts against Gerald (Tooky) Amirault yesterday, finding that he had raped and indecently assaulted nine children at his mother's day-care center.

Judge Elizabeth J. Dolan revoked Amirault's $5,000 cash bail and ordered him held in Middlesex County Jail. He is to be sentenced July 31. He could receive life sentences on the eight rape convictions and 10-year sentences for the seven indecent assaults.

Amirault, 32, of Malden, showed little emotion when the verdicts were returned. His only reaction was to lower his head slightly as each verdict was pronounced.

His wife, family and friends wept and hugged each other. One young woman collapsed and was carried out of the courtroom. She was taken away by emergency medical technicians called by Cambridge police. Another woman had to be supported by two men as she staggered from the courtoom shouting that the witnesses were "all liars," and asking, "How can they do this?" – apparently referring to the jurors.

The parents of the abused children and the parents' friends and relatives sat in stunned silence, remaining long after the defendant's group had left, some weeping and hugging each other and others trying to keep their faces immobile.

Nine children testified, one of them by videotape, during the 12-week trial, saying Amirault had taken them to so-called magic or secret rooms in the Fells Acres Day School in Malden, had undressed them, fondled them indecently, raped them, and made them engage in an obscene game. They also testified that their pictures were taken during these sessions, but Dolan ordered that testimony stricken.

Amirault denied during the trial that he had molested any child, saying that the only time he touched one was when he had to clean up a boy who "had had an accident."

Some of the children may have to testify again because Amirault's mother, Violet Amirault, 61, of Malden, and his sister, Cheryl Amirault Lefave, 28, of Malden, have also been charged with rape and indecent assault and battery.

Assistant District Attorney Laurence Hardoon said yesterday that no decision has been made about prosecution of those cases. He said he and District Attorney Scott Harshbarger would confer on that issue soon.

Hardoon, who directed the prosecution team, sat in subdued silence after the court formalities were over and the judge had retired to her chambers. "I always

AMIRAULT, Page 32

UPI pool photo

Gerald Amirault bows his head yesterday after the jury found him guilty on 15 counts of rape and sexual assault.

Inside

Sox beat Mariners, 9-4

The Red Sox ended a three-game losing streak with a 9-4 victory over the Seattle Mariners last night. Page 49.

Growing up royally

Prince Andrew, now 26 and about to be wed, remains a self-styled rake but he is growing older and wiser, and his decision to marry the eminently acceptable and sensible Sarah Ferguson is being warmly greeted as a step in that direction. So writes the Globe's London bureau chief, Steven Erlanger, on his royal highness only days before Wednesday's royal event in Westminster Abbey. The Globe Magazine.

Bolivian drug raids criticized

US Army troops, operating in Bolivia to help narcotics police in raids on cocaine laboratories, are drawing increasingly sharp criticism from political party leaders, labor unions and students. Page 2.

Brown dropped as ambassador pick

President Reagan has abandoned his plan to name Robert J. Brown as the first black US ambassador to South Africa, administration officials said yesterday. The proposed nomination was dropped after a White House meeting late Friday as a result of information produced by a background investigation, according to a senior official. Page 2.

Negligence blamed for Chernobyl disaster

By Andrew Rosenthal
Associated Press

MOSCOW – The Politburo yesterday attributed the Chernobyl disaster to gross negligence, said four government officials had been dismissed and announced that the death toll from the worst civilian nuclear accident in history had increased to 28.

In a statement distributed by the official Tass news agency, the Politburo also said those who caused the April 26 accident would be put on trial.

The Politburo, the Communist Party's ruling body, said the Chernobyl reactor exploded as workers conducted improperly supervised and badly prepared experiments on a turbine generator without proper safety precautions.

It indicated that safety procedures and technical training also were inadequate at other Soviet nuclear plants. The Soviet Union has 13 graphite-moderated reactors like the one at Chernobyl.

In the most graphic description yet of the scope of the disaster, the Politburo said 28 persons had died, 30 were still hospitalized and 173 others had been stricken by radiation sickness. The previous official death toll was 26.

The accident also caused the equivalent of

CHERNOBYL, Page 10

GOP's Card ponders role in tattered party

By Walter V. Robinson
Globe Staff

WASHINGTON – From behind a desk just 50 yards from the president's White House office, but 429 miles from the fratricidal battlefield of the Massachusetts Republican Party, Andrew H. Card Jr. gauges his political and personal options.

The only prominent Massachusetts Republican in the Reagan White House, he is asking himself whether he should return home as the candidate for governor of a party in disarray, for an election that's just 14 weeks away, against an opponent, Gov. Dukakis, who is seen as virtually unbeatable.

Mass. Republicans yesterday failed to choose a new gubernatorial candidate, and now may take another week or more before making a recommendation. Page 25.

Card is ambivalent, much like the state GOP is about him and others as its party commission looks for a suitable replacement for the two candidates who have abandoned the contest in disgrace.

"Yes, I want it. I want to be governor, but that's not a function of time. I think I'd be the best candidate and the best governor the party could find this year," Card exclaims, but adds, "it's not necessarily the best of times and the best of circumstances for me to be the candidate."

CARD, Page 13

ANDREW CARD
"I want to be governor, but . . ."

Caroline Kennedy met exhibit designer Edwin Schlossberg when she worked at the Metropolitan Museum of Art. Caroline's uncle Senator Edward Kennedy walked her down the aisle.

ALSO IN 1986

The Space Shuttle Challenger *exploded, killing all seven crew members, including school teacher Christa McAuliffe.*

• • • C San Jose Mercury News ■ Wednesday, Nov. 5, 1986 23A

Election '86: The House

U.S. House winners

William Gray III
Pennsylvania

Lindy Boggs
Louisiana

Claude Pepper
Florida

Fred Grandy
Iowa

ALABAMA
1. Callahan (R)
2. Dickinson (R)
3. Nichols (D)
4. Bevill (D)
5. Flippo (D)
7. Harris (D)

ARIZONA
3. Stump (R)

ARKANSAS
1. Alexander (D)
2. Robinson (D)
3. Hammerschmidt (R)
4. Anthony (D)

CALIFORNIA
3. Matsui (D)
4. Fazio (D)
6. Boxer (D)
11. Lantos (D)
12. Konnyu (R)
14. Shumway (R)
15. Coelho (D)
16. Panetta (D-inc.)
19. Lagomarsino (R-inc.)
20. Thomas (R-inc.)
21. Gallegly (R)
22. Moorhead (R-inc.)
24. Waxman (D-inc.)
29. Hawkins (D-inc.)
33. Drier (R-inc.)
35. Lewis (R-inc.)
39. Dannemeyer (R-inc.)
42. Lungren (R-inc.)
43. Packard (R-inc.)
45. Hunter (R-inc.)

CONNECTICUT
1. Kennelly (D)
2. Gejdenson (D)
3. Morrison (D)
5. Rowland (R)
6. Johnson (R)

DELAWARE
Carper (D)

FLORIDA
1. Hutto (D)
2. Grant (D)
3. Bennett (D)
4. Chappell Jr. (D)
5. McCollum (R)
6. MacKay (D)
7. Gibbons (D)
8. Young (R)
9. Bilirakis (R)
10. Higginbotham (D)
11. Nelson (D)
12. Lewis (R)
13. Mack (R)
14. Mica (D)
15. Shaw (R)
16. Smith (D)
17. Lehman (D)
18. Pepper (D)
19. Fascell (D)

GEORGIA
1. Thomas (D)
2. Hatcher (D)
3. Ray (D)
5. Lewis (D)
6. Gingrich (R)
7. Darden (D)
8. Rowland (D)
9. Jenkins (D)
10. Barnard (D)

ILLINOIS
1. Hayes (D)
2. Savage (D)
5. Lipinski (D)
6. Hyde (R)
7. Collins (D)
8. Rostenkowski (D)
9. Yates (D)
10. Porter (R)
11. Annunzio (D)
12. Crane (R)
15. Madigan (R)

INDIANA
2. Sharp (D)
4. Coats (R)
6. Burton (R)
7. Myers (R)
9. Hamilton (D)
10. Jacobs (D)

IOWA
2. Tauke (R)
3. Nagle (D)
4. Smith (D)
6. Grandy (R)

KANSAS
1. Roberts (R)
2. Slattery (D)
3. Meyers (R)
4. Glickman (D)
5. Whittaker (R)

KENTUCKY
1. Hubbard (D)
2. Natcher (D)
3. Mazzoli (D)
4. Bunning (R)
5. Rogers (R)
6. Hopkins (R)
7. Perkins (D)

LOUISIANA
1. Livingston (R)
2. Boggs (D)
3. Tauzin (D)
4. Roemer (D)
5. Huckaby (D)
6. Baker (R)
7. Hayes (D)

MAINE
1. Brennan (D)
2. Snowe (R)

MARYLAND
1. Dyson (D)
2. Bentley (R)
3. Cardin (D)
5. Hoyer (D)
6. Byron (D)
7. Mfume (D)
8. Morella (R)

MASSACHUSETTS
1. Conte (R)
2. Boland (D)
3. Early (D)
4. Frank (D)
5. Atkins (D)
6. Mavroules (D)
7. Markey (D)
8. Kennedy (D)
9. Moakley (D)
11. Donnelly (D)

MISSISSIPPI
1. Whitten (D)
2. Espy (D)
3. Montgomery (D)
4. Dowdy (D)
5. Lott (R)

MISSOURI
1. Clay (D)
3. Gephardt (D)
4. Skelton (D)
5. Wheat (D)
6. Coleman (R)
7. Taylor (R)
9. Volkmer (D)

NEBRASKA
1. Bereuter (R)
2. Daub (R)
3. Smith (R)

NEW HAMPSHIRE
1. Demers (D)
2. Gregg (R)

NEW JERSEY
1. Florio (D)
2. Hughes (D)
4. Smith (R)
5. Roukema (R)
6. Dwyer (D)
7. Rinaldo (R)
9. Torricelli (D)
10. Rodino (D)
11. Gallo (R)
12. Courter (R)
13. Saxton (R)
14. Guarini (D)

NEW MEXICO
1. Lujan (R)
2. Skeen (R)
3. Richardson (D)

NEW YORK
2. Downey (D-inc.)
3. Mrazek (D-inc.)
4. Lent (R-inc.)
5. McGrath (R-inc.)
6. Flake (D)
7. Ackerman (D-inc.)
8. Scheuer (D-inc.)
9. Manton (D-inc.)
10. Schumer (D-inc.)
11. Towns (D-inc.)
12. Owens (D-inc.)
13. Solarz (D-inc.)
14. Molinari (R-inc.)
16. Rangel (D-inc.)
17. Weiss (D-inc.)
18. Garcia (D-inc.)
19. Biaggi (D-inc.)
20. DioGuardi (R-inc.)
21. Fish (R-inc.)
23. Stratton (D-inc.)
24. Solomon (R-inc.)
25. Boehlert (R-inc.)
29. Horton (R-inc.)
31. Kemp (R-inc.)
32. LaFalce (D-inc.)
33. Nowak (D-inc.)

NORTH CAROLINA
1. Jones (D-inc.)
2. Valentine (D-inc.)
3. Lancaster (D)
7. Rose III (D-inc.)
8. Hefner (D-inc.)
9. McMillan (R)

NORTH DAKOTA

NEVADA
1. Ryan GOP

PENNSYLVANIA
1. Foglietta (D-inc.)
2. Gray III (D-inc.)
3. Borski (D-inc.)
5. Schulze (R-inc.)
6. Yatron (D-inc.)
7. Weldon (R)
8. Kostmayer (D-inc.)
9. Shuster (R)
10. McDade (R-inc.)
11. Kanjorski (D-inc.)
12. Murtha (D-inc.)
13. Coughlin (R-inc.)
14. Coyne (D-inc.)
15. Ritter (R-inc.)
16. Walker (R-inc.)
17. Gekas (R-inc.)
18. Walgren (D-inc.)
19. Goodling (R-inc.)
20. Gaydos (D-inc.)
21. Ridge (R-inc.)
22. Murphy (D-inc.)

RHODE ISLAND
1. St Germain (D-inc.)
2. Schneider (R-inc.)

SOUTH CAROLINA
2. Spence (R-inc.)
3. Derrick (D-inc.)
5. Spratt (D-inc.)
6. Tallon (D-inc.)

SOUTH DAKOTA
Johnson (D)

TENNESSEE
1. Quillen (R-inc.)
2. Duncan (R-inc.)
3. Lloyd Dem (I)
4. Cooper Dem (I)
5. Boner (D-inc.)
6. Gordon (D-inc.)
7. Sundquist (R-inc.)
8. Jones (D-inc.)
9. Ford (D-inc.)

TEXAS
1. Chapman (D)
3. Bartlett (R)
7. Archer (R)
11. Leath (D)
12. Wright (D)
15. de la Garza (D)
17. Stenholm (D)
18. Leland (D)
20. Gonzalez (D)
22. DeLay (R)
23. Bustamante (D)
25. Andrews (D)
26. Armey (R)
27. Ortiz (D)

VIRGINIA
1. Bateman (R)
2. Pickett (D)
3. Bliley (R)
4. Sisisky (D)
5. Daniel (D)
6. Olin (D)
7. Slaughter (R)
8. Parris (R)
9. Boucher (D)
10. Wolf (R)

WEST VIRGINIA
1. Mollohan (D)

WISCONSIN
1. Aspin (D)
3. Gunderson (R)
4. Kleczka (D)
5. Moody (D)
6. Petri (R)
8. Roth (R)
9. Sensenbrenner (R)

Despite Clarke's upset victory, Republicans limit House losses

Los Angeles Times

WASHINGTON — Despite a Democratic takeover of the Senate and the historical jinx of an off-year election, House Republicans held their losses to a minimum in Tuesday's elections.

Early today it appeared that Republican losses would not exceed 10, even though the party in the White House has typically lost more than 40 seats in the midterm election six years into the president's term.

Few analysts had expected this year's election to follow that trend. The Republicans were already a badly outnumbered minority in the House with few seats to lose, and House campaigns lacked the national themes that had marked previous off-year elections.

As a result, there will be little change in the balance of power in the next Congress. Democrats already held a 253-180 majority, with two vacancies.

Democrats appeared to be picking up strength in the South, a key battleground where Republicans had made their biggest gains two years ago. Many in both parties had seen this year's House races as a test of whether the trends that had fueled Republican claims to a broad party "realignment" were merely the updraft from President Reagan's huge election victories.

Democrats scored their most important gains in states where the economy has lagged behind the rest of the nation. North Carolina, where Republicans had gained four seats in Reagan's 1984 landslide but whose textile industry has since been ravaged by imports, produced some of the most dramatic finishes again this year.

Democrat Jamie Clarke appeared to have scored the state's biggest upset, when ABC News declared him the winner in his effort to regain the seat he had lost two years ago to Republican Bill Hendon. It was the third match between the two candidates.

Democrat David E. Price also unseated North Carolina Republican Bill Cobey. The race had been marked by a controversy over Cobey's campaign letter asking religious fundamentalists to support him "so our voice will not be silenced and then replaced by someone who is not willing to take a strong stand for the principles outlined in the word of God."

In another show of Democratic strength in the South, South Carolina State Sen. Elizabeth Patterson defeated William D. Workman, the Republican mayor of Greenville. The seat had been vacated by Republican Carroll A. Campbell Jr., who resigned to run for governor — and won.

It remained unclear how strong Democratic gains would be in the depressed farm belt. But in one bellwether race, former Iowa Democratic Chairman Dave Nagle won the seat vacated by Republican incumbent Cooper Evans.

In a rematch of 1984's most bitter House race, Indiana Democratic Rep. Frank McCloskey was holding a slim lead over Republican Richard D. McIntyre, whom McCloskey beat two years ago by four votes after several recounts. The dispute over that election preoccupied the House for five months at the opening of the 1985 session and culminated with a brief Republican walkout when the Democratic-controlled House declared McCloskey the winner.

President Reagan went to Indiana to stump for McIntyre last week in his only campaign appearance of the season exclusively for a House candidate.

Another widely watched Indiana race seemed to belie the value of bigger and bigger campaign spending, which has characterized congressional politics for more than a decade.

Ten-term incumbent Andrew Jacobs Jr., D-Ind., who has intentionally avoided raising a large campaign war chest and spending thousands of dollars on advertising, appeared to be winning an easy victory over real estate manager Jim Eynon, a Republican who outspent him by almost 70-1. Spending by Eynon and by the American Medical Association on his behalf reached $540,000, while Jacobs spent only $8,000.

In one of the most publicized comeback attempts of the year, former New York Democratic Rep. Bella Abzug — moving from her roots in Greenwich Village to suburban Westchester County — failed to unseat incumbent Republican Joseph J. DioGuardi. Known for her floppy hats and vocal feminism, Abzug had surprised most political analysts with her win in the four-way Democratic primary, but the colorful image that made her a national figure was seen as her biggest liability in sedate Westchester.

Among the incoming congressional freshmen will be several whose names are already familiar. But celebrity alone was no guarantee of success.

Joseph P. Kennedy II, the 33-year-old son of the late Sen. Robert F. Kennedy, won over GOP nominee Clark Abt, a Cambridge entrepreneur, in the race for the Massachusetts seat being vacated by retiring Democratic House Speaker Thomas P. "Tip" O'Neill Jr. But even as her brother was claiming victory in Massachusetts, Kathleen Kennedy Townsend, RFK's daughter, appeared to have lost in her bid to unseat Maryland Republican Rep. Helen Delich Bentley.

Kentucky Republicans held on to a House seat by relying on the political appeal of a popular athlete-turned-politician. Jim Bunning, once a star pitcher with the Detroit Tigers and Philadelphia Phillies, soundly defeated Democrat Terry Mann for the seat vacated when Rep. Gene Snyder, R-Ky., decided to end his House career after 11 terms.

Associated Press

Joseph P. Kennedy II, victor in the Massachusetts 8th Congressional District, waves from voting booth after casting his ballot in Boston.

Joseph P. Kennedy II, eldest son of Robert Kennedy, was named after Joseph P. Kennedy, the eldest of Joseph and Rose Kennedy's children. It was Joseph P. Kennedy, not John, who had been groomed for the presidency, but he died during World War II at the age of 29.

The Senate: An Analysis

Poor turnout hurts Republicans

Independents, young voters ignore appeals by Reagan

By Carl M. Cannon
Mercury News Washington Bureau

WASHINGTON — In an election with no national themes, turnout became the crucial factor Tuesday. And when two groups counted on by Republicans — independents and young voters — stayed home, it gave the Democrats a victory in the battle for control of the U.S. Senate.

Independents and voters 18 to 24 years of age supported President Reagan heavily in 1984 and were targeted by the Republican National Committee this year in its bid to retain control of the Senate.

But exit polling by ABC News showed that although Reagan's popularity remains high, these voters simply didn't respond to the president's campaign appeals, and didn't go to the polls in force as they have in recent elections.

Only 5 percent of the electorate Tuesday was made up of voters ages 18 to 24. Voters in this age group cast 12 percent of the votes in 1984 and 10 percent of the votes in 1982.

Even more ominous for Republicans, only 18 percent of those who voted Tuesday identified themselves as independents, a group that in recent years has favored the GOP. In 1984, 26 percent of those who voted were independents and they voted 51-49 Republican.

> ‘That's the story of this election — the people in these two groups who didn't vote.’
>
> — *John Berrigan, ABC pollster and political analyst*

"That's the story of this election — the people in these two groups who didn't vote," said John Berrigan, ABC pollster and political analyst.

In addition, exit polling showed that without Ronald Reagan's name at the top of the Republican ticket, millions of Democrats heeded their party's entreaty to "come home." Two years ago, one-half of the Democrats who said the president was doing a good job voted for Republican congressional candidates, ABC exit polls showed. This year, only one-fourth of the Democrats who like the job Reagan is doing said they voted for Republican congressional candidates.

Democratic strategists sought to give the credit to the strength of their party. "We just had better candidates," said Diane Dewhirst, spokeswoman for the Democratic Senatorial Campaign Committee.

But exit polling of more than 30,000 voters suggested to analysts another explanation. The Democratic Party, which is in the majority, benefited from a campaign that had no compelling national issues and relied heavily on negative advertising. The voters who felt no strong party affiliation — precisely those who helped build the Reagan coalition for Republicans — were not motivated by the issues to get out and vote.

Nearly 4,000 voters were asked after voting if any of seven issues were important in influencing how they voted. All of the seven — the budget deficit, preventing war, reducing unemployment, protecting Social Security, stopping illegal drug traffic, the state of the national economy and the state of the local economy were cited by between 10 and 13 percent of those responding.

The absence of burning national issues also apparently cut into the black vote, which hurt Democrats more than Republicans. Blacks, who vote almost 90 percent Democratic, comprised only 7 percent of those who voted Tuesday, two to three percentage points lower than had been expected, according to the analysts.

One silver lining for Republicans was that the young voters who did turn out continued the trend begun in the Reagan years of voting Republican. First-time voters went 52 to 45 Republican in the Senate races, according to the exit polls.

Washington state voters approve referendum on nuclear waste site

SEATTLE (AP) — Washington state voters approved a referendum Tuesday protesting a federal proposal to locate the nation's first dump for highly radioactive wastes at the Hanford nuclear reservation.

With 12 percent of 6,176 precincts reporting, Referendum 40 was being approved by 125,976 to 26,946, or an 82 percent favorable vote.

Referendum 40 criticized the process the Energy Department used to select Washington's Hanford nuclear reservation, Yucca Mountain, Nev., and Deaf Smith County, Texas, as finalists to permanently store 70,000 metric tons of spent reactor fuel and defense waste byproducts in shafts deep underground.

The referendum directed state officials to use all legal means necessary to convince the government to suspend the site-selection process and to reverse its decision to abandon plans for a second repository in the East.

The referendum also insists on "safe, scientifically justified, and regionally and geographically equitable high-level nuclear waste disposal" and demands congressional budget writers comply with the Nuclear Waste Policy Act.

It also called for a public vote in Washington state if Hanford is picked in 1992 as the dump site, should the governor or Legislature not immediately veto the selection. The state's veto is subject to congressional override.

Lotteries, abortion, taxes on ballots nationwide

Associated Press

Anti-abortion propositions lost Tuesday in Massachusetts, Oregon and Rhode Island, and state lottery issues won in Florida, Montana, South Dakota and Kansas.

In Oregon, voters refused to allow residents to grow their own marijuana. And voters in Roxbury, a poor, mostly black section of Boston, turned back a bid to secede from the city.

In votes on tax limiting measures, Montanans were favoring a freeze on most property taxes, while a Colorado proposition requiring a vote on any new tax or tax increase was losing. In Massachusetts, a measure that would limit state tax collections to a level no higher than the average growth in wages of workers, was leading 55 percent to 45 percent.

With eight of 2,866 Colorado precincts reporting, 4,417 opposed the tax limiting measure and 2,574 favored it.

In Montana, with 7 percent of precincts counted, the tax-freeze measure had 18,715 votes for, or 55 percent, and 15,137 votes, or 45 percent, against. A more radical issue, abolishing property taxes, was losing, 59 percent to 41 percent.

Nebraskans voted to retain the state's mandatory seat belt law. But in a similar vote in Massachusetts, the seat belt law was behind 44,680 to 35,563, or 56 percent to 44 percent, with 112 of 2,193 precincts counted.

Vermont's equal rights amendment appeared to be in trouble. With 10 percent of precincts reporting, 49 percent were for the ERA, while 51 percent were against it.

In Montana, with 7 percent of precincts reporting, the measure was passing 20,104 to 8,367.

In Florida, with 883 of 4,329 precincts reporting, a lottery measure led 279,093 to 198,470. Voters were rejecting a county-option casino gambling measure, 352,346 to 138,852.

Kansas voters were favoring constitutional amendments to create a lottery, to allow pari-mutuel wagering and to leave it up to counties to allow the sale of liquor by the drink.

In South Dakota, with 16 percent of the precincts reporting, voters were favoring a lottery, 45,639 to 23,406.

North Dakota and Idaho also were considering lottery issues.

Oregon voters were choosing among four tax propositions. Measure 7 would create a 5 percent retail sales tax, with 30 percent of the revenue for property tax relief and the rest for schools. Measure 9 would cut property taxes for most people. Measure 11 would exempt half of home values from property taxes. Measure 12 would pay for that exemption by increasing income taxes for some taxpayers.

In Washington state, voters were asked to cast ballots protesting the federal government's decision to include the Hanford nuclear reservation as a finalist to become the federal nuclear waste repository. Under an Oregon measure, the state's only nuclear power plant would have to shut down until a federal nuclear waste repository is operating.

Oregonians rejected the measure that would have allowed residents to grow unspecified amounts of marijuana for personal use, 76 percent to 24 percent.

"Oregonians are independent, but they're not stupid," said state Rep. Paul Phillips, a Republican who helped lead the battle against the measure.

ALSO IN 1986

Americans learned about the Iran-Contra affair involving National Security Council member Oliver North and the sale of weapons in exchange for freeing hostages.

THURSDAY

WISEHART, SCENE, F1
Today's stars don't twinkle

METRO, B1
Let voters rule, 4 on LAFCO say

SPORTS, C2
A bit of Magic in benefit game

The Sacramento Bee

Metro FINAL

©1987 The Sacramento Bee | Volume 261 | Thursday, July 2, 1987 | Founded 1857 | 25¢

Bork nominated to Supreme Court

Foes call him reactionary, promise confirmation fight

By Leo Rennert
Bee Washington Bureau Chief

WASHINGTON — Seeking to extend his conservative legacy, President Reagan on Wednesday nominated federal appeals judge Robert H. Bork, a leading opponent of judicial activism in resolving contemporary problems, to the nation's highest court.

The selection of Bork, 60, who has served on the U.S. Court of Appeals for the District of Columbia since 1982, undoubtedly will evolve into a bruising confirmation fight as Senate liberals and civil rights groups pledged an all-out assault on the nomination.

If confirmed, Bork — best known as the Justice Department official who fired Special Prosecutor Archibald Cox in the 1973 "Saturday Night Massacre" of the Watergate scandal

See BORK, page A22

Associated Press

Reagan announces he is nominating appeals judge Robert H. Bork, left, to succeed Justice Lewis Powell on the Supreme Court.

A conservative judge who doesn't always fit the label

By David G. Savage
Los Angeles Times

WASHINGTON — Although Robert H. Bork, President Reagan's latest nominee to the Supreme Court, was hailed by admirers and denounced by critics Wednesday as a conservative, his opinions reveal a judge less predictable than the label suggests.

As a member since 1982 of the U.S. Circuit Court for the District of Columbia, Bork has proved to be a judge who follows the law and legal precedent — not his personal preferences — in arriving at his opinions.

He has ruled against conservative students who wanted to picket outside the embassies of Nicaragua and the Soviet Union. And he has decided in favor of an artist who sought to put a poster mocking Reagan in Washington subways.

See CONSERVATIVE, page A22

Scoop's on

Bee/Mark Thiessen

Assembly Speaker Willie Brown, a veteran at dishing out political goodies, instead dished out some ice cream cones at Wednesday's Capitol Ice Cream Social. State personalities took turns scooping during the bash, sponsored by the Dairy Institute of California.

Long-awaited budget finally in Duke's hands

By Thorne Gray
Bee Capitol Bureau

By an overwhelming bipartisan vote, the Assembly sent Gov. Deukmejian a $41.2 billion legislative spending plan Wednesday, 16 days late but in time to head off a major fiscal crisis.

The delay of action until after the start of the 1987-88 budget year boosted a state revenue surplus from $700 million to $1.1 billion under a 1979 constitutional spending limit.

Under that limit, lawmakers were free until June 30 to shift some spending authority to schools as a gimmick to raise the state's spending capacity. But that opportunity slipped away at midnight Tuesday as the old fiscal year came to a close.

The result was to leave Deukmejian with the task of vetoing the extra $400 million in spending so the state will not exceed its spending cap and the money can be returned to the taxpayers.

The governor said he would complete his review of the budget "as fast as possible" and sign it into law. "I have no idea yet how much I have to cut," he told reporters after addressing a California Girls State convention Wednesday at California State University, Sacramento.

Under the spending limit, sponsored by tax critic Paul Gann, state and local government growth is restricted to increases in population and inflation. This is the first year

See BUDGET, back page, A24

Budget at a glance

Highlights of the $41.2 billion budget for the 1987-88 fiscal year sent to Gov. Deukmejian by the Legislature:

- Reserve: $953 million, down from the $1 billion sought by Deukmejian.
- Gann limit: The 1986-87 fiscal year ends with the state $1.1 billion over the spending limit.
- Schools: $12.6 billion in state funds.
- Colleges: University of California student fees to go from $1,343 a year to $1,473; California State University fees from $573 to $630 a year; community college fees stay at $100 a year. A 5.7 percent pay raise for UC faculty on Jan. 1, 1988. Immediate 6.9 percent raise for CSU faculty.
- State workers: Six percent wage increases, effective Jan. 1.
- Worker safety: The budget restores $8 million Deukmejian cut to terminate the California Occupational Safety and Health Act.
- Health: One percent cost-of-living increases for most health programs, except 3 percent for the elderly and 10 percent for obstetricians who care for poor women.
- Abortion: Language restricting Medi-Cal abortions for poor women to cases of rape or incest, health of the mother or genetic deformities. The same language has been struck down by courts the last eight years.
- AIDS: $73 million for research, treatment and education programs for acquired immune deficiency syndrome.
- Prisons: $1.21 billion.
- Counties: $89 million in unrestricted grants to counties instead of health and welfare cost-of-living increases.
- Welfare: 2.6 percent cost-of-living increases.

Iacocca: Chrysler was 'dumb'

Company will compensate customers in odometer scandal

By John Holusha
New York Times

HIGHLAND PARK, Mich. — Lee Iacocca, chairman of the Chrysler Corp., conceded Wednesday that the company did things that were "dumb" and "unforgivable" in selling cars that had been driven while their odometers were disconnected.

Iacocca's remarks came as the automaker began a program to counter the unfavorable publicity generated by the case. As part of the program, Chrysler will give new cars to as many as 40 owners of the affected models. Other owners will be offered longer warranties with broader coverage.

Last week, Chrysler was indicted by a federal grand jury for selling 60,000 cars as new, although they had been driven — and in some cases, damaged. Chrysler had failed to tell the buyers about the accumulated mileage or repairs, the indictment said.

Two Chrysler executives were indicted on criminal charges in the matter.

The indictment covers an 18-month period from July 1, 1985, to Dec. 31, 1986. The Justice Department asserted, however, that the disconnecting of odometers went back decades and that millions of cars had been sold with inaccurate mileage readings.

Chrysler's program to compensate customers will apply only to owners of cars sold within the last three years.

The company has argued that it did nothing illegal, and it continued to do so Wednesday. But Iacocca said Chrysler was being damaged in "the court of public opinion."

"Our big concern is for our customers, the people who had enough faith in Chrysler to buy a vehicle from us," Iacocca said. "These charges and the press reports about

See CHRYSLER, back page, A24

Early TV debate showcases little-known Demo hopefuls

By Michael Shanahan and Ricardo Pimentel
Bee Washington Bureau

Seven Democratic presidential candidates, most of them unknown to voters, debated sedately over arms control, taxes and trade Wednesday — 16 months before the 1988 elections.

In the first nationally televised debate of the campaign, the candidates sought to emerge from their blurred collective identity, each of them seeking to become a leading contender while avoiding alienation from major blocs of voters.

But on a special two-hour edition of the Public Broadcasting Service show "Firing Line," the seven experienced politicians failed to assert dramatic differences on what they would do in the White House in the post-Reagan era.

All agreed on opposition to President Reagan's Nicaraguan policies and his proposed "Star Wars" space-based anti-missile program.

The seven candidates also condemned the president's economic and trade policies, but differed somewhat on how to improve the country's economic growth and its place among the other industrialized nations.

At times, the show seemed more of an argument between the candidates and William F. Buckley Jr., the conservative, articulate, occa-

See DEMOCRATS, back page. A24

INSIDE

Business	E1
Classified	D2
Comics	F10
Crosswords	D17, F11
Editorials	B6
Movies	F8
Obituaries	D3
Television	F6

FAIR
Today: high, 79; low 54
Yesterday: high 77; low 53

Soaring jet's engines shut off; dive ends 600 feet above sea

By John Nolan

CINCINNATI (AP) — The crew of a Delta Air Lines jet carrying 205 people told investigators they inadvertently shut down both of its engines, sending the plane to within 600 feet of hitting the Pacific Ocean as terrified passengers inflated life jackets, officials said Wednesday.

Crew members from Tuesday's Flight 810 from Los Angeles to Cincinnati were interviewed Wednesday by investigators from Delta and the National Transportation Safety Board.

The engines of the Boeing 767-232 shut down 10 minutes after the 12:54 p.m. takeoff from Los Angeles, while the plane was over the ocean. After the crew restarted the engines, the flight continued on to Cincinnati, arriving 27 minutes after the scheduled arrival time of 4:28 p.m. PDT.

The crew said the jet was at an altitude of 1,200 to 1,600 feet when the engines were shut down, according to NTSB spokesman Ted Lopatkiewicz in Washington.

At the captain's order, the passengers were told to prepare for a crash while the engines were off.

"They went about a minute without power," he said. "They descended to about 500 or 600

See DIVE, page A22

Kennedy delivered an impassioned Senate floor speech condemning President Reagan's nomination of Robert Bork to the U.S. Supreme Court. His speech began with the words, "Robert Bork's America is a land in which women would be forced into back-alley abortions."

ALSO IN 1987

The world population reached 5 billion on July 11.

DECEMBER 11, 1991
WILLIAM KENNEDY SMITH FOUND NOT GUILTY OF RAPE

William Kennedy Smith was accused of raping a woman at the Kennedy family's Palm Beach compound after meeting her in a bar with his uncle Edward Kennedy and cousin Patrick. Smith, the son of Jean Kennedy Smith, was acquitted of all charges.

ALSO IN 1991

Soviet Union President Mikhail Gorbachev, who initiated the reformist policies of perestroika and glasnost, resigned on December 25 and the Soviet Union was dissolved formally the following day.

SUNNY, WARM The nice days will come to an end at the start of the weekend. Rain and cooler air is expected by Saturday. **WEATHER, 2A**

MOTHER'S VIGIL SITS WITH DAUGHTER THROUGH 22-YEAR COMA **ACCENT, 1D**

SABERHAGEN TRADED TO METS SEATTLE GETS MITCHELL **SPORTS, 1C**

COOKIES FROM CHRISTMAS PAST GRANDMA'S RECIPES **FOOD & DINING, 1FN**

The Palm Beach Post

THURSDAY, DECEMBER 12, 1991 **FINAL EDITION** 148 PAGES 35 CENTS

NOT GUILTY

Jury takes 77 minutes to clear Smith

Jurors say acquittal was easy decision

By GARY KANE and DOUG COHEN
Palm Beach Post Staff Writers

WEST PALM BEACH — The six people selected to decide the fate of William Kennedy Smith shared the same thought as soon as they filed into the jury room to deliberate — there was reasonable doubt.

The jury agreed almost instantly to acquit Smith, said Lea Haller, the youngest juror at 37 and owner of a Texas-based cosmetics wholesaling company.

"We went into the jury room and everybody wrote secretly what they thought so we wouldn't influence each other," she said Wednesday night at her oceanfront condominium in Palm Beach. "It wasn't really a vote. It was just our private opinions."

Up to that point, the jurors were the only people in the country not allowed to read about or discuss the high-profile case. When they weren't in room 411 of the Palm Beach County Courthouse, they were at the Holiday Inn on Belvedere Road near Interstate 95, where they spent nine nights sequestered.

Their free time was spent watching Disney videotapes, playing checkers and eating meals (a two-drink maximum) under the watchful eyes of four Palm Beach County sheriff's deputies to make sure they didn't discuss the case.

As Haller joined the other jurors jotting down their opinions of the evidence, she worried that she would be the only one feeling that Smith was not guilty of the alleged date rape. But she learned her colleagues shared her views.

"Everyone was pretty much in agreement all the way along," she said.

It took them but 77 minutes to render their verdict.

Jurors felt that Smith and the Jupiter woman who accused him of rape both gave compelling and credible testimony, Haller said.

"Her testimony was very touching and it was very believable at the time," she said. "But the evidence in my opinion didn't support the testimony beyond a reasonable doubt."

Please see JURY/20A

LOREN G. HOSACK/Staff Photographer

William Kennedy Smith hugs his mother, Jean Smith, after the verdict Wednesday. Attorney Roy Black is at top left.

Supporters cheer 'happy' defendant outside courthouse

By CHRISTINE STAPLETON
Palm Beach Post Staff Writer

WEST PALM BEACH — William Kennedy Smith hugged his tearful defense attorney Wednesday after a jury quickly decided Smith did not rape a Jupiter woman on the lawn of his family's Palm Beach estate.

"I'm just really, really happy," Smith said as he left the Palm Beach County Courthouse amid dozens of cheering supporters. "Gratitude is the memory of the heart, and I have enough memories in my heart to last a lifetime."

Seventy-seven minutes after the jury began deliberating, Smith clasped his hands as if in prayer and dropped his head in the tense, hushed courtroom as he waited for the verdict to be read.

His four-member defense team and three jury selection experts sat nervously beside him. His mother, Jean Smith, sisters Amanda and Kym, brother Stephen and a friend who is a Jesuit seminarian sat behind him in the crowded gallery.

Circuit Judge Mary Lupo interrupted the reading of the verdict to sternly warn observers and attorneys that she would not tolerate any display of emotion or any movement in the courtroom after the verdict was read.

Please see TRIAL/18A

Smith's accuser: Verdict does not equal innocence

By CHRISTINE STAPLETON and AMY DRISCOLL
Palm Beach Post Staff Writers

WEST PALM BEACH — The woman who accused William Kennedy Smith of rape resumed her silence Wednesday but allowed her attorney to read a prepared statement.

"The jury has spoken," David Roth read. "However, 'not guilty' does not equate to innocence."

Because she was a witness, the woman was not allowed to watch the trial. In the law office of Roth and his partner Douglas Duncan, the woman listened Wednesday for the first time to lead defense attorney Roy Black recite Smith's version of what happened that night.

Roth declined to say how she reacted to the story but sa'd she left before the verdict was returned.

"I hink it's our job to try to explain to our client in more detail what a 'not guilty' verdict means," Roth said. "It means the state did not prove its case beyond every reasonable doubt."

Please see ACCUSER/18A

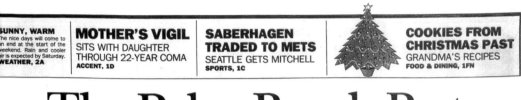

FRANK CERABINO
COMMENTARY

Verdict won't end debate on rape charge

By the time William Kennedy Smith walked out of the courthouse Wednesday, the word of his lightning-fast acquittal had caused the twilight crowd to swell.

Spectators formed like a swollen pool of heads that radiated from a single clump of microphones, his forum for comment during this very public trial.

Those who couldn't cram into the courtyard, hung out office windows or craned their necks from balconies on three levels of the parking garage.

This was goodbye — the last promenade for Smith. He had made this stroll from the courthouse doors to that beat-up Mercury station wagon at the curb for the past six weeks. It's been a 20-yard trip lined with yellow crime-scene tape, a phalanx of cameras and the unanswered questions of shouting reporters.

He had some good days on this stroll, when the bystanders would shout "not guilty" or call his name and applaud. And he's had some bad days when his accuser's testimony would cower the crowd into an eerie silence.

But Wednesday would be his best day, because it would be his last. And you knew that he would wait for the cheers to die down and step up to the microphones to give the talk of the winner.

"Gratitude is the memory of the heart," he began. "I have enough memories in my heart to last a lifetime."

But the man who begins so many of his sentences with the word, "obviously" didn't explain what memories. And when he men-

Please see CERABINO/19A

MORE INSIDE

- **ACCUSER** – After the verdict, WPBF-Channel 25 (ABC) identified Smith's accuser. No other local stations followed suit. **17A**
- **ACCUSED** – William Kennedy Smith's complete statement. **18A**
- **ACQUITTAL** – Smith's defense team toasts their victory — and a juror — at Bradley's Saloon. **19A**

WILLIAM KENNEDY SMITH THE TRIAL

INSIDE

ANN & ABBY	2D	LETTERS	25A
BOND	26A	LOTTERY	2A
BUSINESS	9B	OBITUARIES	8B
CLASSIFIEDS	11C	PEOPLE	2A
EDITORIALS	26A	ROSAFORTE	1C
FLA. NEWS	6,8B	STOCKS	10B
FOOD	1FN	TV SPORTS	2C
LEGIS.	22A	RON WIGGINS	1D

MOVIES, TV LISTINGS . . . IN ACCENT

Vol. 83 No. 217 © 1991 The Palm Beach Post
5 Sections

CANCER – Women are 25% more likely to be diagnosed with breast cancer today than 20 years ago. **STORY, 3A**

Forest Hill student tests positive for TB; 250 checked

By MICHAEL LASALANDRA
Palm Beach Post Staff Writer

WEST PALM BEACH — Some students and teachers at Forest Hill High School are being tested for tuberculosis after health officials learned a student tested positive for the highly contagious disease.

Right now, only classmates and teachers of the student and those who ride on the same school bus are being tested, but the entire school might have to be tested eventually, said Dr. Jean Malecki, medical director of the Palm Beach County Public Health Unit.

About 125 students and teachers were tested at the school on Wednesday. Another 125 are to be tested today. Results will be back in two days.

Worried students lined up in the school gymnasium Wednesday to be tested.

"I'm a little bit worried," said sophomore Shawn McDaniel, 17. "Everybody's been talking about it for the past couple of days."

"I'm scared," said Roger Pitts, 16. "I don't want to die."

Please see TUBERCULOSIS/23A

ABOUT TUBERCULOSIS

- **8 MILLION** new cases occur each year in the world, 22,000 in the U.S.
- **FLORIDA** ranks fourth in the nation with 14.2 cases per 100,000 people.
- **PALM BEACH** County reported 129 cases of TB this year through Oct. 31.

SOURCE: U.S. Centers for Disease Control

July 3, 1992
Senator Edward Kennedy Married Victoria Reggie

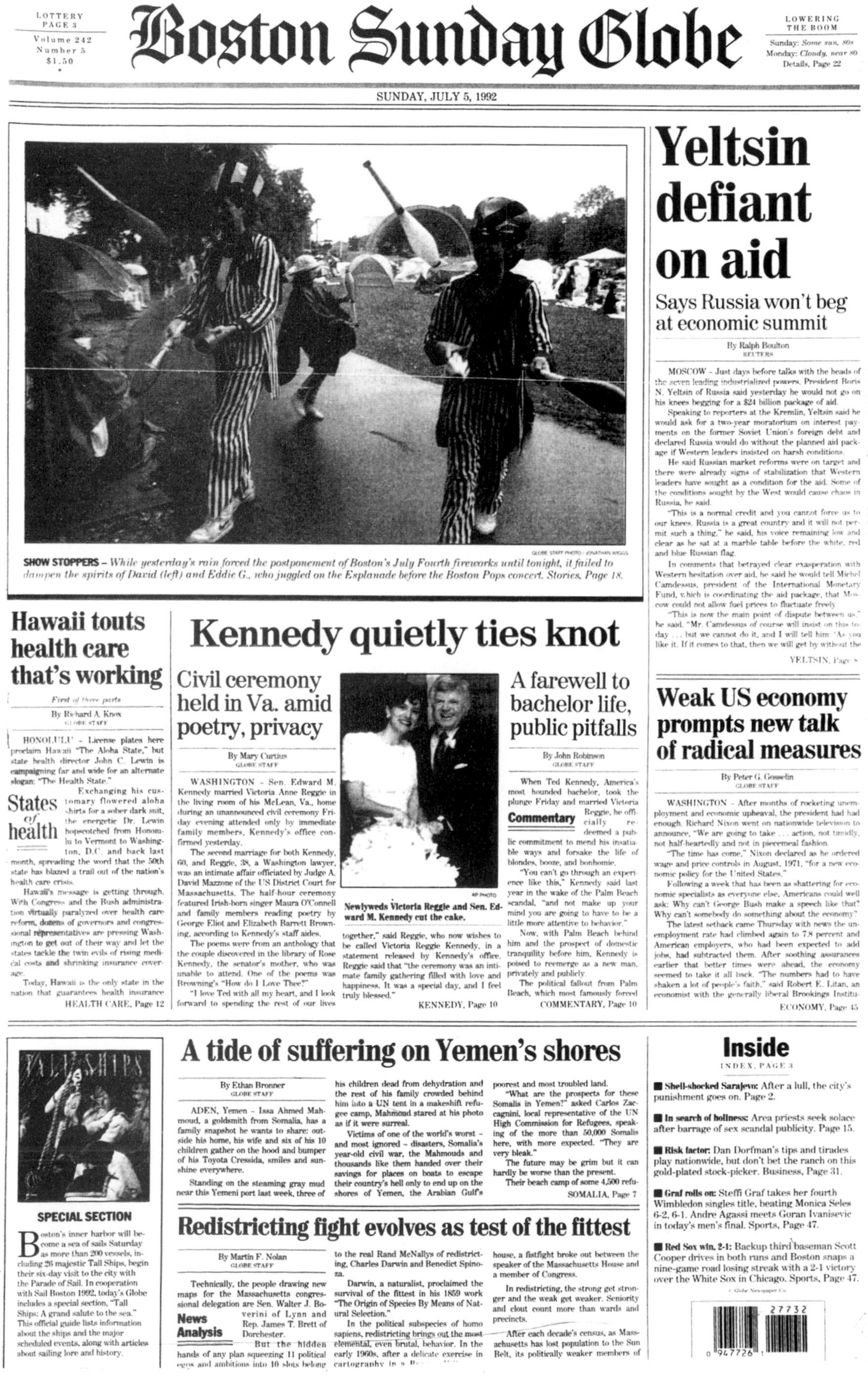

LOTTERY PAGE 3

Volume 242 Number 5 $1.50

Boston Sunday Globe

LOWERING THE BOOM

Sunday: *Some sun, 80s* Monday: *Cloudy, near 80* Details, Page 22

SUNDAY, JULY 5, 1992

GLOBE STAFF PHOTO / JONATHAN WIGGS

SHOW STOPPERS – *While yesterday's rain forced the postponement of Boston's July Fourth fireworks until tonight, it failed to dampen the spirits of David (left) and Eddie G., who juggled on the Esplanade before the Boston Pops concert. Stories, Page 18.*

Yeltsin defiant on aid

Says Russia won't beg at economic summit

By Ralph Boulton
REUTERS

MOSCOW – Just days before talks with the heads of the seven leading industrialized powers, President Boris N. Yeltsin of Russia said yesterday he would not go on his knees begging for a $24 billion package of aid.

Speaking to reporters at the Kremlin, Yeltsin said he would ask for a two-year moratorium on interest payments on the former Soviet Union's foreign debt and declared Russia would do without the planned aid package if Western leaders insisted on harsh conditions.

He said Russian market reforms were on target and there were already signs of stabilization that Western leaders have sought as a condition for the aid. Some of the conditions sought by the West would cause chaos in Russia, he said.

"This is a normal credit and you cannot force us to our knees. Russia is a great country and it will not permit such a thing," he said, his voice remaining low and clear as he sat at a marble table before the white, red and blue Russian flag.

In comments that betrayed clear exasperation with Western hesitation over aid, he said he would tell Michel Camdessus, president of the International Monetary Fund, which is coordinating the aid package, that Moscow could not allow fuel prices to fluctuate freely.

"This is now the main point of dispute between us," he said. "Mr. Camdessus of course will insist on this today ... but we cannot do it, and I will tell him: 'As you like it. If it comes to that, then we will get by without the

YELTSIN, Page 8

Hawaii touts health care that's working

First of three parts

By Richard A. Knox
GLOBE STAFF

HONOLULU – License plates here proclaim Hawaii "The Aloha State," but state health director John C. Lewin is campaigning far and wide for an alternate slogan: "The Health State."

States of health

Exchanging his customary flowered aloha shirts for a sober dark suit, the energetic Dr. Lewin hopscotched from Honolulu to Vermont to Washington, D.C. and back last month, spreading the word that the 50th state has blazed a trail out of the nation's health care crisis.

Hawaii's message is getting through. With Congress and the Bush administration virtually paralyzed over health care reform, dozens of governors and congressional representatives are pressing Washington to get out of their way and let the states tackle the twin evils of rising medical costs and shrinking insurance coverage.

Today, Hawaii is the only state in the nation that guarantees health insurance

HEALTH CARE, Page 12

Kennedy quietly ties knot

Civil ceremony held in Va. amid poetry, privacy

By Mary Curtius
GLOBE STAFF

WASHINGTON – Sen. Edward M. Kennedy married Victoria Anne Reggie in the living room of his McLean, Va., home during an unannounced civil ceremony Friday evening attended only by immediate family members, Kennedy's office confirmed yesterday.

The second marriage for both Kennedy, 60, and Reggie, 38, a Washington lawyer, was an intimate affair officiated by Judge A. David Mazzone of the US District Court for Massachusetts. The half-hour ceremony featured Irish-born singer Maura O'Connell and family members reading poetry by George Eliot and Elizabeth Barrett Browning, according to Kennedy's staff aides.

The poems were from an anthology that the couple discovered in the library of Rose Kennedy, the senator's mother, who was unable to attend. One of the poems was Browning's "How do I Love Thee?"

"I love Ted with all my heart, and I look forward to spending the rest of our lives together," said Reggie, who now wishes to be called Victoria Reggie Kennedy, in a statement released by Kennedy's office. Reggie said that "the ceremony was an intimate family gathering filled with love and happiness. It was a special day, and I feel truly blessed."

KENNEDY, Page 10

AP PHOTO

Newlyweds Victoria Reggie and Sen. Edward M. Kennedy cut the cake.

A farewell to bachelor life, public pitfalls

By John Robinson
GLOBE STAFF

Commentary

When Ted Kennedy, America's most hounded bachelor, took the plunge Friday and married Victoria Reggie, he officially redeemed a public commitment to mend his insatiable ways and forsake the life of blondes, booze, and bonhomie.

"You can't go through an experience like this," Kennedy said last year in the wake of the Palm Beach scandal, "and not make up your mind you are going to have to be a little more attentive to behavior."

Now, with Palm Beach behind him and the prospect of domestic tranquility before him, Kennedy is poised to reemerge as a new man, privately and publicly.

The political fallout from Palm Beach, which most famously forced

COMMENTARY, Page 10

Weak US economy prompts new talk of radical measures

By Peter G. Gosselin
GLOBE STAFF

WASHINGTON – After months of rocketing unemployment and economic upheaval, the president had had enough. Richard Nixon went on nationwide television to announce, "We are going to take ... action, not timidly, not half-heartedly and not in piecemeal fashion.

"The time has come," Nixon declared as he ordered wage and price controls in August, 1971, "for a new economic policy for the United States."

Following a week that has been as shattering for economic specialists as everyone else, Americans could well ask: Why can't George Bush make a speech like that? Why can't somebody do something about the economy?

The latest setback came Thursday with news the unemployment rate had climbed again to 7.8 percent and American employers, who had been expected to add jobs, had subtracted them. After soothing assurances earlier that better times were ahead, the economy seemed to take it all back. "The numbers had to have shaken a lot of people's faith," said Robert E. Litan, an economist with the generally liberal Brookings Institu-

ECONOMY, Page 45

SPECIAL SECTION

Boston's inner harbor will become a sea of sails Saturday as more than 200 vessels, including 26 majestic Tall Ships, begin their six-day visit to the city with the Parade of Sail. In cooperation with Sail Boston 1992, today's Globe includes a special section, "Tall Ships: A grand salute to the sea." This official guide lists information about the ships and the major scheduled events, along with articles about sailing lore and history.

A tide of suffering on Yemen's shores

By Ethan Bronner
GLOBE STAFF

ADEN, Yemen – Issa Ahmed Mahmoud, a goldsmith from Somalia, has a family snapshot he wants to share: outside his home, his wife and six of his 10 children gather on the hood and bumper of his Toyota Cressida, smiles and sunshine everywhere.

Standing on the steaming gray mud near this Yemeni port last week, three of his children dead from dehydration and the rest of his family crowded behind him into a UN tent in a makeshift refugee camp, Mahmoud stared at his photo as if it were surreal.

Victims of one of the world's worst – and most ignored – disasters, Somalia's year-old civil war, the Mahmouds and thousands like them handed over their savings for places on boats to escape their country's hell only to end up on the shores of Yemen, the Arabian Gulf's poorest and most troubled land.

"What are the prospects for these Somalis in Yemen?" asked Carlos Zaccagnini, local representative of the UN High Commission for Refugees, speaking of the more than 50,000 Somalis here, with more expected. "They are very bleak."

The future may be grim but it can hardly be worse than the present.

Their beach camp of some 4,500 refu-

SOMALIA, Page 7

Redistricting fight evolves as test of the fittest

By Martin F. Nolan
GLOBE STAFF

News Analysis

Technically, the people drawing new maps for the Massachusetts congressional delegation are Sen. Walter J. Boverini of Lynn and Rep. James T. Brett of Dorchester.

But the hidden hands of any plan squeezing 11 political egos and ambitions into 10 slots belong to the real Rand McNallys of redistricting, Charles Darwin and Benedict Spinoza.

Darwin, a naturalist, proclaimed the survival of the fittest in his 1859 work "The Origin of Species By Means of Natural Selection."

In the political subspecies of homo sapiens, redistricting brings out the most elemental, even brutal, behavior. In the early 1960s, after a delicate exercise in cartography in a [illegible] house, a fistfight broke out between the speaker of the Massachusetts House and a member of Congress.

In redistricting, the strong get stronger and the weak get weaker. Seniority and clout count more than wards and precincts.

After each decade's census, as Massachusetts has lost population to the Sun Belt, its politically weaker members of

Inside

INDEX, PAGE 3

- **Shell-shocked Sarajevo:** After a lull, the city's punishment goes on. Page 2.
- **In search of holiness:** Area priests seek solace after barrage of sex scandal publicity. Page 15.
- **Risk factor:** Dan Dorfman's tips and tirades play nationwide, but don't bet the ranch on this gold-plated stock-picker. Business, Page 31.
- **Graf rolls on:** Steffi Graf takes her fourth Wimbledon singles title, beating Monica Seles 6-2, 6-1. Andre Agassi meets Goran Ivanisevic in today's men's final. Sports, Page 47.
- **Red Sox win, 2-1:** Backup third baseman Scott Cooper drives in both runs and Boston snaps a nine-game road losing streak with a 2-1 victory over the White Sox in Chicago. Sports, Page 47.

© Globe Newspaper Co.

Divorced in 1982, Kennedy called his second wife "the woman who changed my life." The Reggie and Kennedy families had been friends since John F. Kennedy's presidential campaign.

Senator Edward Kennedy, Jacqueline Kennedy Onassis, John F. Kennedy Jr., and Caroline Kennedy Schlossberg attended the presentation of the Profile in Courage Award, named for President John F. Kennedy's Pulitzer Prize–winning book. (AP Photo/ Stephan Savoia)

ALSO IN 1992

A year after the end of the U.S.-led Gulf War, Iraq refused to allow U.N. inspection teams access to information about its weapons.

SEPTEMBER 22, 1993

SENATOR EDWARD KENNEDY WORKED WITH PRESIDENT CLINTON ON NATIONAL HEALTH INSURANCE PLAN

LIVING
VESTS MAKING A COMEBACK
In style again for men/1C

VENTURE
TRAILS FOR TOMORROW
Cycling on the rails/1F

NEWS
GIANTS WIN; BRAVES LOSE
Ryan's career over?/1F

San Jose Mercury News

MORNING FINAL
35 CENTS

Serving Northern California Since 1851

THURSDAY
SEPTEMBER 23, 1993

'This is our chance'

Clinton outlines his prescription to rebuild the health care system

What reform would save

Here is the White House projection of what national health expenditures would be without any changes and under its reforms. The base line figures are projections from the Congressional Budget Office.

Health care spending (in trillions of dollars)

'94 '95 '96 '97 '98 '99 2000

Fiscal year

Without reform / With reform

ASSOCIATED PRESS

■ Guarantees: The president's plan promises all Americans medical treatment.

Mercury News Staff and Wire Reports

WASHINGTON — Launching his campaign for the centerpiece of his presidency, President Clinton on Wednesday night laid out a radical rebuilding of the nation's health care system that for the first time would guarantee medical care to every American.

In a passionate address that reached beyond dollars and details, Clinton exhorted Congress and the American people to muster the "courage" to change a "badly broken" system as part of the most ambitious social reform since the New Deal.

"At long last, after decades of false starts, we must make this our most urgent priority: Giving every American health security — health care that

See HEALTH, Page 15A

HEALTH CARE REFORM

RELATED STORIES

■ How South Bay people react. PAGE 14A

■ Editorial. PAGE 6B

ASSOCIATED PRESS

Clinton displays a prototype of a health care card.

■ Analysis: Bold vision is fraught with uncertainty.

BY DAVID LAUTER
Los Angeles Times

WASHINGTON — Every so often, usually under the compulsion of crisis, the government collectively braces itself, takes a deep breath and leaps into a largely unknown future.

During the late 1930s, the nation took such a leap, agreeing to give the federal government a whole new set of responsibilities — from providing Social Security for the elderly to establishing a new system of national regulatory agencies to monitor the economy.

In the 1960s, the nation took another such leap, adopting a new code of civil rights laws to change fundamentally the relationship of black and white Americans.

Now, another new president has proposed a sweeping plan.

See ANALYSIS, Page 14A

WHAT'S COVERED
■ Hospital stays.
■ Preventive care.
■ Pregnancy services and family planning.
■ Ambulance services.
■ Vision and hearing care.
■ Preventive dental care for children.

WHAT'S NOT
■ Hearing aids.
■ Cosmetic surgery.
■ Private hospital rooms.
■ Adult eyeglasses and contact lenses.
■ Complete list of benefits. PAGE 15A

New data brightens image of immigrants

BY STEVE JOHNSON
Mercury News Staff Writer

Despite widespread concerns about immigrant contributions to the country, new census data shows them to be extraordinarily diverse and often highly talented — with many sporting educations, incomes and resumes exceeding those of U.S. natives.

Clearly, many immigrants are struggling, according to a government study, made public Wednesday, based on the 1990 census. Immigrants have slightly higher rates of unemployment and welfare use, and considerably higher rates of poverty. And those problems tend to be more noticeable among recent immigrants, especially Mexicans and Southeast Asians who have come to the Bay Area in large numbers.

Those who came to the United States before 1980, however, ap-

See CENSUS, Back Page

Train wreck in the bayou: What happened

A transcontinental Amtrak train reportedly carrying 189 passengers and 17 crew members jumped the tracks outside Mobile, Ala., early Wednesday, plunging into muddy waters and killing at least 40 people.

The Sunset Limited

Locomotives / Baggage / Crew dorm / Coaches / Lounge / Dining / Sleeper

What happened on the bridge

Bayou Cannot Bridge: 500-foot-long, single-track, steel and timber structure, built originally in 1909.

As train derailed on Bayou Cannot Bridge, the three engines plowed into the muddy bayou banks. Survivors reported a fire erupted from a derailed engine.

Coast Guard used helicopters and boats to pull people out of the water; divers began searching for the missing.

Four cars careened into the water; two were coaches that can carry up to 60 people each.

One derailed coach was completely submerged; water in area is about 25 feet deep.

A third coach perched precariously at the edge of the section of bridge that collapsed.

Why the wreck happened

One theory is that a barge hit the bridge just before the train crossed.

KNIGHT-RIDDER NEWS SERVICE/RON CODDINGTON AND JEFF DIONISE

At least 41 dead in Amtrak nightmare

■ Derailment: Weakened bridge collapsed under train.

Mercury News Wire Services

MOBILE, Ala. — Fire danced on the black water while Elizabeth Watts swam for her life. Her husband, Bob, called for her in the darkness.

Together, the Placerville couple found their way to a bridge abutment, and survived the deadliest calamity in Amtrak's 23-year history. More than 40 people died in the wreck, possibly caused when a barge damaged an 84-year-old wood-and-steel bridge.

By late Wednesday night,

See TRAIN, Back Page

Bill Gates reflects on his life, work

BY RORY J. O'CONNOR
Mercury News Staff Writer

SCOTTSDALE, Ariz. — If you were a multi-billionaire at 37, about to be married and had been working at the same job for 18 years, you might think about putting your feet up and settling into a new life of early retirement and world travel.

Gates

You might unless you were Microsoft Corp. Chairman Bill Gates, that is.

Gates, a workaholic who has led Microsoft from a shoestring

See GATES, Back Page

Yeltsin backed in confrontation

■ Standoff: Rebellious Russian parliament hasn't won support.

CRISIS IN RUSSIA

■ Georgia leader Eduard Shevardnadze's new role has danger, not glamour. PAGE 6A

BY MARGARET SHAPIRO
Washington Post

MOSCOW — Russian President Boris Yeltsin, who threw his country into turmoil Tuesday by disbanding parliament and ordering new elections, won crucial backing Wednesday from defense, Interior Ministry and Central Bank officials.

Yeltsin appeared confident and relaxed as he took an impromptu stroll Wednesday with his defense and interior ministers on one of Moscow's main shopping streets.

He promised to avoid bloodshed but also ruled out any dialogue with the conservative parliament, which, he said, no longer exists.

Yeltsin also belittled the parliament's decision Tuesday night to strip him of the presidency and appoint Vice President Alexander Rutskoi in his place.

"This is not serious, this kind of amateurism which has nothing in common with the law or anything else," Yeltsin said.

Legislative leaders, who with Rutskoi have led the opposition to Yeltsin and his reforms, announced they would prosecute anyone who defied

See RUSSIA, Page 7A

INDEX

Court gets tough on Navy's gay ban

■ The federal judge who sided with gay sailor Keith Meinhold, pictured, threatens Secretary of Defense Les Aspin and top Navy officials with contempt charges. PAGE 12A

Silicon Valley favored for consortium headquarters

■ Flat-panel display industry would bring 15,000 manufacturing jobs to the area. BUSINESS PAGE 1E

NEWS SUMMARY

■ Complete summary of today's news. PAGE 2A

Action Line	12C	Ann Landers	2C
Business	1E	Living	1C
California News	3B	Lottery	3B
Classified	3D	Miss Manners	2C
Comics	10C	Movies	4C
Crossword	10C	Obituaries	5B
Editorials	6B	People	4A
Entertainment	3C	Scoreboard	8F
Games	11C	Sports	1F
Garden	1D	Stocks	4E
Bud Geracie	1F	Television	9C
Horoscope	10C	Venture	1F

WEATHER

■ Sunny skies this afternoon, with highs in the mid-70s. Lows tonight in the upper 40s to mid-50s. PAGE 2B

Copyright 1993, San Jose Mercury News

President Bill Clinton found a strong ally in Kennedy when he proposed a comprehensive health care plan to Congress. Kennedy championed other health bills, including the 1985 Consolidated Omnibus Budget Reconciliation Act (COBRA), the 1996 Health Insurance Portability and Accountability Act (HIPAA), and a year later, the State Children's Health Insurance Program (SCHIP).

ALSO IN 1993

Mosaic, the first graphical Web browser, was released and helped popularize the Internet.

May 19, 1994
Jacqueline Kennedy Onassis Died

The Philadelphia Inquirer

City Edition d — Friday, May 20, 1994 — 50 cents outside the eight-county Philadelphia metropolitan area — 35 Cents

Jacqueline Kennedy Onassis Dies

Associated Press / CHARLES KRUPA

Jacqueline Onassis attended ceremonies at the John F. Kennedy Library and Museum in Boston with her son, John F. Kennedy Jr., and President Clinton in 1993. Mrs. Onassis had been fighting cancer for several months. She publicly disclosed her illness in February.

A first lady known for her quiet elegance saw triumph, tragedy

By Jodi Enda
INQUIRER WASHINGTON BUREAU

Jacqueline Bouvier Kennedy Onassis, the soft-spoken, glamorous woman who captured the heart of a nation and came to embody the hope and despair of an era, died at her Manhattan home last night of cancer of the lymph system. She was 64.

Mrs. Onassis returned to her Fifth Avenue apartment Wednesday after doctors at New York Hospital-Cornell Medical Center determined "there was nothing more to do for her," said her longtime friend Nancy Tuckerman. She had entered the hospital Monday, a day after she was photographed walking in Central Park.

Throughout the day yesterday, she was visited by family members and friends. Her daughter, Caroline Kennedy Schlossberg, son, John F. Kennedy Jr., and her longtime companion, Maurice Tempelsman, were among those at her bedside when she died at 10:15 p.m.

Rep. Joseph P. Kennedy 2d, her nephew, had emerged from the apartment earlier in the afternoon, saying, "There's a lot of love in her room and in her apartment."

Doctors had found that the cancer had spread to her liver and brain, according to several news reports. Under terms of a living will she had signed, aggressive treatment of her disease was suspended and she went home to die.

President Clinton issued a statement last night, calling Mrs. Onassis "a model of courage and dignity for all Americans and all the world."

"Even in the face of impossible tragedy, she carried the grief of her family and our entire nation with a calm power that somehow reassured all of us who mourned. We hope that Mrs. Onassis' children, John and Caroline, and her grandchildren find solace in the extraordinary contributions she made to our country."

Born Jacqueline Lee Bouvier on July 28, 1929, in the Long Island resort town of Southampton, she passed gracefully through the stages of her life — from society girl to first lady, to young widow, to wife of a Greek shipping tycoon, to career woman and New York book editor.

In later life, she preferred to be known as Mrs. Onassis. But to her fans she was always Jackie, or Jackie O.

For more than three decades, she was part of the nation's collective consciousness. With her, a generation of Americans dreamed and reveled, ached and mourned.

Together, they watched her children crawl under the Oval Office desk and romp on the White House lawn. Together, they stood at her husband's funeral, as she held tightly to her two young children's hands,

See **ONASSIS** on A22

Family and friends had kept a sorrowful vigil. **A23.**

Associated Press

Jacqueline and then-U.S. Sen. John F. Kennedy cutting their wedding cake in Newport, R.I., on Sept. 12, 1953.

Bell to spend billions on video service

The company will wire this and five other areas to receive video services by fiber-optic lines.

By Michael L. Rozansky
INQUIRER STAFF WRITER

Want to watch a movie at home? As soon as next year, you might be able to forget the video store, skip cable TV and see what's on the telephone.

Bell Atlantic Corp. yesterday laid out an ambitious schedule to wire six major markets, including metropolitan Philadelphia, with a network capable of carrying movies and other video services starting within 18 months.

Bell, which will spend $11 billion on capital improvements over the next five years, named AT&T as primary contractor for its network — giving the larger company the biggest supply contract in telecommunications history.

And it chose General Instrument Corp., a Chicago company that has a major research facility in Hatboro, to supply the set-top converter boxes that will link TV sets with the network.

Although Bell did not release details, AT&T's share has been estimated at $8.5 billion, and General Instrument's contract has been put at $1 billion.

Other regional phone companies have made plans to upgrade their networks, too, but Bell Atlantic's plan to reach 8.5 million homes by 2000 with its interactive network is the most aggressive.

"Bell Atlantic customers will be the first in the nation to receive video services provided by their local-exchange [telephone] carrier over its own network," said Bell Atlantic president Jim Cullen at a Washington news conference.

Bell Atlantic group president Stu Johnson said Bell's programming "will be better than cable TV," with more choices and higher quality. "Finally," he said, "consumers will have a real choice for home video services without being held hostage by a single cable-TV provider, trekking to the video store or settling for the

See **BELL** on A19

For The Inquirer / JOHN BOHN

Phineas P. Gage's skull and bust. Doctors have used his case to back various theories of brain function.

Solving historic medical mystery

By Mark Bowden
INQUIRER STAFF WRITER

It has been 135 years since Phineas P. Gage, a railroad construction foreman, was shot straight through the head — in one side and out the other — by an iron rod longer than a yardstick and more than an inch thick. Afterward, Gage sat up, talked to his men, and even walked part way back to town for treatment.

To the amazement of his doctors and family, who prepared a coffin and made funeral arrangements, Gage recovered. Despite the gaping hole in his head, he fully retained his memory, speech and intelligence. He has gone down in the annals of medicine as the most celebrated frontal-lobe brain injury case in history. The 1984 PBS television series *The Brain* re-enacted the case for millions of viewers.

How could a man shot through the head by a metal rod be relatively unimpaired?

Gage's recovery was so remarkable that at first the 19th-century medical establishment dismissed it as a fabrication. Even after experts at Harvard Medical School satisfied themselves by bringing Gage to Boston for two months of examination, some distant surgeons still called the reports "a Yankee invention." Gage briefly capitalized on his fame by appearing in a P.T. Barnum "freak show."

His lasting fame resulted, however, not just from his surviving, but from the peculiar transformation the accident caused in his personality.

Because Gage's body was never autopsied, and he lived before the age of X-rays and other such diagnostic technology, the exact nature of his injury has remained a mystery. Over the years, his case was used to buttress various and sometimes contradictory theories of brain function.

Now, combining detective work with modern medical imaging techniques, neurologists from Harvard and the University of Iowa have produced what one of them calls "an electronic autopsy" of Gage's damaged brain. Their account, in today's issue of the journal Science, purports to explain, for the first time, exactly which parts of the brain would have been damaged in this bizarre accident, and what neurological effects that damage would have caused.

Given the classic status of the Gage case in neuroscience, it

See **GAGE** on A18

HUD links $15 million to resolution of the Project HOME dispute

Cisneros stopped short of an ultimatum. He said HUD officials would join talks over 1515 Fairmount.

By Amy S. Rosenberg
INQUIRER STAFF WRITER

The U.S. secretary of housing and urban development told Mayor Rendell yesterday that he wants the city to settle its dispute with Project HOME, and that HUD officials will now be part of negotiations over the creation of permanent housing for 48 homeless men.

Henry G. Cisneros said "it would be very difficult" to justify giving the city $15 million in extra funds for the homeless as long as the proposed housing at 1515 Fairmount Ave. is unable to go forward.

The $15 million is set aside for cities that HUD determines have "innovative" programs for the homeless.

The city, however, has been found in violation of the Fair Housing Act for its role in blocking Project HOME's creation of permanent housing for 48 men at 1515 Fairmount Ave.

The dispute was cited in HUD's 100-page national homeless plan released this week in Washington as an example of HUD's commitment to take on cities in fighting discrimination against the homeless.

"I think it's important we get this resolved as directly as possible," Cisneros said in an interview before the meeting with Rendell.

"It would be very difficult to explain to homeless advocates here and in other places that we were funding Philadelphia as an innovative homeless city with a difficult case like that pending."

Cisneros, who was in Philadelphia to speak at the University of Pennsylvania commencement and to tout the Clinton health plan, spent a good part of the day in discussions about 1515 Fairmount.

HUD officials based in Philadelphia have told city officials and advocates for the homeless that HUD

See **SHELTER** on A21

Inside

With no refs, few bad sports and even fewer negative vibes, Ultimate Frisbee is a different type of team sport. And with 20,000 players nationwide, the one-time counterculture sport is coming of age. **Weekend.**

Sections		Features	
National/Int'l	A	Automotive	E13
Metro	B	Classified	E2
Business	C	Comics	F8
Sports	D	Editorials	A24
Real Estate	E	Newsmakers	F2
Magazine	F	Obituaries	B6
Weekend		Puzzles	F9
		Television	F6

Vol. 329, No. 140 © 1994, Philadelphia Newspapers Inc.
Call 215-665-1234 or 1-800-523-9068 for home delivery

Weather

Clouds giving way to some sunshine today. Clear tonight. High 68. Mostly sunny tomorrow. High 77. **Full report, B7.**

N.J. Blue Cross will set up its own health-care centers

By Marian Uhlman
INQUIRER STAFF WRITER

No longer satisfied to be just a financial conduit, New Jersey's largest health insurer transformed itself yesterday into a provider of health care as well.

Blue Cross and Blue Shield of New Jersey said it planned to open 10 family health-care centers statewide, including in Mount Laurel and Burlington. Blue Cross patients who use the centers will save between 10 percent and 15 percent of their annual insurance premiums, according to the nonprofit insurer's estimates.

"It is a fundamental change of who we are," said William J. Marino, president and chief executive.

New Jersey Blue Cross officials said the move was part of a long-term strategy to become a comprehensive managed-care company. A managed-care company provides a wide range of services from doctor care and

See **HEALTH CARE** on A15

Policy shift is breaking a nation's tradition of tolerance.

Dutch crackdown shutting out refugees

By Dick Polman
INQUIRER STAFF WRITER

AMSTERDAM, Netherlands — Coskun Coruz is a native of Turkey, but he feels very Dutch. He speaks Dutch, and he says he even thinks in Dutch. But he doesn't look Dutch, and that could be a big problem after the first of June.

Then the Dutch police will have the authority to stop people at random and demand to see their identification papers.

It's all part of an ambitious crackdown on immigrants, and Coruz is convinced it spells trouble in a land with a reputation as a tolerant haven for the world's homeless.

"Who will they stop?" asked Coruz. "The first reason they try will be because of the skin. Look at my hair. It is dark. And look at my skin. They cannot see, in my head, if I am a foreigner or a Dutchman, so they will focus on my outside."

Echoing the xenophobia that has spread through much of western Europe, the renowned Dutch open door is slamming shut — much to the delight of many white locals, who believe that recession-racked Holland, the most densely populated nation in Europe, has run out of room for newcomers.

The identity checks are aimed primarily at illegal immigrants. But the legal rights of all refugees seeking political asylum are also being sys-

See **NETHERLANDS** on A20

Former first lady Jacqueline Kennedy Onassis, 64, died of cancer at her New York apartment, "surrounded by her friends and her family and her books and the people and the things that she loved," said her son, John F. Kennedy Jr.

Senator Edward Kennedy delivered her eulogy (see pages 113–114) at the church where Jacqueline Bouvier had been baptized as a young girl, New York's Saint Ignatius Loyola Church.

John F. Kennedy Jr. and Caroline Kennedy Schlossberg were surrounded by photographers as they entered their mother's New York apartment building after her death. (AP Photo/Joe Tabacca)

QUOTED

"During those four endless days in 1963, she held us together as a family and a country."

—SENATOR EDWARD KENNEDY, *May 23, 1994*

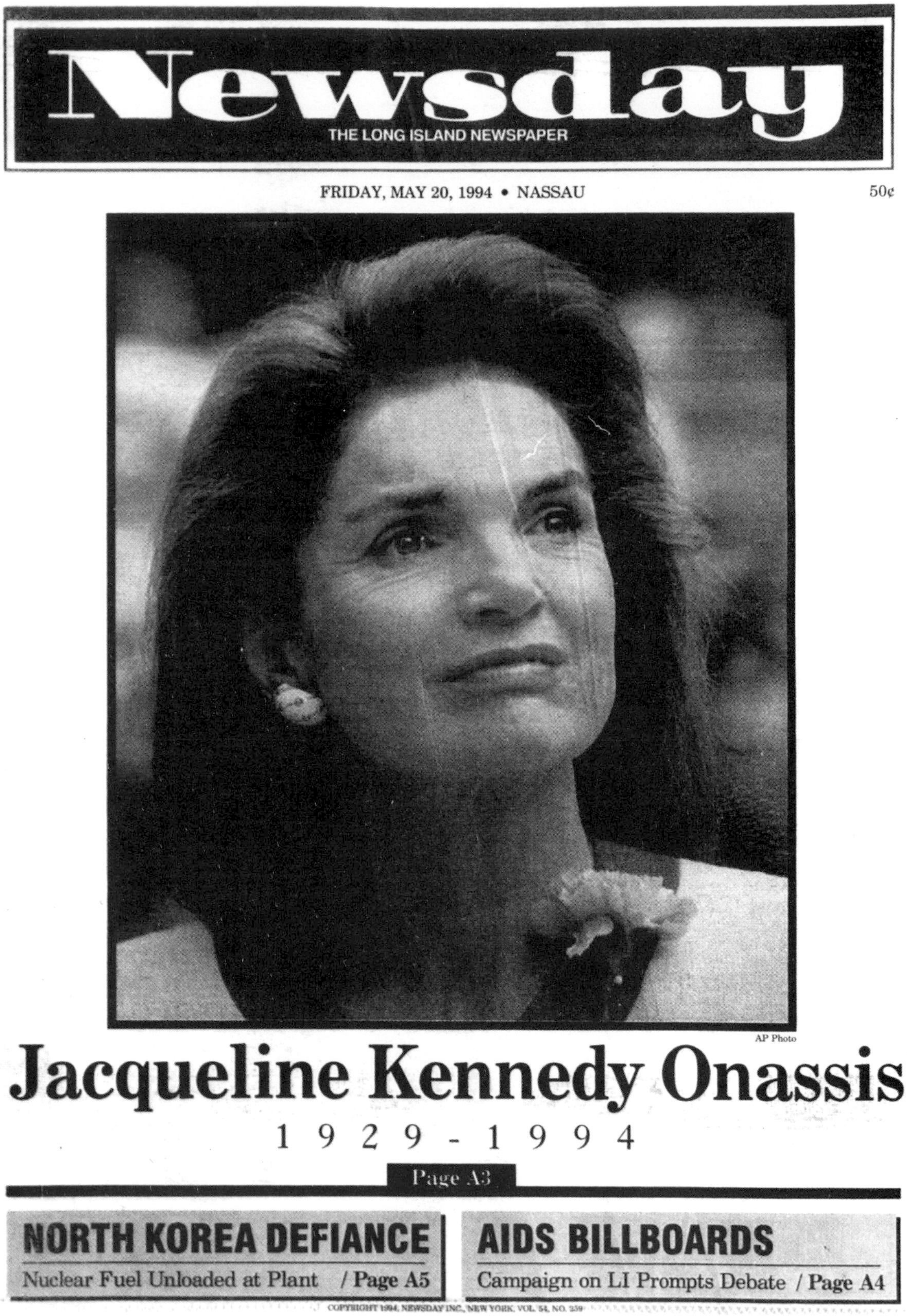

Newsday
THE LONG ISLAND NEWSPAPER

FRIDAY, MAY 20, 1994 • NASSAU 50¢

AP Photo

Jacqueline Kennedy Onassis

1 9 2 9 - 1 9 9 4

Page A3

NORTH KOREA DEFIANCE
Nuclear Fuel Unloaded at Plant / Page A5

AIDS BILLBOARDS
Campaign on LI Prompts Debate / Page A4

COPYRIGHT 1994, NEWSDAY INC., NEW YORK. VOL. 54, NO. 259

Icon of an Era

Jacqueline Kennedy Onassis, 64, dies of cancer

By Ray Sánchez
STAFF WRITER

New York — Jacqueline Kennedy Onassis, who epitomized elegance as the vibrant wife of a young president and later became a symbol of the nation's grief when he was slain, died last night at her home in Manhattan.

The 64-year-old former first lady succumbed at 10:15 p.m. to malignant lymphoma, a form of lymph cancer that had spread throughout her body.

At her bedside were children Caroline Kennedy Schlossberg and John F. Kennedy Jr., as well as her longtime companion Maurice Tempelsman, said her spokeswoman Nancy Tuckerman. Funeral arrangements will be private, she said.

Sen. Edward Kennedy told reporters only hours before her death that his sister-in-law was "enormously grateful to all the people who have been kind enough to send her notes wishing her well. She's resting comfortably and I look forward to seeing her tomorrow." He was on a plane back to Washington when she died, said Melody Miller, his spokeswoman.

* * *

By Anemona Hartocollis
STAFF WRITER

New York — Jacqueline Kennedy Onassis was America's foremost tragic heroine. Beautiful, glamorous and impossibly young when she ascended to the position of first lady, her stoicism and grace after the assassination of President John F. Kennedy more than 30 years ago made her an enduring, and widely revered, cultural icon.

With time, Jackie, as befits a tragic heroine, became not just a woman, but a nostalgic, bigger-than-life reminder of a vanished era in American history: a time of youth, hope and idealism. She was the last, intimate connection to "Camelot," an image that she herself first suggested to characterize her husband's presidency.

"She is now a historic archetype, virtually a demiurge," Norman Mailer wrote a decade ago. "She was ours. She did not belong to herself."

At her death yesterday, Jackie had also triumphed as an intensely private person, a devoted mother and grandmother, with a respected career as a book editor for Doubleday, the New York publishing house.

Images of the tragic Jackie remain seared in America's collective consciousness: still wearing a blood-spattered pink Chanel suit, she stands beside Lyndon B. Johnson as he is sworn in as president; her face obscured by a heavy black veil, she watches as her small son, John-John, salutes the American flag covering his father's coffin.

In the end, she remained aloof from, and relatively untouched by the often negative reappraisals of JFK, as a president and as a man.

In recent years, Jackie Onassis buried herself in her work, becoming a true career woman for the post-feminist age. As a senior editor at Doubleday, working three days a week and earning roughly $50,000 a year, she became kind of a literary rainmaker. Among her best-sellers were Michael Jackson's "Moonwalk," ballerina Gelsey Kirkland's "Dancing on My Grave" and Joseph Campbell's "The Power of Myth."

"To me, a wonderful book is one that takes me on a journey into something I didn't know before," she told Publishers Weekly in April 1993, in a rare personal interview with strict groundrules — no tape-recorder, no camera, no personal questions.

Although she did not seek publicity, and was sometimes compared to Greta Garbo, she was not a true recluse. She could often be spotted frolicking with her grandchildren in Central Park, or escorted by her steady companion, multimillionaire diamond dealer Maurice Tempelsman. Although married, Tempelsman had been linked with Jackie since at least 1979. Recently, he shared her 15-room co-op at 1040 Fifth Avenue, overlooking the Metropolitan Museum of Art, which she bought in 1964. Financially, however, she was independent; the $26 million she inherited from Aristotle Onassis, her second husband, after contesting his will, was said to have grown to an estimated $200-million.

Friends said that her proudest accomplishment was her children, Caroline and John Jr. Both are lawyers, although neither is now practicing. Both escaped the troubled personal lives that dogged many children of the extended Kennedy family. Caroline, an author, and her husband, designer Edward Kennedy Schlossberg, have three children, Rose, 5, Tatiana, 3 and John, 16 months. John Jr., a former assistant Manhattan district attorney, is single.

Jackie could also be seen at benefits for the New York Public Library and the Municipal Art Society. She once commented that she might have liked to become an architect, and she loaned her cachet and clout to causes like saving Grand Central Terminal and defeating plans by St. Bartholomew's Church to erect a skyscraper on Park Avenue.

Last summer, in a rare display of political activism, Jackie, along with Tempelsman and Caroline, hosted President Bill Clinton, Hillary, and their daughter, Chelsea, on a cruise off Martha's Vineyard. During the campaign, Clinton often described a brief youthful meeting with JFK.

Until she was diagnosed with lymphoma, she remained an avid equestrienne, riding to the hounds from her 10-acre house in Peapack, N.J., and keeping two gray geldings at the Upperville, Va., farm of financier Paul and Bunny Mellon. She also owned a 464-acre beachfront estate on Martha's Vineyard.

Portrayals of Jackie always abounded with contradiction. She was the subject of at least 25 biographies, one for almost every year since the assassination. On the one hand she was depicted as elitist, spiteful, emotionally needy, and materialistic, a first lady who, when confronted with a shopping bill for $40,000, could not remember what it was for. On the other hand, friends describe her as witty, playful, inquisitive and modest. Co-workers at Doubleday described how she was not above taking junior editors out to lunch. And of course, under duress, at least in public,

Please see ONASSIS on Page A39

AP Photos

President John F. Kennedy and Jacqueline Kennedy arrive at Love Field in Dallas on Nov. 22, 1963, the day he was assassinated. She is shown below after her marriage on Oct. 20, 1968, to Aristotle Onassis.

One hundred family members and friends attended Jacqueline Kennedy Onassis's burial at Arlington National Cemetery, near the flame she had lit for her husband more than thirty years before. (Page at left from Newsday*)*

ALSO IN 1994

Nelson Mandela, who served twenty-seven years in prison for fighting apartheid, became the first black president of South Africa.

PATRICK KENNEDY ELECTED TO CONGRESS

The Providence Journal

© 1994 THE MORNING EDITION OF THE Providence Journal-Bulletin: SINCE 1829 **ELECTION EDITION** WEDNESDAY, NOVEMBER 9, 1994/50 CENTS/$1.80 PER WEEK BY CARRIER

AM GUIDE

ELECTION '94

559 of 561 polls reporting

U.S. SENATOR

Chafee (R)	213,896	64.4%
Kushner (D)	118,411	35.6%

CONGRESS - DISTRICT 1

P. Kennedy (D)	86,904	54.2%
Vigilante	73,527	45.8%

CONGRESS - DISTRICT 2

Reed (D)	115,246	68.1%
Elliot (R)	53,937	31.9%

GOVERNOR

Almond (R)	164,130	47.2%
York (D)	151,861	43.6%
Healey Jr. (I)	32,108	9.2%

LIEUTENANT GOVERNOR

Weygand (D)	217,862	67.3%
Feroce (R)	86,137	26.6%

SECRETARY OF STATE

Langevin (D)	180,741	55.6%
Leonard (R)	144,100	44.4%

ATTORNEY GENERAL

Pine (R)	255,506	76.0%
Quinn (D)	73,655	21.9%

GENERAL TREASURER

Mayer (R)	211,191	65.6%
James (D)	110,724	34.4%

REFERENDA

1. Supreme Court selection			
Approve 69.9%	Reject	30.1%	
2. Assembly size and pay			
Approve 51.8%	Reject	48.2%	
3. Expansion of gambling			
Approve 67.8%	Reject	32.2%	
4. Constitutional Convention			
Reject 59.4%	Approve	40.6%	
5. Transportation bonds			
Approve 58.2%	Reject	41.8%	
6. Historic preservation			
Reject 55.3%	Approve	44.7%	
7. Prison bonds			
Reject 64.6%	Approve	35.4%	
8. Technical High School bonds			
Approve 50.7%	Reject	49.3%	
9. State House repair bonds			
Reject 55.6%	Approve	44.4%	
10. School aid revenue cap			
Approve 62.3%	Reject	37.7%	
11. Casino gambling tax relief			
Approve 51.2%	Reject	48.8%	
12. Providence casino site			
Reject 77.1%	Approve	22.9%	
13. Pawtucket casino site			
Reject 85.8%	Approve	14.2%	
14. Lincoln casino site			
Reject 71.9%	Approve	28.1%	
15. Coventry casino site			
Reject 85.0%	Approve	15.0%	
16. West Greenwich casino site			
Reject 54.1%	Approve	45.9%	

LOCAL CASINO REFERENDA

17. Providence		
Reject 61.1%	Approve	38.9%
17. Pawtucket		
Reject 67.3%	Approve	32.7%
17. Lincoln		
Reject 52.1%	Approve	37.9%
17. Coventry		
Reject 80.8%	Approve	19.2%
17. West Greenwich		
Reject 63.9%	Approve	36.1%

PROVIDENCE MAYOR

(96 of 96 polls reporting: 100 %)

Cianci (I)	20,510	55.5%
Jabour (I)	14,955	40.4%
Ricci (R)	1,513	04.1%

MASSACHUSETTS

U.S. SENATOR

(1,435 of 2,105 precincts: 68.0 %)

Kennedy (D)	851,065	58.0%
Romney (R)	602,949	41.0%

GOVERNOR

(1,440 of 2,105 precincts: 51.0 %)

Weld (R)	1,037,853	71.0%
Roosevelt (D)	410,265	28.0%

WEATHER

Shower possible today, high in the 60s

A shower possible today. High 66. Low tonight 39. High tomorrow 53. Details on back page of Sports section. **C-12**

INDEX

8 SECTIONS / 96 PAGES

Ann Landers	E-6	Food	G-1
Bridge	E-6	Good Neighbors	G-6
Business	B-1	Legal ads	C-9
Classified	F-1	Lifebeat	E-1
Comics	E-7	People	E-2
Crossword	E-6	Sports	C-1
Death notices	D-21	Television	E-5
Editorial	A-20	What's happening	E-6

State crushes casinos

Rhode Islanders proclaimed a resounding "no" to casino gambling yesterday.

In what loomed as a watershed year for expanded gambling in the Ocean State, voters rejected casinos in all five communities on the ballot, including the leading contender, a Narragansett Indian establishment in rural West Greenwich.

The West Greenwich proposal, Question 16 on the state ballot, was rejected by 54 percent of the state's voters and 64 percent in West Greenwich. The wide differential came as a surprise because recent polls anticipated a cliffhanger.

Tribal leaders vowed last night to proceed with plans for a smaller casino on their reservation, in Charlestown, even as a new governor was threatening to take them back to court to stop them.

"We're down, but we're not out — we go to Charlestown," said Narragansett First Tribal Councilman Matthew Thomas. "We've had to fight for everything that is rightfully ours for 300 years, and we'll keep fighting. Legally, the state has to deal with us."

Voters also said no to a small casino at Lincoln Greyhound Park, no to a mega-casino in Providence, no to a riverboat casino in Pawtucket and no to a gravel-pit casino in Coventry.

None of the five casino questions hit the magic daily double of state

Turn to **GAMBLING**, *Page A-3*

Almond squeaks past York

Journal-Bulletin

GOVERNOR-ELECT: Lincoln Almond greets well-wishers as he arrives at the Marriott last night.

Narrow victory climaxes no-holds-barred campaign

The second time around was magic for former U.S. Attorney Lincoln Almond, who squeaked out a victory over state Sen. Myrth York yesterday in the bare-knuckles fight for governor.

Republican Almond, who failed in his first run for governor, in 1978 against incumbent J. Joseph Garrahy, had a 12,245-vote lead over York after 99 percent of the state's polling stations had reported.

According to unofficial Journal-Bulletin results:

Almond had 47.2 percent of the machine-ballot count; Democrat York had 43.6 percent, and Cool Moose Party candidate Robert J. Healey Jr., who carried the town of Warren, had 9.2 percent. Another 12,000-plus mail ballots have yet to be counted. But given the size of Almond's lead, they have little chance of altering the outcome.

Partisans in the York and Almond camps rode an emotional roller-coaster from the moment Channel 10 declared York the winner at about 8:45 p.m., based on exit polling that projected 47 percent for York and 44 percent for Almond; Channel 6 reported a slight edge for Almond, and Channel 12 declared the race "too close to call."

"We don't want to declare victory or defeat until we actually see the real numbers," a cautious York told reporters.

"This is going to be a long, long night," state Republican chairman John Holmes told a roomful of Republicans milling about the Providence Marriott ballroom to the strains of Gershwin music, shortly after the polls closed.

Almond, watching and waiting in a sixth-floor suite at the Marriott within arm's reach of five unopened bottles of Brut champagne and a bucket of untouched shrimp, cheeses and Almond Joys, fretted over the "Healey factor." But he expressed his faith in the traditionally Democratic Blackstone Valley — where he ended up winning big — to pull him through. Watching with him were his wife, Marilyn, and son, his octogenarian mother, Elsie, and top campaign aides.

By 10:55 p.m., Holmes returned to the podium to announce: "Channel 12 just predicted Lincoln Almond the

Turn to **GOVERNOR**, *Page A-4*

NATION

OLIVER NORTH

NEWT GINGRICH

JEB BUSH

A debacle for Democrats nationwide

Republicans captured control of the Senate yesterday, defeating Democrats across the country.

And they were poised to also take control of the House. Rep. Newt Gingrich of Georgia could be the new Speaker.

The only consolation for Democrats was Sen. Charles Robb's victory over Iran-contra figure Oliver North in Virginia.

In Illinois, former powerful Rep. Dan Rostenkowski was turned out.

There was more bad news in statehouse for Democrats, with New York's Gov. Mario Cuomo being defeated. While Jeb Bush lost in his bid to be elected governor in Florida, his brother George defeated Gov. Ann Richards in Texas. Coverage of this serious setback for President Clinton and Democrats nationwide beings on Page A-14.

THE KENNEDYS

Patrick joins his dad in D.C.

Democrat Patrick Kennedy cruised to victory over Republican Kevin Vigilante yesterday to win the 1st District seat in Congress. He joins his father, Sen. Edward M. Kennedy of Massachusetts, in Washington and becomes at age 27 the youngest Kennedy ever to win a federal office.

Kennedy fashioned his victory in Providence and the traditional Democratic urban strongholds of the Blackstone Valley, including Central Falls, Woonsocket and Pawtucket. Vigilante ran well in the suburban communities, including Barrington, Lincoln, Little Compton and Portsmouth.

With 98.9 percent of the vote tallied, unofficial Journal-Bulletin results showed:

Kennedy, 86,723 votes, or 54.1 percent.
Vigilante, 73,446, or 45.9 percent.

On a day when Republicans were making big gains around the nation, Patrick Kennedy's victory was one of the few bright spots for his party.

Turn to **CONGRESS**, *Page A-6*

Journal-Bulletin Photo

Kennedy reunion

Ambassador Jean Kennedy Smith hugs her nephew Patrick Kennedy yesterday while Sen. Edward M. Kennedy stands by. Massachusetts Senate race, Page A-7.

Cianci cruises to win, calls it a landslide

PROVIDENCE — Elected four years ago by the slimmest of margins, Mayor Vincent A. Cianci Jr. yesterday was cruising to the comfortable victory that had been predicted for him over independent candidate Paul V. Jabour.

"It's the biggest win I've ever had," a jubilant Cianci said last night. "It's a landslide. I'm in the middle of something spectacular."

Cianci, who had been widely expected to win a fifth term in the mayor's office, and who had been ahead in one poll by as much as 28 points just three weeks ago, had swept past Jabour by more than 5,500 votes by the time all of the votes were counted.

According to unofficial Journal-Bulletin returns, Cianci had 20,510 votes to Jabour's 14,955 with all

CIANCI

JABOUR

polling places reporting. Thomas Ricci, the Republican candidate who dropped out Sunday, had 1,513 votes.

The tally Cianci was racking up left him poised to claim the largest margin of victory in his five races for mayor.

Just four years ago, he won the office by 317 votes in a three-way race.

Turn to **MAYOR**, *Page A-17*

Six years before Edward Kennedy's son Patrick won a congressional seat at the age of 27, he had won a seat in the Rhode Island House of Representatives at the age of 21.

ALSO IN 1994

Tom Hanks starred in the Academy Award–winning movie Forrest Gump. *In the film, Forrest met a number of historical figures, including President John F. Kennedy.*

January 18, 1995
Kathleen Kennedy Townsend Became Maryland's Lieutenant Governor

B4 Thursday, January 19, 1995 THE WASHINGTON POST

THE INAUGURATION OF MARYLAND GOV. PARRIS N. GLENDENING

The Governor's 'Vision for Maryland in the 21st Century'

Here are excerpts from Maryland Gov. Parris N. Glendening's inaugural address:

Mr. President, Mr. Speaker, Mr. Attorney General, Madame Treasurer, Mr. Comptroller, Chief Judge, Lieutenant Governor, members of the General Assembly, members of Congress, honored guests, my family, my friends and all Marylanders: Thank you for joining us on this very, very happy day!

My wife, Frances Anne, and my son, Raymond, join me as I stand here today to accept the challenge and the privilege to serve as the governor of our great state.

There is over here an empty chair with a rose, here on the dais. That chair is a symbolic remembrance of our parents—Frances's father, former senator George Hughes, and her wonderful mother, Pat. It is also a remembrance of my parents, Raymond and Jean Glendening. Unfortunately, none of them are any longer with us, but we are absolutely certain they are here in spirit and that they are smiling on us as we share this great day.

We have loving, warm memories of our parents. Frances often speaks of her mother's strength, determination and commitment to family. She has often said that the song "The Wind Beneath My Wings" reminds her of her mother—her mother really was her hero.

Frances Anne, I want to say publicly that you are indeed my hero. You have been "content to let me shine"; you are content here today while "I am the one with all the glory." "I can fly higher than an eagle, because you are the wind beneath my wings." Thank you. This song is dedicated to you: ["The Wind Beneath My Wings" is sung.]

Raymond, and I know you hate this, but I also want to say that your mother and I are very, very proud of you as well. We are proud that you are an honors student at DeMatha; we are proud that you are on the baseball team; and we are proud and blessed that you are our wonderful son—and the first young person in Government House in well over a generation. When he and his friends were running through the halls this morning, no one knew what to think of it.

The rose, the empty chair and the song speak of family. They are symbolic of the legacy and values one generation passes to another. And they are symbolic of how caring and compassion can lead to lives of responsibility and respect.

Today, we reach beyond our personal family to the family of Maryland—people of all ages, all colors, all backgrounds.

We look to those who came before us. Most particularly Governor Schaefer, who embodied—not only for Maryland but also for the nation—the notion that government service can be driven by compassion for people. Our state, our well-being, has been his life's work. We also look to former governor Harry Hughes, whose dignified leadership led our state to focus on things that are really important, like protecting our environment. And we look to former governor Marvin Mandel, who modernized Maryland's structure of government.

For the past two years, I have traveled throughout the Free State, and I have heard the voices of Maryland: the lathe operator in Cumberland struggling to make ends meet, the watermen of the Chesapeake who rise long before dawn to work the bay, the steelworkers, storekeepers and entrepreneurs of Baltimore City, the federal employees who commute from Frederick and the farmers in Kent County.

I have met them all. And they have given me a great gift.

They have taught me that ordinary people can accomplish extraordinary things: that there are certainties in this uncertain world—and that sure as the next sunrise, the decent, hard-working people of Maryland will rise to meet the challenges before us. . . .

In this age of cynicism, I want to earn your faith. I want you to know where we stand, what we stand for and what we hope to accomplish—together.

From the beginning of this effort, I believed I had an obligation to the citizens to clearly state my priorities and my vision to move Maryland forward. That is why we published our plan, the "Vision for Maryland"—to improve education, to create and keep good jobs, to make our communities and streets safe, to protect our unique environment and to make our government efficient and effective; and we offer a practical, common-sense, honest approach. . . .

It can be done!

This is the first of three messages I will deliver over the course of the next 10 days—each part of a three-part package. This inaugural address is my vision for Maryland in the 21st century; the remaining two will address the budget and the details of our legislative programs—in other words, how to make this vision a reality.

Today, we address the basic values and expectations and changes in policies that will lead our Maryland family into the 21st century.

The changes we will experience together will bring both challenges and opportunities.

From preschool to graduate school, we can create a new educational system based on having the highest expectations of our children and young adults—*if* teachers, parents, business people, entire communities join with us to make it happen.

In laboratories and offices and factories, we can create an economy that provides not just jobs, but good, substantive jobs that allow us to support our families—*if* we recognize that business creates wealth and opportunity and that meaningful work provides real independence and hope, that employers have community responsibilities that transcend the paycheck—and *if* business and labor recognize we must work together for jobs to support our families.

We can balance economic growth and the protection of our environment—*if* we recognize they are not and cannot be mutually exclusive.

In our homes, our schools and streets, we can make safety and security the rule and not the exception—*if* we tackle the problem as a community, bound together by common concerns for neighbors and neighborhoods.

And we can make our government work smarter and leaner—*if* state employees help us meet the challenges of re-engineering government.

We must count on everyone to do his or her part. I have faith that *together* we will move Maryland forward. It is already starting to happen; the Maryland I see is not a distant dream.

I see an exciting vision for Maryland as we move into the 21st century. . . .

The changes we will make happen will not be measured overnight, nor in the next four years, nor even in the next eight years. The impact of our changes will be measured over decades.

Change will be measured by what happens in our schools.

Change will be measured by what happens in our communities.

Change will *not* be measured by the laws we pass. It will be measured by the lives we touch.

Change will be measured in the lives and the lifetimes of our children.

I cannot make these changes alone.

Your government cannot make these changes alone.

These changes will come from all of us, throughout the state, working together.

These changes will come when we stop saying we have a problem and then simply asking, "What can government do about it?" . . .

We will build a better Maryland because we believe in each person's right to dignity and independence.

We will build a better Maryland because we believe in family and our Free State family.

Gov. Parris N. Glendening deli

Gov. Parris N. Glendening, right, and his wife, Frances Anne, left, greet soloist Myrick, who performed at the inaugural ceremony. Myrick is from Largo.

Glendening's Ascensi Uplifts Prince George'

PRINCE GEORGE'S, From B1

George's," said Ron Blunck, a computer systems manager from College Park. "If he does a good job for the state, that will reflect favorably on where he came from."

Glendening carefully planned his inauguration day to embrace all of Maryland in every detail.

And yet, an unmistakable part of the soul of Prince George's was threaded throughout the day.

Rabbi Gary S. Fink, of Congregation Oseh Shalom in Laurel, gave the invocation. The Rev. John A. Cherry, pastor of Full Gospel AME, of Temple Hills, gave the benediction.

William E. Kirwan, president of the University of Maryland at College Park, introduced Glendening, a tenured professor at the university. Kirwan quipped that he was granting the new governor "a temporary leave of absence," and he reminded Glendening that political tenure is not as certain as academic tenure.

After the new governor gave his address, the Prince George's County Police Department Bagpipe Band, dressed in kilts that were many shades of mauve, escorted Glendening from the stage.

"What we're doing is taking our county executive and presenting him as the governor of the state," said David McPherson, a county police pipe major.

When Glendening reached the achybreaky part in his speech wh wife, Frances Anne, was his hero, and he had a singer sing a love song to her before he resumed his address, the cynics in the crowd rolled their eyes. But many couples in the audience looked at each other mistily, and one woman started sobbing.

During the Parade of Counties—carefully including student bands from all 24 jurisdictions—Glendening remained sedentary, until the Northwestern High School marching band from Hyattsville passed before him. The boys and girls serenaded their county executive—er, governor—with "Maryland, My Maryland."

Glendening bounced up from his seat and hurried down to shake hands with band members.

Oden Bowie, the 80-year-old grandson of the previous governor from Prince George's, decided it was too wet for him outside, so he watched the ceremony from his office window. He is the secretary of the state Senate.

Standing beneath a portrait of his grandfather, Bowie mused on history. He thought about how his grandfather had been the first governor to occupy the Governor's Mansion, which was a new structure 125 years ago.

"I'm delighted," Bowie said. "Prince George's is entitled to another governor."

Staff writer Michael Abramowitz contributed to this report.

PHOTOS BY NANCY ANDREWS—THE WASHINGTON POST

Lt. Gov. Kathleen Kennedy Townsend greets a well-wisher in the State House in Annapolis after taking the oath of office.

Townsend Adds Glamour, Style to Inauguration Day

By Fern Shen
Washington Post Staff Writer

ANNAPOLIS, Jan. 18—Lt. Gov. Kathleen Kennedy Townsend—along with a sizable contingent of her famous family—brought some glamour, verve and sparkle to Maryland's inauguration day.

At the start of the swearing-in ceremony, when Senate President Thomas V. Mike Miller Jr. said, "Will the Kennedy family please approach the rostrum," Kathleen broke up the room when she replied, aghast, "Not the whole Kennedy family!"

And after Townsend took the oath of office and signed her name, Robert C. Murphy, chief judge of the Maryland Court of Appeals, allowed as how "we had a little historic mishap."

"I signed in the governor's spot," Townsend blurted out, prompting a collective gasp from the crowd and then more laughter.

Murphy later said he pointed Townsend to the wrong spot in the Test book, which contains the official oath of office and is signed by state governors and lieutenant governors. Her name was scratched out to allow Gov. Parris N. Glendening's signature, he said.

The eldest of Robert F. Kennedy's 11 children, displaying her father's smile and apparent candor, Townsend in her dark red suit was a standout in the otherwise somber crowd.

"I looked around the room and said, 'Where's the juice?' and I saw her and I said, 'There's the juice!' " said her brother, Rep. Joseph P. Kennedy II (D-Mass.), who watched, with his wife, Beth, from the Senate gallery, as Townsend was sworn in.

Townsend moved to Maryland in 1984 with her husband, David, who teaches at St. John's College in Annapolis. She has been trying to put to rest criticism of her as a carpetbagger, ever since her unsuccessful attempt to wrest away Republican Helen Delich Bentley's congressional seat in 1986.

Townsend, 43, made family and Maryland history when she took office yesterday: She is the first Kennedy woman to hold elected office and the first female lieutenant governor elected in Maryland.

Her brother was not the only family member to witness the occasion. Also present were her husband, four children, mother Ethel, sister Rory and brother Michael, and her cousin, Mark K. Shriver, the son of former Peace Corps director Sargent Shriver and Eunice Kennedy Shriver, among others.

Family members helped Townsend extensively during the campaign, making public appearances, ringing doorbells and throwing fund-raisers that tapped the Kennedy family's considerable financial resources.

Despite the electorate's recent conservative tilt, 1994 was a banner political year for the liberal-leaning Kennedy clan.

"I think [voters] want lean government, but they don't want meanness," said Rep. Joseph Kennedy, who ran unopposed in Boston. Sen. Edward M. Kennedy (D-Mass.), Townsend's uncle, won the toughest reelection race of his career. And Mark Shriver won a seat in the Maryland House of Delegates, representing Montgomery County.

"You've got as many Kennedys elected here in Maryland as we have in Massachusetts," quipped Joseph Kennedy. "I'm starting to get worried, maybe I should move."

Wanting Meat, Getting Pablum

TWOMEY, From B1

honeymoon, I know. But if you are a lover of words, his speech is an opportunity to underscore the emptiness we get these days from so many who deal in them. Even the most rabid supporter of the self-destructed Ellen Sauerbrey could have swallowed Glendening's speech without indigestion. The first governor from the Washington suburbs in more than a century gave an address that was a perfect reflection of Montgomery and Prince George's counties: comfortable, sort of bland and full of compost.

Glendening called his speech "A Vision for the 21st Century."

This is what he envisioned:

People with decent jobs and decent wages.

Kids going to good schools.

A balance between economic growth and the environment.

Neighborhoods that are safe.

Marylanders working together.

What do you think? Too risky?

Glendening, to be fair, said he was outlining only the broad strokes of his vision, not the specifics. Those will come later. Maybe he'll say something bold then. Maybe he'll say, for instance, that to achieve good schools, all students must stay 10 hours a day.

Now *that* would be saying something.

Somehow, I doubt he will. With the possible exception of people named Newt, the political class fears the specific. It has consequences. A speech today is not meant to lead or inform or enrage or amuse or delight, but simply to be delivered. When it's over, you can't remember a thing the guy said, but you believe you liked it, probably because he came out for continued human existence.

A speech today is wind without wings.

Even the obviously partisan crowd sitting before the new governor yesterday seemed merely whelmed by his remarks, applauding tepidly here and there. Who could be energized by, "Today, we begin an era of unity, a time of inclusion"? Now, if he had said, "Today, we begin an era in which Prince George's and Montgomery get it all and the hell with Baltimore," I'd say that's a speech.

So I propose a new guide to evaluating words: the turnaround rule.

If you want to know the worth of what a politician says, if you want to know whether he or she is giving you pablum or giving you meat, simply take the inverse of what was said. If the inverse makes sense, then you've been given meat. If the inverse is nonsense, you've been given pablum.

For example, imagine if Glendening had said:

As I take office today as your governor, let me sketch my vision. I couldn't care less about families. They've been overrated for centuries, and this administration will have nothing to do with them. As for jobs, you're on your own, people. I don't care whether you work at any wage, decent or otherwise. Nor do I care if your kid does well in school or whether you get mugged, and you can dump your garbage in the Chesapeake as far as I'm concerned.

A politician who comes out for apple pie is offering pablum. And if that's all he can say, why take the job?

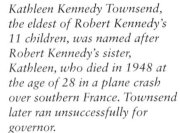

Kathleen Kennedy Townsend, the eldest of Robert Kennedy's 11 children, was named after Robert Kennedy's sister, Kathleen, who died in 1948 at the age of 28 in a plane crash over southern France. Townsend later ran unsuccessfully for governor.

ALSO IN 1995

Timothy McVeigh bombed the Murrah Federal Building in Oklahoma City, killing 168 people.

"All the News That's Fit to Print"

The New York Times

Late Edition
New York: **Today,** cloudy, windy. High 37. **Tonight,** chilly, a snow shower. Low 30. **Tomorrow,** cloudy, a few snow showers. High 36. **Yesterday,** high 37, low 30. Details, page D10.

VOL.CXLIV . . . No. 49,950 — NEW YORK, MONDAY, JANUARY 23, 1995 — 60 CENTS

Simpson Trial Strategies: From Alibi to DNA Tests

By KENNETH B. NOBLE
Special to The New York Times

LOS ANGELES, Jan. 22 — Perhaps not since the kidnapping of the Lindbergh baby has a crime so captivated the American imagination.

And now, after nearly seven months of legal maneuvering, the O. J. Simpson murder trial will finally enter its decisive phase when opening statements begin on Monday.

Two incongruous versions of Mr. Simpson's persona will be given to the 12-member jury, and Mr. Simpson's fate will ultimately depend on which one it decides is closest to the truth.

One is the street-smart San Francisco ghetto kid who overcame tremendous odds to become a beloved star of football and Hollywood, and who is now wrongly accused of a hideous crime.

The other is a hot-tempered, hard-drinking, foul-mouthed bully who for years humiliated and terrorized the mother of his children, the woman he professed to love and cherish.

Prosecutors are expected to depict Mr. Simpson as maniacally jealous of his former wife to the point of stalking and physically abusing her in fits of rage. They will try to persuade jurors that the slayings of Nicole Brown Simpson and her friend Ronald L. Goldman were almost the logical culmination of increasingly violent and obsessive behavior.

The defense strategy, by contrast, is expected to lean heavily on the absence of a murder weapon with Mr. Simpson's fingerprints on it and, even more tellingly, on the lack of an eyewitness who can link him to the crime scene. The defense will raise questions about the victims' characters, suggesting that the killings may have been drug-related.

Prosecutors will have to explain how one man was able to overpower two younger, well-conditioned and physically agile adults without either of them apparently screaming for help. Defense lawyers will argue that it took at least two people to commit the slayings.

A crucial battleground in the case will be the relatively new science of DNA testing, which is used to determine whether blood, semen or tissue came from a victim or suspect. Prosecutors say the results of DNA tests done on samples found at the crime site and at Mr. Simpson's Brentwood estate convincingly identify him as the killer.

To challenge the case on scientific grounds, the defense has amassed a small army of scientific and crime experts, including Dr. Kary Mullins, the Nobel Prize-winning chemist who invented an important DNA test, and Dr. Henry Lee, perhaps the nation's foremost forensic scientist.

Dr. Mullins is expected to testify that DNA analysis is still an imperfect science, and that to convict someone solely on the basis of tiny blood samples is folly. Dr. Lee is expected to testify that the main laboratory that did the DNA testing, Cellmark Diagnostics, may have mishandled blood samples and that the results of the tests are, therefore, unreliable.

But the ultimate verdict is likely to depend at least as much upon which side can capture the sympathies of the jurors. Reasonable doubt is all that 12 jurors need to find Mr. Simpson not

Continued on Page B6, Column 1

SUICIDE BOMBS KILL 19 IN ISRAEL; SHADOW CAST OVER PEACE TALKS

Photographs by Associated Press

Israeli medics giving first aid to some of those wounded by two bombs that killed at least 19 people yesterday.

61 SUFFER WOUNDS

Islamic Holy War Says It Attacked Bus Stop, Packed by Soldiers

By CLYDE HABERMAN
Special to The New York Times

NORDIYA, Israel, Jan. 22 — One or more Muslim suicide bombers set off two powerful explosions today at a bus stop packed with Israeli soldiers, killing at least 19 people, wounding 61 and casting ominous shadows over troubled peace talks between Israel and the Palestinians.

It was a grim scene that has become steadily more familiar to Israelis in recent months: bodies blown apart and sent flying through the air, rescue workers picking up the pieces from the ground and from treetops, victims sobbing in grief or sitting numb in confusion.

Witnesses said the explosions, at an intersection outside an army camp near this farming town in central Israel, were timed several minutes apart. As a result, people who had gone to help casualties of the first blast became victims themselves when the second bomb detonated.

"It was horrible," said a young soldier who gave only his first name, Yuval. "It was full of smoke and human body parts and things flying in the air. Then we thought things had calmed down, and a few minutes later it happened all over again."

It was one of the deadliest terrorist incidents in Israeli history as well as the fifth major suicide bombing since April by Islamic radicals, whose tactics have given their anti-Israel campaign a new, more menacing cast. In the last nine months, a wave of such bombings has killed at least 54 people and wounded nearly 200, the most severe episode being the attack on a Tel Aviv bus that killed 22 passengers in October.

The Islamic Holy War group took responsibility today, saying in a statement that it was carried out by two of its militants from the Gaza Strip, who timed their explosions at a junction known as Beit Lid in a manner intended to make them as lethal as possible.

What made it a special nightmare for Israelis was the fact that the unmistakable target was soldiers going about their normal business, most of them as they were transferring buses at the start of a new work week. In a country where men and women face compulsory military service, often well into middle age as reservists, the attack struck home deeply.

There were also signs that a growing number of Israelis have had enough and that they want to call off talks with the Palestine Liberation Organization that are intended to expand its control over the West Bank and take Palestinian autonomy beyond its present confines of Gaza and the West Bank town of Jericho.

For the first time, President Ezer Weizman called on the Government to suspend negotiations and "rethink which way we're going."

"Right now it's a bloody process, and with bloody processes we don't achieve peace," Mr. Weizman said on a visit to a hospital where victims were taken.

The Israeli President's role is

Continued on Page A6, Column 1

The New York Times

The blasts occurred at an intersection less than a mile from the farming town of Nordiya.

Data Network Is Found Open To New Threat

By JOHN MARKOFF
Special to The New York Times

SAN FRANCISCO, Jan. 22 — A Federal computer security agency has discovered that unknown intruders have developed a new way to break into computer systems, and the agency plans on Monday to advise users how to guard against the problem.

The new form of attack leaves many of the 20 million government, business, university and home computers on the global Internet vulnerable to eavesdropping and theft. Officials say that unless computer users take the complicated measures they will prescribe, intruders could copy or destroy documents or even operate undetected by posing as an authorized user of the system.

For computer users, the problem is akin to homeowners discovering that burglars have master keys to all the front doors in the neighborhood.

The first known attack using the new technique took place on Dec. 25 against the computer of a well-known computer security expert at the San Diego Supercomputer Center. An unknown individual or group took over his computer for more than a day and electronically stole a large number of security programs he had developed.

Since then several attacks have been reported, and there is no way of knowing how many others may have occurred. Officials of the Government-financed Computer Emergency Response Team say that the new assaults are a warning that better

Continued on Page D4, Column 3

An unidentified Israeli soldier wept as he held the uniform shirt of his friend, a victim of the bombing. The fate of the friend was unknown.

Budget Amendment May Be Short Of Enough States for Ratification

By DAVID E. ROSENBAUM
Special to The New York Times

WASHINGTON, Jan. 22 — If Congress approves a constitutional amendment requiring a balanced Federal budget, many state legislatures will probably ratify the measure quickly, but maybe too few to make it part of the Constitution.

A state-by-state survey by correspondents of The New York Times found that some legislatures, afraid of the fiscal consequences, would most likely refuse to ratify the amendment and that the outlook was cloudy enough in others to raise considerable doubt that it will ever be adopted.

To become part of the Constitution, an amendment must be approved by two-thirds majorities in both the House of Representatives and the Senate and then be ratified by the legislatures of three-quarters, or 38, of the states.

A balanced-budget amendment is a top priority of the Republicans now in control of Congress. The House plans to vote on the matter by the end of the month, and two-thirds approval of the amendment in one form or another is expected there, although not absolutely certain.

The Senate will not vote until next month at the earliest, and the prospect there is uncertain. It would take 34 votes in the Senate to block the amendment, and 33 of the 37 senators who voted against such a measure last year are still in office.

The situation in the states is even murkier. Many of the more than 7,400 state legislators are, of course, influenced by public opinion polls showing that 80 percent of Americans favor a balanced-budget amendment. But many state officials, especially governors, are concerned that balancing the Federal budget would force deep cuts in Federal aid to the states and place a heavy burden on the states to raise their own taxes or sharply reduce services.

Expressing the view of other students of state governments, Steven D. Gold, director of the Center for the Study of the States at the State University of New York in Albany, said he believed that support of a

Continued on Page A12, Column 1

Kobe Sows Seeds for a Recovery, But Japan May Reap the Benefits

By JAMES STERNGOLD
Special to The New York Times

KOBE, Japan, Jan. 22 — One island of calm in this smashed, overwhelmingly sad city today was the warmly lit branch of the Bank of Japan, the central bank. Even though it was a Sunday and most of the city remained paralyzed, bank officials in three-piece suits were busy, planting the first seeds of economic regeneration with those brave enough to think of the future.

"Basically, we came through almost untouched," said Shigeru Uebayashi, the assistant branch manager, as he nodded toward the businessmen lining up to withdraw cash inside the squat vault of a building. "I know our outward appearance is rather unimpressive, but this is a strong structure."

His comments aptly summed up the economic prospects that Kobe and Japan face after last Tuesday's earthquake left nearly 5,000 dead and this genial city of 1.5 million devastated.

Kobe's outward appearance is grim indeed. Rain today threatened to touch off landslides and to topple already weakened buildings, complicating the search for those still missing in the rubble and the lives of the nearly 300,000 people now without homes. [Page A8.]

The port here — Japan's second-largest, surpassed only by Yokohama — will not operate properly for months. The central commercial district near the Bank of Japan is a jumble of buildings at twisted angles, hundreds of which will have to be replaced. Takeshi Tsuji, head of the city's economic development bureau, said he believed that the estimated cost of rebuilding — $100 billion — was too low.

But few experts doubt that even with the serious disruptions to trade and life, Japan's economy will be able to absorb the blow and still generate substantial growth in the year ahead. Many agree that the

Continued on Page A8, Column 4

Rose Kennedy, Political Matriarch, Dies at 104

By ROBERT D. McFADDEN

Rose Fitzgerald Kennedy, the mother of President John F. Kennedy and of two United States Senators, the wife of a fabulously wealthy businessman-ambassador and the matriarch of a family whose political triumphs and personal tragedies she carried with quiet dignity for 80 years, died yesterday at the Kennedy family compound in Hyannis Port, Mass. She was 104.

Surrounded by family members at her rambling, white-shingled seaside home on Cape Cod, she died of complications from pneumonia at 5:30 P.M., her son, Senator Edward M. Kennedy of Massachusetts, said. She had been in a wheelchair, partly paralyzed and mostly silent, since 1984, when she suffered the first of a series of debilitating strokes.

"Mother passed away peacefully today," Senator Kennedy said last night. "She had a long and extraordinary life, and we loved her deeply. To all of us in the Kennedy and Fitzgerald families, she was the most beautiful rose of all."

President Clinton extended his condolences last night. "Very few Americans have endured as much personal sacrifice for their country

Continued on Page B7, Column 1

Michael Evans/The New York Times

Rose Fitzgerald Kennedy in 1970.

INSIDE

Psychiatric Patients Escape Through Policy Loopholes

Policies meant to protect psychiatric patients' rights have combined with intense budgetary pressures to cause hospital managers and New York State officials to look the other way as thousands of patients each year run away. Page B1.

Soviet Art Seizures

An international symposium attempts to resolve a Russian-German impasse on settlement of German claims that Soviet troops stole art treasures in World War II. Page C11.

The Price of Wheels

Prices for new vehicles have risen faster than most Americans' wages, and auto makers ask if they have left customers behind. Page D1.

An Eye on Air Fare Ads

The Government is expected to announce that it will begin monitoring advertisements for bargain air fares and other travel deals. Page A10.

NEWS SUMMARY	A2
Arts	C11-16
Business Day	D1-10
Editorial, Op-Ed	A14-15
International	A2-9
Metro	B1-5
National	A10-13, B6
SportsMonday	C1-9
Media	D8
Obituaries	B7-8
TV Listings	C15
Weather	D10
Classified	B8
Auto Exchange	C9

The matriarch of the Kennedy family was 104 when she died at her Hyannis Port home. In his eulogy (see pages 114–117), Edward Kennedy said, "She was ambitious not only for our success, but for our souls."

ALSO IN 1995

John F. Kennedy Jr. and Michael J. Berman launched the politics and lifestyle magazine George, *which folded after Kennedy's death.*

24-PAGE SPECIAL WRAPS MAIN NEWS

SPORTS ★ ★ ★ ★ FINAL

DAILY NEWS

$1.00 www.nydailynews.com NEW YORK'S HOMETOWN NEWSPAPER Sunday, July 18, 1999

LOST

JFK Jr., wife presumed dead in plane crash off Vineyard

RICHARD CORKERY DAILY NEWS

John F. Kennedy Jr., his wife of three years, Carolyn Bessette Kennedy, and her sister Lauren Bessette were killed when their airplane crashed in the Atlantic Ocean as it approached Martha's Vineyard.

Sunday, July 18, 1999 — THE PHILADELPHIA INQUIRER — D A19

JOHN F. KENNEDY JR.

DAVID SWANSON / Inquirer Suburban Staff

Sylvia Rich ties a yellow ribbon outside the TriBeCa home of John F. Kennedy Jr. and his wife, Carolyn Bessette Kennedy in New York City.

Kennedy considered neighbor more than celebrity in New York

By Sudarsan Raghavan
INQUIRER STAFF WRITER

NEW YORK — Some were crying as they placed flowers and notes in front of the TriBeCa apartment building where John F. Kennedy Jr. and his wife live.

It was not an outpouring but rather a slow trickle of affection, as though people were reluctant to believe that Kennedy, his wife, Carolyn Bessette Kennedy, and his wife's sister, Lauren Bessette, could be gone.

To them, Kennedy was not a celebrity. He was a neighbor.

Ivana Trnik, 35, a student at the American Academy of Dramatic Arts in New York, arrived clutching a bouquet of purple flowers. "Purple is a holy color," said Trnik, a Czech who has been in New York for only two weeks. "It's very spiritual."

She heard the news this morning from a friend and, like most who had gathered in front of the eight-story, red-brick building on North Moore Street, was shocked and saddened. "I couldn't believe it when I heard," she said. "It's so tragic."

Asked why she had come, Trnik said: "He carries the legacy of the president. The Kennedy family is the most powerful family in the United States and I wanted to pay my respects.

"Besides," she added, "he was so handsome."

Though his family's roots are in Boston — and its apotheosis was in Washington — New York was John F. Kennedy Jr.'s town.

With all the pictures and sightings of him jogging, skating and strolling through Central Park, New Yorkers felt they knew him intimately — even though he sought and treasured his privacy.

But like his father, Kennedy had the gift of establishing instant rapport.

So Tom Johnston, who works for a courier service and who has delivered packages to Kennedy's apartment building, spoke of Kennedy yesterday as though he were an acquaintance.

But he had never met him: Seeing Kennedy at a museum a few years ago, Johnston said, he had been too nervous to approach Kennedy. But he admired Kennedy from a distance: "He was like his mother — graceful, elegant, with lots of class."

TriBeCa is a newly chic, formerly industrial section of lower Manhattan. Just down the street from Kennedy's building at 20 N. Moore St. is Robert De Niro's TriBeCa Bar and Grill.

TriBeCa is a lot like what SoHo, its immediate neighbor to the north, used to be. In the '70s and '80s, the artistic crowd flocked to cheap lofts in decrepit, decaying Soho. But as the area became one of the trendiest spots in Manhattan, the artists found themselves priced out. So they crossed Canal Street to TriBeCa — the name comes from "Triangle Below Canal Street" — where massive masonry and cast-iron buildings from the last century waited to be rescued.

The upscale residents respect each other's privacy. "This is New York," Johnston said, "so nobody ever gave him a hard time."

Still, Johnston remembers how the New York media loved to cover Kennedy. The day Carolyn Bessette moved in, Johnston said he watched hordes of press trying to get photographs. Yesterday, as he scanned the growing throng of journalists and onlookers outside the building, he said: "It's the same as it was back then." He paused. "But it's a little different now."

Lisa Schiller, 49, an art dealer who lives around the block, said: "I was literally stunned."

Like other neighbors, Schiller often saw Kennedy riding his bike or walking with Carolyn and their black-and-white dog, Friday.

"I literally almost ran into him one day," she said. "He took my breath away. He was so elegant and so handsome." But she never introduced herself because "everyone here respects each other's privacy. It's like the suburbs. They know each other. They recognize each other. They respect each other."

Stuart Farmery, 46, a sculptor who also frequently saw the Kennedys in the neighborhood, lamented: "I'm not going to run into him anymore. I feel the loss."

So will the staff at Socrates Deli, just around the corner from the Kennedys' loft. Kennedy stopped by for breakfast several times a week. Having learned some Greek from his stepfather, Aristotle Onassis, he often tried it out on restaurant workers.

He would say *yasou* — hello — or address the waiters as *filo*, which means friend. And when it came to George Bourountous, the owner, Kennedy would always ask *ti kaneis* — How are you?

"He was such a nice guy. All this is so terrible. I feel so sad," said Bourountous, who remembered one rainy day when Kennedy came in drenched. Bourountous offered him a Socrates Deli T-shirt, which he donned on the spot. After that, Bourountous recalled, he would see Kennedy wearing the shirt biking or walking.

On the Upper East Side last night, there were prayers at the Church of St. Ignatius Loyola on Park Avenue, which Jacqueline Kennedy Onassis attended. Her daughter Caroline's two daughters were baptized there, and in 1994, her funeral was held there.

While his mother was still alive, John Kennedy Jr. and his wife sometimes went to Mass there with her.

Yesterday evening, the church pastor, the Rev. Walter F. Modrys, asked the congregation to pray for a miracle for Kennedy and the others on the plane.

"The Father asked us to pray that anything could be possible and there may be a miracle that they might be found," said Grace Strauber, a 10-year member of the congregation. "If not, we commended his soul to God and prayed for his family.

"I just couldn't believe it," she said. "The family has had so much tragedy. But they're still going strong. I have great faith. It's so wonderful that they have a large family, and I just hope God takes care of them."

DAVID SWANSON / Inquirer Suburban Staff

Throughout the day, people in the New York City neighborhood stop near the eight-story, red-brick apartment building where the Kennedys live.

Years of Tragedies

JONATHAN WILSON / Atheneum

The children of Joseph P. and Rose Kennedy pose with their parents (center) before World War II. They are Eunice (left), John, Rosemary, Jean, Edward, Joseph Jr., Patricia, Robert and Kathleen. Joseph Kennedy accumulated the wealth that made him and his family international celebrities.

Associated Press — United Press International — Associated Press

Joseph P. Kennedy Jr., at left posing with his flight instructor J.S. Dodge (right) in July 1941, later died in a plane crash during World War II. His sister Rosemary, above left in October 1975, is mentally retarded. His sister Kathleen, above right, died in an air crash in 1948.

BORIS YARO / Los Angeles Times — Associated Press

President John F. Kennedy and his wife, Jacqueline, above, ride in a motorcade in Dallas just minutes before he was assassinated on Nov. 22, 1963. Sen. Robert F. Kennedy, left, lies stricken after he was shot in a hotel in Los Angeles on June 6, 1968, while campaigning for the Democratic nomination for president. Robert Kennedy was attorney general while his brother was president.

United Press International

John F. Kennedy Jr. and his mother, Jacqueline, far right, talk at a gathering in June 1990. She died of cancer in 1994. Edward Kennedy Jr., above, is seen training for a handicapped Olympics. He lost his right leg to cancer in 1973. Michael Kennedy, right, a son of Sen. Robert F. Kennedy, died in a skiing accident in Colorado on New Year's Eve 1997.

STEVEN SENNE / Associated Press — MARCY NIGHSWANDER / Associated Press

Crash investigators determined that Kennedy most likely had become disoriented in the hazy night sky and piloted the plane nose-first into the ocean. In another Kennedy tragedy, his cousin Michael Kennedy, son of Robert and Ethel Kennedy, had been killed two years earlier while skiing in Colorado.

JULY 16, 1999
JOHN F. KENNEDY JR. DIED

Sunday, July 18, 1999 — THE PHILADELPHIA INQUIRER — D A17

JOHN F. KENNEDY JR.

Kennedy's deeds a great silencer of critics' jabs

A political mag and a legal stint were among his achievements.

By William R. Macklin
INQUIRER STAFF WRITER

John F. Kennedy Jr., a scion of power with a common man's touch, often endured taunts that he was too good-looking to be smart and too rich to really care.

In his public life, Kennedy rebuked his critics by founding his own magazine and charting a brief but successful course as a New York City prosecutor. Privately, this prince of Camelot never relinquished the pleasure of being a faithful brother, doting uncle and loyal cousin to the famous family he loved.

Kennedy, 38, was flying to the wedding of one of his cousins when the small plane he was piloting disappeared Friday somewhere between Long Island and Martha's Vineyard.

Also aboard the missing Piper Saratoga, which departed Fairfield, N.J., was Kennedy's wife, Carolyn Bessette, 33, and her older sister Lauren Bessette.

The apparent tragedy has brought a national outpouring of sadness over the possible loss of the most visible and charismatic of the younger Kennedys, son of the 35th president and Jacqueline Kennedy Onassis.

Considered by many to be the perfect prince to carry on the Kennedys' Camelot mystique, JFK Jr., as he was often called, inherited his father's bracing good looks as well as the raffish charm of men on his mother's side.

He was People magazine's "sexiest man alive" in 1988 and an irresistible target of tabloid newspapers and the paparazzi, who hungrily chronicled his romance with Daryl Hannah and his dates with Madonna.

"John, although he didn't wish it himself, was born a star," said biographer Wendy Leigh, author of *Prince Charming*.

At times he wore that stardom with all the swaggering confidence his lineage afforded.

He founded George magazine in 1995 and as editor took breezy delight in making it a head-turning, sometimes controversial mix of celebrity glitz and earnest politicism. He even drew fire from relatives for a September 1997 editorial in which he described his cousins Michael and Joseph as "poster boys for bad behavior" after both faced marital scandals.

"John had a great sense of humor and sense of self-deprecation and a trickster side of him," said Douglas Brinkley, a professor of history at the University of New Orleans and a contributing editor at George.

The other side — the side that treated strangers with good-natured ease, that eschewed limos and four-star hotel suites — knew how to conceal his golden-boy persona beneath a veil of commonality.

At the Essex County Airport, from which Kennedy left Friday night, Joe Orlando recalled a chance meeting with Kennedy three months ago. He didn't recognize the man from whom he had borrowed a flashlight.

"I had absolutely no idea who he was," said Orlando, 28, of Hawthorne, N.J.

When Orlando returned the flashlight he introduced himself.

"By the way, I'm Joe," Orlando said.

"Hi, John Kennedy," was the reply.

Orlando was stunned.

DENNIS REGGIE / Associated Press
In a wedding that surprised many, John F. Kennedy Jr. and Carolyn Bessette Kennedy leave a chapel on Georgia's Cumberland Island in 1996.

Associated Press / Look magazine
As his father works at the White House, a 2-year-old John F. Kennedy Jr. peeks out from the presidential desk. This picture of father and son in the Oval Office was taken in 1963. Later that year, the president was killed.

Associated Press
John F. Kennedy Jr. and his sister, Caroline Kennedy Schlossberg, attend the funeral of their mother, Jacqueline Onassis, in May 1994.

"He was very easygoing," he said. "There was never any rudeness. ... I walked back to my plane thinking I was an idiot," for not recognizing him.

Kennedy could be shy, was deeply devoted to his older sister, Caroline Kennedy Schlossberg, 41, and often was reluctant about the demands of celebrity.

When he married Bessette in 1996, the pair, who shared a home in New York, escaped an inevitable media blitz by rounding up a few close friends and heading to a small island off the coast of Georgia where they were wed in the tiny First African Baptist Church. It fell to a cousin, Rhode Island Rep. Patrick Kennedy, to inform the press of the nuptials.

Despite his closeness to his family, Kennedy never exhibited the political ambition of his father, John; his uncles, Robert and Edward; or his cousin, Joseph. Nor did he seem compelled by the activist impulses of another cousin, environmentalist Robert Kennedy Jr.

If the Kennedy mystique required high-profile infusions of public service they did not come from JFK Jr. He preferred seeing his family in personal terms.

In a 1993 interview, JFK Jr. said he found it difficult "to talk about a legacy or a mystique. It's my family. The fact that there have been difficulties and hardships, or obstacles, makes us closer."

Kennedy grew up in a world shadowed by difficulties and awash in hardships.

Born 2½ weeks after his father's 1960 election — the only child ever born to a president-elect — he spent his third birthday watching the funeral procession of his assassinated father. The sight of the boy, known to the world as "John John" standing in front of St. Matthew's Cathedral in short pants, a cool November wind coursing around his bare legs, saluting his father's casket, is one of the most enduring images of the 1960s.

His father's assassination in Dallas on Nov. 22, 1963, happened just four months after the death of his younger brother, Patrick, who was born prematurely and who died on Aug. 7.

Left to rear her two children alone, Jacqueline Kennedy moved to New York, where JFK Jr. and his sister grew up comfortably sheltered from a curious public. He attended private Catholic schools, the Collegiate School, and Phillips Academy in Andover, Mass.

In 1993 Kennedy told Vogue magazine that his mother "never had an agenda for me or my sister. That's probably why we're all so close and have had a relatively normal life. Not being a Kennedy, she could recognize both the perils and the positive aspects. One thing she has done is kept the memory and the character of our father very vivid for us."

Young Kennedy needed the strength afforded by those memories. His uncle Robert Kennedy, gunned down during a political rally in 1968. The car crash on Chappaquiddick, 30 years ago today, that cost the life of a young woman and ended any presidential aspirations for Edward Kennedy. Later, there would be the deaths of his cousin David of a drug overdose in 1984, and then at the end of 1997, of cousin Michael, killed in a bizarre skiing accident.

"It's almost as if there's some ineffable force that demands that they suffer — and suffer nationally," said Neal Gabler, author of *Life: The Movie*, a book that focuses on American celebrity and entertainment culture.

While Jacqueline Onassis could not shield her son from the pain of his losses, nothing, not even the former first lady's marriage to Greek shipping czar Aristotle Onassis and their subsequent divorce, interfered with the tender, protective relationship between the Kennedy children and their mother.

That doesn't mean they always agreed. At Brown University, Kennedy showed a talent for acting and took roles in several plays. He even acted in the Manhattan production of the Brian Friel play *Winners* in 1985.

But when he expressed an interest in pursuing a career on the stage his mother quashed the idea, apparently encouraging her son to pursue a law career instead.

Kennedy, who graduated from Brown in 1983, completed New York University Law School in 1989.

After passing the bar — on his third try — he landed a job with the Manhattan District Attorney's Office. As his law career grew and his visibility mounted, so did the public barbs.

But the open criticism that he was a vainglorious playboy and the whispered innuendo that he lacked intellectual substance were often countered by his performance.

Before ending his tenure at the Manhattan DA's Office in 1993, he had tried six cases and won them all.

Associated Press
Willie Mays, then with the New York Mets, gives John F. Kennedy Jr., 11, batting tips in 1972. At right is a Kennedy friend, Eric Von Huguley.

And on the same day in 1988 that People magazine tagged him the "sexiest man alive," Kennedy offered a passionate introductory speech for his uncle Sen. Edward M. Kennedy at the Democratic National Convention in Atlanta.

As editor of George he handled interviews and did some reporting, filing a compelling profile of late Alabama Gov. George Wallace, among others.

University of New Orleans historian Brinkley, an occasional contributor to George, called Kennedy a "terrific editor" who lionized the Rev. Dr. Martin Luther King Jr., Czech President Vaclav Havel, and farm labor leader Cesar Chavez.

Brinkley said that Kennedy took his responsibility to society seriously and "was circling around how he could best enter the public arena as a reformer."

Still, it was not easy for him to shed his slightly wifty image, and his playful nature didn't help.

He spent many afternoons tossing a Frisbee in Central Park or gliding along on in-line skates near his home in TriBeCa. Newspapers carried photographs of him skating to his mother's apartment shortly after her death on May 19, 1994.

The leg cast he was believed to have been wearing at the time of Friday's crash may have been for the ankle he fractured while playing on Martha's Vineyard last month.

Yesterday, as fans at Yankee Stadium paused to reflect on the man he was and the boy he had been, as President Clinton called for prayers and evangelist Billy Graham spoke hopefully of his "personal friend," millions took comfort from that image of a small boy raising tiny fingers to his forehead on that chilly autumn day in 1963.

Inquirer staff writer Leonard N. Fleming contributed to this article, which includes information from the Associated Press.

Major Events in the Life of John F. Kennedy Jr.

John F. Kennedy wheels his wife out of the hospital in 1960. A nurse carries John Jr.

Nov. 25, 1960 Born in Washington, D.C.

Jan. 20, 1961 His father, John F. Kennedy, becomes president.

Nov. 25, 1963 Salutes his father's casket as the funeral cortege of the assassinated president passes by a Washington church.

Fall of 1964 Moves from Washington to New York, where he attends a Catholic private school then the Collegiate boys' school.

Pulling on his mother's necklace at the White House in 1962.

Fall of 1976 Enters the Phillips Academy in Andover, Mass.

Spring of 1983 Graduates from Brown University in Providence, R.I.

Prior to graduation ceremonies at Brown University in 1983.

August 1985 Makes his professional acting debut in Brian Friel's drama "Winners" in Manhattan.

Fall of 1986 Enrolls at New York University Law School.

July 1988 Addresses Democratic National Convention in Atlanta to introduce his uncle, Sen. Edward M. Kennedy.

August 1989 Hired as a Manhattan prosecutor. He resigns in July 1993, after attaining a 6-0 conviction record.

Speaking to George advertisers in 1996.

John and his wife, Carolyn Bessette, arrive at the Minskoff Theater in New York in 1998.

May 19, 1994 His mother, Jacqueline Kennedy Onassis, dies.

September 1995 Launches George magazine.

Sept. 21, 1996 Marries Carolyn Bessette on Cumberland Island in Georgia. They make their home in Manhattan.

SOURCE: Associated Press

The plane was traveling to the July 17 wedding of Rory Kennedy, the youngest of Robert and Ethel Kennedy's children, in Hyannis Port. Her wedding was postponed and she later married in a private ceremony in Athens, Greece.

QUOTED

"We dared to think . . . that this John Kennedy would live to comb gray hair. . . . But like his father, he had every gift but length of years."

—SENATOR EDWARD KENNEDY,
July 23, 1999
(see pages 117–119)

Caroline Kennedy addressed the convention on the fortieth anniversary of John F. Kennedy's presidential nomination in Los Angeles. "I thank all Americans for making me and John, and all of our family, a part of your families."

Jacqueline Kennedy's style was on display at a Metropolitan Museum of Art exhibit featuring her first lady fashions. (AP Photo/Suzanne Plunket)

ALSO IN 2000

George W. Bush defeated Al Gore in the 2000 presidential election following several recounts and a final decision by the U.S. Supreme Court.

Los Angeles Times

ON THE INTERNET: WWW.LATIMES.COM
CIRCULATION: 1,111,705 DAILY / 1,386,681 SUNDAY

WEDNESDAY, AUGUST 16, 2000
COPYRIGHT 2000/CC. 134 PAGES

DAILY 25¢
DESIGNATED AREAS HIGHER

COLUMN ONE

'Sky Shelves' Can Be Lethal for Shoppers

■ Thousands have been hurt and some killed by falling lumber, detergent boxes and other items. Stores have been sued for millions, but the toll continues to mount.

By DAVAN MAHARAJ
TIMES STAFF WRITER

Few of the millions of shoppers who each day crowd into the retail canyons of big discounters such as Home Depot and Wal-Mart expect to be crushed in an avalanche of merchandise.

But that's exactly what happened to Mary Pentuff.

The 75-year-old Santa Monica woman was looking for lattice to stake her morning glories in November at a Los Angeles Home Depot when a 19-year-old forklift operator accidentally tipped a load of lumber stacked several feet above her. She was crushed to death in front of her horrified daughter.

"You expect to die or get injured if you go to war or if you speed on the freeway," said the daughter, Rebecca Hamilton. "The last thing you expect when you enter your neighborhood store is that you won't come out alive."

Pentuff's accident was just one of thousands of injuries and deaths involving shoppers that resulted from falling merchandise in warehouse-style stores, according to a Times examination of court records from around the country. The incidents have been piling up for at least 15 years, since boxes of Final Touch fabric softener toppled from a shelf at a Sam's Club store near Tulsa, Okla., in 1985, killing a woman who was shopping for cleaning supplies.

Despite numerous lawsuits and millions of dollars in jury awards and settlements against various discount retailers and warehouse superstores, the toll continues to mount. Only last month, a 41-year-old Connecticut man was killed at his neighborhood Home Depot when a 2,000-pound pallet of landscaping timbers fell and pinned him to the ground.

The mushrooming of retail superstores—where forklifts prowl aisles, stacking pallets of merchandise from floor to ceiling—has brought lower prices and convenience to cities and small towns across America. But thousands of consumers who have ventured into these retail centers to run routine errands have encountered tragedy instead.

Wal-Mart has acknowledged in court records that during a six-year period ending in 1996, its claims department reported that falling merchandise was responsible for about 26,000 customer claims and 7,000 employee injuries.

Please see SAFETY, A11

Last 7 Concorde Jets Grounded

As France and Britain prepared to rule Concordes unfit to fly, at least until modifications are made, British Airways grounded its remaining seven. Some analysts predicted the end of supersonic travel. C1

INSIDE TODAY'S TIMES

INSURANCE PACT
A deal averted the possibility Catholic Healthcare would end Blue Cross coverage. C1

WHIRLWIND COURTSHIP
Downtown L.A.'s chapels can crank out shotgun weddings as well as quickie divorces. E1

BEHOLD THE HALL
The heavy work has begun on Disney Hall. A graphic shows what comes next. F1

WEATHER: Hazy sunshine and humid with a few high clouds today; morning fog at the beaches. LA Downtown: 67/88. B5

ON THE INTERNET:
http://www.latimes.com

TOP OF THE NEWS ON A2

Sen. Edward M. Kennedy, with his niece Caroline Kennedy, waves to the crowd after her address at the Democratic National Convention.

MYUNG J. CHUN · Los Angeles Times

LAPD's Response to Protests Shows Its Strength and, Critics Say, Its Faults

By BETH SHUSTER and JIM NEWTON
TIMES STAFF WRITERS

The Los Angeles Police Department that is confronting demonstrators this week is bigger, better-equipped and technologically improved over the force that failed in the face of the 1992 riots.

It also is more resolute—or, in the view of its critics, more reckless.

For the first time, the LAPD's top commanders are using live video feeds from the LAPD's helicopters, as well as cameras positioned on downtown rooftops, to make "real-time" decisions. They have command posts at several locations downtown and have stationed scores of officers—and even the department's mounted unit—in locations close to Staples Center, where the convention is located. They have new, dedicated radio frequencies to improve internal communication, and they are using computers to more rapidly issue cars, weapons and hand-held radios to officers.

In 1992, the LAPD was slow to respond to initial outbreaks of violence after a Ventura County jury returned not-guilty verdicts in the Rodney G. King beating case. The department's early uncertainty was compounded by a series of technological failings—from overloaded 911 lines to cell phones that failed to a communication breakdown that left the Police Department's helicopter over one riot area unable to relay updates to officers waiting to deploy.

"We were just a different department then," said Deputy Chief Martin Pomeroy, who is the LAPD's "incident commander" for the convention. "We're not that department anymore."

In one sense, however, the LAPD in recent days has resembled the one that attracted such

Please see TACTICS, A24

LAPD officers Manuel Melgoza, left, Binnie Phan near Staples Center.

LUIS SINCO / Los Angeles Times

Protests Are Just a TV Show for Delegates

By HECTOR TOBAR
TIMES STAFF WRITER

The most liberal of the Democrats, especially the civil rights activists, are feeling a bit uneasy during their stay in Los Angeles. They don't like the feel of entering a convention hall through phalanxes of police. They don't like the sight of thousands of young people behind fences—"our people," one delegate called them—shouting angry slogans against the party.

"We ran into a bunch of them on the Metro," said Dave Garrity, 51, a self-described gay delegate from Portland, Maine. "They made some good points. But there's a lot of things they don't see."

For 15 minutes in the subway corridors under downtown, Garrity and a group of Maine delegates debated the young protesters about the Supreme Court, civil rights and "the industrial complex." Garrity told them to "go study some history." They told him to vote for Ralph Nader.

It was a rare moment. During these hot, heady days of marches and street battles, delegates and demonstrators have inhabited separate realities, kept apart by the security measures that have sealed off Staples Center. The delegates sit in air-conditioned buses and are waved past checkpoints by police—they hear the voices of the protesters as faint, muffled sounds in the distance.

"I've only seen it on TV," said Claude Baldree, a delegate from Livingston, Texas. In the first two

Please see DELEGATES, A25

2 Kennedys Call on Party to Rekindle JFK's Vision

■ Democrats: 'It is time once again to ask more of ourselves,' president's daughter says in rare political appearance. Other speakers attack Bush and try to rally liberal base.

By MARK Z. BARABAK and CATHLEEN DECKER
TIMES POLITICAL WRITERS

The kin and kindred souls of President John F. Kennedy raised the torch of the New Frontier to summon Democrats on Tuesday night to extend the nation's prosperity to those left behind.

In the city where Kennedy was nominated 40 years ago, his daughter, Caroline, brother Edward and others at the Democratic convention invoked the memory of the slain president—and the vision he called the New Frontier—to urge the election of Al Gore.

"As I look out across this hall and across this country, I know that my father's spirit lives on," said Caroline Kennedy in a rare political appearance that was an emotional high point of a sentimental evening.

"Now, we are the New Frontier. And now, when many of us are doing so well, it is time once again to ask more of ourselves," she said, echoing her father's inaugural address. "As much as we need a prosperous economy, we also need a prosperity of kindness and decency. We need a president who is not afraid of complexity, who believes in an open and tolerant society and who knows the world can be made new again."

Kennedy arrived onstage at Staples Center to the orchestral music

Please see CONVENTION, A23

MORE POLITICAL COVERAGE

PAYBACK TIME—Fat cat backers of the Democrats are treated to festivities at Staples Center sky boxes and celebrity receptions. U1

COURTING LATINOS—Democrats have a strong hold on California's Latinos for now, but Republicans are striving to change that. A3

COMMENTARY—Running mate Joseph Lieberman, who some link in spirit to the Christian Right, would never declare "Moses Day." B9

THE REAL TIPPER—The second lady focuses on what's important to her: family, photography, the homeless and mental health care. E1

Sen. Lieberman 'Clears the Air' With Blacks

By JANET HOOK and MATEA GOLD
TIMES STAFF WRITERS

Hoping to patch up an emerging fissure in the Democratic base, soon-to-be vice presidential nominee Joseph I. Lieberman arrived in Los Angeles on Tuesday and quickly moved to mend fences with black Democrats concerned about his positions on affirmative action, school vouchers and other issues.

In a well-received speech to the party's black caucus, Lieberman said he had been misrepresented as a supporter of Proposition 209, the 1996 California initiative that banned state-funded affirmative action programs.

"I have supported affirmative action, I do support affirmative action and I will support affirmative action," Lieberman said to thunderous applause from the crowd at the Westin Bonaventure Hotel. "Why? Because history and current reality make it necessary."

In his speech and at a private meeting beforehand, Lieberman won over the African American politician who had been most outspoken in questioning his record: Rep. Maxine Waters (D-Los Angeles). She gave Lieberman the endorsement she had been threatening to withhold.

"It clears the air," said Waters after his speech. "He has said enough. He has done enough. I feel comfortable in campaigning for him."

Democratic officials have been worried that disenchantment among Waters and other black leaders would translate into a lack of enthusiasm for soon-to-be presidential nominee Al Gore in the African American community, de-

Please see LIEBERMAN, A22

Amid Tears, Koreans Cross 50-Year Divide

By VALERIE REITMAN
TIMES STAFF WRITER

SEOUL—All of Korea cried Tuesday, or so it seemed.

In extraordinary homecomings filled with wailing and minutes-long group bearhugs, 200 elderly Koreans—100 each from the North and the South—were reunited with their families in Seoul and Pyongyang for the first time since war divided the peninsula half a century ago.

There were plenty of tears at seeing faces long ago given up for dead; tears for the five decades in which they'd had no contact, unaware of whole new lives—wives, babies, grandchildren; tears as some learned for the first time of the deaths of parents and siblings; and tears because they knew that at the end of these three days of reunions, they may never see one another again.

Throughout South Korea, people

Im Hee Kyung, 91, and his son Rim Jae Hyok, 69, of North Korea, separated since the Korean War, meet at a reunion in Seoul.

Agence France-Presse

chattered around TV sets at home and in public places weeping, as much for their own families as for the poignant stories they saw unfolding before them on live television, the result of a historic summit between the leaders of the two Koreas in June.

Kang Young Won, 86, began sobbing when he caught sight of his 90-year-old mother and 62-year-old sister in the Seoul civic center where they awaited him.

All wept, their arms locked tightly around one another, for at least 10 minutes.

"Mother, Mother," Kang, who left South Korea for the North when he was 16, sobbed again and again. When they finally sat down, he dropped to his knees, leaning on his mother's lap, never letting go of her hand. "You're alive, you're alive."

Nearby, North Korean Lee Jong Pil, 70, was weeping too, as he tried to communicate with his 100-year-

Please see KOREAS, A14

Russians Battle Weather, Race Clock to Save Sub

By ROBYN DIXON
TIMES STAFF WRITER

MOSCOW—Rescuers attempted a desperate and tricky operation late Tuesday and early today to save the crew of a stricken Russian nuclear submarine trapped at the bottom of the Barents Sea, but poor weather and swirling currents frustrated their efforts.

With time and oxygen running out for the 116-member crew, the operation was complicated by near-zero visibility in the inky seas.

Repeated efforts overnight failed to attach a piloted rescue apparatus above the submarine's hatch to enable the crew's evacuation.

A naval spokesman said this morning that it was not clear if the crew was still knocking on the hull to communicate with rescuers. After rescue attempts Monday and Tuesday.

Please see SUBMARINE, A12

A Mother Prays Her Son Will 'Not Lose Heart'

By ROBYN DIXON
TIMES STAFF WRITER

MOSCOW—Dmitri Starosyeltsev had to overcome some tough competition to win a position on the nuclear submarine Kursk after he was drafted in November.

The contest was fierce: Two of every three candidates were rejected. But Starosyeltsev, who graduated with good marks from the Railway College in the city of Kursk, won out.

One of the novices in the 116-member crew, he was aboard the ship which gave the vessel its name, working over the weekend in the Barents Sea. Efforts to rescue the

Please see SAILOR, A12

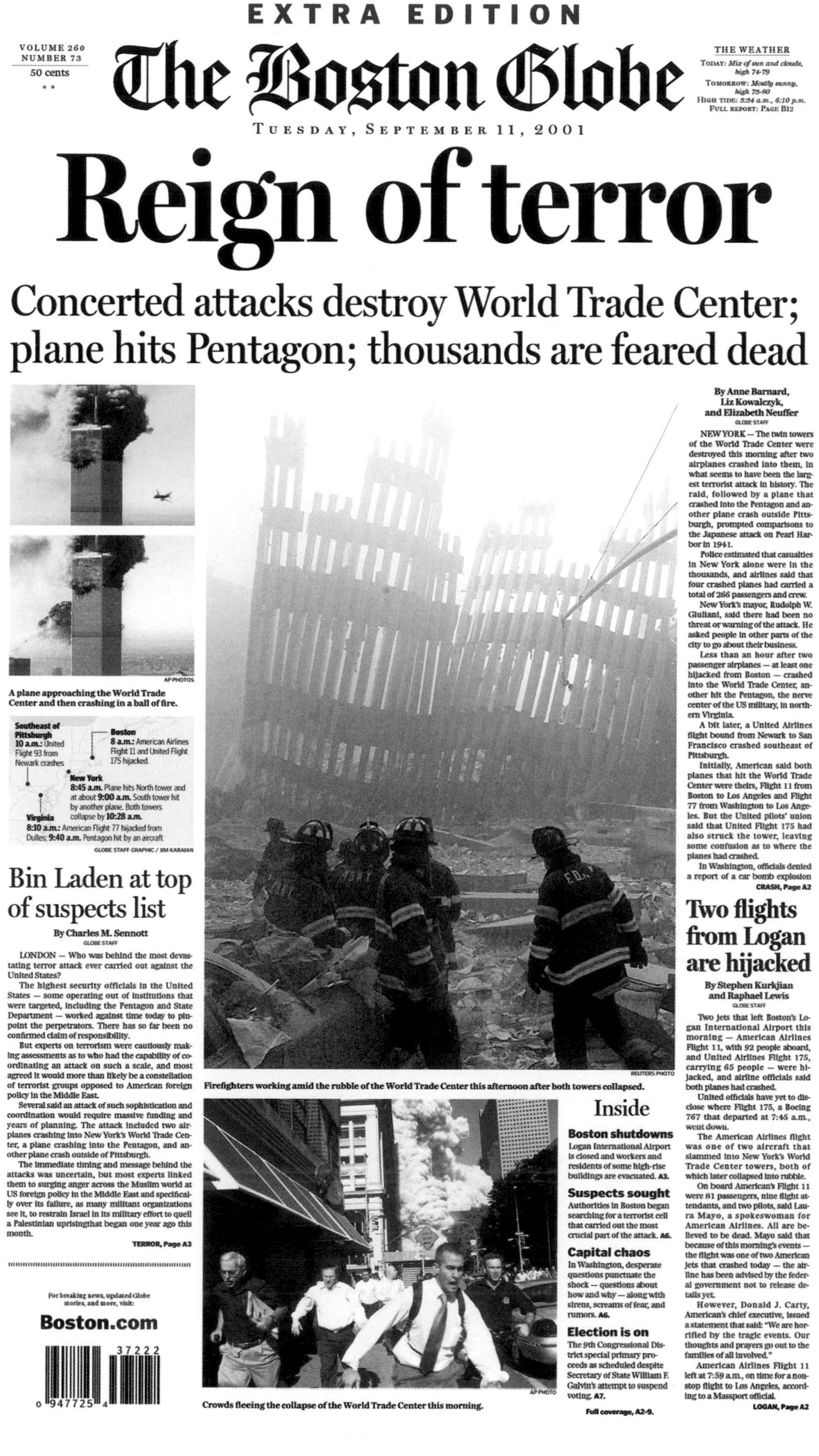

EXTRA EDITION

VOLUME 260
NUMBER 73
50 cents
* *

The Boston Globe

THE WEATHER
TODAY: *Mix of sun and clouds, high 74-79*
TOMORROW: *Mostly sunny, high 75-80*
HIGH TIDE: *5:54 a.m., 6:10 p.m.*
FULL REPORT: PAGE B12

TUESDAY, SEPTEMBER 11, 2001

Reign of terror

Concerted attacks destroy World Trade Center; plane hits Pentagon; thousands are feared dead

By Anne Barnard, Liz Kowalczyk, and Elizabeth Neuffer
GLOBE STAFF

NEW YORK — The twin towers of the World Trade Center were destroyed this morning after two airplanes crashed into them, in what seems to have been the largest terrorist attack in history. The raid, followed by a plane that crashed into the Pentagon and another plane crash outside Pittsburgh, prompted comparisons to the Japanese attack on Pearl Harbor in 1941.

Police estimated that casualties in New York alone were in the thousands, and airlines said that four crashed planes had carried a total of 266 passengers and crew.

New York's mayor, Rudolph W. Giuliani, said there had been no threat or warning of the attack. He asked people in other parts of the city to go about their business.

Less than an hour after two passenger airplanes — at least one hijacked from Boston — crashed into the World Trade Center, another hit the Pentagon, the nerve center of the US military, in northern Virginia.

A bit later, a United Airlines flight bound from Newark to San Francisco crashed southeast of Pittsburgh.

Initially, American said both planes that hit the World Trade Center were theirs, Flight 11 from Boston to Los Angeles and Flight 77 from Washington to Los Angeles. But the United pilots' union said that United Flight 175 had also struck the tower, leaving some confusion as to where the planes had crashed.

In Washington, officials denied a report of a car bomb explosion

CRASH, Page A2

AP PHOTOS

A plane approaching the World Trade Center and then crashing in a ball of fire.

Southeast of Pittsburgh
10 a.m.: United Flight 93 from Newark crashes

Boston
8 a.m.: American Airlines Flight 11 and United Flight 175 hijacked.

New York
8:45 a.m. Plane hits North tower and at about 9:00 a.m. South tower hit by another plane. Both towers collapse by 10:28 a.m.

Virginia
8:10 a.m.: American Flight 77 hijacked from Dulles; 9:40 a.m. Pentagon hit by an aircraft

GLOBE STAFF GRAPHIC / JIM KARAIAN

REUTERS PHOTO

Firefighters working amid the rubble of the World Trade Center this afternoon after both towers collapsed.

AP PHOTO

Crowds fleeing the collapse of the World Trade Center this morning.

Bin Laden at top of suspects list

By Charles M. Sennott
GLOBE STAFF

LONDON — Who was behind the most devastating terror attack ever carried out against the United States?

The highest security officials in the United States — some operating out of institutions that were targeted, including the Pentagon and State Department — worked against time today to pinpoint the perpetrators. There has so far been no confirmed claim of responsibility.

But experts on terrorism were cautiously making assessments as to who had the capability of coordinating an attack on such a scale, and most agreed it would more than likely be a constellation of terrorist groups opposed to American foreign policy in the Middle East.

Several said an attack of such sophistication and coordination would require massive funding and years of planning. The attack included two airplanes crashing into New York's World Trade Center, a plane crashing into the Pentagon, and another plane crash outside of Pittsburgh.

The immediate timing and message behind the attacks was uncertain, but most experts linked them to surging anger across the Muslim world at US foreign policy in the Middle East and specifically over its failure, as many militant organizations see it, to restrain Israel in its military effort to quell a Palestinian uprisingthat began one year ago this month.

TERROR, Page A3

Inside

Boston shutdowns
Logan International Airport is closed and workers and residents of some high-rise buildings are evacuated. A3.

Suspects sought
Authorities in Boston began searching for a terrorist cell that carried out the most crucial part of the attack. A6.

Capital chaos
In Washington, desperate questions punctuate the shock — questions about how and why — along with sirens, screams of fear, and rumors. A6.

Election is on
The 9th Congressional District special primary proceeds as scheduled despite Secretary of State William F. Galvin's attempt to suspend voting. A7.

Full coverage, A2-9.

Two flights from Logan are hijacked

By Stephen Kurkjian and Raphael Lewis
GLOBE STAFF

Two jets that left Boston's Logan International Airport this morning — American Airlines Flight 11, with 92 people aboard, and United Airlines Flight 175, carrying 65 people — were hijacked, and airline officials said both planes had crashed.

United officials have yet to disclose where Flight 175, a Boeing 767 that departed at 7:45 a.m., went down.

The American Airlines flight was one of two aircraft that slammed into New York's World Trade Center towers, both of which later collapsed into rubble.

On board American's Flight 11 were 81 passengers, nine flight attendants, and two pilots, said Laura Mayo, a spokeswoman for American Airlines. All are believed to be dead. Mayo said that because of this morning's events — the flight was one of two American jets that crashed today — the airline has been advised by the federal government not to release details yet.

However, Donald J. Carty, American's chief executive, issued a statement that said: "We are horrified by the tragic events. Our thoughts and prayers go out to the families of all involved."

American Airlines Flight 11 left at 7:59 a.m., on time for a nonstop flight to Los Angeles, according to a Massport official.

LOGAN, Page A2

For breaking news, updated Globe stories, and more, visit:
Boston.com

Senator Edward Kennedy contacted all 177 Massachusetts families who lost loved ones in the attacks, many of whom had been on the two hijacked planes that left Boston's Logan airport. Kennedy stayed in touch with many of these families until the final months of his life.

First Lady Laura Bush and Senator Edward Kennedy made brief public statements after their scheduled education hearing was canceled due to the September 11 attacks. (AP Photo/Kenneth Lambert)

JUNE 7, 2002
MICHAEL SKAKEL FOUND GUILTY OF MURDER

LAKERS DEFEAT NETS 106-83; YANKEES WIN, RED SOX LOSE · SPORTS, C1

America's Oldest Continuously Published Newspaper

Hartford Courant.

WEATHER
Partly Cloudy.
High Near 76. B6

VOLUME CLXV, NUMBER 159 COPYRIGHT 2002, THE HARTFORD COURANT CO. SATURDAY, JUNE 8, 2002 6/7★ Sports Final NEWSSTAND 50¢

Dorthy Moxley said she had prayed Friday morning,
"Dear Lord, again today, like I've been doing for 27 years, I'm praying that I can find . . ."

'JUSTICE FOR MARTHA'

Lawyers Praise State's Case

By RICK GREEN
And JESSE LEAVENWORTH
COURANT STAFF WRITERS

The confident hand of a veteran prosecutor, assisted by shrewd audiovisual theatrics, delivered the surprising Skakel guilty verdict, lawyers and prosecutors said Friday.

"People compare the flamboyance of Mickey Sherman with the steadfastness of Jonathan Benedict. In the courtroom, slow and steady from the prosecutor is what wins the race," said former U.S. Attorney Stanley Twardy. "Methodically, step by step he led the jurors through this and he got the [desired] result."

Though numerous courtroom veterans expressed surprise at a guilty verdict in a case crafted on so much circumstantial evidence, many pointed to the vivid images of Martha Moxley projected on the courtroom wall and the recordings of Michael Skakel as indelible.

"They stuck with the facts that they had and they made it very simple," said lawyer Brian J. Woolf. "The prosecution didn't try to over-reach with the evidence. [Benedict's] summation was brilliant."

The 12 jurors were not available for comment after the verdict. But alternate juror Anne Layton said that during the trial she was leaning heavily toward conviction. For her, Benedict's closing argument was the clincher.

"I think he did an incredible job," she said.

New Haven lawyer Hugh Keefe said Benedict deftly took "a thin case" and turned in "a masterful job."

Also, more than one witness remembered Skakel's movements on the night of the killing — but could not recall any other details. Such testimony weakens a witness's credibility, Keefe said.

"Any witness who firmly remembers what's good for you but has trouble remembering everything else is not a good witness," he said.

Todd D. Fernow, a University of Connecticut Law School professor, said the state astutely realized that "it's the classic whodunit, where they don't have enough evi-

PLEASE SEE LAWYERS, PAGE A6

BOB MACDONNELL / THE HARTFORD COURANT

DORTHY MOXLEY and her son, John, lay flowers on the grave of Martha Moxley at Putnam Cemetery in Greenwich Friday, the day Michael Skakel was found guilty of Martha's murder in 1975. "I wanted to find justice for Martha," Dorthy Moxley told reporters after the verdict. "It's all about Martha." Below, Skakel is helped into a van behind Norwalk Superior Court for transport to prison.

More Coverage Inside

➤ **RELIEF:** In Greenwich, especially at the police department, the conviction brings relief. **Page A4**

➤ **PUNISHMENT STARTED BEFORE VERDICT:** In a packed courtroom awaiting the verdict, Michael Skakel was more alone than ever. **Page A5**

➤ **A LONG WAIT:** Graciousness, not bitterness, marks Dorthy Moxley's reaction to the verdict. **Page A7**

➤ **WHAT'S NEXT:** Skakel — living today in an 8 1/2-foot by 10 1/2-foot prison cell in Suffield — will be sentenced July 19. **Page A7**

ALAN CHANIEWSKI / THE HARTFORD COURANT

A 'Bittersweet' Victory Brings Relief, But Also Grief

By LYNNE TUOHY
And EDMUND H. MAHONY
COURANT STAFF WRITERS

NORWALK — A guilty verdict in the Michael Skakel murder case had seemed as improbable as the likelihood that a vivacious teenaged girl could be bludgeoned to death within the confines of a gated Greenwich community.

But as the handcuffs tightened audibly on Skakel's wrists and several of Martha Moxley's childhood friends sobbed softly but uncontrollably, the weight of reality dropped.

For additional coverage of the case and complete transcripts of the closing arguments, see ctnow.com.

The toll was heavy and harsh, the grief fresh.

Skakel, 41, the father of a 3-year-old son, was led off to prison to await his sentencing on July 19 for the 1975 murder of the girl he had a crush on, but who favored his brother and nemesis, Tommy.

Martha was beaten savagely with a golf iron nearly 27 years ago and died at age 15. One needed only to look at the tears streaming down the face of her brother, John Moxley, to be reminded that Friday's verdict cannot erase the loss.

"It's bittersweet," he rasped, moments after Skakel was led from the courtroom. "It's a hollow victory," Moxley said. But, he added, "my heart stopped beating" when jury foreman Kevin Cambra uttered the word "guilty."

Dorthy Moxley, Martha's mother, never flagged in her pursuit of justice and smiled graciously in the face of despair. But when she entered the courtroom Friday morning, as anxious as everyone else that a verdict was near, she appeared sad and deflated.

Her voice quavered as she whispered, "I've decided this is a solemn day," she said. Asked why, she said, "Well, if we win, it's a solemn day for them. And if they win . . ."

The verdict brought tears and opened a floodgate of emotions.

"I didn't think this day would ever come," she said. "I just feel so blessed and so overwhelmed. This is Martha's day."

Outside court, several of Skakel's brothers stressed their belief in him and in his innocence, and they vowed to secure his release. David Skakel likened the trial to "a witch hunt."

"We are a family with a bedrock of faith, and our faith has been tested today immeasurably," he said.

Prosecutor Jonathan Benedict, too, is a man of faith. He had faith in his case when many did not, and he poured his

PLEASE SEE A DAY, PAGE A6

Bush Makes His Pitch
Predicts 'Tough Battle' Over Homeland Security Plan

By NICK ANDERSON
And RICHARD SIMON
SPECIAL TO THE COURANT

WASHINGTON — President Bush mobilized the power of his office Friday to press for approval of his Department of Homeland Security. But his plan faces the twin dangers of jealousy over legislative power and a tight congressional calendar.

The president, bracing for fierce turf battles, met with prominent lawmakers and then took to the people of Iowa his case for consolidating a wide range of homeland security agencies into a single Cabinet department.

Although Bush assigned the utmost urgency to his proposal, it was headed toward a congressional review that is ordinarily anything but speedy. In particular, many congressional committees could resist the prospective loss of jurisdiction over agencies moving to the new department.

"There's going to be a lot of turf protection in the Congress," Bush said before meeting at the White House with congressional supporters of a new department. "But I'm convinced

PLEASE SEE BUSH, PAGE A8

INSIDE

Business	E1
Classified	F1
Connecticut	B1
Crossword	D7
Editorial	A10, A11
Life	D1
Lottery	A4
Movies	D5
Obituaries	B4, B5
Public Notices	F6

U.S. HAD A HAND IN PHILIPPINES PLAN

By PAULINE JELINEK
And JIM GOMEZ
ASSOCIATED PRESS

WASHINGTON — U.S. forces helped plan the operation in which Philippine troops hunted down Abu Sayyaf rebels who had been holding hostages for more than a year, the Pentagon said Friday.

Conflicting reports about how a gun battle between soldiers and rebels unfolded also left unclear how two of the three hostages died.

"It's not an easy thing to do," Secretary of Defense Donald H. Rumsfeld said, refusing to criticize the rescue attempt.

Martin Burnham, 42, a missionary from Wichita, Kan., was killed during a shootout Friday after Philippine forces found extremist Muslim rebels who had been holding Burnham, his wife,

PLEASE SEE U.S., PAGE A9

Michael Skakel, nephew of Ethel Kennedy, was found guilty of the 1975 murder of 15-year-old Martha Moxley, his friend and neighbor, who was beaten to death with a golf club.

ALSO IN 2002

U.S. military troops and Afghan militia fought al-Qaeda and Taliban forces in eastern Afghanistan.

Los Angeles Times

On The Internet: WWW.LATIMES.COM | TUESDAY, NOVEMBER 18, 2003 | COPYRIGHT 2003/CC†/104 PAGES | 50¢ Designated Areas Higher

Schwarzenegger Sworn In, Rescinds Car Tax Increase

GARY FRIEDMAN *Los Angeles Times*

READY FOR ACTION: *Gov. Arnold Schwarzenegger and his wife, Maria Shriver, stand beneath the seal of California at the conclusion of swearing-in ceremonies at the Capitol in Sacramento.*

After the ceremonies, the new governor moves quickly to tackle state problems, including calling for special legislative sessions.

By PETER NICHOLAS AND JOE MATHEWS
Times Staff Writers

SACRAMENTO — Arnold Alois Schwarzenegger took the oath as California's 38th governor on Monday, vowing to upend the political culture and humble the special interests through decisive action that would amount to the "Miracle of Sacramento."

The audience of 7,500 invited guests, including thousands standing and watching on big-screen televisions, interrupted Schwarzenegger for applause 24 times during the course of his 12-minute inaugural speech, with the loudest ovation coming when he renewed his promise to roll back the state's car tax.

Shortly after the 45-minute ceremony on the west steps of the Capitol, the new governor delivered on that promise, issuing Executive Order 1, which repealed the $4-billion increase that had been approved by the man he replaced — Gray Davis. It was the first of a series of rapid-fire actions meant to draw a clear contrast with a Davis administration renowned for its caution.

Schwarzenegger issued proclamations to convene a trio of special sessions of the Legislature aimed at overturning a new law that allows illegal immigrants to obtain driver's licenses, cutting workers' compensation costs and capping state spending. In the sessions, which will begin today, Schwarzenegger hopes that lawmakers will place two measures on the March ballot — a constitutional amendment that would cap state spending and a bond issue to pay off the deficit accumulated during the last years of the Davis administration.

Schwarzenegger also issued an order suspending 85 packages of regulations still pending from the Davis administration, and called for a review of Davis' handling of all regulations.

"Makeup, please," Schwarzenegger said while signing the repeal of the car tax hike in the governor's Ronald Reagan Conference Room. "Just joking. Very important to know, a friend of mine asked me before I left Los Angeles; he said, 'Are you going to miss the action in the movies?' I said, 'No, I am going to have enough action up in Sacramento.' Well this is action, not just dialogue, this is action."

Schwarzenegger took the oath of office at 11:20 a.m., his left hand on a Bible published in 1911 and held by his wife, Maria Shriver. Inaugural officials had incorrectly described the Bible as an 1811 edition that belonged to Schwarzenegger's family. It

[See Inauguration, Page A18]

RELATED STORIES

Media: Press corps of 700 from 14 nations covers the event. **A19**
Analysis: Schwarzenegger must get a grip on budget gap. **A20**
Money: The governor has raised $1 million since election. **A20**

Mediation Plan Ends MTA Strike

Service will gradually resume after the two sides agree to let a panel draft a compromise.

By KURT STREETER, SHARON BERNSTEIN AND CAITLIN LIU
Times Staff Writers

The Metropolitan Transportation Authority and its mechanics union agreed Monday to settle their remaining contract differences through mediation, ending a 35-day transit strike that has left an estimated 400,000 daily passengers without bus or train service.

A few limited bus routes began running Monday night, and partial rail service on the Red Line subway and light-rail Blue Line was expected to resume this morning. Officials said full countywide service would probably not be restored until Friday.

Negotiators reached a tentative settlement shortly before midnight Sunday after what both sides characterized as several grueling bargaining sessions since Friday.

The agreement was quickly and unanimously approved Monday by the MTA board. It must still be ratified by the Amalgamated Transit Union, Local 1277, which has scheduled a vote for Wednesday. But union President Neil Silver, who is recommending the deal to his members, urged them to go back to work immediately as a show of good faith.

The key sticking point during more than a year of negotiations, the provision of health benefits for active and retired mechanics, remains to be settled. It will be presented now to a panel of three mediators — one picked by each side, the other chosen jointly — who will draft a compromise proposal that can be rejected by either side.

That process could take months, officials said, but both

[See Transit, Page A22]

COLUMN ONE

Where Eye for an Eye Is Justice

■ Revenge shootings are common, even expected, on the streets of South L.A. Police race to find suspects before the gang on the victim's turf does.

Mortal Wounds: One in a series of occasional stories about murder in Los Angeles.

By JILL LEOVY
Times Staff Writer

Four days after his cousin was gunned down a few blocks away, a 14-year-old youth sat alone in a dark house, thinking.

He had spent sleepless nights since a man had walked up to his cousin, Anthony Brown, 16, at 8th and Vernon avenues, and fired repeatedly into his chest at close range. Anthony, a tall, skinny, popular boy who loved practical jokes, stumbled a few feet, then fell, bleeding to death on the pavement.

Now, his cousin wondered, would the killer ever pay? Would someone take revenge?

The question hovers around many killings in South Los Angeles, where one homicide often means another in a ruthless pattern of payback.

As old as humanity, as modern as drive-by shootings, revenge propels the cycle of violent deaths on L.A. streets. Retaliation shootings are so common that some police view them as inevitable. "You get one shooting, and you can count on it: It will prompt one back," said LAPD Officer Kyle Remolino. "One shooting, then another. Back and forth."

Anthony Brown's close friends were not in gangs, nor were he and his cousin. But in the week after Anthony's death, this 14-year-old talked about why he was certain there would be retaliation.

Even though Anthony had resisted the pressure to join gangs, he knew gang members; it's nearly impossible to grow up in the neighborhood without knowing them, his cousin said.

[See Revenge, Page A16]

Muhammad Convicted in Sniper Slayings

By DAVID LAMB AND STEPHEN BRAUN
Times Staff Writers

VIRGINIA BEACH, Va. — A jury on Monday convicted John Allen Muhammad of murder in the serial sniper slayings that targeted innocent victims and spread panic last year across the Washington, D.C., area. The jury of seven women and five men immediately turned to Muhammad's fate, deciding whether he should be put to death.

Deliberating less than seven hours after an exhaustive five-week trial, the jurors found Muhammad guilty on two counts that could carry the death penalty in Virginia.

One was for committing multiple murders over a three-year period, and the second was for killing Dean H. Meyers, a Maryland civil engineer, during an act of terrorism. Though Muhammad was specifically found guilty of Meyers' murder, he was also convicted under a special Virginia statute that allowed prosecutors to bring in evidence of other killings to qualify the crime for the death penalty.

Muhammad, 42, was linked to 11 sniper slayings and five other shootings, including the Oct. 9,

[See Sniper, Page A11]

Immediate Anxiety, Delayed Gratification From Rollback

By EVAN HALPER AND SUE FOX
Times Staff Writers

SACRAMENTO — The $4-billion tax cut ordered by Gov. Arnold Schwarzenegger on Monday brought relief to California car owners, but left open how state lawmakers might now help local agencies pay for police, fire and other services.

Asked where the Legislature would find money to reimburse cities and counties as Schwarzenegger has promised, Senate President Pro Tem John L. Burton (D-San Francisco) said, "He ain't getting it from me.

"We don't have the money," Burton said. "That's a problem between him and local government."

Local governments have relied on the vehicle license fee to help pay for police, fire and other services. But many residents objected over the summer when former Gov. Gray Davis hiked the fee by 200%. Without the increase, Davis had said, the state would not have enough money to keep making the payments.

On Monday, Schwarzenegger made good on his campaign pledge to roll back the so-called car tax, lowering by $158 the amount paid by typical California motorists based on the value of their cars. The tax cut takes effect immediately, but because of administrative and legal issues, it could be 90 days before drivers see lower rates in their registration and renewal bills.

Schwarzenegger's executive order also directed that refunds go to the 3.1 million drivers who have already paid the higher rates — which have been in effect for only a month — and that the state continue paying local governments the monthly allotments they were getting from the tax. To do either, however,

[See Fee, Page A21]

ROBERT DURELL *Los Angeles Times*

A TIME FOR GOOD CHEER: *With former Gov. Pete Wilson behind him, Gray Davis applauds Gov. Arnold Schwarzenegger after he was sworn in as the 38th leader of California.*

Politics Aside, Sacramento Gets Into a Party Mood

By JENIFER WARREN
Times Staff Writer

SACRAMENTO — Gov. Arnold Schwarzenegger starred Monday in a glitzy and historic inauguration that was part political debut, part Hollywood premiere.

Although only 7,500 hand-picked guests — and several hundred journalists from around the world — had passes to witness the event up close, hundreds of other Californians massed on the Capitol's western flank, some crushing up against a chain-link security fence, some gathering half a football field away to watch the ceremony on a giant screen.

By the start of the program, the crowd on the sidewalks was five deep. Fathers hoisted children on their shoulders. Some onlookers climbed trees. Others griped about being stuck in the cheap seats, far from the action.

Samantha Guzman, 43, hopped a bus downtown to catch the show. "If I can just hear his voice from here, I'll be happy," Guzman said, hovering outside the security barrier. "I already saw him drive by in his limousine. He rolled down the window, waved and gave me that gorgeous smile."

At least she could hear the music, an eclectic program that mixed mariachis with Japanese

[See Scene, Page A19]

Limbaugh Returns to Air After Stay in Drug Rehab

By BOB BAKER
Times Staff Writer

Like many recovering addicts fresh from rehab, he was bursting with new personal insights. His vaunted confrontational vocabulary had taken on an unexpected dimension — self-empowerment references and the occasional reminder that you cannot feel responsible for other people's happiness.

Only this time the recovering addict was a rich and famous 52-year-old man sitting inside a Manhattan radio studio, speaking to millions of people.

Rush Limbaugh, who has become a cultural and political force as America's most popular radio host, returned to the air Monday after five weeks in an unnamed Arizona rehabilitation facility where he was treated reportedly for addiction to the painkiller OxyContin.

Associated Press

ON THE JOB: *Rush Limbaugh dates his addiction to 1995 or '96.*

His departure had been forced by a National Enquirer exposé in which a former housekeeper claimed Limbaugh bought and hoarded tens of thousands of pills. Lim-

[See Limbaugh, Page A23]

INSIDE

Mystery at Yellowstone
Scientists are studying a huge and potentially explosive underwater dome. **A10**

AARP Backs GOP Plan
The seniors group adds its support to the Medicare prescription measure. **A14**

Cutting the Music
Record executives hope fewer tracks per album will improve their value in fans' minds. **C1**

Weather
Warmer with clear skies tonight. L.A. Downtown: 76/54. **B14**

News Summary A2

7 85944 00050 6

As a Kennedy and a news anchor, Maria Shriver had a place in both political and journalism worlds. After her husband was elected governor of California, politics took precedence.

ALSO IN 2003

The U.S.-led invasion of Iraq began in March.

Rosemary Kennedy, the developmentally disabled daughter of Joseph and Rose Kennedy, inspired her sister Eunice to start the Special Olympics. Her sister Pat, who once was married to actor Peter Lawford, a member of Frank Sinatra's "Rat Pack," would pass away in 2006 at the age of 82. (Page at right from Newsday*)*

OBITUARIES

NEW YORK

Constance Driscoll, planning pioneer

BY JOSEPH MALLIA
STAFF WRITER

In some ways the story of Constance Wicks Driscoll's life was the story of Floral Park, a village on the Queens border that retains aspects of its once-rural charm. Born and raised on her grandfather's potato farm, Driscoll stayed in her hometown as it grew into a green suburb of comfortable homes built, in part, on the Wicks family acreage.

She raised three children, became one of the first women to serve on the Nassau Republican Committee, became a county planning commissioner, and established a tax-preparation business.

Driscoll, 78, died Monday of respiratory failure at a nursing clinic near her Meredith, N.H., vacation home.

"Connie was a pioneer in the field of planning. She and her family saw our county evolve from its early years, and she was committed to preserving our county's heritage and its intrinsic values for future generations," said former Nassau Executive Thomas Gulotta, who appointed her planning commissioner for several terms during the 1990s. "Her passing is a great loss for all who knew her."

Constance Wicks Driscoll

After graduating from Sewanhaka High School in 1944, she toured the country as part of a USO singing trio called Connie, Grace & Jean entertaining troops. On her return to Floral Park, she received a scholarship at Hofstra College, where she attended for a year. It was while working as a Coty Girl — an in-store model for the cosmetics company at Loesers Department Store in Garden City that she met Joseph H. Driscoll Jr., whom she married in February 1950.

They made a home in Floral Park and raised their three children, Kathryn, Joseph III and David.

A frequent community volunteer, she was PTA president and was active in politics through the Republican and Floral Park Citizens parties, working at polling places and serving as a county committeewoman in the late 1960s and a planning commissioner in the 1990s.

She assisted her husband in his political life as police commissioner and mayor of Floral Park, deputy Nassau County executive under Ralph Caso, chief deputy county executive under Francis Purcell, District Court judge and State Supreme Court justice.

"Connie was quite a woman. She was warm, caring, very generous. She always had time to listen to people and to help," recalled Nancy McLoughlin, who was Floral Park village administrator from 1982 to 1999. "I always felt she was an incredible role model for young women. There was nothing pretentious about her yet she accomplished so much."

In the 1970s Driscoll returned to college, graduating from Nassau Community College and earning a degree in accounting from Hofstra University in 1979.

Finishing college was a great personal achievement for her, and her family displayed her Hofstra diploma during visiting hours Thursday night at the Dalton Funeral Home in Floral Park.

"We have the diploma here because it meant something to her," said her daughter, Kathryn Driscoll Hopkins, chief clerk of the Nassau State Supreme Court.

She was divorced from Joseph Driscoll in the early 1970s and, in 1981, assisted by her close friend Robert H. Niklas, her daughter Kathryn and daughter-in-law Dyan, she started a business in Floral Park, Driscoll & Hopkins Income Tax Services Inc. She sold the business seven years ago and, seeking warmer winters, she moved to Seaford, Del., with Niklas.

"She was an incredibly good person. She always felt it was better to look for the good as opposed to the evil," Kathryn Wicks Driscoll said. "She was always there for us. My friends and my brothers' friends feel this loss almost as much as I do, because she was a friend to them, too."

In addition to Niklas and her daughter Kathryn, Driscoll is survived by sons, David and Joseph III, both of New Hampshire.

A religious service will be held at 9:15 a.m. Saturday at Christ Evangelical Lutheran Church, a Floral Park church built by her grandfather, Carl Kaufmann. She will be buried beside her parents, Harry Wicks and Anna Kaufmann Wicks, at Flushing Cemetery.

NATION

Rosemary Kennedy, 86, JFK's sister

THE ASSOCIATED PRESS

WASHINGTON — Rosemary Kennedy, a sister of John F. Kennedy who was born mentally retarded and lived most of her life in an institution after undergoing a lobotomy, died Friday, her family said. She was 86.

Kennedy, the inspiration for the Special Olympics spearheaded by the Kennedy family, had been a patient since 1949 at St. Coletta School for Exceptional Children in Jefferson, Wis.

She was the third child and first daughter of Joseph and Rose Kennedy.

In 1941, Joseph Kennedy, worried his daughter's mild mental retardation would lead her into situations that could damage the family's reputation, arranged for Rosemary to have a lobotomy. She was 23.

"Rosemary was a woman, and there was a dread fear of pregnancy, disease and disgrace," author Laurence Leamer wrote in his book "The Kennedy Women: The Saga of an American Family."

He wrote that Rosemary, whose retardation possibly stemmed from brain damage at birth, had taken to sneaking out of the convent where she was staying at the time.

Doctors told Joseph Kennedy that a lobotomy, a medical procedure in which the frontal lobes of a patient's brain are scraped away, would help his daughter, Eunice Kennedy Shriver, Rosemary's younger sister, recalled later.

Psychosurgery was in its infancy at the time, and only a few hundred lobotomies had been performed.

The procedure was believed to be a way to relieve serious mental disorders. Rosemary was reduced to an infant-like state, mumbling words and sitting for hours staring at walls, Leamer wrote.

AP PHOTO

The Kennedy kids, from left: Eunice, Jack, Joe Jr., Rosemary and Kathleen. Below, Rose Kennedy with her kids, including Rosemary, center, who was mentally retarded.

NATION

Sugerman, manager of The Doors

THE ASSOCIATED PRESS

WEST HOLLYWOOD, Calif. — Danny Sugerman, who went from an adolescent Doors groupie to manager of the rock group, has died of lung cancer at age 50.

Sugerman, who also cowrote the acclaimed 1980 biography of lead singer Jim Morrison, "No One Here Gets Out Alive," died Wednesday at his home, according to a statement posted on the band's Web site.

A confidante of Morrison and the other musicians, Sugerman promoted their music years after the band's fame peaked.

He consulted on Oliver Stone's 1991 film "The Doors" and put out two compilations of song lyrics, Morrison poetry and articles about the band.

A native of the Los Angeles area, Sugerman was hooked on the Doors after seeing a concert at age 13. He was hired by Morrison a year later to put together a band scrapbook, and fell into the excesses of the rock 'n' roll lifestyle.

Sugerman is survived by his wife, Fawn Hall Sugerman, and a brother and sister.

ALSO IN 2005

Hurricane Katrina, one of the costliest and deadliest hurricanes ever, hit the United States in late August, devastating the Mississippi Gulf Coast and New Orleans.

JANUARY 28, 2008
SENATOR EDWARD KENNEDY ENDORSED SENATOR BARACK OBAMA

The Washington Post | **POLITICS** CAMPAIGN 2008 | Tuesday, January 29, 2008 **A7**

Yesterday
"We will miss him as a family, respect him as a man of great character and courage, but particularly his humility and ability to touch the lives of each individual is something for which he will long be noted."
— **Mitt Romney,** *commenting to reporters in Florida about the death of Mormon Church President Gordon B. Hinckley, right*

Today
Florida voters go to the polls in a contest that means little on the Democratic side and a lot for the GOP. While the Republican candidates have been fighting for Sunshine State votes, the Democrats, for the most part, have skipped campaigning in a state where no delegates will be awarded.

Tomorrow
Sen. Barack Obama heads to Feb. 5 voting state Colorado, where 71 Democratic delegates are at stake, for an event at the University of Denver.

7
DAYS TO SUPER TUESDAY

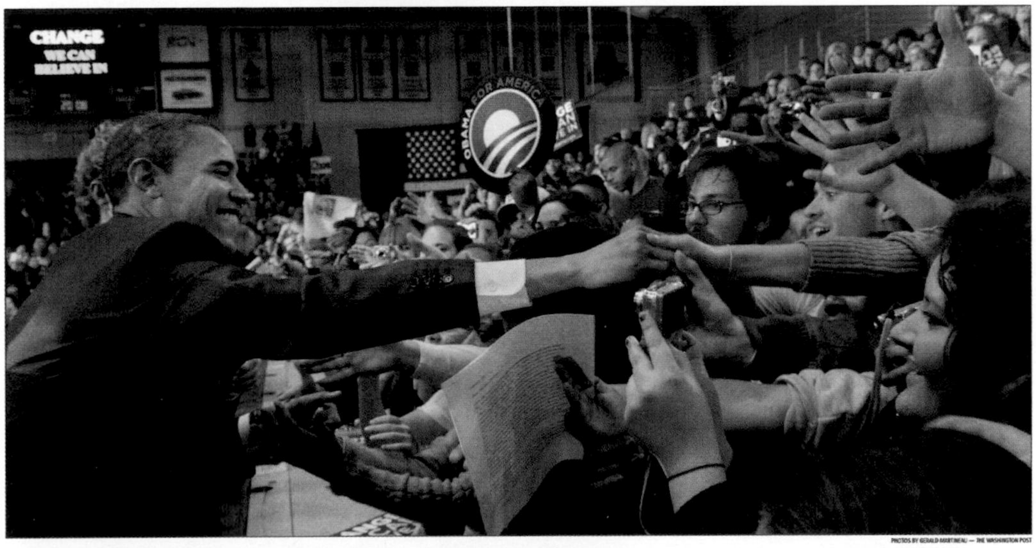

PHOTOS BY GERALD MARTINEAU — THE WASHINGTON POST

Sen. Barack Obama told supporters at his rally at American University that they could help write "the next great American story." "Someday we can tell our children that this was the time when we healed our nation," he said.

At American University in Washington, Sen. Barack Obama listens to Sen. Edward M. Kennedy endorse him for the Democratic nomination for president. Caroline Kennedy, Sen. Kennedy's niece, and Rep. Patrick J. Kennedy, his son, also gave their support to Obama.

DEMOCRATIC ENDORSEMENTS

Obama Ready on 'Day One,' Kennedy Says

By Anne E. Kornblut
and Shailagh Murray
Washington Post Staff Writers

Sen. Edward M. Kennedy delivered a highly prized endorsement for Sen. Barack Obama yesterday as well as a pointed rebuttal to the main lines of attack used against him by Sen. Hillary Rodham Clinton and her husband, Bill Clinton.

In a clear reference to the criticism repeated by the Democratic senator from New York and the former president that Obama (D-Ill.) does not have the experience for the White House, Kennedy — borrowing one of the Clintons' favorite phrases — said Obama is "ready to be president on Day One."

He also rebutted their contention that Obama has been inconsistent in his opposition to the war in Iraq and said Obama represents a new era and a rejection of "old politics."

"From the beginning, he opposed the war in Iraq. And let no one deny that truth," Kennedy (D-Mass.) said.

Kennedy praised Hillary Clinton and the third candidate for the Democratic presidential nomination, former senator John Edwards of North Carolina, describing them as "friends" and declaring he would support the party's nominee.

But he was backing the candidate, who, he said, "has extraordinary gifts of leadership and character, matched to the extraordinary demands of this moment in history."

The Kennedy endorsement gave a fresh boost to Obama as the campaign entered its most competitive phase, with primaries in 22 states up for grabs on Super Tuesday next week. It also overshadowed the arrest in Chicago of Tony Rezko, a major contributor to Obama over the years, on charges that he ran a major kickback scheme.

Rezko, who is accused of a bond violation, was arrested by federal agents yesterday morning at his Wilmette, Ill., home. The Chicago Tribune reported that federal investigators had become concerned in recent weeks about the movement of some of his finances. The Clinton campaign has sought to make an issue of the relationship between Obama and Rezko, and Hillary Clinton referred to him in a debate last week as a slumlord.

Kennedy's endorsement dismayed and angered many Clinton supporters, who had hoped he would remain neutral. Adding to the awkwardness, Clinton appeared yesterday in Massachusetts, where the political establishment is split between the former first lady and Obama. Boston Mayor Thomas M. Menino is a Clinton supporter, along with two popular members of Congress, Reps. Jim McGovern and Barney Frank. Gov. Deval L. Patrick, and now both U.S. senators, are supporters of Obama.

Clinton also campaigned in Connecticut, where Sen. Joseph I. Lieberman (I) has endorsed Sen. John McCain (R-Ariz.), and Sen. Christopher J. Dodd (D) has remained neutral after dropping out of the race.

The endorsement seemed to underscore the tensions the presidential campaign has caused in the Democratic Party establishment, especially in the Senate, where 11 members publicly back Clinton, and eight now support Obama.

That tension was on display late yesterday afternoon, when Obama and Clinton returned to the Senate and a pair of votes brought them together in rare proximity on the floor. Obama glided from desk to desk and was greeted by his colleagues like a returning prizefighter. Standing at the back of the chamber, he joked with Sens. James Webb (Va.) and Jon Tester (Mont.), both uncommitted in the Democratic nomination battle.

Sen. Claire McCaskill (Mo.) and Sen. Kent Conrad (N.D.) joined the group, and Conrad, who endorsed Obama weeks ago, took the roll. "Obama, Obama, Obama," Conrad said, to himself, McCaskill and the Illinois senator.

"We're for Obama," he said, looking at Tester and Webb. "What about you?"

McCaskill will campaign tomorrow in Missouri with Obama, and before walking away she told him "Get some sleep." Clinton remained out of view, having stepped into the cloakroom during the first vote. There she ran into Kennedy, and the two exchanged greetings, according to people familiar with the conversation.

Senate Majority Leader Harry M. Reid (D-Nev.) refused to offer any observations about Kennedy's endorsement. "I'm staying out of the race between Obama and Clinton," Reid said. But others appeared to be wavering. "I'll be letting you know in the next couple of days," said Sen. Patty Murray, a member of the Democratic leadership, whose home state of Washington will hold its Democratic caucuses Feb. 9.

Several senators from highly contested states said they were reluctant to weigh in because their states are likely to be key battlegrounds in the general election. Sen. Robert P. Casey Jr. (D), whose father, the late Pennsylvania governor, had a bitter feud with Bill Clinton in the 1990s over abortion politics, said he became close to Clinton and Obama when they stumped for him in 2006, leading him to stay on the sidelines in the endorsement game.

Sen. Sherrod Brown (D-Ohio), whose home state played an important role in the 2004 general election, said he may yet make an endorsement before the March primary, but he wants to hear more from Hillary Clinton and Obama on free trade and jobs.

In the House, Clinton has secured 72 endorsements; Obama has 44, and Edwards has 15. That leaves 100 or so Democratic House members who have yet to choose sides.

In D.C., an Endorsement And a Crowd for Obama

OBAMA, *From A1*

extraordinary gifts of leadership," Edward Kennedy said in a speech with lofty comparisons of Obama to his brother and pointed responses to criticism of the Illinois senator. "I am proud to stand here today and offer my help, my voice, my energy and my commitment to make Barack Obama the next president of the United States."

Obama told supporters they could help write "the next great American story."

"Someday we can tell our children that this was the time when we healed our nation," he said to applause and screams.

The university said the crowds spilled over to several places on the campus, including a post-rally event outdoors at which Obama and Edward Kennedy made an appearance.

Some professors suspended classes, opting to turn on televisions so students could watch the event, a university spokeswoman said.

Other students simply ditched classes, and workers took the day off and brought their children along. Retirees and others braved the January cold as they lined up waiting for the arena's doors to open. Students began queuing up as early as 5 a.m. for the rally, which started shortly after noon, the school reported.

The crowd inside the arena represented a broad swath of races, ages and religions. Eager 17-year-olds talked about their plans to vote for Obama in the primary — the law permits it in Maryland and Virginia as long as they are 18 by November. And some in their 60s recalled the inspiration they drew from another Kennedy in their youth.

For decades, candidates have strived for comparisons to John F. Kennedy, but yesterday his relatives bestowed that legacy to the 46-year-old Obama.

Edward Kennedy rebutted some of the criticism of Obama by his main rival for the Democratic nomination, Sen. Hillary Rodham Clinton, and her husband, former president Bill Clinton — that he lacks the experience to be president and that he has not been consistent in his opposition to the war in Iraq.

"I know he's ready to be president on Day One," Kennedy said, borrowing a description the New York senator often applies to herself.

The endorsement by Kennedy, the Democratic Party's leading liberal, gave a boost to Obama eight days before the Super Tuesday primaries, when 22 states and a U.S. territory will vote. The Clintons had tried hard to persuade Kennedy to remain neutral; the Massachusetts senator called Hillary Clinton on Sunday to tell her of his decision.

At the rally, Kathleen Kilpatrick, 65, a retired bus driver, wrapped her coat a little tighter and said, "I can't remember this much excitement or energy." She has lived in the District for nearly 40 years.

"The main thing is, this is history for us as a people," said Kilpatrick, who, like Obama, is black. "And today, the Kennedys played such a big part in political history."

Doug Kendall, 43, said he pulled his 8-year-old daughter, Miracle, out of Stoddert Elementary School to attend the event. "I wanted to have Miracle be inspired by Obama," he said. "I always wished I had seen President Kennedy. I wanted to give her a chance."

"To have the experience you didn't have," Miracle chimed in.

Howard University students Ashleigh Hairston and Monique Holmes and recent graduate Askale Shiteraw wore matching T-shirts bearing Obama's face and the words "Obama for Your Mama." They posed for photos with strangers impressed by their attire.

"We bought them . . . yesterday," said Hairston, 21, of Seattle. "I said these will be perfect for the rally."

At 11:30 a.m., officials announced that the arena was filled to capacity, prompting moans from the hundreds still standing in the cold. University security guards instructed people to go across the street to a makeshift overflow room at the Mary Graydon Center. About a third of the crowd refused to move, however, hoping officials would reconsider.

Inside Graydon, two small televisions were set up on carts as about 500 people squeezed into the room.

A few families and dozens of students grabbed chicken nuggets and fries from a stand in the corner. A handful of students sat at a table watching a CNN feed of the rally on a computer. Some did homework, reading textbooks or writing in their notebooks.

The overflow room got so crowded that officials directed more people down the quadrangle to the library, where people crowded around five televisions, including one screen that offered no sound.

"Lots of people were skipping class, and most of the government classes were canceled today," said Nicole Bazik, 20, an AU sophomore in Graydon who had rushed over from her child psychology class after her professor ended the day early because so few students were present.

The Secret Service set up another rally site at an outdoor amphitheater, where Kennedy and Obama treated the frozen faithful to a small second rally all their own.

"My daughter is in school in South Carolina, and she just voted for him, so I took a serious look," said Jeanne Fitzpatrick, 57, of the District, who was among those outside. She recently changed the political signs in her yard. "I had been a Hillary supporter until the past few weeks," she said.

Kennedy sympathized with those in the shivering crowd, describing his childhood as the youngest of nine.

"Whenever we had a crowd, I was always put on the outside," Kennedy said. "So, I love you. When we have Barack Obama as president, everyone will be on the inside."

Staff writer Petula Dvorak contributed to this report.

Edward Kennedy, along with Caroline Kennedy and Patrick Kennedy, announced his support for Barack Obama at an American University rally in Washington, D.C. At a subsequent Obama rally, Kennedy said, "I ask each and every one of you to do for Barack Obama what you did for John F. Kennedy and Robert Kennedy."

ALSO IN 2008

Caroline Kennedy wrote a January 27 New York Times *editorial about Obama titled "A President Like My Father."*

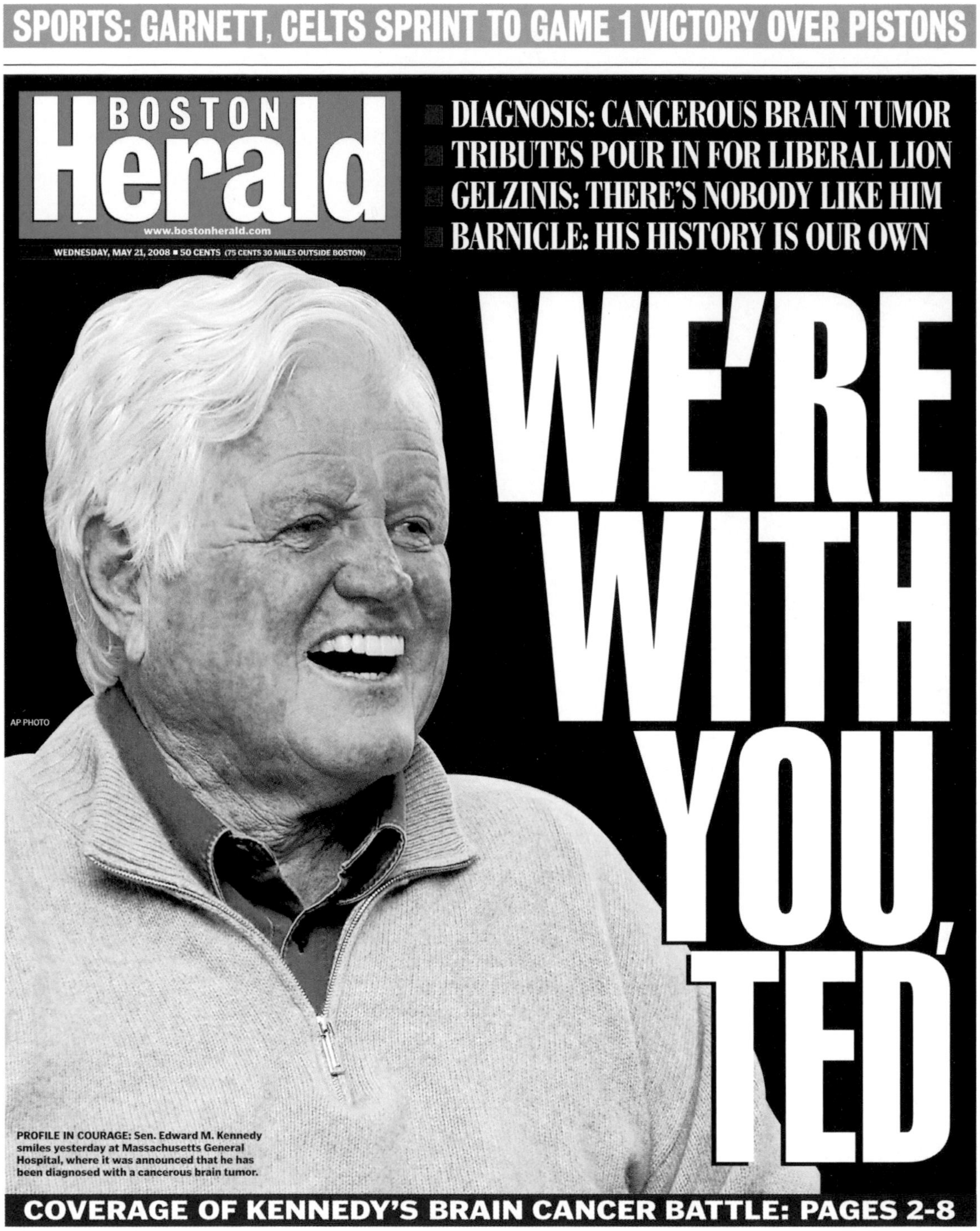

SPORTS: GARNETT, CELTS SPRINT TO GAME 1 VICTORY OVER PISTONS

BOSTON Herald
www.bostonherald.com
WEDNESDAY, MAY 21, 2008 ■ 50 CENTS (75 CENTS 30 MILES OUTSIDE BOSTON)

DIAGNOSIS: CANCEROUS BRAIN TUMOR
TRIBUTES POUR IN FOR LIBERAL LION
GELZINIS: THERE'S NOBODY LIKE HIM
BARNICLE: HIS HISTORY IS OUR OWN

WE'RE WITH YOU, TED

AP PHOTO

PROFILE IN COURAGE: Sen. Edward M. Kennedy smiles yesterday at Massachusetts General Hospital, where it was announced that he has been diagnosed with a cancerous brain tumor.

COVERAGE OF KENNEDY'S BRAIN CANCER BATTLE: PAGES 2-8

After suffering a seizure at home, Kennedy was taken from Cape Cod Hospital to Massachusetts General, where doctors discovered a malignant brain tumor.

Inside Today: The Latest Issue Of Mystic Country, Your Guide To Eastern Connecticut

The Day

theday.com
Chat > Connecticut Sun Coach Mike Thibault will be online today from 2 to 4 p.m. to answer your questions.

WEDNESDAY, MAY 21, 2008, NEW LONDON
VOL. 127, No. 325 32 PAGES **50 CENTS**

Kennedy news brings deep sadness to D.C.

Senate giant's illness could leave a major void on the national stage

By **PETER S. CANELLOS**
The Boston Globe

Washington — News about the Kennedys has so often come in shocking bursts, such as plane crashes and gunfire, that Tuesday's revelation that the senior senator from Massachusetts is suffering from a deadly illness had a quiet poignancy all its own.

Days when Democrats worried that an assassin might try to remove the last Kennedy brother have long since receded, and Ted Kennedy carries a new image as the Senate's indefatigable warrior. So it was a surprise that something as ordinary as cancer would be what slows down Kennedy's relentless drive to promote liberal causes, build coalitions, and pass legislation.

ANALYSIS

And yet, as many grimly noted, Kennedy is 76, and brain cancer is often deadly. So there was profound sadness throughout the Capitol. Democratic senators gathering for their weekly policy lunch said a prayer. Republicans at their weekly lunch described a deep feeling of sorrow.

Many spoke of how Kennedy's

See **KENNEDY** *page* **A3**

SEE RELATED STORIES ON **A3, A5**

'Obviously it's tough news for any son to hear. He's comforted by the fact that his dad is such a fighter, and if anyone can get through something as challenging as this, it would be his father.'

Robin Costello, a spokeswoman for U.S. Rep. Patrick Kennedy, D-R.I.

Sen. Edward M. Kennedy, D-Mass., smiles as he sits with his daughter, Kara Kennedy, in a family room at the Massachusetts General Hospital in Boston on Tuesday afternoon after it was announced earlier in the day that Kennedy has been diagnosed with a brain tumor.

STEPHAN SAVOIA/AP

Kennedy's close Senate friend, Dodd takes news especially hard

STEPHEN CROWLEY/The New York Times

Sen. Chris Dodd, D-Conn., talks about his friend and colleague, Sen. Edward Kennedy, on Capitol Hill in Washington on Tuesday after it was announced that Kennedy has a malignant brain tumor.

By **TED MANN**
Day Staff Writer

For a man much in love with words, a single silent photo seemed to speak for Chris Dodd on Tuesday afternoon.

This was after the senator's usually stentorian voice had failed him, dissolving into something close to tears, as Dodd declared himself "very confident" that his friend, Sen. Edward M. Kennedy, would survive the brain cancer doctors have diagnosed.

"He's a strong guy and has great heart, and we're confident he's going to be back here," Dodd said of Kennedy, the man he calls his "brother" in the U.S. Senate.

But Dodd's lip trembled as he spoke, and as a press conference broke up in the Capitol hall, a photographer captured him, eyes downcast and lips slightly apart, with the arm of the majority leader, Sen. Harry Reid, D-Nev., draped over one shoulder.

There are likely few colleagues clos-

See **DODD** *page* **A5**

Scouts Hope DOT Will Wake Up And Smell The Coffee

New rules could stop Labor Day tradition of free roadside drinks

By **LEE HOWARD**
Day Staff Writer

After 25 years of serving motorists around the clock during Labor Day weekend at the Interstate 95 weigh stations in Waterford, Merton W. Ferguson is ready to pull the plug on free coffee and doughnuts.

New Department of Transportation rules requiring groups using state highway stops to supply their own electricity and water — and to suspend operations overnight, when Ferguson said motorists need free coffee most — have made it difficult to conduct fundraisers there.

"We can't do it under those conditions — we'd have to quit," said Ferguson, longtime organizer of the free coffee stop for Boy Scout Troop 24 in Niantic, which he serves as a scoutmaster assistant.

"Can we still do it? Maybe, but I doubt it," said J. William Brubaker, scoutmaster of Troop 66 in Niantic, which also takes part in the effort.

The problem, Ferguson said, is that suspending free coffee between 9 p.m. and 6 a.m. would mean spending hours packing up and setting up supplies and equipment each of the four days the troop holds the free-coffee event. To provide its own electricity, the troop would have to run a generator all day.

Ferguson said the exterior electrical outlets were installed in August 2002 "specifically for our coffee stop usage."

Ferguson suggested in a letter to the DOT that the Boy Scouts pay a fee for using the on-site electricity. But Jeffrey J. Wilson, transportation maintenance director for the Bureau of Engineering and Highway Operations, did not respond to the idea in a February letter to Ferguson.

"I am disappointed with your decision ... for not being able to comply with the few regulations set forth regarding this activity," Wilson said in a letter to that referred to nine different

See **DOT** *page* **A8**

Campaign 2008

AL BEHRMAN/AP

Far left, *Sen. Hillary Rodham Clinton, D-N.Y., acknowledges supporters during her Kentucky primary victory rally in Louisville, Ky., Tuesday evening.*

Left, *Sen. Barack Obama, D-Ill., speaks to supporters at a rally in downtown Des Moines, Iowa, on Tuesday, where he declared himself "within reach" of the Democratic nomination. Obama posted an easy victory in Tuesday's Oregon primary. See story on* **A4**.

KEVIN SANDERS/AP

A celebration of 40 years of saving 'special places'

Avalonia Land Conservancy takes stock on anniversary

By **JUDY BENSON**
Day Staff Writer

WALKING ONE OF THE MAIN TRAILS through the Pine Swamp Wildlife Corridor in Ledyard on Monday, Anne Pearson caught the call of a prairie warbler, and clusters of white buds on a waist-high shrub captured her passing glance.

"The blueberries are going to be good this year," she said, cradling a cluster in her cupped hand.

The 317-acre Pine Swamp corridor, comprising several parcels pieced together over the last decade, is the largest owned by one of the region's oldest land trusts, the Avalonia Land Conservancy, and is the portion of its 2,640 acres Pearson knows best.

During a visit to the site with Mike Goodwin, like Pearson a volunteer steward of the Pine Swamp property, she pointed out the sand mounds where turtles nest, the glacial moraines that distinguish one of the hillsides, the evidence of the land's former use as a gravel mine, and the rare ladyslippers flowering in a hidden corner near one of the ponds.

"This is a pretty interesting place, for people with a variety of interests, if you're into rocks and geology, if you're a birder, or if you're into fishing," said Pearson, who figures she visits about twice a month. "Every time you come here there's something new, something different."

As the Avalonia Land Conservancy celebrates its 40th anniversary at its annual meeting tonight,

See **AVALONIA** *page* **A3**

INSIDE TODAY

NEWS

Quake Leaves Millions Homeless
Eight days after a massive, deadly earthquake, China begins to grapple with what to do with as many as 5 million homeless. **A2**

Cooking Oil In Big Demand
Restaurants from California to Kansas are reporting thefts of old cooking oil by rustlers who are refining it into biofuel. **A4**

WEATHER

Not Much Improvement
Today, mixed clouds and sun, chance of a shower. High 58. Thursday, variable cloudiness, chance of a shower. High 57. **B8**

INDEX

Business C7
Calendar B2
Classified D5
Comics D4
Daybreak D1
Editorials A6
Movies D2
Nation A4
Obituaries B4
Police logs B2
Region B1
Sports C1
State B5
Television D3
World A2

www.theday.com

Within days of returning from the hospital in May, Kennedy competed in the annual Figawi regatta. Kennedy and the crew on his sailboat, including wife Vicki and sons Edward Jr. and Patrick, finished second. The following month Kennedy underwent successful brain surgery to remove the tumor.

Also in 2008

An ailing Fidel Castro resigned as president of Cuba.

AUGUST 25, 2008
SENATOR EDWARD KENNEDY
ADDRESSED DEMOCRATIC NATIONAL CONVENTION

Kennedy's ill health did not prevent him from attending his final convention, where he said, "This November the torch will be passed again to a new generation of Americans." At Coretta Scott King's funeral in 2006, Ethel Kennedy, Robert Kennedy's widow, leaned over to Senator Barack Obama and whispered similarly, "The torch is being passed to you," Newsweek *reported.*

CAPE COD TIMES

The Cape and Islands' Daily Newspaper

capecodONLINE.com

YANKEE STADIUM FAREWELL
SPORTS B1

HIGH TECH TOOLS FOR SCHOOL
Business C1

Vol. 72, No. 206 — TUESDAY, AUGUST 26, 2008 — 75 cents

INSIDE

AMPHIBIOUS VEHICLE OFFERS TRIP TO THE '60s

David Tubman has been turning heads since he restored a 1965 "Amphicar" and began visiting ponds across the Cape.

Cape & Islands /A3

NATION & WORLD /A8

Latest tropical storm bears down on Haiti

Gustav is expected to make an eventual turn toward Florida, which is still reeling from being drenched by Tropical Storm Fay.

NEW ENGLAND /A9

Petition will challenge voiding of 1913 law

An effort has been launched to restore a law that bans the marriage of gay couples from out of state. If enough signatures are obtained the question will appear on the ballot in November 2010.

WEATHER

Sunny, with highs in the 70s. /B8

TAKE NOTE

VOTERS FACE DEADLINE FOR STATE PRIMARY

Massachusetts residents who intend to vote in the Sept. 16 state primary must be registered to vote by the close of business tomorrow. Secretary of State William Galvin says registrars in city and town halls will be open until 8 p.m. to accommodate late registrants. U.S. citizens, residents of Massachusetts and anyone who will be at least 18 years old on or before primary day are eligible to register.

INDEX

Advice	C6
Arts & Entertainment	B7
Business	C1
Cape & Islands	A3
Comics/Crossword	C5
Movies	B7
New England	A9
Nation & World	A8
Obituaries	C7
Opinion	A10
Television	B6

ELECTION 2008 — DEMOCRATIC NATIONAL CONVENTION

Kennedy: 'The hope rises again, and the dream lives on.'

RON EDMONDS/ASSOCIATED PRESS

"Nothing is going to keep me away from this special gathering tonight," said Sen. Edward Kennedy, addressing the Democratic National Convention in Denver.

Resolute senator electrifies convention

BY DAVID ESPO
THE ASSOCIATED PRESS

DENVER – Ailing and aging, Sen. Edward M. Kennedy issued a ringing summons to fellow Democrats to rally behind Barack Obama's pioneering quest for the White House last night in a poignant opening to a party convention in search of unity for the fall campaign.

"Barack will finally bring the change we need," seconded Obama's wife, Michelle, casting her husband – bidding to become the first black president – as a leader with classic American values.

She pledged he would end the war in Iraq, revise a sputtering economy and extend health care to all.

Democrats opened their four-day convention in the shadow of the Rocky Mountains as polls underscored the closeness of the race with Republican John McCain. And there was no underestimating the challenges confronting Obama.

He faces lingering divisions from a fierce battle with Hillary Rodham Clinton for the nomination, tough ads by McCain and his Republican allies, and a reminder that racism, too, could play a role.

"There are people who are not going to vote for him because he's black," said James Hoffa, president of the Teamsters union. "And we've got to hope that we can educate people to put aside their racism and to put their own interests No. 1."

Kennedy and Obama's wife were the bookends of an evening that left the delegates cheering, one representing the party's past, the other its present.

"The work begins anew, the hope rises again, and the dream lives on," Kennedy said in a strong voice, reprising the final line of a memorable 1980 speech that brought a different convention to its feet. The

see DEMOCRATS, page 12

CAPE BLOGGERS POST FROM THE CONVENTION

Follow the Democratic National Convention this week with Times' bloggers in Denver at **www.capecodline.com/dnc.** *And read along next week for dispatches from the Republican National Convention in St. Paul.*

Eric Turkington is a delegate to the Democratic National Convention and is an elected state representative for the Barnstable, Dukes and Nantucket district of Cape Cod.

Kate Singletary is a regional organizer of Massachusetts for Barack Obama, coordinator of Cape and Islands for Barack Obama and an elected delegate to the DNC.

GHOSTS OF NOMINEES PAST ROAM CONVENTION

Losing presidential candidates stay mostly in the background. **/A2**

PAUL SANCYA/ASSOCIATED PRESS

Michelle Obama pledged last night that her husband would end the war in Iraq, revise a sputtering economy and extend health care to all.

U.S. plan would slow ships to protect right whales

By MARY ANN BRAGG
mbragg@capecodonline.com

A federal plan to help restore the endangered North Atlantic right whale population in waters along the East Coast took a step forward yesterday.

National Oceanic and Atmospheric Administration officials released their final analysis on five options to implement the plan, which includes slower ship speeds and use of shipping routes that avoid whale grounds.

An analysis of what would happen if no changes were made was also considered, according to federal documents.

North Atlantic right whales migrate along the East Coast, using New Eng-

see WHALES, page 7

NEW ENGLAND AQUARIUM

A proposed federal plan would help protect right whales, like the one that washed ashore in 1999 in Wellfleet.

State agency cites TLT pattern of 'misleading' bids

By AARON GOUVEIA
agouveia@capecodonline.com

FALMOUTH – TLT Construction Corp. – the general contractor for the Falmouth High School building project – has a history of lying to procure publicly funded jobs, according to state officials.

Last week, the state Division of Capital Asset Management banned TLT from bidding on any public construction projects for the next 18 months. In a letter to TLT dated Aug. 20, the state agency – which certifies all general contractors in the state – claims TLT lied about completion dates on three separate projects and failed to include necessary information about pending lawsuits and fines.

"DCAM's investigation reveals that TLT engages in a pattern of repeatedly providing misleading and ambiguous information, or simply omitting infor-

see CONTRACTOR, page 6

THE GAMES BEGIN
Flores nets Dems endorsement for UC president in first day of campaign. *3*

LIN CARRIES CRIMSON TO TWO HOME WINS
JUNIOR POSTS 54 POINTS IN TWO-GAME STRETCH. *11*

NBER SAYS U.S. IN RECESSION
Economy has been in a recession since Dec. 2007, according to the Cambridge-based think thank. *7*

The Harvard Crimson

THE UNIVERSITY DAILY SINCE 1873 | TUESDAY, DECEMBER 2, 2008 | CAMBRIDGE, MASSACHUSETTS

Harvard Awards Kennedy Honorary Degree

RAQUEL RODRIGUEZ—CRIMSON PHOTOGRAPHER

By LAUREN D. KIEL
CRIMSON STAFF WRITER

Senator Edward M. Kennedy '54-'56, the liberal lion who has represented Massachusetts for nearly a half century and was diagnosed with brain tumor in May, received an honorary degree from Harvard at a convocation ceremony in Sanders Theatre yesterday afternoon.

Over 50 years after he graduated from the College with a degree in Government, the youngest member of the famous political family was honored for his lifetime commitment to public service.

"I hope that in all the time since then I have lived up to the chance Harvard gave me," Kennedy said after he received a doctorate of laws from University President Drew G. Faust.

Any fears the senator may have had were likely assuaged yesterday by the words of praise from the ceremony's speakers and multiple standing ovations he received from the packed theatre.

"He's one of a kind," Senator John F. Kerry, who has been Kennedy's colleague for 24 years, said in a brief interview after the ceremony. "It's a privilege to serve with him."

Kennedy was originally scheduled to receive the honor during Commencement last spring in a surprise announcement that came two weeks after the senator was diagnosed with the malignant brain tumor.

See KENNEDY Page 4

FROM THE CEREMONY

RAQUEL RODRIGUEZ—CRIMSON PHOTOGRAPHER

THE GUEST LIST *Left: Senator Edward Kennedy pauses for reflection during his speech. Kennedy, who is battling a brain tumor, was given an honorary degree yesterday at Sanders Theater. Top Right: Senator Kennedy and his wife, Victoria Reggie Kennedy, wave to the crowd. Middle Right. Yo-Yo Ma '76 gives a stirring performance on his cello. Bottom Right: Senator Kennedy shares a laugh with University President Drew G. Faust.*

Students Protest Jan. 20 Exams

Petition seeks make-up option for finals scheduled for inauguration day

By ANITA B. HOFSCHNEIDER
CRIMSON STAFF WRITER

For Ryan D. Zampardo, a senior in Mather House, the first difficulty in attending the upcoming presidential inauguration is getting a ticket. A Democrat from Michigan, he has contacted his local representative in Congress but has not yet received a response.

But even if he succeeds, he will face a possibly more difficult situation than national politics: January 20, the day of the inauguration, is in the middle of the College's final exam period, and Zampardo happens to have a test that day, one that counts for 40 percent of his grade for the class and may prevent him from witnessing a significant moment in American history.

The class?

Government 1540: "The American Presidency."

Over 2,000 undergraduates are set to sit for exams on January 20 for almost 40 different classes. Several of them who hoped to go down to Washington, D.C. for the inauguration have had to make different plans.

For some, these different plans include resigning to remain on campus and watch the recaps later that night. For others, however, different plans means taking action.

On November 18, the day after he saw the final exam schedule, Jason Y. Shah '11 formed the Facebook group "Petition for Make-Ups of Harvard College Exams on Inauguration Day 2009," and within a week, the group grew to over 250 members. That day, working with Shah, Tanuj D. Parikh '09 created an online petition of the same name. The petition now has almost 600 electronic signatures.

In addition to the Facebook group and the petition, Shah and Parikh have been collaborating with other students to speak with professors and work with the Undergraduate Council to resolve the issue favorably before winter break. Last night, the UC passed a position paper advocating that students who have proof that they are attending the inauguration should be eligible for make-up exams on the Sunday before the inauguration. It will be circulated to different administrators.

"Through our efforts, we hope to

See EXAMS Page 7

Study Examines AIDS Casualties

By ANITA B. HOFSCHNEIDER
CONTRIBUTING WRITER

An estimated 330,000 people died as a result of the South African government's lack of implementation of a "timely and feasible" antiretroviral treatment program between 2000 and 2005, according to a study by Harvard researchers published yesterday in the Journal of Acquired Immune Deficiency Syndromes.

The study, conducted by Pride Chigwedere, a graduate of the Harvard School of Public Health, and four other researchers from the school, also found that the infection of 35,000 newborns with HIV could have been prevented with widespread use of ARV drugs.

In total, the number of "person-years"—the number of years that people would have lived with ARV treatments—lost by the South African government is estimated at 3.8 million.

ARV drugs are accepted therapy for HIV/AIDS in the global scientific community.

"When antiretroviral drugs are given in combination, HIV replication and immune deterioration can be delayed, and survival and quality of life improved," according to the World Health Organization.

But the government of former South African president Thabo Mbeki, who succeeded Nelson Mandela in 1999, argued that ARV drugs were dangerous and ineffective. Mbeki's organization restricted

See AIDS Page 6

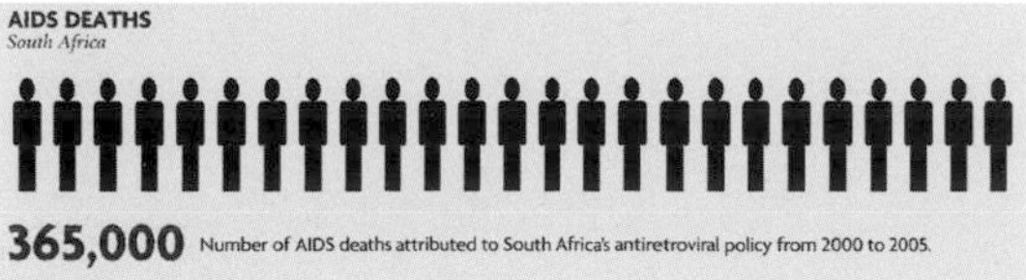
AIDS DEATHS
South Africa
365,000
Number of AIDS deaths attributed to South Africa's antiretroviral policy from 2000 to 2005.

Four Students Win Marshalls

By SOFIA E. GROOPMAN
CONTRIBUTING WRITER

A crossword-puzzle whiz, an activist for human rights in Latin America, a budding neuropsychologist, and an aspiring scholar of contemporary China comprise the four Harvard seniors rewarded Marshall Scholarships for the two academic years following graduation. Kyle A. Mahowald '09, John M. Sheffield '09, Emma Y. Wu '09, and Andrew C. Miller '09 all received the prestigious scholarship, which will fund two years of study for a graduate level degree at any university in the United Kingdom.

Harvard's triumph in racking four scholarships marks a significant surge from years past. No more than two Harvard students have won over the past five years.

Nationally, up to 40 recent American undergraduates are granted the scholarship every year. All applicants must have a minimum GPA of 3.7.

Mahowald, an English concentrator, plans to study linguistics at Oxford University. "I'm interested in words and language," said the Winthrop House resident, who was the youngest cruciverbalist to ever publish a puzzle in the Sunday New York Times.

Sheffield, a social studies concentrator, said that he was motivated to apply for what he called "a really great scholarship" because it was "a way to get to Oxford to study applied statistics."

Sheffield additionally plans to study political science in his second year abroad and come back to the U.S. for a Ph.D. in that field.

Sheffield found out he had received the scholarship only a day after his interview in Atlanta.

"My flight was delayed in Baltimore so I showed up at Harvard, sleep deprived and angry that I had to spend time in Baltimore," Sheffield said. "It felt like the beginning of a horror movie—trapped in a hotel in Baltimore. But then I came back and I walked up to my dorm room and I found out."

Wu, a linguistics and mind, brain, and behavior concentrator, who plans to study experimental psychology and cognitive neuropsychology at University College in London, said he relishes the "opportunity to dip my toes in research

KYLE A. MAHOWALD '09 | *ANDREW C. MILLER '09* | *JOHN M. SHEFFIELD '09* | *EMMA Y. WU '09*

See MARSHALL Page 7

INSIDE THIS ISSUE
VOLUME CXXXV, NO. 123
50 CENTS
CMM <3 Casablanca

REAL WORLD 2 | CORRECTIONS 2 | COMICS 2 | PUZZLE 2 | MENU 2

FOR BREAKING NEWS AND UPDATED STORIES, VISIT WWW.THECRIMSON.COM

TODAY'S FORECAST
PARTLY CLOUDY
HIGH: 44 | LOW: 27

Upon receiving his honorary degree, Kennedy said, "It was exactly one hundred years ago this September that my father entered Harvard College as a freshman—to be followed in the next generation by Joe, Jack, Bobby, and then by me."

ALSO IN 2008

Senator Barack Obama defeated Senator John McCain in the presidential election, becoming the nation's first African American president.

New York Governor David Paterson confirmed that Caroline Kennedy was seeking his appointment to the U.S. Senate seat vacated by Hillary Clinton, who would become secretary of state. The Senate seat was held by Robert Kennedy, Caroline's uncle, from 1965 until his assassination in 1968. (Pages at right from New York Daily News*)*

ALSO IN 2008

The social networking Web site Facebook hit the 100 million users mark and Google celebrated its tenth anniversary.

Caroline turned out to support Barack Obama at a rally in the Meadowlands last February.

GETTY

FAVORITE

Caroline Kennedy, from

Look at the face of Caroline Kennedy, and you'll see a woman of enormous and varied accomplishment — a lawyer, writer, wife and mother. Now the 51-year-old New Yorker is poised to expand that list to include U.S. senator as she seeks Hillary Clinton's soon-to-be-vacant seat.

Embracing public office marks a distinct about-face for Kennedy, who has been famous all her life but meticulously maintained her privacy. In spite of her being camera-shy and low-profile, the world has always been fascinated with the ex-President's daughter.

Kennedy's life in pictures — from her girlhood days to getting married (and shushing onlookers while she was at it) to commanding center stage during Barack Obama's bid for 1600 Pennsylvania Ave. (her old address, of course) — reveals a fascinating woman ready to follow her father and uncles into the family business.

Joe Dziemianowicz and Gina Salamone

▲Caroline smooches her dad during a quiet pre-White House moment in the summer of 1960. AFP

AP

AP

▲ A carefree Caroline (r.) marches off to her first day of school at the Convent of the Sacred Heart in New York with cousin Sydney Lawford in 1965. She hauls her own book bag; Jackie (behind her) sought to keep life normal for her famous family.

◀ A 6-year-old Caroline at the funeral for her dad. Her little brother, John Jr., salutes the casket in this famous Daily News photo, which also shows widow Jackie Kennedy and Caroline's uncles, Sen. Edward Kennedy on the left and Robert Kennedy on the right. Robert went on to hold the Senate seat Caroline is now seeking.

AP

▲Caroline graduates from Concord Academy in Massachusetts in 1975. Helping her celebrate are brother John (l.), grandmother Rose and uncle Ted Kennedy. After high school, Caroline got her bachelor's degree from Harvard and her J.D. from Columbia Law School, and even interned at the Daily News.

◀ The News covered Caroline — in a Carolina Herrera gown — giving photographers the "shush" signal at her 1986 Massachusetts wedding to Edwin Schlossberg. Ted Kennedy is at left.

DAILY NEWS

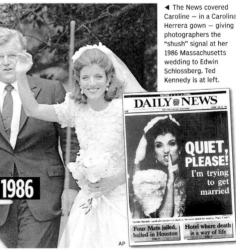

QUIET, PLEASE!
I'm trying to get married

Four Mets jailed, bailed in Houston

Hotel where death is a way of life

AP

DAUGHTER

JFK's little girl to Senate hopeful

RETNA

▲Caroline has juggled motherhood with her other activities (she has three kids, Rose, Tatiana and John, now 20, 18 and 15). Seven years after this scene was snapped, she edited the book "Profiles in Courage for Our Time." It celebrates what she calls "the most admirable of human virtues – courage."

AP

◀When John Kennedy Jr. (above, in 1996 with Ted and Caroline); his wife, Carolyn Bessette; and Carolyn's sister, Lauren, died in a 1999 plane crash off Martha's Vineyard, the tragedy was front-page news around the world. At l., Caroline attends a ceremony at sea.

RICHARD CORKERY/DAILY NEWS

▲Caroline married a man who shares her humanitarian interests. She joined her husband, Edwin Schlossberg, as he hosted the opening reception in Battery Park City in October for Mercy Corps' Action Center to End World Hunger.

ELISABETH A. ROBERT

◀A champion of education (she has helped raise more than $65 million for arts programs in NYC schools), Caroline was on hand for a performance by the Queens-Brooklyn Conservatory of Music.

REUTERS

▲In Los Angeles with Michelle Obama, cousin Maria Shriver (2nd from r.) and Oprah Winfrey, Caroline spoke at a rally for then-candidate Barack Obama. She said: "I am here today because I have never had a candidate who inspires me the way people say that my father inspired them. But I do now."

THE FIRST FAMILY OF DEMOCRATIC POLITICS

Caroline Kennedy's family tree has deep roots in American politics and government spanning three generations, with branches that reach all the way to the White House:

■**GRANDFATHER Joseph P. Kennedy (1888-1969)** The patriarch of the clan, he was founding chairman of the SEC and U.S. ambassador in London at the start of World War II. He groomed his sons for political careers.

■**FATHER John F. Kennedy (1917-1963)** The 35th President of the United States. Assassinated when Caroline was not quite 6 years old.

■**MOTHER Jacqueline Bouvier Kennedy (1929-1994)** A fierce guardian of her children, she became synonymous with culture, class and style as First Lady.

■**BROTHER John F. Kennedy Jr. (1960-1999)** Caroline's brother died tragically in a plane crash, months after deciding against a run for the Senate seat that Caroline is now pursuing.

■**UNCLES Sen. Ted Kennedy (D-Mass.)** A lion of the Senate, elected in 1962, Kennedy is fighting terminal brain cancer but hopes there will soon another Sen. Kennedy. **Robert F. Kennedy (1925-1968)** Dad's former attorney general, was elected in 1964 to the same Senate seat Caroline now seeks. Assassinated in 1968 while running for President. **Robert Sargent Shriver** The husband of Aunt Eunice, he was driving force behind the creation of the Peace Corps.

■**COUSINS Maria Shriver** First Lady of California, wife of the Governator, Arnold Schwarzenegger. **Kathleen Kennedy Townsend** Uncle Bobby's eldest, she's a former lieutenant governor of Maryland. **Joseph Kennedy 2nd** Bobby's son and a Massachusetts congressman from 1987 to 1999, Kennedy now runs a nonprofit providing discounted heating oil to low-income families. **Bobby Kennedy Jr.** An environmental lawyer, Bobby Jr. has emerged as one of Caroline's most vocal supporters. **Patrick Joseph Kennedy** A congressman from Rhode Island since 1995, he is Uncle Ted's youngest child.

Senator Edward Kennedy encouraged Caroline Kennedy to pursue the Senate seat for New York. However, awkward meetings with the media and confusion about her ambitions made critics wonder whether she was suited for political office.

SENATOR EDWARD KENNEDY COLLAPSED AFTER SEIZURE AT INAUGURATION LUNCHEON

Kennedy collapsed after a seizure during a post-inaugural luncheon in the U.S. Capitol's Statuary Hall. "We believe the incident was brought on by simple fatigue," said a doctor at Washington Hospital Center. (Clipping at right from The Seattle Times*)*

Kennedy seizure attributed to fatigue

INAUGURATION DIGEST |

WASHINGTON – Sen. Edward Kennedy, D-Mass., 76, who had surgery for a brain tumor in June, was hospitalized Tuesday but quickly reported feeling well after a seizure at a post-inauguration luncheon for President Obama.

Sen. Edward Kennedy was hospitalized.

"After testing, we believe the incident was brought on by simple fatigue," Dr. Edward Aulisi, chairman of neurosurgery at Washington Hospital Center, said. "He will remain ... overnight for observation."

Robert Byrd, 91, who was seated next to him at the lunch, grew emotional and left the room after his colleague was taken out, aides said. That led to rumors that Byrd, D-W.Va., might have suffered a health problem, but staff members said he was fine.

Medical experts said a seizure in a brain-cancer patient was not unusual and ordinarily had no serious consequences.

QUOTED

"I would be lying to you if I did not say that right now, a part of me is with him . . . And my prayers are with him and his family and Vicki."

—PRESIDENT BARACK OBAMA, *January 20, 2009*

TIMES UNION ■ Albany, New York   Friday, January 23, 2009 ■ A3

EMPIRE STATE

STATE EDITOR
Casey Seiler
454-5619
cseiler@timesunion.com

AROUND NY

Midlevel court upholds gay marriage benefits

ALBANY — A midlevel appeals court Thursday upheld New York's policy granting health benefits to spouses of gay state workers legally married outside the state.

Five Appellate Division justices, in two concurring decisions, rejected claims that the state Department of Civil Service exceeded its statutory authority in granting health insurance benefits to same-sex partners legally married elsewhere.

The justices upheld a 2008 ruling from a lower court in Albany, rejecting a challenge on behalf of four upstate taxpayers brought by attorney Brian Raum, who is also counsel for the Christian-based Alliance Defense Fund.

— *Associated Press*

Teen accused of attacks on 3 peers, teachers

BETHPAGE — A Long Island high school student is accused of attacking three fellow students and threatening to kill a teacher and striking another.

Police say they arrested Bethpage High School student Charles P. Sheridan on charges of assault, menacing, attempted robbery and robbery. Sheridan pleaded not guilty at his arraignment Thursday and was released without bail.

Police say the 17-year-old attacked one student Wednesday afternoon, striking him more than a dozen times. They say he pushed two other students, and stole $40 from one of them. Police say he then threatened a teacher and left another with an eye injury.

The school district says Sheridan has been suspended.

— *Associated Press*

Insurance agent, 71, accused of bank heist

PEEKSKILL — A 71-year-old insurance agent was arrested in his Rockefeller Center office and charged with a knifepoint bank robbery in the suburbs, police said Thursday.

The getaway car was a Lexus SUV, police said.

Edward Solomon of Ossining was accused of stealing $5,900 from the Trustco bank in a Peekskill shopping center last Friday, said Lt. Eric Johansen. He said Solomon used a knife to force an employee to let him into the teller area, where he rifled the cash registers.

Solomon officially retired two years ago as an agent for Prudential Financial Inc., but was allowed to continue working with his established clients, said Prudential spokesman Bob DeFillippo.

— *Associated Press*

Hospitals, doctors start digitizing patient records

BUFFALO — Hospitals and doctors in western New York have a new, electronic way to share patient records.

Officials say digitizing medical information is a goal of both Gov. David Paterson and President Barack Obama.

PATERSON

The new HEALTHeLINK clinical information exchange in western New York is a collaboration of hospitals and community organizations. Its goal is get every doctor in the region to participate.

Health authorities say allowing doctors to share information will save money by avoiding duplicative testing when patients are seen by multiple doctors, and save lives by reducing errors.

Paterson in March announced $105 million in grants to help develop a statewide system.

— *Associated Press*

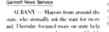

DON'T MISS

Full coverage of a crazy day of activity surrounding the Senate selection ... video of Michael Bloomberg talking (sort of) about Caroline Kennedy and the A.M. Roundup

Breaking political news throughout the day on Capitol Confidential: http://blogs.timesunion.com/capitol

Panel: 'Troopergate' showed flaws

State Commission of Investigation recommends merger

By RICK KARLIN
Capitol bureau

ALBANY — If you're looking for a new smoking gun in the 18-month-old and all-but-over travel records scandal dating from the Eliot Spitzer-Joseph L. Bruno era, you won't find it in Thursday's report from the state Commission of Investigation.

But while the commission offers no new insight on the affair, it does offer some provocative suggestions on how the state should handle future political investigations. It's also ignited angry words from the leaders of two other investigative agencies, which the report suggests folding into the commission.

The scandal erupted in 2007 after the Times Union raised questions about then-Republican Senate Majority Leader Joseph L. Bruno's use of a state helicopter for trips to New York City which included political fund raisers.

That prompted Bruno to accuse then-Gov. Spitzer of spying on him, leading to a months-long battle.

At least five groups investigated the affair: the state inspector general, Attorney General Andrew Cuomo, the Commission on Public Integrity, Albany County District Attorney David Soares and the Senate Investigations Committee.

The bottom line: No laws were found to be broken, but some of Spitzer's inner circle may have acted improperly by drawing the State Police into a political dust-up.

The state Commission of Investigation entered the fray late, saying at the outset it would investigate the investigators, and that's what it did. It found the whole affair quickly devolved into what Commission member George Friedman described as a "circus-like atmosphere."

"That's why we made this recommendation," said Friedman, referring to the commission's call for the governor to merge the inspector general and Commission on Public Integrity into his commission.

A merger, the report concluded, would save money and be more efficient, as well. "Clearly, had there been a single agency with broad jurisdiction, the matter could have been resolved in a more efficient and timely manner at much less cost to the taxpayer," the commis-

Please see REPORT A9 ▸

2 children die in Chinatown

MARY ALTAFFER/ASSOCIATED PRESS

EMERGENCY SERVICE personnel work at the scene Thursday of an accident on East Broadway in the Chinatown neighborhood of Manhattan. Authorities say two children were killed and another was seriously injured after a van mounted a sidewalk and struck them in the world-famous tourist area where sidewalks are often crowded with people.

Loan shark fed on victims

Inspector general cites $13,000 in loans; man sought sex, drugs

BY ROBERT GAVIN
Staff writer

ALBANY — A former state employee spent nine years moonlighting as a loan shark, at times seeking sex and drugs as repayment instead of cash, the state Inspector General's Office said Thursday.

Alan R. West, 47, a onetime customer service representative with the New York State Higher Education Services Corp., lent roughly $13,000 to nine colleagues between 1999 and 2008, according to a report from Inspector General Joseph Fisch's office.

West "victimized one borrower by soliciting sexual favors in lieu of $150 in interest payments," the report said. His targets made partial loan payments in the form of "burnables," the report said, adding it "appears in context to have been a reference to illegal drugs."

West resigned May 30, three days after he was suspended from his $37,469-a-year job. West's loans allegedly ranged from $20 to $3,000, with most arranged on the workplace e-mail system.

He began work at the Higher Education Services Corp. in the mail room in 1991.

The loans took place face-to-face, "usually at a secluded location in the HESC offices, such as in a stairwell or on the loading dock," the report said.

All of the borrowers said their requests were voluntary with no threats made, the report said.

The inspector general's office found West loaned one employee $3,000 with a biweekly 7 percent interest rate, which would equal an annual rate of 182 percent. He gave another worker $30 under the agreement the employee would give him $40 two weeks later, which would be a rate of 865 percent, the office said.

The case has been referred to Albany County District Attorney David Soares, whose office declined comment. At present, West faces no charges. Under state law, a person who seeks the equivalent of more than 25 percent annual interest without legal authority can be charged with felony usury.

A certainty: Kennedy withdraws

Reports from JFK daughter and governor vary about her exit from Senate consideration

By IRENE JAY LIU
Capitol bureau

In its final days, the two-month saga to pick a replacement for Hillary Rodham Clinton has devolved into a morass of innuendo, mudslinging and contradictory accounts from the camps of Caroline Kennedy and Gov. David Paterson.

Hours after Kennedy released a statement that she had withdrawn her name from consideration, an aide to Caroline Kennedy said Thursday that it was a "personal situation, not involving Sen. Ted Kennedy" that prompted her action.

Kennedy called the governor Wednesday, asking to be withdrawn from consideration, the aide said. The governor "graciously" suggested that Kennedy think about it for 24 hours before making her final decision. At the end of the conversation, the matter was still very much open, according to the aide.

In the early evening, the New York Post and The New York Times posted Web stories stating unequivocally that she had dropped out — news that created a scramble among Kennedy's press team and the governor's communications staff.

Between 10 and 11 p.m. Wednesday, Kennedy told the governor that she was no longer interested, the Kennedy aide said.

A source close to the governor disputed Kennedy's timeline of the events.

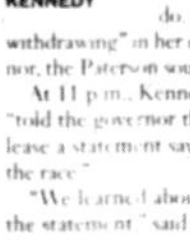

KENNEDY

According to the source, Kennedy's Wednesday call to Paterson included the notice she was feeling "overwhelmed" about her candidacy and asked the governor for 24 hours to decide what she wanted to do. "She never talked about withdrawing" in her conversation with governor, the Paterson source said.

At 11 p.m., Kennedy called Paterson and "told the governor that she was going to release a statement saying that she was still in the race."

"We learned about her decision through the statement," said the source, referencing Kennedy's statement of withdrawal released around midnight Thursday morning.

There were issues that were "potentially problematic" for her candidacy, but the source would not specify the nature of the issues.

Nearly identical quotes from sources "close to Paterson" turned up in a number of media outlets. In those stories, the sources also alleged Kennedy's candidacy was troubled by alleged tax matters, marital issues and problems involving a household employee; no direct evidence was provided.

Responding to the allegations, Kennedy spokesman Stefan Friedman said, "Caroline Kennedy withdrew her name for consideration from the United States Senate for personal reasons. Any statements to the contrary are false. The governor set up a fair and deliberative selection process. This kind of mudslinging demeans that process and all those involved."

The governor's press office released a statement Thursday afternoon calling Kennedy a "friend" and effectively contradicting the unnamed Paterson sources.

The statement said that none of the information gathered during the selection process "created a necessity for any candidate to withdraw. Any speculation to the contrary is both inaccurate and inappropriate."

▸ *Irene Jay Liu can be reached at 454-5081 or by e-mail at iliu@timesunion.com*

Mayors want options, taxing authority

Local leaders want aid, mandate relief, ability to raise more municipal revenues

By JAY GALLAGHER
Gannett News Service

ALBANY — Mayors from around the state, who annually ask the state for more aid, Thursday focused more on state help in raising money on their own and holding down expenses.

With the state facing a $15.4 billion deficit of its own, the chief executives of local governments urged lawmakers to give them more flexibility to both raise taxes and spend the money they have more efficiently.

New levies on motorists and cell-phone users, sales taxes on a broader array of services and reduced pension benefits for future employees were among the ideas embraced by many of the municipal chief executives, who were making their annual comments on the proposed state budget before the Legislature's fiscal committees.

"The combination of local aid, relief from state mandates and expanded revenue options will go a long way towards helping our struggling communities," said Cohoes Mayor John McDonald, who is president of the state Conference of Mayors.

Despite the state's financial problems, Paterson has proposed holding aid to most local governments steady, with the exception of New York City, from whom the governor wants to take $328 million in local aid. Mayor Michael Bloomberg called that unacceptable, especially since about 50 percent of all tax revenues the state collects comes from New York City residents and businesses, and the city sends about $12 billion more a year to Albany than it gets back in aid and services.

The biggest problem for towns in Paterson's budget plan is a proposed cut of 20 percent, or $59 million, in highway aid, Association of Towns Executive Director Jeffrey Haber told lawmakers.

MIKE GROLL/ASSOCIATED PRESS

NEW YORK Mayor Michael Bloomberg testifies Thursday before the Senate Finance and Assembly Ways and Means Committee.

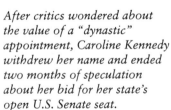

After critics wondered about the value of a "dynastic" appointment, Caroline Kennedy withdrew her name and ended two months of speculation about her bid for her state's open U.S. Senate seat.

QUOTED

"I informed Governor Paterson today that for personal reasons I am withdrawing my name from consideration for the United States Senate."

—CAROLINE KENNEDY,
January 22, 2009

SENATOR EDWARD KENNEDY ATTENDED WHITE HOUSE HEALTH CARE CONFERENCE

SPORTS: Friars fall to No. 11 Villanova Wildcats, 97-80. **C1**

MILD ARRIVES
Mostly cloudy but much milder today, with highs near 50; patchy fog tonight.
Forecast, B8

The Providence Journal
projo.com
FRIDAY
MARCH 6, 2009
75¢
Home Delivery 401.277.7600

A plan to put state panel at the center of sports disputes

But state Sen. John Tassoni says he is "getting hammered" over his idea to oversee recreation leagues.

BY TOM MOONEY
JOURNAL STAFF WRITER

You're the mother of 11-year-old Little Suzie who wants to make the town's mite football cheerleading squad. The problem, as you see it, is Suzie's coach. She wouldn't know talent if it hit her upside the head.

So you have words with Ms. Coach about Suzie's lack of participation. Next thing you know, Suzie's off the squad and you're stuck without recourse to right such an injustice.

Enter state Sen. John Tassoni Jr., a Democrat from Smithfield, who says it's time for some government oversight over youth recreational leagues to end the practices of favoritism and vindictiveness. Tassoni said several constituents approached him about the issue.

"My focus is on the leagues," said Tassoni yesterday. "Who's friends with who, people who get suspended and have no recourse. I think every parent is protective of their child if they think they are being railroaded and there is nowhere to go with it. I know a lot of people are complaining about how these rec leagues are being run. We need something to keep an eye of them."

So Tassoni has proposed legislation that would create a seven-member council appointed by the governor to lend some "transparency" to the workings of such sports leagues and to "increase access and improve [the] quality of youth sports programs."

The idea, Tassoni admitted yesterday on his drive back from a Boston television station to discuss his idea, isn't going over well.

"I'm getting hammered," he said.

SEE **SPORTS, A5**

Championing change

MCT / ZBIGNIEW BZDAK

President Obama and Massachusetts Sen. Edward M. Kennedy at yesterday's forum on health-care reform.

At a White House conference on health care, Sen. Edward M. Kennedy says, "this time, we will not fail."

BY JOHN E. MULLIGAN
JOURNAL WASHINGTON BUREAU

WASHINGTON — President Obama yesterday launched his campaign to overhaul the nation's medical system at a White House conference that featured expressions of support from across the industry and the political spectrum.

Mr. Obama declared after the half-day gathering of about 150 public officials, medical experts and business leaders from around the country that it had produced "a clear consensus that the need for health-care reform is here and now."

The gathering also featured an emotional welcome for one of the nation's most persistent champions of health-care reform, the ailing Sen. Edward M. Kennedy. There were hints, however, of battlelines forming among the dozens of interested groups represented at the event.

"Sir Edward Kennedy," Mr. Obama said to laughter as a beaming Kennedy entered the East Room, cane in hand, to a warm ovation — with his son, Rep. Patrick J. Kennedy, among those applauding. "That's the kind of greeting a knight deserves," said the president, referring to the honor

SEE **HEALTH CARE, A4**

'Substantial' doubt over GM's future

BY NICK BUNKLEY
THE NEW YORK TIMES

DETROIT — Auditors for General Motors, in one of the bleakest assessments yet of the automaker's prospects, said yesterday that the company's survival was in "substantial doubt" even if it received all $30 billion it hoped to borrow from the federal government.

The report by the auditing firm Deloitte & Touche also raised the possibility that GM could have to liquidate its operations if its loan request is denied.

GM's acknowledgment that it is perilously close to bankruptcy — its auditors made a similar announcement last fall — was not unexpected. But the report stirred

SEE **GM, A4**

Economic snapshot

- Investors fled Wall Street yesterday, driven by worries about the nation's big banks and General Motors Corp. The Dow fell 281.40, or 4.1 percent, to 6,594.44, its lowest close since April 1997. **Details, A11**
- A report released yesterday shows that 48 percent of the nation's homeowners who have a subprime, adjustable-rate mortgage are either behind on their payments or in foreclosure.
- Shares in Citigroup Inc. , once the nation's most powerful bank, yesterday traded at below $1 a share before closing at $1.02. The bank, which had a market capitalization of around $270 billion in 2007, is now valued at about $6.2 billion. (AP)

Bishop guilty in 2007 murder

A jury takes less than two hours to find convicted murderer Alfred "Freddie" Bishop guilty of killing Gabriel Medeiros.

BY TALIA BUFORD
JOURNAL STAFF WRITERS

WARWICK — Alfred "Freddie" Bishop sat with his cheek resting on his right fist as the jury read its verdict yesterday in Kent County Superior Court.

He'd heard it all before.

"Guilty," the foreman repeated to each of the seven counts lodged against Bishop for the 2007 murder of Gabriel Medeiros.

The victim's family quietly celebrated behind the prosecution

SEE **BISHOP, A5**

THE PROVIDENCE JOURNAL / BOB THAYER

Alfred "Freddie" Bishop as a jury finds him guilty of murder yesterday.

Days after the health care conference, the senator was honored at the Kennedy Center and was named a recipient of the Profile in Courage Award, with tribute to his work on health care reform.

CREATING A STICKY SITUATION

THE PROVIDENCE JOURNAL / BOB BREIDENBACH

Driver Alison Cumens, right, pushes her midget racer to a space in the Dunkin' Donuts Center. Helping her are crew members Colin Martin, left, and Sean Moyer.

For the first time in 50 years, auto racing comes to Providence — at The Dunk.

BY PETER C.T. ELSWORTH
JOURNAL STAFF WRITER

PROVIDENCE — Spilled popcorn and soda are a given at sports events.

But workers at the Dunkin' Donuts Center yesterday were busy deliberately spraying Cherry Coke syrup on the concrete floor as they prepared the arena to host Rhode Island's first professional auto races in 50 years.

Tonight and tomorrow night, more than 40 Three-Quarter Midgets will be tearing round the sticky track at speeds of up to 70 mph. Seven races are scheduled for each night: four qualifying heats, two consolation races and a main feature with 20 cars running 20 laps.

Racing fans can expect noisy thrills and spills. "When they tumble, they tumble good," said promoter Len Sammons standing in the infield yesterday. The drivers are well protected, however, and even minor injuries are rare, he said.

The 8-foot, 130-horsepower cars are open framed with their engines mounted next to the driver for inside weight. The outside tires are 2-inches bigger than the inside ones so they lean into the curves. Fans will look down on the action as the front seating sections at The Dunk have been folded up behind sand-filled barriers.

The state's last professional auto race featured TQ Midgets at the old Rhode Island Auditorium in 1959.

Race time is 7:30 both nights, with time trials starting tonight at 6:30.

pelsworth@projo.com / (401) 277-7403

'It was crazy that day' at Roger Williams school

Assistant principal Robert Perkins speaks out on the Dominican Republic flag incident.

BY LINDA BORG
JOURNAL STAFF WRITER

PROVIDENCE — As assistant principal Robert Perkins tells it, last Friday was a frustrating day at Roger Williams Middle School.

It began badly. Perkins was in the corridor when he saw three students racing down the hallway waving a Dominican flag, which got quite a response from other students who were celebrating Dominican Independence Day. Perkins took the flag away and told the boys that he wouldn't tolerate any behavior that would disrupt the school day. He told the students that he would keep the flag until

SEE **SCHOOL, A5**

QUOTED

"This is the cause of my life . . . it's always been deeply personal, because the importance of health care has been a recurrent lesson throughout most of my 77 years."

—SENATOR EDWARD KENNEDY, Newsweek, *July 27, 2009*

INSIDE TODAY

© 2009 Published daily since 1829
4 SECTIONS

Ask Amy	D6	Lifebeat Movies	D1
Bridge	D6	Lotteries	C4
Business	A9	Obituaries	B5
Classified	C6	People	D1
Comics	D7	Sports	C1
Crossword	D6	Television	D8
Editorial	B6	Today's events	D6
Legal ads	B2		

MARTINEAU SEEKS SENTENCE REDUCTION

Former House majority leader Gerard M. Martineau wants his jail sentence reduced and is basing his appeal on a Superior Court decision that found the state Constitution protects legislators from prosecution based on their votes or other legislative activities. **B1**

CALIF. COURT CONSIDERS GAY MARRIAGE BAN

A skeptical California Supreme Court hears arguments from lawyers seeking to overturn a constitutional amendment approved by voters last year that bans same-sex marriage. **A2**

LAFFEY NOT RUNNING

Former Cranston Mayor Stephen P. Laffey says he will not run for governor next year, while former U.S. Sen. Lincoln Chafee says he is "very, very seriously" considering entering the race. **B1**

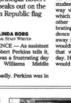

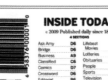

FAITHFUL WATCHMEN

If anything, the screen version of *Watchmen* as directed by Zack Snyder is too faithful to the graphic novel created by Dave Gibbons and Alan Moore. **D1**

June 12, 2009
Representative Patrick Kennedy Entered Treatment Facility

BUMMER
Rain and thunderstorms today with highs in the 70s; more rain tonight.
Forecast, B8

The Providence Journal

projo.com

FRIDAY
JUNE 12, 2009
$1.00
Home Delivery 401.277.7600

Kennedy decides to 'step away' for medical treatment

The congressman and his friends release few details.

BY JOHN E. MULLIGAN
JOURNAL WASHINGTON BUREAU

WASHINGTON — Rep. Patrick J. Kennedy, a public face of recovery from addiction since an automobile accident spurred him into rehabilitation three years ago, has entered an undisclosed medical facility for treatment.

Sean Richardson, a former aide to Kennedy who has remained a close friend, said the Rhode Island Democrat is out of Washington but not, strictly speaking, away from work because he is in continual contact with his congressional office and keeping track of such legislative priorities as health care.

Richardson said he could not spell out how long Kennedy will be at the out-of-town medical facility. But he hinted at a range: Kennedy will probably be gone for more than a few days, returning in time for the hoped-for debate on a national health-care overhaul later in the summer.

While close friends of Kennedy gave few details of what the congressman called a temporary "step away from my normal routine," they stressed that this chapter in his recovery was not prompted by any sort of accident, injury, or trouble with the law.

Three Kennedy intimates said in separate interviews that they either did not know or would not discuss whether he has had an episode of drinking or drug abuse.

"As Patrick's friend, I am very happy to see him prioritize his long-term health and recovery," said former Minnesota Republican Rep. Jim Ramstad, who spoke in a telephone interview after Kennedy issued a statement describing his decision in the most general terms.

Ramstad, a recovering alcoholic of long standing, has helped Kennedy on the road to sobriety since soon after the Rhode Island Democrat had a highly publicized car crash on Capitol Hill on May 5, 2006.

Ramstad and Dr. Ronald E. Smith,

SEE **KENNEDY, A4**

JOURNAL FILES
CONNIE GROSCH

Rep. Patrick Kennedy says he has "decided to temporarily step away from my normal routine to ensure that I am being as vigilant as possible in my recovery."

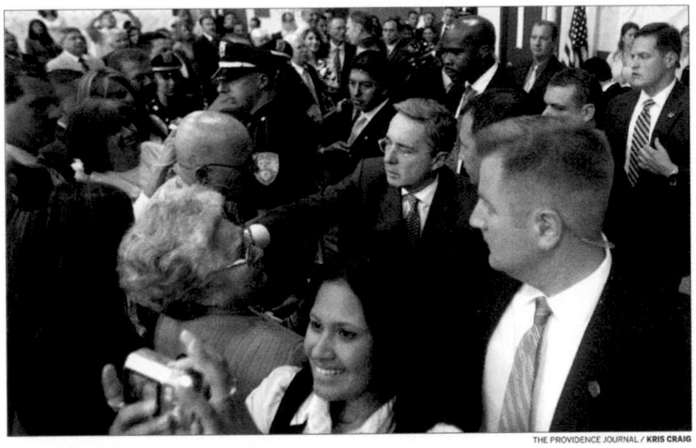

THE PROVIDENCE JOURNAL / **KRIS CRAIG**

Colombian President Alvaro Uribe Velez reaches into a crowd during an appearance at Central Falls High School where he addressed the region's Colombian community. It was the first visit to the state by a sitting president of Colombia.

A president in Central Falls

Supporters cheer as Colombian President Alvaro Uribe Velez enters the gymnasium at Central Falls High School on Thursday.

Colombian community gives a warm welcome to Uribe

BY TATIANA PINA
JOURNAL STAFF WRITER

CENTRAL FALLS — Andres Taborda, 16, and his aunt waited in the long line that snaked down Illinois Street on Thursday to hear Colombian President Alvaro Uribe Velez speak at Central Falls High School.

Andres attends St. Raphael Academy, in Pawtucket, where his family lives. He was born here but his parents emigrated from Colombia, and family conversation over coffee after Sunday Mass often focuses on the president of their homeland.

Uribe has been widely credited with transforming the nation as his security policies have weakened guerillas, made paramilitaries less active and reduced crime. In office since 2002, he enjoys a 70 percent approval rating. He is in Rhode Island this week to address the annual meeting of the U.S. Conference of Mayors, which opens Friday in Providence.

Nothing was going to keep Andres Taborda from hear-

SEE **URIBE, A4**

U.S. CONFERENCE OF MAYORS

How plans for meeting unraveled

From the Obama administration to officials with the mayors' organization, everyone assumed the contract dispute between Providence and its firefighters would be resolved. They were all wrong.

BY JOHN E. MULLIGAN
JOURNAL WASHINGTON BUREAU

WASHINGTON — Three weeks ago, Providence Mayor David N. Cicilline and his colleagues from around the country were celebrating the kind of coup that local politicians dream about.

For a national convention built around President Obama's promise of jobs and money for their cities, the mayors had landed Vice President Joe Biden, more than a dozen top White House staff and Cabinet secretaries, and almost 100 of the federal bureaucrats who are dispensing a $787-billion antidote to the hardest times since the Great Depression.

The annual meeting of the U.S. Conference of Mayors was going to be an Obama "love fest," said Tom Cochran, the organization's longtime chief executive. "We had giant pictures of Barack Obama. We had the big flat-screen TV" to broadcast speeches by Biden, senior adviser Valerie Jarrett, Housing and Urban Development Secretary Shaun Donovan and other administration brass.

But with announcements from Cicilline and the White House last Friday, the love fest was off.

Under the threat of a firefighters' union picket line, the Obama administration sent regrets, not only from Biden, but also from

SEE **MEETING, A8**

THE PROVIDENCE JOURNAL / **FRIEDA SQUIRES**

Providence Firefighter Stephany Blackwell and others gather Thursday at the union hall to assemble picket signs.

ACLU takes issue with protester registration

BY RANDAL EDGAR
JOURNAL STAFF WRITER

PROVIDENCE — As if the protests and cancellations weren't enough, this weekend's U.S. Conference of Mayors gathering drew more unwanted attention Thursday when the Rhode Island Affiliate of the American Civil Liberties Union called on Mayor David N. Cicilline to stop using an online registration form for people who plan to protest or picket

SEE **PROTESTS, A6**

On the inside

- Without the presence of Obama administration officials, conference organizers are forced to revise the meeting's focus. **A8**
- Health-care costs, pension benefits and personnel assignments are among the key contract issues dividing the city and firefighters. **A8**
- An Boston-based advocacy group hopes to persuade the mayors to stop spending money on bottled water. **A6**

Traffic snarls foreseen in Rte. 195 change

The new section of Route 195 west will open next week and traffic officials warn drivers to expect disruptions.

BY BRUCE LANDIS
JOURNAL STAFF WRITER

PROVIDENCE — Governor Carcieri acknowledged yesterday that a major highway opening next week will make traffic worse, not better, for drivers entering the city from the eest on Route 195.

The change will shift westbound Route 195 traffic to a new section of highway providing a link to southbound Route 95. Officials say the arrangements for that switch, which will last for several months, will disrupt traffic, but they contend it's unavoidable because of the way construction has to be sequenced.

The governor said that the $610-million Route 195 relocation is a "hugely, hugely important project" that's worth the inconvenience, one that will improve the state's economy and make its capital city more attractive while making the highways safer and helping traffic flow better.

The governor said, though, that he looks forward to the fall, when the next phase of the pro-

SEE **RTE. 195, A4**

projoVIDEO

Video: The DOT is getting ready for phase three of the relocation of Route 195: opening the new 195 westbound to Route 95 south. For a sneak peak at the new highway, watch the video at projo.com/video

INSIDE TODAY

© 2009 Published daily since 1829
4 SECTIONS

Ask Amy	D8	Lifebeat Movies	D1
Bridge	D8	Lotteries	C2
Business	A9	Obituaries	B5
Classified	C6	People	D1
Comics	D10	Rhode Island	B1
Crossword	D8	Sports	C1
Editorial	B6	Television	D9
Legal ads	B2	Today's events	D8

The Providence Journal
SUMMERTIME FUND™

Mail your donation to
The Providence Journal
Summertime Fund
75 Fountain Street
Providence, RI 02902

REGULATING TOBACCO

The Senate approves giving the FDA sweeping powers over tobacco products, allowing the agency to limit the amount of nicotine in cigarettes, regulate how the products are advertised and require a graphic warning on each pack. **A2**

SWINE FLU A PANDEMIC

U.N. health officials formally declare the worldwide outbreak of swine flu a pandemic, meaning that the spread of the virus is considered unstoppable. **A2**

BESSETTE SENTENCED

Andrew T. Bessette, 18, is sentenced to a year in prison, 15 months of home confinement and 7 years of probation for a car crash that killed his 15-year-old cousin, Marissa Lorea. **B1**

Congressman Patrick Kennedy, the youngest son of Edward Kennedy, battled and sought treatment for alcoholism, bipolar disorder, and drug addiction.

A L S O   I N   2 0 0 9

Michael Jackson, regarded by many as the King of Pop and one of the most successful musicians in the world, died at the age of 50.

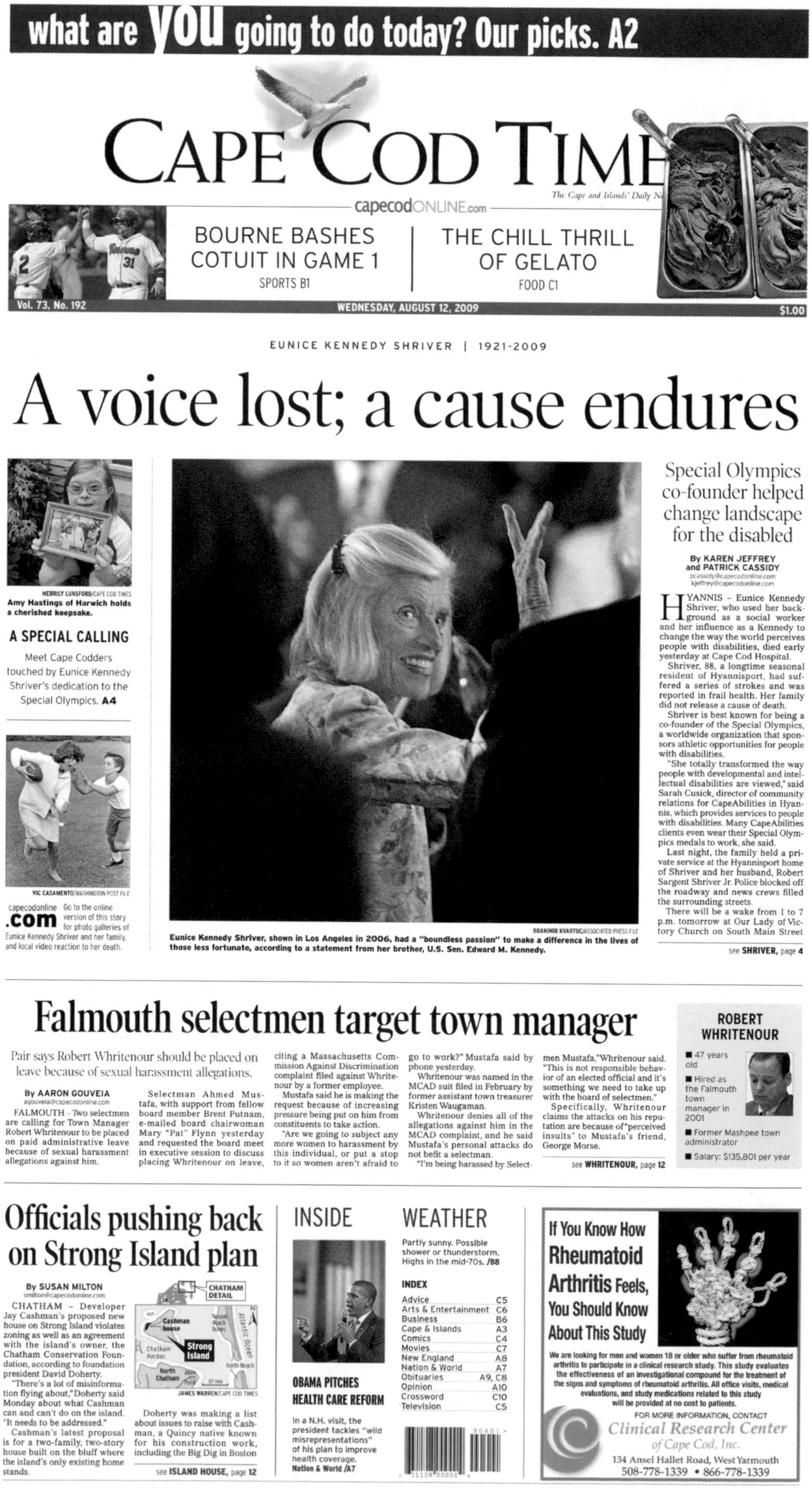

what are YOU going to do today? Our picks. A2

CAPE COD TIMES

The Cape and Islands' Daily N[...]

capecodONLINE.com

BOURNE BASHES COTUIT IN GAME 1
SPORTS B1

THE CHILL THRILL OF GELATO
FOOD C1

Vol. 73, No. 192 | WEDNESDAY, AUGUST 12, 2009 | $1.00

EUNICE KENNEDY SHRIVER | 1921-2009

A voice lost; a cause endures

MERRILY LUNSFORD/CAPE COD TIMES

Amy Hastings of Harwich holds a cherished keepsake.

A SPECIAL CALLING

Meet Cape Codders touched by Eunice Kennedy Shriver's dedication to the Special Olympics. **A4**

VIC CASAMENTO/WASHINGTON POST FILE

capecodonline .com Go to the online version of this story for photo galleries of Eunice Kennedy Shriver and her family, and local video reaction to her death.

BRANIMIR KVARTUC/ASSOCIATED PRESS FILE

Eunice Kennedy Shriver, shown in Los Angeles in 2006, had a "boundless passion" to make a difference in the lives of those less fortunate, according to a statement from her brother, U.S. Sen. Edward M. Kennedy.

Special Olympics co-founder helped change landscape for the disabled

By KAREN JEFFREY and PATRICK CASSIDY
pcassidy@capecodonline.com
kjeffrey@capecodonline.com

HYANNIS – Eunice Kennedy Shriver, who used her background as a social worker and her influence as a Kennedy to change the way the world perceives people with disabilities, died early yesterday at Cape Cod Hospital.

Shriver, 88, a longtime seasonal resident of Hyannisport, had suffered a series of strokes and was reported in frail health. Her family did not release a cause of death.

Shriver is best known for being a co-founder of the Special Olympics, a worldwide organization that sponsors athletic opportunities for people with disabilities.

"She totally transformed the way people with developmental and intellectual disabilities are viewed," said Sarah Cusick, director of community relations for CapeAbilities in Hyannis, which provides services to people with disabilities. Many CapeAbilities clients even wear their Special Olympics medals to work, she said.

Last night, the family held a private service at the Hyannisport home of Shriver and her husband, Robert Sargent Shriver Jr. Police blocked off the roadway and news crews filled the surrounding streets.

There will be a wake from 1 to 7 p.m. tomorrow at Our Lady of Victory Church on South Main Street

see **SHRIVER,** page **4**

Falmouth selectmen target town manager

Pair says Robert Whritenour should be placed on leave because of sexual harassment allegations.

By AARON GOUVEIA
agouveia@capecodonline.com

FALMOUTH – Two selectmen are calling for Town Manager Robert Whritenour to be placed on paid administrative leave because of sexual harassment allegations against him.

Selectman Ahmed Mustafa, with support from fellow board member Brent Putnam, e-mailed board chairwoman Mary "Pat" Flynn yesterday and requested the board meet in executive session to discuss placing Whritenour on leave, citing a Massachusetts Commission Against Discrimination complaint filed against Whritenour by a former employee.

Mustafa said he is making the request because of increasing pressure being put on him from constituents to take action.

"Are we going to subject any more women to harassment by this individual, or put a stop to it so women aren't afraid to go to work?" Mustafa said by phone yesterday.

Whritenour was named in the MCAD suit filed in February by former assistant town treasurer Kristen Waugaman.

Whritenour denies all of the allegations against him in the MCAD complaint, and he said Mustafa's personal attacks do not befit a selectman.

"I'm being harassed by Selectmen Mustafa," Whritenour said. "This is not responsible behavior of an elected official and it's something we need to take up with the board of selectmen."

Specifically, Whritenour claims the attacks on his reputation are because of "perceived insults" to Mustafa's friend, George Morse.

see **WHRITENOUR,** page **12**

ROBERT WHRITENOUR

- 47 years old
- Hired as the Falmouth town manager in 2001
- Former Mashpee town administrator
- Salary: $135,801 per year

Officials pushing back on Strong Island plan

By SUSAN MILTON
smilton@capecodonline.com

CHATHAM – Developer Jay Cashman's proposed new house on Strong Island violates zoning as well as an agreement with the island's owner, the Chatham Conservation Foundation, according to foundation president David Doherty.

"There's a lot of misinformation flying about," Doherty said Monday about what Cashman can and can't do on the island. "It needs to be addressed."

Cashman's latest proposal is for a two-family, two-story house built on the bluff where the island's only existing home stands.

CHATHAM DETAIL
28
Cashman house
Nauset Beach Dunes
Atlantic Ocean
N
Chatham Harbor
Strong Island
North Beach
North Chatham
Allen Point
½ mile

JAMES WARREN/CAPE COD TIMES

Doherty was making a list about issues to raise with Cashman, a Quincy native known for his construction work, including the Big Dig in Boston

see **ISLAND HOUSE,** page **12**

INSIDE

OBAMA PITCHES HEALTH CARE REFORM

In a N.H. visit, the president tackles "wild misrepresentations" of his plan to improve health coverage.
Nation & World /A7

WEATHER

Partly sunny. Possible shower or thunderstorm. Highs in the mid-70s. **/B8**

INDEX

Advice	C5
Arts & Entertainment	C6
Business	B6
Cape & Islands	A3
Comics	C4
Movies	C7
New England	A8
Nation & World	A7
Obituaries	A9, C8
Opinion	A10
Crossword	C10
Television	C5

Dozens of Special Olympians joined the procession leading Eunice Kennedy Shriver's casket to the church. The procession included her daughter Maria Shriver and her husband, Sargent Shriver, the first director of the Peace Corps, who was George McGovern's vice presidential running mate in 1972, and in 1976 sought the Democratic nomination for president.

ALSO IN 2009

Former CBS Evening News *anchorman Walter Cronkite, remembered for his coverage of President John F. Kennedy's assassination, died at 92.*

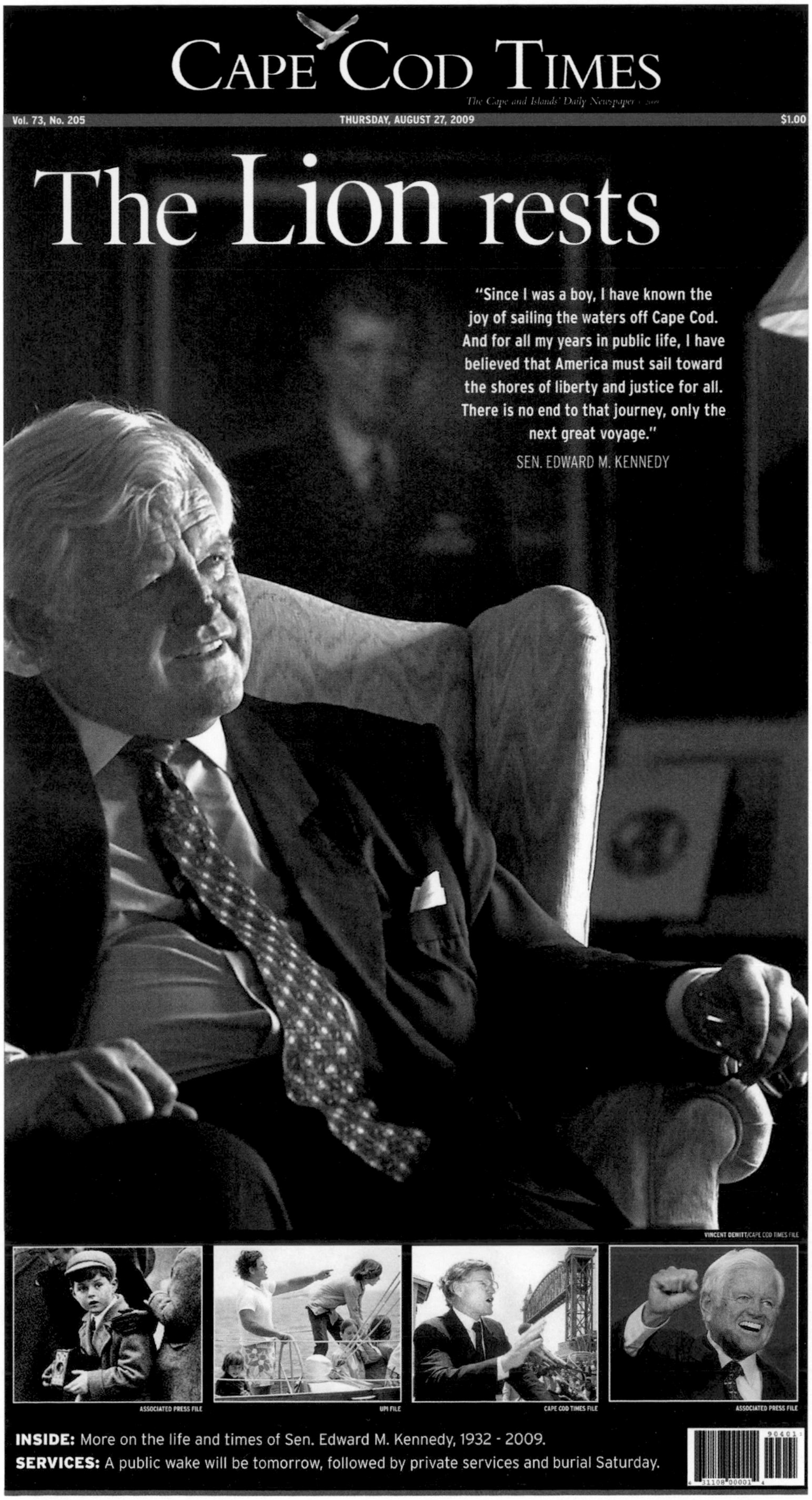

CAPE COD TIMES

The Cape and Islands' Daily Newspaper

Vol. 73, No. 205 | THURSDAY, AUGUST 27, 2009 | $1.00

The Lion rests

"Since I was a boy, I have known the joy of sailing the waters off Cape Cod. And for all my years in public life, I have believed that America must sail toward the shores of liberty and justice for all. There is no end to that journey, only the next great voyage."

SEN. EDWARD M. KENNEDY

VINCENT DEWITT/CAPE COD TIMES FILE

ASSOCIATED PRESS FILE

UPI FILE

CAPE COD TIMES FILE

ASSOCIATED PRESS FILE

INSIDE: More on the life and times of Sen. Edward M. Kennedy, 1932 - 2009.

SERVICES: A public wake will be tomorrow, followed by private services and burial Saturday.

Senator Edward Kennedy moved into his parents' house on the Kennedys' Hyannis Port compound in the 1980s, and it was there that he died at the age of 77. During the final months of his life, Kennedy continued to visit with friends and family on the house's porch and sail on his 50-foot blue-hulled schooner, the Mya.

SENATOR EDWARD KENNEDY DIED

The Boston Globe

Wednesday, August 26, 2009

Kennedy dead at 77

Liberal lion of the Senate, symbol of family dynasty succumbs to brain cancer

Home prices, sales on rise in Boston area

US inspects Boston's language instruction

Top officer offers a dire assessment on Afghanistan

In protesting the president, civility rules

WEDNESDAY, AUGUST 26, 2009

Los Angeles Times

Edward Kennedy dies at 77

MAJOR SHIFT FOR L.A. SCHOOLS

Election uncertainty may hamper Afghan war effort

Forecast bleak for Obama agenda

It never sleeps, but now it sits

Call today. (888) 327-5065

3.875%*

President Obama awarded Edward Kennedy the Presidential Medal of Freedom thirteen days before his death. Kennedy was unable to attend the ceremony due to his health and the death of his sister the day before. His daughter, Kara, accepted the award on his behalf.

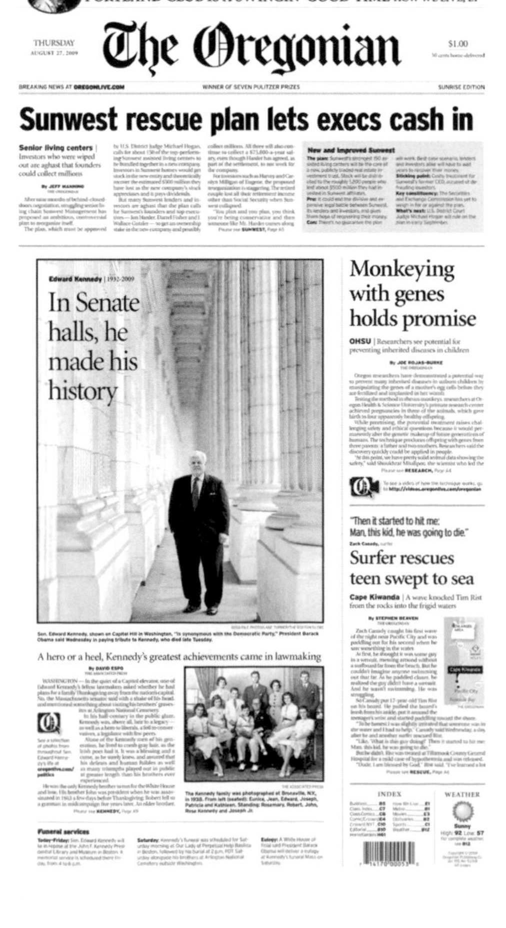

PORTLAND CLUB IS A SWINGIN' GOOD TIME HOW WE LIVE, E1

THURSDAY AUGUST 27, 2009

The Oregonian

Sunwest rescue plan lets execs cash in

Edward Kennedy | 1932-2009

In Senate halls, he made his history

Monkeying with genes holds promise

"Then it started to hit me: Man, this kid, he was going to die."

Surfer rescues teen swept to sea

A hero or a heel, Kennedy's greatest achievements came in lawmaking

"All the News That's Fit to Print"

The New York Times

NEW YORK, FRIDAY, AUGUST 28, 2009

ABUSE ISSUE PUTS THE JUSTICE DEPT. AND C.I.A. AT ODDS

Weighing Hope and Reality in a Cancer Battle

Despite Church's Push on Issue, Some Bishops Assail Health Plan

Flooded Iowa City Rebuilding And Feeling Just a Bit Ignored

War and Family Left Behind, Afghan Youths Seek a Life in Europe

San Jose Mercury News

mercurynews.com VALLEY FINAL 103 | Thursday, August 27, 2009 | THE NEWSPAPER OF SILICON VALLEY 75 cents

SEN. EDWARD M. KENNEDY | 1932-2009

A dynasty's end

Eunice	John	Rosemary	Jean	Joseph Sr.	Edward	Rose	Joseph Jr.	Patricia	Robert	Kathleen
Complications from stroke 2009	Assassinated in Dallas 1963	Natural causes 2005	Remaining survivor, age 81	Complications from stroke 1969	Cancerous brain tumor 2009	Complications pneumonia 1995	Killed in WWII plane crash 1944	Complications pneumonia 2006	Assassinated in Los Angeles 1968	Plane crash in France 1948

JFK LIBRARY VIA NEW YORK TIMES/PHOTO TAKEN AT U.S. EMBASSY IN LONDON IN 1938, WHEN KENNEDY SR. WAS AMBASSADOR TO THE U.K.

Blazing light of a political family flickers out with the passing of Ted Kennedy

By Allen G. Breed
Associated Press

BOSTON — Hundreds of photographs line the walls of the John F. Kennedy Presidential Library & Museum. For the moment, one in particular has captivated a visitor from New Hampshire.

In the black-and-white image, taken in the late 1930s, proud parents Joe and Rose Kennedy march toward the camera, flanked by their nine children, all grinning, arms interlocked, a united front. Teddy, the youngest, is in the center, skipping along as if trying to keep up or, perhaps, pull ahead.

To 50-year-old Shelly Huelsman of Nashua, N.H., this remarkable generation — one that produced a president, of course, but also congressmen and senators, an ambassador and the founder of an international organization for the disabled — was like "a shooting star," but one whose afterglow continues to illuminate and inspire.

"They're a legacy, you know?" Huelsman, who was born the year before JFK's election, says as the wail of sirens and the mournful drone of bagpipes drift in from a neighboring room dedicated to his assassination. "I think even when they're gone, it'll live on for hundreds of years. Don't you?"

One generation. It seems so much more deeply rooted than that, but that's really how

See **KENNEDY**, *Page 12*

Last of a breed
A keen knack to draw bipartisan support on controversial legislation. PAGE A14

A rallying point
Health care reform was a personal passion for Kennedy. PAGE A12

Enduring lessons
San Jose consultant recalls his time working for the senator. PAGE B1

Online Extra
See slide shows and videos of Kennedy, and share condolences in our guest book.

HIGH-SPEED RAIL

Train project may be delayed

Environmental report 'inadequate,' state judge rules

By Gary Richards and Jessica Bernstein-Wax
Bay Area News Group

California's proposed high-speed rail project hit a major bump Wednesday when a judge called into question the environmental report backing a controversial route that would bring the bullet trains over Pacheco Pass into the South Bay and up the Peninsula.

The ruling, which could significantly delay the $40 billion project and add billions more to its price tag, has opponents celebrating because they hope it will renew calls for alternative routes. Yet, supporters say the judge's decision only strengthens their position because it describes other routes, such as over the Altamont Pass and across San Francisco Bay, as too expensive.

The ruling comes at a critical time. About $8 billion in federal stimulus dollars are about to be doled out to high-speed routes across the country, and California seemed poised to capture much of that money. A delay of any significance could erase about $3 billion in aid and increase construction costs. Any significant delay could also threaten Caltrain's plans to electrify its trains down the Peninsula, because the two projects are connected.

The ruling Wednesday from a California Superior Court judge in Sacramento who said the state's High-Speed Rail Authority's environmental impact report was "inadequate" because it failed to address Union Pacific's recent announcement that it would not allow the speedy

See **HIGH-SPEED**, *Page 13*

Jean Kennedy Smith, who served as U.S. ambassador to Ireland during the Clinton administration, is the last surviving child of Joseph and Rose Kennedy's nine children.

SOCIAL NETWORKING

Your Facebook data may be an open book

ACLU says quizzes expose just about everything

By Scott Duke Harris
sdharris@mercurynews.com

Privacy advocates have long warned that users of Facebook and other social networks who seek amusement from quizzes like "What Simpsons Character Are You?" might be mortified by the way creators of such applications can access and potentially "scrape" personal information — not just about the quiz-takers, but their friends as well.

Take the quiz
See the first link to full quiz. PAGE 11

Now, engaging in some online jujitsu, the ACLU of Northern California is employing a cautionary Facebook quiz of its own to illustrate how quizzes that may seem "perfectly harmless" can release an array of data to the wider world — including users' "religion, sexual orientation, political affiliation, photos, events, notes, wall posts, and groups."

The app, titled "What Do Facebook Quizzes Know About You?" delivers its answer by opening a window that scrolls biographical data, attributed comments and photos.

More than 8,000 participants have taken the ACLU's

See **PRIVACY**, *Page 11*

MULTITASK OVERLOAD

Stop scanning the page. Focus!

Researchers say high-tech task jugglers cannot pay attention as well as those who do one job at a time

By Lisa Fernandez
lfernandez@mercurynews.com

Hey, concentrate for a second here. We know you *think* you can simultaneously text your boss, e-mail your girlfriend, post a school photo to your Facebook page and shop for shoes online better than doing it the old-fashioned way — one task at a time.

Sorry. A team of Stanford University researchers says you can't.

More specifically, the team found that people who are HMM (heavy media multitasker in research parlance) do not pay attention, cannot control their memory or cannot switch easily from one job to another as adeptly as low-tech people who concentrate on one job at a time.

"I found it very surprising," said Eyal Ophir, the study's lead researcher at Stanford's Communication Between Humans and Interactive Media Lab who is admittedly a one-thing-at-a-time kind of guy. "We thought that multitaskers would have some kind of special ability. All we found were deficits."

See **MULTITASK**, *Page 13*

LOCAL » B1
Court: Toss evidence in steroid case

BUSINESS » B9
Bay Area home sales trail nation

BUSINESS » B9
In Beijing, they move into Ikea

NATIONAL » A4
Health firms fund Blue Dogs

103

SUBSCRIBE » 1-800-870-NEWS (6397) or mercurynews.com/subscribe

WEATHER » 12B
Patchy fog
H: 86-92 L: 65-72

INDEX

Business+Tech B9
Classified CL1
Comics Eye 40
Crossword CL9
Dear Abby Eye 40
Lottery A2
Movies Eye 22
Obituaries B7
Opinion A14-A15
Stocks B11
Television Eye 46

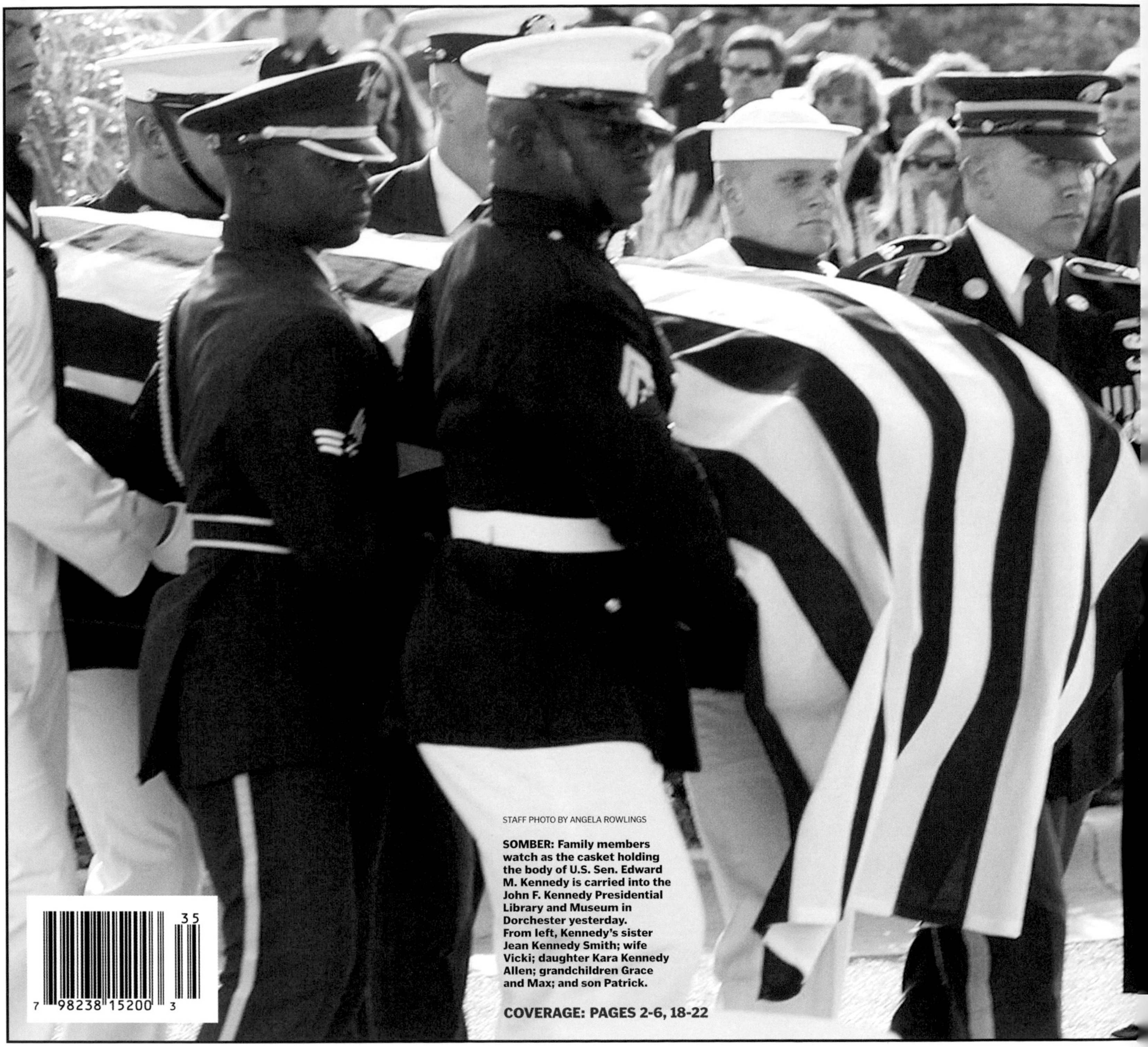

STAFF PHOTO BY ANGELA ROWLINGS

SOMBER: Family members watch as the casket holding the body of U.S. Sen. Edward M. Kennedy is carried into the John F. Kennedy Presidential Library and Museum in Dorchester yesterday. From left, Kennedy's sister Jean Kennedy Smith; wife Vicki; daughter Kara Kennedy Allen; grandchildren Grace and Max; and son Patrick.

COVERAGE: PAGES 2-6, 18-22

BOSTON Herald

FRIDAY, AUGUST 28, 2009 ■ $1.00

Ted K comes home to Hub

A FAMILY'S FAREWELL

A seventy-mile memorial motorcade and procession for the casket of Senator Edward Kennedy began at the family home in Hyannis Port and ended at the John F. Kennedy Library in Boston. Thousands lined the memorial route in Boston, where Rose Kennedy's father, John Francis "Honey Fitz" Fitzgerald, served as mayor during the early twentieth century.

EL PAÍS

www.elpais.com

EL PERIÓDICO GLOBAL EN ESPAÑOL

DOMINGO 30 DE AGOSTO DE 2009 | Año XXXIV | Número 11.762 | EDICIÓN NACIONAL | **Precio: 2,20 euros**

Hallado el cadáver de Laura Alonso
La Guardia Civil investiga el asesinato de la joven **PÁGINA 36**

El Real Madrid vence al Deportivo
Los nuevos 'galácticos' exhiben su potencial (3-2) **PÁGINA 42**

"Aún lloro mucho"
Retrato del auténtico Cristiano Ronaldo **EL PAÍS SEMANAL**

EFE

Cuatro presidentes se despiden de Edward Kennedy

Estados Unidos se despidió ayer del último patriarca de una dinastía clave para entender el último medio siglo estadounidense. Al funeral de Edward Kennedy, que falleció el martes pasado a los 77 años, acudieron el presidente Barack Obama y tres ex mandatarios: George W. Bush, Bill Clinton y Jimmy Carter (en la fotografía, en la iglesia de Nuestra Señora del Perpetuo Socorro, en Boston). El *león del Senado* iba a ser enterrado anoche en el cementerio de Arlington, el más simbólico del país. **PÁGINAS 4 Y 5**

Zapatero subirá los impuestos a las rentas del capital

El presidente busca el pacto con la izquierda y los nacionalistas

LUIS R. AIZPEOLEA, **Madrid**

El presidente del Gobierno, José Luis Rodríguez Zapatero, ha ordenado que la subida de impuestos se centre en las rentas del capital, es decir, aquellos ingresos que no proceden del trabajo, como intereses bancarios, dividendos, ganancias por ventas de acciones o fondos de inversión, plusvalías por compraventa de casas y otros bienes, seguros de vida... El objetivo, con el que trabaja el Ministerio de Hacienda, es paliar el déficit público sin afectar las rentas del trabajo, muy sensibles políticamente. Para sacar adelante la reforma fiscal buscará el apoyo en la Ley de Presupuestos de la izquierda (IU, ICV, ERC) y algunos partidos nacionalistas, como BNG, PNV y CC. **PÁGINAS 12 Y 13**

Negocios

Tributos de crisis

Las arcas del Estado viven su peor momento. Para frenar su deterioro, Zapatero se ha lanzado a una misión de alto riesgo político: subir los impuestos. EL PAÍS analiza las opciones que maneja el Ejecutivo

Feijóo sustituye a Camps como principal barón del PP tras el 'caso Gürtel'

El presidente de la Xunta, Alberto Núñez Feijóo, se ha convertido en el principal barón regional de Mariano Rajoy, una condición que ha perdido Francisco Camps por culpa del *caso Gürtel*. **PÁGINAS 14 Y 15**

Identifíquese, es usted negra

La ONU falla contra España en un caso de discriminación racial

Tras 17 años de lucha judicial, Rosalind Williams, de 66 años, ha logrado que el Comité de Derechos Humanos de la ONU le dé la razón con un dictamen que le saca los colores al Tribunal Constitucional. El mensaje para el Estado español es bien claro: la policía no puede tratar de modo distinto a alguien por el color de su piel. **PÁGINA 34**

More than a thousand mourners attended the funeral Mass at the Basilica of Our Lady of Perpetual Help, including former presidents Jimmy Carter, Bill Clinton, and George W. Bush. President Barack Obama delivered the eulogy (see pages 119–122). Following the service, Kennedy's casket was transported to Washington, D.C.

QUOTED

"He was given the gift of time that his brothers were not. "

—PRESIDENT BARACK OBAMA, *August 29, 2009*

"All the News That's Fit to Print"

The New York Times

Late Edition
New York: **Today**, partly sunny, pleasant, high 83. **Tonight**, clear skies, low 61. **Tomorrow**, mostly sunny, cooler, high 73. Yesterday, high 72, low 64. Details, Page 20.

VOL. CLVIII . . No. 54,783 | © 2009 The New York Times | NEW YORK, SUNDAY, AUGUST 30, 2009 | $6 beyond the greater New York metropolitan area. | $5.00

DOUG MILLS/THE NEW YORK TIMES

Kennedy family members and friends gathered around the grave site at the funeral on Saturday for Senator Edward M. Kennedy at Arlington National Cemetery.

U.S. SAYS PAKISTAN ALTERED MISSILES SOLD FOR DEFENSE

CHARGE TESTS RELATIONS

Illegal Changes Said to Expand Capability to Strike on Land

By ERIC SCHMITT and DAVID E. SANGER

WASHINGTON — The United States has accused Pakistan of illegally modifying American-made missiles to expand its capability to strike land targets, a potential threat to India, according to senior administration and Congressional officials.

The charge, which set off a new outbreak of tensions between the United States and Pakistan, was made in an unpublicized diplomatic protest in late June to Prime Minister Yusuf Raza Gilani and other top Pakistani officials.

The accusation comes at a particularly delicate time, when the administration is asking Congress to approve $7.5 billion in aid to Pakistan over the next five years, and when Washington is pressing a reluctant Pakistani military to focus its attentions on fighting the Taliban, rather than expanding its nuclear and conventional forces aimed at India.

While American officials say that the weapon in the latest dispute is a conventional one — based on the Harpoon antiship missiles that were sold to Pakistan by the Reagan administration as a defensive weapon in the cold war — the subtext of the argument is growing concern about the speed with which Pakistan is developing new generations of both conventional and nuclear weapons.

"There's a concerted effort to get these guys to slow down," one senior administration official said. "Their energies are misdi-

Continued on Page 10

Tide Turning, Florida Sees Itself Shrink

By DAMIEN CAVE

HOLLYWOOD, Fla. — The smiling couple barreling ahead on the cover of Liberty magazine in 1926 knew exactly where to go. "Florida or Bust," said the white paint on the car doors. "Four wheels, no brakes."

So it has been for a century, as Florida welcomed thousands of newcomers every week, year after year, becoming the nation's fourth-most-populous state with about 16 million people in 2000.

Imagine the shock, then, to discover that traffic is now heading the other way. That's right, the Sunshine State is shrinking.

Choked by a record level of foreclosures and unemployment, along with a helping of disillusionment, the state's population declined by 58,000 people from April 2008 to April 2009, according to the University of Florida's Bureau of Economic and Business Research. Except for the years around World Wars I and II, it was the state's first pop-

Continued on Page 21

Kennedy Mourners Memorialize 'Soul of the Democratic Party'

By DAN BARRY

ARLINGTON, Va. — The nation said final farewell on Saturday to Edward M. Kennedy, who used his privileged life to give consistent, passionate voice to the underprivileged for nearly a half-century as a United States senator from Massachusetts. He was the only one of four fabled Kennedy brothers to reach late adulthood, and he was remembered for making the most of it.

Along the rain-dappled roadways of Boston in the late morning, and then in the sweltering humidity of Washington in early evening, people waited for the fleeting moment of a passing hearse so that they could pay respects to the man known simply as Ted. At the United States Capitol, where Mr. Kennedy had served for so long, his wife, Victoria Reggie Kennedy, stepped out of a limousine to receive hugs, bow her head during prayers, and to hear the singing of "America the Beautiful."

The gray rainy day began with a funeral Mass at a working-class Roman Catholic church in Boston where the senator had sometimes sought comfort, without entourage or advance notice. Where he once reflected amid the hush of empty oak pews, there now sat hundreds gathered in his honor, including President Obama; three of the four living former presidents; dozens of foreign dignitaries and members of Congress; and, of course, people so familiar to Americans simply because they are Kennedys.

And it was during that portion of the Mass, when prayers of hope are shared, that his grandchildren, nieces and nephews stepped up to the microphone to express once more Ted Kennedy's political and human desires:

That human beings be measured not by what they cannot do but by what they can do. That quality health care becomes a fundamental right and not a privilege. That the old politics of race and gender die away. That newcomers be accepted, no matter their color or place of birth. That the nation stand united against violence, hate and war. And, in echo of his famous words, that the work begins anew, the hope arises anew, and the dream lives on.

"We pray to the Lord," each petitioner concluded.

And each time the mourners answered as one, "Lord, hear our prayer."

After Holy Communion, Mr. Obama delivered the eulogy for the man whose endorsement in the 2008 campaign was like the passing of a sword from Camelot, helping enormously in giving this country its first African-American president.

"Today we say goodbye to the youngest child of Rose and Joseph Kennedy," Mr. Obama said. "The world will long remember their son Edward as the heir to a weighty legacy, a champion for those who had none, the soul of the Democratic Party, and the lion of the United States Senate — a man whose name graces nearly 1,000 laws, and who penned more than 300 laws him-

Continued on Page A14

Justices to Revisit 'Hillary' Film, And Corporate Cash in Politics

By ADAM LIPTAK

WASHINGTON — The Supreme Court will cut short its summer break in early September to hear a new argument in a momentous case that could transform the way political campaigns are conducted.

The case, which arises from a minor political documentary called "Hillary: The Movie," seemed an oddity when it was first argued in March. Just six months later, it has turned into a juggernaut with the potential to shatter a century-long understanding about the government's ability to bar corporations from spending money to support political candidates.

The case has also deepened a profound split among liberals, dividing those who view government regulation of political speech as an affront to the First Amendment from those who believe that unlimited corporate campaign spending is a threat to democracy.

At issue is whether the court should overrule a 1990 decision, Austin v. Michigan Chamber of Commerce, which upheld restrictions on corporate spending to support or oppose political candidates. Re-arguments in the Supreme Court are rare, and the justices' decision to call for one here may have been prompted by

Continued on Page 15

Students Get New Reading Assignment: Pick Books You Like

By MOTOKO RICH

JONESBORO, Ga. — For years Lorrie McNeill loved teaching "To Kill a Mockingbird," the Harper Lee classic that many Americans regard as a literary rite of passage.

But last fall, for the first time in 15 years, Ms. McNeill, 42, did not assign "Mockingbird" — or any novel. Instead she turned over all the decisions about which books to read to the students in her seventh- and eighth-grade English classes at Jonesboro Middle School in this south Atlanta suburb.

Among their choices: James Patterson's adrenaline-fueled "Maximum Ride" books, plenty of young-adult chick-lit novels and even the "Captain Underpants" series of comic-book-style novels.

But then there were students like Jennae Arnold, a soft-spoken eighth grader who picked challenging titles like "A Lesson Before Dying" by Ernest J. Gaines and "The Bluest Eye" by Toni Morrison, of which she wrote, partly in text-message speak: "I would have N3V3R thought of or about something like that on my own."

The approach Ms. McNeill uses, in which students choose their own books, discuss them individually with their teacher

DAVID WALTER BANKS FOR THE NEW YORK TIMES

Lorrie McNeill gives her middle school students a wide choice of reading in Jonesboro, Ga.

FUTURE OF READING
Children's Choice

and one another, and keep detailed journals about their reading, is part of a movement to revolutionize the way literature is taught in America's schools. While there is no clear consensus among English teachers, variations on the approach, known as reading workshop, are catching on.

In New York City many public and private elementary schools and some middle schools already employ versions of reading workshop. Starting this fall, the school district in Chappaqua, N.Y., is setting aside 40 minutes every other day for all sixth, seventh and eighth graders to read books of their own choosing.

In September students in Seattle's public middle schools will also begin choosing most of their own books. And in Chicago the public school district has had a pilot program in

Continued on Page 18

INTERNATIONAL 4-10
Chechnya Suffers a Relapse
A period of relative calm has ended in the former Soviet republics of Chechnya, Ingushetia and Dagestan with an outburst of violence. PAGE 4

NATIONAL 12-21
Clash Over Coal Ash Disposal
An Alabama landfill is taking millions of cubic yards of coal ash from a spill in Tennessee. Some see a windfall in the ash; others are skeptical. PAGE 12

METROPOLITAN
Paddling in Hudson's Wake
A reporter set out in a kayak to mark the 400th anniversary of Henry Hudson's exploration of the majestic waterway that now bears his name. PAGE 1

SPORTSSUNDAY 1-16
2009 College Football Preview
The spread offense, the star quarterback Tim Tebow, Heisman hopefuls, team rankings, conference prospects and bowl game predictions. PAGE 1

OP-ED IN WEEK IN REVIEW 7-10
Nicholas D. Kristof PAGE 8

0 354713 8

Hundreds of congressional staff members and others honored Kennedy as his hearse passed the Capitol building on its way to Arlington National Cemetery. With John F. Kennedy's eternal flame in view, a small group gathered for the burial service of his brother Edward.

Edward Kennedy Jr. kissed his father's casket at funeral services for the senior senator from Massachusetts and Kennedy family patriarch. (AP Photo/ Alex Brandon)

ALSO IN 2009

Longtime family friend Paul Kirk Jr. was appointed to Kennedy's Senate seat until a special election in January 2010—fifty years after Senator John F. Kennedy announced he would be a candidate for president of the United States.

EULOGIES

Senator Edward Kennedy delivered eulogies for his brother Robert Kennedy, his sister-in-law Jacqueline Kennedy Onassis, his mother, Rose Fitzgerald Kennedy, and his nephew John F. Kennedy Jr. Those tributes are reprinted here as prepared, along with the eulogy delivered by President Barack Obama at Senator Kennedy's funeral service.

Tribute to SENATOR ROBERT KENNEDY

Delivered by Senator Edward Kennedy
St. Patrick's Cathedral, New York City,
June 8, 1968

On behalf of Mrs. Robert Kennedy, her children and the parents and sisters of Robert Kennedy, I want to express what we feel to those who mourn with us today in this Cathedral and around the world. We loved him as a brother and father and son. From his parents, and from his older brothers and sisters—Joe, Kathleen and Jack—he received inspiration which he passed on to all of us. He gave us strength in time of trouble, wisdom in time of uncertainty, and sharing in time of happiness. He was always by our side.

Love is not an easy feeling to put into words. Nor is loyalty, or trust or joy. But he was all of these. He loved life completely and lived it intensely.

A few years back, Robert Kennedy wrote some words about his own father and they expressed the way we in his family feel about him. He said of what his father meant to him: "What it really all adds up to is love—not love as it is described with such facility in popular magazines, but the kind of love that is affection and respect, order, encouragement, and support. Our awareness of this was an incalculable source of strength, and because real love is something unselfish and involves sacrifice and giving, we could not help but profit from it.

"Beneath it all, he has tried to engender a social conscience. There were wrongs which needed attention. There were people who were poor and who needed help. And we have a responsibility to them and to this country. Through no virtues and accomplishments of our own, we have been fortunate enough to be born in the United States under the most comfortable conditions. We, therefore, have a responsibility to others who are less well off."

This is what Robert Kennedy was given. What he leaves us is what he said, what he did and what he stood for. A speech he made to the young people of South Africa on their Day of Affirmation in 1966 sums it up the best, and I would read it now:

"There is a discrimination in this world and slavery and slaughter and starvation. Governments repress their people; and millions are trapped in poverty while the nation grows rich; and wealth is lavished on armaments everywhere.

"These are differing evils, but they are common works of man. They reflect the imperfection of human justice, the inadequacy of human compassion, our lack of sensibility toward the sufferings of our fellows.

"But we can perhaps remember—even if only for a time—that those who live with us are our brothers; that they share with us the same short moment of life; that they seek—as we do—nothing but the chance to live out their lives in purpose and happiness, winning what satisfaction and fulfillment they can.

"Surely this bond of common faith, this bond of common goal, can begin to teach us something. Surely, we can learn, at least, to look at those around us as fellow men. And surely we can begin to work a little harder to bind up the wounds among us and to become in our own hearts brothers and countrymen once again.

"Our answer is to rely on youth—not a time of life but a state of mind, a temper of the will, a quality of imagination, a predominance of courage over timidity, of the appetite for adventure over the love of ease. The cruelties and obstacles of this swiftly changing planet will not yield to obsolete dogmas and outworn slogans. They cannot be moved by those who cling to a present that is already dying, who prefer the illusion of security to the excitement and danger that come with even the most peaceful progress. It is a revolutionary world we live in; and this generation at home and around the world, has had thrust upon it a greater burden of responsibility than any generation that has ever lived.

"Some believe there is nothing one man or one woman can do against the enormous array of the world's ills. Yet many of the world's great movements, of thought and action, have flowed from the work of a single man. A young monk began the Protestant reformation, a young general extended an empire from Macedonia to the borders of the earth, and a young woman reclaimed the territory of France. It was a young Italian explorer who discovered the New World, and the thirty-two-year-old Thomas Jefferson who proclaimed that all men are created equal.

"These men moved the world, and so can we all. Few will have the greatness to bend history itself, but each of us can work to change a small portion of events, and in the total of all those acts will be written the history of this generation. It is from numberless diverse acts of courage and belief that human history is shaped. Each time a man stands up for an ideal, or acts to improve the lot of others, or strikes out against injustice, he sends forth a tiny ripple of hope, and crossing each other from a million different centers of energy and daring, those ripples build a current that can sweep down the mightiest walls of oppression and resistance.

"Few are willing to brave the disapproval of their fellows, the censure of their colleagues, the wrath of their society. Moral courage is a rarer commodity than bravery in battle or great intelligence. Yet it is the one essential, vital quality for those who seek to change a world that yields most painfully to change. And I believe that in this generation those with the courage to enter the moral conflict will find themselves with companions in every corner of the globe.

"For the fortunate among us, there is the temptation to follow the easy and familiar paths of personal ambition and financial success so grandly spread before those who enjoy the privilege of education. But that is not the road history has marked out for us. Like it or not, we live in times of danger and uncertainty. But they are also more open to the creative energy of men than any other time in history. All of us will ultimately be judged and as the years pass we will surely judge ourselves, on the effort we have contributed to building a new world society and the extent to which our ideals and goals have shaped that effort.

"The future does not belong to those who are content with today, apathetic toward common problems and their fellow man alike, timid and fearful in the face of new ideas and bold projects. Rather it will belong to those who can blend vision, reason and courage in a personal commitment to the ideals and great enterprises of American Society.

"Our future may lie beyond our vision, but it is not completely beyond our control. It is the shaping impulse of America that neither fate nor nature nor the irresistible tides of history, but the work of our own hands, matched to reason and principle, that will determine our destiny. There is pride in that, even arrogance, but there is also experience and truth. In any event, it is the only way we can live."

This is the way he lived. My brother need not be idealized, or enlarged in death beyond what he was in life, to be remembered simply as a good and decent man, who saw wrong and tried to right it, saw suffering and tried to heal it, saw war and tried to stop it.

Those of us who loved him and who take him to his rest today, pray that what he was to us and what he wished for others will some day come to pass for all the world.

As he said many times, in many parts of this nation, to those he touched and who sought to touch him:

"Some men see things as they are and say why. I dream things that never were and say why not."

Tribute to
JACQUELINE KENNEDY ONASSIS

Delivered by Senator Edward Kennedy
Church of St. Ignatius Loyola, New York City,
May 23, 1994

Last summer, when we were on the upper deck on the boat at the Vineyard, waiting for President and Mrs. Clinton to arrive, Jackie turned to me and said: "Teddy, you go down and greet the President."

But I said: "Maurice is already there."

And Jackie answered: "Teddy, you do it. Maurice isn't running for re-election."

She was always there—for all our family—in her special way.

She was a blessing to us and to the nation—and a lesson to the world on how to do things right, how to be a mother, how to appreciate history, how to be courageous. No one else looked like her, spoke like her, wrote like her, or was so original in the way she did things. No one we knew ever had a better sense of self.

Eight months before she married Jack, they went together to President Eisenhower's Inaugural Ball. Jackie said later that that's where they decided they liked inaugurations.

No one ever gave more meaning to the title of first lady. The nation's capital city looks as it does because of her. She saved Lafayette Square and Pennsylvania Avenue.

Jackie brought the greatest artists to the White House, and brought the arts to the center of national attention. Today, in large part because of her inspiration and vision, the arts are an abiding part of national policy.

President Kennedy took such delight in her brilliance and her spirit. At a White House dinner, he once leaned over and told the wife of the French Ambassador, "Jackie speaks fluent French. But I only understand one out of every five words she says—and that word is DeGaulle."

And then, during those four endless days in 1963, she held us together as a family and a country. In large part because of her, we could grieve and then go on. She lifted us up, and in the doubt and darkness, she gave her fellow citizens back their pride as Americans. She was then 34 years old.

Afterward, as the eternal flame she lit flickered in the autumn of Arlington Cemetery, Jackie went on to do what she most wanted—to raise Caroline and John, and warm her family's life and that of all the Kennedys.

Robert Kennedy sustained her, and she helped make it possible for Bobby to continue. She kept Jack's memory alive, as he carried Jack's mission on.

Her two children turned out to be extraordinary, honest, unspoiled, and with a character equal to hers. And she did it in the most trying of circumstances. They are her two miracles.

Her love for Caroline and John was deep and unqualified. She reveled in their accomplishments, she hurt with their sorrows, and she felt sheer joy and delight in spending time with them. At the mere mention of one of their names, Jackie's eyes would shine brighter and her smile would grow bigger.

She once said that if you "bungle raising your children nothing else much matters in life." She didn't bungle. Once again, she showed how to do the most important thing of all, and do it right.

When she went to work, Jackie became a respected professional in the world of publishing. And because of her, remarkable books came to life. She searched out new authors and ideas. She was interested in everything.

Her love of history became a devotion to historic preservation. You knew, when Jackie joined the cause to save a building in Manhattan, the bulldozers might as well turn around and go home.

She had a wonderful sense of humor—a way of focusing on someone with total attention—and a little girl delight in who they were and what they were saying. It was a gift of herself that she gave to others. And in spite of all her heartache and loss, she never faltered.

I often think of what she said about Jack in December after he died: "They made him a legend, when he would have preferred to be a man." Jackie would have preferred to be just herself, but the world insisted that she be a legend too. She never wanted public notice—in part I think, because it brought back painful memories of an unbearable sorrow, endured in the glare of a million lights.

In all the years since then, her genuineness and depth of character continued to shine through the privacy, and reach people everywhere. Jackie was too young to be a widow in 1963, and too young to die now.

Her grandchildren were bringing her new joy to her life, a joy that illuminated her face whenever you saw them together. Whether it was taking Rose and Tatiana for an ice cream cone, or taking a walk in Central Park with little Jack as she did last Sunday, she relished being Grandjackie and showering her grandchildren with love.

At the end, she worried more about us than herself. She let her family and friends know she was thinking of them. How cherished were those wonderful notes in her distinctive hand on her powder blue stationery!

In truth, she did everything she could—and more—for each of us.

She made a rare and noble contribution to the American spirit. But for us, most of all she was a magnificent wife, mother, grandmother, sister, aunt and friend.

She graced our history. And for those of us who knew and loved her—she graced our lives.

Tribute to
ROSE FITZGERALD KENNEDY

Delivered by Senator Edward Kennedy
St. Stephen's Church, Boston, January 25, 1995

On my office wall, there is a note from Mother, reacting to a comment I once made in an interview. "Dear Teddy," she wrote in the note, "I just saw a story in which you said: 'If I was President. . . .' You should have said, 'If I were President . . . ,' which is correct because it is a condition contrary to fact."

Mother always thought her children should strive for the highest place. But inside the family, with love and laughter, she knew how to put each of us in our place. She was ambitious not only for our success, but for our souls. From our youth, we remember how, with effortless ease, she could bandage a cut, dry a tear, recite from memory the "The Midnight Ride of Paul Revere," and spot a hole in a sock from a hundred yards away.

She sustained us in the saddest times—by her faith in God, which was the greatest gift she gave us—and by the strength of her character, which was a combination of the sweetest gentleness and the most tempered steel.

She was indomitable for all her days. Each summer for many years, we would gather 'round at night, and sitting at the piano, Mother would play "Sweet Rosie O'Grady," the song that became her own special ballad:

Just around the corner of the
street where I reside,
There lives the cutest little girl
that I have ever spied.
Her name is Rosie O'Grady,
and I don't mind telling you,
That she's the sweetest little Rose
the garden ever grew.
I love sweet Rosie O'Grady,
and Rosie O'Grady loves me.

When she finished, her voice would lilt, and her eyes would flash, and she would ask if we would like to hear it one more time. And we always would.

All her life, Mother also loved learning, and she was an excellent student herself. We still have her report card from Dorchester High School. In her 3 years there, she received 71 A's, 22 B's, and 1 C. I asked her about that C, which was in geometry. She said there must be some mistake. She didn't remember anything but A's.

One spring some years ago, when she was in her nineties, I took her on Good Friday to the Three Hours devotion. But the nurse warned me in advance that Mother had to eat, so we would have to leave after only an hour.

At one o'clock, I whispered: "Mother, it's time to go." She looked at me and sternly said: "Not yet, Teddy." So I asked a second time, and her answer came in a tone that was distinctly not a whisper: "Teddy, the service is not over yet."

By now, the congregation was discreetly staring at us and clearly thinking: See, he's trying to get out of Church early, but that sainted Mother of his—isn't she wonderful?—just won't let him.

Later that night, of course, Mother and I said the Rosary, as she did every night, by herself or with any of her children or grandchildren who happened to be home. In the Kennedy family, you learned the glorious Mysteries at an early age.

You learned just as early how to catch a pass, sail a boat or serve a tennis ball. All her life, Mother was interested in our games. The summer she turned 101, I went into her room and showed her my tennis racket. She said, "Are you sure that's your racket, Teddy? I've been looking all over the house for mine."

Jack once called her the glue that held the family together. We learned a special bond of loyalty and affection, which all of us first came to know in the deep and abiding love that Mother shared with Dad for 57 years.

From both of them together, we inherited a spirit that kept all their children close to each other and to them. Whatever any of us has done—whatever contribution we have made—begins and ends with Rose and Joseph Kennedy. For all of us, Dad was the spark, and Mother was the light of our lives. He was our greatest fan; she was our greatest teacher.

She was born in 1890, the year of the Battle of Wounded Knee, when Benjamin Harrison was in the White House. And she never let us forget that she had lived so much of the history that we only read about. Our dinner table was her classroom, and the subject was the whole world of human events.

One evening early in 1984, when Mother was 93, she asked if we thought President Reagan would run again. One of our guests replied, "Of course he'll run, Mrs. Kennedy. After all, he's very young. He's only 73." Mother looked at the guest for a second and then answered him with a twinkle in her voice: "You're just trying to flatter me. I know that he's the oldest President in American history." Unless it came from her, there was no blarney when Mother was around.

So what now secures for Rose Fitzgerald Kennedy the high place in history that she will have? I think it is most of all the warm place she holds in the hearts of so many people everywhere, from Boston to Dublin, from Berlin to New Delhi to Buenos Aires. Millions who never met her sensed the kind of rare and wondrous person she was, a shining example of the faith that sustained her through even the hardest sorrow. She had an inner strength that radiated from her life. She was a symbol of family in this country and around the world. She cared for a retarded child as much as for the most powerful statesman. She truly did believe that we are all, royalty and disability alike, created in the image and likeness of God.

She was the granddaughter of immigrants who saw her father become the first Irish-Catholic Congressman from Boston, and her son and grandson succeed him. She saw three sons serve in the Senate—actually she was sure that it was her campaigning that put us there—and we all thought that as usual she was right. She saw the son who proudly carried her Fitzgerald name become the first Irish-Catholic President of the United States.

And she was just as proud to see a new generation of her family carrying on her belief in public service.

But Mother also taught us that you do not have to run for office to make a difference. She was equally proud of her daughters and the contributions they have made. Jean—the founder of Very Special Arts and now, like our father before her, the Ambassador. Pat, for the pioneering support she has given to young writers. Eunice, founder of Special Olympics and the leader of a global revolution of human rights for the retarded and disabled.

And Mother had a special place in her heart and prayers for our sister Rosemary, for her bravery and the things she taught us all.

Mother gave not only to her children, but she gave her children, fired with her own faith, to serve the Nation and the earth. To us, she was the most beautiful Rose of all the roses in the world. Her life shows us the truth and the way.

Mother knew this day was coming, but she did not dread it. She accepted and even welcomed it, not as a leaving, but as a returning. She has gone to God. She is home. And at this moment she is happily presiding at a heavenly table with both of her Joes, with Jack and Kathleen, with Bobby and David.

And as she did all our lives, whether it was when I walked back through the rain from school as a child, or when a President who was her son came back to Hyannis Port, she will be there ready to welcome the rest of us home someday. Of this I have no doubt, for as they were from the beginning, Mother's prayers will continue to be more than enough to bring us through.

Not long ago, I found a beautiful poem that symbolizes what all of us feel today. Its title is "The Rose Still Grows Beyond the Wall":

Near a shady wall a rose once grew,
  Budded and blossomed in God's free light,
Watered and fed by morning dew,
  Shedding its sweetness day and night.

As it grew and blossomed fair and tall,
  Slowly rising to loftier height,
It came to a crevice in the wall,
  Through which there shone a beam of light.

Onward it crept with added strength,
  With never a thought of fear or pride.
It followed the light through the crevice's length
  And unfolded itself on the other side.

The light, the dew, the broadening view
  Were found the same as they were before;
And it lost itself in beauties new,
  Breathing its fragrance more and more.

Shall claim of death cause us to grieve,
  And make our courage faint or fail?
Nay! Let us faith and hope receive;
  The rose still grows beyond the wall,

Scattering fragrance far and wide,
  Just as it did in days of yore,
Just as it did on the other side,
  Just as it will for evermore.

Tribute to
JOHN F. KENNEDY JUNIOR

Delivered by Senator Edward Kennedy
Church of St. Thomas More, New York City,
July 23, 1999

Thank you, President and Mrs. Clinton and Chelsea, for being here today. You've shown extraordinary kindness throughout the course of this week.

Once, when they asked John what he would do if he went into politics and was elected president, he said: "I guess the first thing is call up Uncle Teddy and gloat." I loved that. It was so like his father.

From the first day of his life, John seemed to belong not only to our family, but to the American family.

The whole world knew his name before he did.

A famous photograph showed John racing across the lawn as his father landed in the White House helicopter and swept up John in his arms. When my brother saw that photo, he exclaimed, "Every mother in the United States is saying, 'Isn't it wonderful to see that love between a son and his father, the way that John races to be with his father.' Little do they know—that son would have raced right by his father to get to that helicopter."

But John was so much more than those long ago images emblazoned in our minds. He was a boy who grew into a man with a zest for life and a love of adventure. He was a pied piper who brought us all along. He was blessed with a father and mother who never thought anything mattered more than their children.

When they left the White House, Jackie's soft and gentle voice and unbreakable strength of spirit guided him surely and securely to the future. He had a legacy, and he learned to treasure it. He was part of a legend, and he learned to live with it. Above all, Jackie gave him a place to be himself, to grow up, to laugh and cry, to dream and strive on his own.

John learned that lesson well. He had amazing grace. He accepted who he was, but he cared more about what he could and should become. He saw things that could be lost in the glare of the spotlight. And he could laugh at the absurdity of too much pomp and circumstance.

He loved to travel across this city by subway, bicycle and roller blade. He lived as if he were unrecognizable—although he was known by everyone he encountered. He always introduced himself, rather than take anything for granted. He drove his own car and flew his own plane, which is how he wanted it. He was the king of his domain.

He thought politics should be an integral part of our popular culture and that popular culture should be an integral part of politics. He transformed that belief into the creation of *George*. John shaped and honed a fresh, often irreverent journal. His new political magazine attracted a new generation, many of whom had never read about politics before.

John also brought to *George* a wit that was quick and sure. The premier issue of *George* caused a stir with a cover photograph of Cindy Crawford dressed as George Washington with a bare belly button.

The "Reliable Source" in *The Washington Post* printed a mock cover of *George* showing not Cindy Crawford, but me dressed as George

Washington, with my belly button exposed. I suggested to John that perhaps I should have been the model for the first cover of his magazine. Without missing a beat, John told me that he stood by his original editorial decision.

John brought this same playful wit to other aspects of his life. He campaigned for me during my 1994 election and always caused a stir when he arrived in Massachusetts. Before one of his trips to Boston, John told the campaign he was bringing along a companion, but would need only one hotel room.

Interested, but discreet, a senior campaign worker picked John up at the airport and prepared to handle any media barrage that might accompany John's arrival with his mystery companion. John landed with the companion all right—an enormous German shepherd dog named Sam he had just rescued from the pound.

He loved to talk about the expression on the campaign worker's face and the reaction of the clerk at the Charles Hotel when John and Sam checked in.

I think now not only of these wonderful adventures, but of the kind of person John was. He was the son who quietly gave extraordinary time and ideas to the Institute of Politics at Harvard that bears his father's name. He brought to the institute his distinctive insight that politics could have a broader appeal, that it was not just about elections, but about the larger forces that shape our whole society.

John was also the son who was once protected by his mother. He went on to become her pride—and then her protector in her final days. He was the Kennedy who loved us all, but who especially cherished his sister, Caroline, celebrated her brilliance and took strength and joy from their lifelong mutual admiration society.

And for a thousand days, he was a husband who adored the wife who became his perfect soul mate. John's father taught us all to reach for the moon and the stars. John did that in all he did—and he found his shining star when he married Carolyn Bessette.

How often our family will think of the two of them, cuddling affectionately on a boat, surrounded by family—aunts, uncles, Caroline and Ed and their children, Rose, Tatiana, and Jack—Kennedy cousins, Radziwill cousins, Shriver cousins, Smith cousins, Lawford cousins—as we sailed Nantucket Sound.

Then we would come home—and before dinner, on the lawn where his father had played, John would lead a spirited game of touch football. And his beautiful young wife—the new pride of the Kennedys—would cheer for John's team and delight her nieces and nephews with her somersaults.

We loved Carolyn. She and her sister, Lauren, were young, extraordinary women of high accomplishment—and their own limitless possibilities. We mourn their loss and honor their lives. The Bessette and Freeman families will always be part of ours.

John was a serious man who brightened our lives with his smile and his grace. He was a son of privilege who founded a program called Reaching Up to train better caregivers for the mentally disabled.

He joined Wall Street executives on the Robin Hood Foundation to help the city's impoverished children. And he did it all so quietly, without ever calling attention to himself.

John was one of Jackie's two miracles. He was still becoming the person he would be, and doing it by the beat of his own drummer. He had only just begun. There was in him a great promise of things to come.

The Irish ambassador recited a poem to John's father and mother soon after John was born. I can hear it again now, at this different and difficult moment:

We wish to the new child
A heart that can be beguiled
By a flower
That the wind lifts
As it passes.
If the storms break for him

May the trees shake for him
Their blossoms down.

In the night that he is troubled
May a friend wake for him
So that his time may be doubled,
And at the end of all loving and love,
May the Man above
Give him a crown.

We thank the millions who have rained blossoms down on John's memory. He and his bride have gone to be with his mother and father, where there will never be an end to love. He was lost on that troubled night—but we will always wake for him, so that his time, which was not doubled, but cut in half, will live forever in our memory, and in our beguiled and broken hearts.

We dared to think, in that other Irish phrase, that this John Kennedy would live to comb gray hair, with his beloved Carolyn by his side. But like his father, he had every gift but length of years.

We who have loved him from the day he was born, and watched the remarkable man he became, now bid him farewell.

God bless you, John and Carolyn. We love you and we always will.

Tribute to
SENATOR EDWARD KENNEDY

Delivered by President Barack Obama
Our Lady of Perpetual Help Basilica,
Roxbury, Massachusetts, August 29, 2009

Mrs. Kennedy, Kara, Edward, Patrick, Curran, Caroline, members of the Kennedy family, distinguished guests, and fellow citizens:

Today we say goodbye to the youngest child of Rose and Joseph Kennedy. The world will long remember their son Edward as the heir to a weighty legacy; a champion for those who had none; the soul of the Democratic Party; and the lion of the U.S. Senate—a man whose name graces nearly one thousand laws, and who penned more than three hundred himself.

But those of us who loved him, and ache with his passing, know Ted Kennedy by the other titles he held: Father. Brother. Husband. Uncle Teddy, or as he was often known to his younger nieces and nephews, "The Grand Fromage," or "The Big Cheese." I, like so many others in the city where he worked for nearly half a century, knew him as a colleague, a mentor, and above all, a friend.

Ted Kennedy was the baby of the family who became its patriarch; the restless dreamer who became its rock. He was the sunny, joyful child, who bore the brunt of his brothers' teasing, but learned quickly how to brush it off. When they tossed him off a boat because he didn't know what a jib was, six-year-old Teddy got back in and learned to sail. When a photographer asked the newly elected Bobby to step back at a press conference because he was casting a shadow on his younger brother, Teddy quipped, "It'll be the same in Washington."

This spirit of resilience and good humor would see Ted Kennedy through more pain and tragedy than most of us will ever know. He lost two siblings by the age of sixteen. He saw two more taken violently from the country that loved them. He said goodbye to his beloved sister, Eunice, in the final days of his own life. He narrowly survived a plane crash, watched two children struggle with cancer, buried three nephews, and experienced personal failings and setbacks in the most public way possible.

It is a string of events that would have broken a lesser man. And it would have been easy for Teddy to let himself become bitter and hardened; to surrender to self-pity and regret; to retreat from public life and live out his years in peaceful quiet. No one would have blamed him for that.

But that was not Ted Kennedy. As he told us, ". . . [I]ndividual faults and frailties are no excuse to give in—and no exemption from the common obligation to give of ourselves." Indeed, Ted was the "Happy Warrior" that the poet William Wordsworth spoke of when he wrote:

As tempted more; more able to endure,
As more exposed to suffering and distress;
Thence, also, more alive to tenderness.

Through his own suffering, Ted Kennedy became more alive to the plight and suffering of others—the sick child who could not see a doctor; the young soldier sent to battle without armor; the citizen denied her rights because of what she looks like or who she loves or where she comes from. The landmark laws that he championed—the Civil Rights Act, the Americans with Disabilities Act, immigration reform, children's health care, the Family and Medical Leave Act—all have a running thread. Ted Kennedy's life's work was not to champion those with wealth or power or special connections. It was to give a voice to those who were not heard; to add a rung to the ladder of opportunity; to make real the dream of our founding. He was given the gift of time that his brothers were not, and he used that gift to touch as many lives and right as many wrongs as the years would allow.

We can still hear his voice bellowing through the Senate chamber, face reddened, fist pounding the podium, a veritable force of nature, in support of health care or workers' rights or civil rights. And yet, while his causes became deeply personal, his disagreements never did. While he was seen by his fiercest critics as a partisan lightning rod, that is not the prism through which Ted Kennedy saw the world, nor was it the prism through which his colleagues saw him. He was a product of an age when the joy and nobility of politics prevented differences of party and philosophy from becoming barriers to cooperation and mutual respect—a time when adversaries still saw each other as patriots.

And that's how Ted Kennedy became the greatest legislator of our time. He did it by hewing to principle, but also by seeking compromise and common cause—not through deal-making and horse-trading alone, but through friendship, and kindness, and humor. There was the time he courted Orrin Hatch's support for the Children's Health Insurance Program by having his Chief of Staff serenade the Senator with a song Orrin had written himself; the time he delivered shamrock cookies on a china plate to sweeten up a crusty Republican colleague; and the famous story of how he won the support of a Texas Committee Chairman on an immigration bill. Teddy walked into a meeting with a plain manila envelope, and showed only the Chairman that it was filled with the Texan's favorite cigars. When the negotiations were going well, he would inch the envelope closer to the Chairman. When they weren't, he would pull it back. Before long, the deal was done.

It was only a few years ago, on St. Patrick's Day, when Teddy buttonholed me on the floor of the Senate for my support on a certain piece of legislation that was coming up for vote. I gave him my pledge, but expressed my skepticism that it would pass. But when the roll call was over, the bill garnered the votes it needed, and then some. I looked at Teddy with astonishment and asked how he had pulled it off. He just patted me on the back, and said "Luck of the Irish!"

Of course, luck had little to do with Ted Kennedy's legislative success, and he knew that. A few years ago, his father-in-law told him that he and Daniel Webster just might be the two greatest senators of all time. Without missing a beat, Teddy replied, "What did Webster do?"

But though it is Ted Kennedy's historic body of achievements we will remember, it is his giving heart that we will miss. It was the friend and colleague who was always the first to pick up the phone and say, "I'm sorry for your loss," or "I hope you feel better," or "What can I do to help?" It was the boss who was so adored by his staff that over five hundred spanning five decades showed up for his 75th birthday party. It was the man who sent birthday wishes and thank you notes and even his own paintings to so many who never imagined that a U.S. Senator would take the time to think about someone like them. I have one of those paintings in my private study—a Cape Cod seascape that was a gift to a freshman legislator who happened to admire it when Ted Kennedy welcomed him into his office the first week he arrived in Washington; by the way, that's my second favorite gift from Teddy and Vicki after our dog Bo. And it seems like everyone has one of those stories—the ones that often start with "You wouldn't believe who called me today."

Ted Kennedy was the father who looked after not only his own three children, but John's and Bobby's as well. He took them camping and taught them to sail. He laughed and danced with them at birthdays and weddings; cried and mourned with them through hardship and tragedy; and passed on that same sense of service and selflessness that his parents had instilled in him. Shortly after Ted walked Caroline down the aisle and gave her away at the altar, he received a note from Jackie that read, "On you the carefree youngest brother fell a burden a hero would have begged to be spared. We are all going to make it because you were always there with your love."

Not only did the Kennedy family make it because of Ted's love—he made it because of theirs; and especially because of the love and the life he found in Vicki. After so much loss and so much sorrow, it could not have been easy for Ted Kennedy to risk his heart again. That he did is a testament to how deeply he loved this remarkable woman from Louisiana. And she didn't just love him back. As Ted would often acknowledge, Vicki saved him. She gave him strength and purpose; joy and friendship; and stood by him always, especially in those last, hardest days.

We cannot know for certain how long we have here. We cannot foresee the trials or misfortunes that will test us along the way. We cannot know God's plan for us.

What we can do is to live out our lives as best we can with purpose, and love, and joy. We can use each day to show those who are closest to us how much we care about them, and treat others with the kindness and respect that we wish for ourselves. We can learn from our mistakes and grow from our failures. And we can strive at all costs to make a better world, so that someday, if we are blessed with the chance to look back on our time here, we can know that we spent it well; that we made a difference; that our fleeting presence had a lasting impact on the lives of other human beings.

This is how Ted Kennedy lived. This is his legacy. He once said of his brother Bobby that he need not be idealized or enlarged in death beyond what he was in life, and I imagine he would say the same about himself. The greatest expectations were placed upon Ted Kennedy's shoulders because of who he was, but he surpassed them all because of who he became. We do not weep for him today because of the prestige attached to his name or his office. We weep because we loved this kind and tender hero who persevered through pain and tragedy—not for the sake of ambition or vanity; not for wealth or power; but only for the people and the country he loved.

In the days after September 11th, Teddy made it a point to personally call each one of the 177 families of this state who lost a loved one in the attack. But he didn't stop there. He kept calling and checking up on them. He fought through red tape to get them assistance and grief counseling. He invited them sailing, played with their children, and would write each family a letter whenever the anniversary of that terrible day came along. To one widow, he wrote the following:

"As you know so well, the passage of time never really heals the tragic memory of such a great loss, but we carry on, because we have to, because our loved one would want us to, and because there is still light to guide us in the world from the love they gave us."

We carry on.

Ted Kennedy has gone home now, guided by his faith and by the light of those he has loved and lost. At last he is with them once more, leaving those of us who grieve his passing with the memories he gave, the good he did, the dream he kept alive, and a single, enduring image—the image of a man on a boat; white mane tousled; smiling broadly as he sails into the wind, ready for what storms may come, carrying on toward some new and wondrous place just beyond the horizon. May God Bless Ted Kennedy, and may he rest in eternal peace.

ACKNOWLEDGMENTS

We are most indebted to the journalists whose work appears in this book and the organizations that gave us permission to reprint their newspaper's pages. We relied especially on some newspapers for their comprehensive coverage of the Kennedys over the last fifty years: *The Boston Globe*, *The New York Times*, *The Washington Post*, and the *Los Angeles Times*. This book would not have been possible without their participation.

We are grateful to the Associated Press for permission to reprint its photographs and stories that appear on the newspaper pages included here, along with some additional iconic images of the Kennedy years. Thanks to Jim Baltzelle for facilitating our request.

For research, we used multiple sources, including each of the participating newspapers, especially *The Boston Globe* **and** *The New York Times*; Wikipedia; and the John F. Kennedy Presidential Library and Museum.

For newspaper pages, we called on librarians, photo department staffs, industrious administrators, and others. Patty Smail at ProQuest managed our multiple archival orders with grace and attention to detail.

We are grateful to Bob Schieffer, who immediately agreed to write the introduction and then wrote it just as immediately and beautifully.

At Andrews McMeel Publishing, we thank Chris Schillig, whose patience we required and warmth we enjoyed. We also thank John Carroll, Holly Camerlinck, Cliff Koehler, Tim Lynch, and David Shaw for doing everything possible to make this a book readers will treasure.

We turned frequently to our Poynter co-workers for help in many ways. We work in such a collegial place that even those we do not thank by name are a part of this book. We asked many to share memories of the Kennedy years; seek permissions; write, rewrite, and proof captions; and market and sell this book. For all they've done and will do to support this effort, we thank Cathy Campbell, Roy Peter Clark, Karen Dunlap, Rick Edmonds, Chrissy Estrada, Howard Finberg, Jill Geisler, Kathy Holmes, Maria Jaimes, Kelly McBride, Jessica Sandler, Jennette Smith, Mallary Tenore, Butch Ward, and Keith Woods.

Several colleagues played particularly critical roles. We always give Bill Mitchell the most difficult tasks and he always comes through.

ACKNOWLEDGMENTS

Sandy Johnakin managed all the permissions with great care. Becky Bowers found time to copy edit as if there are more than twenty-four hours in a day. Steve Myers made himself available to coach and coax and check.

We thank our families—Gary and Colter Moos; Dawn, Will, Robert, and Bryan Shedden; Marty, Jim and Ike Hartford; and Jean Dickenson. They tolerated our distracted attention and took care of each other so we could take care of this book.

And finally, we thank each other. If not for our coeditors we would have collapsed under the weight of this project. Instead, we encouraged and focused each other to create a well-researched, readable second draft of history with the sort of serendipity only time and attention can provide.

David Shedden, Director, Eugene Patterson Library
Sara Quinn, Poynter Faculty
Julie Moos, Director, Poynter Online and Poynter Publications
The Poynter Institute

About The Poynter Institute

The Poynter Institute is a school dedicated to teaching and inspiring journalists and media leaders. Through its seminars, publications, and Web site (poynter.org), the Institute promotes excellence and integrity in the practice of craft and in the practical leadership of successful businesses. Poynter stands for a journalism that informs citizens, enlightens public discourse, and strengthens the ties between journalism and democracy.

The school offers training at its Florida campus throughout the year in the areas of online and multimedia, leadership and management, reporting, writing, and editing, TV and radio, ethics and diversity, journalism education, and visual journalism. Poynter's e-learning portal, News University (newsu.org), offers newsroom training to journalists, journalism students, and educators through faculty-led, online seminars, Webinars, and over eighty self-directed courses. Most of these courses are free or low cost and are open to the public.

The Institute was founded in 1975 by Nelson Poynter, chairman of the *St. Petersburg Times*. Before his death, Mr. Poynter willed controlling stock in his companies to the school. As a financially independent, nonprofit organization, The Poynter Institute is beholden to no interest except its own mission: to help journalists seek and achieve excellence.